Theory and Applications of Ontology: Philosophical Perspectives

Roberto Poli · Johanna Seibt
Editors

Theory and Applications of Ontology: Philosophical Perspectives

Springer

Editors
Roberto Poli
University of Trento
Department of Sociology
and Social Research
26 Verdi str.
38100 Trento
Italy
roberto.poli@unitn.it

Johanna Seibt
University of Aarhus
Department of Philosophy
Jens Chr. Skousvej 7
8000 Aarhus C
Nobelparken Bldg. 1467
Denmark
filseibt@hum.au.dk

ISBN 978-90-481-8844-4 e-ISBN 978-90-481-8845-1
DOI 10.1007/978-90-481-8845-1
Springer Dordrecht Heidelberg London New York

Library of Congress Control Number: 2010932551

Printed on acid-free paper

Springer is part of Springer Science+Business Media (www.springer.com)

Preface

After a long period of decline, ontology is back at the forefront of philosophy, science and technology. These days ontology comes in at least two main fashions: the traditional philosophical understanding of ontology has been recently flanked by a new – computer-based – understanding of ontology.

There are scholars from both fields contending that ontology in knowledge engineering and ontology in philosophy are two completely different disciplines. On the one hand there is analysis closely tied to the concrete problems of domain modeling; on the other, difficult and usually very abstract speculations on the world and its most rarified structures. For this reason, it is claimed, those scientists who occupy themselves with ontology in knowledge engineering should not be concerned with what philosophers have to say (and vice-versa).

The thesis defended by *Theory and Applications of Ontology* is exactly the opposite. We shall try to show in this work that – despite their different languages and different points of departure – ontologies in knowledge engineering (let's say: ontology as technology) and ontology in philosophy (let's say: ontology as categorial analysis) have numerous problems in common and that they seek to answer similar questions. And for this reason, engineers and philosophers must devise ways to talk to each other.

The current resurgence of interest in ontological issues displays a number of novel features, both among philosophers and among information technologists. Among philosophers, the revival of a genuine interest in ontology requires the removal of certain prejudices that have profoundly influenced the analytic and the continental camps, both of which have in recent decades systematically delegitimized ontological inquiry in favour of its epistemological transformation (not to say reduction). To this shared error of broadly Kantian (or more properly neo-Kantian) stamp, analytic philosophy has added a linguistic prejudice, and the continental one styles of inquiry and writing that can be described as devoid of methodological rigour.

Behind these obstructions to ontological investigation one perhaps discerns the consequences of another feature common to both camps: the fact that the most influential thinkers of the last 100 years – the reference unquestionably goes back to Wittgenstein and Heidegger, however different their philosophical views may have been – both embraced an a-scientific approach; both, that is, delegitimized alliances, or at least serious contact, between science and philosophy. In consequence, the revival of interest in ontology also provides an opportunity for renewed discussion of the relationships between science and philosophy.

Science continuously advances, and that which it proves to be valid endures. Problem-oriented thinkers try to follow problems, not to anticipate conclusions or to presuppose an image of the world. This perspective is largely correct. It should, however, be qualified if one is not to commit the ingenuous error of believing that it is only 'solutions' that advance knowledge. Also attempts and failures, in fact, are instructive. For all these reasons we may accept Aristotle's contention that ontology is *philosophia prima* as regards the problems it seeks to resolve, as long as we remember that it can only be *philosophia ultima* as regards the elaboration of results. And it is here that we discern how ontology concretely operates in harness with science, because it 'presupposes the accumulated knowledge of centuries and the methodical experience of all the sciences' (N. Hartmann, *Der Aufbau der realen Welt*, 2nd ed., Meisenheim am Glan, 1949, p. 26).

Besides points of contact, of course, there are also a number of differences, perhaps most notably the fact that ontology in knowledge engineering is a discipline still in its infancy, while ontology in philosophy is as old as philosophy itself. Consequently, the history of philosophy contains ideas, tools and proposals of use for contemporary developments; and it also indicates the options that will lead us into dead ends or nowhere at all. When things are viewed in the light of such a long and articulated history, one knows from the outset that ontology does not permit ingenuous simplifications. For these reasons, philosophical ontology may usefully contribute to ontology in knowledge engineering.

It is true, though, that philosophical ontology addresses questions of a more general nature, ones apparently of no relevance to ontology in knowledge engineering. Consequently, it may appear that certain components of philosophical ontology could be ignored in the passage to ontology as technology. Nevertheless, one should always bear in mind the greater explanatory value and the broader structuring capacity of more general schemes and more comprehensive theories. For this less overt reason, too, philosophical ontology is useful for ontology in knowledge engineering.

The philosophical codification of ontology has often restricted itself to organization of its general architecture, without delving into the details of minute categorization. On the other hand, the concrete, situated practice of ontology as technology may conversely prove useful for the development of philosophical ontology.

For these and other reasons, there is mounting interest in the development of standards, modeling principles, and semantically transparent languages. Ontology thus comes into play as one of the strategies available to developing the semantic web, construct robust data-bases, managing huge amounts of heterogeneous information because ontologically founded knowledge of the objects of the world is able to make codification simpler, more transparent and more natural. The belief is that ontology can give greater robustness to computer-based applications by providing methodological criteria and categories with which to construct and build them, as well as contexts in which to set and re-categorize different data-bases so that they become more mutually transparent. In this way ontology directly contributes to standardization of the life-cycle model, and can therefore serve as an innovative and possibly unexpected component of software quality assurance.

These problems are dramatically magnified by the fact that unlike all the societies of the past, modern societies are no longer afflicted by a lack of information. If anything they suffer from its excess, from having to cope with too much unused and unusable information. It becomes increasingly difficult, in fact, to find the information that one needs, when one needs it, to the extent that one needs it and in the appropriate form. Although the information may be stored somewhere, all too often one does not know where; and even when one is aware of how to find the information, it is often accompanied by further information irrelevant to one's purposes. And when information is available, it is often forthcoming in the wrong form, or else its meaning is not explicitly apparent.

However broad the range of information already gathered may be, a great deal more has still to be assembled and codified. And this inevitably complicates still further the problem of the functional, flexible, efficient and semantically transparent codification of information.

Broadly speaking, the two research communities of philosophers and engineers have still not found a way to relate to each other systematically. While philosophers tend unilaterally to emphasize the need for a conceptual complexity that matches the complexity of the subject-matter, engineers tend equally unilaterally to stress the drawbacks of the tools available and the presence of insuperable computational problems. One side is perhaps too theoretical, the other too pragmatic. In short, taken as they stand, the two views seem difficult to reconcile.

However, in dynamic terms, one easily foresees mounting social and institutional pressure for the development of tools able to model fragments of reality in terms that are both adequate and efficient. And from this point of view, we are all at fault. Those colleagues who concern themselves with technologies seemingly pay closer attention to manipulation than to knowledge. Likewise, those who concern themselves with philosophy suffer from the reverse problem, that of navigating in a sea of theories for which the rationale is sometimes unclear.

For our part, we have grown increasingly convinced that the same problems will force engineers to address theories, and philosophers to address the limitations of our current capabilities. Provided, however, that both sides have the will, the ability, the desire and the courage to do so. If they decide to tackle these problems, it will become reasonable to identify and systematically develop those areas of convergence and contact now existing.

In this sense, the two volumes of *Theory and Applications of Ontology* may play a role in paving the way for a better mutual understanding between engineers and philosophers. Since the two communities are still very different as to their own languages, conceptual tools and problem-sets, we thought that collecting papers within one single volume would have been too constraining. We therefore devised two different volumes, one dedicated to the philosophical understanding of ontology and one to the computer-based understanding of ontologies. Both volumes contain both papers describing the state of the art in their respective topics and papers addressing forefront, innovative and possibly controversial topics.

Trento, Italy Roberto Poli

Contents

1 Ontology: The Categorial Stance . . . 1
Roberto Poli

2 Particulars . . . 23
Johanna Seibt

3 The Ontology of Mereological Systems: A Logical Approach . . . 57
Heinrich Herre

4 Causation . . . 83
Asbjørn Steglich-Petersen

5 Actualism Versus Possibilism in Formal Ontology . . . 105
Nino B. Cocchiarella

6 Dispositions and Response-Dependence Theories . . . 119
Eline Busck Gundersen

7 Properties . . . 135
Frédéric Nef

8 Boundary Questions Between Ontology and Biology . . . 153
Pietro Ramellini

9 The Ontology of Perception . . . 177
Liliana Albertazzi

10 Interactive Knowing: The Metaphysics of Intentionality . . . 207
Mark H. Bickhard

11 The Role of Logic and Ontology in Language and Reasoning . . . 231
John F. Sowa

12 Ontologies in the Legal Domain . . . 265
Laurens Mommers

13 Ontology in Economics . . . 277
Jason Potts

14 Ontology and Phenomenology 287
Angela Ales Bello

15 Phenomenology and Ontology in Nicolai Hartmann and Roman Ingarden 329
Nicoletta Ghigi

16 Ontology and Methodology in Analytic Philosophy 349
John Symons

17 Hermeneutic Ontology 395
Daniel O. Dahlstrom

Contributors

Liliana Albertazzi Cimec (Centre for Mind and Brain), and Department of Cognitive Sciences and Education, University of Trento at Rovereto, Rovereto, Italy, liliana.albertazzi@unitn.it

Angela Ales Bello Lateran University, Piazza S. Giovanni in Laterano 4, 00120 Città del Vaticano, Italy, alesbello@tiscali.it

Mark H. Bickhard Lehigh University, Bethlehem, PA, USA, mhb0@lehigh.edu

Nino B. Cocchiarella Indiana University, Bloomington, Indiana, USA, cocchiar@indiana.edu

Daniel O. Dahlstrom Department of Philosophy, Boston University, Boston, MA, USA, dahlstro@bu.edu

Nicoletta Ghigi University of Perugia, Perugia, Italy, nicoletta.ghigi@unipg.it

Eline Busck Gundersen Centre for the Study of Mind in Nature, University of Oslo, Oslo, Norway; Department of Philosophy and History of Ideas, Aarhus University, Denmark, e.b.gundersen@csmn.uio.no

Heinrich Herre Research Group Onto-Med, IMISE, University Leipzig, Leipzig, Germany, heinrich.herre@imise.uni-leipzig.de

Laurens Mommers Centre for Law in the Information Society, Leiden University, Leiden, The Netherlands, l.mommers@law.leidenuniv.nl

Frédéric Nef EHESS, Institut Jean-Nicod, Paris, France, frederic.nef@ehess.fr

Roberto Poli Department of Sociology and Social Research, University of Trento, Trento, Italy, roberto.poli@unitn.it

Jason Potts School of Economics, University of Queensland, Brisbane, QLD, Australia; ARC Centre of Excellence for Creative Industries and Innovation, Queensland University of Technology, Brisbane, QLD, Australia, j.potts@uq.edu.au

Pietro Ramellini Pontifical University 'Regina Apostolorum', Rome, Italy, ramellini.pietro@inwind.it

Johanna Seibt Department of Philosophy, University of Aarhus, Aarhus C, Denmark, filseibt@hum.au.dk

John F. Sowa VivoMind Intelligence, LLC, Rockville, MD, USA, sowa@bestweb.net

Asbjørn Steglich-Petersen Institute for Philosophy and History of Ideas, University of Aarhus, Aarhus C, Denmark, filasp@hum.au.dk

John Symons Department of Philosophy, University of Texas, El Paso, TX, USA, jsymons@utep.edu

Introduction

After two centuries of mainstream denial, ontology is back again. In fact, the past two or three decades have seen the slow resurgence of ontology as a progressively accepted and even respected field of philosophical inquiry. Ontology has come back in many different flavours. To mention but a couple of cases ontology has come back as the effort to establish the basic categorial grid of being, or the effort to dig deeper into the intricacies of specific groups of entities, such as organisms or minds. Furthermore, recent events in information technology have led to a new manifestation of the philosophical field of ontology. In this new manifestation, ontology is also a technological discipline. The development of knowledge-based systems has lead to computer applications written to manage knowledge expressed in symbolic form, in a variety of domains such as diagnostics and manufacturing engineering and in a variety of programming languages. The use of different rules, languages and terminologies, however, makes interoperability difficult if not intractable. The philosophical notion of ontology suggests a possible solution in the form of a system-neutral repository of abstract knowledge which can be refined to specify system rules and artifacts in the domains to be modeled, accompanied by automated translators mediating between each knowledge system and the repository.

The two volumes of Theory and Applications of Ontology (TAO) are intended to inform the scholar in philosophy or the researcher in the sciences, information technology, or engineering, of the present state of the art in philosophical ontology and the systems available for the study, development, and application of ontology as technology. While Volume 2 addresses the recent flowering of ontology as an all-encompassing field of study and application, which provides a declarative semantic framework for mutual understanding and interoperability between technological system components, models and processes, Volume 1 addresses philosophical ontology. The present volume, Volume 1 is intended as a snapshot of much, although not all, of the work in progress on ontology in philosophy. Nevertheless, each of the two volumes is self-contained and can be studied independently.

The chapters in this first volume of TAO are grouped in three parts. We consider this grouping necessary, in order to help the reader deal with the large volume of knowledge contained in the book. Of course, this grouping does not mean that the chapters are not related or interrelated; in fact, the reader will discover references from chapters that present seemingly different aspects of ontologies to common concepts and entities, which constitutes a proof of the universal application of ontologies. The chapters in the first part of the book present aspects of general ontology. Those in the second part of the book discuss domain or regional ontologies. The final part contributes chapters that shed light into the history of twentieth century ontology.

As we already mentioned, the first part in Volume 1 contains the chapters that provide an overview of various aspects of general ontology. Poli presents an overview of the most general structures than ontology may require. After distinguishing descriptive, categorial and formalized ontologies, Poli notes that most philosophers seem to have adopted one form or another of oversimplified theories of substance, and proposes a general framework for better addressing the nature of substance. Continuing, Seibt investigates notions of particularity, starting from the distinction between *foundational* and *target* particularism. Herre surveys mereological systems, an area of research that is today one of the core topics of ontology. Petersen discusses causation: Despite the undeniable importance of causation, its correct understanding remains subject to considerable controversy. She then presents the two main clusters of proposals in the literature, namely the view that sees causation essentially as a *relation* between facts or events, and the view that focus on the ontology of the *processes* by which causes are connected to their effects. Petersen discusses the most influential varieties of both views and underlines their main difficulties. Cocchiarella analyses the difference between being and existence. The simplest account of the distinction between being and existence is that between actualism and possibilism, where by existence he means physical existence, i.e., existence as some type of physical object; and by being he means possible physical existence, i.e., physical existence in some possible world. According to possibilism, there are objects that do not now exist but could exist in the physical universe, and hence being is not the same as existence. On the other hand, in actualism being is the same as existence. Cocchiarella then clarifies their differences by formally modeling different aspects of actualism and possibilism within a suitable system of formal ontology. Busck Gundersen overviews some of the central issues about dispositions and response-dependence theories. Finally, Nef discusses the difference between concepts, predicates and properties.

The second part groups five chapters that discuss specific domain ontologies, namely biology, perception, language, interactive knowing, law and economics. After a general survey of the most prominent ontological questions lying behind biology, Ramellini studies the case of biological boundaries. The problem is that the various boundaries distinguished by biologists (perceptual, compositional, epithelial, cellular and *sensu lato* processual boundaries) appear to be flawed by theoretical inconsistencies. Ramellini introduces then a new concept of organismic boundary and discusses some of its merits. Albertazzi analyses in details the psychological acts in which visual objects are presented and shows some of their intricacies. She proposes to consider acts of presentation as an irreducible level of the ontology of mind. Addressing the lack of consensus among cognitive scientists about the role of logic and ontology in relating language to the world, Sowa reviews the ongoing research, relates it to the historical developments in logic and philosophy, and proposes a synthesis that can accommodate the full range of language use from casual conversation to precise technical nomenclature. Bickhard defends the idea that a process framework is needed for understanding the emergence of normative function and representation. Mommers discusses the nature and classification of a varying set of ontology models focusing on legal domains, their environments, legal argumentation and other legal and legally relevant phenomena. Potts explores the vast ontological complexity of the economic world. The economic world in fact is an emergent (and massively parallel) process of socially-coordinated individual knowledge. In turn, the organizations and institutions that coordinate economic behavior are themselves subject to self-organization and evolution, showing that the economic world is ontologically complex in a profound way.

The third part includes four chapters dedicated to the reconstruction of the main trends within twentieth century ontology. The two chapters by Ales Bello and Ghigi reconstruct phenomenological ontology. Ales Bello presents Husserl and some of his pupils, notably Reinach, Hering, Conrad-Martius and Stein. Ghigi discusses in some depth the ontological proposals of Ingarden and Hartmann. Symons presents an articulated sketch of the history and methodology of ontology in the analytic tradition. Dahlstrom, finally, offers a vision of hermeneutic ontology, focuses on Heidegger and Gadamer.

The three parts of this volume aim at providing comprehensive coverage of the current status of ontology. They have been structured in a way that guides the reader from overviews of contemporary discussion in ontology to new proposals and suggested developments. This structure reflects the editors' choice of most profitable studying path. However, each part is independent from the others and will equip the reader with updated and complete knowledge under a specific perspective in ontology. Each chapter has been authored by distinguished scholars in the various applications of ontologies. Let them guide you, the reader, in a path of knowledge discovery that we, the volume editors, find to be the most fascinating.

Chapter 1
Ontology: The Categorial Stance

Roberto Poli

1.1 Introduction

Different authors assign different meanings to ontology and metaphysics.[1] Some use ontology and metaphysics interchangeably (most analytic philosophers, Heidegger), others claim that ontology is broader than metaphysics (Meinong, Ingarden), still others that metaphysics is broader than ontology (most traditional philosophers, Hartmann). Furthermore, the reasons for which one may be broader than the other vary. Before any substantial analysis of the field, therefore, a working delimitation of its range is required. To cut a complex story short, I shall propose the following interpretation:

1. *Ontology* deals with what, at least in principle, can be categorized (objectified, i.e. subsumed under distinguishable categories).
2. *Metaphysics* deals with the problem of the totality; generally speaking, there is no way to exclude that the totality could present aspects that we may forever be unable to rationalize, i.e. submit to a rational analysis.

Summarizing briefly: ontology deals with what can be rationally understood, at least partially. According to this interpretation, science in all of its branches is the most successful and powerful ally of ontology. Metaphysics is broader than ontology in the sense that the possibility is admitted of aspects of reality that in principle may go beyond the capacity of any rational enterprise we may happen to develop. Finally, ontics can be thought of as *existential* ontology, that is, the section of ontology dealing with actual existents.

R. Poli (✉)
Department of Sociology and Social Research, University of Trento, Trento, Italy
e-mail: roberto.poli@unitn.it

[1]Thanks to Ion Baianu, Nino Cocchiarella, Claudio Gnoli, Frank Loebe, Leo Obrst, Jerzy Perzanowski, Johanna Seibt, and John Sowa for their comments on previous versions of this chapter.

R. Poli, J. Seibt (eds.), *Theory and Applications of Ontology: Philosophical Perspectives*, DOI 10.1007/978-90-481-8845-1_1,

The distinction between ontology and metaphysics becomes even clearer if one makes reference to the Aristotelian idea of science, according to which there are many different sciences, characterized by specific (types of) objects and their laws: physics is the field of natural movements and transformations, logic the study of (formal) reasoning, politics the analysis of public virtues; rhetoric the study of how to convince others (advertising being its modern facet). Three key questions arise naturally from this perspective point: (1) the categorial structure characterizing each and every science; (2) the mutual connections and forms of dependence and autonomy among sciences; (3) the nature and sense of the whole emerging from them all. The former two questions contribute to defining domain and general ontology, whereas the latter question merges into metaphysics.

1.2 Three Configurations of Ontology

The unity and the variety of the world is the outcome of the complex interweaving of dependence and inter-dependence connections and various forms of autonomy among the many items[2] of which the world is composed. We shall seek to explain the features of this multiplicity by beginning with an apparently trivial question: what is there in the world?

One may say that there are material things, plants and animals, as well as the products of the activities and activities of animals and humans in the world. This first, almost trivial, list already indicates that the world comprises not only things, animate or inanimate, but also activities and processes and the products that derive from them. It is likewise difficult to deny that there are thoughts, sensations and decisions, and the entire spectrum of mental activities. Just as one is compelled to admit that there are laws and rules, languages, societies and customs. We can set about organizing this list of objects by saying that there are *independent items* that may be *real* (mountains, flowers, animals, and tables), or *ideal* (sets, propositions, values), and *dependent items* which in turn may be *real* (colors, kisses, handshakes and falls) or *ideal* (formal properties and relations).

All these are in various respects items that *are*. Some of the real ones are actually exemplified in the world in which we live; others have been exemplified in the past; and yet others will possibly be exemplified in the future. All real items are therefore temporal items. On the other hand, ideal or abstract items are atemporal, i.e. their form of existence is independent of time (Poli 2001b, chap. 5).[3]

Descriptive ontology concerns the collection of such *prima facie* information on types of items either in some specific domain of analysis or in general.

Formal ontology distills, filters, codifies and organizes the results of descriptive ontology (in either its local or global setting). According to this interpretation, formal ontology is formal in the sense used by Husserl in his *Logical Investigations*.

---

[2]On the meaning of “item”, see Section 1.6 below.

[3]Scholars from the Brentanian tradition usually distinguish between existence (for real items) and subsistence (for ideal ones).

Being "formal" in such a sense therefore means dealing with categories like *thing*, *process*, *matter*, *form*, *whole*, *part*, and *number*. These are pure categories that characterize aspects or types of reality and still *have nothing to do with the use of any specific formalism*.

Formal codification in the strict sense is undertaken at the third level of theory construction, that of *formalized ontology*. The task here is to find the proper formal codification for the constructs descriptively acquired and categorized in the way just indicated. The level of formalized constructions also relates to evaluation of the adequacy (expressive, computational, cognitive) of the various formalisms, and to the problem of their reciprocal translations.

The close similarity between the terms "formal" and "formalized" is somewhat unfortunate. One way to avoid the clash is to use "categorial" instead of "formal".[4]

Most contemporary research on methodology in ontology recognizes only two levels of work in ontology and often merges the level of the formal categories either with that of descriptive or with that of formalized analysis. As a consequence, the specific relevance of categorial analyses is too often neglected.

The three configurations of ontology differ from each other but there are multiple dependencies among them. Descriptive findings may bear on formal categories; formalized outcomes may bear on their categorial classification, etc. To set out the differences and the connections between the various ontological levels of theory construction precisely is a most delicate but significant task (Poli 2003).

So far we have simply tried to *prima facie* clarify and delimit the concept of ontology from the related concepts of ontics and metaphysics. Before presenting ontology from the point of view of its contents, two more clarifications are needed.

1.3 Ontological Presentations

The distinction is needed between *pure* ontology and its *presentations*. The latter are related to some point of view (which could be linguistic, cultural or whatever), while pure ontology is independent of the perspectives on it. Otherwise stated, pure ontology is that structural invariant that unifies and underlies all its possible perspective-based variants (ontology as seen from nowhere, as Leibniz would have said). To provide but a sketchy example, a pure ontology may claim that "process" and "object"[5] are the only categories needed and that these are further specified in terms of the distinction, say, between countable and non-countable items.[6] However, for those that are accustomed to the said distinction, a framework

[4] Note the use of "categorial" instead of the more usual term "categorical". The latter will be reserved for the mathematical understanding of category, as for example in Topos Theory.

[5] "Presential", according to the GFO ontology (GFO stands for General Formal Ontology). Presentials exist entirely at a time-point and are seen as dependent boundaries of processes, which then are the only needed independent category. This section of the GFO ontology is based on Brentano's idea of time, space and the continuum. See: http://www.onto-med.de/en/publications/scientific-reports/om-report-no8.pdf .

[6] See Note 9 below.

offering the possibility to distinguish between countable and uncountable items may prove to be cognitively more transparent and in the end easier to use than a system without it. *Ontological presentations* are specific settings of the underlying ontological framework intended to better meet the requirements of a community of users. Unfortunately, it seems that a great deal of the recent ontological work has been conducted in such a way that a specific presentation of ontology (usually in the form of a linguistically-based and furthermore English-based presentation) has been taken as playing the role of pure ontology.

1.4 Ontology vs. Epistemology

Defining the tasks and characteristics of ontology is also important if we are to avoid confusion with epistemology. The difference can be evidenced by listing concepts of ontology and epistemology. Ontological concepts are: object, process, event, whole, part, determination, dependency, composition, etc. Epistemological concepts are: belief, truth, probability, confirmation, knowledge and all its subsequent modulations (uncertain knowledge, wrong knowledge, etc.).

If ontology is the theory of (the structures of) items, epistemology is the theory of the different kinds of knowledge and the ways in which it is used. The mutual or bilateral form of dependence linking ontology and epistemology does not oblige us to conclude that we cannot represent their specific properties and characteristics separately. On the contrary, we should specify both what ontology can say about epistemology (a belief is a kind of item, it has parts and determinations, etc.), and what epistemology can say about ontology (knowledge of items is a kind of knowledge). This is a difficult task and mistakes are always possible, but there is no principled reason for denying its realizability, even if one understands why it is so easy to blur ontological and epistemological issues.

The ontological and epistemological perspectives interweave and condition each other in complex ways. They are not easily separable, amongst other things because they are complementary to each other.

A further difference – similar but not identical to that between ontology and epistemology – is the difference between an ontological reading and an epistemological one. Consider the sentence:

(1) Napoleon was the first emperor of France.

Its untyped formal reading is:

(2) Somebody was the first something somewhere,

while its typed reading is something like

(3) A is/past the first B of C.

From a cognitive point of view, (1) may mean for instance that

(4) The man portrayed by David in the likeness of a Roman Caesar was the first emperor of France (Ushenko 1958).

Neither (2) nor (3) imply (4), whereas (4) does imply (2) or even (3). In general, it is always possible to develop many different cognitive readings of the same sentence. These various readings depend on the information that is implicitly or explicitly added. If we do not add new information, reading (4) above is unjustified because the sentence (1) does not entail the information that Napoleon was portrayed by David.

In general, (2) and (3) (the formal readings) are too poor; they are general but they say too little.[7] On the other hand, (4) is too strong, it is not sufficiently general and it depends on added information. The real difficulty for the ontological reading is that it lies somewhere in between. It is more than the purely logical reading and it is less than the many different cognitive integrations.

The truly ontological viewpoint manifests the many facets of the item. It says not only that somebody was the first something somewhere, but that he performed an important institutional role in some specific part of Europe. It says, moreover, that he was a human being and for this reason that he had a body and a mind, that he was alive, etc.

There is a myriad of information embedded in the sentence "Napoleon was the first emperor of France". The ontological reading should be able to extract and organize this information without resorting to any external source of knowledge (Poli 2001b).

After these preliminaries, it is now time to present ontology from the point of view of its contents.

1.5 Ontology as Theory of Categories

Following the path opened by such thinkers like Husserl, Hartmann, Peirce and Whitehead (and first of all by Aristotle), ontology adopts a categorial framework. Resorting to a categorial framework means looking for "what is universal" (either in general or in some specific domain). Those with a grounding in contemporary mathematics will also recognize here the similar claim advanced by Bill Lawvere some decades ago: the Theory of Category, as a foundational theory for mathematics, is based on "what is universal in mathematics" (Lawvere 1969, p. 281). Ontology searches everywhere for what is universal. This is precisely the meaning of ontology viewed as a theory of categories.

However, categories come in different guises. Some are taxonomic (is-a, or subclass relation) categories, others are prototypical and there may be other frameworks as well. Moreover, there is also no denying that there are many different types of "domain" categories (mathematical, linguistic, biological, economic, etc). However,

[7] Needless to say, the typed reading is much more informative than the untyped one. However, the ontological problem remains as hard as soon one ask how types are structured and one another connected.

since Aristotle ontological categories are broader than any type of domain categories and deal with the most universal distinctions, starting from the one between substance and accident. So understood, most categories are taxonomical categories. A wider perspective point will include not only the classical taxonomical categories we know since Aristotle, but also principles. To remain within a broadly Aristotelian framework, principles include the oppositions between matter and form, power and act, part and whole, being and one. Principles are trans-categorial (where category is taken in the restricted, taxonomical sense) in the sense that they run across the various categories.

As soon as we move from Aristotle to our time, such matters become much more tangled. During the past two centuries the philosophical theory of categories has been subjected to at least six major conceptual revolutions, respectively ascribable to Kant, Hegel, Brentano, Husserl, Peirce and Whitehead. Here we cannot assess all of their pros and cons. However it is noteworthy that all them claim that their main problem is the problem of time, i.e. the problem of the dynamical nature of reality.

1.6 The Main Distinction

We shall adopt item as the universal term. All the subsequent distinctions we are going to consider are distinction among items. Item is more general than the traditional concept *ens*, read as "everything conceivable", even if for any practical purposes the two may be taken as essentially equivalent.[8] The first distinction after item is between substances and their determinations (traditionally called accidents).

Philosophers have struggled for centuries to gain proper understanding of the category substance. As a matter of fact, the history of philosophy is a remarkable repository of the many variations undergone by the category of substance. It has been variously held that substances are not subject to change, are the unknowable sources of our perceptions, come only in pre-established types, etc. However, in the end the Aristotelian theory of substance is still possibly the most intuitive and productive starting point. The original Aristotelian understanding of substance takes it to be "the bearer of accidents". Within his framework, substance refers to whatever is at least partially existentially autonomous (i.e. non-dependent). In this sense, living beings are the best exemplifications of substances. Notwithstanding the many problems lurking behind the surface of the Aristotelian point of view, it should

[8] To be precise, one should distinguish, together with the Stoics, among *soma*, *on* and *ti*, or with some of the Medievals, notably Gregory of Rimini (1300–1358), among *res*, *ens* and *aliquid*, or again, with Meinong (1853–1920), among *real*, *ideal* and *Aussersein* objects. What is termed *soma*, *res* or *real object* is the body, the *on*, *ens* or *ideal object* is an entity, while the *ti*, *aliquid* or *Aussersein object* is something indeterminate. That which actually exists, the genuine object, is only the *soma*, *res* or *real object*. An entity, by contrast, could well be *asomaton* or incorporeal. Thus while the *soma* is subject to the principle of individuation, the *on* admits at most some criterion of identity, and the *ti* admits neither identity nor individuation. For them the *on* can be objective without having to be existent, a *soma*. On these distinctions see Poli 1996a.

however be taken for granted that substances are essentially dynamical realities, i.e. that they change. Furthermore, substances present a number of different "compositions", i.e. they can be seen from different perspective points (matter-form, power-act, part-whole, etc.). It seems fair to acknowledge that Aristotle failed to establish the proper connections among the theory of categories, the role of the principles (the tension between the dynamics of actuality and potency and the principle of the *one* being the main sources of difficulty), the theory of whole and parts, and the theory of the continuum. In the end, Aristotle decided to subordinate both wholes and continua to the dialectics of actuality and potentiality. He therefore asserted that whenever the whole is actual, its parts can only be potential. Similarly, whenever the continuum is actual its points are potential. And vice versa in both cases. The main ground for his claims was that "no substance is composed of substances" (*Metaphysics* 1041 a 5). Similarly, no whole is composed of other wholes. Therefore, parts of wholes are not wholes themselves. "Evidently even of the things that are thought to be substances, most are only potencies – both the parts of animals (for none of them exists separately; and when they are separated, then too they exist, all of them, merely as matter) and earth and fire and air; for none of them is a unity, but as it were a mere heap" (*Metaphysics*, 1040 b 5–9).

The resulting picture has an apparent coherence to it, but the overall structure is highly unstable: as soon as the slightest change is made to the theory of substance, the theory of wholes and parts or the theory of the continua, the entire framework totters. It therefore comes as no surprise to find that Brentano's (and for that matter Leibniz's) innovations to the dialectics between continua and their elements on the one hand, and between wholes and their parts on the other, gave rise to a genuinely new vision (Poli 2004).

Some of the constraints adopted by Aristotle can be loosened, obtaining in such a way a more general theory. First of all, there is no need to maintain that substances should be countable (each substance being a one). Furthermore, not only could it be accepted that substances can be made of other substances, and wholes of other wholes, but it is also possible to admit that accidents may have accidents. This amounts to claiming that substances are not the only things that have accidents; some accidents can be bearers of other accidents. In so doing, beside the substance-accident tie, also the substance-substance and the accident-accident ties should be incorporated within the framework of general ontology.

A further generalization, foreseen by Brentano, is provided by the idea of substances without accidents. For Brentano, "bodies are . . . substances which are not known to have accidents". The idea that bodies do not have accidents is striking. Either Brentano is utterly wrong or our commonsensical ideas of substance and accident are in need of deep revision.

The apparent strangeness of this position fades as soon as one realizes that accidents can be viewed as referring to the results of measuring processes, i.e. as the modifications suffered by an observing system when it is coupled to an observed system. In this sense not only are rods measuring devices, but also seeing and hearing can be taken as such. What is accidental from the point of view of the observing system may and usually is substantial from the point of view of the observed system.

Summing up what we have seen so far, one can sensibly claim that from the point of view of a modernized Aristotelian viewpoint there is no reason to claim that substances must be countable, or possess accidents.

1.7 The Articulation of Substance

Substances can be seen from a number of different frameworks (and requires all them). It may be claimed that one of the reasons for the still unfinished state of the theory of substance is the unsupported oversimplified theory adopted by most philosophers. Our claim is that to properly understand substance we need at least six different theories, five directly dealing with its internal configuration and one dealing with both internal and external aspects. For reasons that will become immediately apparent, we will organize the six theories into three groups: (1) Ground categories; (2) Universal theories, and (3) Levels of reality.

1.7.1 Ground Categories

The information treated in this chapter of the theory of substance concerns the differences among such general categories as object, process, event, state of affairs, stuff, group, and so on. A widely adopted distinction here is between countable and uncountable natures. Some of the above categories are either countable (object, state of affairs) or uncountable (stuff), some other come in both guises (some processes are countable, others uncountable; cfr. Seibt 2004).[9]

1.7.2 Universal Theories

The instances of ground categories can be further categorized according to a number of different dimensions of analysis. Every dimension of analysis is based on a governing relation. As far as general ontology is concerned, it is important that universal theories avoid any form of domain-based bias. I shall return to this problem in Section 7.4 below.

[9]However, a deeper analysis may show that the countable-uncountable opposition is *either* superficial or parochial. It is superficial if the said distinction could be derived from other, deeper categories. On the other hand it may be parochial in the sense that it is a distinction embedded in only some of the world languages. According to Rijkhoff (2002), linguistic data show that six types of nouns can be distinguished: general nouns, sort nouns, mass nouns, set nouns, singular object nouns, and collective nouns. It may also be that the countable-uncountable opposition is *both* superficial and parochial. Ontological categories run the risk of being parochial when they are grounded on only a section of the available scientific and experiential data. On the other hand, the possible superficiality of ontological categories may depend on cognitive or cultural biases, and in this sense categorial superficiality is a deeper phenomenon; see the section on ontological presentations above.

1.7.2.1 Classification

For any kind of item, its instances can be classified. Taxonomies (class-subclass relations or is-a trees, plus instance-of relations) are the best-known forms of classification.[10] Occasionally other types of classification different from is-a classifications are proposed, e.g. the classification of chemical elements or prototypical classifications. However, these latter forms of classification cannot be included in the section of universal classifications because they are based on specific domain biases: structural information for chemical elements and cognitive saliencies for prototypical classifications.

1.7.2.2 Structure

Structure concerns the (1) constitution and the (2) part-whole organization of substances. Constitution is the relation linking a substance to its underlying matter or material. Part-of (in any of its equivalent formal alternatives) provides information about the organization of the item under analysis. Different types of holons (wholes)[11] and parts can be distinguished. I only point out that the classification of holons should distinguish at least among aggregates, wholes in the proper sense, and systems. Aggregates are defined by any appropriate measure of proximity among their parts (e.g. in the forms of similarity or contiguity); wholes require that their parts be linked by some form or other of solidarity ("they move together", as Aristotle said)[12]; systems, finally, are dynamical wholes. Unity by solidarity is stronger than unity by proximity, and dynamic integration, i.e., formation of a dynamic whole is stronger than unity by solidarity and proximity. This means that only some aggregates are also wholes, and that only some of the latter may be systems. Similarly, different types of parts can be distinguished. Here I mention only parts in the sense of constituent parts (what something is made of) and parts as descriptive parts of the whole. As far as organisms are concerned, organs and their cells are constituent parts of the organism, while, say, hands, arms and trunk are descriptive parts. These two different types of part may or may not coincide. Furthermore, analysis by parts as constituent parts may or may not coincide with analysis conducted in terms of the constitution relation. In order to systematically distinguish the different cases, the theory of levels of reality (see below Section 7.4) is required.[13]

---

[10] As usual, relying on an already elaborated classification is a different situation from building a new classification.

[11] "Holon" was initially used by Koestler (1967). While I endorse his vision, here I am using holon only as a convenient substitute for "whole", meant as one of the three subtypes of holons.

[12] However, Aristotle's claim is valid only for solids.

[13] The main difference being between relations between items pertaining or not pertaining to the same level (either as a stratum or layer) of reality.

1.7.2.3 Chronotopoids

Drawing on Brentano, I shall treat the *general* problem of space and time as a problem of chrono-topoids (understood jointly, or separated into chronoids and topoids).[14] Space and/or time are customarily understood in the form of *physical* space-time. As necessary as it may be, the physical understanding of space-time is only one of the many types of ontological spatio-temporal frameworks. Chronotopoids are the most general spatio-temporal frameworks, independently of any material, psychological and social bias.

Development of the theory will require solution of some significant problems. The first of them is establishing which families of chrono-topoids are continuous and which are discrete.

The second problem concerns the cohesion of their structure – the forces, that is, which hold them together. In formal terms, this is the same problem as before: devising a theory of, say, the continuum requires knowing how it is constituted. But in ontological terms it is not the same thing. If the continuum is not only a formal structure but also as real one, there must by something (forces?) holding it together. The solution to this aspect of the question relates to the problem of causal connections (see Section 1.7.2.4 below). Here we find a first interaction between the theory of causes and the theory of chronotopoids.

Much more needs to be added, for something is still lacking from our framework. I shall return to chronotopoids in Section 1.7.4 below.

1.7.2.4 Interactions (Causations)

Interactions are forms of causation. Whatever items are recognized by an ontology, they act upon one another and influence one another. For the time being, as in the previous section, I am obliged to confine myself to this rather minimal description of interaction. I shall resume discussion of interaction in Section 1.7.4 below, after I have introduced the theory of levels of reality.

1.7.3 Levels of Reality

No general consensus exists about how to define, describe or even sketch the idea of level of reality. Not surprisingly, my choice is to adopt a *categorial* criterion: the levels of reality are characterized (and therefore distinguished) by their categories. The main subsequent distinction is between universal categories (those that pertain to reality in its entirety – ground categories and universal frameworks of analysis) and categories that pertain solely to one or some levels of reality.

---

[14] See Poli (2004) and Albertazzi (2005). Bell (2000) and (2005) provide an intuitionistically-based reconstruction of Brentano's theory. A different interpretation is under elaboration by Herre (in preparation).

Most authors prefer instead to adopt an objectual standpoint, rather than a categorial one. Arguing in favor of the objectual standpoint has the undoubted advantage that it yields an elementary definition of level: a level consists of a collection of units. From this point of view, the series of levels is a series of objects interacting at different degrees of granularity. A model of this kind is accepted by large part of the scientific community, because it depicts the widely held view of levels based on a reductionist approach. Higher-order groups of items may behave differently, even to the point that it is impossible to calculate (predict) their specific behaviour, but in the end what matters is that they can all be reduced to the lower *atoms*.

If this were indeed the way matters stand, then the general neglect shown towards the problem of the levels would be justified.

In order to deal with the real complexity of the problem of the levels, the general picture must be altered so that it becomes possible to study not only *linear* hierarchies but *tangled* ones as well. This conclusion bears out the approach which undertakes categorial analysis, compared to the one which studies items in iteration.

An argument in favor of the approach *by objects* is the ease with which it is possible to pass from a object-based description to a process-based one: if a level is defined by items in iteration (where the items can be canonically conceived as objects), then a level can be characterized by a dynamic. A multiplicity of structurally stable dynamics, at diverse levels of granularity, may articulate a multiplicity of levels. However, if it turns out that the structuring in levels does not respect a universal principle of linearity, then one is forced to restrict the multidynamic frames to their linear fragments. Which is precisely the situation of current theories of dynamic systems. On careful consideration, in fact, the predominant opinion is that there is only one multi-dynamic (multi-layered) system: the one described by the natural sciences. Other forms of knowledge are scientific to the extent that they can be located in the progressive series of supraformations (groups of groups of groups of items, each with its specific kinds of interaction). Hence the alternative: a discipline is scientific to the extent that it can be located in the series of aggregation levels – if so it can be more or less easily reduced to the base level – or it cannot be thus located and is consequently not a science: it has no citizenship in the realm of knowledge and is scientifically stateless.

The distinction is widespread among three basic realms or regions (or strata, as I will call them) of reality. Even if the boundaries between them are differently placed, the distinction among the three realms of material, psychological and social phenomena is essentially accepted by most thinkers and scientists. A major source of discussion is whether inanimate and animate beings should be placed in two different realms (this meaning that there are in fact four and not three realms) or within the same realm. The latter option involves the thesis that a phase transition or something similar connects inanimate and animate items.

From a categorial point of view, the problem of how many strata there are can be easily solved. Leaving apart universal categories (those that apply everywhere), two main categorial situations can be distinguished: (a) Types (Items) A and B are categorially different because the description (codification or modeling) of one of them requires categories that are not needed by the description (codification or modeling) of the other; (b) Types (Items) A and B are categorially different because their description (codification or modeling) requires two entirely different groups of categories. Following Hartmann, I term the two relations respectively as relations of over-forming (*Überformung*) and building-above (*Überbauung*).[15] Strata or realms of reality are connected by building-above relations. That is to say, the main reason for distinguishing as clearly as possible the different strata of reality is that any of them is characterized by the birth of a *new* categorial *series*. The group of categories that are needed for analyzing the phenomena of the psychological stratum is essentially different from the group of categories needed for analyzing the social one, which in its turn requires a group of categories different from the one needed for analyzing the material stratum of reality.

Over-forming (the type (a) form of categorial dependence) is weaker than building-above and it is used for analyzing the internal organization of strata. Each of the three strata of reality has its specific structure. The case of the material stratum is the best known and the least problematic. Suffice it to consider the series atom-molecule-cell-organism (which can be extended at each of its two extremes to include sub-atomic particles and ecological communities, and also internally, as needed). In this case we have a clear example of a series that proceeds by levels of granularity. Compared to the material realm, the psychological and social ones are characterized by an interruption in the material categorial series and by the onset of new series of categories (relative to the psychological and social items). More complex types of over-forming are instantiated by them.

A terminological note may be helpful. I use the term "level" to refer in general to the levels of reality, restricting the term "layer" to over-forming relationships, and the term "stratum" to building-above relationships. I shall eventually use the expressions "sub-layer" and "sub-stratum" when analysis requires them.

The question now arises as to how the material, psychological and social strata are connected together. The most obvious answer is that they have a linear structure like the one illustrated by the left side of Fig. 1.1.

On this view, the social realm is founded on the psychological stratum, which in its turn is founded on the material one. Likewise, the material stratum is the bearer of the psychological stratum, which in its turn is the bearer of the social one. The point of view illustrated by the left side of Fig. 1.1 is part of the received wisdom. However, a different option is possible. Consider the right side of Fig. 1.1.

Material phenomena act as bearers of *both* psychological *and* social phenomena. In their turn, psychological and social phenomena reciprocally determine each other.

[15] Cfr. Hartmann (1935). The simplified version presented in Hartmann (1952) is worth reading as well. For an introduction to Hartmann cfr. Werkmeister (1990) and the essays collected in Poli (2001d). Even if my vision is substantially different from Hartmann's, his contribution is a required starting point for anybody interested in the problem of levels of reality.

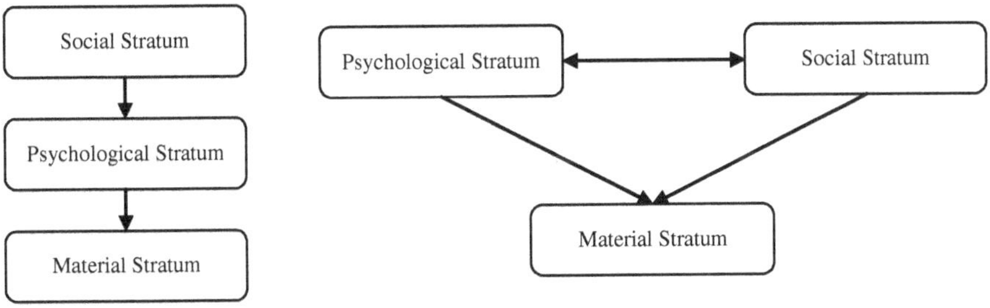

Fig. 1.1 *Left*: Linearly organized strata. *Right*: Strata with bilateral dependence

Psychological and social systems are formed through co-evolution, meaning that the one is the environmental prerequisite for the other (Luhmann 1995).

The next step is to articulate the internal organization of each stratum. Analysis shows that the internal organization of the three strata exhibits different patterns.[16]

1.7.4 Multiplying Universal Theories by Levels of Reality

Universal theories provide highly generic frameworks of analysis. It may well be that specific domain ontologies require some appropriate modifications of those generic frameworks of analysis. Indeed, there is no reason to rule out that the general theory of structures (part-of), chronotopoids or interactions to, say, biological items (organisms) or psychological items (representations, or emotions) or to social items (laws, languages, business situations or objects of art) are too general for in-depth analysis of these domain items. The theory of levels comes in here as the main categorial framework for providing guidance on how to proceed systematically with the domain modifications of universal theories.

I am now in the position to add something more to the analysis of chronotopoids and interactions initiated in Sections 1.7.2.3 and 1.7.2.4 above.

In the course of the twentieth century, numerous scholars sought to defend and elaborate the idea that there are different kinds of time and different kinds of space. The problem is not just the difference between time as the external order of phenomena (clock or calendar time, understood not only informally but specified up to

[16] A proper analysis of the social stratum is still awaited. Aspects of my theory of levels have been presented in Poli (1996b, 1998, 2001a–d, 2002, 2006a, b) and in Gnoli and Poli (2004). Caveat. A major misunderstanding of the theory of levels of reality is interpreting the theory of levels as a theory of items' granularity. That this interpretation is false can be easily seen by considering that the set of physical items comprises both subatomic particles and galaxies and, indeed, the whole *physical* universe. Physics comprises items at all (real) granularities. Nevertheless physics does not describe *all* of reality. Something more is required to describe the non-physical aspects of reality, something that, categorially speaking, goes beyond physics, and in two different senses: as a categorial *extension* of physics (chemistry and biology) and as a categorial *alternative* to physics and its extensions (the psychological and social strata).

the desired level of precision) and the inner, subjective time of psychological phenomena (qualitative or phenomenological time). The difference between "time" and "timing" has been described convincingly by van Gelder and Port (1995), and their work may be consulted for a modern version of the difference between the two types of time. I shall not reiterate their arguments here, because the thesis that I wish to discuss is more demanding than that implicit in the difference between the two families of time just mentioned. Stated simply, I shall argue that that there are *numerous* families of times, each with its own structure. The same applies to space: I shall argue that there are numerous types of real spaces endowed with structures that may differ greatly from each other. The qualifier "real" is essential. I shall not be concerned with the fact – which I consider entirely obvious and not at all disconcerting – that many different abstract (usually mathematical) theories of space and time can be constructed. We shall later need all our mathematical imagination to comprehend the richness of the real; for the time being let us focus on the claim is that there are many *real* times and spaces.

I have said that during the twentieth century various thinkers sought to defend and elaborate the idea that it is proper to distinguish diverse spaces and times – for example in psychological, social, anthropological, historical, and cultural terms. Unfortunately, it seems correct to say that many of these authors substantially failed in their attempts because they were unable to go beyond allusive and metaphorical renditions of their ideas. The thesis that I propose here is that these failures were due mainly to the lack of a theory of the levels of reality. In the case of the time and space problem as well, we can only hope to move forward by devising an adequately generalized version of the corresponding categories.

To restate, drawing on Brentano, I shall treat the general problem of space and time as a problem of chrono-topoids (understood jointly, or separated into chronoids and topoids).

Development of the theory will require solution to three main problems. The first two have already been mentioned and concern the analysis of (1) which family of chrono-topoids are continuous and which are discrete, and (2) the cohesion of their structure – the forces, that is, which hold them together.

The third problem centers on the synthesis among different chronotopoids. However many the differences may be among the multiple chronotopoids required by the items which constitute reality, chronotopoids do not operate independently of each other; they must merge into a synthetic configuration. In this respect, again, the theory of chronotopoids must obviously rely on a theory of the levels of reality.

Some further information may aid the reader in navigating through the complex terrain described. I shall furnish only some basic details. The point to be made most forcefully is that the study of psychological and social phenomena requires a variety of geometric structures (spaces) only some of which are sufficiently known (see e.g. Koenderink and van Doorn 2001). Needed for this purpose are spaces with hierarchical structures (atlases of maps on different scales), spaces with locally unordered structures, point-less continua (whose minimal parts are therefore "infinitesimal"), spaces based on forms of exclusively local organization, and so on. Study will have to be made of multiple relations among these spaces (as well as other types not mentioned). Spaces can be varyingly understood as containers or as structures in which geometric entities are viewed as operators of various kinds. The latter may have inputs, states to be modeled, and corresponding results.

An exemplification which is less abstract and more explicitly tied to the natural articulation of space might comprise the space in which we move, visual space, the visual field, the space of color, various types of parametric space (shapes, phases of movement), and the spaces of meaningful objects (e.g. physiognomies). A large part of the contemporary literature concentrates on structures based on and guided by data, while processual approaches (e.g. of microgenetic type) are very rare (for an exception see Rosenthal 2004). Some of these spaces can be viewed as abstractions of corresponding parametric spaces of physical type (consider the space of colors understood as a three-dimensional subspace of the space of physical radiation), while others have no obvious physical correlate and are apparently authentically mental (hot and cold colors). Of particular interest is the case of pictorial space: that is, the space obtained when an observer looks "into" a painting. Because a painting consists of a surface covered by patches of color in a certain pattern, the pictorial space is a psychic object hallucinated by the observer. Nonetheless, pictorial objects have spatial attitudes, shapes, intrinsic colors and material properties which form a spatial scene. The studies by Koenderink show that pictorial space is a homogeneous space with one isotropic dimension (and is therefore not Euclidean), locally unordered, with a self-similar topological structure.

Passing to interactions, the theory of levels of reality is also the natural setting for elaboration of an articulated theory of the forms of causal dependence. In fact, it smoothly grounds the hypothesis that any ontologically different level has its own type of interactions, or form of causality (or family of forms of causality). Material, psychological and social types of interaction could therefore be distinguished (and compared) in a principled way.

The further distinction between causal dependence/interaction (between items) and categorial dependence (between levels) provides means with which to elaborate a stronger antireductionist vision.

Besides the usual kinds of basic interaction between phenomena of the same nature, the theory of levels enables us to single out upward forms of causality (from the lower level to the upper one). A theory of levels also enables us to address the problem of *downward* forms of causality (from the upper to the lower level). The point was first advanced by Donald Campbell some years ago (see e.g. his 1974 and 1990). Andersen et al. (2000) collects a series of studies on the theme.

The connection between the theory of levels and causality entails recognition that every level of reality may trigger its own causal chain. This may even be taken as a definition of level of reality: A level of reality is distinguished by its specific form of interactions. As a consequence, we thus have a criterion with which to distinguish among levels of reality and levels of description.

This acknowledgement also enables us to develop a theory able to accommodate different senses of causality (distinguishing at least among material, psychological and social causality). However, if the downward option is also available, the direct or elementary forms of causality should have corresponding non-elementary forms.

The theories that are obtained by multiplying universal frameworks of analysis by levels of reality do not pertain to general ontology. By adopting a terminology that has some currency in the field of ontologies as technologies, we may claim that they pertain to core ontologies, i.e. they provide (part of) the interface connecting general to domain ontologies.

1.8 Determinations

The two main distinctions within determination are the difference between determinables and determinates and the difference between intensive and extensive determinates. The former distinction is a generalization of the traditional distinction between genera and species, while the basic difference between extensive and intensive determinates is that the former always exist between two points and are based on the relation "more than", while the latter determinates may be punctiform in nature and are based on "different from" (the following section gives some details on the former distinction).

1.9 The Substance-Determination Relation

Both substances and determinations present individual and universal modes. "Socrates" is the expression used to refer to one single individual substance; "philosopher" refers to Socrates, Plato, and Aristotle (and many others besides). "Socrates" is the name of exactly one individual; "philosopher" is the expression for (possibly) many individuals. The same distinction applies to determinations. There are expressions referring to individual determinations (the unique, individual shade of red of this individual object) and expressions referring to possibly many individuals (red). Expressions that can be applied to possibly many individuals are called universals. As we have just seen, the distinction between individuals and universals applies to both substances and determinations. Universals come in levels of generality: "red" is an universal, and "colour" is as well an universal, but obviously "colour" is wider than (more general than) "red". The same applies to substance-universals: "dog" and "mammal" are both universals, but "mammal" is wider than "dog".

Two different structures arise from this basic framework. Firstly, the connection should be analyzed between individuals and universals pertaining to the same ontological type (i.e. individual and universal substances and individual and universal determinations). It emerges that within each type, the relation linking individual to their universals (to still wider universals) generates a taxonomy (as computer scientists are used to saying, it is an is-a relation: Lassie IS-A dog, a dog IS-A mammal).

Table 1.1 Summarizes these three positions

	Universals are:		
	Linguistic expressions	Concepts	Objects
Nominalism	Y	N	N
Conceptualism	Y	Y	N
Realism	Y	Y	Y

Secondly, the relation between substance and determination should be scrutinized. Some of the most demanding traditional problems in ontology arise from the analysis of this problem. The relation between determination and substance is traditionally called inherence (the usual direction goes from determinations to substances: the claim is that a determination inheres in a substance, not vice versa).

The problem concerns the ontological nature of universals. In this regard, three main positions are usually distinguished: nominalism, conceptualism and realism (Table 1.1).[17] Nominalists claim that universals are linguistic expressions; conceptualists claim that universals result from our cognitive capacities, from our ability to distinguish and categorize our experiences. In this sense universals are concepts. Needless to say, universals as concepts can be named by linguistic expressions; therefore conceptualism seems stronger than nominalism. Realists, finally, claim that universals exist independently of all forms of concrete existence. For the realists, there are both individual and universal objects.

One can then say that nominalists accept only universal expressions, while conceptualists accept both universals expressions and universals concepts, and realists accept universal expressions, universal concepts and universal objects.

1.10 Predication

Before concluding I should briefly mention at least one of the many fruitful interactions between categorial and formalized ontology. The most enlightening case is possibly provided by the study of the connections between universals and (formal) predication. The guiding question runs as follows: what is the ontological basis of (formal) predication? Not surprisingly, one may then answer: (1) linguistic expressions (nominalism); (2) concepts (conceptualism), or (3) (ideal) objects (realism).

The result is that each base requires a proper logical framework. I shall briefly compare them by considering the form of the comprehension principle most

[17] As a matter of fact, each of them comes in a number of different guises. The problem is particularly severe for conceptualism, especially as far as the difference between constructive and holistic concept generation is concerned. Realism too can be articulated in different ways. However, in this paper I shall not consider most of these complications.

appropriate to each position. The reason for considering comprehension principles is that they establish the general form of admissible axiom schemas valid for each framework. In order to articulate the analysis, a second order predicate framework is required. In what follows, I shall rely in particular on Cocchiarella (1989).[18]

1.10.1 Nominalism

According to nominalism universals are linguistic expressions, i.e. "beyond the predicate expressions that occur or can occur in language there are no universals" (Cocchiarella 1989, p. 256). Furthermore, nominalism is committed to extensionality, and the formal theory of predication associated with it is standard first-order predicate logic with identity, which can be extended to standard second order predicate logic with quantifiers interpreted substitutionally. The following is the appropriate comprehension principle for nominalism:

(CPn) $$(\exists F^n)(\forall x_1)...(\forall x_n)[F(x_1,...,x_n) \leftrightarrow \varphi]$$

where (1) φ is a wff in which F^n does not occur, (2) no bound predicate variable occurs in φ, (3) $x_1,...,x_n$ are among the distinct individual variables occurring free in φ. The meaning of condition (2) is that all the instances of φ are only first order wffs.

1.10.2 Conceptualism

The move towards conceptualism requires the idea that it is concepts that account for (mental) reference and predication. One can then distinguish between referential and predicable concepts. Furthermore, referential concepts are complementary to predicable concepts and saturate each other in the unity of a mental sentence. Conceptualism rejects the nominalistic thesis that universals are expressions. For conceptualism, instead, concepts are the semantic ground for the (correct or incorrect) application of predicate expressions.

Generally speaking, conceptualism admits only a potential infinity of concepts. For this reason, the comprehension principle for conceptualism is more restrictive than (CPn) and has the following structure:

(CPc) $$(\forall G_1)...(\forall G_k)(\exists F^n)(\forall x_1)...(\forall x_n)[F(x_1,...,x_n) \leftrightarrow \varphi]$$

where (1) φ is a *pure* second order wff, that is to say, one in which no non-logical constant occurs, (2) neither F^n nor the identity sign occur in φ; (3) φ is predicative in nominalism's purely grammatical sense (i.e., no predicate variable has a bound

[18] For a wider analysis see also Cocchiarella (1986, 1996, 2001).

occurrence in φ), and (4) $G_1, \ldots, G_k$ are all of the distinct predicate variables occurring free in φ, (5) $x_1, \ldots, x_n$ are the only distinct individual variables occurring free in ϕ.

Given (3) it is clear that every instance of (CPc) is as well an instance of (CPn). However, not every instance of (CPn) is also an instance of (CPc).

The following are some of the relevant differences between (CPn) and (CPc): (1) the initial quantifiers of (CPc) are not necessarily required by (CPn); (2) according to (CPn), but not (CPc), φ may contain the identity sign as well as any of the predicate constants of the language in question. Furthermore, nominalism interprets quantifiers substitutionally, while conceptualism interprets them referentially.

The only conceptualistic criterion for deciding whether a well formed formula $\varphi(x_1, \ldots, x_n)$ of an applied theory Σ is predicative is whether $(\exists F^n)(\forall x_1)\ldots(\forall x_n)[F(x_1, \ldots, x_n) \leftrightarrow \varphi]$ derives from Σ. The conceptualist theory of predicativity is then different from the nominalistic theory of predicativity. The reference to Σ is mandatory: in conceptualism, predicativity should always be relativized to an applied theory. Which means that for conceptualism no wff can be shown to be absolutely predicative.

For conceptualism, the formation of concepts proceeds through stages, from structurally simpler stages to structurally more complex ones. Later stages may reorganize the concepts developed by previous stages. Furthermore, previously formed concepts can become the contents of subsequent concepts. Holistic conceptualism considers such an iterated procedure of concept formation "by a new form of closure which is holistic with respect to all of the intermediate stages, i.e., by an idealized transition to a limit at which impredicative concept-formation is finally realized as a state of cognitive equilibrium."

The comprehension principle for holistic conceptualism, i.e. for both predicate and impredicative concepts is as follows:

(CP) $$(\exists F^n)(\forall x_1)\ldots(\forall x_n)[F(x_1, \ldots, x_n) \leftrightarrow \varphi]$$

where (1) ϕ is any wff in which F^n has no free occurrence and in which (2) $x_1, \ldots, x_n$ are free distinct individual variables. For holistic conceptualism, "any open wff is 'predicative' in the semantic sense of having a concept as the semantic grounds for its correct or incorrect application in that domain."

The main result arising from holistic conceptualism is that it is able to close the constructive gap between grammatical and semantical predicativity.

1.10.3 Realism

According to (logical) realism, properties and relations exist independently of all forms of concrete existence, i.e. they are ideal objects. Logical realism accepts a fully impredicative version of the comprehension principle (CP). Both logical realism and holistic conceptualism validate (CP). In this sense they are similar to each other. However, the nature of their universals and the ground each of them provides for validating (CP) are different. In short, the main problem for logical realism is that there is no way for it to provide an ontological (and semantic, for that matter) ground for sustaining the predicative-impredicative distinction.

1.11 From Commutative to Non-commutative Ontology

Ontology has been defined in Section 1.5 above as the theory of what is universal in reality. This is precisely the reason why ontology adopts the categorial stance. However, one should be aware of the three following problems.

Firstly, general ontology should include such recalcitrant phenomena as those pertaining to the quantum, the emotional and the artistic levels of reality. Not by chance, I have mentioned examples respectively pertaining to the material, the psychological and the social strata of reality. Each of them presents specific forms of complexity, which go well beyond customarily accepted types of complexity. A general ontology intrinsically unable to address any of the mentioned subjects is unsuitable as a true general ontology. According to the proposal outlined above, the theory of levels is the conceptual framework needed to address the over-complex domains mentioned.

Secondly, by their very nature, ontological categories do not admit exceptions. Ontological categories, interpreted as the categories of reality, are essential to their instances. For the reason just given, ontological categories are highly abstract. This is true of both general ontology and domain ontologies (say, biology, or works of arts).[19] To distinguish the categories of general ontology from the most general categories of any domain ontology, the latter will be called *core* categories. The framework described by this paper explicitly addresses this problem by distinguishing ground categories and universal theories on the one hand, from levels of reality on the other. Levels behave as interfaces that enrich pure universal ontological categories with groups of core categories. On adopting core categories, the ontological framework becomes richer and in this sense more flexible. The theory of levels of reality not only makes this transformation possible but also provides the means with which to avoid ad hoc solutions.

On the other hand – and this is the third issue – as soon as one descends from pure ontological categories (both as general and core categories) to the specific idiosyncrasies of individual instances, the latter may present irreducible features, either as variations or anomalies. Variations can be easily dealt with, because they have a categorial nature. On the other hand, anomalies, or what can be taken as exclusively individual features, are structurally more resistant to categorial analysis. However, the theory of levels is helpful even for these more difficult cases, because

[19] However, different types of domain ontologies should be distinguished, from categorially closed domains to ad-hoc ones. The claim in the main text applies mainly to the former types of domain ontologies. This problem warrants further analysis.

it helps set domain-specific *typed* forms of differentiation, that is to say, differentiations grounded in the nature of the items composing the level under analysis. As soon as ontological variations and anomalies are recognized (i.e., as soon as reality in its irreducible individuality is recognized) one has therefore moved from an exceptionless categorial framework to a framework admitting variations and anomalies. The theory of levels of reality plays an essential role in both the move from pure universal categories to core categories and from the latter to the variations and anomalies of their instances. Levels are a necessary condition for systematic analysis of these problems. The still unclear issue is the sufficient conditions, *if any*, for systematically grasp ontological individualities.

The three issues just sketched are only some of the reasons for the shift from a mainly abstract to a properly eidetic (or phenomenological) type of ontology. In this context, "abstract" refers to the extraction of categories by abstraction, i.e., by averaging over instances, while "eidetic" means making explicit the internal nature of any possible item of analysis. The issue is that abstraction can be used only when a collection of items is given,[20] while eidetic analysis can be conducted on any single item.[21] Otherwise stated, abstraction is derivative, i.e. secondary, over eidetic analyses.

References

Albertazzi, L. 2005. *Immanent realism. Introduction to Franz Brentano*. Dordrecht: Springer.

Andersen, P.B., C. Emmeche, N.O. Finnemann, and P.V. Christiansen. eds. 2000. *Downward causation. Minds, bodies and matter*. Aarhus: Aarhus University Press.

Bell, J. 2000. Continuity and the logic of perception. *Transcendent Philosophy* 1(2):1–7.

Bell, J. 2005. *The continuous and the infinitesimal in mathematics and philosophy*. Monza: Polimetrica.

Campbell, D.T. 1974. Downward causation in hierarchically organised biological systems. In *Studies in the philosophy of biology*, eds. F.J. Ayala, and T. Dobzhansky, 179–186. London: Macmillan.

Campbell, D.T. 1990. Levels of organization, downward causation, and the selection-theory approach to evolutionary epistemology. In *Theories of the evolution of knowing*, eds. G. Greenberg, and E. Tobach, 1–17. Mahwah, NJ: Erlbaum.

Cocchiarella, N. 1986. Logical investigations in predication theory and the problem of universals. Naples: Bibliopolis.

Cocchiarella, N. 1989. Philosophical perspectives on formal theories of predication. In *Handbook of philosophical logic*, eds. D. Gabbay, and F. Guenther, vol. IV, 254–326. Dordrecht: Reidel.

Cocchiarella, N. 1996. Conceptual realism as a formal ontology. In *Formal ontology*, eds. R. Poli, and P. Simons, 27–60. Dordrecht: Kluwer.

Cocchiarella, N. 2001. Logic and ontology. *Axiomathes*12:117–150.

Gnoli, C. and R. Poli 2004. Levels of reality and levels of representation. *Knowledge organization* 31(3):151–160.

Hartmann, N. 1935. *Zur Grundlegung der Ontologie*. Berlin: W. de Gruyter.

---

[20] About which one must ask *how* any given collection has been formed.

[21] It may be worth nothing that a similar movement from abstract to eidetic structures is taking place in contemporary mathematics under the heading "commutative vs. non commutative mathematics".

Hartmann, N. 1952. *The new ways of ontology*, Chicago.
Herre, H. (in preparation). "Ontology of Time in GFO". Onto-Med Report Nr. 9. Research Group Ontologies in Medicine (Onto-Med), Leipzig University.
Koenderink, J.J. and A.J. van Doorn. 2001. Pictorial space. In *Looking into pictures: an interdisciplinary approach to pictorial space*, eds. H. Hecht, R. Schwartz, and M. Atherton, 239–299. Cambridge, MA: The MIT Press.
Koestler, A. 1967. *The ghost in the machine*, 1990 reprint edition. London: Penguin Group.
Lawvere, W. 1969. Adjointness in foundations. *Dialectica* 23:281–296.
Luhmann, N. 1995, *Social systems*. Stanford: Stanford University Press.
Poli, R. 1996a. *Res, ens*, and *aliquid*. In *Formal ontology*, eds. R. Poli, and P. Simons, 1–26. Dordrecht: Kluwer.
Poli, R. 1996b. Ontology for knowledge organization. In *Knowledge organization and change*, ed. R. Green, 313–319. Frankfurt: Indeks.
Poli, R. 1998. Levels. *Axiomathes* 9(1–2):197–211.
Poli, R. 2001a. The basic problem of the theory of levels of reality. *Axiomathes* 12(3–4):261–283.
Poli, R. 2001b. *Alwis. Ontology for knowledge engineers*. PhD Thesis, Utrecht.
Poli, R. 2001c. Foreword. *Axiomathes* 12(1–2):5–9.
Poli, R. 2001d. Special issue on Hartmann, *Axiomathes* 12:3–4.
Poli, R. 2002. Ontological methodology. *International Journal of Human-Computer Studies* 56:639–664.
Poli, R. 2003. Descriptive, formal and formalized ontologies. In *Husserl's logical investigations reconsidered*, ed. D. Fisette, 193–210. Dordrecht: Kluwer.
Poli, R. 2004, Approaching Brentano's theory of categories. In *Phenomenology and Analysis. Essays in Central European philosophy*, eds. A. Chrudzimski, and W. Huemer, 285–321. Frankfurt: Ontos Verlag.
Poli, R. 2006a. Levels of reality and the psychological stratum. *Revue Internationale de Philosophie* 61(2): 163–180
Poli, R. 2006b. First steps in experimental phenomenology. In *Artificial cognition systems*, eds. A. Loula, R. Gudwin, and J. Queiroz, 358–386. Hersey, PA: Idea Group Publishing.
Rijkhoff, J. 2002. *The noun phrase*. Oxford: Oxford University Press.
Rosenthal, V. 2004. Microgenesis, immediate experience and visual processes in reading. In *Seeing, thinking, and knowing*, ed. A. Carsetti, 221–243. Dordrecht: Kluwer.
Seibt, J. 2004. Free process theory: Towards a typology of occurrings. *Axiomathes* 14:23–5.
Ushenko, A.P. 1958. *The field theory of meaning*. Ann Arbor: University of Michigan Press.
van Gelder, T. and R.F. Port. 1995. It's about time: An overview of the dynamical approach to cognition. In *Mind as motion*, eds. R.F. Port, and T. van Gelder, 1–43. Cambridge, MA; London: MIT Press.
Werkmeister, W. 1990. *Nicolai Hartmann's new ontology*. Tallahassee, FL: Florida State University.

Chapter 2
Particulars

Johanna Seibt

As any other field of inquiry, ontological research is guided by fundamental premises pertaining to method and content. One of the content-related premises, and arguably the most fundamental and decisive one, consists in the claim that particulars are ontologically 'prior' in two senses of the term. They are either taken to be the natural choice for the type of *basic entities*, i.e., entities that are in their being and their identity so straightforwardly intelligible that ontological definitions ideally should be formulated only in terms of (structures, classes, or mereological relationships) of such entities. Alternatively, particulars are sometimes considered the prior *object of ontological investigation*, since in cognition and action we focus on things, it is claimed, which are particulars par excellence.

Let us call the first sort of commitment, i.e., the thesis that particulars are primary *explanantia*, 'foundational particularism' and the second sort of commitment, i.e., the thesis that particulars are primary ontological *explananda*, 'target particularism'. The majority of contemporary ontologists endorse either foundational particularism or target particularism. In fact, particularism is not the only unreflected presupposition operative in current ontological theory construction. Particularism is part of a more comprehensive network of assumptions that twentieth century ontology has imported from the ontological tradition by adopting the semantic standard interpretation of predicate logic, its main analytical tool. Some of these traditional assumptions have been challenged, opening the path to so-called 'revisionary' ontologies, but by and large the premises of the ontological tradition operate like the constraints of a Kuhnian research paradigm, restricting the domain of legitimate problems and the space of legitimate solutions. Elsewhere I have called this network of unreflected presuppositions 'the myth of substance' or 'the substance paradigm,' and I have shown in which ways these hidden premises of (a large part of) the contemporary debate are hampering ontological theory construction. Put in a somewhat simplified fashion, it can be shown that at least three of the central ontological questions: the problem of individuation, the problem of universals, and the problem

J. Seibt (✉)
Department of Philosophy, University of Aarhus, Aarhus C, Denmark
e-mail: filseibt@hum.au.dk

R. Poli, J. Seibt (eds.), *Theory and Applications of Ontology: Philosophical Perspectives*, DOI 10.1007/978-90-481-8845-1_2,

of persistence, receive most of their dilemmatic character from the presuppositions of the substance paradigm – without these presuppositions, these questions are not 'problems' but tasks with a wide range of alternative solutions.[1]

In the following I will discuss notions of particularity and investigate the viability of foundational particularism; certain implications for target particularism will become apparent but I will not take issue here with this aspect of the traditional methodological bias for the particular.[2] I will show that foundational particularism is a highly problematic, if not untenable, position as long as it is combined with certain premises of the myth of substance, as the current research paradigm has it. In Section 2.1 I offer a brief reconstruction of the methodology of analytical ontology. In Section 2.2 I list some core elements of the substance paradigm and illustrate in which ways the standard interpretation of predicate logic surreptitiously has hampered the innovative efforts of the early analytical ontologists, playing into the hands of the myth of substance. In Sections 2.3 and 2.4 I discuss the two most commonly used sorts of basic particulars, namely, so-called 'bare particulars' and 'tropes'. As shall become apparent, current accounts of particulars are thwarted with difficulties precisely to the extent to which they incorporate the constructional principles of the substance paradigm. Thus in conclusion I suggest that the notion of particularity should be separated from the network of constructional principles in which it has been traditionally embedded, or, alternatively and preferably in my view, be replaced with a modally weakened version of the term that should better be called 'contingent uniqueness'.

2.1 Ontology – the Theory of Categorial Inference

Twentieth century ontological research has been methodologically highly diversified, more, in fact, than ever before, and one of the aims of this volume is to document this methodological breadth. My focus here is on the method of mainstream analytical ontology, which begins with R. Carnap's idea – formulated in the early 1920s – of using modern logic for the precise description of the structure of denotational domains. This program – in its various adaptations and modifications by W.v.O. Quine, N. Goodman, and W. Sellars took centerstage in American philosophy during the 1940–1950s, and continuously grew more sophisticated with respect to both its formal resources and the target of its reconstructive efforts, especially in interaction with the development of philosophical logic and formal semantics since the 1970s. Since that time analytical ontologists have been in the comfortable position to apply a 'standard methodology' and to swim with the mainstream instead of engaging in foundational methodological reflections. However, as shall become apparent in the course of this paper, it is questionable whether contemporary ontology can afford such methodological complacency typical of what

[1] Cf. e.g., Seibt 1990, 1995, 1996a, 1997b, 2000a, 2005, 2007.

[2] On this see in particular Seibt 2004a, b and 2008.

T. Kuhn called ‘normal science’. I will argue here that this is not so, and this section and the following will offer some methodological reflections that prepare the general ground for specific arguments to follow. Here I begin with a reconstruction of the most general methodological commitments of analytical ontology as theory of categorial inference, before turning to more specific and problematic additions in Section 2.2.

According to the analytical mainstream the task of ontology is to explore various ways of structuring the referential domain of a language or theory L. The entities in the referential domain of L are nowadays often called the ‘truthmakers’. The term ‘truthmaker,’ originating from Husserl, was brought again into currency to denote any kind of entity ‘in virtue of which sentences and/or propositions are true’, e.g., objects, properties, events, states of affairs; it contrasts with the familiar notion of a ‘truth-bearer’, which is any kind of entity that can be said to be true or false, e.g., a sentence or proposition.[3] The contrast between truth-makers and truth-bearers also signals – and that I consider to be the decisive theoretical advancement of Carnap’s program – that the ontological investigation of truthmakers can be undertaken quite independently of any metaphysical investigation into the nature of truth and the status of ‘reality’ as discovered or constructed.[4]

In a pithy formulation, ontology might be thus called ‘the theory of truthmakers.’ More precisely, an ontological theory has the form of the quadruple $<M, T_M, f, L>$: it specifies an assignment f which correlates the elements of a class *L* of true (i.e., taken as true) L-sentences with structures of the domain of interpretation M as described by a domain theory T_M.[5] T_M describes simple and complex ontological correlates for sentences and parts of sentences of L. Strictly speaking, truthmakers are the ontological correlates of whole sentences of L, but to simplify terminology let ‘truthmaker’ refer to not only to ontological correlates of true L-sentences but also to ontological correlates of their components. The assignment function f, which is rarely explicitly defined, abides by the following requirements.

First, the assignment should be such that it can be used to explain, in terms of suitable structural descriptions of the domain of a language L, why L-speakers are justified in drawing material inferences of a certain type. These inferences, which I call *categorial inferences*, define the meaning of the ‘ultimate *genera* terms’ of L (e.g., ‘thing,’ ‘property,’ ‘person’ etc.). Mostly the justification at issue takes the form of an entailment from the definition of the truthmaker for an L-sentence S to

---

[3] Cf. Mulligan, et al. 1984, p. 287.

[4] For historical and systematic reconstruction of Carnap’s influence on analytical ontology cf. e.g., Seibt 1996, 1997c.

[5] Unlike semantical theories, ontologies are not developed specifically for *one* language (conceptual scheme) only but aspire to articulate structures of the world as viewed from *any* language (conceptual scheme). Elsewhere (e.g., Seibt 2000b) I discuss the possible scope of ontological theories, given the possibility of ontological and linguistic relativity, and the relationship of language and conceptual schemes. Here the variable ‘L’ should simply be read as ‘L or any language functionally equivalent to L’ and expressions such as ‘our concept C’ should be read as ‘the concept C consisting in the inferential role R of L or functional equivalents of R in other languages.’

the inferences licensed by S in L. That is, the domain theory provides definitions for basic types of entities (categories) in terms of certain features (category features); the inferences licensed by a sentence S are justified if they can be shown to follow from the category features of the truthmakers of S. For example, consider the English sentences:

[1] This is an aggressive dog.
[2] This is a 1970s color.
[3] This is an exciting journey we are on right now.

Sentence [1] licenses the inference:

[4] The dog to the left of this dog is not identical with this dog.

but [2] does not license the interference analogous to [4]:

[5] The color to the left of this color is not identical with this color.

Furthermore, sentence [3] licenses [6]:

[6] Whatever I will see of this journey in five minutes from now will not be identical with this journey.

while sentence [1] fails to entail the interference analogous to [6]:

[7] Whatever I will see of this dog in five minutes from now will not be identical to this dog.

That [1] licenses [3] has traditionally been explained by the fact that the ontological correlate (truthmaker) of the demonstrative in [1] is a substance, which has the category feature of particularity, i.e., it cannot occur in two places at the same time, and thus entails [3]. In contrast, in order to explain why [2] does not entail [5], the ontological correlate of the demonstrative in [2] traditionally has been described as an attribute, an 'universal' or 'repeatable' entity that may – in some fashion or other – 'occur multiply' in space at the same time. Similarly, to explain that [1] does not licence [7], ontologists determined that the category substance not only has the category feature of particularity, but in addition also the category feature of persistence (later called 'endurance') or identity through time understood as being wholly present at any moment in time at which the substance exists.

Second, ontological interpretations are restricted by the desideratum that the number of explanantia, i.e., the number of categories and category features, should be kept at a minimum. This is Occam's well-known 'principle of parsimony,' whose full rationale and justification comes into view only if ontology is understood as an explanatory theory, as I am suggesting here.

Third, given that ontology is an explanatory theory, the basic categories in the domain theory T_M must be chosen according to their explanatory potential. Ontological categories, as much as theoretical concepts in science need a *model* to serve their explanatory function. In physics, water current or an ideal spring serve as cognitive models for the theoretical entities of an electrical current or a harmonic oscillator, respectively. Similarly, in ontology the notion of a substance is frequently introduced by way of comparing it to a thing, monads are compared to minds, or

Whiteheadian occasions are compared to events. The models of ontology stand in a slightly different relationship to the theoretical terms they elucidate, however. In the sciences the relationship between theoretical term and cognitive model is one of analogical illustration – there are structural similarities between the empirical properties of the model and the theoretical properties of the theoretical entity, but the model is not an instance of the kind of entity introduced by the theoretical term. In contrast, the models of a theoretical entity in ontology are specific instances of the category or entity type they are to elucidate and literally possess many (though not all) features of that category. The model must be familiar to L-speakers or, as I say, *founded* in their agentive experience.[6] Only if T_M operates with founded categories, L-speakers will be able to *understand* what kind of entities make their true sentences true, and only then L-speakers can accept the T_M-descriptions of such entities as explanations for why they are justified in entertaining certain concepts, i.e., in drawing the associated inferences.

In short, then, the *data* of an ontology are patterns of categorial inferences determining the inferential role of the ultimate genera terms of L; the *task* of an ontology is to offer structural descriptions of truthmakers for L-sentences that involve certain ultimate *genera* terms of L (and, optionally, more specific kind terms of L belonging to these *genera* in L); and the *goal* of an ontology is to operate with structural descriptions that use only founded categories, i.e., that L-speakers can accept as a *plausible* description of what it is that makes their sentences true.

So far my reconstruction of the general methodology of mainstream analytical ontology; even though the terminology may be partly unfamiliar, I trust that in content the reconstruction is an uncontroversial description of the actual procedure of analytical ontologists. Let us now look at some of the additional assumptions that standardly enter into the concrete implementation of this methodology.

2.2 The Myth of Substance and the 'Dirty Hands' of Logic

The explanatory tasks of ontology introduce a problematic psychological element into theory choice in ontology: the greater the familiarity of the model of an ontological entity (category), the greater the latter's initial plausibility. Whether the initial plausibility of a category is ultimately warranted depends on whether it can be used to formulate coherent structural descriptions of truthmakers. But even if the relevant theory of truthmakers displays obvious short-comings, the initial plausibility of the

---

[6]This is a new way to read the Carnapian postulate of foundedness in the *Aufbau*, for further details on the methodological claims sketched here see Seibt 1997b and 2000b. The 'model' of the ontological category is denoted by an *ulimate genera* term of L (e.g., of English). One of the primary difficulties for theories of tropes (or 'moments') consists in the fact that the category 'trope' lacks a model in this sense – in English there is no term expressing the ultimate genus of 'this red' versus 'that red.' This lacuna is covered up by the tropist's quick move to technical jargon like 'property instances' or 'exemplifications of attributes,' which does not 'found' the category in the required sense.

category will incline researchers to try and fix the specifics of the theory rather than to abandon the category altogether.

The history of Western ontology – in Hegel's quip 'the tendency towards substance' – provides a striking illustration of this principle. Aristotle's search for a suitable conception of 'ousia' centered on an investigation of our reasoning about material things, non-living and living. In this way denotations of the kind term 'thing' became the model of the theoretical entity Aristotle aimed to introduce. Given the central practical significance of things in our everyday interactions, the model for ousia endowed the postulated theoretical entity substance with very high initial plausibility. Aristotle famously experimented with various notions ousia which he assigned various sets of category features. In one of its characterizations ousia was said to be a particular, persistent, the locus of change, countable or one of its kind, non-instantiable, independent, discrete, simple, unified.[7] This version of the category was later translated as 'substance' which turned out to be incoherent. But instead of abandoning the category of substance metaphysicians tinkered with the specifics of a theory of truthmakers based on substances.

More precisely, the history of Western ontology since Aristotle is striking in three regards. First, the term 'substance' is faithfully traded and consistently applied as label for the most basic ontological category in an ontological domain theory. Second, the intensional and extensional definitions of the category 'substance', i.e., its definitions in terms of lists of category features or in terms of paradigmatic instances, differ so widely that there is no 'least set of common denominators' or intersection of extensions of all or even only the main historical notions of substance. To put it poignantly, there is 'no substance to the notion of substance.'[8] (Facile references to 'the traditional notion of substance' or 'substances in the old sense', as these can often be found in recent texts, are thus strictly speaking semantically empty if the term is not further historically contextualized). Third, while there is no notion of substance common to all substance ontologies, there are certain restrictions on how substance-ontological domain theories are constructed. As I have shown elsewhere, there are around 20 characteristic principles about linkages between category features that substance ontologists typically employ in the construction of their domain theories. As I shall elaborate presently, the core elements of this set of principles establish in combination the ontological primacy of concrete individual particulars.

---

[7]Cf. Aristotle *Metaphysics* 1042a34, *Physics* 200b33, *Metaphysics* 1038b35f, ibid. 1017b16ff, *Categories* 2a13ff, *Metaphysics* 1037b1ff, *Categories* 3b33, *Metaphysics* 1041a4f, and ibid. 1041b11ff, respectively.

[8]Cf. Seibt 1990, cf. also Stegmaier 1977, who summarizes the situation in similar terms. The lack of internal semantic integration of the historical notions of substance is both documented and obscured in classical and more recent studies (e.g., by L. Prat, B. Bauch, E. Cassirer, R. Jolivet, J. Hessen, M. Latzerowitz, A. Reck. D. Hamlyn, A. Leschbrand, B. Singer, T. Scaltsas), which typically retreat to a purely inventatory approach. Rosenkrantz/Hoffmann 1991 and Simons 1994 offer definitions of independent particulars called 'substance' without, however, discussing whether the definiendum is representative for the notion of substance in a wider historical perspective.

Thus, even though not every historical definition of substance explicitly stipulates that substances are particulars, particularism (both in the sense of foundational and of target particularism) is nevertheless an effect of the longstanding 'tendency towards substance' since it is implied by traditional domain principles that have been operative in Western ontology since Aristotle. These principles form a research paradigm in the Kuhnian sense: they direct the collection and the interpretation of the data, and restrict the space of legitimate problems and solutions. In fact, since most of these traditional assumptions have sunk deeply into the systematic sediment of ontological debate and appear nowadays as 'laws of thoughts' that do not need further reflection, we may speak not only of a 'substance paradigm' but even of a theoretical 'myth' akin to the 'myth of the ghost in the machine' or the 'myth of given': the 'myth of substance.'[9]

If particularism is part and parcel of the myth of substance, any discussion of particularism and particulars should aim, first, to identify those aspects of current accounts of particulars that are not implied by the notion of particularity itself but are dispensable additions due to the presuppositions of the substance paradigm; in a second step one should then investigate to what extent these additional aspects hamper the formulation of a coherent conception of a particular. This is what I aim to do in this contribution. Let me thus first highlight some of the principles of the traditional systematic embedding of the notion of particularity, before I trace out the damaging effects of these additional principles for some current accounts of particulars.

The notion of particularity as such is rather easily determined: it is a category feature that applies to various entity types (object, event, property, relation, mode etc.) and expresses a form of uniqueness that contrasts with generality. There are two ways to formulate such uniqueness:

Particularity-1: Something is particular if by necessity it occurs in one spatiotemporal location only.[10]

Particularity-2: Something is particular if by necessity it occurs in one entity only.[11]

The second definition of particularity is obviously wider than the first, since the entity in which the candidate particular is said to occur might exist as whole at several points in time, or it might be spatially scattered at some time t. Nevertheless,

---

[9]Cf. Seibt 1990, 1996a, 1996c, 2005.

[10]Throughout this essay I will use the notion of a spatiotemporal location or region not in the sense of relativity theory but more generally to denote the pair of a spatial region and a certain temporal period; something occurs in the spatiotemporal region $r = \langle S, T \rangle$ if it occupies the spatial region S during T. Here and hereafter I simply speak of a 'location', with the understanding that such locations are extended regions that are connected (possibly multiply connected, i.e., containing holes).

[11]The predicate 'x occurs in y' is here used as a placeholder for a variety of more specific ontological relations such as spatiotemporal inclusion, exemplification, constitution, parthood, containment in the ontological assay, etc.

ontologists use both definitions interchangeably, as we shall see below, and thus apparently proceed from two hidden assumptions. The two definitions of particularity are co-extensional only if one adopts (a) an a-temporal perspective and (b) considers only spatially connected ('unified') entities. The first of these restrictions reflects the traditional bias against change and becoming, the idea that true being is the domain of the eternal, which has been prevalent in Western metaphysics and ontology since Parmenides onwards. The second restriction is, in fact, one of the core elements of the substance paradigm or myth of substance and can be formulated as a linkage between the category features of 'individuality' and 'unity':

(P1) *Principle of Unity*: All concrete individuals are unified.

The precise sense of the envisaged unification or unity is notoriously a matter of debate, but one underlying shared intuition is clearly that the relevant sense of unity should imply that individuals occur in topologically connected regions.

Principle (P1) is one of about 20 principles that derive from linkages between category features introduced by Aristotle's investigations into the notion of ousia. Here are eight further principles creating a rich systematic embedding of the notion of particularity.

(P2) *Principle of Concreteness:* All particulars are concrete.
(P3) *Principle of Independence*: All particulars are independent.
(P4) *Principle of Individuality*: All and only concrete particulars are individuals.
(P5) *Principle of Countability:* All (and only) individuals are countable.
(P6) *Principle of Determinateness*: All and only individuals are fully determinate.
(P7) *Principle of Subjecthood*: The properties that are truly attributed to an entity are attributed to the ontological factor that individuates the entity.
(P8) *Principle of Categorial Dualism*: Ontological structures consist of (simple and complex) particular entities or (simple and complex) universal or multiply occurrent entities, or combinations of both.
(P9) *Principle of Endurance*: All concrete individuals are identical through time; they do not have temporal parts.[12]

This is, I submit, the characteristic systematic context of the notion of particularity in the Western ontological tradition. Of course, there are many different ways to formulate the relevant linkage principles, some less and some more redundant in inferential regards, and one might question the content of the principles as long as

[12]For other examples and the full list of characteristic Aristotelian presuppositions to be found in the ontological tradition and the contemporary debate see Seibt 1990, 1995, 1996a, 1997b, 2005, 2007. Note that the simple version of (P2), the principle of particularism: all and only individuals are particulars, has been championed in the substance-ontological tradition but it seems not by Aristotle himself (cf. Gill 1994).

the meaning of the linked category features is not further specified. But precisely in the given vague formulation working ontologists will recognize in (P1) through (P9) some of the 'core intuitions' of their discipline. In fact, in the course of the historical hegemony of the substance-ontological tradition principles like (P1) through (P9) gradually received the status of 'laws of thought' that could also serve as constraints for the task of finding precise definitions for the category features mentioned in (P1) through (P9).

Taken in combination principles (P1) through (P9) generate a concept of particularity that hereafter I shall call 'substantial particularity', contrasting the latter with 'particularity *per se*' or necessary uniqueness as defined above in 'Particularity-1'. Substantial particulars are unique, concrete, fully determinate individuals that are unified, persisting subjects. As I shall argue below, such a category is, prima facie at least, multiply incoherent and the fact that, to the present day and with few exceptions only, ontologists operate with the notion of substantial particularity can only count as a striking illustration of Bergson's observation that 'the human mind has the tendency to consider the concept it uses most frequently to be the clearest.'

Most striking in this regard is the fact that even though the *notion* of substance is no longer popular, the myth of substance is alive and well in the very tools that analytical ontology has introduced in the twentieth century to rid metaphysical research from murky principles and chase shadowy assumptions into the light of reason. For instance, as W. Sellars noted, our default reading of the existential quantifier as 'there is *an* x' clandestinely introduces a problematic restriction to countable items; 'in logic', he concluded, 'we come always with dirty hands.'[13] In fact, not only countability is a built-in feature of individuals in our standard interpretation of predicate logic, but also assumptions about linkages between individuality, identity, particularity, unity, and concreteness. Consider the following passages from Quine's *Methods of Logic*. Quine reminds us that 'despite its simplicity, identity invites confusion'[14] and without further ado equates identity and sameness:

> [8] *Identity* is such a simple and fundamental idea that it is hard to explain otherwise than through mere synonyms. To say that x and y are identical is to say that they are the *same* thing.[15]

He continues to explain that the essential function of identity statements is to establish informative redundancies among (complex) names.

> [9] For the truth of a statement of identity it is necessary only that '=' appear between names of the same objects. (...) If our language were so perfect a copy of its subject matter that each thing had but one name, then statements of identity would indeed be useless.[16]

---

[13]Sellars 1960, p. 502. See also Puntel's criticism of the "object ontological dogma" of analytical ontology in Puntel 1990, 1993.

[14]Quine 1952, p. 208.

[15]Op. cit.

[16]Op. cit. p. 209.

Finally, Quine translates quantified identity statements, e.g. '(x)(y)(x is a god . y is a god.→.x=y),' as numerical statements, e.g., 'There is one god at most.'[17] Altogether these – uncommented – transitions yield the following result. The notion of identity to be introduced is the notion of sameness *simpliciter*; it is not the relation 'x is the same substance or physical object as y' but rather the supra-categorial or transcendental (in the scholastic sense) notion of sameness that is the target here.[18] And yet, the subsequent elucidations of this general relation of sameness introduce conceptual linkages that are unproblematic only if such a restriction to substances or physical objects is already in place. For in [9] the relation of sameness is said, without further explanation, to be functionally exhausted in the indication of coreference of *names*, i.e., expressions that denote particular 'objects', and so reveals that all and only particular entities stand in the relation of sameness. Moreover, in the final elucidation, the relation of sameness is read as the relation of numerical oneness, which has the effect that all and only countable and unified entities stand in the relation of sameness. Altogether, then, entities standing in the relation of sameness are said to be countable particulars – identity in the sense of sameness is effectively linked to countability, unification, and particularity, just as principles (P1) through (P5) prescribe.

In sum, contemporary ontological inquiry is still profoundly influenced by the theoretical presuppositions of the traditional research paradigm in ontology, which I call the substance paradigm or, more polemically, the myth of substance. Since these presuppositions have entered the standard readings of logical constants, i.e., the existential quantifier and the identity sign, the myth of substance is written into the formal tool of analysis most commonly used by contemporary ontologists. The default interpretation of logical individual constants and variables are entities that are 'substantial particulars' in the sense defined above: they are concrete, unified, countable, individual, enduring, independent, and determinate entities that are 'particulars-per-se', i.e., that have exactly one spatial occurrence at any point in time at which they exist. In the following section I will now investigate whether the category of a 'substantial particular' at all forms a coherent notion – as I shall argue, the longstanding conviction that 'particular objects' or 'substances' are an unproblematic type of basic entities is quite unfounded.

2.3 Particulars and the Debate About Individuality

References to 'particulars' are ubiquitous in ontological discussion but there are two main areas of debate that anchor the term systematically: the debate about universals and the debate about individuality or identity. Both of these debates, in past and current versions, are infused with the presuppositions of the myth of substance

[17] Op. cit. p. 211.

[18] The expression 'thing' occurring in [8] is supposed to have the wide reading as 'item' or 'entity', it is not to carry any categorial restrictions to physical things.

and thus, by default, references to 'particulars' invoke the notion of what I called above 'substantial particulars', i.e., entities that are not only necessarily unique (particular-per-se) but also unified, concrete, individual, independent, determinate, and enduring logical subjects, in accordance with (P1) through (P9) above.

This is most palpable perhaps in the debate about universals with its typical association of the general and the abstract. Often the problem at issue is couched in terms of an exclusive theoretical alternative: 'do we need universals, i.e., abstract and general entities, in addition to concrete particulars, in order to make sense of the fact that the same predicate can be truthfully applied to several things?' Such a set-up of the problem of universals immediately restricts the solution space, in accordance with (P8), (P6) and (P4). If particulars and universals are the only categories to choose from, and if particulars are 'apriori' taken to be concrete and determinate, then the additional category to be taken into consideration must consist of abstract and determinable or general entities. Aristotle himself postulated general entities called 'forms' that were *concrete* repeatables, but in the subsequent scholastic discussion the option of operating with concrete repeatables receded into the background; the dispute between 'realists' and 'nominalists' polarized the debate into the opposition between those supporting and those denying the existence of universals that by default were taken to be general and abstract. The traditional linkage between the general and the abstract was further reinforced by the contemporary revival of the debate about universals in the first half of the twentieth century, when metalogical results and arguments from the discussion about the foundations of mathematics (questionable status of the axiom of choice, incompleteness of second order theories etc.) were used to make a case for or against interpreting predicate constants in terms of abstract entities such as classes or functions.

The debate about individuality on the other hand is less palpably biased in its very set-up, but it provides the richest material for an analysis and critical discussion of traditional presuppositions in the current use of the term 'particular'. The classic expository gambit for postulating 'particulars' is a pointer to violations of Leibniz' so-called 'principle of the identity of indiscernibles'. Leibniz assumed that any difference between 'substances' is not 'solo numero' but based on descriptive features–if substances are distinct, there is at least one attribute that is had by one but not by the other. In this formulation the principle pertains to substances and attributes and thus is a *prescriptive* principle governing the domain of ontological interpretation. In an alternative formulation by means of 'semantic ascent', the principle says that if we can truly ascribe the same predicates to two names, then these names are coreferential. In this formulation the principle makes a *descriptive* claim about the truth-conditions of L-sentences, i.e., about the *data* that an ontological theory must try to accommodate. The second reading dominates in the contemporary debate and thus it shall be adopted here.[19] If the Leibniz principle holds, the

---

[19]The two readings are frequently conflated and little attention has been paid to the fact that in addition the principle may be read either as a principle of individuation (stating conditions of distinctness) or of numerical identity (stating conditions of plurality), cf. Seibt 1996a.

ontological correlate for the *ultima genera* L-term 'thing' or 'object' could make do with nothing else but a 'bundle' of attributes (properties, relations), i.e., with a suitable collection of those general entities that are the ontological correlates of our common talk about features. If the Leibniz principle fails, i.e., if there are cases of numerical distinctness or two-ness without descriptive difference, then the ontological correlate of an object must include at least one additional ontological constituent besides general entities (otherwise the data of an ontological theory of things or objects, i.e., the inferential role of the common sense term 'thing' or 'object', would not be adequately accounted for). Consider the following passage:

> [10] 'How shall we define the diversity which makes us count objects as two in a census?' We may put the same problem in words that look different, e.g., 'What is meant by' a particular'?' or 'What sorts of objects can have proper names?'[20]

The author of this passage in effect declares that particulars are to account for (i) numerical difference as well as (ii) distinctness (diversity), and that particulars are the ontological correlates of proper names, assigning them thus (iii) the role of logical subjects (cf. P4, P5, P7 above). The following passage connects individuality and particularity-per-se or uniqueness as in (P4) above:

> [11] To be an individual is to be at a place at a time...thus the individuality or uniquess of individuals is ensured... This guarantees the genuine individuality of most of what we should ordinarily call 'individuals.'[21]

In fact, contributions in the debate about the Leibniz principle typically connect in their initial characterizations of the problem (i) numerical identity ('oneness,' 'numerical distinctness', 'numerical difference'), (ii) individuality, ('difference', 'thisness' (versus 'thatness')) and (iii) logical subjecthood ('thisness' (versus 'suchness')), compare [12] through [15]:

> [12] "A: ...*Different* things have at least one property not in common. Thus, different things must be discernible; and hence, by contraposition, indiscernible things must be identical. Q.E.D.
> B: ...Do you claim to have proved that *two* things having all their properties in common are identical?
> A: Exactly."[22]
> [13] "Assume that there are *two* things both of which have the same non-relational characters. What accounts for their being (numerically) *different*? That is the problem of individuation. To grasp it as well as to solve it, one must attend to the uses of 'same' and 'different.'...[The problem of individuation is the problem of] how to account for the *thisness* of *this*."[23]
> [14] [The proponent of the Leibniz Principle] "doubts whether there can be any sense in talking of a *plurality* of objects unless it is a way of talking about differences of properties...If [a certain rule] is valid, the principle of the identity indiscernibles becomes analytic;

---

[20] Russell 1911 (1984), p.

[21] Stove 1921 (1984), p. 183.

[22] Black 1952 (1976), p. 282, emphasis supplied.

[23] Allaire 1965 (1984), pp. 305 and 309.

for it will then be necessarily true that there is no *difference* between things that cannot represented as a difference between properties."[24]

[15] [The question at issue in the Leibniz Principle is whether] "thisnesses are primitive and nonqualitative... In order to establish the distinctness of *thisnessses* from all suchnesses, therefore, one might try exhibit possible cases in which *two* things would possess all the same suchnesses, but with different thisnesses."[25]

The authors of these quotations take themselves to explicate basic and uncontroversial intuitions, but in effect endorse powerful traditional principles pertaining to the linkages of category features. To my knowledge only one author protested against the habitual identification of the explanatory tasks of accounting for individuality qua subjecthood and accounting for numerical plurality:

[16] *Nous-A* and *Nous-B* [two copies of a certain issue of *Nous*] are two individuals. Each one is an individual. Even if the other disappeared, *each* one is an individual, a possessor of properties, whether qualities or not, and itself not a property...The distinctness or diversity that creates a problem about individuality is the contrast between individuals and non-individuals, and it has *nothing* to do with a plurality of individuals.[26]

Even more problematic, however, might be the fact that contributors to the debate about individuality commonly assume that 'one' and 'the same' of re-identification is 'one and the same'.[27] But what matters most for present purposes, as witnessed by the passages just quoted, contributors to the debate about individuality presuppose that a particular or necessarily unique entity can and should fulfill also a number of additional explanatory roles. A particular is an ontological constituent that can and should also serve as the 'individuator' of a thing, as logical subject for what we predicate of a thing, should help us to explain in which sense the features of a thing depend on the thing but not vice versa, etc. But as I will argue now, it is questionable whether any one constituent could fulfill all these explanatory roles at once.

2.3.1 The Bare Particular Theory

Let us assume, then, in line with the debate about individuality, (i) that there are scenarios with two or more objects with exactly the same descriptive features, (ii) that these cases are violations of the Leibniz Principle, and (iii) that these cases therefore imply that the ontological correlate of an object must contain not only general entities but also a constituent warranting necessary uniqueness and distinctness.

[17] [One way] of solving the problem of individuation is to make the further constituent a *bare particular*. This notion...has two parts. Bare particulars neither are nor have natures. Any two of them, therefore, are not intrinsically but only numerically different. That is their

---

[24] Ayer 1953 (1976), p. 264, emphasis supplied.

[25] Adams 1979, pp. 10 and 12; emphasis supplied.

[26] Castañeda 1989, p. 132.

[27] See Seibt 1996a.

> bareness. It is [impossible in the sense of yielding an ill-formed ontological statement] for a bare particular to be 'in' more than one ordinary thing. That is their particularity. . .....A bare particular is a mere individuator.[28]

The bare particular theory has a venerable history in similar stipulations of constituents without qualitative determinations, such as Aristotle's (report on a) notion of bare matter, Aquinas' *materia signata*, or Locke's 'unknown support'. But the bare particular theory is more advanced in its formulation and thus the historical dialectics repeats itself only to some extent. Critics of bare particulars target the 'bareness' of the postulated particular constituents with two sorts of objections. The first objection is epistemological: bare particulars are ontological components which are either empirically inaccessible or even unknowable. Given that epistemological complaints of this kind are not relevant in ontology – even though they might matter in metaphysics – I will not take them into account here.[29] The second objection is semantical: bare particulars amount to an "obscure metaphysical commitment,"[30] or even to outright "absurdity,"[31] since the very concept is unsound. These are the criticisms I will consider here and fortify with a new argument.

Let us reconstruct the two basic arguments in favor of particular individuators in greater detail. The first argument has two strands, one in which the Leibniz Principle is shown to fail, and one in which this failure is presented as implying the introduction of individuating particular constituents. Let us call ontological constituents that account for the descriptive aspects of a thing, i.e., traditionally speaking its qualities, properties, and relations, its 'descriptors.' The first argument which I call the 'duplication argument' thus aims to establish that something else is needed beyond descriptors in order to account for the individuality – taken to be tantamount with the numerical identity – of a thing. In an informal and abbreviated reconstruction the duplication argument runs as follows.

(I) The Duplication Argument

Premise 1: There are things which are exact qualitative duplicates.
Premise 2: Duplicates are different individuals.
Premise 3: The 'properties' or 'characters' of a thing are 'literally the same.'
Inference 1: In certain cases the individuality of a thing cannot be accounted for in terms of the thing's descriptors alone.
Premise 4: The Leibniz Principle postulates that the individuality of a thing is determined by its descriptors.

---

[28] Bergmann 1967, p. 24.

[29] Proponents of the bare particular view agree that we may not 'directly recognize a particular as the same' or 'as such' but claim that we are acquainted with them 'when we see two indistinguishable white billard balls' (Grossman 1983, p.57; cf. also Allaire 1963).

[30] Kripke 1980, p. 18.

[31] Sellars 1952, p. 282.

Conclusion 1: Exact qualitative duplicates present counterexamples to the Leibniz Principle–the individuality of a thing cannot in all circumstances be accounted for in terms the thing's descriptors.[32]

Premise 5 (partly supported by conclusion 1): The ontological analysis of 'individuation' must introduce an additional constituent besides the descriptors of a thing.

Premise 6: The additional individuating constituent is either a particular or a descriptor.

Premise 7 (partly supported by premise 3): The additional individuating constituent cannot be a descriptor.

Conclusion 2: The additional individuating constituent is a particular.

For present purposes let us simply accept the duplication argument, noting that premise 1 may be supported either by the claim that duplication scenarios are conceivable or factually given in the quantum-physical domain, where certain measuring results may be described as reflecting pluralities of indistinguishable 'particles' (bosons). Furthermore, it should also be kept in mind that bare particular theorists do have an argument in support of premise 3:

> [18] [I]t appears that two characters [i.e., qualificators] may be merely numerically different. But we cannot give a sense to such difference without either putting characters in space or blurring the difference between characters and things.[33]

While the duplication argument aims to show that we need particulars as ontological constituents establishing the individuality (numerical identity) of a thing, the second argument is to evince that these individuating particulars must be bare.

(II) The Exemplification Argument

Premise 1: The ontological factor that individuates an entity is also the logical subject of the entity's predicates.

Premise 2: Predication is exemplification.

Conclusion: The logical subject that exemplifies a descriptor (attribute) may exhibit features but must itself be something without any features.

---

[32] Cf. Bergmann 1967, 7ff, Allaire 1963, p. 293, Allaire 1965, 305ff.

[33] Allaire 1963, p. 299. The passage contains a rather compressed reduction argument, to be unfolded into something along the following lines. (i) Descriptors are either universal or particular. (ii) Two things α and β can be thought to be exact qualitative duplicates, i.e., to be qualitatively identical. (iii) The qualitative descriptors of the two things are numerically different, since they occur in numerically different things, i.e., in two different space-time locations. (iv) In order to account for the numerical difference of the qualitative descriptors of α and β we would need to choose between the following two options: (a) descriptors are universals but nevertheless they are individuated by their space-time location; (b) descriptors are particulars. (v) Neither option in (iv) is acceptable; therefore thesis (iii) is to be rejected – the qualitative descriptors of α and β are not numerically different but are 'literally the same.' See also Allaire 1968.

Michael Loux offers the following reconstruction of this argument.

> The dialectic which leads to this view takes as its starting point the assumption that where P is an exemplified property, the possessor of P is something that can be apprehended independently of P; it is a thing such that whatever it is its being that does not presuppose its possessing P. According to this assumption, then, properties are something added to their possessors; in itself, the possessor of a property has a being that is distinct from and independent of the property it possesses...Let us consider a small red ball...That assumption forces us to say that whatever it is that possesses the color associated with the ball, it is something which in itself is not red. It is such that the property of being red is something added to it, so as to characterize it as red. But while the possessor of this property is not in itself red, it is not something which in itself is some color other than red; for we associate with the ball not just the color red, but also the generic property of being colored, so that whatever possesses the color red also possesses the generic property of being colored. But, then, the assumption just stated forces us to say that the possessor of the properties associated with the ball is something which in itself has no color at all; it is something to which the property of being colored is added.[34]

And so on for every attribute of the ball, however specific or general. In this reconstruction the argument indeed is 'likely to appear shocking.'[35] Let me supply some considerations and further premises which should make the argument somewhat more palatable, in an effort to 'strengthen the opponent'.

First, it is important to realize that the proponent of the reported argument must be taken to operate with a specific account of predication. The subject whose bareness is to be demonstrated is a relatum of the relation of *exemplification*; it is not a relatum of Tarski's relation of satisfaction, holding between the referent of the subject-term and the predicate-term, and it is not the argument of predicative functions in the Fregean sense. Second, proponents of the argument can recommend their analysis of predication on two counts, showing its superiority to both the Tarskian and Fregean analysis. On the one hand, unlike functional application, the relation (or 'tie', 'nexus') of exemplification accounts for the unity of a thing since it ties the constituents of a thing into a complex.

(EX1) Exemplification generates a unified complex.

On the other hand, the relation of satisfaction does not express a definite type of connectedness which could *explain* why we call a sentence 'a is F' true if the referent of 'a' satisfies 'F'. But the relation of exemplification answers to this explanatory demand – 'a is F' is true insofar as the referent of 'a' is an *example* of the feature or kind denoted by 'F'.

(EX2) A predicate–term 'F' is truly predicated of a subject-term 'a' iff the referent of 'a' is an example of the attribute denoted by 'F'.

---

[34] Loux 1978, p. 108.

[35] Ibid. p. 110.

As we shall see presently, one might refrain from such a literal, essentially Platonist, reading of the relation of exemplification and assign it a more technical interpretation, thereby again losing the explanatory asset of the literal account. But insofar as the Platonist reading as in (EX2) is retained, this implies, so one might argue, that logical subjects must be logically independent of the attributes they exemplify. For assume (EX2) as a premise.

Premise 3: = (EX2)

Now consider a tennis ball T which is round, white, weighs 48 g, and has a certain degree of elasticity *d*. What exemplifies the attribute whiteness cannot be anything which is essentially round, weighs essentially 48 g, or has essentially degree of elasticity *d*. For an example of whiteness must 'in itself' be just white and nothing else. Thus what exemplifies whiteness cannot be the ball T which *qua* ball is in itself essentially round, but it must be something about T which can fail to be round. Let's call that α. Factor α cannot be 'in itself' or essentially white, however, for otherwise α could not be an example of roundness. Now assume the following premise holds:

Premise 4: every thing has more than one descriptive aspect and the subject of predications about it always exemplifies several attributes.

The subject in premise 4 cannot in itself, or essentially, be an example of any one of them. Assume we further accept the equivalence stated in premise 5:

Premise 5: 'x is in itself an example of y' is true ⇔ 'x exemplifies y essentially' is true.

Then we reach another version of the conclusion stated above:

Conclusion: The subject of the predicate F-ness is the denotatum of the predicate-term 'F' is not in itself but only contingently an example of F-ness.

In this, more differentiated formulation, the conclusion of the exemplification argument will appear less scandalous. Thus, before dismissing the exemplification argument all too quickly, one should ask whether one's interpretation of 'bare' individuators as 'lacking in all properties,'[36] – which is certainly correct for the historical notion of bare matter – indeed represents the commitments of today's bare particularists. Contemporary defendants of the bare particular view have vividly rejected the common reading as an overly puritanic reaction that blurs a sensitive distinction in types of bareness. 'Those who claim that there are bare particulars, Russell, Bergmann, Allaire, et al., claim that they are nude of natures, not that they are naked of properties.'[37] Let us get clearer on this distinction. The proponent of *naked particulars* champions either one of the following conceptions of 'bareness.'

(BP1a) The individuator of α is logically independent of any attribute of α.
(BP1b) The individuator of α is a factor which is entirely dissociated of attributes, i.e., it does not have or exemplify any attribute.

---

[36] Loux 1978, p. 110. Loux himself does go some way to investigate this question.
[37] Baker 1967, p. 211.

The proponent of *nude particulars* on the other hand is content with more modest forms of exposure.

> (BP2a) The individuator of α is logically independent of each attribute.
> (BP2b) "Bare particulars neither are nor have natures [i.e., essential attributes]."[38]

Thus it will not do to argue against bare particulars along the following lines:

> Perhaps the neatest way in which to expose the absurdity of the notion of bare particulars is to show that the sentence, 'Universals are exemplified by bare particulars,' is a self-contradiction. As a matter of fact, the self-contradictory character of this sentence becomes evident the moment we translate it into the symbolism of *Principia Mathematica*. It becomes, '(x).(∃F) Fx.2019; ¬(∃F)Fx', or in other words, 'If a particular exemplifies a universal, then there is no universal which it exemplifies.[39]

But even if we may rescue bare particulars *qua* nude particulars from objections against naked particulars, ultimately the notion is fraught with incoherence, as I will show now.

2.3.2 Paradise Lost: Incoherent Nude Particulars

Even though immune against some of the arguments put forth against the naked particular approach, the notion of a nude particular becomes suspect once we step back from the specific dialectics of the debate and take a more general angle. Would not any entity about which we can say anything at all – for instance that it is a particular, concrete, and nude – seem to need *some* essential attributes? Some opponents of nude particulars have thus argued that we cannot coherently claim that the definitional trait of being nude is something that a nude particular exemplifies only contingently: could nude particulars be logically independent even of their nudity and particularity-?[40]

There is, thus, the problem about the modal status of the definitional features of nude particulars. The difficulty I want to draw attention to resides at an even more general plane. As I shall argue now, it is the very idea of having individuating constituent *also* perform the role of a logical subject that renders the nude particular approach inconsistent. To begin with another look at the principle of exemplification that has proved so useful in defending the bare particular view.

> The nexus ...will be represented by 'ε' and called *exemplification*. '*a* ε A' is a well-formed sentence if and only if '*a*' and 'A' stand for a bare particular and a universal, respectively; it is true if and only if *a* is *the* bare particular and A is *one* of the universals 'in' *an* ordinary thing.[41]

---

[38] Bergmann 1967, p. 24.
[39] Sellars 1952, p. 282f.
[40] See for example, Loux 1978, p. 110ff.
[41] Ibid., p. 26.

According to this definition the bare particular α of a thing u exemplifies all and only those attributes that are constituents of u. For instance, if u is a square thing, then squareness and α are both constituents of u, u is said to be square, and α exemplifies squareness. Thus, according to the definition of exemplification just cited there are two ways in which an attribute can be related to another entity which is not an attribute.

(R1) x has attribute F iff x is a thing and there is a bare particular y which is the bare particular of x and α exemplifies F.
(R2) x exemplifies F iff there is a thing u and x is the bare particular of u and x and F are constituents of u.

As we noted previously, bare particulars must be assumed to be essentially concrete and particular-per-se, i.e., necessarily uniquely occurrent, entities, if they are to play of individuators. But how can we predicate of a particular α that it is bare, or a particular entity, or is a constituent of a thing? How are we to understand the relationship between α and these attributes? It seems that we have three possibilities in order to explain how the bare (nude) particular α and, say, the attribute of being a bare particular, are related.

(a) α neither has nor exemplifies the attribute of being a bare particular.
(b) α has the attribute of being a bare particular in the sense of (R1).
(c) α exemplifies the attribute of being a bare particular in the sense of (R2).

If the proponent of the bare particular view were to choose the first option, the position would remain obscure. The second option amounts to assimilating the ontological structure of things and bare particulars. This option is not open to bare particularists, since they insist things belong into the ontological category of 'facts' and thus are structurally very different that the category of bare particulars. Thus, we are left with the third option in order to specify the relationship between bare (nude) particulars and their attributes.

Let us assume then that bare particulars exemplify the attribute of being a bare particular. The following difficulty arises. Bare particulars exemplify all and only those attributes which are said to be true about things or which are had by things. But a thing, which is within the bare particular view categorized as a fact, cannot be said to be a bare particular. Thus, against our initial assumption, bare particulars cannot exemplify the attribute of being a bare particular. To restate the arising inconsistency more formally:

(1) Assumption: Definition of predication.
'a is F' is true iff the denotatum of 'a' has a bare particular constituent which exemplifies the denotatum of 'F.'

(2) Assumption: Definition of exemplification.
Entity x exemplifies attribute F iff there is a thing A and there is an entity x which is the bare particular of A and x and F are constituents of A.

(3) Assumption: Definition of a bare particular:
(x) (x is a bare particular iff

$x \in \{y|\ (\exists z)\ (y \text{ is a constituent of } z\ \&$
$(f)\ (f \text{ is a constituent of } z \leftrightarrow y \text{ exemplifies } f))\}).$

(4) Assumption:
Some predications about things, i.e., some sentences of the form ′a is F′ are true.

(5) From (1), (2), (3), (4):
There are bare particulars, i.e.,
$(\exists x)(x \in \{y|\ (\exists z)\ (y \text{ is a constituent of } z\ \&$
$(f)\ (f \text{ is a constituent of } z \leftrightarrow y \text{ exemplifies } f))\}).$

(6) From (3):
There is the attribute BP of being a bare particular:
$\text{BP} := \lambda y\ [(\exists z)\ (y \text{ is a constituent of } z\ \&$
$(f)\ (f \text{ is a constituent of } z \leftrightarrow y \text{ exemplifies } f))\})].$

(7) Assumption: An entity which is a thing is not a bare particular.

(8) From (7):
The predicate which denotes the attribute BP cannot be truly predicated of any thing.

(9) From (1), (2), (8):
There is no entity x which exemplifies the attribute BP.

(10) From (9):
The class *BP* which consists of all and only things exemplifying the attribute BP, is empty:
$\neg(\exists x)(x \in \{y|\ (\exists z)\ (y \text{ is a constituent of } z\ \&$
$(f)\ (f \text{ is a constituent of } z \leftrightarrow y \text{ exemplifies } f))\}).$

There are two ways in which proponents of bare particulars could try to rebut this argument. First, they might try to question the overall strategy of the argument, namely, the idea of applying the bare particularist's account of predication (see assumption 2) both for predications about things, i.e., at the level of the 'object language' or language to be analyzed, *and* for predications about bare particulars, i.e., at the level of the ontological meta-theory. This line of rebuttal is not promising in my view since ontological theories of predication are commonly taken to be self-applicatory. The analysis of predication as stated in the metalanguage normally can also be applied to the assertions of the metalanguage, by entering the level of a meta-metalanguage. But precisely this step up into the meta-metalanguage is not possible with the account of predication stated in assumption 2 and, for that matter, with any account of predication that postulates that the logical subject of the predicates of a thing is not the thing but an ontological constituent of the thing that has a different ontological make-up that the thing itself.

Second, proponents of bare particulars might reject the equivalence in assumption 3, i.e., the postulate that *all and only* those attributes are constituents of a thing that are denoted by the thing's predicates. Instead a bare particularist might postulate that all the denotata of predicates which are truly predicated of a thing A are constituents of A, allowing for attributive constituents that are exemplified by the bare particular of A but are not features predicated of A. In other words, bare particularists may argue that assumption 3 should be formulated as an implication:

$$(x)\ (x \text{ is a bare particular iff } x \in \{y|\ (\exists z)\ (y \text{ is a constituent of } z\ \&\ (f)\ (f \text{ is a constituent of } z \rightarrow y \text{ exemplifies } f))\}).$$

Such a change, however, would remove an essential constraint on the notion of exemplification and render the term all but semantically empty – for example, the bare particular α of grey cube A could then be said to exemplify also the attributes of redness and triangularity and, in fact, any available attribute.[42]

In sum, even though 'knock-down-drag-out' arguments are very rare in ontology, even though there might be epicycles that one could add to the bare particular view to undercut the stated argument, postulating bare particulars does not seem a promising strategy to arrive at an account of the individuality of things. However, what our brief discussion also should have shown is that main difficulties of the bare particular view do not stem from the notion of particularity itself, but from the fact that the particular constituents of things were also assigned other explanatory functions. Some linkages between category features turned out to be more problematic than others. The traditional link between particularity and logical subjecthood is clearly at the center of the problems arising for the bare particular view.[43]

2.4 Alternative Conceptions of Particulars

Particularism is the conviction that particular entities enjoy 'ontological primacy' either as ontological explanantia or explananda, i.e., either as basic ontological entities or as primary targets of ontological investigation. The argument in Section 2.3 was to show that the notion of a bare particular is not a promising candidate for

---

[42]There are additional difficulties for Bergmann's account of a bare particular. Since Bergmann's bare particulars are 'momentary entities' (1967, p. 34), they could in fact exemplify only very few of the attributes which we ascribe to things with predicates like 'three years old' or 'getting colder' or 'doubled in size.' Bergmann would need to hold that common-sense predicates of things express very complicated structures of attributes for momentary entities. Another sort of problem arises with relational properties. Consider the predicate 'bigger than thing *B*' predicated of *A*; if the attribute expressed by this predicate were to contain the ontological correlate of *B*, as this would be commonly constructed, the ontological description of A would contain two bare particulars, that of *A* and, embedded, that of *B*. But by definition a bare particular 'cannot be "in" more than one ordinary thing' (1967, p. 24).

[43]The link between particularity and individuality on the other hand is more innocuous. Initially Bergmann postulates just one explanatory function for bare particulars: 'A bare particular is a mere individuator. Structurally that is its only function. It does nothing else'(1967, p. 25) If bare particularists had taken this modest characterization to heart, the theory might be in better shape. Unfortunately, however, the mono-functional entity apparently struck Bergmann and others as explanatorily shallow and thus the traditional linkages between individuality and other category features made their way into the functional characterization of bare particulars.

a basic ontological category. Is there any other type of particular, then, that one could postulate as basic ontological category? Wilfrid Sellars introduced in 1952 the notion of a 'basic particular' or 'instance of one quale' and in effect formulated an early version of what nowadays is known as 'trope ontology', i.e., the view that 'property particulars' are all there is.[44] Tropes theories come in many different varieties, with more or less striking deviations from the presuppositions of the substance paradigm or myth of substance. Tropes are particular entities that are often taken to be concrete, enduring, and determinate; in some frameworks, however, they are defined as abstract particulars (against P2 above), or as instantaneous particulars (against P9), or as determinable particulars (against P5). Most importantly, all trope theories reject (P3) and (P6), the presupposition that particulars are to be independent and logical subjects – tropes are dependent entities, where this dependence is often, but not always, characterized as the dependence of logical predicates.

However, trope theories do retain the presuppositions (P1), (P4), and (P5) – tropes are unified, countable, and individuals, i.e., each a distinct 'this', and it is precisely here where again some of the main difficulties of the trope theory can be located. Critics of tropes have charged that since tropes are supposed to be simple (without internal complexity), we cannot make coherent sense of a relation of exact similarity holding among the tropes of what is intuitively the 'same character' but in different locations.[45] This also spells trouble for a coherent elucidation of their individuality and particularity. Since tropes may spatially superposed – for instance, a red-trope and a round-trope may be co-located on the skin of a tomato – most trope theorists consider them to be abstract (holding on to the traditional principle of non-superposition for concrete particulars). But then the particularity of tropes cannot consist in the unique spatial occurrence in the sense of the definition of 'Particularity-1' above. The alternative account of 'Particularity-2' above, postulating that a particular is an ontological constituent that occurs in one (complex ontological correlate of a) thing only, is not amenable to the trope theorist who considers things to be trope structures. Thus the only way to establish that tropes are particulars would be in terms of Particularity-1 together with the postulate that tropes with the same (exactly similar) character may not be spatially superposed. The particularity of tropes thus stands and falls with a convincing definition of the exact similarity among tropes.

In fact, the problem just highlighted for the particularity of tropes is quite general. Any theory that (a) treats things as 'bundles' of 'unanalyzable units of 'located suchness', e.g., particular tropes, events, or states of affairs, *and* (b) retains the principle (P4) that all and only concrete particulars are individuals, must give an account

[44]Present-day trope ontologists (See e.g., Campbell 1990 and Keinänen 2005) are wont to trace their roots back to Williams 1953, or, more rarely, to G. F. Stout's 'particular characters' postulated in the early 1920s. Sellars' attempt at logical atomist trope theory is largely overlooked.
[45]Cf. Hochberg (1992).

of the distinctness of these particular constituents. In this way some internal complexity is grafted onto the particular constituents, which conflicts with the demand that they be simple.

Finally, let us briefly consider the thesis that particulars are 'bundles' of universals. Proponents of the 'universalist' sort of bundle theory obviously reject foundational particularism. But, like trope theorists, they have not succeeded in renouncing the myth of substance altogether. Participants in the debate about the universalist bundle theory agree that the theory has the following three tasks. (i) The theory must show that 'thing-like' bundles of universals (i.e., the complexes of universals that are the ontological correlates of things) are necessarily uniquely located in space, i.e., are particulars in the sense of Particularity-1. (ii) It must be shown that such particulars also can play the role of the logical subject for a thing's predicates. (iii) The theory must warrant that any two of such complexes of universals necessarily are distinct. The latter two tasks derive directly from presuppositions (P4) and (P5) above and, again, generate the main difficulties for the position: how to ensure the possibility of accidental predications, and how to exclude duplication scenarios in support of the Leibniz Principle.[46] These difficulties are so notorious that I can perhaps make do with a quick pointer here. For present purposes it is important to have a brief look at the first task, namely, of how to account for the particularity of those universal complexes (bundles) that are the ontological correlates of things. Proponents of the universalist bundle theory cannot resort to particularity-2 (i.e., particularity in the sense of being necessarily unique to one entity), since the constituted particulars precisely do not enter as ontological constituents into any further entities, or if do, then only contingently so. This leaves particularity in the sense of particularity-1, but how could the co-occurrence of general entities establish necessary spatial uniqueness of occurrence? The traditional bundle theorist is faced with the choice of either having to include particular spatio-temporal locations within the bundle or to give up on the necessity of spatial uniqueness.[47] Russell famously is among those who opt for the latter, thereby in effect introducing a new notion of particularity[48]:

> 'Particularity'-3: An entity is particular iff it occurs (contingently) in a single spatial location at any point in time at which it exists.

But does 'particularity-3' really deserve the name? Particularity-3 merely formulates a notion of 'contingent uniqueness'. Given that some traditional universals also may fulfill this definition – compare for instance the extension of the universal of 'center of a circle that is concentric to the dome of St. Peter's Cathedral in Rome' – the categorial difference between particulars and universals is profoundly compromised. In one sense the universal-based bundle theories of particularity and substantial particulars thus can be said to fail relative to their reductional aims. In

[46]Cf. Russell 1948, Van Cleve 1985, Losonsky 1987, Casullo 1988.

[47]Cf. Casullo 1988, p. 133, Long 1968, p. 197, Jones 1950, p. 68f.

[48]Russell 1948, pp. 298, 304ff.

another sense, however, they point towards an eliminative solution of the problem of particularity.

Before elaborating on this – essentially Leibnizian – idea of doing ontology without particulars, let us quickly review the result of this section. In the contemporary ontological literature we find two main alternatives to the traditional presumption that 'substantial particulars' are ontological primary, namely, theories based on tropes and theories based on universals. These two strategies differ profoundly regarding the role of the notion of particularity – trope theorists subscribe to foundational particularism and take particularity to be a primary, undefined category feature, while universal theorists try to define the unique locatedness of things without resorting to traditional particulars. However, at the presuppositional level there are striking similarities between both strategies. Both tropists and universalists retain the traditional substance-ontological linkages between the category features of particularity, individuality, countability, unification, and – in the case of the universalists – also logical subjecthood. Interestingly, the main problems arising for each theory type can be traced directly to these substance-ontological presuppositions.

2.5 Non-particular Individuals

In the preceding sections I have highlighted difficulties arising from an unreflected commitment to foundational particularism, the thesis that particulars have ontological primacy at least in the sense that they form a basic ontological category, in combination with unreflected commitments to the myth of substance, i.e., to certain traditional linkages between category features. The arguments presented may not suffice to shatter particularist intuitions – few, if any, arguments in ontology are inescapable – but may at least lead us to review the notion of particularity and its role in ontology. This might even benefit foundational particularism, since once we are clear on the contrast between 'substantial particularity' and 'particularity *per se*', foundational particularism can be extended into new domains. For example, P. Teller has suggested that the field quanta of quantum-physical field theory (Fock space formulation) should be categorized as non-individual particulars.[49]

On the other hand, reflections on the notion of particularity might also lead us to reject the notion altogether. If we follow the line of the universalist bundle theorists we also can entertain the research hypothesis that the classical binary contrast between particularity and universality is altogeter ill-conceived – all we need in ontology in order to model our inferences about things and persons are entities which are *de facto* or contingently unique. Separating the traditional linkage between individuality and particularity provides an effective heuristics for the construction of new non-particularist ontologies: will a theory based on non-particular individuals serve the explanatory aims of ontologies not equally well or even better? Will it not be preferable, for a reconstruction of our reasoning about the world in

[49]Cf. Teller 1983, 1995a.

common sense and science, to replace the traditional contrast between universals and particulars by a gradient field of more or less general entities, with contingently unique individuals – Leibniz' *infima species* – as one extremal point of the scale?

To provide at least a pointer to a non-particularist ontology that may support a first, and affirmative, answer to these questions, let me outline the main ideas of General Process Theory (hereafter 'GPT'), an ontology based on 'dynamics' or generic processes that are individuals but not particulars in the sense of particularity-1 or particularity-2.[50] GPT operates with a conception of individuality that focuses not on location but on 'specificity-in-functioning' in the widest sense of 'functioning', i.e., on the dynamic role of an entity (e.g. an activity) within a certain dynamic context. The practice of individuating in terms of *what* is happening or going-on, rather than *where,* is just as well-entrenched in our common sense and scientific reasoning as the practice of individuating by location. The following sentences about concrete occurrences of activities and stuffs, for example, clearly involve a function-based notion of individuation: 'it is snowing, not raining,' 'the radiation has decreased by 50%,' 'the erosion runs all along the coast,' or 'the fire spread rapidly,' 'there's water in the next valley,' or 'you can't see the gin in your glass, since it is just as transparent as the tonic.'[51]

Concrete activities come in two kinds. Some, like swimming or sliding, are the doings of a person or a thing (or of collections thereof), while others, so-called 'pure' or 'subjectless' activities, like snowing, raining, lightening cannot be attributed to logical subjects and are typically expressed with impersonal constructions such as 'it is snowing' etc.[52] The basic category of GPT, a new category labeled 'general processes,' is *modelled* on the common sense notion of a subjectless activity or pure dynamics in the sense described above in Section 2.1: even though general processes are theoretical entities that are axiomatically defined, their explanatory power derives to a large extent from their model or prime illustration, subjectless activities, which exhibit the most characteristic features of of the new, postulated entity type.[53] Here, then, are seven characteristics of subjectless activities

[50] Cf. Seibt 1996a, b, c, 1997a, b, 2004a, b, 2007, 2008.

[51] Historically viewed, this second sense of individuality as specificity-in-functioning has been discussed in the Aristotelian tradition in individualistic interpretations of the 'to ti en einai', such as Duns Scotus' 'haecceitas'. Leibniz' so-called principle of the identity of indiscernibles can count as an attempt to revive the understanding of individuality or thisness as specificity-in-functioning, against the more prevalent understanding of thisness as determined by unique location that enabled, and was supported by, the Cartesian geometrical approach to the physical world.

[52] Sellars, following C.D. Broad, takes 'subjectless' or 'pure' activities to be expressed by sentences with 'dummy subject', cf., 'it is snowing,' 'it is lightening' (Sellars 1981). Even though this might be helpful for illustrational purposes, it cannot serve as a criterion since many activities that cannot be understood as the 'doings' of a thing (or a collection of things) are expressed by nouns.

[53] In earlier expositions of the new ontological framework the basic category was called 'dynamic masses' and 'free processes,' but due to the ubiquitous presumption of foundational particularism it became increasingly necessary to highlight more clearly that the basic individuals of the new scheme are non-particular, i.e., general entities. The reader should note that even though GPT is a process ontology, general processes have little in common with Whiteheadian 'actual occasions'; in fact, the closest categorial cognates to general processes are E. Zemach's concrete 'types' (Zemach

that can illustrate the theoretical properties of general processes entailed by the axiomatics of GPT. (i) Subjectless activities are occurrences in their own right rather than modifications of persons or things – like things, and unlike properties and relations, they are *independent* in the sense that their occurrence in space and time does not necessarily require the existence of a different sort of entity they occur in or qualify (they may of course be constituted or caused by other entities). (ii) Subjectless activities are *temporally extended* – there are no instantaneous activities.[54] (iii) However, quite unlike things, and much like stuffs (water, wood, etc.) subjectless activities occur in space and time both with indeterminate and with determinate locations (cf. 'there is lots of rain in Denmark' vs. 'on Oct. 12 it rained in Aarhus between 8 am and 1 pm'). Most importantly, a subjectless activity does not necessarily occur in a unique spatiotemporal location – ontologically speaking, a subjectless activity is *not a particular*. While things are located at any time in one place only, subjectless activities are multiply locatable like properties and stuffs – they can, and mostly do, occur in many places at the same time: 'it is snowing' can be true of many different scattered regions at the same time. (iv) Subjectless activities also resemble stuffs in that they are not 'countable', i.e., they do not come in 'natural' countable units' but are measurable in portions or amounts (e.g., an hour of snowing, 1,000 lumens of light), which then may be counted. (v) Like stuffs and properties, subjectless activities are not necessarily determinate in all of their qualitative or functional aspects – ontologically speaking, they are *determinables.* (vi) Subjectless activities are *individuated in terms of their roles within a dynamic context*, rather than by their location in space and time. (vii) Subjectless activities are *dynamic* but they are not changes. Constitutive 'phases' of their overall dynamicity (for example: the change of place of every single flake constituting the dynamicity of the snowing) contribute to the functionality of the activity but not *as* temporal stages or phases. In contrast to developments, activities have no internal temporal differentiation. These seven aspects of subjectless activities dovetail with the main category features of general processes: they are *independent, individual, concrete, spatiotemporally extended, non-particular, non-countable, determinable, and dynamic* entities. Each of the mentioned category features is well-known from the ontological debate, but their combination is new (in fact, it is outright inconceivable as long as one chooses to remain spellbound by the presuppositions of the substance paradigm).

1970). The predicate 'x is a model for category y' is defined in Seibt (2004b, Chap. 1). To simplify I use here 'semantic descent' and characterize subjectless activities directly in terms of ontological features (independent, concrete, non-particular etc.); the proper methodological procedure would be to show how the *logical* role of sentences about subjectless activities dovetails with *ontological* features of the entities in terms of which these sentences are interpreted. Cf. Seibt 2004b, chaps. 2 and 3.

[54]That is, there are no instantaneous activities in the sense of stages constituting temporally extended activities. GPT certainly acknowledges – and, in fact, makes much of this – that in common sense reasoning we do assume that activities exist continuously in time, and thus are dynamic features that can be ascribed to any point in the time period during which they are going on.

However, GPT is not only a framework designed to show that ontology can do well without particular entities, it is also to show that non-particular entities are all we need in ontology. That is, GPT is a *monocategoreal ontology* in the sense that general processes are the ontological counterparts not only of statements about subjectless activities but also of statements about things, stuffs, events, properties, actions, relations, persons, etc. In other words, *any concrete individual can be said to be a general process*, since the logical differences between statements about, say, things and stuffs, or activities and events, can be accounted for in terms of ontological differences among varieties of general processes. These differences are articulated within a typological matrix based on the values of five classificatory dimensions, four of which can be straightforwardly described. First, the *participant structure*of a dynamics specifies the number and type of causal agents and patients involved in the dynamcis. Second,general processes are classified relative to basic varieties of *dynamic constitution* or process architecture, such as sequences, forks, joints, cycles etc. Third, the parameter of *dynamic shape* classifies dynamics according to their typical (part of) trajectories in phase space, some of which correspond with distinctions familiar from linguistic theories of 'Aktionsarten' and verbal aspects. (telic/atelic, ingressive, egressive, repetitive, conative etc.). Finally, the parameter specifying the *dynamic context* of a dynamics classifies a dynamics (e.g. a biological organism) relative to its influence on its generative environment (e.g., the organism's ecosystem).

The most important of these classificatory dimensions, relating to the so-called *homomerity and automerity pattern* or *mereological signature* of a dynamics, requires special elaboration. Already Aristotle observed that common stuffs such as water and flesh are 'like-parted (homoeomerous) bodies': they are 'composed of parts uniform with themselves.'[55]. As various contemporary authors observed, there is an analogous mereological condition for activities, holding with respect to time – they are 'monotonous' or 'homogenous' occurrences where beginning, middle, and end of the interval of their duration are 'of the same nature as the whole'.[56] Just as any spoon of a puddle of water is like the whole, namely, an expanse of water, so any minute of an hour of snowing is like the whole, namely, a period of snowing. Thus we can formulate the following general mereological condition:

> *Like-partedness or homomerity*: An entity of kind K is homomerous iff all of its spatial or temporal parts are of kind K.

Upon a closer look, however, activities express an even more remarkable mereological condition than like-partedness. Since activities are purely 'functionally' individuated, it does not make sense to distinguish between an activity and its nature – an activity *is* a concrete type of dynamics. Of course we may say that every minute

[55]Cf. *History of Animals*, 487a2. Aristotle speaks of 'homoeomerous' entities, which could be translated as 'similar-parted' (of a similar kind) and contrasted with 'like-parted' (homomerous, of the same kind). This difference has been neglected in the discussion of 'homogeneous' entities and here I will do so as well.

[56]Cf. e.g., Vendler (1957), Verkuyl (1978, p. 224), Mourelatos (1978, p. 431).

of an hour of snowing is of the same nature as the whole, but then we are talking not about the activity of snowing at all, but rather about a particular spatiotemporal amount of snowing. For the activity itself, the following holds:

> *Self-partedness or automerity:* An entity E is automerous iff for any spatio-temporal interval r it holds that if r is a subregion of a spatiotemporal region R in which all of E occurs, then r is a region in which all of E occurs.[57]

Some entities are less homogenous or monotonous than others, (e.g., mixtures such as fruit salad and repetitive sequences such as folding shirts), and there are entities for which it holds that there are *no* parts like them or containing them, namely, things and events (developments). For example, computers and symphonies are not like-parted: no spatial part of my computer is a computer, and no temporal part of a baptism or a symphony is again a baptism or symphony.

The features of like-partedness and self-partedness can be generalized in two respects: first, with respect to dimensionality, and, second, with respect to degree:

> *Maximal, normal, minimal homomerity*: An entity α of kind K is maximally / normally / minimally like-parted in space (/time) iff *all / some / none* of the spatial (/temporal) parts of the spatiotemporal extent of α are of kind K.
> *Maximal, normal, minimal automerity:* An entity α is maximally / normally / minimally self-contained in space (/time) iff a spatiotemporal region in which α exists has *only / some / no* spatial (/temporal) parts in which all of α exists.

Figure 2.1 offers a graphical illustration of different degrees of spatial and temporal automerity.

General processes in GPT are sorted into different types in terms of their like-partedness (homomerity) and self-partedness (automerity) in space and time.

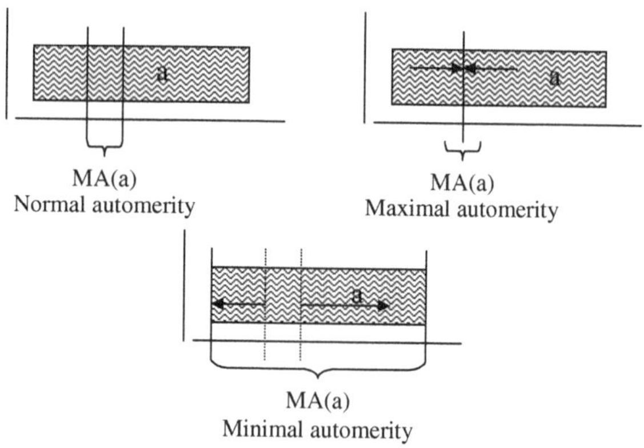

Fig. 2.1 Graphical illustration of degrees of spatial or temporal self-partedness (automerity). 'MA(a)' denotes the minimal amount of the dynamics denoted by 'a'. The *horizontal* and *vertical axes* represent orderings in space and time, here on purpose unassigned: if the horizontal dimension is time, the graphics represent temporal automerity, and vice versa.

[57] Self-partedness is a coherent concept only within a mereology with non-transitive part-relation; for a brief exposition see Seibt 2008; for a theory of persistence based on self-partedness see Seibt 2007.

For example, (i) general processes denoted by statements about activities (e.g. the process denoted by 'it is snowing') are *type-1 processes*, that is, they are temporally maximally automerous (and spatially unmarked); (ii) general processes denoted by statements about stuffs (e.g., the process denoted by '...is water' and 'Water (is)...') are *type-2* processes, i.e., they are spatially normally automerous and temporally maximally automerous; (iii) general processes denoted by statements about spatial *amounts* of stuffs ('this expanse of water') are *type-3* processes, i.e., they are spatially normally homomerous but minimally automerous, and temporally maximally automerous; (iv) general processes denoted by statements about developments (e.g., the process denoted by 'the explosion' and 'it exploded') are *type-4 processes,* i.e, they are temporally minimally homo- and automerous, (v) general processes denoted by statements about things (e.g. the process denoted by 'this cup' and 'is a cup') are *type-5 processes,* i.e., they are spatially minimally homo- and automerous but temporally maximally automerous. Since homomerity and automerity patterns can be embedded, we can define more complex 'recurrence profiles' for the processes that are the denotations of statements about series of developments, collections of things, and so forth.

All general processes are thus self-parted and like-parted, but to different degrees in the three spatial dimensions and one temporal dimension. In a sense, then, GPT precisely inverts the traditional bias of the substance paradigm and its commitment to foundational particularism. According to foundational particularism, it is 'most natural' to analyze non-countable, non-particular entities such as stuffs and activities (e.g., *water* or *snowing*) in terms of countable and uniquely located entities such as portions or quantities of stuff and bounded developments (as denoted by e.g., 'this puddle of water', 'a dl of water', or 'snow flake's S_1's moving from p_1 to p_2'). In contrast, in GPT the countable is treated as a subform of the stuff-like or non-countable: a thing is treated as the minimal amount of an extremely inhomogenous stuff, and a development as the minimal amount of a least monotonous activity.

In sum, general processes are concrete dynamics that are best understood on the model of subjectless activities. The theory of general processes, GPT, takes the 'route to individuality less traveled': traditional substance ontology typically has tied individuality to particularity-1 or necessary uniqueness of location, and consequently could ascribe individuality *only* to concrete entities that are determinately located in bounded regions and occur in countable units. But individuality may also be grounded in an entity's 'specificity-in-functioning'. This is the strategy pursed in the construction of the theory of general processes, GPT, whose basic individuals are concrete entities that are multiply locatable and 'stuff-like', i.e., do not occur *per se* in countable units nor in determinate regions. Once we adopt a notion of individuality based on 'specificity-in-functioning', the traditional entity dualism between particular individuals and universal non-individuals dissolves, and the path is open to a monocategoreal framework where subtypes of basic individuals is all there (concretely) is for the interpretation of common sense and scientific reasoning.

2.6 Conclusion

Foundational particularism, the assumption that all ontological basic entities are particulars, is a longstanding but questionable premise of ontological theory construction. The viability of foundational particularism obviously depends on how the notion of a particular is defined. The main aim of this paper was to draw attention to the fact that many contemporary ontologists conceive of particularity from within the 'substance paradigm', a network of powerful traditional presuppositions about linkages between category features; they associate with the notion of particularity systematic connections to other category features that are rooted in theoretical habituation rather than the meaning of particularity per se. Thus common references to 'particulars' are *de facto* references to 'substantial particulars', i.e., to entities that necessarily occur in a unique spatial location at any point in time at which they exist, but are also concrete entities, individuals, logical subjects, determinate, and enduring. That this combination of category features – and in particular the combination of particularity with independence, individuality, and logical subjecthood – does not seem to form a coherent category was shown with reference to the debate about bare and nude particulars. I also highlighted that the most recent versions of particularist ontologies, such as trope theory, relinquish some of the presuppositions of the myth of substance and thus circumvent objections familiar from the debate about bare and nude particulars. But I also adumbrated that these approaches inherit traditional problems precisely to the extent to which they retain the traditional presuppositions of the substance paradigm. The same holds for the 'universalist bundle theory of individuals' and more generally any non-particularist ontology that aims to construct particulars out of general entities.

There are two overall conclusions one might draw from the foregoing observations. First, in order to entitle oneself to a coherent use of the notion of a particular one needs to separate between the explanatory roles of particularity, subjecthood, individuality, and deteminateness even more than trope theorists have done so far. As the reader may have noticed, much of the literature cited in this paper is from the middle of the twentieth century up to the 1980s, and this is not by accident. During the last two decades other topics such as reduction, causation, persistence, and parthood have been in the center of attention of the ontological discussion and the notion of a 'particular' is used with disturbing casualty. But the problem of particulars that exercized authors in the 1960s has merely been forgotten, not solved, and thus the current facile recourse to 'particulars' does not yet seem legitimate.

Second, once we can contrast 'substantial particularity' with 'particularity per se', foundational particularism can be extended into domains where entities notoriously do not fit our reasoning about things, e.g., quantum physics. Vice versa, the contrast between substantial and pure particulars and the separation of the traditional linkage between individuality and particularity provides an effective heuristics for the construction of new non-particularist ontologies. To illustrate this claim I sketched basic ideas underlying the construction of General Process Theory (GPT) whose basic entities are generic dynamics that are individuals but not particulars in the sense of particularity-1 or particularity-2. GPT is a scheme designed to show not only that ontology can do without particulars, but also that non-particular entities are all we need – once we give up on foundational particularism, ontological frameworks can operate one basic category only.

The fact that the 'ontologies' used in recent knowledge representation software are based on concepts or descriptions, i.e., on terms for general entities, suggests strongly, I believe, that foundational particularism is more a matter of a longstanding theoretical habituation in philosophy than a transcendental requirement of thought – it does not seem to be a condition for the possibility of making sense of the world we reason about in common sense and science that this world is an assembly of particulars. To be sure, this is a research hypothesis to be explored by non-particularist ontologies in computer science and philosophy alike, and the sense of 'possibility' will differ in each field. Unlike computer scientists philosophers will have to pay attention to the larger systematic context of a notion of individuality that is based on specificity rather than on location. For example, intimately connected with the two strategies for defining individuality – as implying necessary uniqueness vs. qualitative/functional distinctness – are two intuitions of the meaning of concrete being – being as being placed vs. being as 'acting' or 'functioning'. Or again, if all individuals and in particular also you and I could, in principle, occur multiply in space or recur in time, this may bruise our egos, or it might create some theological difficulties for the necessary uniqueness of souls. But one person's modus tollens is another modus ponens and so philosophers might choose to adapt the systematic context to the new commitment to non-particular individuals. The thought of everything being merely contingently unique is existentially just as challenging and comforting as the traditional presumption of necessary uniqueness or particularity.

References

Adams, R.M. 1979. Primitive thisness and primitive identity. *The Journal of Philosophy* 76:5–26.

Allaire, E. 1963. Bare particulars. In Blackmann 1984, 293–300.

Allaire, E. 1965. Another look at bare particulars. In Blackmann 1984, 305–311.

Allaire, E. 1968. Relations and the problem of individuation. *Philosophical Studies* 19:61–63.

Baker, R. 1967. Particulars: Bare, naked, and nude. *Nous* 1:211–212.

Bergmann, G. 1967. *Realism. A critique of brentano and meinong*. Madison: The University of Wisconsin Press.

Black, M. 1978. The identity of indiscernibles. In Loux 1976, *Universals and particulars*. Notre Dame, In: University of Notre Dame Press 250–263.

Blackmann, L. 1984. *Classics of analytical metaphysics*. Lanham, MD: University Press of America.

Campbell, K. 1990. *Abstract particulars*. Oxford: Blackwell.

Castañeda, H.N. 1989. *Thinking, language, and experience*. Minneapolis, MN: University of Minnesota Press.

Casullo, A. 1982. Particulars, substrata, and the identity of indiscernibles. *Philosophy of Science* 49:591–603.

Casullo, A. 1988. A fourth version of the bundle theory. *Philosophical Studies* 54:125–139.

Grossmann, R. 1983. *The categorial structure of the world*. Bloomington, IN: University of Indiana Press.

Hochberg, H. 1992. Troubles with tropes. *Philosophical Studies* 59:18–19.

Jones, J.R. 1950. Simple particulars. *Philosophical Studies* 1:65–74.
Keinänen, M. 2005. *Trope theories and the problem of universals*. Ph.D. Dissertation, Philosophical Studies from the University of Helsinki.
Kripke, S. 1980. *Naming and necessity*. Dordrecht: D. Reidel.
Long, D. 1968. Particulars and their qualities. *The Philosophical Quarterly* 18(72):193–206.
Losonsky, M. 1987. Individuation and the bundle theory. *Philosophical Studies* 52:191–198.
Loux, M. 1978. *Substance and attribute*. Dordrecht: Reidel.
Mourelatos, A. 1978. Events, processes, and states. *Linguistics and Philosophy* 2:415–434.
Mulligan, K., P. Simons, and B. Smith. 1984. Truthmakers. *Philosophy and Phenomenological Research* 66:287–321.
Puntel, L. 1990. *Grundlagen einer Theorie der Wahrheit*. Berlin: de Gruyter.
Puntel, L. 1993. The context principle, universals, and primary states of affairs. *American Philosophical Quarterly* 30:123–135.
Quine, W.v.O. 1952. *Methods of logic*. London: Routledge & Kegan.
Rosenkrantz, G., and J. Hoffman. 1991. The independence criterion of substance. *Philosophy and Phenomenological Research* 51:835–853.
Russell, B. 1911. On the relations between universals and particulars. In: Blackmann 1984, *Classics of analytical metaphysics*. Lanham, MD: University Press of America 157–175.
Russell, B. 1948. *Human knowledge: Its scope and its limits*. New York, NY: Simon and Schuster.
Seibt, J. 1990. *Towards process ontology: A critical study in substance-ontological premises*. Ph. D. Dissertation Pittsburgh: UMI-Dissertation Publication.
Seibt, J. 1995a. Individuen als Prozesse: Zur prozess-ontologischen Revision des Substanzparadigmas. *Logos* 5:303–343.
Seibt, J. 1996a. Non-countable individuals: Why one and the same is not one and the same. *Southwest Philosophy Review* 12:225–237.
Seibt, J. 1996b. The myth of substance and the fallacy of misplaced concreteness. *Acta Analytica* 15:61–76.
Seibt, J. 1996c. Der Umbau des 'Aufbau': Carnap und die analytische ontologie. *Deutsche Zeitschrift für Philosophie* 44:807–835.
Seibt, J. 1997a. The 'Umbau': From constitution theory to constructionism. *History of Philosophy Quarterly* 14:305–351.
Seibt, J. 1997b. Existence in time: From substance to process. In *Perspectives on time. Boston studies in philosophy of science*, eds. J. Faye, U. Scheffler and M. Urs, 143–182. Dordrecht: Kluwer.
Seibt, J. 2000a. The dynamic constitution of things. In *Facts and events*, eds. J. Faye et al., 241–279. Amsterdam: *Poznan Studies in Philosophy of Science*.
Seibt, J. 2000b. Ontology as theory of categorial inference. In *Wahrheit-Sein-Struktur. Auseinandersetzungen mit Metaphysik*, eds. D. Greimann, and C. Peres, 272–297. Hildesheim: Olms Verlag.
Seibt, J. 2004a. Free process theory: Towards a typology of processes. *Axiomathes* 14:23–57.
Seibt, J. 2004b. *General process theory*. Habilitationsschrift at the University of Konstanz.
Seibt, J. 2005. Der Mythos der Substanz. Substanz, ed. K. Trettin, 197–229, Klostermann, Frankfurt.
Seibt, J. 2007. Beyond endurance and perdurance: Recurrent dynamics. In *Persistence*, ed. C. Kanzian, 133–165. Frankfurt: Ontos-Verlag.
Seibt, J. 2009. Forms of emergence in general process theory. *Synthese*, 166:479–517.
Sellars, W. 1960. Grammar and existence. *Mind* 69:499–533.
Sellars, W., 1952. Particulars. Philosophy and Phenomenological Research 13:184–199.
Simons, P. 1994. Particulars in particular clothing: Three trope theories of substance. *Philosophy and Phenomenological Research* 54:553–575.
Sellars, W. 1981. Foundations for a metaphysics of pure processes. *The Monist* 64:3–90.
Stegmaier, W. 1977. *Substanz: Grundbegriff der Metaphysik*. Stuttgart: Fromann-Holzboog.
Stout, G. 1921. The Nature of Universals and Propositions. Reprinted in Blackman 1984, 175–191.

Teller, P. 1983. Quantum physics, the identity of indiscernibles, and some unanswered questions. *Philosophy of Science* 50:309–319.

Teller, P. 1995. *An interpretive introduction to quantum field theory*. Princeton, NJ: Princeton University Press.

Van Cleve, J. 1985. Three versions of the bundle theory. *Philosophical Studies* 47:95–107.

Vendler, Z. 1967. *Linguistics and philosophy*. Ithaca, NY: Cornell University Press.

Verkuyl, H. 1978. Thematic relations and the semantic representation of verbs expressing change. *Studies in Language* 2:199–233.

Williams, D.C. 1953. On the elements of being. *Review of Metaphysics* 7:3–18; 171–192.

Zemach, E. 1970. Four ontologies. *The Journal of Philosophy* 23:231–247.

Chapter 3
The Ontology of Mereological Systems: A Logical Approach

Heinrich Herre

3.1 Introduction and Preliminaries

Mereology is the theory of parthood relations. These relations pertain to part to whole, and part-to-part within a whole. This area of research is today some of the core topics of ontology and of conceptual modelling in computer science and artificial intelligence. Mereology can be traced back to ancient philosophy. In computer science and artificial intelligence the term ontology became popular since the beginning of the 1990. The mereological theory set forth in this paper is presented as a logical theory which is formalized in first-order logic. These theories are included in the General Formal Ontology (GFO) which is a top level ontology being developed by the research group Onto-Med (Herre et al. 2006).

Subsequently we review and summarize standard notations of the field of logic, model theory and set theory, as presented in Hodges (1993), Mendelson (2001), Chang and Keisler (1977). A logical language L is determined by a syntax, specifying its formulas, and by a semantics. Throughout this paper we use first order logic (FOL) or monadic second order logic as a framework. The semantics of FOL is presented by relational structures, called Σ-structures, which are interpretations of a signature Σ consisting of relational and functional symbols. We use the term *model-theoretical structure* to denote first-order relational structures, but also monadic second structures. For a model-theoretic structure $\Im$ and a formula φ we use the expression "$\Im \models \varphi$" which means that the formula φ is true in $\Im$. A structure $\Im$ is called a model of a theory T, being a set of formulae, if for every formula $\varphi \in T$ the condition $\Im \models \varphi$ is satisfied. Let Mod(T) be the class of all models of T. The logical consequence relation, denoted by $\models$, is defined by the condition: $T \models \varphi$ if and only if $\mathrm{Mod}(T) \subseteq \mathrm{Mod}(\{\varphi\})$. For the first order predicate logic the completeness theorem is true: $T \models \varphi$ if and only if $T \vdash \varphi$, whereas the relation $\vdash$ is a suitable formal derivability relation. The operation Cn(T) is the classical closure operation which is defined by: $\mathrm{Cn}(T) = \{\varphi \mid T \models \varphi\}$. Monadic second order logic allows for quantification on subsets or unary relations. Second order logics do not satisfy

H. Herre (✉)
Research Group Onto-Med, IMISE, University Leipzig, Leipzig, Germany
e-mail: heinrich.herre@imise.uni-leipzig.de

R. Poli, J. Seibt (eds.), *Theory and Applications of Ontology: Philosophical Perspectives*, DOI 10.1007/978-90-481-8845-1_3,

a completeness theorem. A theory T is said to be decidable if there is algorithm Alg (with two output values 0,1) that stops for every input formula and satisfies the condition: For every φ of L(T): T $|= \varphi$ if and only if Alg(φ) 1.

An extension S of a theory T is said to be complete if for every sentence φ either S $|= \varphi$ or S $|= \neg\varphi$. A complete and consistent extension of T is called an *elementary type* of T. Assuming that the language T is countable then there exists a countable set X of types of T such that every sentence φ which is consistent with T is consistent with a type from X. In this case we say that the set X is dense in the set of all types of T.[1] The classification problem for T is solved if a reasonable description of a countable dense set of types is presented.

In the present paper we give an overview about the ontology of mereological systems based on the part-of relation $\leq$. There are several approaches and theories describing this relation. The minimal consensus about the properties of the relation $\leq$ exhibits it as a partial ordering. The paper is organized as follows. Section 3.2 presents an overview about the relevant abstract mereological systems. These are described as sets of axioms in a formal language, mainly in first order logic. The notations draws partly on the standard literature as in Simons (1987), Varzi (1996), Burkhardt and Dufour (1991). The presentation in this section adds some further results. Furthermore, limitations of the classical systems are presented, which are discussed in the literature. In Section 3.2.3 some ideas are reviewed about definable relations and implicit axioms. In Section 3.3 some basic relations between mereology and set theory are discussed. This section is based mainly on the results of Lewis (1991). We add some further ideas and remarks about the ontology of singletons. Section 3.4 is devoted to a systematic classification of mereological systems. We present a partial classification of the consistent complete extensions of two theories, of the general extension mereology (GEM) including the second order variant, and of the classical merereology CM. It turns out that the classical mereology in the framework of first order logic is decidable, whereas the second order variant is undecidable. Then, we present some new systems which are extensions of the ground mereology M by introducing the notion of the tree-skeleton of a partial ordering. In Section 3.5 domain-specific mereologies are presented and discussed. A complete and general description of the notion of whole and part which works for every situation seems to be impossible, at least in the present stage of research. Hence, we propose a logical framework which allows to formally capture the main aspects of parts and wholes.

3.2 Abstract Mereology

In section the basic theories on mereology are exposed, further limitations are studied, and some other theories different from the basic theories are set forth and

[1]This notion of *being dense in a set* derives from a well-known topological interpretation used in model theory where the types are points in a topological space which is called the Stone Space of the theory (Chang and Keisler 1973, Hodges 1993).

discussed. The word "part" has many different meanings in natural language usage which reveals that the parthood-relation is not uniquely determined. The considered examples lead to a common core, i.e. to principles which are applicable to most of the considered and analysed examples. We expose a formal basis of mereology by starting with a ground theory and then extend this theory by number of principles which lead to a system of theories mirroring the richness of the many facets of this topic. We present these theories as abstract, formally axiomatized mathematical theories.

3.2.1 Basic Theories

The basic mereological theories start with a partial ordering and extend this theory by adding a number of further principles. One of these extensions exhibits a theory whose models are semi-boolean algebras. In this section we give an overview about the abstract mathematical theory of mereological systems. A basic mereological system $M = (E, \leq)$ is given by a domain E of entities and a binary relation $\leq$.

3.2.1.1 Basic Axioms and Ground Mereology

The relation $\leq$ satisfies the condition of a partial ordering. Every partial ordering $(E, \leq)$ can be, from this perspective, considered as a mereological system. This minimal system is called *ground mereology* and is denoted by M. The system M is specified by the following axioms:

(M1) $\forall x\,(x \leq x)$, (reflexivity)
(M2) $\forall xy\,(x \leq y \wedge y \leq x \rightarrow x = y)$, (anti-symmetry)
(M3) $\forall xyz\,(x \leq y \wedge y \leq z \rightarrow x \leq z)$, (transitivity)

The ground mereology M is the first order theory of partial orderings; it is a rather weak theory that will be extended by a number of further axioms. To formulate the most important mereological standard theories we introduce several definitions.

(D1) $x < y := x \leq y \wedge x \neq y$ (proper part)
(D2) $ov(x, y) := \exists z\,(z \leq x \wedge z \leq y)$ (overlap), $disj\,(x, y) := \neg ov(x, y)$ (x and y are disjoint)
(D3) $sum(x, y, z) := \forall w\,(ov\,(w, z) \leftrightarrow ov\,(w, x) \vee ov\,(w, y))$ (mereological sum)
(D4) $intersect(x, y, z) := \forall w(w \leq z \leftrightarrow w \leq x \wedge w \leq y)$(mereological intersection)
(D5) $compl(x, y) := \forall w\,(w \leq x \leftrightarrow \neg\, ov\,(w, y))$ (x is absolute complement of y)
(D6) $relcompl(x, y, z) := \forall w(w \leq z \leftrightarrow w \leq y \wedge \neg\, ov\,(w, x))$ (z = y-x, relative complement).

For any of these definitions we may find a domain D such that all these relations can be satisfied, in the sense that the existential closure of these definitions is true on D, i.e. for example, $D \models \exists\, x\; y\; z\; sum\,(x,y,z)$; hence, these definitions are not vacuous.

The subsequent axioms belong to the abstract core theory of mereology. They are divided into axioms pertaining to several version of supplementation and in axioms related to the fusion or mereological sums of entities.

3.2.1.2 Principles of Supplementation and Extensionality

(M4) $\forall xy\,(y < x \rightarrow \exists z\,(z < x \wedge \text{disj}\,(z, y)))$ (weak supplementation principle)
(M5) $\forall xy\,(\neg y \leq x \rightarrow \exists z\,(z \leq y \wedge \text{disj}\,(z, x)))$ (strong supplementation principle)

Minimal mereology, denoted by MM, is the theory containing exactly the axioms {M1,M2,M3,M4}. In (Simons 1987) minimal mereology is considered as constitutive for understanding the *part-of* relation. The theory which includes exactly the axioms M1,M2,M3,M5 is called *extensional mereology* and is denoted by EM.

There are inter-relations between these axioms: M4 is derivable from $M \cup \{M5\}$, but not conversely, hence $M \cup \{M5\}$ |- M4, and not ($M \cup \{M4\}$ |- M5).

From the extensional mereology the following theorem is derivable:

Ext: $\exists z\,(z < x) \vee \exists z\,(z < y) \rightarrow (x = y \leftrightarrow \forall z\,(z < x \leftrightarrow z < y))$. Hence, Ext says that two objects are equal if they have the same proper parts, under certain minor restrictions captured in the premise of this formula. The following formula (Ext1) is derivable from the extensional principle.

Proposition 1 (Ext1) $\forall z(z \leq x \rightarrow \text{ov}(z, y)) \rightarrow x \leq y)$ (overlap of all parts yields part-of).

Proof Assume the premise is true, but the conclusion does not hold; then not($x \leq y$). We consider two cases. Case 1: disj(x,y). In this case there is part of x, x itself which does not overlap with y. Case 2. ov(x,y) and not(x=y); then there exists, according to strong supplementation, a part of x which is disjoint to y; hence, again, the premise does not hold. Q.e.d.

From EM follows the principle $\forall xy\,(\forall z(\text{ov}(z, x) \leftrightarrow \text{ov}(z, y)) \rightarrow x = y)$.

3.2.1.3 Fusion Principles and Closure Axioms

In this section we consider two further extensions of extensional mereology EM which pertain to the notion of fusion. The mereological sum of two entities is the simplest case of the mereological fusion. This fusion may be easily extended to the case of mereological fusion of a finite set of entities. We achieve a strong extension of CM if we allow for mereological fusions of infinite sets of entities. There are two versions of the general fusion axiom, one of them is formulated in FOL, the other needs a monadic second order logic.

The following axioms state the existence of the mereological sum and intersection.

(M6) $\forall xy\,\exists z\,(\text{sum}(x, y, z))$ (existence of the mereological sum)
(M7) $\text{ov}(x, y) \rightarrow \exists z\,(\text{intersect}(x, y, z))$ (existence of intersection if y and x overlap)

By the extensionality principle the results of sum and intersect are uniquely determined, hence they are partial functions. The axiom (M6) can be weakened by assuming that x and y are parts of an entity. We, then get the following variant

$$(M6')\ \forall xy(\exists u\,(x \leq u \wedge y \leq u) \rightarrow \exists z\,(\text{sum}(x, y, z)))$$

The operation of relative complement uses the strong supplementation axiom.

(M8) $\forall xy(\neg x \leq y \rightarrow \exists z\,(\mathrm{relcompl}(x, y, z)))$ (existence of relative complement)

Again, the relation relcompl(x,y,z) is a partial function. Classical mereology, denoted by CM, is defined by CM = EM ∪ {M6, M7, M8}. Hence, the existence of the mereological sum, intersection, and the relative complement is postulated. There is a relation between the models of CM and Boolean algebras. For any elements a, b such that $a \leq b$, the set $\{c \mid a \leq c, c \leq b\}$ defines with respect to the relations sum, intersect, and relcompl a Boolean algebra. Hence, every model of CM is a distributive lattice with relative complements (Grätzer 1998). If we postulate, in addition to CM, the existence of a greatest and a least element then the resulting theory describes the class of Boolean algebras.

Let φ (x) be a formula with the free variable x (and perhaps some more free variables). Then the fusion-axiom for φ has the form:

$$\mathrm{Fus}\,(\varphi) := \exists x \varphi\,(x) \rightarrow \exists\, z\,(\forall y(\mathrm{ov}(y, z) \leftrightarrow \exists\, w\,(\varphi\,(w) \wedge \mathrm{ov}(y, w)))$$

And a weaker form: $\mathrm{Fus}^*\,(\varphi) :=$

$$\left[\exists x \varphi\,(x) \wedge \exists\, u \forall \vee\,(\varphi\,(v) \rightarrow v \leq u)\right] \rightarrow \exists z(\forall y(\mathrm{ov}\,(y, z) \leftrightarrow \exists\, w\,(\varphi\,(w) \wedge \mathrm{ov}(y, w)))$$

Note that further free variables in φ are quantified in front of Fus(φ) by the universal quantifier ∀. The elementary fusion schema FUS is the set FUS := {Fus (φ) | φ is a formula of FOL of signature $\{\leq\}$, and the weak schema FUS* is defined accordingly. .It turns out that CM, augmented with FUS, is logically equivalent to a finite set of axioms. The addition of the full fusion schema yields the *General Extensional Mereology*, denoted by GEM. The axioms M6, M7, M8 are derivable from EM ∪ FUS. The models of GEM include quasi-boolean algebras (Boolean algebra with the zero element removed). The theory GEM is not complete, nothing can be derived about the existence of atoms. In Section 3.4 we will classify the complete extensions of several of the considered mereologies.

3.2.1.4 Bottom and Top

We consider some other axioms which are not included in all mereological theories. The following axiom is usually accepted in most mereological systems.

(M9) $\neg\exists\, x \forall y\,(x \leq y)$ (there is no least element w.r.t. $x \leq y$) .

There are two further axioms which might be interesting from viewpoint of algebraic systems (Boolen algebras). These axioms are not included in most systems, though there are some exceptions (Bunge 1966).

(Bottom) There exist a least object, i.e. an entity that is part of every entity.

(Top) There exist a greatest object, i.e. an entity that contains every entity as a part.

3.2.2 Limitations of the Basic Systems

In this section we show that the basic systems presented in Section 3.2.1 leads to certain problems in applications to conceptual modelling. In turns out that abstract mereology reveals many problems that make it hard, even impossible, to apply it directly to situations in reality. The abstract mereology is, as a logical theory, too strong, but at the same time it is too weak because relevant distinctions of the part-of relation cannot be expressed and explicated. From model-theoretical view-point full abstract mereology GEM strongly restricts the classes of models, hence many models that are important in conceptual modelling are excluded.[2] We consider and analyse objections that pertain the Ground Mereology, in particular to the transitivity axiom, furthermore, we consider objections against extensional mereology, and finally, we discuss problems that arise when applying the full mereology GEM. We divide the following discussions in several subsection, considering several groups of axioms separately.

3.2.2.1 Ground Mereology

Even the axioms of ground mereology M are not entirely uncontroversed.

Objections Against the Transitivity Axioms

There is a number of authors criticizing the transitivity axioms M3. The pattern of arguments is given by the following representative example:

Example 1. The hand is a part of a violinist, the violinist is part of an orchestra, hence, the hand is a part of an orchestra.

The application of transitivity in this example is counter-intuitive. Several authors criticised this axiom by varying this example in several directions (Rescher 1955a, Moltmann 1997, Cruse 1979, Gerstle 1995, Pribbenow 2002).

Example 2. Berlin is a part of Germany. Germany is a part of the European Union. Hence, Berlin is a part of the European union.

In both examples the role that parts play are not taken into consideration.

Example 3. A cell is a part of an organ, a nucleus is a part of a cell, hence, a nucleus of a cell is a part of an organ.

In Example 3 the granularity plays an important role. The other axioms of M, reflexivity and anti-symmetry are less controversial, although there are some phenomena in the context of part-hood that must further be analysed.

---

[2]The stronger a theory the smaller the class of models, i.e. the following principle is satisfied for arbitrary theories T, S in first-order logic: $Cn(T) \subseteq Cn(S)$ if and only if $Mod(S) \subseteq Mod(T)$. Cn(T) is the deductive closure of the theory T.

Objections Against Reflexivity and Symmetry

Objections against reflexitivy are minor, because the theory of non-reflexive part-of is logically equivalent to the reflexive version if some definitions are added to the axioms. Let us consider the proper part version of ground mereology denoted by M'.

$$(M1')\ \neg x < x$$
$$(M2')\ x < y \rightarrow \neg y < x$$
$$(M3')\ x < y \wedge y < z \rightarrow x < z.$$

Then M and M' are equivalent in the following sense. Consider the following definitions:
df1: $x < y \leftrightarrow x \leq y \wedge x \neq y$, df2: $x < y \leftrightarrow x < y \vee x = y$. Then, the following conditions hold:

(a) $M \cup \{df1\} \models M'$
(b) $M' \cup \{df2\} \models M$.

There are also arguments against the anti-symmetry axiom, because it excludes circularities (Sanford 1993). This might be relevant if mereology is used as a foundation for mathematics. Then, set theories without the foundation axiom must be taken into consideration (Devlin 1993).

3.2.2.2 Extensional Mereology and Supplementation Principles

There is a number of arguments objected against extensional mereology EM, i.e. against the extensionality axiom and the supplementation principles.

Objections Against the Supplementation Principles

Is it, for example, reasonable to assume that every entity is the mereological sum of its proper parts? If the entity e has a proper part f , does there exist a part of f which is disjoint with f ?

The system $M \cup \{M4\}$ implies the following condition S: Every entity is the least upper bound (w.r.t to $\leq$) of its proper parts. The converse does not hold, i.e. $M \cup \{S\}$ does not imply M4. There arises the question whether there are entities which are more than the sum of its proper part.

We consider examples that contradict the principle S, and in turn the weak supplementation principle M4.

*Example*1 Brentano claims in (Brentano 1968) that a non-thinking soul is a part of a thinking soul, but there is no proper part of a thinking soul which differs from the non-thinking soul.[3]

[3]It is stated on p. 53 (Brentano 1968). 'Unter den Wesen welche Teile zeigen, finden sich einige, deren Ganzes sich nicht aus einer Mehrheit von von Teilen zusammensetzt; es erscheint vielmehr als eine Bereicherung eines Teiles, aber nicht durch Hinzukommen eines zweiten Teils.'

Example 2 Let us consider the series of von Neumann-ordinals [Set Theory cited, Devlin, Jech], say the ordinals 0,1,2,3. We stipulate that for ordinals α, β the ordering $\alpha < \beta$ is interpreted as a proper part relation. Then 0,1,2 are all proper parts of 3 but the union of these proper parts does not yield the ordinal 3. This can be seen by representing the numbers as transitive sets: $0 = \varnothing, 1 = \{\varnothing\}, 2 = \{\varnothing, \{\varnothing\}\}, 3 := \{\varnothing, \{\varnothing\}, \{\varnothing, \{\varnothing\}\}\}$. This example does not satisfy, furthermore, the weak supplementation principle.

Objections Against the Extensionality Principle

Concerning the extensionality principles there are objections against both directions of this axiom.

Let us consider both implications of the extensionality principle, and assume in the following consideration the basic premise: $\exists z\,(z < x) \vee \exists z\,(z < y)$.

$$\text{(a)}\ \forall z\,(z < x \leftrightarrow z < y) \rightarrow x = y.$$
$$\text{(b)}\ x = y \rightarrow \forall z\,(z < x \leftrightarrow z < y)\,.$$

Some typical objections against (a) are as follows. Two objects may be different, but may have the same proper parts. Obviously, starting with a set of components that can be used to assemble more complex objects, for example to construct a house from a set of bricks, but also numerous other objects with the same set. Then, the resulting objects may exhibit different forms, hence they are different. Other examples: A bunch of flowers may depend crucially on the arrangement of the individual flowers (Eberle 1970).

A reply to this objection might be that the form of an object can be also considered as part. In any case, we must define the set of admissible parts. And then the question arise, whether there are counterexamples against (a) for every type of parts. We could say, for example, that every property of an object is a part of it. Then the condition (a) would claim the two entities with the same properties are identical.

The condition (b) seems to be acceptable, since it is a form of Leibniz's identity principle: if two entities are identical they have the same properties. This seems to be a trivial basic principle.

But, if the identity relation is taken over time then the possibility of mereological change implies that sameness of parts is not necessary for identity, i.e. there can be two equal identities with different parts. If a cat survives the lost of its tail, then the cat with tail (before the accident) and the cat without tail (after the accident) are numerically the same in the spite of their having different proper parts. Though, a careful analysis shows that this argument is not convincing, because it does not clarify which kind of entity the cat is. In fact, the term "cat" is used here as denoting different entities: a process, presential, and a perpetuant. We hold that the condition (b) must be accepted by any correct top level ontology. In particular, in GFO (Herre 2006) the principle (b) is true, i.e. is considered as an axiom.

3.2.2.3 Fusion Principles and Algebraic Operations

The general fusion axiom in GEM allows to create for every definable set of entities a new object by taking the mereological sum of its members. Such constructions may yield entities which are outside of the human cognition. We argue that humans accept a mereological sum of individuals only if the set can be completed to a comprehensible whole. This whole can be, according to GFO, an object, a process, or a situation.

3.2.3 Definable Relations and Implicit Axioms

In the final part of this section we consider secondary properties of part-of relations. These are relations and properties which are introduced by definitions. Let D = (E, $\leq$) a model of the ground mereology M, and $\varphi(x(1), \ldots, x(n))$ a formula the of the first-order language L($\leq$). Then, the formula $\varphi(x(1), \ldots, x(n))$ defines a new relation in the model M by the following stipulation:

$$\{(a(1), \ldots, a(n)) \, |M| = \varphi[a(1), \ldots, a(n)]\}.$$

Examples of such definitions are the property of being an atom atom(x), or being the mereological sum of atoms, atomic(x) which are specified by the following conditions:

$$\text{atom}(x) \leftrightarrow \neg\exists y\, (y < x)\, ; \text{atomic}(x) := \sup\{a | \text{atom}\,(a) \wedge a \leq x\} = x.$$

Explicit definitions over L($\leq$) can be understood as axioms of the following sort:

$$R(x\,(1), \ldots, x(n)) \leftrightarrow \varphi\,(x\,(1), \ldots, x(n)),$$

where the formula φ is from the language L($\leq$).

The addition of explicit definition does not change the underlying theory (in our case GM), i.e. the following proposition is true (Chang 1977, Hodges 1993).

Proposition 2 *Every definitional extension S of a theory T is conservative over T, hence, every sentence of signature of T which is derivable from S is already definable from T.*

The situation changes if we add, in addition to the explicit definitions, further axioms which pertain to the new introduced relation symbols. Particular structures are linear orderings and part-of relations which are build upon linear orderings. We show some examples of conservative and non-conservative extensions of ground mereology. We now consider the following explicit definition of a relation which is called exclusive part-of Guizzardi (2005).

$$(D): x <(e)\, y \leftrightarrow x < y \wedge \forall z\, (x < z \rightarrow z \leq y \vee y \leq z)\,.$$

The addition of (D) to M yields a conservative extension. The relation x <(e) y defines a sub-relation in every model of M. Obviously, x <(e) y is again partial ordering.[4] The sub-relation x <(e) y satisfies additional properties, besides being a partial ordering. In fact, it defines a partial ordered tree (briefly called tree) within the system (E, $\leq$). A partial ordering (D, $\leq$) is called an *ordered tree* if for every element a in E the set $\{b \mid a \leq b\}$ is a linear ordering. A *linear ordering* (D, $\leq$) is a partial ordering satisfying the additional axiom $\forall xy\,(x \leq y \vee y \leq x)$, hence it does not contain any branching point.

Proposition 3 *For every partial ordering L = (E, $\leq$) the relation x <(e) y defines a tree in E, denoted by Tree(L). Tree(L) is called the tree-skeleton of L.*

The tree-skeleton Tree(M) of a partial ordering is a disjoint union of connected trees, whereas tree T is connected if every two elements of T are connected by a tree-path. This condition holds if any two elements have an upper bound, i.e. $\forall xy\,\exists u\,(x \leq u \wedge y \leq u)$. Obviously, the tree-skeleton of a partial ordering is uniquely determined. If M is a tree, then tree(M) = M; this holds, in particular for linear orderings. Using the Proposition 3 we may introduce two interesting extensions of M: the theory of ordered tree, denoted by T, and the theory linear orderings, denoted by LO. Then, obviously, $M \subseteq T \subseteq LO$. Both theories satisfy the axioms of mereological sum and intersection. Also, the axiom of extensionality is true. But the supplementation axioms are false.

3.2.4 Contextually Based Parthood-Relations

In the preceding section we considered several limitations of the part-of relations. It turns out that for every axiom of the basic theories one may find a situation in reality which contradicts this axiom. One consequence of this fact could be to reject all these axioms, but then only logically true axioms remain, and such tautologies express nothing relevant about the part-of relation. Another, more reasonable consequence proposes the adaptation of part-of relations to relevant situations in the world. For this purpose that must take into consideration the context of the relations' usage. For every relevant context we must develop a context-dependent version of the part-of relation. For this reason we need a library of part-hood relations which covers the relevant situations. There are many dimensions which determine the specificity of a context or of a situation. These include the granularity, the roles which an entity plays, and the level of reality.

We hold that the Ground mereology M should be accepted. The considered examples do not really disprove the usage of the transitivity axiom, but it shows that the mereology must be adapted to specific domains. And such an adaptation can be, we believe, realized in such a way that the Ground axioms in M becomes true. The problems described in Sect 3.2 arise if the wholes and their admitted parts

---

[4] This is not the case for every definable binary relation. In fact, every binary relational system can be defined within a suitable partial ordering.

are not adequately described. Hence, we must add a predicate Wh(x) which captures the wholes of a domain, and then a further domain-specific part-of relation must be introduced. A framework for domain-specific mereologies is proposed in Section 3.5.

3.3 Set Theory and Abstract Mereology

In this section we review some results about the relation between set theory and mereology. There have been several attempts to found set theory, and hence mathematics, on mereology. The first systems of this kind were developed by Lesniewski during 1913–1931 (Lesniewski 1929). Recent approaches of a foundation set theory were carried out by Lewis (1991). The current section summarizes the work by Lewis (1991); the formalizations of the axioms are due to Ridder (2002). It turns out, as Lewis expounded in (Lewis 1991), that abstract mereology together with a fragment of set theory (pertaining to the existence of singletons) yields full set theory. Hence, mathematics can be, in principle, developed on the basis of mereology (extended by a small fragment of set theory). This section is included, on the one hand for completeness, on the other hand to describe a bridge between ontology and set theory which itself can be understood as a basis for mathematics.

3.3.1 Sets and Classes

We present here a sketch of a system which is formalized in monadic second order predicate logic. This formalization is mainly due to Ridder (2002). This language, denoted by L(MS) (MS abbreviates "Mereology plus Singletons"), has two basic relations $\leq$ (part-of relation), singl(x,y) (y is singleton of x), = (is considered as a logical symbol). Furthermore, L(MS) admits variables for unary predicates X, Y, Z, (capital letters) and for items x, y, z (small letters). Atomic formulas have the form $X(z), X = Y, x = y, x \leq y$, singl(x,y). Arbitrary formulas are built up from atomic formulas by the following rules: if φ, ψ formulas then $\varphi \wedge \psi, \varphi \vee \psi, \varphi \rightarrow \psi, \varphi \leftrightarrow \psi, \neg\varphi$ are formulas (closure with respect to propositional connectives); if φ is a formula then $\exists X\varphi$, $\forall X\varphi$ and $\exists x\varphi$, $\forall x\varphi$ are formulas.

We assume the logical axioms for L(MS) and in addition the following comprehension schema:

For every formula φ: we admit the following formula

$$\text{Compr}(\varphi)\text{: } (\exists x\, \varphi(x) \rightarrow \exists P \forall x (P(x) \leftrightarrow \varphi(x)) .$$

The comprehension schema is denoted by Compr, whereas

$$\text{Compr} = \{\text{Compr}(\varphi) \mid \varphi \text{ is a formula in } L(MS)\} .$$

Some definitions (w.r.st $\leq$). The definitions for ov(x,y), and disj(x,y) are as in Section 3.2. The second order fusion is defined as follows:

$$\mathrm{fus}(X, a) =_{df} \forall y\,(\mathrm{ov}(y, a) \leftrightarrow \exists z\,(X(z) \wedge \mathrm{ov}(z, a))$$

with the meaning: a is the fusion of X, i.e. of the items contained in X. The axioms in the sequel are denoted by A(1), A(2),... The axioms A(1),A(2),A(3) represent the ground mereologyM.

$$\begin{aligned}
&A(1): x \leq x \\
&A(2)\; x \leq y \wedge y \leq x \rightarrow x = y \\
&A(3)\; x \leq y \wedge y \leq z \rightarrow x \leq z \\
&A(4)\; \forall P\,(\exists x\, P(x) \rightarrow \exists y\,(\mathrm{fus}(P, y)) \\
&A(5)\; \forall P \forall x\, y\,(\mathrm{fus}(P, x) \wedge \mathrm{fus}(P, y) \rightarrow x = y)
\end{aligned}$$

A weaker form of A(4) is the following axiom A'(4):

$$A'\,(4)\; \forall P([\exists x\, P(x) \wedge \exists v \forall u\,(P(v) \rightarrow u \leq v)] \rightarrow \exists y(\mathrm{fus}\,(P, y)))$$

Let us denote the axioms Compr $\cup$ {A(1), A(2), A(3), A(4), A(5)} by the symbol MSO(M), this is the monadic second order theory of mereology with second order fusion axiom. From A(4) and A(5) follows that the fusion of P exists and is uniquely determined. Hence, we may introduce a function symbol Fus(X) which is defined by the following condition: Fus(X) = a $=_{df}$ fus(X,a). The fusion axiom implies the existence of a greatest entity, denoted by W, containing all entities as a part.

From these axioms we may prove the existence and uniqueness of the mereological sum, of the intersection and the relative complement. The theorems are numbered accordingly by T(1), T(2),...

$$\begin{aligned}
&T(1)\; \forall x\, y\, \exists z\,(\mathrm{sum}(x, y, z)) \\
&T(2)\; \forall x\, y\, u\, v\,(\mathrm{sum}(x, y, u) \wedge \mathrm{sum}(x, y, v) \rightarrow u = v)\,. \\
&T(3)\; \mathrm{ov}(x, y) \rightarrow \exists z\,(\mathrm{intersect}(x, y, z)) \\
&T(4)\; \forall x\, y\, u\, v\,(\mathrm{intersect}(x, y, u) \wedge \mathrm{intersect}(x, y, v) \rightarrow u = v) \\
&T(4)\; \exists u\;(u \leq y \wedge \neg u \leq x)) \rightarrow \exists z\,(\mathrm{relcomp}(x, y, z))\,. \\
&T(5)\; \forall x\, y\, u\, v\,(\mathrm{relcomp}(x, y, u) \wedge \mathrm{relcomp}\,(x, y, v) \rightarrow u = v)
\end{aligned}$$

The proof uses the comprehension principle and the fusion axiom. We sketch the typical reasoning. In proving T(2) let be given the items x, y, and consider $\varphi\,(z) := z = x \vee z = y$. By comprehension there exists a predicate P such that P(x) and P(y). The fusion of P yields an item u such that sum(x,y,u).

The reconstruction of set theory needs a formalization of the infinity by mereological terms. The infinity axioms are based on infinite entities introduced by the condition (Ridder 2002):

$$\mathrm{inf}(x) =_{df} \exists P\,(\exists y P(y) \wedge x = \mathrm{Fus}(P) \wedge \forall y\,(P(y) \rightarrow \exists z\,(P\,(z) \wedge y < z))))$$

An entity e is infinite, if e is the fusion of a set P of entities such that the system (P,<) has no maximal elements, i.e. for every a: P(a) there is a b, P(b), such that a<b. The notion of as finite entity is derived from infinity: finite(x) $=_{df} \neg$ inf(x). Atoms are defined as usual, at(x) $=_{df} \neg\exists$ y (y < x) , i.e. a has no proper parts. There are several axioms that refer to the notions of *many* and *few*.

An entity e is large if there is a set X of entities such that for all a,b $\in$ X, a $\neq$ b, $\neg$ ov(a,b) and Fus(X) = W, and for all a $\in$ X, a contains exactly one atom y such that y $\leq$ e and at most a second atom. This condition can be formalized by the following expression:

$$\text{large}(x) := \exists P\,(\exists y(P(y) \wedge W = \text{Fus}(P) \wedge \forall a\, b\,(P(a) \wedge P(b) \wedge a \neq b \rightarrow \neg \text{ov}(a, b)) \\ \wedge \forall\, y\left[(P\,(y) \rightarrow \exists!!z \text{ at}\,(z, y)\text{ at}(z, x) \wedge \exists!(2)z(\text{at}(z, y))\right].^5$$

$$\text{small}\,(x) := \neg\text{large}(x)\,.$$

We now introduce the notions of *few* and *many*, these are predicates which are defined for predicates, few(X), many(X). Assume a set P is given and *a* is a large entity that does not overlap with any element from P. Then a set X is *few* if there exists a small entity x and a set Y of entities such that x does not overlap with the fusion of X , every element in Y is the binary sum of an element of X and an atom of x, for every element *b* of X there exists an element y of Y such that y is the sum of *b* and an atom of x and every atom of x is part of at most one element of Y.

This can be formalized as follows, according to (Ridder 2002)

$$\forall P\,(\exists\, x\, P(x) \wedge \exists\, y\,(\text{large}(y) \wedge \forall\, x\,(P(x) \rightarrow \neg\text{ov}(x, y)) \rightarrow [\text{few}(X) : \\ =\exists Y x\,(\text{small}\,(x) \wedge \exists y Y\,(y) \\ \wedge \neg\text{ov}(x, \text{Fus}(X)) \wedge \forall z\,(Y\,(z) \rightarrow \exists rs\,(X\,(r) \wedge \text{At}(s, x) \wedge z \\ = r{+}s)) \wedge \forall z\,(X(z) \rightarrow \exists r\, s\,(Y(r) \wedge \\ \text{At}(s, x) \;\wedge r = r + z)) \wedge\neg\exists\, y\, u\, v\,(\text{At}(y, x) \wedge y \leq u \wedge y(u) \wedge Y(v) \wedge u \neq v)\right].$$

$$\text{many}(X) := \neg\,\text{few}(X)\,.$$

A(6): Small-Few-Principle. An entity x is small if and only if it has few atoms.

$$\text{small}(x) \leftrightarrow \exists\, P(\exists y\, P(y) \wedge \text{few}(P) \wedge \forall y(P(y) \leftrightarrow \text{at}(y, x))$$

In capturing the whole set theory we must introduce a replacement schema in the framework of L(MS). For a formula φ (x,y) with first-order variables x,y we define

$$\text{Repl}(\varphi) := \forall P\, Q\,(\exists x\, P(x) \wedge \exists x\, Q(x) \wedge \forall\, x\,(P(x) \rightarrow \exists!!y\,(Q\,(y) \wedge (\varphi(x, y) \vee \varphi(y, x))) \wedge$$

---

[5] $\exists!!$(n) x has the meaning "there exists exactly n many x", whereas $\exists!$(n) x has the meaning "there exist at most n many x". The index (n) is ommitted if n=1.

$$\forall x\,(Q\,(x) \rightarrow \exists\, y(P(y) \wedge (\varphi\,(x, y) \vee \varphi\,(y, x)) \wedge \mathrm{few}(X)) \rightarrow \mathrm{few}(Y)\,.$$

Now, the relation singl(x,y) (y is singleton of x) is considered. The idea behind the relation singl(x,y) is the condition: $y = \{x\}$.

$$\mathrm{A}(7)\ \mathrm{singl}(x, u) \wedge \mathrm{singl}(x, v) \rightarrow u = v\ (\mathrm{singl}(x, y)\ \text{is a functional relation})\,.$$

Now, several further relations and predicates are introduced. The relation singl(x,y) is functional, hence we may introduce a functional symbol $\mathrm{Sg}(x) = y \leftrightarrow$ singl(x,y).

An entity x is a singleton if there an entity y such that singl(y,x); we introduce a symbol sing(x) defined by $\mathrm{sing}(x) \leftrightarrow \exists\ y\ (\mathrm{singl}(y,x))$. The interpretation of set theory in the theory Mon(SM) needs definitions of set, class, and membership. The following condition defines the empty set. Since N(x) is uniquely determined we may introduce a constant symbol $\varnothing$.

$$N(x) := \exists\, P\, \exists\, y\, (y = \mathrm{Fus}(P) \wedge \forall w\, (P(w) \leftrightarrow \forall z\, (z \leq w \rightarrow \neg \mathrm{sing}(z)))$$

$$x = \varnothing := N(x)\,.$$

$$\mathrm{Cl}(x)\ := x\ \text{is the mereological sum of its singletons}\ \ (x\ \text{is a class})$$

$$\mathrm{Set}(x) := x = \varnothing \vee (\mathrm{Cl}(x) \wedge \exists\, y\, (y = \mathrm{Sing}(x)))\,.$$

The membership relation can be introduced as follows:

$$x \in y := \mathrm{Cl}(y) \wedge \exists\, z\, (\mathrm{singl}(x, z) \wedge z \leq y))\,.$$

From these axioms the classical axioms of set theory ST can be derived, hence the theory ST is interpretable in the theory MS.

3.3.2 Interpretability of Set Theory in Mereology and Models of Th(Mer)

We need a translation tr: $L(ST) \rightarrow L(MS)$, such that certain conditions are satisfied. The translation function tr is based on the notion of interpretability between theories as expounded in (Ershov 1965, Tarski 1935).

The function tr is defined inductively on the complexity of the formulas.

$$\mathrm{tr}(x\ \in\ y) := \mathrm{Cl}(y) \wedge \exists z(\mathrm{singl}(x, z) \wedge z \leq y))\,.$$

$$\mathrm{tr}(\forall x \varphi) := (\mathrm{Set}(x) \rightarrow \mathrm{tr}(\varphi))$$

$$\mathrm{tr}(\exists x \varphi) := (\mathrm{Set}(x) \wedge \mathrm{tr}(\varphi))$$

Now, one may prove the following theorem, essentially carried out in Ridder (2003).

Proposition 4 For every sentence φ of ZFC holds: ZFC $\models \varphi$ if and only if MS $\models \mathrm{tr}(\varphi)$.

The theory MS is a monadic second order theory of basic signature $\{\leq, \mathrm{singl}(x, y), =\}$; hence there are (besides $=$), two non-logical binary relation symbols $\leq$, singl,. This theory is undecidable which follows from standard results in logic (Ershov 1965). Furthermore, the models of the sub-theory restricted to $\leq$ alone exhibits a distributive lattice with relative complements.

3.3.3 The Ontology of Singletons

In this section we discuss the ontology of singletons. There are two different approaches to establish the ontology of singletons: one of them is the method of reduction, the other consists in the introduction of a new kind of ontological entity. The reductive method consists in explaining and defining singletons by other well-established ontological entities and principles. The non-reductive method stipulates singletons as a new kind of entity which must be characterized axiomatically.

Sets are introduced in an informal manner. According to Cantor (1932), a set is a many which can be thought of as one, it is a totality of definite objects that can be combined into a whole by a law. In Shoenfield (1967) a set is considered as a collection of objects which is formed by gathering together certain objects to form a single object. Kleene (1967) holds that a set is constituted by objects thought of together. Robbin (1969) states that a set is a collection of objects and is thought to have an independent existence of its own. Further and similar definitions of a set are expounded in Devlin (1993) and (Halmos 1960).

Categories are abstract, non-temporal entities, which may be represented by linguistic expressions denoting concepts (Herre 2006). We may assume that every communicable category is a concept.[6] For every concept C we may consider the collection $\{a \mid a :: C\}$ of instances of C, denoted by Ext(C). Ext(C) and C are, obviously, different kinds of entities. We consider Ext(C) as a set which satisfies the axiom of extensionality with respect to the membership relation. The extensions Ext(C) of categories, considered as sets, are compatible with Cantor's definition: the conditions presented in a specification of C can be understood as a law combining the elements of Ext(C) to a whole. In Kleene's definition of a set a law is not necessarily assumed, it is required only that a collection of objects can be thought together, can be comprehended as a whole.

The naive understanding of a set exhibits two aspects, one is related to a law specifying the set, the other concerns with the membership relation which captures the relation between objects and the set. The specification of a set by a condition

[6]Universals are sometimes considered as categories being independent from any subject; they are associated to invariants of reality. Such universals cannot be immediately communicated, concepts must be related to them which, in turn, may be communicated by using symbols and tokens denoting them.

pertains to a feature of categories, and, hence, does not grasp the essence of a set. On the other hand, a set is understood to be a whole. According to the approach of Lewis (1991) these wholes are the mereological fusion of singletons being atomic parts. Given a material object Ob we may consider the set Parts(Ob) of parts of Ob. The set Parts(Ob) as a whole is different from the object Ob. Ob is the mereological fusion of the elements of Parts(Ob); on the other hand, the set Parts(Ob), as a whole, is the mereological sum of the singletons which are associated to the parts of Ob. We take the position of D. Lewis that an understanding of a set is, finally, reduced to an understanding of the notion of a singleton. We add our particular opinion that singletons capture those features of a set which have no relation to the notion of a category. Hence, singletons exhibit the essence of sets in general.

In the subsequent consideration we present a new approach to singletons which is compatible with the top level ontology GFO. A singleton has a double-sided nature. On the one hand, it is a cognitive construction of the mind based on a view. On the other hand, we hold, it is an ideal entity which has an objective existence. Furthermore, there is a relation between set theory in general and the realm of spatio-temporal entities. Additionally, singletons capture a facet of what is called reification. Reification of a thing T means- in this context – to consider T as an element without looking at its parts. Considering an entity as an element needs the existence of a set of which this entity is an element. This set can be interpreted as a meta-level entity from which one looks at its members.

Let Obj be a thing, a spatio-temporal entity, say a chair or a house. By an intentional act we perceive the object immediately. But, there is also a meta-level of contemplation. Looking from meta-level at the object is different from its immediate perception.[7] The meta-level perspective is a basic step for creating sets, and the simplest set which satisfies this condition is the singleton of a thing. If subsets are parts of a set, then a singleton has no proper parts. To reify is to treat an entity as a thing, but what is really done (in most cases) is to treat it as an element of a meta-level entity considered as a set.

3.4 Classification of Mereological Systems

In this section we continue the investigation of abstract mereological systems, and present a preliminary classification of those theories that might be relevant for real domains. This section uses theories about Boolean algebras and distributive lattices with relative complements.

[7] There is a relation between singletons and the process of bracketing in the sense of Husserl (1985). This term describes the process of thinking away the natural interpretation of an experience to capture its intrinsic nature. The natural interpretation refers to the immediate perception, the intrinsic nature to its pure existence.

3.4.1 Lattices, Ideals and Filters

In this section we review the basics of lattice theory and provide the tools to carry out the classification of the elementary types of the theories CM (classical mereology) and GEM (general extension mereology). Models of the classical system CM can be represented as structures $M = (E, \cup, \cap, -1)$. $\cup$ denotes mereological sum, $\cap$ mereological intersection, and – the difference between entities. In GEM we may assume that a greatest element exists because we may construct the mereological sum of all entities providing the greatest element. In CM the existence of the greatest element is not derivable.

3.4.1.1 Lattices and Partial Orderings

A lattice $M = (E, \cup, \cap)$ is an algebraic structure with two binary operations $\cup$, $\cap$ satisfying the following conditions:

$$L1 : x \cup x = x; x \cup x = x$$

$$L2. x \cup y = y \cup x; x \cup y = y \cap x$$

$$L3. x \cup (y \cup z) = (x \cup y) \cup z; x \cap (y \cap z) = (x \cap y) \cap z$$

$$L4. x \cup (x \cap y) = x; x \cap (x \cup y) = x$$

Let be defined: $x \leq y := x \cup y = y$ or $x \leq y := x \cap y = x$. Then, if $(E, \cup, \cap)$ is a lattice then $(E, \leq)$ is a partial ordering satisfying the additional condition that any two elements have a least upper bound (l.u.b.) and a greatest lower bound (g.l.b.). Conversely, if $(E, \leq)$ is a partial ordering such that for any two elements the supremum and the infimum exist, we may introduce operations $\cup$, $\cap$ by following definitions: $a \cup b = \sup\{a, b\}$, $a \cap b = \inf\{a, b\}$. Then, $M = (E, \cup, \cap)$ is lattice.

3.4.1.2 Ideals and Factor Lattices

Let $(E, \cup, \cap)$ be a lattice. A subset $I \subseteq E$ is an ideal in M if: 1. if $a \in I$ and $b \leq a$ then $b \in I$; 2. $a, b \in I$ implies that $a \cup b \in I$..

For every ideal I in M we may introduce an equivalence relation as follows: a $\equiv$(I) b iff there exists an element $c \in I$ such that $a \cup c = b \cup c$. Let E^* be the factor set of E modulo $\equiv$(I), also denoted by $E^* = E/\equiv(I)$. Let $[a]_I$ be the equivalence class associated to the element a, i.e. $[a]_I = \{b | a \equiv(I) b\}$. The function $f(a) = [a]_I$ is a homomorphism from M onto M^*. The system $M^* = (E^*, \cup, \cap)$ is called the factor lattice of M w.r.t. the ideal I. The operations $\cup$, $\cap$ are defined for equivalence classes as follows: $[a] \cup^* [b] = [a \cup b]$; $[a] \cap^* [b] = [a \cap b]$.

3.4.1.3 Distributive Lattices, Complements, and Boolean Algebras

A lattice $D = (E, \cup, \cap)$ is distributive if the following conditions are satisfied: $x \cap (y \cup z) = (x \cap y) \cup (x \cap z)$; $x \cup (y \cap z) = (x \cup y) \cap (x \cup z)$. Distributive lattices with relative complement are defined as follows. Let 0 be the least element of a distributive lattice, hence D = (E, ∪, ∩, 0). Assume a,b ∈ E and a ≤ b. An element c ∈ E is a complement of a with respect to b iff c ∩ a = 0 and a ∪ c = b. A system D = (E, ∪, ∩, 0,1) is a Boolean algebra iff it is a distributive lattice with least and greatest elements 0,1, and for every a ∈ E there exists an b such that a ∩ b = 0 and a ∪ b = 1. This element b is uniquely determined and is called the complement of a. Because of uniqueness we may introduce a unary operation c(x); c(x) is the complement of x.

3.4.1.4 Generalizations

Relative complements may be generalized to lattices without 0 and 1. Let D = (E, ∪, ∩) be distributive lattice, and $a, b \in E, a \leq b, a \leq c \leq b$. An element d, $a \leq d \leq b$, is called a relative complement of c with respect to a and b if and only if $c \cup d = b, c \cap d = a$. D is said to be relatively complemented if for every $a, b \in E, a \leq b$, and c: $a \leq c \leq b$, there exists a relative complement d of c with respect to a,b. Obviously, if D is a distributive relatively complemented lattice then for every, a,b ∈ E, the sub-system $\{c|a \leq c \leq b\}$ defines a Boolean algebra.

Lattices can be generalized to *weak lattices*. A weak lattice is a partial ordering satisfying the subsequent conditions:

$$\forall x\, y\, (\exists z\, (x \leq z \wedge y \leq z) \rightarrow \exists v\, (v = \sup\{x, y\}))$$
$$\forall x\, y\, (\exists z\, (z \leq x \wedge z \leq y) \rightarrow \exists v\, (v = \inf\{x, y\}))$$

Mereological system do not satisfy, in general, the existence of suprema and infima for finite sets, though, the classical systems are distributive weak lattices.

3.4.1.5 Properties of Elements in Distributive Weak Lattices

Let D = (E, ≤) be a weak distributive, and relatively complemented lattice. An element a ∈ E is an *atom*, if $\neg\exists y\, (y < a)$; a is said to be *atomic* if $a = \sup\{b|b \leq a, \text{a is atom}\}$. The predicates at(x) denote atoms, atomic(x) atomic elements. An element a is said to be atomless if there is no atom b such that b ≤ a; hence a does not contain an atom as part. An element a is called separable if is either atomic or atomless or the union of an atomic and an atomless element. Hence, the predicate sep(a) is definied by the condition: $\text{sep}(x) \leftrightarrow \text{atomic}(x) \vee \text{atomless}(x) \vee \exists y\, z\, (\text{atomic}(y) \wedge \text{atomless}(z) \wedge x = y \cup z)$.

3.4.1.6 Separability Ideals

Let D = (E, ≤) be a weak distributive relatively complemented lattice. The set Sep(D) is defined by Sep(D) = { a | a is separable}. Sep(D) is an ideal, hence the factor lattice D/Sep(D) is uniquely determined. The *separability sequence* of D is inductively defined as follows. D(0) := D, D(1) := D(0)/Sep(D(0)), D(n+1) := D(n)/Sep(D(n)), n = 0,1,2,. . .,n,. . . Associated to this sequence is an increasing sequence of ideals $S(0) \subseteq S(1) \subseteq \ldots \subseteq S(n) \subseteq \ldots$ such that S(0) := Sep(D). If S(n) = S(n+1), then S(n) = S(n+ k) for every $k < \omega$. Since we assume that D is a countable

the sequence $S(\alpha)$ stabilizes at a countable ordinal.[8] The *separability degree* of D is the least ordinal at which the sequence S stabilizes. The *separability characteristics* of D, denoted by char(D)= (α, β, γ), is determined according to (Ershov 1980) as follows.

(1) $\alpha = \infty$, if $S(\delta)$ stabilizes at an ordinal $\delta \geq \omega$, in this case: $\beta = \infty, \gamma = \infty$
(2) $\alpha = n$, n <, the separability degree of D equals n. If D(n-1) has k many atoms, $0 \leq k \leq \omega$, then $\beta = k$; if D(n-1) has infinitely many atoms then $\beta = \infty$; if D(n-1) has atomless elements, then, otherwise, $\gamma = 0$.

The components of the separability characteristics of a distributive relatively complemented weak lattice can be expressed by first order formulas. Hence, these formulas can be used to elementarily distinguish models of mereological theories, and to define extensions of them.

3.4.2 The Systems with General Fusion Principles

Any of the considered systems is an extension to classical mereology. Firstly, we consider GEM (General Extension Mereology with the elementary fusion schema FUS). We investigate two forms of FUS. Fus(φ) as usual, and a restrictied version, denoted by

$$\mathrm{Fus}^*(\varphi) := \left[\exists u\, \varphi(u) \wedge \exists u \forall v\, (\varphi(v) \rightarrow v \leq u)\right] \rightarrow \mathrm{Fus}(\varphi).$$

Fus*(φ) allows fusion only if the elements satisfying φ have an common upper bound. It is obvious, that GEM implies the existence of a greatest entity if we take $\varphi(v) := v = v$. The weaker system GEM* does not imply the existence of a greatest element. The models of GEM* satisfy a number of conditions. Every model D of GEM* has the seperability degree 0, because every element is separable. This is implied by the fusion schema FUS*. Hence $\alpha(D) = 0$, i.e., it is true $\forall x$ (sep(x)). There might be the following possibilities: $\beta = k, \infty, \gamma =, 0, 1$, The any of these characteristics we my find a first order formula, abbreviate them by Ch(α), Ch(γ), whereas Ch(k) says that there are exactly k many atoms, and Ch(∞) is an infinite axiom schema saying that there exist k many atoms for every k. Ch(γ) says that there are accordingly atomless elements or not.

[8] We take account of in the present paper only natural numbers, not arbitrarly ordinals. This restriction is sufficient since we consider elementary classifications of mereological systems, i.e. classifications based on the language of first order predicate logic.

If we assume the strong fusion schema FUS then there exists a greatest element, but there must not exist a least element. Again we may distinguish the possible models with respect to their separability characteristics. In both cases there is infinite number of different consistent extensions of the theories GEM resp.. GEM*. These extensions may be proved to be consistent by constructing models satisfying the respective conditions. Here, we may use the results in (Ershov 1980), where Boolean algebras were constructed satisfying these conditions. These described extensions are, in general, not complete because further conditions must be taken into account.

3.4.3 Classical Mereology

In this section we describe a classification of some consistent extensions of mereological systems which satisfy the condition of a lattice with relative complements. In (Simons 1987) only atomic or atomless mereologies are considered. In this section we show that the possible systems are much richer if we assume as a classification framework first order logic. The classification is based on a similar classification of lattices with a relative complement. A basic notion in this classification is the degree of separability. This field of research is associated to a classification of partial orderings.

We consider the classical basic theory CM without the elementary fusion schema. Then the classification of all complete extensions of this theory is more complicated. We sketch an overview about them. The classification of complete extensions or CM uses some definitions. An entity is atomistic, denoted by atomist(x), iff x is the supremum of all atoms below x. An element is separable if it is atomic or atomless or the mereological sum of an atomist entity and an atomless entity. We again describe elementary properties, using the characteristics of a lattice, according to Section 3.4.2, to define different consistent extensions of the classical mereology.

One may prove that for every characteristics δ there is a model of CM satisfying this characteristics δ. This follows from the classification of the elementary types of Boolean algebras, as expounded by Tarski and completely elaborated and generalized by Ershov (1980) which gives the deepest insights in the structure of classical mereological systems. Semi-Boolean algebras result from Boolean algebras by removing 0 or 1 or both. Every semi-Boolean algebra is a model of CM. But, the converse is not true. Hence, the classification of the elementary types, using the characteristics set forth in Section 3.4.1 is not complete and must be refined and extended.

We sketch a basic construction for models of CM. Let D = (M, $\leq$) be a linear ordering, and Int(D) the set of all half-open intervals (a,b], for a < b. BA(D) is the smallest system of sets which contains the system Int(D) as a subset and is closed (within Pow(D)), the power-set over D), and which is closed with respect to union intersection and complements. BA(D) is a Boolean algebra with a linear ordered basis isomorphic to D.

3.4.4 *Extensions of the Ground Mereology*

There are relevant extensions of the ground mereology M which are incompatible with the classical system CM. Among these extensions belong: the linear orderings and the ontology of ordered trees. Both theories are decidable. Linear orderings exhibit some particular phenomena. If the linear ordering has no least element then this system must be infinite. We may now classify partial orderings M with respect to the tree-skeleton tree(M) as introduced in Section 3.2.3. We consider those M whose tree-skeleton is connected, hence the axiom is true that for arbitrary elements belonging to the domain of the relation <(e) there exists an upper bound.

An element *a* belongs to the domain of tree(M), denoted by D(tree(M)), if there exists an x such that a<(e)x or x<(e)a. Usually, D(tree(M)) $\neq$ M. Mereological systems M may be classified with respect the elementary properties of their tree-skeletons D(tree(M),<(e)), denoted by TSK(M). Two mereological systems M, N are tree-equivalent if their tree-skeletons TSK(M), TSK(N) are elementary equivalent. A mereological system M is tree-like if M = TSK(M) = M. If a tree-like mereological system M is a linear ordering we may use the results of (Läuchli 1966) to achieve a further classification pertaining to their elementary properties.[9] A classification of the elementary types of all tree-like mereological systems is an open problem.

3.5 Domain-Specific Mereologies

Any foundational ontology includes a number of basic relations. We assume that the part-of-relation is included in every reasonable domain.

3.5.1 *Domains*

We hold that a domain D = (Obj, V, CP) is determined by a set Obj(D) of objects[10], a set V of views, and a set CP of classification principles. A conceptualization Concept(D) is defined by a set Conc(D) of concepts, and a set Rel(D) of relations. The concepts Conc(D) are defined by a selection of views of V and a choice of classification principles of CP. Furthermore, a set of relations Rel(Concept(D)) must be introduced. We emphasize that a domain has usually more than one conceptualization. We assume that the relations Rel(Concept(D)) include the part-of relations p(x,y). Usually, the elements of Obj(D) have an internal structure. For every kind of object one must clarify what the parts of it are. Furthermore, we must distinguish between those objects which are considered as wholes, and those which a parts of

---

[9]The elementary classification of linear orderings is more complicated than for Boolean algebras because their are uncountably many elementary types of linear orderings.

[10]In most cases the objects are individuals.

wholes, but not being wholes. Furthermore, we must take into consideration the level of granularity. We stipulate that within a domain D for any level of granularity there exists wholes which are associated to this level.

3.5.2 *Parts and Wholes*

Formally, the wholes of a domain D – in the framework of a formal mereological theory – can be represented by a unary predicate Wh(x) whose instances are the wholes of D. We consider the notion of whole as primitive, hence it cannot be reduced to other notions. In general, the whole is more than the set or the mereological fusion of its parts.[11] The understanding of the relation between parts and wholes must take into consideration both the analytical and the synthetic approach. How parts may be defined and derived from wholes (analysis), and how wholes are constructed from entities which occur in the resulting wholes as parts (synthesis)? In both approaches the notion of a whole resists a complete explanation. The synthetic approach to wholes tries to find restrictions of the fusion principle which assure the existence of wholes. D. Lewis doubts whether such principles can ever be found, (Lewis 1986). We hold that one reason for this difficulty is that wholes in most situations cannot be completely separated from cognition. We claim, furthermore, that the understanding of wholes is related to the levels of reality. We now collect a number of examples about wholes which show the diversity of phenomena in which wholes come into appearance.

3.5.2.1 Gestalts

This area presents many examples about the fact that the whole is more than the collection of its parts. The first examples were presented and discussed by von Ehrenfels (1890), Wertheimer claims that the Gestalt is a whole which is perceptually primary and that the parts are derived from it (Wertheimer 1922, 1923). Rescher and Oppenheim (1955b) provides a basis for a clear and simple terminology for investigation and discussion of wholes, parts and their inter-relationships.

3.5.2.2 Material Objects and Natural Boundaries

Natural boundaries of material objects can be contribute to a whole, in particular, if the objects have a closed natural boundary. Material objects which are perceived as a whole have usually a natural boundary (as defined in the top level ontology GFO). We claim that natural boundaries are cognitively biased, though we assume that material objects belong to the material stratum of the world. Examples are an individual organism or a crystal.

---

[11] This remark does not contradict the supplementation principle because wholeness adds features to the entity that cannot captured by pure mereology.

3.5.2.3 Systems

The notion of a system is very general. In principle, even heaps of unspecified materials can be understood as systems. It seems to be reasonable to restrict this very general understanding and to impose a number of restrictions to the most general notion of a system. We consider systems S as wholes satisfying at least the following conditions: a) there exists a boundary for S that allows to discriminate the interior of the system from the outside environment. b) the parts of the system, called components, are related by specific relations, c) the system S can be comprehended as a whole. We may distinguish several kinds of systems, material systems as machines, software-systems and material objects, organisms (biological systems), environmental systems, social systems, and cognitive systems.

3.5.2.4 Situations, Situoids, and Sets

Situations are introduced as parts of the world that can be comprehended as wholes. Sets exhibit a particular type of wholes whose parts are subsets. Sets are atomistic, i.e. they are the mereological sum of its atomic parts which are singletons.

3.5.3 General Framework

In this section we sketch a *general framework* for presenting and analysing domain-specific mereological systems. For this purpose the abstract mereologies must be refined by including granularity levels and a predicate Wh(x,L) expressing that the entity x is a whole of granularity level L. Then, the set Obj(D) of underlying objects exhibits a much more complex structure.

For every domain D we may introduce a mereological system M(D) which is specified as follows. Let Obj(D) be the class of objects belonging to the domain D. Then we take the closure of Obj(D) with respect to the objects of D. Not every (unrestricted) part of an object O of D is a domain-specific part of O.

We consider systems M(D) = (E, E(0),..,E(k), Wh(0), ..., Wh(k), p(1),...,p(k), p). Here, the set E is the union of the E (i) , i.e .E = E (0) ∪ ... ∪ E (k).E (i) includes the objects of a certain granularity level. Wh(i) are the wholes of the granularity level i, p(i) is the part-of relation which is defined for the level i. The relation p contains all the relations p(i) as sub-relations, but in addition further links between the levels i,j. Consider the set Wh(i) of wholes of the level i. Trans(Wh(i)) is the smallest set of objects containing the wholes Wh(i) and closed with respect of taking parts based on the relation p(i), i.e. closed with respect to the condition: if e is an element of Trans(Wh(i)) and p(i)(f,e), then f, too, is an element of Trans(Wh(i)). We assume that E(i) $\supseteq$ Trans(Wh(i)). The systems Trans(Wh(i)) exhibit those parts of the domain D that can be captured by the specification of wholes and their parts.[12]

---

[12]There can be, of course, many other entities that belong to the domain which cannot be generated in this mereological way, for example, those entities which are individual properties that inhere

There can be, of course, many other entities that belong to the domain which cannot be generated in this mereological way, for example, entities which are individual properties that inhere in objects. These entities may be captured by considering relations, different from the part-of relation. By construction, the systems Trans(Wh(i)) are partial orderings (w.r.t. p(i)) and one may ask which types of partial orderings are realized in real domains. In particular the systems Trans(Ob) for some object Ob in Wh(i) can be considered. An elementary condition on the objects in Wh(i) might be that two different wholes have no common parts. This seems to be true for organisms with a natural boundary. A further condition to be taken into consideration is the type of individuals. Wh(i) could be presentials (at a certain time point) or processes, or both. Finally, we consider the problem of axiomatization of domain-specific mereological systems of the form M)D). For the sake of simplicity we assume one level of granularity only, hence the structure M(D) has the form (E, Wh(x), p(x,y)). The axioms are formalized in FOL based on the vocabulary V = (Wh(x), p(x,y)). The complete theory of M(D), denoted by Th(M(D)), is defined by Th(M(D) = {F | F belongs to FOL(V) and F is true in D}. For complex domains D a complete axiomatization can hardly be achieved. Furthermore, it can be expected that only few axioms hold in any of these mereological systems M(D). We collect some axioms that might be interesting in classifying these systems M(D).

1. The relation p(x,y), restricted to Wh(x) yields a partial ordering

$$\forall x\,(Wh(x) \rightarrow p(x,x))$$
$$\forall xy\,(Wh(x) \wedge Wh(y) \wedge x \leq y \wedge y \leq x \rightarrow x = y)$$
$$\forall xyz(Wh(x) \wedge Wh(y) \wedge Wh(z) \wedge x \leq y \wedge y \leq z \rightarrow x \leq z)$$

2. Covering axiom: every entity is a part of a whole.

$$\forall x\,\exists y\,(Wh(y) \wedge x \leq y)$$

3. Every whole is the fusion of its proper parts.

$$\forall x\,(Wh(x) \rightarrow x = Fus(\{a|a < x\})$$

   A whole is said to be simple if it satisfies condition 3.
4. Disjointness of wholes.

$$\forall xy\,(Wh(x) \wedge Wh(y) \wedge \text{not}\,(x{=}y) \rightarrow disj(x,y))$$

Formally, we may apply the axioms M4,M5,M6,M7,M8 to wholes, or to the set of all entities of M(D). An exhaustive overview about the possible reasonable combinations of these axioms is a project for future research.

---

in objects. These entities may be captured by considering relations which are different from the part-of relation.

Acknowledgment Many thanks to F. Loebe, and R. Hoehndorf for diverse discussions about several topics of mereology. I am grateful to R. Poli and anonymous reviewers their critical remarks that contributed to the quality of paper.

References

Brentano, F. 1968. *Kategorienlehre*. Felix Meiner: Hamburg.

Brentano, F. 1973. *Raum, Zeit, und Kontinuum*. Hamburg: Meiner Verlag.

Bunge, M. 1966. On null individuals. *Journal of Philosophy* 63:776–778.

Burkhardt, H., and C.A. Dufour. 1991 Part/whole I: History. In *Handbook of metaphysics and ntology*, eds. H. Burkhardt, and B. Smith, 663–673. München: Philosophia.

Cantor, G. 1932. *Gesammelte Abhandlungen mathematischen und philosophischen Inhalts*. ed. Zermelo E. Berlin: Springer.

Chang, C.C., and H.J. Keisler. 1977. *Model theory*, Amsterdam: North-Holland Publishing Company.

Chisholm, R.M. 1878. Brentano's conception of substance and accident. *Grazer Philosophische Studien* 5:197–210

Cruse, D.A. 1979. On the ransitivity of the part-whole relation. *Journal of Linguistics* 15:29–38.

Devlin, K. 1993. *Set theory: The joy of sets*, 2nd ed. New York, NY: Springer.

Eberle, R.A. 1970. *Nominalistic systems*. Dordrecht: Reidel.

Ehrenfels, C. 1890. von: Über Gestaltqualitäten. *Vierteljahresschrift für wissenschaftliche Philosophie* 14:249–292.

Ershov, Y. 1980. *Problemi Rasreshimost i Konstruktivnije Modeli*. Moskva: Nauka,

Ershov, Y., I. Lavrov, A. Taimanov, and A.D. Taitslin. 1965. .Elementarnie Teorii. *IMN* 20(4): 37–108.

Gerstl, P., S. Pribbenow. 1995. Midwinters, end games, and bodyparts. A classification of part-whole relations. *Interntional Journal of Human-Computer Studies* 43:865–889.

Grätzer, G. 1998. *General lattice theory*. Boston, MA: Birkhäuser.

Guizzardi, G. 2005. *Ontological foundations for structural conceptual models*. Ph.D. thesis, Enschede, Telematica Institut, The Netherlands.

Halmos, P.R. 1960. *Naïve set theory*. Princeton, NJ: Van Nostrand.

Herre, H. 2010. This volume. The ontology of medical terminological systems. Towards the next Generation of Biomedical Ontologies.

Herre, H., P. Burek, F. Loebe, F. Hoehndorf, and H. Michalek. 2006. *General formal ontology (GFO) – A foundtional ontology integrating objects and processes*, Onto-med report Nr. 8 , IMISE, Universität Leipzig.

Hodges, W. 1993. *Introduction to model theory*. Cambridge: Cambridge University Press.

Husserl, E. 1985. *Die phänomenologische Methode. Ausgewählte Texte I*. Stuttgart: Reclam

Husserl, E. 1992a. *Logische Untersuchungen., 2. Bd. Untersuchungen zur Phänomenologie und der Theorie der Erkenntnis*. Hamburg: Verlag Felix Meiner.

Husserl, E. 1992b. *Ideen zu einer reinen Phänomenologie*. Hamburg: Verlag Felix Meiner.

Inwagen, van P. 1993 Naïve mereology, admissable valuations, and other matters. *Nous* 27: 229–234.

Johnston, M. 1992. Constitution is not identity. *Mind* 101:89–105

Kleene, S.C. 1967. *Mathematical logic*. New York, NY: Wiley.

Kleinknecht, R. 1992. Mereologische strukturen der welt. *Wissenschaftliche Zeitschrift der Humboldt-Universität zu berlin, Reihe der Geistes- und Sozialwissenschafteb* 41: 40–53

Läuchli, H., and L. Leonard. 1966. On the elementary theory of linear order. *Fundamenta Mathemat-icae* 59:109–116.

Lesniewski, S. 1929. Grundzüge eines neuen Systems der Grundlagen der Mathematik, *Fundamenta Mathematicae* IXV:1–81

Lewis, D. 1986. *On the pluraty of the world*. Oxford: Blackwell.

Lewis, D. 1991. *Parts and classes*. Oxford: Blackwell
Lewis, D. 1993. Mathematics is megethology. *Philosophia Matematica* 3:3–23.
Markosian, N. 1998. Bruatl composition. *PhilosOphical Studies* 92:211–249.
Martin, R.M. 1965. Of time and the null individual. *Journal of Philosophy* 62:723–736.
Mendelson, E. 2001. *Introduction to mathematical logic*. London: Chapman and Hall.
Moltmann, R. 1997. *Parts and wholes in semantics*. Oxford: University Press.
Oliver, A. 1992. The metaphysics of singletons. *Mind* 101:129–140.
Oliver, A. 1994. Are subclasses pats of classes? *Analysis* 54/4:215–223.
Pribbenow, S. 2002. Meronymic relationships. In R. Green, and C.A. Bean, ed. Dordrecht: Kluwer Publication
Rescher, N. 1955a. Axioms for the part relation. *Philosophical Studies* 6:8–11
Rescher, N., and P. Oppenheim. 1955b. Logical analysis of gestalt concepts. *British Journal for Philosophy of Science* 6:89–106
Ridder, L. 2002. *Mereology*. Frankfurt am main: Vittorio Klostermann
Robbin, J.W. 1969. *Mathematical logic*. Menlo Park: W. A. Benjamin.
Sanford, D. 1993. The problem of the many. Many composition quantifiers, and naive mereology. *Nous* 27:219–228
Shoenfield, J.R. 1967. *Mathematical logic*. Reading, MA: Addison Wesley.
Sider, T. 1997. *Four dimensionalism. An ontology of persistence and time*. New York, NY: Oxford University Press.
Simons, P. 1987. *Parts – A study in ontology*. Oxford: Clarendon Press.
Tarski, A. 1935. Zur Grundlegung der Booleschen Algebra I. *Fundamenta Mathemat-icae* 24: 177–198.
Tarski, A., A. Mostowski,, and R.M. Robinson. .1953. *Undecidable theories*. Amsterdam: North Holland
Tversky, B.1989. Parts, partonomies, and taxonomies. *Development Psychology* 25:983–995
Varzi, A. 1996. Parts, wholes and part-whole relations: The prospects of mereotopology. *Data and Knowledge Engineering* 20(3):259–286.
Wertheimer, M. 1922. Untersuchungen zur Lehre von der Gestalt I. *Psychologische Forschung* 1:,47–58.
Wertheimer, M. 1923. Untersuchungen zur Lehre von der Gestalt II. Psychologische *Forschung* 4:,301–350
Zimmermann, D.W. 1996. Could be extended objects be made out of simple parts? An argument for “Atomless gunk”. *Philosophy and Phenomenological Research* 56:1–29

Chapter 4
Causation

Asbjørn Steglich-Petersen

4.1 Introduction

Causation is of undeniable importance to our understanding of, and interaction with our surroundings. Its importance is evidenced by our reliance on causal concepts in tasks of the following sorts:

- *Explanation.* Knowledge of causal relationships allows us to explain courses of events.
- *Prediction.* Knowledge of causal relationships allows us to predict future events.
- *Manipulation.* Knowledge of causal relationships allows us to manipulate our surroundings.

To these 'connotations' of causation, some authors add further notions, such as *evidence* for the occurrence of both causing and caused events (e.g. Mellor 1995), the placing of moral *responsibility* for events (e.g. Kim 1973), and *statistical relevance* (e.g. Schaffer 2004).

Despite its undeniable importance, the correct understanding of causation remains subject to considerable controversy. There are two main clusters of proposals in the literature. The first, and perhaps dominant view, sees causation essentially as a *relation* between facts or events, where the occurrence of the caused event is somehow *conditional* or *dependent* upon the causing event. This conditionality of the effect upon the cause can be a matter of strict determination or mere probability raising, and there is a plethora of ways in which the view has been spelled out in detail. The view originated with the immensely influential regularity theory of David Hume, but has since evolved and bifurcated into ever growing varieties,

---

A. Steglich-Petersen (✉)
Institute for Philosophy and History of Ideas, University of Aarhus, Aarhus C, Denmark
e-mail: filasp@hum.au.dk

R. Poli, J. Seibt (eds.), *Theory and Applications of Ontology: Philosophical Perspectives*, DOI 10.1007/978-90-481-8845-1_4,

including the so-called necessary and sufficient conditions approach, the counterfactual dependence approach, and various indeterministic varieties of these theories. I will call this broad family of views *the conditional approach*.[1]

The second main cluster of theories, in part motivated by the perceived failure of the conditional approach, does not necessarily deny that effects are often conditional on their causes, but does not see this as essential to causation. Instead, they focus on the ontology of the *processes* by which causes are connected to their effects, and attempt to single out causation by the various characteristics processes must have in order to qualify as causal. I will call this family of views the *process approach*.

Both approaches face serious problems, and it is fair to say that there is no real consensus about their relative plausibility. Nevertheless, the discussion that has led to the current state of the field has been immensely rich in insight. In this article, I present some of the most influential varieties of these views, and try to provide an overview the main difficulties that led to the currently most influential versions. I will first consider various versions of the conditional approach in Section 4.2. In Section 4.3 I move on to introduce a number of theories within the process approach. Finally, in Section 4.4 I look at what is currently the most volatile battleground between the two approaches, namely the question of whether there can be causation by omission and prevention.

4.2 Conditional Theories of Causation

In this section I introduce some of the main versions of what I called the conditional approach to causation. For better or worse, David Hume's discussion of causation in his *Treatise of Human Nature* (1739–1740) largely defined the subsequent philosophical discussion of causation. I shall therefore begin by introducing his views, before moving on to consider contemporary theories.

4.2.1 Hume on Causation

Hume's discussion is cast within his empiricist epistemological framework, and a short summary of it is therefore needed to appreciate the subsequent arguments about causation. According to Hume, all mental states with cognitive content derive their content from *impressions*, which are direct sense experiences. He coins the term 'simple ideas' as 'fainter' copies of the impressions themselves. There cannot, therefore, be any simple ideas, which do not derive from the senses. Simple ideas are thus by definition guaranteed some degree of correspondence with empirical

[1] This approach is also sometimes named the *epistemic* approach, because of its initial motivation by epistemic concerns. As we shall see, however, in more recent developments of the conditional approach, the focus on epistemic concerns has receded, making the more neutral term 'conditional' more appropriate.

experience. *Complex* ideas, on the other hand, are combinations of simple ideas. Although this means that complex ideas derive from experience, they do so in a derivative way and are not, therefore, guaranteed to correspond directly to empirical experiences. The idea of a unicorn, for example, does not correspond to any sense experience, but the simple ideas it is made up from do so correspond. This gives rise to two corresponding sources of knowledge: direct perception, which is simply the formation of simple ideas on the basis of perception, and reasoning, being the combination of simple ideas, or of complex ideas made up from simple ones. In other words, whether it derives from reasoning or not, there can be *no idea without a preceding impression*. An idea is epistemically legitimate only if it can be traced back to direct sense impressions.

Hume framed his philosophical method around this notion. The method is this: for any given philosophical idea, ask from which impression it derives, and reduce the idea itself to those impressions. I will call this philosophical method, descendants of which are still popular, 'Humean reduction'. To make matters more precise, some relation, property, state of affairs, etc., can be given a Humean reduction if it can be reduced to a property, relation, or state of affairs, which is directly observable, i.e. immediately given in experience (Tooley 2003).

Returning now to our main topic, this method gives rise to Hume's famous question about causation (which is interesting whether we agree with Hume's epistemological framework or not):

> Let us therefore cast our eyes on any two objects, which we call cause and effect, and turn them on all sides, in order to find that impression, which produces an idea of such prodigious consequence. (*Treatise*, I.iii.2)

The guiding idea is that one can have causal thoughts (thoughts about causal relations) only if causal relations have impinged upon experience. Causal thoughts can only be what such experience gives rise to. So we can get a theory of causation by investigating what impressions of causation we could possibly have.

The procedure in practise is to distinguish the elements which enter into the common idea of the causal relation, and then look for the impressions from which they might have derived – a form of mental archaeology. Hume finds three elements in the common idea of causation:

- Spatial and temporal contiguity between cause and effect
- Temporal precedence of cause to effect
- A 'necessary connection' between cause and effect

The first two ideas are rather unproblematic from an empiricist point of view – one can, in principle at least, readily observe the relations of contiguity and temporal order. It is more doubtful whether they in fact form necessary conditions of causal relations. Hume's arguments for this are somewhat inconclusive, although they do seem to give expression to a very common line of thought. The necessity of spatial and temporal contiguity for causal relations is argued for as follows,

> tho' distant objects may sometimes seem productive of each other, they are commonly found upon examination to be link'd by a chain of causes, which are contiguous among themselves and to the distant objects; and where in any particular instance we cannot discover this connexion, we still presume it to exist. (*Treatise*, I.iii.2)

The argument for temporal precedence of cause to effect is less clear, and most modern authors deny that such precedence can or should be established on purely conceptual grounds. His argument seems to have the following structure, starting with considering simultaneous effects: suppose that event C causes event E. The only temporal part of C that can cause E is the last temporal part of C that *could* have done so, for the passage of time is not itself causally efficacious. But if the last possible temporal part of C that can cause E is simultaneous with E, then *only* what is simultaneous with E can cause E. But this would also apply to C itself, so if any causes are simultaneous with their effects, all must be, resulting in the absurd consequence that everything happens at once (*Treatise*, I.iii.2). As for causes that happen *later* than their effects, Hume simply builds it into his definition of cause that this is impossible – a move which modern theorists have taken great pains to avoid (e.g. Lewis 1973b).

Whether these epistemically unproblematic elements are necessary for causation or not, however, they are clearly not *sufficient*. Otherwise any two events that are spatially and temporally contiguous, such that the one precedes the other, would stand in a causal relationship to each other[2]. What is needed in addition is what Hume calls a 'necessary connection' between the causally related events. In investigating what the content of this idea may be, Hume deploys a method of exclusion, examining in turn three main candidates, *viz.* logical connection, powers, and constant conjunction.

4.2.1.1 Necessary Connections as Logical Relations?

Hume denies the possibility of logical connections between distinct objects: *there is nothing in any object, considered by itself, which can afford us a reason for drawing a conclusion beyond it* (*Treatise*, I.iii.14). In making this claim, Hume relies on the principle that reasoning cannot by itself arrive at any conclusion about matters of fact, which does not derive from impressions. The only independent principle constraining reasoning is the principle of non-contradiction, and our guide to non-contradiction is intelligibility: *Whatever is intelligible, and can be distinctly conceived, implies no contradiction, and can never be proved false by any demonstrative argument or abstract reasoning a priori* (*Treatise*, I.iii.14).This is a very powerful principle in the present regard, since there is typically no *logical* contradiction in supposing one event not to follow another. According to Hume, there is even no rational compulsion to think that there are causes *at all.*

[2] Ducasse (1926) actually defends a version this view, but it has few modern adherents.

4.2.1.2 Necessary Connections as 'Powers of Objects' Considered in Themselves

The most influential account of causation prior to Hume was in terms of 'inner powers' of objects. This has to do partly with the peculiarity that causal language is associated strongly with *agency* – causal change was for a long time explained as a form of volition, either of God or of humans, or, according to Aristotle, of the objects themselves (Anscombe 1971, Pearl 2000). So when one object causes change in another, it is because of some 'inner power' of that first object to affect the change. Hume denies any talk of 'inner powers' on the grounds that we have no impression whatsoever of such inner powers, and hence no legitimate idea of such powers: *all ideas are derived from, and represent impressions. We never have any impression, that contains any power or efficacy. We never therefore have any idea of power* (*Treatise*, I.iii.14).

4.2.1.3 Necessary Connection as 'Constant Conjunction'

Having found that there is nothing besides contiguity and precedence of cause to effect to be observed in any *singular* instance of causal relations, then, Hume turns to the *repetition* of causal relations:

> 'Tis not, therefore, from any one instance, that we derive the idea of cause and effect, of a necessary connection of power, of force, of energy, and of efficacy. Did we ever see any but particular conjunctions of objects, entirely different from each other, we shou'd never be able to form any such idea. (*Treatise*, I.iii.14)

So the idea of a necessary connection could only arise from impressions of repeated instances of similar relations. The crucial question is: is the idea arising from such repeated impressions an idea of a property *in the objects*, or is it merely a property of *the mind observing* the repeated instances? Hume argues that constant conjunction cannot give rise to an idea of necessity 'in the objects'. The argument is twofold: we neither *discover* anything new in the objects with the repetition of conjunction, nor does the repetition *produce* a new property in the objects:

> . . .the repetition of like objects in like relations of succession and contiguity discovers nothing new in any of them; since we can draw no inference from it, nor make it a subject of our demonstrative or probable reasoning. [. . .] This repetition of similar objects in similar situations produces nothing new either in these objects or any external body. For t'will readily be allow'd, that the several instances we have of the conjunction of resembling causes and effects are in themselves entirely independent. . . (*Treatise*, I.iii.14)

If we allow Hume these two arguments, the conclusion follows inevitably that the necessity of causation is a mere projection of the mind arising from the experience of repeated instances of conjunction of like events. Hume offers the following definition of cause:

> An object precedent and contiguous to another, and where all the objects resembling the former are plac'd in a like relation of priority and contiguity to those objects that resemble the latter. (*Treatise*, I.iii.14)

We now have a rough outline of Hume's basic theory of causation, and the method and arguments that led him to accept it. His lasting legacy can be summarised in two important and extremely influential strands of thought.

First, *singular* causal relations, i.e. the relations that obtain between any two particular instances of cause and effect, are understood in terms of *general* causal relations, i.e. the relations that hold between the *types* of events to which the particular events belong. Singular causal relations are causal, in other words, by virtue of being instances of general *causal laws*. Second, general causal relations are analysed in terms of *constant conjunction* of instances of such types of events. What makes it true that a particular event of type 1 causes another particular event of type 2 is that events of type 1 are *always* and *invariably* followed by events of type 2. In sum, singular causal relations depend on general causal relations, or causal laws, which in turn are to be understood as true generalisations about particular conjunctions of types of events. So even though particular causal relationships depend on general ones, they can still be given a Humean reduction to particular, directly observable matters of fact. With this in place we can move on to consider some modern developments of the strategy[3].

4.2.2 Modern Regularity Views

The modern heirs of Hume's regularity account are the various theories that analyse causation in terms of conditional statements linking cause and effect. Early versions of this theory construe causal relations in terms of general *necessary* and/or *sufficient conditions*[4]. When translated into these terms, Hume's account becomes something like this, where *c* and *e* denote singular events and capital letters *C* and *E* denote the event types to which *c* and *e* belong respectively:

> *c* causes *e* iff *c* and *e* both occur, and as a matter of natural law *E* occurs if and only if *C* occurs.

There are a number of well-known problems with this simple account, which have led to a succession of ever more sophisticated versions. I will note some of the most important difficulties in the following.

A first problem has to do with the sufficiency requirement. When we make causal claims, we rarely if ever intend to assert that the relevant cause is by itself sufficient for its effect. When we say that Sally's smoking caused her lung cancer, we presumably don't mean to imply that her smoking was by itself *sufficient* for her getting lung cancer. Other factors are needed, such as cells that are prone to mutation, etc. Instead we usually mean to say that the relevant cause was one of a number of factors that together sufficed for the given effect. So instead of saying that *C* must be

---

[3] For a recent exposition and discussion of Hume's theory of causation, see Beebee (2006)

[4] For a selection of such theories, see Mill (1843), Braithwaite (1953), Hempel (1965) and Hart and Honere (1959).

sufficient for *E*, we should instead say that *C* form part of a set of factors *S*, such that as a matter of natural law *S* collectively suffice for *E*.

A second problem has to do with the necessity requirement. There is some plausibility in saying that any singular event is such that it wouldn't have come about, had it not been for its cause, such that the cause was in that sense necessary for the effect. But it seems much less plausible when this requirement is reflected as above in general relations between the types of causally related events. To go back to the previous example, when we assert that Sally's smoking caused her lung cancer, we do not mean to imply that *any* instance of lung cancer requires smoking. Other causes of lung cancer, such as inhaling asbestos particles, are not only possible, but quite common. A similar problem of a more technical nature is that the necessity requirement, when coupled with sufficiency, creates a *symmetric* relation, whereas the causal relation is typically *asymmetric*. One possible reaction would be to completely drop the necessity requirement, which some philosophers indeed have opted for. But that would be to give up the thought that effects somehow depend on their causes. Another option is to incorporate the necessity requirement into the set of conditions that collectively suffice for the given effect. One way of doing this would be by restricting the above set *S* to the *minimal set* of factors that collectively suffice for *E*. Another option along the same lines would be to adopt a more complicated condition like the so-called *INUS* condition developed by Mackie (1965). Ignoring certain subtleties, this account can be represented thus,

> *c* causes *e* iff *c* and *e* both occur and *C* is an *I*nsufficient but *N*ecessary part of an occurrent set of conditions *S* that, as a matter of natural law, is *U*nnecessary but *S*ufficient for *E*.

This account clearly does solve the above two worries. Even with this more sophisticated version of the regularity account, however, serious problems remain. One complaint has to do with the possibility of indeterministic causation, to which I shall turn now. Others are of a more general nature, which I shall turn to after discussing probabilistic causation.

4.2.2.1 Probabilistic Corrections to the Regularity View

As it stands, the regularity view is incompatible with cases of indeterministic causation. Even if the more sophisticated version of the regularity account allows that sufficient conditions tend to be quite complex, they do require that the complex set of factors jointly suffice for the effect, such that effects of the relevant sort invariably follow such sets. But we often speak of causes that *tend* to result in certain effects, rather than doing so invariably; causes that cause in virtue of raising the probability of the relevant effect, rather than rendering them inevitable.

Some such cases might be thought to be compatible with the sophisticated version of the regularity account. For example, smoking is a cause of lung cancer, but does not invariably result in lung cancer – it merely raises the probability of lung cancer. But rather than indicating an example of indeterministic causation, this might be taken merely to show that for a large proportion of smokers, other factors are present such that when smoking is added, it forms a set of conditions that invariably, i.e. deterministically, results in lung cancer. So even if a general statement about the relationship between smoking (S) and cancer (C), such that for all x (if Sx then Cx), fails, there must be some more complicated general law, for example: for all x (if (Sx and Fx) then Cx), which holds.

Some authors, e.g. Anscombe (1971), has criticised this move as begging the question on behalf of the regularity account, claiming there is simply no evidence of the existence of such complicated regularities. Be that as it may, however, a more serious problem arises from the possibility genuinely indeterministic causation.

Consider Anscombe's example of a Geiger counter placed next to a piece of radioactive material, and wired to a bomb that will explode if the Geiger counter reaches a certain number. Anscombe argues that you can make two such arrangements as identical as you like, and the one might go off without the other, concluding that neither necessitates its effect. Anscombe in fact goes as far as concluding that causal relationships aren't even *nomic*, but it is not obvious that this is the only possible conclusion. Rather than concluding that causal relationships aren't nomic, perhaps we should merely conclude that they instantiate *probabilistic laws* rather than *deterministic* ones. Perhaps causes are the kinds of things that *invariably raise the probability of their effect*. A simple candidate theory would be as follows, where Pr(E|C) denotes for the probability of E conditional on C:

$$\text{C causes E iff } \Pr(\text{E} \mid \text{not-C}) < \Pr(\text{E} \mid \text{C})$$

So, for example, smoking causes cancer if and only if the probability of cancer is higher conditional on smoking, than it is conditional on not smoking. This simple account suffers from problems analogous to the simple regularity analysis: it states a symmetric relation between E and C, since the relation would hold as well if E had been the cause of C; because of that, it also allows spurious correlation, where C and E have a common cause rather than being causally related themselves. Many strategies have been proposed to rule out spurious correlation[5]. All of these exploit the thought that a common cause A of C and E probabilistically 'screens off' C as a cause E, in the sense that Pr(E|C & A) will be less or equal to Pr(E|A). So we need the definition to ensure that the putative cause is not screened off in this way by a common cause, as in the following:

$$\text{C causes E iff } \Pr(\text{E} \mid \text{not-C} \;\&\; S) < \Pr(\text{E} \mid \text{C} \;\&\; S) \text{ for any relevant set of conditions } S$$

This approach seems more plausible, but has the same weakness as the *INUS* condition of it being very difficult to specify the relevant set of conditions *S* to hold constant. For more on this, see in particular Hitchcock (1993).

This probabilistic variant of the regularity view handles both deterministic and indeterministic causation well, and thus completely replaces the deterministic version of the regularity account, but more general problems remain. Even if it can be

[5] For a selection of influential proposals, see Reichenbach (1956), Salmon (1980a), Cartwright (1979), and Hitchcock (1993).

harnessed to rule out spurious correlation where C and E have a common cause, it still doesn't rule out symmetry. The above condition does not decide if C is the cause of E, rather than vice versa. Another problem we have not introduced yet is that of epiphenomenal causation, where some cause C first causes an epiphenomenal event E and then a further event A, without E being the cause of A. Although there have been several ingenious proposals at how to solve them within the broad regularity framework, it was these difficulties that motivated the counterfactual theory of causation. Instead of delving further on these problems, I will therefore now turn to explore this next variant of what I called the overarching conditional approach to causation.

4.2.3 Counterfactual Theories of Causation

A new beginning for the Humean, conditional program for causation was initiated with David Lewis' 1973 paper 'Causation'. In it, he proposed to give up the traditional regularity account altogether, and instead embrace an account that took as its core a different and more complex kind of conditional – the *counterfactual* conditional, i.e. a conditional statement in the subjunctive mode. In its simplest version, which was mentioned with endorsement by Hume in passing, the theory says that,

> *c* causes *e* iff *c* and *e* are actual events, and had *c* not occurred, *e* would not have occurred.

For a number of reasons that I will review shortly, this simple version is far from watertight, but first we need to understand why a proposal of such deceiving simplicity didn't come into prominence before the publication of Lewis' paper.

As we have seen, the main motivation behind Hume's regularity theory of causation, and the subsequent empiricist theories described above, has been to avoid reference to mysterious relations and necessities. The regularity account achieved this by deploying a conditional statement (albeit of growing complexity), the truth conditions of which are settled by the actual truth-values of the component propositions, which in turn are settled in an unproblematic way by whether or not events of the relevant types co-occur. Counterfactual conditionals, on the other hand, has seemed less palatable to the empiricist agenda.

The problem is that in order to settle the truth-value of propositions of the form 'If A had happened, B would have happened' (hereafter abbreviated 'A □→ B'), we need to look beyond the truth-value of the component propositions. In other words: counterfactual conditionals are not truth functional. This is easy to see by considering the following two propositions:

1. If I had been in Canada, I would have been in Asia
2. If I had been in Canada, I would have been in North America

Both of these complex propositions take atomic propositions that are *in fact* false. It is false that I am in Canada, false that I am in Asia, and false that I am in North America. Yet, while the first *conditional* proposition is false, the second is true. So the truth-values of counterfactual propositions are underdetermined by the truth-values of the atomic propositions they relate.

Prior to Lewis, there had been various failed attempts at giving an analysis of counterfactuals in terms that are palatable to the empiricist. Perhaps in saying that 'A □→ B' we are saying that there is a set of statements *S*, such that it is true that '(S & A) → B', where '→' stands for the normal material conditional. But it is all but clear how we should specify such sets *S*.

An account that takes this into account is the *possible worlds analysis* of counterfactual conditionals, first proposed by Stalnaker (1968) and developed later by Lewis (1973a). This account is essentially as follows:

> 'A □→ B' is true in the *actual world* if and only if (i) there are no *possible worlds* in which 'A' is true, or (ii) some possible world in which 'A' is true and 'B' is true is closer to the actual world than any possible world in which 'A' is true and 'B' is false.

The first possibility (i) is only fulfilled when a counterfactual takes an impossible proposition as its antecedent, and since nothing is caused by something that is impossible, it is (ii) we must focus on. The intuitive idea here is quite simple: 'A □→ B' is true if one has to move farther away from reality to find a situation in which A is true and B false, than to find a situation in which A is true and B is true. For example, most people think that the following counterfactual statement is true:

> If Oswald had not shot Kennedy, Kennedy would have survived his visit to Dallas.

Why do we think this is true? Because it would require more of a departure from reality to find a world in which Oswald didn't shoot, but someone else killed Kennedy in Dallas, than to find a world in which Oswald didn't shoot, and Kennedy survived his trip to Dallas. Of course, if you believe in conspiracy theories according to which Oswald had a backup team, then you should *disbelieve* the statement, and the reason is clear: according to you, it would now take a smaller departure from reality to find a world where Oswald didn't shoot, but Kennedy got killed nonetheless by one of Oswald's accomplices, than to find a world where he didn't shoot and Kennedy survived.

This account presupposes a number of things about possible worlds. Most importantly that all possible worlds can be *ordered* according to how close they are to the actual world, allowing that two possible worlds might be equally close, thus forming a strict partial order. Important questions turn on *how* to judge which possible worlds are more similar to actuality. According to Lewis, the most important criteria are resemblance in natural laws and space-time distribution of matter. However, no strict method is supplied for judging or weighing these factors against each other. Sufficiently large similarity is space-time distribution of matter may sometimes trump similarity of natural laws, although he seems to think that natural laws are more weighty comparison measures. Another important question is how to understand the nature of possible worlds, and whether they indeed can be part of an empiricist ontology.

Leaving ontological qualms aside for now, however, we can begin to appreciate the benefit of the analysis. On the possible worlds analysis, counterfactual conditionals turn out to be truth-functional. The truth-value of the conditional statement is determined by the truth-value of the component propositions, albeit their truth-value throughout the vast multiplicity of possible worlds.

Having clarified the semantics of counterfactuals, we can return to the main issue of defining causal relations in terms of them. According to the simple version above, the causation of one event by another *simply is* counterfactual dependence. But this will not do, for two reasons. The first reason is that while the causal relation appears to be *transitive*, counterfactual dependence is *non-transitive*. The second reason is that the simple account would be unable to account for pre-emptive causes. I will return to this later point in a moment, but will first look at the transitivity problem. Consider the following two inference patterns. While the first of these patterns seems valid, the second pattern is not:

Pattern 1	*Pattern 2*
C is the cause of E	$A \mathrel{\Box\!\!\rightarrow} B$
E is the cause of R	$B \mathrel{\Box\!\!\rightarrow} C$
∴ C is the cause of R	$\therefore A \mathrel{\Box\!\!\rightarrow} C$

To see that the second pattern is invalid, consider the following example:

If Hoover had been a Russian, then Hoover would have been a communist
If Hoover had been a communist, then Hoover would have been a traitor
∴ If Hoover had been Russian, then Hoover would have been a traitor

This argument has arguably true premises, but an arguably false conclusion. So while counterfactual dependence may be *necessary* for causation, it cannot be *sufficient* for it. Recently, some theorists have claimed that causation is not in fact a transitive relation. Here's a putative example from Kvart (1991). A persons finger is cut off in an accident; she is rushed to the hospital and a surgeon reattaches it; the surgeon does such a good job that a year later, the finger functions perfectly. Here we have step-wise causation from the accident to the operation, from the operation to the reattachment, and from the reattachment to the finger working perfectly. But it seems wrong to claim that the accident caused the finger to work perfectly a year later. It is debated how successful such cases are as counterexamples. As Lewis (2000) has pointed out, examples such as this seem convincing because a type of event *C* that *usually* prevents event types *E* (having one's finger cut off does not *usually* cause it to function perfectly a year later, but rather prevents it), is made to cause an intermediate event that in turn causes an event of type *E*. This produces an unusual and anti-intuitive result, but if we focus on the particular case rather than general causal patterns, we can accept it (however, see Hall 2004b). Anyone convinced of Lewis' argument is still left with a problem, however: causation is transitive, but counterfactual dependence is not. So the simple account fails.

Another problem arises from the possibility of pre-emptive causes. Consider the famous case of Billy and Suzy, each about to throw a stone at a bottle. Suppose that Suzy throws her stone before Billy, and shatters the bottle. Seeing that Suzy was quicker than he was, Billy never throws his stone. Clearly, Suzy's throw was the cause of the bottle shattering. But even this being so, the shattering did not depend counterfactually on Suzy's throw, since if Suzy hadn't thrown her stone, Billy would, thus shattering the bottle after all. So the simple counterfactual analysis fails for this reason as well. The transitivity problem shows that counterfactual dependence is not sufficient for causation; the pre-emption problem shows that it is not necessary.

To solve these two problems of transitivity and pre-emption, Lewis first defines a relation different from causation, that he names 'causal dependence'. He offers several versions of the definition, but we might just define it as follows:

> *e* causally depends on *c* iff *e* and *c* are actual events, and had *c* not occurred, *e* would not have occurred.

So causal dependence is just counterfactual dependence between actual events. Causal dependence is then used to provide necessary and sufficient conditions for causation in the following way:

> *c* causes *e* iff there is some chain of events e1, e2, ... e*n*, such that the first causally depend on *c*, each depends on the preceding one, and *e* depends on the last event in the chain.

This account can be extended in an easy way to handle indeterministic causation (Lewis 1986): first define *probabilistic* dependence in a way analogous to the definition of causal dependence above, and then define chains of probability raising events and ultimately probabilistic causality in terms of it[6]:

> *e* probabilistically depends on *c* iff *e* and *c* are actual events, and had *c* not occurred, the probability of *e* would have been much lower.

How does the detour via chains of causal dependence solve the problems of missing transitivity and pre-emptive causation? Transitivity comes automatically, since the chain of causal dependence defining causation is made transitive by the actuality constraint on the events making up the chain. The idea of causal chains also solves the pre-emption case. Think back to Billy and Suzy: Suzy's throw was the cause of the bottle shattering, but the shattering did not depend counterfactually on the throw, since Billy would have thrown his stone at the bottle if Suzy had failed to do so. But the revised account requires that there is a chain of causally dependent events leading from the cause to the effect, and while there is no such chain leading from Billy's throw to the shattering, there is one leading from Suzy's.

With this in place, we can return to review the main advantages of the counterfactual approach over its regularity based predecessors. For the regularity accounts, the main stumbling blocks turned out to be that they could not distinguish between cause and effect (symmetry), and that they could not distinguish epiphenomenal from genuine causation.

---

[6] For a recent discussion and modification, see Ramachandran (2004).

Take the problem of symmetry as it arises for the counterfactual account first. Suppose that Sally's throw is the cause of the bottle shattering. On the counterfactual account, what this amounts to is that the chance of the bottle shattering would have been much lower than it was, had Sally not thrown the stone, which is indeed the case. But if that is the case, the reverse counterfactual seems to hold as well: the probability of Sally throwing the stone would have been much lower, had the bottle not shattered, thus making it seem that the shattering is the cause of her throw. But Lewis denies that this latter counterfactual is in fact true. For the closest possible world in which the bottle doesn't shatter is not a world in which Sally doesn't throw the stone. For, *ex hypotesi*, in the actual world Sally's throw precedes the shattering, so finding a world with no throw requires that we change a larger portion of the space-time distribution of matter, than we would have to in order to find a world that merely lacks the shattering. Throw/non-shattering worlds are thus more similar to actuality than non-throw/non-shattering worlds. But what about natural laws? If the throw was the actual cause of the shattering, altering actuality to find a throw/non-shattering world would seemingly require violation of natural laws, or at least supposing something unlikely to happen. But, Lewis argues, the same would go for *any* change we make from reality in the space-time distribution of matter, including the throw, so the more we change the actual course of events, the more we will have to change on the natural law side of things as well. So overall, the throw/non-shattering world is closer to reality than any non-throw/non-shattering worlds. If this move is accepted, epiphenomenal causation can be distinguished from genuine causation in a similar way[7].

4.2.3.1 Problems for the Conditional Approach

Two main groups of objections have riddled modern versions of the conditional approach in general, and the counterfactual approach in particular. The first group of objections pertain to show that dependence of the effect upon the cause, whether this dependence is deterministic or probabilistic, is not a necessary condition for causation. The most important of these arguments build on certain problematic 'second generation' cases of *pre-empting* causes that cause their effects without the effects depending on the cause. The second main group show that such dependence is not sufficient for causation either. The most important of these arguments build on problematic cases of *fizzling*, where a factor affect the likelihood of an event without being the cause of it. Despite numerous attempts at repairing the theory, there is some consensus that both of these problems are as yet unsolved.

We have already seen how simple cases of pre-emptive causes might be accounted for by the counterfactual approach by defining causation in terms of stepwise chains of causally dependent events. But a series of increasingly hard cases of pre-emptive causation seem to elude this original solution. The original example

[7] For more on Lewis' ban on 'backtracking conditionals', see Lewis (1979; 1986); for criticism, see in particular Fine (1975), Horwich (1989), and Price (1992).

was a case of 'early' pre-emption. Suzy's throw prevented Billy's throw altogether. But imagine now that Billy throws his stone too, albeit shortly after Suzy, so that his stone arrives at the bottle nanoseconds later than Suzy's, thus being a 'late' pre-empted cause. For these cases, Lewis' original solution in terms of chains of causally dependent events will not be of help, because there will be no intermediary event, such as the stone's trajectory in mid air, dependent on Suzy's throw, which the shattering in turn depends upon. If we imagine the full trajectory of Suzy's stone as a series of events stretching from it being thrown to it hitting the bottle, there is no event in this series that the bottle shattering depends upon, since for each of those events it holds that had it not happened, Billy's stone would have shattered the bottle nonetheless.

Early attempts at dealing with late pre-emption focused on adding more structure to the chain of events required to qualify it as causal. The best-known version was developed in Lewis (1986). However, as ingenious as these proposals are, they are thwarted by a special case of pre-emption named *trumping*, first described by Schaffer (2000a). Trumping is pre-emption, but with no intermediary process. In the original version of this case, we are asked to imagine a fairy tale land in which two wizards, Merlin and Morgana, each cast a spell on the prince that will turn him into a frog by midnight. By the laws of magic, the first spell cast in a day will be the effective one. Merlin casts his spell at dawn, and Morgana casts his at nightfall. By midnight, the prince duly turns into a frog. As the example is set up, Merlin's spell is the cause. But there is no dependence upon Merlin's spell since, had he not cast it, Morgana's spell would have done the same work. But there is no intermediary chain of events leading from Merlin's spell to the prince's unfortunate destiny.

Lewis' most recent version of the counterfactual theory, presented first in his (2000) and expanded in (2004a), was designed to handle trumping cases, but is widely believed to be independently implausible. The core of the theory is that the notion of dependence invoked in the definition of causation should be expanded from being a mere 'whether-whether' dependence, where the occurrence of one event depends on the occurrence on another, to also being a dependence of the time and manner of the occurrence of the caused event on the time and manner of the occurrence of the causing event. This more complicated notion of dependence, Lewis calls causal *influence*:

> Where c and e are distinct events, c *influences* e if and only if there is a substantial range $c1$, $c2$, ... of different not-too-distant alterations of c (including the actual alteration of c) and there is a range of $e1$, $e2$, of alterations of e, at least some of which differ, such that if $c1$ had occurred, $e1$ would have occurred, and if $c2$ had occurred, e2 would have occurred, and so on (Lewis 2004a, p. 91)

This can then be used to define causation in the following manner, analogous to the definition in terms of the more simple kind of causal dependence, in a way that ensures transitivity: *c causes e* if and only if there is a chain of stepwise influence from c to e.

On the face of it, this handles the hard cases of late pre-emption and trumping quite well. If we alter Merlin's spell, making it a toad-spell rather than a frog-spell for example, what happens to the prince will change accordingly, but no change of Morgana's spell will affect what happens to the prince in the same way. One objection to this move is that if we change Morgana's spell sufficiently, altering its content and time to be earlier than Merlin's spell, Morgana's spell will influence the prince too. One possible answer here is that such larger alterations run afoul of the 'not-too-distant' requirement in the definition. But it has proven hard to specify how distant alterations are allowed to be, since in some cases, very small alterations on the pre-empted cause can tip the balance of influence. It also will not do to identify the cause with the event that takes *the least* amount of alteration to tricker alterations in the caused event, since there is typically not a single unique cause of an event.

Because of these difficulties, many theorists have accepted that dependence is not necessary for causation. It is nonetheless commonly held that dependence is sufficient for causation. This is equivalent to giving up the counterfactual account as an *analysis* of causation, but many insist that dependence is an important aspect of causation nonetheless. Counter-examples to sufficiency remain more controversial. The currently most debated counter-example turns on whether or not to allow cases of double-prevention and omissions as genuine causes of events. If we cannot allow such events as causes, counterfactual dependence seems insufficient for causation. On the other hand, if we *do* allow them as causes, the process approach to causation, which I will consider in the next section, will be in trouble. Since the possibility of such cases bear on both approaches, I will therefore postpone discussion of them until I have introduced the process view.

4.3 Process Theories of Causation

I now move on to discuss the second main group of proposals for a theory of causation. I will first introduce some early versions of the theory, but quickly move on to what is widely regarded as the most plausible and worked out version, namely that defended by Wesley Salmon in his most recent works (1998), and by Phil Dowe in his (2000).

4.3.1 Early Process Theories: Mark-Transmission

Central to the early process theories of causation is the attempt to find a way of distinguishing 'pseudo-processes' from genuine ones. To illustrate this distinction, consider the following example described by Salmon (1980b). Suppose we have a large circular building with a spotlight at its centre. The spotlight turns on and off such that the light travels in pulses casting spots of light on the inside of the building. This, Salmon calls a 'paradigm of a causal process' (p. 156). There is a causal process flowing from the spotlight to the spots of light on the ceiling. On the other hand, the spotlight circulates so that the light spots travel the ceiling in circles. The pattern created by the travelling spots of light, Salmon calls a paradigm of a 'pseudo-process' (p. 156). For Salmon, the central property distinguishing causal processes from pseudo-processes is the ability to *transmit a mark*. By mark-transmission, Salmon means the ability of a process to preserve a modification of some quality over space-time points, such that it is transmitted from some point in space-time point to another. For example, the light travelling from the spotlight to the ceiling is a genuine process, because it is able to transmit modifications introduced at any stage to any later stage. If a red-coloured piece of glass is inserted into the light cone, for example, the light will become red from that stage onwards, thus 'transmitting' this modification all the way to the ceiling if uninterrupted. On the other hand, the resulting red spot on the ceiling will not be transmitted in the pseudo process to the next spot unless the red glass is introduced in the process leading to that spot as well. The *production* of mark-transmitting processes is given a probabilistic definition, but I will not dwell on that here. The important point is that causation is a matter of cause and effect being connected by the right kind of mark-transmitting process.

There are several problems with this theory, however. One problem is that it seems overly *restrictive* about the identity of 'marks' transmitted from one space-time point to another, and from one process to another, both quantitatively and qualitatively. Another problem is that it seems overly *inclusive* about the 'marks' it allows being of significance to whether or not we should count a given process transmitting those marks as causal. For example, the theory might allow the shadow of a flagpole to be a causal process in virtue of transmitting the mark of pointing in the opposite direction of the place of the sun on the horizon. The next generation of process theories were designed in part to improve on these difficulties.

4.3.2 The Conserved Quantity Theory

The currently most worked out process theory is the so-called 'conserved quantity' theory. This theory builds in large part on the mark-transmission theory, but improves it in certain crucial respects. Most importantly, it avoids the problems facing its predecessor of being at once overly restrictive about identity of marks, and overly inclusive about the kinds of marks allowed to be of significance.

The basic structure of the theory as developed in Dowe (2000) is this[8]: First it is assumed that regions of space can be divided into genuine objects on the one hand (broadly construed to include both everyday objects such as tables and chairs, and slightly more ephemeral ones such as waves and cells), and 'gerrymandered' space-regions on the other hand, such as random conjunctions or disjunctions of objects. A *process* is then defined as a 'world-line' of an object, i.e. the unique path of an object as it travels through four-dimensional space-time. *Causal* processes are then defined as a world-line of an object that *possesses a conserved quantity*. The quantity conserved can be any quantity that is governed by the law of conservation,

[8] Wesley Salmon develops a very similar theory in his (1998).

such as energy or charge. This takes over the basic idea from the mark-transmission theory, but improves it in two crucial regards addressing the basic worries expressed above. It avoids being overly *restrictive* because there is no requirement of identity across time of the relevant quantities. It avoids being overly *inclusive*, because the quantities that are allowed to make a difference as to whether a process is causal are restricted to those governed by the law of conservation. In addition to the concept of a causal process, which by itself explains many cases of causation, for example 'immanent' causation whereby a single object, such as a chair, persists, Dowe also defines causal *interactions*, which include most common sense instances of causation. Such interactions are defined as an intersection of world-lines in which an exchange of conserved quantities takes place, for instance by transferring energy from one world-line to another. Dowe (2004, p. 189) thus summarises the Salmon-Dowe theory of causation in the following two propositions:

1. A *causal process* is a world-line of an object that possesses a conserved quantity.
2. A *causal interaction* is an intersection of world-lines that involves exchange of a conserved quantity.

To illustrate, let us return once again to the case of Suzy and Billy. Take first Suzy alone, throwing a stone at the bottle, thus shattering it at the impact. According to the conserved quantity story, this counts as Suzy causing the bottle to shatter since there is a causal process, namely the stone's trajectory with a certain amount of conserved energy, which links Suzy's throwing the stone to the bottle shattering. Further, both the throw and the impact on the bottle constitute causal interactions. Suzy's accelerating arm, itself a process with a conserved quantity, intersects with, and thus transfers momentum to the stone, which in turn transfers this to the bottle, thus shattering it. The theory also allows an easy distinction between the genuine causal process whereby Suzy shatters the bottle, and the spurious link from Billy's pre-empted throw to the shattering, even for cases of late pre-emption: Even if Billy's stone is well underway towards the bottle, there is never an intersection between this process and the bottle, and therefore no causal connection either.

4.3.3 Problems for Process Theories

Two main groups of objections have riddled modern versions of the process account. The first denies that the relevant processes are *necessary* for causation. These focus mostly on alleged cases of causation by prevention and omission. Since the plausibility of such cases is highly relevant for the conditional view of causation as well, I will devote a separate section to them next.

The second group of objections pertain to show that the presence of a process of the kind proposed above is not a *sufficient* condition for causation. One such objection focuses on putative cases of causally irrelevant processes that are nonetheless connected to the effect in the appropriate way (Hitchcock 1995, Schaffer 2001).

Think back to Billy and Suzy. This time Suzy throws the stone, and Billy merely watches. But inevitably, innumerable photons will be emitted from Billy, which will be absorbed both by the stone in mid-air, and by the bottle in the instant it shatters. It seems as if the world-lines of these photons constitute causal processes, and it seems as if they interact with the shattering in the appropriate way, both directly and indirectly by way of photons absorbed by the stone. But it seems that they are nonetheless causally irrelevant to the shattering. There have been several responses to this sort of objection. The most promising of these, advocated in particular by Salmon (1998), claims that the processes, in this case the photons, *are* in fact causally relevant to the effect, but in a negligible proportion. The world-lines of the photons *do* possess a conserved quantity, which *is* transmitted to the bottle, thus making a causal impact, which is so small, however, as to be negligible to any causal explanation. The challenge to this type of response, of course, is to qualify what it takes to be negligible in a way that avoids appeal to counterfactual dependence or probability-raising; no convincing account has been offered for this so far.

4.4 Causation by Absence

I mentioned earlier that one of the main battleground between those who favour the process theory, and those who want to, at the very least, hold on to counterfactual dependence as a *sufficient* condition for causation, are to be found in cases of causation by omission and prevention. If these are genuine cases of causation, processes of the kind described above are not necessary for causation. If they are *not* genuine cases of causation, dependence is not sufficient for causation.

There are many kinds of (putative) causation involving absent events. Some basic variants, which can be combined in various ways, can be discerned by combining the different places an absent event can be located in a causal structure:

- *Causation by simple omission*: the absence of an even type C causes the occurrence of an event e. Example: a gardener failing to water the plants causes the plants to die.
- *Causation by simple prevention*: the occurrence of an event c causes the absence of an event type E. Example: Billy catching Suzy's stone midair causes the bottle not to shatter.
- *Prevention by omission*: the absence of an event type C causes the absence of an event type E. Example: Suzy not throwing the stone causes the bottle not to shatter.
- *Causation by disconnection*: the occurrence of an event c causes the absence of an event type D; the absence of an event type D causes the occurrence of event e. Example: Billy shooting Suzy through the heart prevents oxygen supply to Suzy's brain, causing her to die (Schaffer 2004).

Of these cases, the first three are by far the most controversial. Consequently, those opposed to causation by absence tend to focus on these first three cases, while those defending it tend to focus on the last case. If we begin by focusing on the case *against* causation by absence, one basic problem is that it creates *too many* causes for any given event (Menzies 2004). We might find it intuitive that the gardener's failure to water the plants caused them to die, but since the neighbour, and any other person in a certain proximity *could* have watered the plants as well, the failure of these people to water the plants must also be counted as causes for the plants' death as well. On the other hand, some cases of causation by absence, particularly cases of disconnection, seem highly plausible, and are indeed recognized as causal in the sciences and in the law. Schaffer (2004) provides a list of legal and scientific cases of disconnection that are treated as causal and satisfy all of the causal connotations mentioned at the outset of this article. I will return to one such example shortly. If we accept such cases as genuinely causal, it would be difficult not to also accept the other species of causation by absence as causal, since they all depend on absences.

4.4.1 Causation by Absence and Counterfactual Dependence

Technically, the dependence theory is not committed to counting cases of causation by simple omission, simple prevention, and prevention by omission as genuine cases of causation, since on the dependence theory, causally related events are required to be *actual*. However, the dependence theory can easily be harnessed to count such cases as genuine causation. One way of doing so would be to construe the absence of an event as itself a kind of event (Hall 2004a, p. 248), but many would oppose commitment to such 'spooky' entities (e.g. Beebee 2004). Lewis (2004b) proposes another procedure that avoids such commitment. This works by first defining a more primitive relation *biff*, which for our purposes can simply be identified with counterfactual dependence between *actual* events[9], and then re-defining causation in terms of this more primitive notion in a way that is compatible with causation by omission in the following way,

- *Causation*: event *c* directly causes event *e* iff *c biffs e*.
- *Causation by simple omission*: the absence of any event of type *C* causes event *e* iff, had there been an event *c* of type *C*, *c* would have *biffed* some event *d* incompatible with *e*.
- *Causation by simple prevention*: event *c* causes the absence of any event of type *E* iff *c biffs* some event *d* incompatible with any event of kind *E*.

---

[9] Lewis employs a more complicated definition of *biff*, designed to satisfy the further desiderata of making causation an intrinsic relation, but I will not go into that here. For more on *biff* and intrinsicness, see Menzies (1999) and Lewis (2004b).

- *Prevention by omission*: the absence of any event of kind *C* causes the absence of any event of kind *E* iff, had there been an event *c* of kind *C*, *c* would have *biffed* some event *e* of kind *E*.

Even without this move, however, the dependence theory does seem committed to counting causation by *disconnection* as a case of genuine causation, since the events *c* and *e* are actual and counterfactually dependent in the suitable sense. Suzy's death is counterfactually dependent on Billy's shooting her, even if the dependence comes about by preventing an event midway. So the plausibility of counting counterfactual dependence as sufficient for causation does seem to depend on whether or not such cases are indeed cases of causation.

4.4.2 Causation by Absence and Process Theories

Putative cases of causation by absence pose a problem for process theories insofar as they contain no process of the required sort between cause and effect. The most common strategy has been to simply deny that these are indeed cases of causation, but whereas some cases, especially cases of causation by omission, are intuitively easy to deny, denying others, especially cases of disconnection, seems to come at a high price in common sense. Some process theorists that recognise this cost have tried to develop theories that explains our causal intuitions without being committed to causation by absence. Dowe (2001) develops such an account in the following way, where different sorts of causation by absence are defined in terms of genuine causation and relationships of counterfactual dependence[10]:

- *Quasi-causation by simple omission*: the absence of any event of type *C* quasi-causes event *e* if *e* occurred and no event of type *C* occurred, and there occurred an event *d* such that *d* caused *e*, and if an event of type *C* had occurred, it would have prevented *e* by interacting with *d*.
- *Quasi-causation by simple prevention*: event *c* quasi-causes the absence of any event of type *E* if *c* occurred and no event of type *E* occurred, and there occurred an event *d*, and there was a causal interaction between *c* and *d* such that had *c* not occurred, *d* would have caused an event of type *E*.
- *Quasi-prevention by omission*: the absence of any event of type *C* quasi-causes the absence of any event of type *E* if no events of type *C* and *E* occurred, and had an event of type *C* occurred, it would have caused an event of type *E* to occur.

Critics of this strategy have noted that in many cases there is nothing 'quasi' about causation involving absences. Many such cases, particularly cases of disconnection, exhibit all of the causal connotations mentioned in the beginning of this article, and are frequently characterised as 'causal' in the sciences that invoke them.

[10] I have changed his notation in accordance with the convention adopted in this article.

We would be hard pressed, for example, in denying that Suzy's death upon being shot through the heart by Billy could not be *explained* and *predicted* by the shooting; that the shooting was not an effective way of *manipulating* Suzy state of health; that Billy would not be *responsible* for Suzy's death; that being shot through the heart is not *statistically relevant* to death, etc. As Schaffer (2004) notes, it is difficult to see what more it could take to convince oneself that such a case indeed is a case of genuine causation. In lieu of a stronger explanation of why they should be classified as 'quasi' rather than as 'genuine' causation, it is thus fair to say that such cases remain a major obstacle to the process approach's claim to have found necessary conditions for causation.

Acknowledgements I wish to thank Johanna Seibt for helpful comments on an earlier draft of this article, and the Danish Research Council for Culture and Communication for financial support.

References

Anscombe, G.E.M. 1971. *Causality and determination.* Cambridge: Cambridge University Press.
Beebee, H. 2004. Causing and nothingness. In *Causation and counterfactuals*, eds. J. Collins, et al. Cambridge: MIT Press.
Beebee, H. 2006. *Hume on causation.* London: Routledge.
Braithwaite, R.B. 1953. *Scientific explanation.* Cambridge: Cambridge University Press.
Cartwright, N. 1979. Causal laws and effective strategies. *Nous* 13:419–439
Dowe, P. 2000. *Physical causation.* New York, NY: Cambridge University Press.
Dowe, P. 2001. A counterfactual theory of prevention and "causation" by omission. *Australasian Journal of Philosophy* 79:16–26.
Dowe, P. 2004. Causes are physically connected to their effects: why preventers and omissions are not causes. In *Contemporary debates in philosophy of science*, ed. C. Hitchcock. Oxford: Blackwell.
Ducasse, C.J. 1926. On the nature and observability of the causal relation. *Journal of Philosophy* 23:57–68
Fine, K. 1975. Review of counterfactuals by David Lewis. *Mind* 84:451–458.
Hall, N. 2004a. Two concepts of causation. In *Causation and counterfactuals*, eds. J. Collins, et al. Cambridge, MA: MIT Press.
Hall, N. 2004b. Causation and the price of transitivity. In *Causation and counterfactuals*, eds. J. Collins, et al. Cambridge, MA: MIT Press.
Hart, H.L.A., and A.M. Honore. 1959. *Causation in the law.* Oxford: Clarendon Press.
Hempel, C.G. 1965. *Aspects of scientific explanation.* New York, NY: The Free Press.
Hitchcock, C. 1993. A generalized probabilistic theory of causal relevance. *Synthese* 97: 335–364
Hitchcock, C. 1995. Salmon on explanatory relevance. *Philosophy of Science* 62:304–320
Horwich, P. 1989. *Asymmetries in time.* Cambridge, MA: MIT Press.
Hume, D. 1978. *A treatise of human nature.* ed. L.A. Selby-Bigge (orig.), 1739–1740. Oxford: Clarendon Press.
Kim, J. 1973. Causes and counterfactuals. *Journal of Philosophy* 70:570–572
Kvart, I. 1991. Transitivity and preemption of causal impact. *Philosophical Studies* 64:125–160
Lewis, D. 1973a. *Counterfactuals.* Oxford: Blackwell.
Lewis, D. 1973b. Causation. *Journal of Philosophy* 70:556–567
Lewis, D. 1979. Counterfactual dependence and time's arrow. *Nous* 13:455–476
Lewis, D. 1986. Postscripts to "causation". *Philosophical Papers II.* New York, NY: Oxford University Press.

Lewis, D. 2000. Causation as influence. *Journal of Philosophy* 97:182–197

Lewis, D. 2004a. Causation as influence (expanded version). In *Causation and counterfactuals*, eds. J. Collins, et al. Cambridge, MA: MIT Press.

Lewis, D. 2004b. Void and object. In *Causation and counterfactuals,* eds. J. Collins, et al. Cambridge: MIT Press.

Mackie, J.L. 1965. Causes and conditions. *American Philosophical Quarterly* 2/4:245–255; 261–264

Mellor, D.H. 1995. *The facts of causation.* London: Routledge.

Menzies, P. 1999. Intrinsic versus extrinsic conceptions of causation. In *Causation and laws of nature*, ed. H. Sankey. Dordrecht: Kluwer.

Menzies, P. 2004. Difference-making in context. In *Causation and counterfactuals*, eds. J. Collins, et al. Cambridge, MA: MIT Press.

Mill, J.S. 1843. *A system of logic.* London: Longmans.

Pearl, J. 2000. *Causality. Models, reasoning, and inference.* Hardcover: Cambridge University Press.

Price, H. 1992. Agency and causal asymmetry. *Mind* 101:501–520, New York: New York Academy of Sciences.

Ramachandran, M. 2004. A counterfactual analysis of indeterministic causation. In *Causation and counterfactuals*, eds. J. Collins, et al. Cambridge: MIT Press.

Reichenbach, H. 1956. *The direction of time.* Berkeley: University of California Press.

Salmon, W. 1980a. Probabilistic causality. *Pacific Philosophical Quarterly* 61:50–74

Salmon, W. 1980b. Causality: production and propagation. In *Oxford readings in philosophy: Causation*(Reprinted), eds. E. Sosa, et al. Oxford: Oxford University Press.

Salmon, W. 1998. *Causality and explanation.* New York, NY: Oxford University Press.

Schaffer, J. 2000a. Trumping preemption. *Journal of Philosophy* 97:165–81

Schaffer, J. 2000b. Causation by disconnection. *Philosophy of Science* 67:285–300

Schaffer, J. 2001. Causes as probability raises of processes. *Journal of Philosophy* 98:75–92

Schaffer, J. 2004. Causes need not be physically connected to their effects: The case for negative causation. In *Contemporary debates in philosophy of science*, ed. C. Hitchcock. Oxford: Blackwell.

Stalnaker, R. 1968. A theory of conditionals. In *Studies in logical theory*, ed. N. Rescher. Oxford: Blackwell.

Tooley, M. 2003. Causation and supervenience. In *Oxford handbook of metaphysics*, eds. M. Loux, et al. Oxford: Oxford University Press.

Chapter 5
Actualism Versus Possibilism in Formal Ontology

Nino B. Cocchiarella

Comparative formal ontology is the study of how different informal ontologies can be formalized and compared with one another in their overall adequacy as explanatory frameworks. One important criterion of adequacy of course is consistency, a condition that can be satisfied only by formalization. Formalization also makes explicit the commitments of an ontology.

There are other important criteria of adequacy as well, however, in addition to consistency and transparency of ontological commitment. One major such criterion is that a formal ontology must explain and provide an ontological ground for the distinction between *being* and *existence*, or, if the distinction is rejected, an adequate account of why it is rejected. Put simply, the problem is: Can there *be* things that do not exist? Or is being the same as existence? Different formal ontologies will answer these questions in different ways.

The simplest account of the distinction between being and existence is that between actualism and possibilism, where by *existence* we mean physical existence, i.e., existence as some type of physical object; and by *being* we mean possible physical existence, i.e., physical existence in some possible world. According to *possibilism*, there are objects that do not now exist but could exist in the physical universe, and hence *being* is not the same as *existence*. In *actualism* being is the same as existence.

> Possibilism: There are objects (i.e., objects that have being or) that possibly exist but that do not in fact exist.
> Therefore: Existence $\neq$ Being.
> Actualism: Everything that is (has being) exists.
> Therefore: Existence $=$ Being.

Now the implicit understanding in formal ontology of both possibilism and actualism is that the objects that the quantifier phrases in these statements range over are values of the variables bound by the first-order quantifiers $\forall$ and $\exists$ (for the universal

N.B. Cocchiarella (✉)
Indiana University, Bloomington, Indiana, USA
e-mail: cocchiar@indiana.edu

R. Poli, J. Seibt (eds.), *Theory and Applications of Ontology: Philosophical Perspectives*, DOI 10.1007/978-90-481-8845-1_5,

and existential quantifiers, respectively), and hence that what has being (on the level of objects) is a value of the (object) variables bound by these quantifiers. In other words, *to be* (an object, or thing) in both actualism and possibilism is to be a value of the bound object variables of first-order logic. This means that in possibilism, where being is not the same as existence, existence must be represented either by different quantifiers or by a predicate, e.g., *E*!, which is the predicate usually chosen for this purpose.

Another criterion of adequacy for a formal ontology is that it must explain the ontological grounds, or nature, of modality, i.e., of such modal notions as *necessity* and *possibility*, and in particular the meaning of possible physical existence. If the modalities in question are strictly formal, on the other hand, as is the case with logical necessity and possibility, then it must explain the basis of that formality. This criterion cannot be satisfied by a set-theoretic semantics alone, especially one that allows for arbitrary sets of possible worlds (models) and so-called accessibility relations between those worlds. Such a semantics may be useful for showing the consistency of a modal logic, or perhaps even as a guide to our intuitions in showing its completeness; but it does not of itself provide an ontological ground for modality, or, in the case of logical modalities, explain why those modalities are strictly formal.

We restrict our considerations here to how physical existence, both actual and possible, is represented in a formal ontology. This does not mean that the formal ontologies considered here cannot be extended so as to include an account of how abstract objects might be represented as well, if allowed at all.

5.1 Logical Atomism

One ontology that is a paradigm of actualism is logical atomism. Logical atomism is also probably the only ontology in which a strictly formal interpretation of logical necessity and possibility can be given. This is because it is only in an ontology of simple objects and simple properties and relations as the bases of logically independent atomic states of affairs that the absolute totality of possible worlds is determined; it is only with respect to this totality, in other words, as opposed to arbitrary sets of possible worlds, that logical necessity and possibility can be made sense of as modalities.

Reality, according to logical atomism, consists of the existence and nonexistence of atomic states of affairs, where the existence of a state of affairs is 'a positive fact' and its nonexistence 'a negative fact'.[1] The actual world, in other words, consists of all that is the case, namely the totality of facts, whether positive or negative.[2] Every other possible world consists of the same atomic states of affairs that make up reality, except that what are positive facts in one world can be negative facts in another,

[1]Wittgenstein (1961, 2.06). For a fuller discussion of logical atomism as a formal ontology, see Chaps. 6 and 7 of Cocchiarella 1987.

[2]Wittgenstein (1961, P. 1). It is an issue of debate as to whether the *Tractatus* allowed for negative facts. But there definittely are negative facts in Russell's version of logical atomism.

with every possible combination of atomic states of affairs being realized in some possible world or other. The totality of possible worlds, in other words, is completely determined by all the different combinations of the existence or nonexistence of the atomic states of affairs that make up reality. The direction of this determination is important. Atomic states of affairs do not have *being* (the-case-or-not-the-case) because they exist (are the case) in some possible worlds; rather, possible worlds are possible because they are resolvable into the atomic states of affairs that make up reality.

Every atomic state of affairs is a configuration of objects, and therefore because every state of affairs is a positive or negative fact in each possible world, each possible world consists of the same totality of objects as every other possible world. There is no distinction, in other words, between the existence and the being of objects. That is why logical atomism is a paradigm of actualism. Also because the totality of all possible worlds is completely determined by the different combinations of atomic states of affairs, then an invariance through this totality, which is what is meant by *logical necessity*, has a precise and clear meaning. That is, necessity as what holds through all the logically possible worlds of this ontology amounts in effect to none other than logical necessity.

Another observation about the ontology of logical atomism is that the number of objects in the world is part of its logical scaffolding.[3] That is, for each positive integer n, it is either logically necessary or impossible that there are exactly n objects in the world; and if the number of objects is infinite, then, for each positive integer n, it is logically necessary that there are at least n objects in the world. This is true in logical atomism because every possible world consists of the same totality of objects.

One important consequence of the fact that every possible world (of a given logical space) consists of the same totality of objects is the logical truth of the Carnap-Barcan formula (and its converse)

$$(\forall x)\Box\varphi \leftrightarrow \Box(\forall x)\varphi.$$

Carnap, it should be noted, was the first to actually give an argument justifying the logical truth of this principle in terms of his state-description semantics for logical atomism.[4]

5.1.1 The Modal Thesis of Anti-essentialism

One condition regarding a strictly logical or formal notion of necessity is that it must satisfy the modal thesis of anti-essentialism; that is, the thesis that for any condition φ, if φ *must be* true of some objects, then φ must be true of all objects, or dually, if φ *can be* true of some objects, then φ *can be* true of all objects. In other words, no condition is essential to some objects that is not essential to all, which is as it

[3]This observation was first made by Ramsey in his adoption of logical atomism. Cf. Ramsey 1960.
[4]Cf. Carnap 1946, pp. 37 and 1947, Section 40. Unlike Carnap, Barcan assumed the formula as an axiom, and gave no explanation or reason why it should be assumed.

should be if necessity means logical necessity. That is, logically necessity does not discriminate between objects and their properties or relations. This thesis, as we have shown elsewhere, is in fact valid in the framework of logical atomism. It was Rudolf Carnap, incidentally, who in 1946 first formulated a version of this thesis.[5] It was formulated again much later in 1969 by Terence Parsons. However, whereas Carnap showed that the thesis is logically true (in his state-description semantics for logical atomism), Parsons showed only that the thesis is consistent (in a 'cut down' semantics of arbitrary sets of possible worlds).

Several conditions must be satisfied in the formal characterization of this thesis. One is that proper names, i.e., constants for objects, must not occur in the condition φ being specified.[6] Another condition is that φ must satisfy an identity-difference condition with respect to the object variables occurring free in it. This condition can be dropped if nested quantifiers are interpreted exclusively and not inclusively as we assume here, where, e.g., it is allowed that the value of y in $(\forall x)(\exists y)\varphi(x, y)$ can be the same as the value of x, as for example in $(\forall x)(\exists y)(x = y)$.[7] When nested quantifiers are interpreted exclusively, then identity and difference formulas are superfluous.[8]

Retaining the inclusive interpretation and identity as primitive, however, an *identity-difference condition* is defined as follows.

Definition 1 *If* $x_1, ..., x_n$ *are distinct objectual variables, then* identity-difference condition *for* $x_1, ..., x_n$ *is a conjunction of one each but not both of the formulas* $(x_i = x_j)$ *or* $(x_i \neq x_j)$, *for all* i,j *such that* $1 \leq i < j \leq n$.

Because there are only a finite number of nonequivalent identity-difference conditions for $x_1, ..., x_n$, we can assume an ordering, $ID_1(x_1, ..., x_n), ..., ID_j(x_1, ..., x_n)$, is given of all of these nonequivalent conditions.

The modal thesis of anti-essentialism may now be stated for all formulas φ in which no object constants occur as follows: for all positive integers j such that $1 \leq j \leq n$, every formula of the form,

$$(\exists x_1)\ldots(\exists x_n)[IDj(x_1,\cdots,x_n) \wedge \Box\varphi] \rightarrow (\forall x_1)\ldots(\forall x_1)[IDj(x_1,\cdots x_n) \rightarrow \Box\varphi]$$

is to be logically true, where $x_1, ..., x_n$ are all the distinct object variables occurring free in φ. As already noted, we can also phrase this thesis in terms of its equivalent contrapositive form:

$$(\exists x_1)\ldots(\exists x_n)[IDj(x_1,\cdots,x_n) \wedge \Diamond\varphi] \rightarrow (\forall x_1)\ldots(\forall x_1)[IDj(x_1,\cdots x_n) \rightarrow \Diamond\varphi]$$

Where n=0, the above formula is understood to be just $(\Box\varphi \rightarrow \Box\varphi)$; and where n=1, it is understood to be just $(\exists x)\Box\varphi \rightarrow (\forall x)\Box\varphi$, or equivalently $(\exists x)\Diamond\varphi \rightarrow$

[5]Carnap 1946, T10-3.c, p. 56.

[6]If object constants do occur in a formula, they can be replaced uniformly by distinct new object variables not already occurring in the formula.

[7]See Hintikka, 1956 for a development of the exclusive interpretation.

[8]Cf. Wittgenstein (1961), and Cocchiarella (1987, Chap. V1).

$(\forall x)\Diamond\varphi$. The first of these last formulas state that if something is essentially φ, then everything is essentially φ.

One of the consequences of this thesis, it should be noted, is the reduction of all *de re* formulas to *de dicto* formulas. (A *de re* formula is one in which some individual variable has a free occurrence in a subformula of the form $\Box\psi$). A *de dicto* formula is a formula that is not *de re*.) Naturally, such a consequence is another indicator that we are dealing with a strictly formal, logical notion of necessity.

Theorem 1 *(*De Re *Elimination Theorem)* For each *de re* formula φ, there is a *de dicto* formula ψ such that $(\varphi \leftrightarrow \psi)$ is valid in the ontology of logical atomism.

5.2 Actualism and Possibilism Across Temporal Modalities

Though claims have been made that all of the complexity in the world can be reduced to the atomic states of affairs of logical atomism, that thesis is at best dubious if not obviously false. How plants, animals, and complex physical objects in general can be reduced to such states of affairs is only part of the problem. There is also the question, for example, of how space and time are to be accounted for as well.

Assuming an ontology with complex physical objects within a space-time manifold as opposed to the simple (space-timeless?) objects of logical atomism, we can represent another view of the distinction between actualism and possibilism. Given a local time (*Eigenzeit*) of a world-line in the space-time manifold and a moment of that local time we can distinguish between the past, the present and the future (of that local time), and with that distinction we can then represent the further distinction between past, present and future existence. Past, present and future objects will then certainly be considered as values of the bound object variables in possibilism, whereas actualism can be taken as restricting quantification to what exists in the present. *Being,* in other words, encompasses past, present, and future objects with respect to a local time, whereas existence encompasses only those objects that presently exist.[9] No doctrine of *merely possible* existence is needed in such a framework to explain the distinction between existence and being. Thus, we can interpret modality so that it *can* be true to say that some things do not exist, namely past and future things that do not now exist. In fact, there are potentially infinitely many different modal logics that can be interpreted within the framework of tense logic and the space-time manifold. In this respect, tense logic provides a paradigmatic framework within which possibilism can be given a logically perspicuous representation as a formal ontology.

Tense logic provides a paradigmatic framework not just for possibilism but for actualism as well. Instead of possible objects, for example, actualism assumes that

[9]For some philosophers, e.g., Arthur Prior, being encompasses only past and present objects, apparently because, unlike the past and the present, the future is as yet undetermined in their ontology. See Prior (1967, Chap. viii).

there can be vacuous proper names, i.e., proper names that name nothing. Some names, for example, may have named something in the past, but now name nothing because those things no longer exist; and hence the statement that some things do not exist can be true in a semantic, metalinguistic sense, i.e., as a statement about the denotations, or lack of denotations, of proper names. What is needed, according to actualism, is not that we should distinguish the concept of existence from the concept of being, but only that we should modify the way that the concept of existence (being) is represented in standard first-order predicate logic with identity.

On this view, a first-order logic of existence should allow for the possibility that some of our singular terms might fail to denote an existent object, which, according to actualism, is only to say that those singular terms denote nothing, rather than that what they denote are objects (beings) that do not exist. Such a logic for actualism amounts to what today is called a *logic free of existential presuppositions*, or simply *free logic*.[10] Thus, whereas the logic of possibilism can be taken as standard first-order logic (with identity) with past, present and future objects (with respect to a given local time) as the values of the bound object variables, the logic of actualism is a free logic, i.e., logic free of existential presuppositions regarding the denotations of singular terms.

The distinction between actualism and possibilism can be seen in part by how each represents existence. Possibilism, as already noted, must assume some way by which to distinguish existence from being, and one standard way is by means of a predicate for existence, e.g., $E!$. Quantification over existing objects would then be represented by restriction to this predicate. Thus, actualist quantifiers can be defined in possibilism as follows:

$$(\forall^e x)\varphi x =_{df} (\forall x)[E!(x) \to \varphi x]$$
$$(\exists^e x)\varphi x =_{df} (\exists x)[E!(x) \wedge \varphi x].$$

In actualism, on the other hand, the quantifiers $\forall^e$ and $\exists^e$ would be taken as basic, and existence would then be defined as follows:

$$E!(x) =_{df} (\exists^e y)(x = y),$$

where x and y are distinct object variables. As noted above, the logic of these quantifiers is free of existential presuppositions. In possibilism we have as a theorem,

$$(\forall x)\varphi x \to (\forall^e x)\varphi x$$

but of course not its converse.[11]

---

[10]See Lambert (1991) for a collection of papers on free logic and its philosophical applications.

[11]See Cocchiarella, 'Quantification, Time and Necessity,' in Lambert (1991) for axiomatizations of both actualism and possibilism, as well as axioms for tense logic and the modal logics analyzable in terms of tense logic.

5.3 Modality Within Tense Logic

The first modal concepts ever to be discussed and analyzed in the history of philosophy are concepts based on the distinction between the past, the present, and the future. The logician Diodorus of Megaris, for example, is reported as having argued that the possible is that which either is or will be the case, and that the necessary is that which is and always will be the case.[12] Where $\mathcal{F}$ is the future-tense operator, the Diodorean modalities can be defined as follows:

$$\Diamond^f \varphi =_{df} (\varphi \vee \mathcal{F}\varphi)$$
$$\Box^f \varphi =_{df} \varphi \wedge \neg\mathcal{F}\neg\varphi$$
$$\therefore \Box^f \varphi \leftrightarrow \neg\Diamond^f \neg\varphi$$

Aristotle also explained necessity and possibility in terms of time, but, unlike Diodorus, he included the past as part of what is possible; that is, for Aristotle the possible is that which either was, is, or will be the case in what he assumed to be the infinity of time, and therefore the necessary is what is always the case[13]. Using $\mathcal{P}$ for the past-tense operator, Aristotle's modalities can be defined as follows:

$$\Diamond^t \varphi =_{df} \mathcal{P}\varphi \vee \varphi \vee \mathcal{F}\varphi$$
$$\Box^t \varphi =_{df} \neg\mathcal{P}\neg\varphi \wedge \varphi \wedge F\neg\varphi$$
$$\therefore \Box^t \varphi \leftrightarrow \neg\Diamond^t \neg\varphi$$

Both the Diodorean and Aristotelian temporal modalities are understood to be *real modalities* based on the reality of time. In fact they provide a paradigm by which we might understand what is meant by a real, as opposed to a merely formal, modality such as logical necessity. In addition, these temporally-based modalities contain an explanatory, concrete interpretation of what is called the accessibility relation between possible worlds in modal logic, except that worlds are now construed as momentary states of the universe as described by the models associated with the moments of a local time. That is, where possible worlds are momentary descriptive states (models) of the universe with respect to the local time (*Eigenzeit*) of a given world-line, then the relation of accessibility between worlds is ontologically grounded in terms of the earlier-than relation of that local time.

The Aristotelian modalities are stronger than the Diodorean, of course, and in fact they provide a complete semantics for the quantified modal logic known as **S 5**. The Diodorean modalities, on the other hand, provide a complete semantics for the quantified modal logic known as **S4.3**. The Carnap-Barcan formula is valid in the possibilist form of both systems; that is, both of the following

[12]See Prior (1967, Chap. 2), for a discussion of Diodorus's argument.

[13]See Hintikka, 1973, Chaps. V and IX.

$$(\forall x)\Box^t \varphi x \leftrightarrow \Box^t (\forall x)\varphi x$$
$$(\forall x)\Box^f \varphi x \leftrightarrow \Box^f (\forall x)\varphi x$$

are provable in **S5** and **S4.3**, respectively, with respect to the possibilist quantifiers. On the other hand, both fail with respect to the actualist quantifiers. That is, both of the following

$$(\forall^e x)\Box^t x \leftrightarrow \Box^t (\forall^e x)\varphi x$$
$$(\forall^e x)\Box^f \varphi \leftrightarrow \Box^f (\forall^e x)\varphi$$

are invalid in the corresponding actualist systems.

5.3.1 Relativity Theory and the Light-Signal Relation

As temporal modalities based only on a local time, Aristotle's and Diodorus's notions of possibility and necessity exclude certain situations that are possible in special relativity theory. These situations are possible because of the finite limiting velocity of causal influences, such as a light signal moving from one point of space-time to another. Relative to the present of a given local time, for example, a state of affairs can come to have been the case, according to special relativity, without its ever actually being the case.[14] That is, where $\mathcal{FP}\varphi$ represents φ's coming (in the future of the given local time) to have been the case (in the past of that future), and $\neg\Diamond^t\varphi$ represents φ's never actually being the case, the situation envisaged in special relativity might be represented by:

$$\mathcal{FP}\varphi \wedge \neg\Diamond^t\varphi. \qquad \textbf{(Rel)}$$

This conjunction is incompatible with the connectedness assumption of the local time in question; for on the basis of that assumption,

$$\mathcal{FP}\varphi \rightarrow \mathcal{P}\varphi \vee \varphi \vee \mathcal{FP}$$

is provable, and therefore, by definition of $\Diamond^t$,

$$\mathcal{FP}\varphi \rightarrow \Diamond^t\varphi$$

is also provable. That is, $\mathcal{FP}\varphi$, the first conjunct of **(Rel)**, implies $\Diamond^t\varphi$, which contradicts the second conjunct of **(Rel)**, $\neg\Diamond^t\varphi$. The connectedness assumption cannot be given up, moreover, without violating the notion of a local time or of a world-line as an inertial reference frame upon which that local time is based. The notion of a local time is a fundamental construct not only of our common-sense

---

[14]Cf. Putnam (1967), for a fuller discussion of this type of situation.

framework but of natural science as well, as in the assumption of an *Eigenzeit* in relativity theory.

One way to represent this situation is by introducing special future-tense and past-tense operators, $\mathcal{P}_c$ and $\mathcal{F}_c$, based on a light-signal relation that connects space-time points of both the same and different world-lines.[15] The only constraint that should be imposed on such a signal relation is that it be a strict partial ordering, i.e., transitive and asymmetric.[16] We can then distinguish the causal past with respect to a space-time point on a world line from the simple past, with the causal past represented by $\mathcal{P}_c$ and the simple past represented by $\mathcal{P}$. Similarly, we can also distinguish the causal future, as represented by $\mathcal{F}_c$ from the simple future as represented by $\mathcal{F}$. The causal past includes not just the past with respect to a here-now of a local time of a world-line, but also the past with respect to any momentary state of any other world-line that can send a light-signal to that here-now; and similarly the causal future includes not just the future of that here-now but also the future of any momentary state of any world-line to which a light-signal can be sent from that here-now. The geometric structure at a given momentary state of a world-line is a Minkowski light-cone. That is, at each momentary state X of a world-line there is both *a prior light cone (the causal past)* consisting of all the momentary states (or space-time points) of world-lines that can send a signal to X and *a posterior light cone (causal future)* of all the momentary states (or space-time points) of world-lines that can receive a signal from X. Momentary states are then said to be *simultaneous* if no signal relation can be sent from one to the other.

Now because the light-signal relation has a finite limiting velocity, simultaneity will not be a transitive relation. As a result any one of a number of momentary states of one world-line can be simultaneous with the same momentary state of another world-line. What this allows according to special relativity theory is the possibility of a state of affairs coming to have been the case without its ever actually being the case, a possibility that should be represented of course in terms of the signal tense-operators $\mathcal{F}_c\varphi$ and $\mathcal{P}_c\varphi$—i.e., in terms of the causal past and causal future—and not in terms of the simple past-tense and future-tense operators $\mathcal{P}$ and $\mathcal{F}$. In addition, because there is a causal connection from the earlier to the later momentary states of the same local time, the signal relation is assumed to contain as a proper part the connected temporal ordering of the moments of each of the local times. The following, in other words, are valid theses of such a causally connected system:

$$\mathcal{P}\varphi \rightarrow \mathcal{P}_c\varphi$$
$$\mathcal{F}\varphi \rightarrow \mathcal{F}_c\varphi$$

[15]For a formalization of the topology of space-time based on the light-signal relation see Carnap (1958,§§48–50).

[16]See Cocchiarella 1984, Section 15, for the details of a semantics for these operators. The signal relation, incidentally, provides yet another example of a concrete interpretation of an accessibility relation between possible worlds, reconstrued now as the momentary states of the universe at different space-time points.

Of course, because the signal relation has a finite limiting velocity, the converses of these theses will not also be valid. Were we to reject the assumption of relativity theory that there is a finite limit to causal influences, namely, the speed of light–as was implicit in classical physics and is still implicit in our commonsense framework where simultaneity is assumed to be absolute across space-time–then we would validate the converses of the above theses, in which case the signal-tense operators would be completely redundant, which explains why they have no counterparts in natural language, which, prior to the special theory of relativity, allowed for unlimited causal influences.

One important consequence of the divergence of the signal-tense operators from the standard ones is the invalidity of

$$\mathcal{F}_c\mathcal{P}_c\varphi \rightarrow \mathcal{P}_c\varphi \vee \varphi \vee \mathcal{F}_c\varphi$$

and therefore the consistency of

$$\mathcal{F}_c\mathcal{P}_c\varphi \wedge \neg\Diamond^t\varphi.$$

Unlike its counterpart in terms of the standard tenses, this last formula is the appropriate representation of the possibility in special relativity of a state of affairs coming (in the causal future) to have been the case (in the causal past) without its ever actually being the case (in a given local time). Indeed, not only can this formula be true at some moment of a local time of a causally connected system, but so can the following formula[17]:

$$[\mathcal{P}_c\Diamond^t\varphi \vee \mathcal{F}_c\Diamond^t\varphi] \wedge \neg\Diamond^t\varphi.$$

Quantifiers in possibilism now range over things that exist in space-time with respect to any local time and not just with respect to a given local time. Note that just as some states of affairs can come to have been the case in the causal past of the causal future without their actually ever being the case, so too there can be things that do not exist in the past, present or future of a here-now of a given local time, but which nevertheless might exist at a space-time point of another world-line that is simultaneous with that here-now.

Finally, we note that there is also a causal counterpart to Diodorus's notion of possibility as what either is or will be the case, namely, possibility as what either is or will be the case with respect to the $\mathcal{F}_c$-operator:

$$\Diamond^s\varphi =_{df} \varphi \vee \mathcal{F}_c\varphi.$$

[17]This formula would be true at a given moment t of a local time X if in either the prior cone or posterior cone of that moment there is a space-time point t' of a world-line Y such that φ is always true in Y, even though φ is never true in X. See Putnam (op. cit.) for an example of how this is possible in relativity theory.

Instead of the modal logic **S4.3**, this Diodorean notion of possibility results in the modal logic **S4**. Moreover, if we assume, as is usual in special relativity, that the causal futures of any two moments t, t' of two local times *eventually intersect*, i.e., that there is a moment w of a local time such that both t and t' can send a signal to w, then the thesis

$$\mathcal{F}_c\neg\mathcal{F}_c\neg\varphi \rightarrow \neg\mathcal{F}_c\neg\mathcal{F}_c\varphi$$

will be validated, and the new Diodorean notion of possibility will then result in the modal system **S4.2**, i.e., the system **S4** plus the thesis

$$\Diamond^s\Box^s\varphi \rightarrow \Box^s\Diamond^s\varphi.$$

Many other modal concepts can also be characterized in terms of a signal-related system of local times, including, e.g., the notion of something being necessary because of the way the past has been. What is distinctive about them all is the unproblematic sense in which they can be taken as ontologically grounded modalities. In addition, they also provide clear examples of the distinction between being and existence.

5.3.2 The Many-Worlds Model of Quantum Mechanics

There are notions of possible worlds, and with them forms of modality and distinctions between being and existence, that go beyond the space-time manifold. Philosophers sometimes speak, for example, of metaphysical modalities, and with them a metaphysical distinction between being and existence. But, aside from giving at best a purely set-theoretic semantics, no real ontological grounds have been described for such modalities, though apparently something more than just a physical modality is intended. Having restricted ourselves here to physical existence, both actual and possible, we will also restrict ourselves to physical modalities.

One example of a physical modality with a clear ontological basis is implicit in the many-worlds interpretation of quantum mechanics (**QM**). Each particle in the universe is associated in **QM** with a probability wave that specifies the different probabilities of where that particle might be located anywhere in the universe at each moment. Whether a particle is the same as its wave function, or whether the wave function is merely a mathematical construct that describes the particle's motion is one of the issues that distinguishes different versions of **QM**. In standard quantum mechanics, when a measurement is made and a particle is observed at a given location, then the probability of finding it at that location becomes 100% while the probability of finding it at any other location at that time drops to zero. This is what is meant in saying that the wave function 'collapses'. The many-worlds interpretation denies that a particle's wave function ever collapses.

Instead of a collapse of the wave function, what happens according to the many-worlds interpretation is that every potential outcome described in the particle's probability function is realized in a separate parallel world, so that anything that could happen in the sense of being physically possible according to **QM** in fact does happen in some parallel world.[18] All of the worlds accessible in this way from a given world when a measurement is made at a given moment have the same past up to that moment, but, except for the laws of nature, they differ thereafter in some way. An infinite number of parallel worlds populated by copies of ourselves is assumed in this way, where all of the worlds 'co-exist' in a quantum superposition.[19]

Although the objects in those worlds are not ' real' in the same sense in which the objects of our universe are real, nevertheless, they have an ontological status as objects of the multiverse. This type of situation is represented in a formal ontology in terms of an **S4** modal logic in which necessity and possibility are based on what is physically possible in **QM**. The modal logic is **S4** because the accessibility relation between possible worlds is a partial ordering determined by the wave functions that split each universe into its related parallel universes. The result in effect is a branched-tree model of the universe something like the semantics for **S4** in terms of the signal-tense operators described in the previous section. The result, in other words, is a version of possibilism in which we can distinguish between quantifying over the real objects of our universe from quantifying over the objects in other possible (parallel) worlds. Actualism would be restricted to quantifying only over the objects that exist in our world at a given moment of a local time.

In addition to the many-worlds interpretation of **QM** there are other cosmological models of the universe in which a multiverse of possible parallel worlds are described. One such, for example, is the concordance model.[20] There are other models as well, and in fact a number of different theories of parallel worlds can be described in clear scientific terms.[21] The important point about all of these theories is that unlike metaphysical theories they provide scientifically viable ontological grounds for the notion of a possible world, and with that the notion of possible, as opposed to actual, objects as well.

References

Cocchiarella, N.B. 1984. Philosophical perspectives on quantification in tense and modal logic. *Handbook of philosophical logic*, vol. II, 309–354. Dordrecht: D. ReidelPub. Co.

Cocchiarella, N.B. 1987 *Logical studies in early analytic philosophy*, Columbus: Ohio State University Press.

---

[18]In Everett's original version of the axioms of the many-worlds interpretation no account was given of how the branching into different parallel worlds takes place. Later proposals by Graham and DeWitt introduce the complicated notion of a measuring device that results in observations (by humans or automata) upon which the splitting into parallel worlds is based. See De Witt and Graham (1973).

[19]For a fuller account of the many-worlds interpretation see De Witt and Graham (1973).

[20]See Tegmark (2003).

[21]See, e.g., Kaku (2005).

Cocchiarella, N.B. 1991. Quantification, time and necessity. In *Philosophical Applications of Free Logic*, ed. K. Lambert, 242–256. Oxford: Oxford University Press.
Carnap, R. 1946. Modalities and quantification. *Journal of Symbolic Logic* 11: 33–64
Carnap, R. 1947. *Meaning and Necessity*, Chicago: University of Chicago Press.
Carnap, R. 1958. *Introduction to symbolic logic and its applications*. New York; NY: Dover Publication.
De Witt, B. and N. Graham. eds. 1973. *The many-Worlds interpretation of quantum mechanics*. Princeton: Princeton University Press.
Hintikka, J. 1956. Identity, variables and impredicative definitions. *Journal of Symbolic Logic* 21:225–245.
Hintikka, J. 1973. *Time and necessity, studies in Aristotle's theory of modality*. London: Oxford University Press.
Lambert, K. ed., 1991. *Philosophical applications of free logic*. New York and Oxford: Oxford University Press.
Kaku, M. 2005. *Parallel worlds*. New York, NY: Doubleday.
Parsons, T. 1969. Essentialism and quantified modal logic. *Philosophical Review* 78:35–52.
Prior, A.N. 1967. *Past, present and future*. Oxford: Oxford University Press.
Putnam, H. 1967. Time and physical geometry, *The Journal of Philosophy* LXIV: 8; reprinted in Putnam's *Mathematics, Matter and Method, Philosophical Papers, vol. 1*, Cambridge University Press, 1975.
Ramsey, F.P. 1960. *The foundation of mathematics*, ed. R.B. Braithwaite. Paterson, NJ: Littlefield, Adams.
Tegmark, M. 2003. Parallel Universes. In *Science and ultimate reality: From quantum to cosmos*, honoring John Wheeler's 90th birthday, eds. J.D. Barrow, P.C.W. Davies, and C.L. Harper. Cambridge: Cambridge University Press.
Wittgenstein, L. 1961. *Tractatus logico-philosophicus*. New York, NY: Routledge & Kegan Paul.

Chapter 6
Dispositions and Response-Dependence Theories

Eline Busck Gundersen

This chapter offers a taste of some central issues concerning dispositions and response-dependence theories. The first part focuses on the conditional analysis of dispositions and the problem posed by finkish, masked and mimicking counterexamples. The second treats the relationship between dispositions and their bases, and summarises some of the central argument types relevant to the assessment of this issue. The third part provides an overview of response-dependence theories. It also contains a brief discussion of some questions that connect the three themes of the chapter. These concern conditional fallacy problems for response-dependence theses, the relationship between dispositional and subjunctive formulations of response-dependence theses, and the implications for (dispositional) response-dependence theses of which view one takes on dispositions in general.

Dispositions are ubiquitous, familiar, puzzling, and, according to some, metaphysically suspect. Let me try to unpack this strange claim. As for ubiquity and familiarity, dispositional properties and vocabulary are familiar from many contexts, everyday and theoretical. We all know that if a substance is poisonous, one might come to harm if ingesting it; that if a china vase is fragile, one should pack it carefully when moving house; that if one's friend is courageous, one can trust her to act appropriately in dangerous situations. These are paradigmatic examples of dispositional properties. Features like these seem very real; they seem to be genuine respects in which things (broadly understood) can be similar and different. Dispositional concepts are also widespread and important in science; think of e.g. the concepts of power and radioactivity. In philosophy, dispositions are ubiquitous too. Dispositional accounts have been offered of a wide range of phenomena; examples include knowledge, linguistic meaning, mental states, colours and other traditional secondary qualities, and aesthetic and ethical values. A new development in dispositional or dispositional-like theories is response-dependence theories. These, too, have been applied to a wide range of subject matters (see Section 6.3).

E.B. Gundersen (✉)
Centre for the Study of Mind in Nature, University of Oslo, Oslo, Norway;
Department of Philosophy and History of Ideas, Aarhus University, Denmark
e-mail: e.b.gundersen@csmn.uio.no

R. Poli, J. Seibt (eds.), *Theory and Applications of Ontology: Philosophical Perspectives*, DOI 10.1007/978-90-481-8845-1_6,

So there are good reasons to take an interest in understanding dispositions and disposition ascriptions.[1]

As for 'puzzling' and 'metaphysically suspect', dispositions are special in that they concern what *would* or *might* happen in certain circumstances, not (or not primarily) how the object actually behaves. A fragile glass might exist forever without breaking but still be fragile; what is important is what *would* happen if it was struck or dropped. For this reason, dispositions have been thought to be metaphysically suspect, and many have attempted to analyse or account for them in terms of more acceptable properties. This has turned out to be no easy task. The result is a long-standing and interesting dispute about the nature of dispositions and disposition ascriptions.

In a paper of this format, many important issues from debates on dispositions must be left out or only briefly touched on. One issue that we shall have to leave out is the question whether dispositions are intrinsic properties.[2] Another is the possibility of bare (base-less) dispositions (though a few remarks and references on this issue can be found in Section 6.2). I will also leave out early discussions about the legitimacy or existence of dispositional properties, since most people are now happy to acknowledge that dispositional properties exist. It seems better to focus on a few of the central issues than to attempt a superficial overview of everything.

6.1 The Conditional Analysis and Its Problems

Intuitively, to say that something has a disposition is to say that it can be expected to react in a certain way in certain situations. If an object is fragile, it will normally break if struck. If a substance is poisonous, it will cause harm if ingested. If a person is brave, she will act appropriately in the face of danger. Accordingly, dispositions have traditionally been analysed in terms of counterfactual dependencies. A general recipe for conditional analyses of dispositions (or, more accurately, of disposition ascriptions) can be stated as follows:

(CA) Something, x, is disposed at time t to give response r to stimulus s iff, if x was exposed to stimulus s at time t, x would give response r[3]

A simplified, specific example would be this toy analysis of fragility:

(FRAG) x is fragile at t iff, if x was struck at t, x would break

Of course, this is an over-simplification; the fragility of eggs, china vases and thin icicles would manifest in slightly different ways, and how to capture all the

---

[1]This point is stressed by Fara (2005), p. 43. See also his excellent survey article, Fara (2006).

[2]Most take dispositions to be intrinsic properties (e.g. Lewis 1997), but see McKitrick (2003a) for arguments that some dispositions are extrinsic properties.

[3]This formulation is taken from Lewis (1997). It does not cover all dispositions; some adjustment would be needed to accommodate e.g. dispositions to elicit certain responses in other beings and things, or dispositions for which no particular stimulus is specifiable (e.g. radioactive decay). But it will do for current purposes.

variety is a difficult question. But we shall be concerned, not with the question how to capture specific dispositions like fragility, but with general questions concerning the CA, so we shall ignore these complications for now.

Despite its intuitive appeal, the conditional analysis of dispositions has been targeted by four kinds of counterexamples. Two of these exploit the idea that an object's dispositions might change as a result of the very stimuli characteristic of those dispositions. One class of counterexamples is based on *finkish dispositions*: dispositions that are lost when the characteristic stimulus occurs so the response is never manifested.[4] A frequently used example involves a sorcerer who has decided to protect his favourite fragile vase by making it solid if it is struck, thereby preventing it from breaking. As long as the vase is not struck, it remains exactly as it would have been without the sorcerer's protection; intuitively, it remains fragile. So the analysandum is true. But if the vase were struck, it would change and become solid, and so would not break; the analysans is false. A non-supernatural, everyday example of a finkish disposition is Martin's original example of a circuit breaker.[5]

A second group of counterexamples are based on *finkish lacks of dispositions*. In these cases, the object lacks the disposition, but would gain it if the stimulus occurred, and would do so in time for the stimulus to trigger the response. An example would be a solid stone vase which a bad-tempered sorcerer has decided to make fragile if it is struck. The vase would intuitively remain solid until the interference of the sorcerer; the analysandum of (FRAG) is false. But thanks to the sorcerer, the vase would break if struck; the analysans is true. Again, we have a counterexample to the analysis.

The third and fourth kinds of counterexamples concern cases where the disposition itself does not change, but where the manifestation of the disposition is masked or mimicked by external factors. In *masking* examples, the object has and retains the disposition, and the stimulus occurs, but external factors prevent the response. So the analysandum is true, the analysans false. A standard example of a masked disposition is a fragile vase which is packed with polystyrene during transport to prevent it from breaking if accidentally struck.[6] Intuitively, the vase remains fragile; it is intrinsically exactly like other, unpacked vases from the same production line, and these would certainly break if struck. But if our vase were struck, it would not break, thanks to the protective packing. So, as in the case of finkish dispositions, the analysandum is true, but the analysans comes out false.

---

[4]Finkish counterexamples are often credited to Martin (1994), but are also discussed by Shope (1978) in a more general form. The term 'finkish' is, as far as I know, due to David Lewis. 'Altering' is a common alternative label.

[5]Martin (1994), p. 3. In a bit more detail, the example is this: A wire has the dispositional property of being live iff it is the case that if the wire were touched by a conductor, electrical current would flow through it to the conductor. But Martin's 'electro-fink' switches off the electricity whenever such contact is made.

[6]The example is due to Johnston (1992). Johnston coined the term 'masking' and was the first to present masking cases as problems for the conditional analysis of dispositions.

In *mimicking* cases, the object does *not* have the disposition, but if the stimulus were to occur, the response would be brought about anyway by factors external to the object. An example would be a solid stone vase filled with nitro-glycerine that would explode and break the vase if it were struck. In such cases, the analysandum is false, the analysans true.

The four types of counterexamples are closely related. Masking and mimicking seem more or less parallel, since an instance of masked fragility could also be viewed as an instance of mimicked solidity, and vice versa. Likewise for finkish dispositions and finkish lacks of dispositions: a finkishly fragile object finkishly lacks solidity, and vice versa.

Evaluations of the relative strength of the counterexamples vary in the literature. Lewis (1997) takes finkish dispositions and lacks, but not masking and mimicking, to pose serious problems for the analysis. Mumford (1996) proposes a remedy against masking and finkish cases, but leaves mimicking and finkish lacks as open questions. But given the very similar structures of the counterexamples, it might seem reasonable to expect all four kinds of cases to be addressed in a roughly uniform way.

The counterexamples based on finkish dispositions, finkish lacks of dispositions, maskers and mimickers are not easily deflected. For example, it won't do to solve the problems about finkish dispositions and lacks by requiring that the intrinsic nature of x remains unchanged when s occurs. This would indeed prevent a fragile vase from losing its fragility when it is struck. But it would also prevent it from breaking. So adding this requirement would not help us capture the way dispositions work.[7] Inserting a clause like 'x would r on s *unless somehow prevented*' won't do the trick either. Such a move would yield too many dispositions, as we might arguably say that anything is disposed to break if struck unless somehow prevented, but that stones, metals etc. are normally somehow prevented.[8] Other varieties such as a 'no masker or fink is operating'-clause would make the analysis circular, as maskers and finks will presumably have to be defined in dispositional terms.[9]

Nor will it do to reject the problem cases as speculative toy examples of no real importance. The phenomena exploited by these four kinds of counterexamples are more than speculation; they are familiar from everyday life, and turn on the same sort of pragmatic considerations that support the conditional analysis itself. In order to survive and succeed in our various projects, we need to be able to predict how things and people will react in various circumstances that might arise. Ascribing dispositional properties to things helps us do exactly that. The conditional analysis owes its intuitive strength to capturing this crucial aspect of dispositions. One reason that it is important to know what to expect is that it is often useful or necessary to manipulate dispositions, especially those with unpleasant manifestations.

---

[7]Lewis (1997), p. 158.

[8]Bird (1998), p. 231 and Gundersen (2002), p. 391.

[9]Martin (1994), p. 6. It may be that some sort of ceteris paribus clause can solve the problems, but if so, more needs to be said. See e.g. Mumford (1996).

Sometimes, this can be done by removing unwanted dispositions or by preventing the stimuli that cause their manifestations. But in other cases, the best or only option is to mask the disposition – to make sure that, though the disposition remains in place and the stimulus occurs, the response is not manifested. An example would be anti-histamines; they work, not by allowing the patient to avoid the unpleasant stimulus (grass-pollen, say), and not by curing the allergy, but by giving temporary relief from its unpleasant manifestations. So masking is a very real phenomenon that an account of dispositions had better accommodate. Similarly for mimicking; greenhouses mimic the effects of warmer climates, contact lenses mimic the visual ability of normal-sighted humans, etc. Everyday examples of finkish dispositions and finkish lacks are less widespread, but they exist; think again of Martin's circuit breaker.[10]

Most philosophers take the counterexamples to refute the classical conditional analysis. In response, some have proposed amendments supposed to deal with the counterexamples. The most famous proposal of this kind is David Lewis' revised conditional analysis, which we shall look at in some detail.

Lewis proposes to solve the problems with finkish dispositions and lacks by building into the analysis an appeal to the causal bases of dispositions. A disposition's base can be characterised as the property, or complex of properties, of the object that, together with the stimulus, is causally responsible for the response. Lewis's revised conditional analysis is this (in his own words, an unlovely mouthful):

> (LEWIS) Something x is disposed at time t to give response r to stimulus s iff, for some intrinsic property B that x has at t, for some time t' after t, if x were to undergo stimulus s at time t and retain property B until t', s and x's having of B would jointly be an x-complete cause of x's giving response r (1997, p. 157)
> (An x-complete cause means a complete cause as far as x's intrinsic nature is concerned.)

The problem with finkish dispositions is that the disposition, and with it the base property B, might be lost as a result of the stimulus, so that s would not give rise to r. Lewis's solution is, roughly, to replace claims of the form 'if s were to occur, r would follow', or 'x has a property B which would join with s to cause r', with something along the lines of 'x has a property B which, *assuming it stayed long enough after s to cause r*, would join with s to cause r'. In non-finkish cases, B stays and causes r; in finkish cases, it does not. In both cases, x has a property B which would have done the appropriate causal job if it had stayed long enough. So in both cases, the analysans is true like the analysandum.

The problem with finkish lacks of dispositions is solved by requiring that *B is a property that x already has at t*, not one it acquires as a result of s. This makes the analysans come out false as expected for any object that lacks the disposition, finkishly or otherwise.

Lewis's proposal is widely recognised as a solution to the problems with finkish dispositions and lacks. However, as Bird (1998) has pointed out, Lewis's revised

[10] I am indebted to Crispin Wright for discussion and suggestions about these issues.

analysis is as vulnerable to masking counterexamples as the simple conditional analysis. Bird argues this point by way of examples. In one example, a person has taken an antidote to a poisonous pill. Though the pill retains its usually fatal property B, nothing would happen if the person ingested it, which means that the analysans of the CA for 'poisonous' comes out false even though the pill is still poisonous.

But there is a more general way to make the point than by examples like Bird's. Lewis's addition to the simple conditional analysis is the appeal to base properties, and this move deals efficiently with finkish cases. But in masking cases, the dispositions, and so their bases, remain unaltered, while the manifestation is prevented by external factors. So the move with bases does nothing to address the problem with masking, and hence it is not surprising that Lewis's analysis inherits the problems of the simple CA. A different approach seems needed, and it is not clear from Lewis's discussion of masking cases what should be done.[11]

There is no agreement in the literature about the correct reaction to the counterexamples to conditional analyses of dispositions. Some have concluded that conditional analyses of dispositions should be given up, e.g. Martin (1994), Bird (1998), and Fara (2005). But even among this group of philosophers, very different lessons are drawn from the failure. While Martin supports a primitivist view of dispositions as unanalysable but real, Bird advises us to forget about analysing dispositions and turn our attention to the non-dispositional physical properties that serve as their bases. Fara proposes a (non-conditional) analysis in terms of habituals – claims about how an object typically, though not exceptionlessly, behaves.

Others (Gundersen 2002, 2004, Bonevac et al. 2006) have argued that the problems are due to inadequacies in the standard (Lewis/Stalnaker) semantics for subjunctive conditionals. On their view, finkish, masked and mimicked dispositions can be accommodated, and the conditional analysis redeemed, by making appropriate adjustments to the semantics for the conditionals. This is a discussion that is still very far form concluded.

6.2 Dispositions and Their Bases

We shall now turn to another issue: the relation between dispositions and their bases. Above, I characterised bases as the properties or complexes of properties of an object that, jointly with the stimulus, are causally responsible for bringing about the manifestation of the disposition. In principle, bases could themselves be dispositional properties – some think that a disposition could even be its own base – but when people talk about bases, the often mean the basic bases, as it were: the micro-physical properties thought to be ultimately responsible for the causal work associated with the disposition. Some argue that every disposition must have such a base (Armstrong 1968, Prior et al. 1982, Smith and Stoljar 1998); others argue

[11] Lewis's discussion of masking cases (1997, pp. 152–153) has been interpreted in many ways, none of which seem to solve the problem. See e.g. Choi (2003).

that does not have to be the case (McKitrick 2003b). The relationship between dispositions and their bases is an interesting and hotly debated issue.

A whole spectrum of views familiar from the philosophy of mind are available. Some use causal exclusion arguments and/or arguments from ontological economy to support an identity theory of dispositions: a theory that dispositions are identical with their bases. Examples of identity theories are found in Armstrong, who defends a type–type identity thesis, and Mumford, who argues for a thesis of token–token identity.[12] Another alternative is a functionalist theory like Prior, Pargetter and Jackson's (1982). On this view, dispositions are second order (role) properties of having certain (realiser) properties, i.e. the bases. Thus, to be fragile is to have a certain property – a certain molecular structure, perhaps – in virtue of which the object would break if struck. (Mumford's (1998) view is also a version of functionalism, but one that identifies dispositions with the realiser properties.)

Other alternatives are eliminativist positions that take talk of dispositions to be a flawed way of talking about bases, and primitivist positions that take dispositions to be irreducible but real properties that should not be accounted for in any terms but their own (Martin 2007). Finally, fully-fledged dualism would be an option, though there are not many current examples of such a view.

Many of the core arguments from the philosophy of mind can be, and have been, applied to dispositions (and indeed to lots of other areas where physical 'bases' are in play, e.g. colours). I shall give a brief overview of the most important such arguments in the following. We should note that the dialectical situation is somewhat different for dispositions than it is for mental states. For example, an eliminativist position with respect to dispositions ('skip dispositions and focus on bases') or a conclusion of causal impotence are far less unpalatable than the analogous conclusions about mental states.

One (type of) argument that carries over neatly to the case of dispositions is the *causal exclusion argument*.[13] It shows that there is an inconsistency across the following claims:

(1) Dispositions are causally efficacious
(2) The base of a disposition is sufficient to do the causal work associated with the disposition
(3) Dispositions and their bases do not over-determine their effects
(4) Dispositions are distinct from their bases

Or, in a bit more detail: We standardly describe dispositions as causes; explanations of the form 'the cup broke because it was fragile' make sense and are commonly accepted. But whenever causal work is ascribed to a (based) disposition, this work could also be described as done by its base property. This property is by

---

[12] Armstrong (1968) and Mumford (1998).

[13] For the causal exclusion argument for mental states, see e.g. Kim (1998). The statement of the argument given here is inspired by Crane (2001). For a causal exclusion argument regarding dispositions, see Prior et al. (1982), pp. 255–256.

itself sufficient to bring about the effects ascribed to the disposition – most notably, its manifestation. Thus, even if it seems natural to say that the vase broke because it was fragile and fell to the floor, we could also justifiably say that the bonds between the molecules in the vase were of a certain kind, and this was sufficient to cause it to shatter upon hitting the floor. So we have two competing explanations. Furthermore, what happens in the case of dispositions and their bases is not happily described as a case of causal over-determination (as when two stones hit a window simultaneously and both are sufficient to cause it to break). Invited conclusion: unless you think that dispositions are identical with their bases – in which case there is really only one candidate for the causal job – you must acknowledge that dispositions are causally impotent.

As noted, the conclusion that dispositions are causally impotent is easier to accept than the analogous view with respect to mental states, and is endorsed by many (e.g. Prior et al. 1982). An alternative option is to argue that some innocent sort of over-determination is in play, though it is relevantly different from standard cases of over-determination like the stones-break-window-case. Or one can deny 4 and go for an identity theory. This would also have an advantage in terms of ontological economy. But as we shall see, it has its own problems.

Other arguments from the philosophy of mind have applications to dispositions too. For example, a local version of the *multiple realisation argument* might run as follows: poisonousness has different bases in different poisonous substances. But yet we would like to say that poisonous things have something in common in virtue of which they are, well, poisonous. Since they do not share the same base property, the disposition – the property they have in common – can't be identical with the bases.

Or, in a different version targeting type–type-identifications only, and due to Prior et al.:

> We cannot say both that being fragile = having molecular bonding α, and that being fragile = having crystalline structure β, because by transitivity we would be led to the manifestly false conclusion that having molecular bonding α = having crystalline structure β.[14]

A possible response from an identity theorist would be to take poisonousness to be the disjunction of different possible bases for the disposition. Any fragile object would have the property of having either molecular bonding α or crystalline structure β or . . ., and thus they would share a property after all. But this would invite the counterargument that disjunctions are just as causally impotent as dispositions. The causal work is done by the disjuncts, not the disjunction, and thus if the disposition is identified with the disjunction, the disposition is still not the cause. So an identity theory motivated by arguments from causal exclusion would lose its underpinning by the disjunction move.[15]

---

[14]Prior et al. (1982), p. 253.

[15]For a statement of this argument (though for colours, not dispositions), see Johnston (1992), pp. 135–136.

An analogue of *Kripke's argument against identity theories* for mental states[16] can also be employed for dispositions. The argument would be something like this[17]: Names for dispositions are exactly that – names – and as such they are rigid designators; they designate the same thing in all worlds in which they designate anything at all. So 'fragility' refers to the same property in all worlds. Take a name for the physical property purportedly identical with fragility, say, molecular structure α. This name, too, is a rigid designator. An identity claim between rigid designators is necessary if true, so if fragility is identical with molecular structure α, then they are necessarily identical. But there are worlds in which fragile objects do not have molecular structure α, and where objects with molecular structure α are not fragile, for it is contingent what the causal basis of a disposition is. So the identity claim is not necessary, and hence, by rigidity, it can't be true.

All these types of arguments invite counterarguments and deserve much more attention. But this brief exposition should at least serve to give a flavour of the discussion.

Note that your view on the relation between dispositions and their bases has strong implications for any dispositional theories you might hold about particular subject matters (colours, values, whatnots). For example, if you are a type–type identity theorist about dispositions and hold a dispositional theory of colours, then your view will have more in common with colour physicalism than with different varieties of colour dispositionalism. You will identify the colour with a disposition – a disposition to elicit colour experiences of a certain kind, or a disposition to reflect light with certain distributions of wavelengths – and you will identify this disposition with its base, presumably a complex of microphysical properties of the surfaces of objects. So your view will be a version of colour physicalism, and will be very different from those dispositional views that identify response-patterns or reflectance spectra as the central features of colours.

This point is surprisingly often ignored. The notion of a disposition is generally taken for granted in dispositional accounts of other subject matters. The same is true of response-dependence theories. In the discussion of these in the next section, we shall revisit the implications of different views on the relationship between dispositions and their bases.

6.3 Response-Dependence Theories

A new development within the field of dispositional and similar theories is the idea, or ideas, of response-dependence. The term response-dependence was coined by Mark Johnston in 1986,[18] and has subsequently been used to cover a variety of loosely related but very different theories. Response-dependence theses have

---

[16] Kripke (1972), pp. 144–155.

[17] Again, based on Prior et al. (1982), pp. 253–254.

[18] Johnston (1989), p. 146, fn. 8; Wright (1992), p. 109, fn. 16.

been proposed for many subject matters. Examples include colours (e.g. Johnston 1992), moral values (e.g. Lewis 1989, Smith 1994, Johnston 1989, Lopez De Sa 2003), aesthetic values (Zangwill 2001), modality (Menzies 1998), abstract objects/mathematics (Divers and Miller 1999), rule-following/meaning (Pettit 1990, Wright 1989), and social institutions (Hindriks 2005).

Two overall paradigms of response-dependence theories can be distinguished. For one paradigm, the core idea can be described in terms of a difference in the order of determination between certain response-patterns in appropriate subjects and facts about the matter (or extensions of the concepts) in question. Johnston's original suggestion was that moral values resemble traditional secondary qualities like colours in that things are good because they are perceived as good in favourable conditions, whereas with qualities like shape it is the other way around: things are perceived as square in favourable conditions because they *are* square. In his papers on response-dependence, Johnston gave his view an overtly dispositional formulation and characterised response-dependent concepts as concepts of dispositions to produce certain responses in certain subjects in certain (non-trivially specifiable) conditions.[19]

The order of determination idea was further developed by Crispin Wright into a distinction between concepts that have their extensions determined by judgements made in favourable conditions and concepts for which such judgements merely track independently constituted extensions.[20]

Response-dependence accounts of this first paradigm are generally motivated by their potential to combine a moderate realist stance towards their subject matter with the view that it is closely related to a human perspective. This combination is attractive in many domains. For morality, for example, there is a moderate realist intuition that there are facts of the matter as to which actions are right or wrong (though these may not be as objective as e.g. facts about shape and mass). Yet moral features seem related to subjects in a way that e.g. mass and shape are not, and tend to go missing if we consider things in abstraction from the perspective of acting or experiencing subjects. A response-dependence account can accommodate both features. Very roughly, if there are facts about how the relevant subjects would respond, there are facts about the relevant response-dependent properties (and the extensions of response-dependent concepts), and thus a moderate realism is vindicated. But these facts are closely related to – indeed, constitutively dependent on – the response-patterns of subjects. So the realism in question is indeed a moderate one; response-dependence theses of this kind construe their very subject matter as dependent on the response-patterns of subjects.

A very different kind of response-dependence theory was developed by Philip Pettit in response to a challenge posed by (Kripke's) Wittgenstein's rule-following considerations[21]: How can a finite set of sample applications of a rule, e.g. a rule

[19] Johnston (1993), p. 103; see also Johnston (1989).

[20] Wright (1992), appendix to Ch. 3, pp. 108–139.

[21] See Pettit (2005), in which his most important papers on the topic are reprinted. Wittgenstein (1953) and Kripke (1982).

governing the correct use of a concept, guide a learner to the correct applications in new cases, given that it is in principle possible to extrapolate from a finite set of examples in indefinitely many ways?

In response, Pettit offers the following genealogy of concepts: Some concepts are acquired by way of other concepts, but a class of basic concepts must be acquired in a different way, based on ostension or something similar. The challenge is to explain how these concepts could get off the ground. Pettit's explanation is based on the idea that people's response-dispositions make certain salient similarities stand out between sample cases, and make it natural to classify new cases in certain ways – e.g. to classify Danish post-boxes with blood and ripe tomatoes rather than with grass and leaves. A second crucial element in the story is a second-order disposition to seek constancy in verdicts across different people and different times. When conflicting verdicts arise, we are disposed to seek explanations of what has gone wrong, and to count verdicts made in similar circumstances as less reliable in the future. This is how favourable conditions are picked out: they are the ones that survive the practice of discounting conditions that yield conflicting verdicts.

This brand of response-dependence is ontologically neutral; a response-dependent concept of this kind could refer to a natural kind, or it could be response-dependent in the stronger (Wright/Johnston) sense as well. Unlike the latter, Pettit-style response-dependence does not imply a limitation on the level of realism; it concerns aetiology, not ontology.[22] Thus, Pettit can, and does, accept a thesis of global response-dependence (all basic concepts are acquired in the way described above) without inviting strongly anti-realist conclusions.

Response-dependence theses have traditionally been stated in terms very similar to those employed in conditional analyses of dispositions. Most authors agree that response-dependent concepts underwrite non-trivial, a priori true biconditionals of something like the following form:

(RD) Something, x, is F (/falls under concept F) if and only if x would elicit certain responses R in certain subjects S in certain favourable conditions C

This formula provides ample scope for variation. Some authors, including Johnston, replace the 'would' with 'is disposed to', thus yielding an explicitly dispositional account. Also, very different accounts can be obtained by varying the specifications of R, S and C, or by imposing further conditions on the equations (e.g. necessity, or Wright's independence and extremal conditions[23]). The responses could be e.g. judgements, phenomenal responses such as colour experiences, or emotional responses. The subjects and conditions could be idealised, statistically typical, actually statistically typical, etc. Different choices with respect to these variables make for very different theories.

The philosophical content that the biconditionals are employed to capture varies enormously. In fact, even Pettit employs the traditional biconditionals in stating his

---

[22]See Devitt (2006) for an argument – in my view, an unsuccessful one – that this claim is false.

[23]Wright (1992), app. to Ch. 3.

view, and argues that even for response-dependent concepts that refer to natural kinds, the biconditionals will be a priori because response-patterns fix the reference of the concepts in question.[24] For theses of the Wright/Johnston paradigm, the biconditionals are almost universally used, with variations such as those mentioned above.

Response-dependence theses raise many interesting issues, most notably issues about realism, objectivity, and subjectivity. We only have space to examine a few. Given the contents of Sections 6.1 and 6.2, it will be natural to choose the following questions for closer examination: First, are response-dependence theses vulnerable to counterexamples like those that threaten the conditional analysis of dispositions? Secondly, what is the difference between overtly dispositional response-dependence theses and those formulated in terms of subjunctive conditionals? Finally, what implications does the stance taken on the relationship between dispositions and their bases have for response-dependence views, particularly those of the dispositional variety?[25]

Not surprisingly, it is possible to construct finkish counterexamples to response-dependence biconditionals as well as to the conditional analysis and other accounts based on subjunctive conditionals.[26] Let us assume for the sake of the argument that colours are response-dependent, and consider the following simple response-dependence thesis:

(WHITE) x is white if and only if x would look white to standard subjects (say, statistically typical humans) in standard conditions (normal daylight, proper distance to the object, etc.)

Suppose x is a piece of photo-sensitive paper, waiting to be used for making photographs in a darkened lab. We would normally say that the paper is white; presumably it has a surface structure that would normally go with white appearance, and in the soft, reddish light of the lab, it looks the same colour as the lab assistant's white T-shirt and coffee mug. But if the paper was taken outside and placed in normal daylight, it would look black, as the light would change its surface structure. Indeed, if it was later returned to the lab, it would resemble the coffee more than the mug, and would be useless for making photographs. So the left-hand-side of (WHITE) is true, and the right-hand-side false; we have a counterexample of exactly the same shape as the finkish counterexamples discussed above.[27]

---

[24] I argue elsewhere (Gundersen 2006) that Pettit would do better without the biconditionals, and that they can't be a priori for his version of response-dependence.

[25] In the following, I rely on my own work on response-dependence, rather than summarising common ground from the literature. All points are elaborated in Gundersen (2006).

[26] Finkish counterexamples pose a challenge to any theory based on theses of the form $P \leftrightarrow (Q \Box\!\!\rightarrow R)$, where $\Box\!\!\rightarrow$ is a subjunctive conditional, and where Q's becoming the case could make it the case that not P, so that R would not follow if Q occurred. For a general treatment of such 'conditional fallacy' problems, see Shope (1978).

[27] For another standard example, Johnston's chameleon, see Johnston (1992), p. 231, and (1993), p. 119.

The literature on response-dependence offers a number of responses to this problem. We shall consider two of them, Wright's and Johnston's.[28] A very visible difference between Johnston's and Wright's accounts of response-dependence is that Johnston's is formulated in dispositional terms, while Wright employs subjunctive conditionals. Ironically, both motivate their choice by arguing that it, as opposed to the other, can deal with conditional fallacy problems.[29]

Wright's response to the problem is to change the shape of the equations. He replaces 'basic equations' like

(BE) x is white $\leftrightarrow$ if standard conditions were to obtain, a standard subject S would judge that x is white

with 'provisional equations' where the standard (or favourable) conditions are placed in a proviso:

(PE) If standard conditions were to obtain, then: x is white $\leftrightarrow$ S would judge that x is white

Basic equations are vulnerable to conditional fallacy problems, since the standard conditions' coming to obtain might sometimes alter the truth value of 'x is white'. But provisional equations say only what would happen in cases where the standard conditions are already met; any changes in x induced by their coming to obtain will already have taken place, and so will not give rise to counterexamples. This move creates problems of its own,[30] but seems efficient against finkish counterexamples.[31]

We shall not rest with this conclusion, however, since Johnston's alternative suggestion raises interesting issues connected with the last two of the advertised questions. Johnston takes finkish counterexamples to refute both the simple conditional analysis of dispositions and response-dependence accounts formulated in terms of subjunctive conditionals. He thinks the problems for response-dependence theses should be addressed by seeking a better account of dispositions that avoids the counterexamples. Once such an account is found, it can be employed in formulating response-dependence theses that are immune to conditional fallacy problems. Johnston does not, however, offer such an account in his published work.

Until a fink-free account of dispositions is provided, what is the status of Johnston's approach? The thought might be that, pending a suitable account of dispositions, the dispositional idiom can function as a place-holder for the correct account, and that this allows us to bracket the problems with finks etc. until we have an account of dispositions that avoids them.

---

[28] See Blackburn (1993) for an interesting alternative.

[29] Wright (1992), pp. 117–120. Johnston (1992), p. 231.

[30] For example the 'univocity' objection raised and discussed by Wright (1992), pp. 125–127.

[31] What about maskers and mimickers? Such cases would not be ruled out by Wright's move. However, masking and mimicking cases do not present specific problems for response-dependence theses, since they can presumably be avoided by appropriate specifications of the favourable conditions. Or, at any rate, maskers and mimickers are not harder to rule out than other perturbing factors that must be ruled out by the specifications of the favourable conditions. But this is an issue too large to be treated here.

Such an approach seems unsatisfactory for two reasons. The first is that we straightforwardly help ourselves to an account of dispositions that we don't yet have. Unless this move is supported by reasons to believe that an account of dispositions is forthcoming that would solve the problems, this strategy contains an element of wishful thinking. Secondly, and worse, it is far from clear that the correct account of dispositions, once discovered, will fulfil the expectations. Not all possible accounts of dispositions would be suited as a basis for response-dependence theories. This brings us to the questions about the relationship between dispositional and subjunctive response-dependence accounts, and about the implications for response-dependence of the view taken on dispositions.

The relationship between dispositional and conditional formulations of response-dependence theses depends heavily on one's view of dispositions. Given a simple *conditional analysis* of dispositions, the two will be equivalent. The dispositions in question will be analysed in exactly the terms of a response-dependence thesis formulated by way of subjunctive conditionals. But on other accounts of dispositions, these two varieties of response-dependence views come apart.

If you take dispositions to be *identical* with their bases, a dispositional response-dependence account will have a very different flavour from response-dependence accounts as they are usually understood. Response-dependence theses of the Wright/Johnston paradigm are generally theses that the subject matter under discussion is essentially related to response-patterns, rather than whatever base properties might underlie these in the actual world. So an identity theory of dispositions does not sit well with a dispositional response-dependence account of this kind.

A *functionalist* view of dispositions might work as a basis for a response-dependence thesis of sorts. A view like Mumford's that identifies dispositions with the realiser properties (bases) would presumably inherit many of the problems of a simple identity theory. But a functionalist position that identifies dispositions with role properties (as in Prior et al.) might constitute an interesting combination with response-dependence theses, and deserves to be explored.

On a *primitivist* view of dispositions, a dispositional response-dependence account will be correspondingly uninformative. Or, better: it will result in a sort of primitivist view with respect to response-dependent properties too. In comparison, the subjunctive formulation would give more information about what characterises response-dependent properties, and how they differ from other properties.

An *eliminativist* view of dispositions would be a poor basis for interesting dispositional response-dependence theses. But then again, an eliminativist about dispositions would presumably be equally sceptical about response-dependent subject matters, and so would not see this as a problem.

To sum up, the stance taken with respect to dispositions has wide-ranging implications for dispositional response-dependence theses. Dispositional and conditional formulations of response-dependence theses will be equivalent if dispositions are given a conditional analysis, but otherwise they will be very different. Many views on dispositions are badly suited as basis for response-dependence theses. These points, like the parallel point about dispositional theories in general, have, surprisingly, been completely ignored in the literature.

With respect to the strategy of fink-proofing response-dependence theses by formulating them in dispositional terms, we must conclude that it is unsatisfactory unless backed by an appropriate account of dispositions. Pending an account of dispositions, there is no guarantee that a complete understanding of the nature of dispositions, once achieved, would provide an appropriate basis for response-dependence theses.

In one respect, though, the approach might point us in the right direction. Many of the strategies employed to defend, amend, or replace the conditional analysis of dispositions in the face of the counterexamples can be employed in defence of response-dependence accounts too. So a response-dependence theorist seeking to defend her account against finkish counterexamples would be right to look to research on dispositions for inspiration. Conversely, the discussion about the conditional analysis of dispositions and its counterexamples might be enriched by suggestions from the debate about response-dependence. Characteristic features of response-dependence accounts – e.g. the notion of standard or favourable conditions – might suggest solutions that would otherwise have gone unnoticed. But this is a matter for another day and another paper.

In this paper, I hope to have given the reader a taste of some of the issues and problems surrounding dispositions and response-dependence theses. The appropriate conclusion seems to be this: there is a lot of work to do in this area, and a lot of interesting issues to be explored.[32]

References

Armstrong, D.M. 1968. *A materialist theory of the mind*. London: Routledge.

Bird, A. 1998. Dispositions and antidotes. *Philosophical Quarterly* 48:227–234.

Blackburn, S. 1993. Circles, finks, smells and biconditionals. In *Philosophical perspectives*, ed. J.E. Tomberlin, Language and logic, vol. 7, 259–279. Atascadero, CA: Ridgeview Publishing Co.

Bonevac, D., J. Dever, and D. Sosa. 2006. The conditional fallacy. *Philosophical Review* 115(3):273–316.

Choi, S. 2003. Improving bird's antidotes. *Australasian Journal of Philosophy* 81(4):573–580.

Crane, T. 2001. *Elements of mind*. Oxford: Oxford University Press.

Devitt, M. 2006. Worldmaking made hard: Rejecting global response dependency. *Croatian Journal of Philosophy* 6(16):3–26.

Divers, J. and A. Miller. 1999. Arithmetical platonism: Reliability and judgement-dependence. *Philosophical Studies* 95:277–310.

Fara, M. 2005. Dispositions and habituals. *Nous* 39:43–82.

Fara, M. 2006. Dispositions. *Stanford encyclopaedia of philosophy*. http://plato.stanford.edu/entries/dispositions/

Gundersen, L.B. 2002. In defence of the conditional account of dispositions. *Synthese* 130(3):389–411.

Gundersen, L.B. 2004. Outline of a new semantics for counterfactuals. *Pacific Philosophical Quarterly* 85(1):1–20.

[32]Thanks to Lars Bo Gundersen and Crispin Wright for many inspiring discussions of the subjects treated in this paper.

Gundersen, E.B. 2006. *Making sense of response-dependence.* Ph.D. thesis, University of St. Andrews, http://hdl.handle.net/10023/211.

Hindriks, F. 2005. *Rules and institutions – Essays on meaning, speech acts and social ontology.* Ph.D. thesis, Erasmus University Rotterdam, Rotterdam.

Johnston, M. 1989. Dispositional theories of value. *Proceedings of the Aristotelian Society* 63(Suppl.):139–174.

Johnston, M. 1992. How to speak of the colours. *Philosophical Studies* 68:221–263.

Johnston, M. 1993. Objectivity refigured: Pragmatism without verificationism. In *Reality, representation and projection,* eds. J. Haldane and C. Wright, 85–133. Oxford: Oxford University Press.

Kim, J. 1998. *Mind in a physical world.* Cambridge, MA: MIT Press.

Kripke, S. 1972. *Naming and necessity.* Cambridge, MA: Harvard University Press.

Kripke, S. 1982. *Wittgenstein on rules and private language.* Oxford: Basil Blackwell.

Lewis, D. 1989. Dispositional theories of value. *Proceedings of the Aristotelian Society* 63(Suppl.):113–138.

Lewis, D. 1997. Finkish dispositions. *Philosophical Quarterly* 47(187):143–158.

Lopez de Sa, D. 2003. *Response-dependencies: Colors and values.* Ph.D. thesis, University of Barcelona, Barcelona, accessible on the author's webpage.

Martin, C. 1994. Dispositions and conditionals. *Philosophical Quarterly* 44(174):1–18.

Martin, C. 2007. *The mind in nature.* Oxford: Oxford University Press.

McKitrick, J. 2003a. A case for extrinsic dispositions. *Australasian Journal of Philosophy* 81(2):155–174.

McKitrick, J. 2003b. The bare metaphysical possibility of bare dispositions. *Philosophy and Phenomenological Research* 66:349–369.

Menzies, P. 1998. Possibility and conceivability: A response-dependent account of their connections. *European Review of Philosophy* 3:255–277.

Mumford, S. 1996. Conditionals, functional essences and Martin on dispositions. *Philosophical Quarterly* 46:86–92.

Mumford, S. 1998. *Dispositions.* Oxford: Oxford University Press.

Pettit, P. 1990. The reality of rule-following. *Mind* 99:1–21.

Pettit, P. 2005. *Rules, reasons, and norms.* Oxford: Oxford University Press.

Prior, E., R. Pargetter, and F. Jackson. 1982. Three theses about dispositions. *American Philosophical Quarterly* 19:251–257.

Shope, R. 1978. The conditional fallacy in contemporary philosophy. *Journal of Philosophy* 75(8):397–414.

Smith, M. 1994. *The moral problem.* Oxford: Blackwell.

Smith, M. and D. Stoljar. 1998. Global response-dependence and noumenal realism. *The Monist* 81:85–111.

Wittgenstein, L. 1953. *Philosophical investigations.* Oxford: Blackwell.

Wright, C. 1989. Wittgenstein's rule following considerations and the central project of theoretical linguistics. In *Reflections on Chomsky*, ed. A. George, 233–265.Oxford: Oxford University Press.

Wright, C. 1992. *Truth and objectivity.* Cambridge, MA: Harvard University Press.

Zangwill, N. 2001. 'Skin deep or in the eye of the beholder?': The metaphysics of aesthetic and sensory properties. *Philosophy and Phenomenological Research* 61(3):595–618.

Chapter 7
Properties

Frédéric Nef

7.1 Introduction

> What are properties? Do any exist?[1] These are surprisingly difficult questions to answer satisfactorily. One might suppose that a property is whatever is denoted by a meaningful predicate and that, since there are many such predicates, there are many properties. But we know that matters cannot be as simple as that, because the supposition that every meaningful predicates denotes a property apparently leads to a paradox (Lowe 2002, p. 137)

The paradox Lowe is referring to is the following. If P is the predicate 'non-predicable', then if for any predicate, there is a property of non-predicability, but if P has this property, we can use P as a predicate and there is no property. We have a paradox, because P is such that in order to be a property it is not a property, which is self-contradictory. This version of Russell's paradox can therefore be used against the reduction of properties to predicates. But if properties are not identical to predicates, there is an 'intimate connection' (Lowe) between them and a part of the difficulties caused by the formal treatment of properties is located in the subtlety of the relations between predicates and properties. We usually establish a correspondence between the two by means of formal transformations. Among these transformations we can enumerate:

– nominalization. Ex.: wise -> the property of wisdom -> wisdom
– pseudo-nominalization. Ex: wise -> the property of being wise
– pseudo nominalization + raising of 'property'. Ex.: red -> the property of being red -> the red
– abstraction with a suffix '-ness'. Ex: red -> redness

F. Nef (✉)
EHESS, Institut Jean-Nicod, Paris, France
e-mail: frederic.nef@ehess.fr

[1] As properties are either general or particular, some philosophers introduce an ontological distinction between two different *modi essendi*. Moore in the *Principia Ethica* attributed 'being' to the universals and 'existence' to the particulars (and therefore to the quality instances); Meinong declared the universals subsist (*bestehen*) and the particular properties exist. Russell in the *problems of Philosophy*, used this meinongian distinction (see Hochberg 2002, p. 108 ff. for a summary of the development of these notions).

R. Poli, J. Seibt (eds.), *Theory and Applications of Ontology: Philosophical Perspectives*, DOI 10.1007/978-90-481-8845-1_7,

As Swoyer (2000) declared 'English contains a plethora of suffixes', besides -ness, we find: -hood, -ship, -cy etc. Suffix belong to the category of SN/<SN/SN>: they take nominal modifiers and give nominal phrases (singular terms).

7.2 Preliminary Distinctions

7.2.1 Concepts, Predicates and Properties

Some preliminary distinctions have to be drawn between CONCEPTS, PREDICATES and PROPERTIES. We grasp a concept, we attribute a predicate to a subject and we instantiate a property. Concepts are mental, predicates are linguistic and properties are both. These distinctions are usually accepted, but they are no more than a starting point, because to make a distinction between these items is not equivalent to a theory of the relations between them. The relation between properties and predicates is crucial, in so far as possessing a good understanding of their relation is a condition for a realism of properties. To affirm that properties are meanings of predicates is not enough:

> One reason for denying this is of course that, if they were, they could not give our predicates their meanings, any more than particulars could give the meanings of names or other singular terms, if that was all they were (Mellor 1982, p. 257)

Properties do not give the meaning of predicates and predicates do not refer to properties. Concepts express rules of connection between predicates and properties: to possess the concept of red, brings together the property of redness and the predicate 'red' (but also 'rouge' or 'rot'). But this does not imply that conceptualism is a true doctrine. Conceptualism is defined in that way. Objects possessing some property fall under concepts of this property and the essence or meaning of properties is given by the conditions for objects falling under concepts. For example the meaning of 'red' is given by conditions of the concept 'red'. As Armstrong (1978, pp. 22–27) noticed conceptualism is incoherent, because the notion of 'falling under' appeals to a property (a universal in Armstrong's words cf. Armstrong 1997). Conceptualism cannot eliminate properties through the relation of 'falling under', because this notion appeals to properties, it was supposed to push away (see Denkel 1996, p. 157).

7.2.2 Classification of Properties

Several types of properties may also be distinguished: natural vs. non natural ones, essential vs. accidental, monadic vs. relational. A NATURAL PROPERTY, according to D. Lewis[2] carves reality at its articulations,[3] ESSENTIAL properties define the essence of a thing. A MONADIC PROPERTY is expressed by a one place predicate: the property of whiteness expressed by 'white' is monadic, whereas the property of being fifty miles from Paris, expressed by 'fifty miles from Paris', is a RELATIONAL PROPERTY attributed for example to Chartres. Relational properties are called 'relations', when are considered the relational properties with the *relata*. For example we can obtain the relation: 'to be at a distance of 50 miles <a,b>' applied to Chartres and Paris. Some philosophers (like Leibniz in some of his writings) have tried to eliminate relations and reduce them to relational properties and even to monadic properties. For example they propose to analyze 'John loves Mary' as 'John is a lover of Mary in so far as Mary is loved by John'. We will not discuss this point, connected with deep issues of ontology.

A STRUCTURAL PROPERTY is a property belonging to a set of objects – the color blue attributed to a set of blue points is a structural property of the points and of the set, but the geometrical form of the distribution of the points on a sheet of paper is an EMERGENT PROPERTY of the set of points (no point possesses this property of having this geometrical form). It seems that relational properties are always structural and that emergent properties are natural. Properties pertain to mental, physical or mathematical domains. In the last one, structural properties are prevailing.[4] Some properties emerge from the physical to the mental (but not conversely). In the mental very few relational properties exist. The mental domain is either individual, or social and we can make a distinction between individual properties (to have a size or a mass) and social properties (to have an extension, for a group). All these observations call for a careful empirical description.

---

[2]For a presentation of Lewis's theory of natural properties, see Oliver (1996, pp. 38–44). D. Lewis introduced a distinction between sparse and abundant theories of properties. If properties are sets of particulars, we obtain an abundant theory of properties. In order to obtain a sparse theory of properties, D. Lewis proposed to select a minority elite of properties, the natural ones. What remains a bit mysterious is the selection method for natural properties.

[3]According to H. Hochberg, Moore introduced in 1903 the distinction between natural and non-natural properties in the context of his fight against naturalism in ethics. Hochberg assumed that this distinction has in fact a Brentanian origin:

> The key to understanding Moore's early view was his acceptance of a familiar theme in the Brentanist school at the turn of century — the analysis of objects as bundles of quality instances (tropes, Husserl's 'moments' (...) For Moore, at that time, a natural property like yellow was a universal which had quality instances or tropes that were constituents of ordinary objects (or sense data) — yellow objects (Hochberg 2002, p. 107)

[4]There is a strong overlap between formal theories of properties and philosophy of mathematics. The main topics discussed at the intersection of the two are: typed or untyped properties (in case of higher order properties), compound properties, reduction of mathematics to logic and therefore the possibility of a general and formal theory of properties. For a recent survey of property theory (cf. Jubien 1989; U. Mönnich)

7.2.3 Realism and Anti-realism

Properties theories break up into two camps or form two sides: property realism and property anti-realism. As we have learned from M. Dummett, realism is modular: we can be moral realists and metaphysical anti-realists. Moreover realism is sub-modular: we can be facts realists and properties anti-realists. Property realists consider properties as independent entities. But they can be thought of either as functions from possible worlds to individuals, or as abstract and structured objects. The classical view of model theoretic semantics is the first of the two. D. Lewis broke with this somewhat artificial construction, but as he usually considered properties as sets of individuals, his position concerning property realism is not deprived of ambiguity. A. Plantinga considering that the admission of both property and object is a criteria of realism (property and object realism) criticized several times Lewis' conception of properties. According to Plantinga, Lewis is not a property realist (as he is not a genuine modal realist), but according to Lewis almost all philosophers are property ersatzists, because they reduce properties to concepts, words or magical items. It is not the place here to settle this question out of hand, but we have to underline the fact that property[5] realism is not an easy matter. What is clearer, but not automatically more convincing, because clarity could be a form of superficiality and self-satisfaction, is property anti realism. In that camp, property existence is denied. Properties simply do not exist, in any sense of 'exist', for example to be in space-time, to have a causal power etc. They do not seem to have a nature; they seem to fill explanatory roles (cf. Chris Swoyer 2000). But what are they then? There is no univocal answer either to this question. Nominalists declare that properties are nothing but extensions in classes of individuals (cf. supra) and conceptualists declare that properties are nothing but concepts (they contract therefore the obligation to precisely define concepts, which is not easy). These two camps have no clear cut frontiers: a philosopher like Armstrong does not belong clearly to either camp. He is not a property realist, for his substantive ontology forbids him from giving an ontological role to properties in metaphysical structures. However he cannot be enlisted or enrolled in the antirealist army, for he very sharply refuses to identify properties with predicates. In some sense, Armstrong's realism of universals is closer to property realism than to conceptualism (Kant, Strawson) or nominalism (Quine 1961, Goodman). I ought to stress the fact that nominalism can not be a definitive solution to the vexing question of property realism, in so far as giving whatever answer to this unsettled question: 'how do we constitute or recognize classes of individuals?' leads necessarily to face the much disputed unavoidability of properties. In the case of classes, it may be maintained that the carving of the classes implies to possess and master natural properties.

---

[5]Ersatzism according to D. Lewis is a form of anti-modal realism. Whereas modal realists assume the existence of possible worlds, on the same footing as our brave actual world, ersatzists reduce possible worlds e.g. to linguistic ersatz (sets of sentences) or to other ersatz. We may call properties ersatzist philosophers who reduce properties to predicates, concepts etc (cf. Marcus 1993).

7.2.4 *Instantiation and Exemplification*

There is another conceptual difficulty concerning the basic definitions relative to properties. This difficulty, which is by no means purely formal or verbal, is caused by the confusion in current literature between exemplification and instantiation. These two relations have apparently the same *relata*: universals and particulars, but in fact they are deeply different. Let us define exemplification and instantiation:

a instantiates F iff a is F
If a is F, then the F of a exists
the F is then an exemplification of F

For example 'this apple instantiates 'red' or 'redness' (if we tolerate scotist formalities)' is equivalent to 'this apple is red'. If this 'apple' is red, then the red (or redness), of this apple exemplifies 'red' (or 'redness'). This distinction between instantiation and exemplification is characteristic of realism, and especially of Platonism of Hochberg 1968. Philosophers of nominalist persuasion interpret predicative statements attributing properties differently. For example the statement 'a is F' is interpreted as 'a belongs to the class of F's'. The opposition Nominalism vs. Platonism is an opposition between two extremities of a spectrum:

Nominalism	conceptualism	realism of universals	Platonism
ANTI-REALISM			REALISM

7.3 Ontology of Properties

7.3.1 *Existence*

Realists attribute existence to properties; anti-realists deny it. But what is existence for a property? Do properties exist like objects? We will examine later the dependent character of properties. We will now examine some existence criteria. The first criterion is the causal one. A property could be defined as something that causes an effect. For example the property of viscosity denotes a type of causation. If a is viscous and if a draws, the viscosity of a causes a slackening of the liquid. It could be objected that not all properties have a causal potential. For example what is the causal potential of beauty, or symmetry? What is the causal potential of a mental property? Perhaps emergent properties do not necessarily have a causal potential, which could be a privilege of a part of structural properties.[6] In any case, the causal

[6]But we have to notice that in some definition of emergence it is specified that there is an influence of the emergent property on the behavior of the parts of the basis of the emergence. For example: a property P is an emergent property from on object O mereologically complex iff P supervenes upon properties of the parts of O, iff P is a property not possessed by any of the parts of O, iff P is distinct from any structural property of O, and P has a determining influence on the parties of O (I underline). As a matter of fact, the term 'influence' is vague, and we should have to analyze this concept.

criterion is not clear for the existence of properties. Moreover the causal criterion, even if it works, meets another difficulty, concerning the identity of properties. If two properties cause the same effect, they are not necessarily identical; are they at least analog? For example density and impenetrability causing the same effect in some contexts are not identical precisely for this reason. Causal criteria cannot be used as criteria of identity of properties. Quine banished properties partly for this reason: it is difficult to secure tests of identity for these entities (pseudo-entities according to Quine). But the semantic content of properties is intuitively accessible to any English speaker, who is able to draw a line between density and impenetrability, even if in some causal contexts they have the same power. What we have to do is to analyze and formalize the rules of detecting semantic differences. We are not sure that two properties that can be substituted in every context are identical for this reason. This failure of substitutability is not limited to properties; it is a characteristic of intensional expressions or entities. We have the choice between three solutions: (a) elimination of properties, (b) extensionalization of properties, (c) intensionalization of logic. (a) is not a solution, for we have many good reasons to think that properties are an important part of our ontological apparatus (the same could be said about objects: objects and properties are in the same boat, as Plantinga has shown[7]). (b) is a hopeless task, because properties are deeply intensional. We ought to therefore explore the feasibility of (c). But even in the absence of such a guide for resolving controversies, we have to clarify basic issues regarding properties.

7.3.2 *Concrete vs. Abstract Existence*

Is it possible to be certain about properties existence? We can obtain certitude about the existence of something either by means of demonstration, or by inference to the best explanation.[8] It is obviously not possible to ascertain the existence of properties through demonstration. We are able to give proof of existence for $\underline{a}$, but we are not able to demonstrate the existence of properties F, G, H ... of $\underline{a}$. We are able to give a demonstration of the attribution of F, G, H ... to $\underline{a}$, but we cannot prove that F, G, H ... exist in the true sense of 'exist'. If existence is defined as presence in space-time, the search for some test relative to properties existence implies the clarification of their conditions of localization. Only concrete things are present in space-time. Abstract ones, like numbers, sets, facts, propositions are therefore deprived of localization conditions. Are properties abstract or concrete? If they are abstract, they exist

[7]In 'Objets et propriétés' (Nef 2004) I have explored the complex relations between objects and properties. Cf. also Nef (2005, 2006, 2009) for a continuation of the same theme.

[8]Swoyer (2000, 2.1.) contrasts very sharply different types of arguments concerning the existence of properties: transcendental and demonstrative arguments, on one hand, and inference to the best explanation, on the other hand. He urges that 'most of the arguments advanced on behalf of properties appear anemic when jugged by the demonstrative ideal, but that they look much better when viewed as inferences to the best explanations'.

either as platonic entities, or they supervene upon concrete entities. Each branch of the alternative has its own difficulties. Platonic properties possess a strong tendency towards an endless multiplication, and supervening upon concrete entities is not natural for very abstract properties. In order to explore the predicament of abstraction, we ought to analyze the relations between objects and properties.

7.3.3 Objects and Properties

Properties are usually defined either as mereological parts of objects, or as ways of being. In the first case objects are usually defined as bundles of properties. We can very often read that the metaphor, or the model of tying properties in bundles is a weak one, and that it does not possess any descriptive or explanatory power. But, this image of bundles was precisely chosen in virtue of its flexibility and for the few constraints it would impose on the relation between properties inside bundles. A bundle is even weaker than a set, relative to this type of constraints. However an image is not formal enough, and if sets for different reasons, concerning notably the strength of the relation of membership are excluded, we face the choice of embrassing mereological formalism. If the use of metaphorical language is allowed, we might say that properties do not belong, strictly speaking, to objects, but adhere to them, if we want to express this relation of gluing between properties and objects (and between properties themselves, see below). But some tropes theoreticians have argued persuasively against mereological sums of properties (Simons 1994). If we may use a structural vocabulary (Bacon 1995, Puntel 2006), metaphysical structures using mereology are not rich enough, if it is beneficial to represent and eventually formalize the genuinely metaphysical relations between properties and objects (dependence, foundation etc.).

For these reasons it has been proposed (Levinson 1980, Lowe 2002, p. 140 s.) to define properties simply as ways of being.[9] If a is F, F is then a way of being for a. For example, if this apple is red, 'red' (or 'redness') is a way of being. We ought to notice that the intuitive appeal of this concept strongly depends on the type of properties it is applied to which it is applied. If I say that Dion's walking is slow, it seems intuitively appealing to paraphrase that statement with this semi technical expression 'ways of being'. But if I consider the mass of an electron, it is blatantly counter-intuitive to paraphrase the statement 'the electron e has a mass m' with ways of being: to have such a mass is not a way of being ! It is not a way of being; it is simply being. Another difficulty: the concept of 'way' is relative to our apprehension of what there is. This concept is compatible with Kantian's anti-realism (subjectivity

[9]Lowe (2002, p. 140) accepts both particular and universal ways of being. He calls the universal ways of being «properties» and the particular way of being «modes», a tribute to Locke's metaphysics.

plus limitation to the phenomenal part of reality), but much less easily compatible with realism. Last problem: how to tie together the ways of a being? If this apple is red, juicy and small, how does one connect the way of being red, the way of being juicy and the way of being small?

But there is a much more serious difficulty arising from the ontology underlying this 'way of being' metaphor. This difficulty is that we have to assume the existence of substrata, if we want to give the ways some ontological respectability, because if w is a way of being of a, expressed by a F, a has to be considered as being naked. We ought to reason by subtraction. Let us consider a particular a with the properties F, G, H ... F is way of being of a, G and H too ... But that implies that a is without property. (cf. Loux 2002) If a is not qualified, it is a substratum, and even worse, a bare particular, the *monstrum horrendum* of ontology (cf. Allaire 1963). Armstrong introduced a type of bare particular, the thin particular, a sort of coat hanger for properties, a particular without any property, but the property of being identical to itself (and then different from any other particular).

If we weigh the pro and the con of drawbacks brought by the two solutions briefly discussed (bundles or substrata), I consider that a better solution can be based on the tradition of constitution ontology, that is the solution en terms of bundles. I recall that according Loux (2006) and other writers two main types of ontology exist: constituent ontology and relation ontology. My own position would be to favor a constituent ontology, but without substrata and as little substance as possible .

7.3.4 Modal and Epistemic Components of Properties

Another point of the ontology of properties we have to discuss concerns the modal and epistemic components of properties. Properties are contingent or necessary, possible or impossible. An impossible property is for example 'to go faster than light'. A possible property: 'to be a song heard by the Queen Victoria the last day of her life' (perhaps she heard no song that unfortunate day, but nothing prevents the possibility of such a hearing). A contingent property does not affect the identity of its bearer, whereas a necessary property does: water not boiling at 100°C at an altitude of 0 m is not water. In other words, a is necessarily F iff a is F in every possible world. Besides modal characteristics, we have epistemic ones, closely related to each other. A priori properties are in general necessary properties and a posteriori properties are either necessary or contingent, because Kripke has shown that important natural properties are both necessary and a posteriori (cf. Kripke 1980). Some philosophers do not accept applying the distinction a priori vs. a posteriori to properties, because these terms should not strictly speaking characterize the properties themselves, but the access to them. A priori would mean that the property is attributed on the sole basis of the definition of the bearer (for example we attribute a priori the property of extension to a body, and therefore we say that extension is an a priori property of bodies). It is probably true, but this confusion has, as far as we can see, no harmful consequences.

7.3.5 Ontological Economy

It is evident that properties are threatened by skepticism. We can doubt their existence, their utility, and their innocuity. But we can oppose to this skepticism some robust methodological principles. Perhaps the most important of these principles concerns ontological economy. Nominalists identify the admission of properties with extravaganza and waste. They reason with the following mood: 'Why use such ineffective tools, when we have efficient predicates at our disposition? Are not properties anything but shadows of predicates?' The opposite is true: there are innumerable predicates and just a handful of natural properties. Nothing prevents the multiplication of predicates, but we can stop the multiplication of properties. First we can eliminate the higher order properties; second we can eliminate unnatural properties. Armstrong (1978) argued forcefully in consideration of ontological parsimony against identity between predicates and properties.

What is ontological economy? How can one not misuse Occam's razor? We know of some applications of this tool: elimination of derivative entities and synonym terms. A behavior governed by ontological economy may lead to dangerous or useless results, if the norms of theoretical and ontological minimalism are not carefully defined. How can one decide that an ontology is minimal? In the Polish tradition this question was much debated. Some of its representatives developed minimalist ontologies, with only *concreta* (Kotarbinski's pansomatism, second Brentano's ontology (cf. Smith 1987). Following this path, we encounter at least two problems: How to determine the size and the cardinality of an ontological domain? How to decide which ontological domain is minimal? Quantitative and qualitative economy are not the same. We have to at least make a distinction between the number of entities and the number of types of entities pertaining to a domain. We also have to take into account the explicative power of the model. Let us contemplate a model M with a domain D of size x, and a model M′ with a domain D′ of size x′, x′ larger than x (we leave undecided if it means that D′ has more entities, or more types of entities; let us suppose both for the sake of the argument). If M′ has a significantly larger explicative power, we could chose M′ instead of M, even if M seems at first sight more economical. The almost general rejection of Lewis' so to speak modal realism is a well-known case of ontological jurisprudence. Several philosophers justified this rejection by a critical consideration about the fantastic size of the ontological domain, because almost anything could be a possible world (in technical terms, any mereological sum). But D. Lewis himself rightly replied that we have to make a strong distinction between types and occurrences: in his ontology we have indeed a large number of occurrences (that is possible worlds, alien properties etc.), but in fact a very small number of types (probably two: worlds and properties). There could be an argument based on scientific realism if multiverse cosmological models could be ever empirically validated. In that case, the richness of Lewis' ontology would be positively appreciated. These questions lead to an even more general question: what is a metaphysical program? What do we expect of an ontology of properties? A metaphysical program can be defined in two very different ways. It could be considered as a description of existing entities, and in that case, many complicated decisions have to be taken concerning the existence of such and such type of entity. It could also be identified with conceptual analysis of ultimate conceptual schemes governing our apprehension and reality, through perception and science (cf. Sellars and in general Kantian anti-realism). Indeed conceptual analysis augments ideological economy, because it tries to eliminate all the parasitic predicates (I use here Quine's distinction between ideology and ontology, the first of the two being constituted with primitive ideas of a theory, whereas ontology is the set of primitive entities relative to the same theory). It is however less certain that conceptual analysis *ipso facto* brings with it ontological economy. Even if there is no special mode of knowledge within metaphysics – metaphysical intuition and all other fancies are nothing but dreams – there is on the other hand a specific rationality of metaphysical investigation, besides general principles common to all sorts of knowledge. Metaphysics obeys reflective equilibrium norms common to physical and moral sciences, but, like mathematics, metaphysics is a general theory of structures (Bacon 1995) and therefore there is an abstraction inherent to its method. Is it possible to naturalize ontology? Even if we adopt naturalist norms of explanation, (for example if we adopt an evolutionary concepts of norms themselves, trying to envision ontology as a set of adaptive processes), a large difference will subsist between metaphysical and epistemological naturalism, caused by the problem of causally inert kinds in metaphysics. Does metaphysics rest upon a causal explanation? We cannot discuss this point any further, but it is important to underline that an ontology of properties faces considerable blocks of methodology.[10] These blocks are a special case of the difficulties we face whan we look for an explanation in ontology (cf. Swoyer 2000 2.1.).

7.3.6 Three Ontologies of Properties

Let us come back to the definition of properties, in order to justify our choice of the tropist ontology thereof. We have the choice between three ontologies of properties: (a) the classical ontology of the standard model theory, (c) the ontology of moderate realism, (b) the tropist ontology. In the STANDARD MODEL THEORY properties obey the axiom of extensionality. Properties are sets (or classes, I will not develop this point), and identity conditions on sets cause the problem of co-extensional properties with different meanings:

(i) a property F is a set E of entities having F
(ii) if a property F and a property G are the same set of entities having from another side F and G from the other side, F and G are identical
(iii) F and G can have different meanings and same extension
(iv) if F and G are identical, they cannot have different meanings

[10]See A. Oliver's development on methodology for metaphysicians, especially what concerns a difference between ideological economy and ontological economy (Oliver 1996, pp. 2–5).

(v) there is a contradiction between (iii) and (iv) therefore there is something false in (i) or (ii)
(vi) as (ii) is a sound consequence of (i) there is something false in (i)
(vii) therefore a property F is not a set of entities having F.

The ontology of MODERATE REALISM defines properties as instances of universals. For example the red(ness) of this apple is an instantiation of the universal 'red'. This ontology is based on an opposition between universal and particular. It is derived from the platonic notion of participation: the F of a̲ is an instance of F iff a̲ participates in F. Moderate realism does not recognize the validity of this equivalence, because it finds the notion of participation somewhat obscure, but in fact it is not evident that the notion of instantiation is any clearer. Armstrong himself repeatedly conceded that instantiation relation is indeed obscure. For this reason he proposed qualifying this relation as a 'non relational tie' (this phrase is borrowed from Strawson). But even if this last phrase is perhaps a step in the right direction, it is not much clearer. It says instantiation is not strictly speaking a relation, but it does not say much about the nature of the non relational tie instantiation is supposed to be. From my perspective, on this point faithful to G. Bergmann, it means that instantiation is a nexus or a connection (cf. Bergmann 1967, 1968, 1992). So far, so good. But to affirm that there is a connection between particular and universal and that this very connection constitutes the essence of the states of affairs looks like an unconditional surrender to massive evidence.

The TROPIST ONTOLOGY OF PROPERTIES (Williams 1953, Campbell 1990, Bacon 1995, Simons 1994) takes as basic the instances themselves of properties and adopts the nominalist stance defining universals as resemblance classes of particulars. The metaphysical definition of 'trope' (by D.C. Williams) is cryptic: 'occurrence of an essence'. Other denominations are available on the ontological market. Bergmann used the term 'quality instance'. D.W. Mertz preferred to call them 'unit attributes' (cf. Mertz 1996). But Bergmann was an opponent to tropes, and Mertz is a moderate realist who considers unit attributes as instantiations of universals, which is contrary to the trope theory. For example Bacon (1995) underlines that tropes are not exemplifications of universals – they are bits of properties:

> A trope is an instance or bit (not an exemplification) of a property of a relation; e.g. Clinton's eloquence, Sydney's beauty, or Pierre's love to Heloïse. Clinton's eloquence is understood here not as Clinton's participating in the universal eloquence, nor as the peculiar quality of Clinton's eloquence, but simply as Clinton's bit of eloquence, the eloquence that he alone has (Bacon 1997, p. 1)

In fact the tropist ontology possesses however at least two big advantages. First: to propose a one-category ontology (advantage of simplicity); second: to be in harmony with our apprehension of reality through perception, language and science (advantage of naturalness). Traits of perception, demonstratives of language and particles of physics are nice epistemic replicas of tropes. Particularism does not seem to be an ontology forged artificially and thereafter imposed on semantic and psychological intuition. There is nothing mysterious in tropes, perhaps because there is nothing mysterious in the world.

7.3.7 Instantiation and Exemplification

I have sketched in § 4 the difference between instantiation and exemplification. I will now adopt this usage until the end of this chapter. Instantiation is a formal relation . For example 'x' is an instance of the variable 'x' (or more accurately: this x (i.e. this trace of ink on the page) is an instance of the variable denoted by the letter type 'x'). The smiling of Madonna is an instance of smile. In that sense Madonna's smiling is a trope, that is an abstract particular, as far as we take this smiling out of Madonna (so to speak). This instantiation relation is both very close and very far away from inherence (as reinterpreted by Brentano, cf. Smith 1987). In inherence ontology Madonna's smiling inheres Madonna's substance and in Brentano's version the accident of Madonna's smiling contains more than Madonna's substance unmodified by *this* smile. What they have in common is the fact that the particular individuating the whole (substance or bundle) contains in fact the whole out of which it was taken. What is different is that the trope is not a modification of the substance, as accident is a modification of the substance. We might dare to say that trope ontology is a kind of Aristotelian constituent ontology, even if there is too strong a relational aspect in it, very close to the platonic tradition. But trope ontology does not conserve the modification scheme, which is perhaps a projection of grammatical structures (see next § for the predication). EXEMPLIFICATION is a genuine ontological relation in platonic tradition. Socrates' courage exemplifies courage, the Form of courage which constitutes the transcendent unity of the class of exemplified courages. Some trope theoreticians strongly reject exemplification in virtue of its platonic pedigree. But it is possible to turn exemplification upside down and understand exemplification in the following way. Let us consider Socrates' courage, Aurelia Scholl's courage .... We can conceive of a modified exemplification relation as the abstraction of all the courages of Socrates, A. Scholl .... As soon as we attribute courage to a, whoever it is, we make two distinct things: we attribute this courage to a and we attribute courage in general. The exemplification relation is an abstraction upon the attribution of a trope. If a trope is an occurrence of an essence, to exemplify a property is to abstract the essence from the occurrence of attribution. In other words, we take out of context of attribution the content of what is attributed. In that sense exemplification is the opposite of Whitehead's notion of concretion. In Whitehead's terms, to exemplify a trope is to make it an 'eternal object'. But the difference with Platonism is striking. Plato said that even if there were no Socrates, no A. Scholl's ... courage will still exist, but in trope theory it would no longer be the case. What is common to Platonism and trope theory is that exemplification is a two-term relation necessarily requiring the existence of the *relata*.

Two separate sorts of issues diminish the clarity of trope theory. From one side, it is not clear to characterize tropism. Is it a nominalism? A realism? A naturalism or even a physicalism? In my short exposition I have implicitly given a nominalist presentation of tropism, but is it impossible to give a non nominalist one? After all, some writers (like C.B. Martin, if I understand his extremely dense papers) have proposed to combine universals with tropes. In that case, tropism is no longer a variety of nominalist doctrine because we no longer need resemblance classes. It seems at first sight that it is possible to combine water with fire, so to speak, but I would consider that form of combination more like a very interesting interpretation of Platonism and not as an extension of nominalism.

But anyway the nature of tropes is not very clear, even if tropism can explain exemplification (Bacon 1995) because tropism explains exemplification as an overlapping: the compresence class of Socrates overlaps partly the set of courage tropes

7.3.8 Nominalism and Tropism

Predication is the heart of the ontology of properties. Realist arguments are based on the nature of predication. a is F is analyzed: among a's properties there is at least F. Predication is implicitly considered as a quantification of properties. Nominalists analyze predication as a class membership: a is F is analyzed: a is a member of F's class. Predication is then interpreted as an implicit quantification of classes. Trope theory is not committed to nominalist analysis of predication. The tropist analysis of a is F is the following. A class of compresence[11] of tropes, a, contains the trope F or the class of tropes F. This apparently cumbersome analysis has the advantage of covering complicated cases such as 'This smiling is Emma's smiling' (meaning that the smiling aforementioned is typical of Emma's way of smiling). As D. Mertz has demonstrated in his indexed predicates calculus, if we introduce particular properties (expressed by indexed predicates) we become capable of formally interpreting sentences like 'John is a better musician than Peter', which are a source of well known problems in traditional logic.

7.4 Semantics

7.4.1 Modeltheoretic Semantics and Tropist Semantics

Model-theoretic semantics depends upon the classical notion of properties. Semantics for tropes would be different. A first reason is given by the fact that tropes are cross-categorical: they are expressed by words or groups of words belonging to a variety of categories. For example different types of phrases in the following sentences denote tropes (I underline the phrases):

---

[11] The relation of compresence is a Russellian one (Russel 1948). A and B are compresent iff a and b are located at the same moment. This relation is used by tropists in order to provide unification of thick particulars constituted of tropes. Some writers (e.g. P. Simons, A. Denkel) disbelieved the possibility of accounting for unification in terms of compresence and turn themselves to 'internal foundation relation' (cf. Mertz 2002, p. 169). Russelian compresence is very close to Whitehead's 'togetherness'. (cf. *Process and Reality*, p. 20)

I prefer the blue of the book to the blue of the gown.
The sudden paleness of her face scared the earl.
This flash makes me blind.
My love for you is everlasting.

In classical model theoretic semantics a model is defined as:

$$M = < D, I, V >$$

Where D is a domain of entities, usually individuals, I a function of interpretation assigning entities to expressions of the language and V a function of valuation.

In a tropist semantics the model is defined as:

$$M^* = < P^*, I, V >$$

where P^* is a set of abstract particulars (or tropes). In order to obtain individuals necessary for the interpretation of SN and NP, I have to add a relation taking tropes and giving individuals. In literature, compresence is this relation and I will later discuss thereupon.

Is there in M^* a homomorphism between language and reality? What is the size of P^*? If $P^* \geq \aleph_0$ then quantification is no longer objectual. Is tropist semantics based on set theory (Bacon) or mereology (P. Simons)? I shall not discuss these questions, I shall only say a few words about Kripkean semantics and tropist semantics. Kripke's semantics are usually set theoretic and defend on one hand an homomorphism between language and reality and on the other hand neutral quantification. Tropist semantics is usually mereological, and does not defend the aforementioned homomorphism and neutral quantification. Semantics pursues reference and meaning. It analyses relations between language and reality (through modeling) and gives the meaning of sentences (through truth conditions). All this becomes dramatically problematic when tropes are substituted for individuals. Reference to tropes is not systematic and the compositional meaning of the sentences has to be defined in another way. It seems more reasonable in this ontological framework to consider directly tropes as truthmakers. I shall not develop tropist semantics as a research program but I will turn back to properties in general, after having shown the importance of the particularist turn in semantics and ontology.

7.4.2 *Abstract vs. Concrete and Universal vs. Particular*

Properties are either abstract or concrete and either universal or particular. The opposition between concrete and particular is as important as that which exist between particular and universal. We then have four classes of properties:

1. Abstract and universal. Ex.: the red, the wisdom
2. Abstract and particular. Ex.: Socrates wisdom

3. Concrete and universal. Ex.: to have a mass of m.
4. Concrete and particular. Ex.: to have this mass.

Classes 2 and 4 correspond to tropes. If we adopt a trope ontology, with the category of trope as basic and unique, we ought to derive the two other classes. It is fascinating to note that in order to refer to a trope we must use the nominalization of a property (cf. Moltmann 2004, p. 1). A's wisdom denotes the particular property consisting for A to be wise. 'Socrates wisdom' denotes then a particular property a trope. Does 'wisdom' denote a trope, as F. Moltmann argued for? She sustained in fact that 'wisdom' refers to a 'kind of trope'. But what is a kind of trope is not clear: 'By this I mean a universal whose instances are concrete property manifestations, but which does not have the status of an object' (op. cit. p. 2) If a kind of trope is a universal, then there is no strict delimitation between the two. It seems that it is the syntactic context which gives to nominalized adjectives a sense or the other: In 'Wisdom is a virtue' 'wisdom' has a sense different from that other context: 'Socrates wisdom is gloomy': in the first case 'wisdom' refers to a concept; in the second case 'wisdom' refers to a trope, because as a matter of fact in 'wisdom is a virtue', 'wisdom' refers to what is common to a class of tropes, relative to individuals at different moments.

7.4.3 Describing Properties: From Physical Rigidity to Divine Simplicity

I will now sketch a descriptive framework for a general theory of properties. Properties belong at least to three different domains: they can be physical (rigidity, viscosity ...), moral (good vs. bad, courageous ...) or metaphysical, which can be first order properties (simplicity ...) or second order one (positivity ...). Relations of supervenience, dependence, foundation ... connect sets of properties and fasten ontological structures. Properties are nuclear or extra-nuclear. Extra-nuclear properties are properties of properties. For example 'to be incomplete' is a property of an object, but it is a property of property in so far as to be incomplete is said of a set of properties. *Dramatis personae* are incomplete because they are relative to descriptions, which cannot be complete by definition. Hamlet is incomplete, but to be incomplete for Hamlet is very different from being fat or apparently mad. 'Incomplete' is a property but this property means to have an incomplete set of properties. We would have the same type of problem with 'contradictory'. Imagine a bad novelist attributing two contradictory properties. 'Contradictory' is in that case a property of the set of properties, which says that this set contains two contradictory properties. Meinong coined the phrase 'extra-nuclear property'. We have not to admit non-existing objects if we want to use this phrase. It is true that for Meinong non-existing objects are incomplete and may be even contradictory, but this distinction between the two types of properties is immune to the admission or non-admission of non-existing objects. If we restrain ourselves to existing objects, we will however obtain extra-nuclear properties, as 'complete', 'non-contradictory' etc. This leads to another characterization of properties, a purely ontological one, tracing to classical metaphysics, as purely positive. Let us define a property as partly privative, partly affirmative or positive. If I say that Gandhi is morally good, this attribution implies an affirmation of something relatively positive and presupposes a privation – he cannot be said absolutely good. But according to theologians when we say that God is morally good, we imply that He is absolutely good and we presuppose that there is absolutely no privation of His goodness. In that case 'positive' is a property of any divine property. The same could be said of 'simplicity': divine simplicity is a positive property, whereas simplicity is for us a relative property.

7.4.4 An Ontology of Properties

Living and conscious organisms are composed of the three types of properties – of matter, life and mind. At each level properties are tied by compresence relations. Sets of properties of a superior level supervene on sets of inferior level. Is the relation of supervenience transitive? Does mind supervenes upon matter? If emergence is the converse of supervenience, transitivity of supervenience would imply a transitivity of emergence and it is doubtful that emergence is transitive. Anyhow, there seems to be a hierarchical organization of properties. Properties of matter exhibit characteristics not present in properties of mind (for example matter is extended, whereas the mind is not, and on the contrary the mind is reflexive, whereas matter is not). At every level appear essential properties of characteristics emerging at that level. All these rapid considerations show at least that we ought to make a distinction between properties of entities belonging to a level and properties of a level of reality considered as a whole.

References

Allaire, E. 1963. Bare particulars. *Philosophical Studies* 14:1–8
Armstrong, D. 1977. *A world of states of affairs*. Cambridge: Cambridge University Press.
Armstrong, D. 1978. *Universals and scientific realism, vol. II: A theory of universals*. Cambridge: Cambridge University Press
Bacon, J. 1995. *Universals and property instances: The alphabet of being*. Oxford: Blackwell
Bacon, J. 1997. Tropes. *Stanford encyclopedia of philosophy*, on the web, 1997
Bergmann, G. 1967. *Realism*. Madison: University of Madison Press.
Bergmann, G. 1968. *Meaning and existence*. Madison: University of Wisconsin Press
Bergmann, G. 1992. *New foundations of ontology*. W. Head ed., Foreword by E. Allaire. Madison: The University of Madison Press
Campbell, K. 1990. *Abstract particulars*. Oxford: Blackwell
Denkel, A. 1996. *Object and property*. Cambridge: Cambridge University Press
Hochberg, H. 1968. Nominalism, platonism and being true of. *Noûs* 2:413–419
Hochberg, H. 2002. Individuation of individual properties: A study of metaphysical futility. *The Modern Schoolman* 79:107–136 (January/march)

Jubien, M. 1989. On properties and property theory. In *Properties, types and meanings*, eds. G. Chiercchia, B.H. Partee, and R. Turner, vol. I, 159–175. Dordrecht: Kluwer.
Kripke, S. 1980. *Naming and necessity*. Cambridge, MA: Harvard University Press
Levinson, J. 1980. The particularization of attributes. *Australasian Journal of Philosophy* 58: 102–115
Lewis, D. 1986. *On the plurality of worlds*. Oxford: Blackwell.
Loux, M. 2002. *Metaphysics*, 2nd edn. London: Routledge
Loux, M. 2006. Aristotle's constituent ontology. *Oxford studies in metaphysics*, vol. 2, 207–250. Oxford: Clarendon Press
Lowe, E.J. 1999. Abstraction, properties and immanent realism. *Proceedings of the twentieth world congress of philosophy. Volume 2: metaphysics*, ed. T. Rockmore, 195–205. Bowling Green, OH: Philosophy Documentation Center.
Lowe, E.J. 2002. Properties, modes and universals. *The Modern Schoolman* 74:137–150 (January/march)
Marcus, R.B. 1993. Essentialism in modal logic. In *Modalities. Philosophical essays*. Oxford; New York: Oxford University Press.
Martin, C.B. 1980. Substance substantiated. *Australasian Journal of Philosophy* 58(1):3–10
Mellor, H. 1982. Properties and predicates. In *Matters of metaphysics*, 170–182. Cambridge: Cambridge University Press
Mertz, D.M. 1996. *Moderate realism and its logic*. New Haven: Yale University Press.
Mertz, D.M. 2002. Combinatorial predication and the ontology of attributes. *The Modern Schoolman* 79:163–198
Moltmann, F. 2004. Properties and kinds of tropes: new linguistic facts and old philosophical insights. *Mind* 113(449):1–41
Nef, F. 2004. Objet et propriété. *La structure du monde. Objets, propriétés, états de choses. Le renouveau de la métaphysique dans l'école australienne de philosophie*, ed. Jean-Maurice Monnoyer, 277–298. Paris: Vrin.
Nef, F. 2005. *Les propriétés des choses. Expérience et logique*. Paris: Vrin
Nef, F. 2006. *qu'est- ce que la métaphysique*? Paris: Gallimard
Nef, F. 2009. *Traité d'Ontologie*. Pairs: Gallimard
Oliver, A. 1996. The metaphysics of properties. *Mind* 105(417):1–80
Oliver, A.éd. 1997. *Properties, Oxford readings in philosophy*. Oxford: Oxford University Press
Puntel, L. 2006. *Struktur und Sein*. Tübingen: Mohr Siebeck.
Quine, W.V.O. 1961. On what there is. In *From a logical point of view*, 2nd edn. New York: Harper and Rowe.
Russell, B. 1912. *The problems of philosophy*. London: Home University Library
Russell, B. 1948. *Human knowledge, its scope and its limits*. London: Allen and Unwin
Simons, P. 1994. Particulars in particular clothing: Three trope theories of substance. *Philosophy and Phenomenological Research* 54(3):553–575.
Smith, B. 1987. *Austrian philosophy. The Brentanian legacy*. Chicago: Open Court
Swoyer, C. 2000. Properties. *Stanford encyclopedia of philosophy*, on the web, 2000
Williams, D.C. 1953. The elements of being. *Review of Metaphysics*, I 7:3–18, 171–192, II, id. 171–192

Chapter 8
Boundary Questions Between Ontology and Biology

Pietro Ramellini

8.1 Introduction: Ontology and Biologists

Many biologists do not care at all for ontology[1]: either they simply choose not to tackle the ontological premises and underpinnings of biological phenomena, or they firmly claim that ontology is merely a residual of superseded superstitions, if not a true obstacle to research.

In my opinion, however, not to have an ontology is to have a bad ontology; so, I think it preferable to positively address the ontological questions whenever and wherever they appear in the course of biological research, instead of obscuring or denying them.

Obviously, it is the general and theoretical biologist who must, in a way or another, explicitly take into consideration such questions, while the experimenter may simply accomplish his work without forgetting how many ontological problems hide behind it, with but a hope at a glimpse beyond his specialised field of investigation from time to time.

8.2 Ontological Questions in Biology

Now, what are such most prominent ontological questions lying behind biology?

If we skim some papers and treatises of ontology, looking for those chapters which would be worth the attention of a biologist, we can easily discover many links between these two fields of knowledge. I shall thus list some of them, mainly in the field of organismic biology and along the lines of the eighth chapter of Mahner and

P. Ramellini (✉)
Pontifical University 'Regina Apostolorum', Rome, Italy
e-mail: ramellini.pietro@inwind.it

[1] Nor did they care for it in past decades, as Woodger showed *ad abundantiam* and repeatedly (1929[1], 1967[2]).

R. Poli, J. Seibt (eds.), *Theory and Applications of Ontology: Philosophical Perspectives*, DOI 10.1007/978-90-481-8845-1_8,

Bunge (1997), which is explicitly devoted to the ontological fundamentals of biophilosophy[2]; however, a glance at other handbooks (e.g. Jacquette 2002) would have yielded – if surely not the same ontological framework – a similar list of ontological items.

Mahner and Bunge's starting point is given by the analysis of (concrete) *things*, and actually in most cases biologists deal with (concrete) bodies, their parts and/or the bodies they are part of. Here, the conceptual opposition[3] part/whole is involved, with all the subtle problems posed by the dissection (be it factual or conceptual) of living bodies into their parts, or by the relations between part and part (e.g. horizontal coordination) and between part and whole (vertical subordination); a very delicate question, which still lies largely unsolved, is that of an organism's proper parts: given a pregnant woman, it is rather easy to recognize that the foetus is not a proper part of its mother, but in some cases it is very difficult to distinguish an organism's proper parts from bodies having accidentally or temporarily penetrated from outside, like some symbionts (Ramellini 2006a).

Things are characterized by their *properties* (accidents, qualities), whose study is linked to the biological analysis of characters, states of characters or traits of phenotypes (Laubicher and Wagner 2000). Relational properties are particularly important in biology (Rashevsky 1961, Rosen 2000), to the point that Mayr (1982) has qualified it as quintessentially a science of relations.

When properties hold constant relations among themselves, Mahner and Bunge claim *laws* obtain, and everybody knows that biological laws or quasi-laws, as well as their extension and generality, often stir hot debates in the philosophy of biology (Brandon 1997).

The totality of properties of a thing at a given instant constitutes its *state*, a concept which also links biology to physics, particularly to thermodynamics, with the endless and somewhat boring debate on an (alleged) steady or non-equilibrium state of living bodies (see Ageno 1986 for a convincing setting-up of the question).

Changes in/of things are of the utmost importance for biology (Salthe 1993), as one can assess by merely listing the questions involved:

- the close association usually asserted between life and dynamism or metabolism, with the ensuing problems in cases of metabolic reduction or standstill;
- the importance of both ontogenetic (please note the etymological root *onto-*) and phylogenetic change;
- the debate on the historical character of living bodies;
- the question whether biological change is merely quantitative or also qualitative.

---

[2]I address the reader to this book for further references on the following items. For an extremely interesting list of keywords in theoretical biology see the Konrad Lorenz Institute Theory Lab website at http://www.kli.ac.at/theorylab/index.html.

[3]Conceptual oppositions are of particular interest in biology: '[b]iology is a science of antitheses' (Woodger 1967: 11). See Gil (1978) for a general survey on conceptual oppositions.

From a traditional vantage point, change also implies a passage from *potency* to *act*; this conceptual opposition has obvious counterparts in biology, like all developmental potencies (from totipotency to unipotency, or even to the ontologically problematic notion of nullipotency; see NIH 2006), or the distinction between a biological possibility/capacity and its actual implementation (as with the problematic notion of the metabolic capacities of a cryoconserved tissue).

Finally, change implies a reference to a *spacetime* framework (for a Whiteheadian viewpoint see Woodger 1967, 299 ff.). In this respect, the synchrony/diachrony couple is spread everywhere in biology, sometimes rather hidden as in the opposition between (spatial) anatomy and (temporal) physiology, sometimes patent as in the nondimensional/multidimensional concept of biological species, or in the debate between historical and ecological biogeography.

Differences between things then call for the notion of *individuality*, notoriously at the core of hot disputes about the ontological status of the human embryo (see for instance the debate after the publication of Ford 1988), or of taxonomic species (since Ghiselin 1974).

In turn, individuality involves questions of *identity* (Wilson 1999):

- the numerical identity of biological entities: for instance, what we call human body actually is a symbiotum, where human cells are numerically a small minority of all cells present in that body's place (see below);
- qualitative identity, with the huge biodiversity of organisms and taxa, and problems of natural kinds, species and classification (Schuh 2000, Coyne and Allen Orr 2004); diversity takes also the appearance of anomalies-abnormalities, opening the door to pathology (which after all is a chapter in general biology) and its discussions on the ontological status of diseases (Thagard 1999);
- diachronic identity, with problems of identity maintenance through time during development, especially when a metamorphosis occurs, or during processes of body division or fusion, like in autotomy or fertilization (Boniolo and Carrara 2004).

Things do not occur alone, but compose either aggregates or *systems*. The above mentioned debate on the ontological status of embryos mainly lies in considerations about its being a system: is a human morula a mere aggregate of blastomeres (i.e. not an embryo but at most a pre-embryo), or since the very fusion of gamete plasmalemmas does it constitute a system (i.e. first a unicellular and then a multicellular organism)?

A system is always set apart from a background, i.e. its environment (Ramellini 2007): thus, we find here the mereological and topological problems posed by *boundaries* between living bodies (be them unicellulars, cells inside multicellulars, or multicellulars) and their surrounding environment (more on this below); boundaries are even more problematic in the case of systems composed of spatially scattered components, like ecological communities, biological populations and ecological niches (Smith and Varzi 2002).

Other boundaries are found in respect to time, when system *emergence* or submergence occurs. In this respect, two fundamental ontological concepts appear to me largely underestimated by biophilosophy, namely:

- the concept of genesis, which lies at the root of primary biological notions like epigenesis, genetics, phylogeny and abiogenesis (Ramellini 2003);
- the concept of corruption (in the sense of the Greek phthrà), which results nearly forgotten, obviously apart from the case of organismic death.

Often emergence occurs by assembly and self-*organization*, two concepts that intervene in developmental biology and above all in the origin(s) of life, one of the greatest unsolved problems in biology (Fry 2000, Luisi 2006). The term organization contains the Aristotelian etymological root *organ-*, which is very fertile in biology, from organelles to superorganisms, or from organs to organisms and, indeed, to organization and self-organization themselves (Schiller 1978). In general, self-properties are of the utmost importance in biology,[4] and have prompted in the last decades a vast literature, especially about self-organization (Kauffman 2000).

Processes of organization may lead to the emergence of new *levels of reality* (Poli 2001). In biology, handbooks and treatises are usually arranged according to a hierarchy of levels of organization, but the question stands as to which and how many levels to recognize or establish (Ramellini 2001).

The concept of *cause* or causation is to be found in the old question of final causes and teleology, recently revived by the concept of teleonomy, and undoubtedly associated with the notion of physiological function (Allen et al. 1998); also the couples proximate/ultimate causes in evolution (Mayr 1982), and downward/upward causation (Campbell 1974) stir countless debates in literature and congresses.

The possibility of uncaused events is at the core of the concepts of *chance* and probability: the role of chance in biology is often underlined, be it in terms of chance and necessity (Monod 1970), order from noise (Foerster 1960) or complexity from noise (Atlan 1979). However, equally often biologists underestimate the philosophical troubles raised by the concept of chance (Boniolo 2003).

Last but not least, the very concept of *life* has important links with ontology (Ramellini 2006a). Some biologists have asked themselves why the definition of life, though sometimes considered the central problem in theoretical biology (Rizzotti 1996), is so scarcely palatable to their colleagues. Unquestionably, a part of the answer is that life is not a truly biological concept, being on the contrary a scientific-ontological question: as Bunge correctly put it, regarding concepts like life or time, 'science just borrows them leaving them in an intuitive or presystematic state. Only ontology is interested in explicating and systematizing concepts which, since they are used by many sciences, are claimed by none. For example, physics asks not "What is time?", biology "What is life?", psychology "What is

[4] My personal collection of biological terms starting with the prefixoid *auto*-includes more than fifty entries, see Ramellini (2006b: 111 ff).

the mental?", and sociology "What is sociality?". It is the task of ontology, jointly with the foundations of science, to try and supply answers to such questions and, in general, to clarify whatever idea science takes for granted or leaves in the twilight' (Bunge 1977, p. 20).

As it can easily be seen, biology (as indeed any other science, i.e. – if you want – any other regional ontology) offers a rich crop of questions in material and formal ontology, many of which closely related to each other, and reciprocally overlapping.

Being impossible to even survey all these questions, I shall now focus on the subject of the boundary of a living body.

8.3 A Case Study: Biological Boundaries

The topic of boundaries has always raised some interest in both ontology (see Varzi 2004 and the references therein) and biology. The difference is that biologists have rarely tackled this question theoretically, so to the best of my knowledge the following survey is a pioneer work, which explains its conjectural and provisional character.

To begin with, if we want to address the question of the boundary of a living body, we previously need to define the term 'living body', a notoriously puzzling topic. To cut a long story short, I shall simply suggest here a definition developed elsewhere (Ramellini 2006a): a living body is a macroscopic body possessing a canalizing capacity largely determined by those carbon polymers which largely compose it (above all, its proteins and its deoxyribonucleic acids, whose sequences almost completely determine the sequences of its proteins). By canalizing capacity I mean the capacity of a macroscopic body to canalize an exchange (with its surrounding environment) and a largely assimilative-dissimilative replacement (inside it) of material particles such that the body maintains itself (with its canalizing capacity). The life of a living body is its possessing the canalizing capacity, while its death is the irreversible cessation of its life.

So, we are interested in the boundary of a (concrete) body which is macroscopic, i.e. showing a conduct largely following the laws of classical physics. I claim that the vast majority of biologists, when thinking of, speaking about and interacting with the living, refer to living (macroscopic and concrete) bodies. And when they tackle the question of the boundary of such bodies, biologists refer to different types of boundary, namely: perceptual (above all visual ones), compositional (above all at molecular levels), epithelial (both as epidermises and mucous membranes), cellular (above all biomembranes) and processual (in their various versions) boundaries.[5] As often happens, also in biology the question of boundaries is strongly linked

[5]Compare these types with Woodger's list of the modes of biological analysis: perceptual (usually visual), genetical, manual (above all visual and tactual), physiological and chemical (1967: 274–275).

to the psychology and philosophy of perception (see e.g. Gibson 1950), to problems of spatial properties and deformations (i.e. to topology; see e.g. von Foerster 1982 and Edelman 1988 for biological development; Stroll 1988 for surfaces) and to part-whole relations (i.e. to mereology; see e.g. Woodger 1937 for biological applications, with an appendix by Alfred Tarsky; Simons 1987 and Casati and Varzi 1999 for a general framework); this obviously implies that the different viewpoints are to be carefully distinguished, without confusing ontological with biological or mereological arguments.

8.3.1 Perceptual Boundaries

The term 'perceptual boundary' mainly refers to visual and haptic, i.e. tactile or better somatosensory, boundaries (Ramellini 2002).

Though many biologists and, indeed, laymen, found their naive notion of boundary on optical surfaces and visual perception, rarely this preconception is explicitly dealt with.[6] Apart from experimental studies on mimicry, camouflage and vexillary functions, only here and there do we find in literature theoretical hints on visible surfaces; for instance, according to Portmann (1965), an animal's surface – when opaque – becomes a new organ, largely independent from inner structures: not only a protective envelope or a means of exchange between body and environment, but a very window to launch messages and establish relationships.

Let us see what such a visual surface could consist of. If you look, at some distance and from various slants, at a naked man floodlighted in clean air, you will see a variously coloured surface, undergoing changes according to his moving (e.g. breathing) and being moved (e.g. by wind). Now, if you get closer to him, some problems will arise:

– some shallow parts are nearly transparent[7]: through his nails you will see the derma lying below them, with its blood vessels, though under slanting light you will perceive their shallow, light-reflecting surface; again, being his corneas and eye lenses also transparent (due to the peculiar arrangement of their collagen and crystallin polymers), an optical illusion in the form of two black discs, i.e. the pupils, will appear[8]; however, eye surfaces shine when conjunctives reflect light;

[6]On the importance of optical boundaries in the genesis of the concept of cell see however Woodger (1967^2: 158).

[7]I also recall the case of «glassy» fishes like *Parambassis ranga*, whose thoraco-abdominal muscles are nearly transparent, making their «visible» boundary invisible to predators (interestingly, glassy fishes are often sold after injections of fluorescent dyes into their bodies, to make them more appealing to aquarists, who evidently are not predators). Transparent living bodies account for Portmann's caveat about opaque surfaces. The physical basis of transparency is still poorly understood (Johnsen and Widder 1999).

[8]This optical illusion is also due to a photoabsorbent layer, the choroid, behind the pupil. However, many animals – like dogs – possess a light-reflecting layer behind or within the retina, i.e. the *tapetum lucidum*, allowing them a better night vision.

- many shady wrinkles and pits make it difficult to locate the visual boundary: nostrils look as a dark zone not further distinguishable, while at closer inspection hair turns into the surface of each single hair. In general, where there are orifices like the mouth, the visual boundary seems located at the rima separating an «external» horny epithelium and an «internal» mucous membrane (except in cases like the hard palate, which is lined by horny epithelium, or the glans penis and the inside of the prepuce, which are covered by a mucosa). Needless to say, these mucocutaneous rimae can be treated of as parts of their own, with their peculiar properties.[9]

From a physical viewpoint, the visual perception of this boundary is linked to complex interactions among light photons, the air as a medium, the chemical components of the living body and the eye of the observer, with all the theoretical problems associated with each of these items.

Passing to somatic senses, if a woman moves her right hand towards the rest of her body, sooner or later the hand will bang into it, meeting with her haptic boundary. It is a wavy surface, changing through time; if something presses it, the surface broadens or reduces in various ways. Here also some problems arise:

- following the haptic boundary, she will arrive at her mouth, where the boundary goes on with the oral mucosa and, beyond it, the digestive and respiratory mucous epithelia, as well as the ducts of the glands associated with them; and indeed, a probe performing such a stochastic walk could even find itself again on the visual surface, for instance passing from the skin on her face, through the mouth cavity, the pharynx and the nostrils, again to the skin on her face;
- here and there one meets liquid or moist materials, like mucus or gastric fluids, so the question arises as whether the haptic boundary coincides with these materials or with the epithelium beneath them; besides, some touchable surfaces pertain to bodies which are in some sense detached from the remainder of the body, like in the case of dandruff, sebum or single hairs, so we must ask ourselves if the haptic boundary includes each dandruff flake's surface, or passes beneath them.

Here again, the haptic boundary results from complex interactions between an haptic sensor and the materials the living body consists of (*and* is surrounded by: think of a living body so strictly set against other bodies, be them living – as in the case of colonies – or not – as for endolithic organisms living inside stones, that the probe cannot touch it without having touched and even penetrated the others).

In general, perceptual boundaries may also be grasped through instruments. For instance, if we look at a human body with the help of an infrared viewer (i.e. one which transduces invisible inputs into visible outputs), a strange surface will appear, vanishing as it is where the body surface temperature equals that of its background;

---

[9] Notably, their being erogenous zones due to the presence of superficial nerve networks; see the classical paper by Winkelmann (1959).

and, if our binoculars were to detect only neutrinos, that body would not appear at all, being it perfectly transparent to such particles. Another example is given by the images provided by schlieren systems, which make the layer of warm air around human skin visible, thus enlarging the boundary beyond its visible limits, and giving to it a peculiar character of incessant trembling.

8.3.2 Compositional Boundaries

Let us now consider a probe travelling through space while recording the chemical composition of what it meets. If the probe travels through a room where our naked man is, it will detect:

- first of all, a mixture of gasses, i.e. the air;
- at a certain point, it will register a sudden compositional change, finding keratin, sebum or lactic acid, i.e. the epidermis, in the place of nitrogen or argon;
- then, a complex mixture of water, ions, molecules and polymers will follow, i.e. human cells but also intercellular matrices like blood plasma;
- finally, air will come back, when the probe leaves the man.

After a stochastic walk through the room, we shall be able to resume the probe's records by saying that there is a body plunged into air, whose boundary corresponds to the surface of maximum compositional change.

Yet, we must remember that:

- composition may be related either to elements (Ar, C, etc.) or to pure substances (Ar, but also O_2, H_2O, Na^+, while it is controversial whether polymers are pure substances) or to different kinds of material particles (atoms, ions, micromolecules, polymers; sure, even organelles or hairs are material entities, but let us now focus on chemistry), and so on;
- the degree of resolution must be declared: the composition per cube decimetre is a rather different matter from that per cube nanometre;
- a choice is to be made between qualitative (e.g. a list of the elements present), quantitative (e.g. the number of atoms for each element, or the volume occupied by each element's atoms) or qualiquantitative composition.

If we were to ignore such questions, curious outcomes would result. For instance, let a probe enter a room where a man is sitting in damp air and smoking, and let the probe record the qualitative composition per cube millimetre in kinds of material particles of circamolecular size. Then, its result will be that the room is homogeneously filled up with atoms, molecules and polymers: in fact, each cube millimetre of the air surrounding the man contains atoms (e.g. of argon), molecules (e.g. of water vapour) and polymers (the smoke's soot); but quite similarly, also each cube millimetre of the human body contains atoms (e.g. sodium cations or argon atoms), molecules (e.g. of liquid water or water vapour) and polymers (e.g. proteins in his liver, or the smoke's soot in his lungs).

So, countless compositional boundaries result from simply combining different types of composition and degrees of resolution, while in some cases no boundary will be detected by the chemical probe.

8.3.3 Epithelial Boundaries

One is tempted to merge the preceding observations by saying that, all considered and some minor inconsistencies apart, visual, haptic and compositional boundaries coincide with an epithelium lining both the surfaces exposed to an «outer» medium and those of «inner» body cavities[10]; with which we enter the field of biological boundaries proper.

A first problem is that all unicellulars and many multicellulars lack tissues, hence epithelia; as to unicellulars, in a moment we shall examine cellular boundaries, while in cases like multicellular fungi, either cells are directly exposed to their surrounding environment, or pseudotissues are built.

Then, epithelia are often provided with discontinuities, like orifices or even open wounds. The case of leaves is particularly challenging: here, the cuticle of the leaf is interrupted by small openings called stomata, whose rimae open on intercellular spaces filled with air (an obvious adaptation to gas exchanges during photosynthesis); so, a spongy tissue results, with cells and many air spaces among them; in other words, differently from e.g. lung epithelia, leaves do not possess a continuous sheet of epithelial cells.

Either through orifices or vesicles, epithelia perform an often intense trafficking of matter with their surrounding environment; for instance, many glandular epithelia let out whole cells or cellular parts as their secretions, raising the problem of where and when these detached parts cross the epithelial boundary.

Finally, not in all cases does an epithelium constitute a significant (functional) boundary: plant roots are composed of a central cylinder of tissues, surrounded by a monolayer of cells called endodermis, and by a peripheral cortex, surrounded by the root epidermis. Now, the endodermis separating the cylinder from the cortex shows no intercellular gaps, since its cells are strictly in contact with one another: in fact, strips of suberin (i.e., roughly speaking, cork) stick together the endodermal cells, constituting an effective barrier against uncontrolled or undesired throughputs of substances through roots; this is why, while the peripheral cortex may contain toxic chemicals, infectious bacteria or mutualistic symbionts, the central cylinder is maintained clean and sterile. Thus, the endodermis seems a stronger (functional) boundary then the root epidermis.

---

[10]Sometimes (e.g. Smith and Varzi 1997), the surface of skin alone is considered as the outer boundary of the human body, pointing out that such boundary has discernible sub-boundaries, like the edge-line of mouth or surgery-scars.

8.3.4 Cellular Boundaries

To account for cases where tissues are lacking, one could resort to cells and their boundaries, that is – *prima facie* – to cell biomembranes, i.e. plasmalemmas.

This position is held for instance by Mahner and Bunge, who write that '[a]lthough every system has a more or less definite boundary separating it from its environment ..., the boundary of living systems is peculiar in that it ultimately involves a biomembrane – even if it is overlain by a cellulose wall, a horn or wax layer, a shell, or what have you. As this comparatively sharp boundary restricts the exchange of substances with the environment, biosystems are semi-open systems, although they are usually said to be open systems. In general, a *semi-open system* is a system which has a boundary that restricts the class of exchanges between the components of the system and the items in its environment. This is why biosystems interact *selectively* with environmental items' (1997, p. 143).

Let us take a closer look at the suggestion that the *ultimate* boundary of a living body is a biomembrane: namely, a biomembrane boundary. Obviously, here we are thinking of plasmalemmas, which however do not exhaust the vast array of biomembranes, leaving for instance apart all intracellular biomembranes.

If we consider a unicellular, the theoretical problems posed by its plasmalemma are more or less the same as for a multicellular in respect to its epithelia: for instance, a cell may produce and let out vesicles (a process called exocytosis), or it may let in environmental materials again through vesicles (endocytosis); or there are discontinuities in the plasmalemma, like temporary pores or stable protein channels. Particularly challenging is the envelope of some bacteria, consisting of an «inner» biomembrane, a middle space containing a thin cell wall, and a second, «outer» biomembrane; here, one could ask Mahner and Bunge what the ultimate biomembrane boundary is.

As to multicellulars, let us consider one more time an adult living body *B* belonging to *Homo sapiens*, developed from a human fertilized egg, i.e. a zygote *Z*. Let us call human eczygotic cell (*EC*) every cell of *Homo sapiens* derived from *Z*[11]: that is, for the sake of discussion let us exclude all cells of other species (like the bacteria living in symbiosis in the gut) and all cells of *Homo sapiens* coming from other humans (like the cells of a foetus living in *B*'s womb, or the white blood cells implanted into *B* by blood-transfusion). An *EC*'s plasmalemma, or at least a part of it, may be either in contact with another *EC*'s plasmalemma (like for two epithelial cells in contact), or free (like for a white blood cell inside blood plasma).

We have at least the following possibilities:

1. A first possibility is to locate the biomembrane boundary in correspondence with the surface resulting from all free *EC*'s plasmalemmas.

---

[11] The set of all the *EC*s of a human, plus *Z*, could be compared with the set *zgdend* as introduced by Woodger (1937: 90).

According to this option, *B*'s boundary proves to be extremely fragmented, given the huge number of environmental prolongations and exclaves, as well of body enclaves. In fact, let us follow the record of a biomembrane probe: starting to move from the air surrounding *B*, in order to meet the cellular boundary, the probe must first pass through *B*'s epidermal keratinized layers (which are made of cell corpses), to reach the first epithelial (living) cells with their free plasmalemmas; then it will meet a mass of (living) cells with their plasmalemmas in close contact, often reinforced by intercellular junctions; so, the probe will travel through the body, remaining inside its cellular boundary, until it will meet other epithelial cells, whose free plasmalemmas constitute another part of *B*'s boundary (either because the probe will have completely crossed the body, emerging from the skin on the other side, or because it will still be «inside» *B*, but where a mucous membrane lines a body cavity).
Now, this is only a rough account of the situation, since on closer inspection the biomembrane boundary appears to be much more fragmented. For instance, wherever there is a connective tissue, its cells are more or less free inside a matrix (like blood plasma or cartilage matrix), hence their plasmalemmas are free and constitute part of the biomembrane boundary: so, in a blood vessel the biomembrane boundary is located in correspondence with the free plasmalemmas of its endothelium (i.e. the wall of the vessel, directly in contact with blood), blood plasma being outside such boundary; but plunged into the plasma there are countless blood cells, which are *EC*s and whose countless free plasmalemmas are parts of *B*'s boundary ... So, not only the lumina of *B*'s cavities, but even all *B*'s intercellular spaces and mediums constitute countless environmental prolongations or exclaves that fragment to excess *B*'s biomembrane boundary.[12]
Another problem is presented by those body parts which actively leave, or are passively detached from, *B*: what about the plasmalemma of a *B*'s spermatozoon, when it is ejaculated outside *B*: does it become an exclave of *B*? And if a blood droplet falls to the ground from a wound, do its white blood cells' plasmalemmas still constitute a part of *B*'s boundary?[13]

2. A second possibility is to consider, as parts of the cellular boundary, also all the remnants of plasmalemmas (i.e. all the limiting biomembranes of the corpses of what had been *EC*s): in such case, among the plasmalemmas which make boundary we will also find the free plasmalemma remnants of cell remnants (e.g. cell corpses and apoptotic bodies, see below); so, the boundary will be located in correspondence with the epidermal surface and its cell remnants (horny epithelium,

---

[12]Note that after all the human body is a simple case, since its (living) cells occupy the bulk of the body; in other cases, cells occupy only a small minority of the total volume: for instance, in a trunk of a spermatophyte, almost only its vascular cambium and phloem are composed of (living) cells.

[13]Such question, apparently so bizarre, stirred hot debates during the Middle Ages, as to whether Jesus' blood drops, felt down on the *Via Crucis*, had resurrected with him.

hairs etc.). However, many enclaves would still persist, now also surrounding cell remnants like blood platelets; besides, the question of the detached parts would become complicated, since the detachment of «dead» parts (dandruff, hairs, etc.) is more frequent than for living parts.

3. Let us then also add all the derivatives of *EC*s: thus, the «cellular» boundary will shift to encompass all cells and/or their remnants and/or their derivatives: gut fluids, glandular secretions like milk, sweat or insulin, intercellular matrices, gasses (either those about to be exhaled or those otherwise produced by the body, like in the swim bladder of fishes) and extracellular annexes of some organs (like the gelatinous matrix in the inner ear, with the little «stones» or otoliths it contains).
   Also in this case, some problems will follow, like the fact that usually gas masses do not show spatial boundaries.
4. Finally, we could extend the «cellular» boundary to include not only possible non-eczygotic human cells but, above all, all nonhuman (and *a fortiori* non-eczygotic) cells, and/or their remnants, and/or their derivatives. Actually, we must not forget that human cells, in a human body, are in number a very small minority of all the cells there present: on a total number of about 10^{13} human cells, even in perfectly healthy humans we find about 10^{14} bacteria, just to leave apart the members of hundreds of species of protists (e.g. gut protozoa), fungi (e.g. spores), plants (e.g. pollen grains) and animals (e.g. the tiny mites happily living in our eyebrows), be them passively or actively, temporarily or permanently installed in our «human» bodies (Wilson 2005, De Rossi 2006).
   But in such case, could we still consider such an expanded boundary, which more or less coincides with the optic-haptic boundary, as the boundary of a *human* body?

8.3.5 *Sensu Lato* Processual Boundaries

Maybe as an attempt to circumvent all these difficulties, many biologists appeal to various types of *sensu lato* processual boundaries, often called processual proper, dynamic, functional or operational boundaries.

According to Foucault (1966), it is quite the conceptual shift from the visible boundaries of plants and animals to their organic unity of processes and functions to mark – with Cuvier – the epistemic breakthrough from natural history to biology at the end of the eighteenth century: the object of natural history 'is given by surfaces and lines, not by functioning or invisible tissues. The plant and the animal are to be seen less in their organic unity than through the visible carving of their organs' (1966, p. 149, my transl.); on the contrary, Cuvier opens the doors to biology when he 'gives large prominence to functions in respect to organs, and subjugates the disposition of the organ to the sovereignty of the function' (*ivi*: 276, my transl.). In sum, 'during the classical age life was standing upon an *ontology* which concerned the same way all material beings, subjugated to extension, weight, movement; ...

from Cuvier onwards, the living escapes, at least at first sight, the general laws of the extended being' (*ivi*: 286, my transl., emphasis added).[14]

After Cuvier, processual boundaries have been proposed repeatedly, either as a negation of static-spatial boundaries (e.g. Piaget 1967, p. 63, Bertalanffy 1968, p. 215) or as a positive claim (e.g. Maturana and Varela 1980, pp. 81, 90–91, Kauffman 1995, p. 62).

There is probably a strict link between the argument for processual boundaries and the concept of living system (as opposed to the concept of living body): in fact, contrarily to a body, a system may be composed of spatially scattered components, in which case it would be difficult to speak of a topologically continuous boundary (much like in the case of the boundary rigorously established on plasmalemmas). In this respect, Wimsatt (1976) has even claimed that evolutionary increases of complexity are characterized by 'a trend away from 1 to 1 mappings between functions and recognizable physical objects', whence a 'failure of functional systems to correspond to well-delineated and spatially compact physical systems' (1976, p. 185).

Again, processual boundaries may not coincide with other boundaries, like the cellular ones. For instance, the propagation of action potentials in a neuron depends, among other items, on the salt solution surrounding its plasmalemma; thus, a «processual» neuron will be composed of the «cellular» neuron *and* the muff of aqueous solution containing the ions co-responsible for impulse propagation; that is, a neuron's cellular boundary will be located in correspondence with its plasmalemma, while its processual boundary will correspond to that layer of solution around its plasmalemma where certain ionic concentrations begin to conform to a particular chemical equilibrium called the Gibbs-Donnan equilibrium.

To see which problems emerge from the processual approach, let us scrutiny Ageno's position, by which the boundaries of a coherent system are the boundaries of the coherence of its inner processes (1986, p. 407), so that coherent systems are delimited by the extension of their coherent processes in space and time (Ageno 1992, p. 143). Here Ageno makes reference to his distinction between bound and coherent systems: while a bound system (like an atom, a stone or a cluster of galaxies) is kept united by the attractive forces among its parts, a coherent system (like a Bénard cell, a tornado or a man) owes this to a reserve of internal energy granting the coherence of its molecular movements.

Apart from the difficulty of understanding what exactly Ageno means by coherence (see Ramellini 2006a), here the main problem relates to the very concepts of

---

[14]According to Foucault, '[L'objet de l'histoire naturelle] est donné par des surfaces et des lignes, non par des fonctionnements ou d'invisible tissus. La plante et l'animal se voient moins en leur unité organique que par la découpe visible de leurs organs' (1966: 149). Cuvier 'fait déborder – et largement – la fonction par rapport à l'organe, et soumet la disposition de l'organe à la souveraineté de la fonction' (*ivi*: 276). In sum, "tout au long de l'âge classique la vie relevait d'une *ontologie* qui concernait de la même façon tous les êtres matériels, soumis à l'étendue, à la pesanteur, au mouvement; ... à partir de Cuvier, le vivant échappe, au moins en première instance, aux lois générales de l'être etendu" (*ivi*: 286, emphasis added).

boundary of a coherence, or boundary of a process. Briefly, while we can surely speak of the temporal boundaries of a process, its spatial boundary cannot be but the boundary of the body (or bodily or concrete system) undergoing that process; consequently, what Ageno holds is that the boundary of a coherent system *S* is the boundary of that (concrete) system *S* whose processes are coherent, which is a true but rather unfruitful assertion.

In other words, despite the appeal that various process ontologies have on biologists, it seems to me that only an ontology based on the bearers of processes can satisfy their needs, be them experimental or theoretical (Mahner and Bunge 1997, pp. 20–21).

8.3.6 The Organismic Boundary

Despairing of the prospects to find out *the* boundary of a living body, some authors have declared that simply it does not exist, or that it is at most a *fiat* rather than a *bona fide* boundary.[15]

For instance, Haldane (1931) wrote that the organism and the external environment are so intimately entangled that '[t]here is no spatial limit to the life of an organism' (1931, p. 74). A peculiar version of this position holds that all what a living system needs to live or develop is part of it, hence inside its boundary: if even a mathematician like Thom (1998) claimed that a prey, though outside the predator, is an integrating part of its vital dynamic totality, so that the border between predator and environment is rather fluid (1998, p. 279), it is undoubtedly the Developmental Systems Theory (DST) to have stressed that the bearer of development is not an organism, but a developmental system encompassing 'not just genomes with cellular structures and processes, but intra- and interorganismic relations, including relations with members of other species and interactions with the inanimate surround as well' (Oyama 1985, p. 123).

Others authors have however (correctly) criticized these positions. For instance, Needham criticized Haldane saying that 'if no line can be drawn between organism and immediate surroundings, no better line can be drawn between immediate surroundings and far-off surroundings', so we can but contemplate the whole universe, the 'analysis of living things being laid aside' (Needham 1936, p. 11); and exactly the same comment has been advanced about DST by Mahner and Bunge, when they claim that expanding 'further and further nested developmental systems would lead us directly to holism, that is, to the assumption that the entire universe is *the* developmental system' (Mahner and Bunge 1997, p. 301).

On the opposite side, some have maintained that boundaries are at the very core of life. Jonas (1966), for instance, claims that a most deep characteristic of life is 'its being self-centered individuality, being for itself and in contraposition to all

[15] For these two technical terms see Smith (1994) and Varzi (2004).

the rest of the world, with an essential boundary dividing "inside" and "outside" – notwithstanding, nay, on the very basis of the actual exchange' between organism and environment (1966, p. 79); Hoffmeyer (1998) says that life is organized around those nested sets of membranes we call organisms; Keller (2001) writes that boundaries like cell membranes are 'a cornerstone of biological organization ... with absolutely vital significance' (2001, p. 301).

From my ontological and biological viewpoint, the boundary of a living body cannot be but the boundary of a (concrete) body, and of a body *qua* living.

To be more precise, let us first draw a distinction between a living body and an organism, or organismically living body, as set out elsewhere (Ramellini 2006a): an organism is a living body which is biologically subordinated to itself and only to itself, since it possesses the capacity to biologically regulate itself and only itself, through its concrete parts regulating both themselves and each other. Thus, a bacterium in a test-tube is both a living body and an organism; a human white blood cell in a test-tube is a living body but not an organism; a human white blood cell in a human body is neither a living (free) body nor an organism, being rather a living (concrete) part of an organism.

Now, how to decide which (concrete) parts of a living body do constitute together an organism? The methodological way is: take a living body *L*; take a concrete part *P* of *L*, and look for the parts *P* subordinates to itself (regulates) and for the parts *P* is subordinated to (by which *P* is regulated); repeat the same inspection for these last subordinated-subordinating (regulated-regulating) parts, until you will obtain a closed network of inter-subordinating (inter-regulating) parts: this will be your organism *O*.[16] For instance, if we consider a human hepatocyte *P* inside a «human body» *L* (actually, and more precisely, a human symbiotum), we shall discover that *P* subordinates – and is subordinated to – the other hepatocytes; then we shall discover that these hepatocytes subordinate – and are subordinated to – the lymphocytes, and so on, until we shall arrive to a closed system of reciprocally subordinating parts, which neither subordinate other parts of *L* (for instance, gut bacteria) nor are subordinated to them; this closed system will be the human organism *O* inside the human symbiotum *L*.

As it is clear, the organism *O* will sometimes coincide with the entire living body *L* from which one started, while sometimes *O* will be smaller than *L*; that is, some organisms are living bodies (like the bacterium in a test-tube), while others are living parts of living bodies (like the same bacterium inserted into the intestine of a man, or the human organism inside a «human body»).

Now, let us focus on the organismic boundary of an organism *O*, i.e. of a body *qua* organismically living.[17] Let us ask ourselves whether a quantity of matter

[16]For a thorough discussion see Ramellini (2006).

[17]That is, I shall not tackle here the problem of the boundary of a living part of an organism, like a hepatocyte or possibly a heart. Actually, while the boundary of a cell inside a multicellular seems rather clear, with tissues or organs it becomes far more blurry, to the point that I doubt that we can recognize a heart as a *living* part (Ramellini 2006a).

M (be it an atom or a macroscopic system, a quantity of gas or a solid, and so on) is a (concrete) part of *O*, hence inside its organismic boundary.

A first, provisional condition for *M* to be a part of *O* follows from the fact that every part of *O* is, at the same time, a part of *L* (while the converse not always holds). Thus *M*, in order to be a part of *O*, must simultaneously be a part of *L*; that is, *M* must be not only physically close to, or in contact with, *O*, but also «attached» to it, in the sense of co-moving with *O*.[18]

For instance, a beech leaf *M*, fallen down to the stump of the beech from which it had budded, is not a part of that beech *qua* body, hence a fortiori it is neither a part of that tree *qua* living body nor *qua* organismically living body (though it may contribute, when on the ground at that beech's stump and with the rest of its litter, to protect its roots from winter cold, thus performing some «function» for that beech). But what about the same leaf *M* when, though still on that beech, it is about to fall to its stump? Or what about a leaf that happens to have fallen into a hole in a branch of that beech and now is rotting there?

Another example is provided by cobwebs. Once completed, a cobweb is not a part of the spider that has woven it (*pace* Diderot 1769), since it is not attached to it. But what about a cobweb when it is still attached to a spider's abdomen during its weaving? And what about those single cobweb threads, attached to the abdomen of «flying» spiders in order to make them soar thanks to air currents (sometimes as far as hundreds of kilometres)?

These considerations show that *M*'s being attached to *O* is not a sufficient condition for *M* to be inside *O*'s organismic boundary: inter-subordination (inter-regulation) between *M* and *O*'s parts is also required; in other words, the (concrete) parts of an organism are characterised not only by concreteness, but also by inter-subordination (inter-regulation).

For instance, a growing leaf budded by an organismic tree is inter-subordinated with the rest of that tree, thus it is an organismic part inside its organismic boundary (or better, the deep part of that leaf is inside the organismic boundary, while its shallow part is at the same time a part of the organismic boundary). In contrast, the petiole of a leaf about to fall usually contains a layer of substances which occlude its vessels; if so, this implies that the leaf has lost inter-subordination with the rest of the tree, then the fact that it is still attached is simply a mechanical matter, with no significance as regards its biological and ontological status of being a part of the relevant organism inside its organismic boundary. In other words, a tree in autumn carrying the last leaf *M* about to fall is a living body *L*, composed of *M* and of the rest *R* of *L*: if *R* is an organism *O* (i.e. if all *R*'s parts are inter-subordinated), then its organismic boundary will exclude *M*; that is, *M* will be inside *L*'s boundary but outside *O*'s organismic boundary.

---

[18]Though concepts like co-movability or solidarity still need in my opinion a better explication (for an interesting approach see Hoffman and Rosenkrantz 1997: 80 ff.), it is at least clear that here I am speaking of a physical, rather than a topological, closeness, contact or attachment. For an alternative viewpoint, according to which attachment is not so important, see the concept of extended phenotype in Dawkins (1982).

As to cobwebs, I am prepared to consider the thread of a «flying» spider as a part of the relevant organism, while the cobweb still attached to a spider's abdomen during its weaving seems to me insufficiently inter-subordinated with the spider's parts as to be inside the relevant organismic boundary.

In other words, an *M* can enter or leave *O*'s organismic boundary by gaining or losing inter-subordination (inter-regulation) with *O*'s parts.

For instance, a sand grain on the cuticle of a *Palaemon* shrimp is not inside its organismic boundary, but some sand grains cross the boundary when after each moult the shrimp introduces them into its newly formed statocysts, using them as statoliths[19]; another illustration would be the stones that poultry ingest (as well as dinosaurs did) to aid food grinding in the gizzard, and obviously a bite of food itself. Now, when does a mouthful of bread cross the organismic boundary? When it is attacked by the enzymes inside the mouth, or when it becomes a part of chyme and then of chyle, or when glucose – the end product of its digestion – crosses the intestinal mucosa? The answer is: when mouthfuls, or better the products of their gradual digestion, become inter-subordinated with the parts of the organism, i.e. more or less when they are absorbed by intestinal villi.

To look at yet another illustration, when it is inside blood plasma, a single particle of uric acid (a catabolic substance of humans deriving from the oxidization of certain organic molecules) contributes to plasma osmotic pressure, and may have a protective role as an antioxidant[20]; in the meantime, it is subject to the general regulation of osmotic pressure. Thus, we can admit that such a particle is inter-subordinated with *O*'s parts, thus being a part of *O* inside its organismic boundary; now, the fact is that at high concentration uric acid becomes a toxic waste, to be eliminated by kidneys. Once expelled into the urine, but before urination, a particle of uric acid is no longer inter-subordinated with *O*'s parts, though it is still attached to *O*. Hence, uric acid particles cross *O*'s organismic boundary when they cross the free plasmalemmas of certain kidney cells called podocytes, i.e. where they lose inter-subordination with *O*'s parts.

The topological catastrophes of organismic boundary generation, merging and corruption are currency in biology. I shall set aside here well known examples such as cell division or fertilization, to tackle other biological phenomena that may be more intriguing to the ontologist.

During human early development, for causal reasons that are not yet well understood, it may happen that an embryo split into two embryos, generating two monozygotic twins; before the division, there is one organism possessing one organismic boundary, while afterwards there are two organisms bounded by two organismic boundaries: in fact, though the cells of the two twins are *EC*s derived

---

[19]The statocyst is an organ capable of sensing the gravitational field, thanks to little stones made of sand grains called statoliths; this has obviously tempted biologists to give the shrimps tiny magnets instead of sand, inducing them to orientate according to the resultant of magnetic and gravitational fields.

[20]Besides, in plants uric acid is a precursor of ureids, organic compounds which play an important role in transporting nitrogen from roots to other organs of the plant.

from the same zygote, being there no metabolism at a distance, the two twins are not inter-subordinated, hence they constitute two organisms. The fact is, however, that rarely the division is not complete, so that the embryo splits only partially, and Siamese twins result: how to consider them? Undoubtedly, the twins do constitute a single living body, but how many organisms are there? Again, it all depends on inter-subordination: if the bodily conjunction between the twins is so little that it implies no inter-subordination,[21] then there will be one living body and two organisms, hence two organismic boundaries. On the other hand, if conjunction is so extensive as to imply inter-subordination,[22] then there will be one living body and one organism (usually doomed to early death), hence one organismic boundary.

An extraordinary case of organismic boundary merging occurs in the parasitic worms belonging to *Diplozoon paradoxum*. Hatching from eggs, their larvae settle on fish gills as ectoparasites; when two larvae meet on the same fish, they fuse their bodies and become sexually mature adults: in fact, their hermaphrodite reproductive apparatuses develop, in such a way that the testicle ducts of the first open onto the oviduct of the second, and vice versa; the intestine too branches out in both partners. From such process onwards, the «two» partners remain permanently fused, and probably neither could survive alone (supposing it could free itself from its partner). The partners assume an X shape, since body fusion involves only their middle regions: so, there are two heads (with two mouths) and two tails; reproductive organs are doubled as well, with their ducts intercommunicating. In this case, inter-subordination seems so deep that this «diplozoon» (from the Greek: double animal) can be considered one living body and one organism, with one organismic boundary[23]; to realize the difference, the fish carrying it, though attached to the parasite, is undoubtedly a distinct organism, with its distinct organismic boundary.

It is easy to assess that inter-subordination (inter-regulation) is a matter of degree, thus it is not at all easy to recognize the threshold between two organisms *A* and *B* which are merely «attached» to each other, and two organisms *A* and *B* which share so much of their life processes as to generate one (new) organism *C* by fusion (while *A* and *B* themselves die *qua* organisms). However, it is clear that neither part contiguity nor body continuity are sufficient conditions for one living body to constitute one organism; rather, inter-subordination is absolutely necessary.

That is, we know many cases where a physical link is established or maintained between two (or more) living bodies, without implying organismic continuity

---

[21] Like in the famous xiphopagus twins Chang and Eng Bunker (1811–1874), whose conjunction simply involved a band of cartilage in the xiphoid process of their chests.

[22] Like in cephalothoracopagus twins, with sharing of head, neck, chest, and hence usually heart and brain.

[23] However, if it were shown that, say, digestive processes in the fused intestine are physiologically separated, this would cast doubt on the diplozoon being only one organism.

and organismic boundary merging: apart from the above mentioned examples, a bacterial cell conjugating through the channel called pilus with its partner does not combine with the latter sufficiently tightly as to constitute one organism; in mice, the so-called polar cell is not inside the zygote's organismic boundary, despite its being attached to the zygote by a thin extensible tether; a slender strawberry stolon sooner or later produces an independent offshoot, which constitutes a new organism, though still attached to its mother plant.

Organismic boundary corruption occurs whenever an organism dies. Defining organismic life as the possession of the regulatory capacity by an organism, we receive the result that organismic death is the irreversible cessation of its organismic life (Ramellini 2006a). So, a bacterial cell infected by viruses appropriately called bacteriophages starts to synthesize viral components which self-assemble and build new bacteriophages; at this point, the bacterium usually dies, its plasmalemma disintegrates, and the cell content is released into the surroundings (bacterial lysis); such events obviously imply the corruption of the bacterial organismic boundary. It is worth noting that not always the corruption of the organismic boundary of an organismically living body (*qua* organism) coincides with the corruption of the boundary of that body (*qua* body): for instance, during apoptosis or «cell suicide», when the cell dies its plasmalemma forms spheroidal protrusions (blebbing), so that the cell body fragments into small spheroids (apoptotic bodies), each of them bounded by a part of what had been the cell plasmalemma; that is, the organismic boundary generates, on its corruption, the body boundaries of numerous apoptotic bodies. In other words, according to the motto *corruptio unius generatio alterius*, plasmalemma corruption leads either to plasmalemma debris or to the generation of biomembranes of other kinds.

And now we can pause, to sum up our considerations. The relevant boundary of an organism is neither the boundary of that organism *qua* percept, nor *qua* mixture of chemicals, nor *qua* biological body bounded by biological envelopes, nor *qua* bearer of processes, but *qua* an organismically living body: the organismic boundary is the boundary of an organism *qua* organism.

So, I stipulate the following explicit intensional definition by genus and difference:

> organismic boundary of the organism $O =_{df}$ (concrete) part of O which spatially encompasses all and only the other (concrete) parts of O

The boundary here addressed is *the* boundary *of* the organism, and not *a* boundary *for* it; that is, we are speaking of the maximal boundary of the organism, i.e. the sum of all the boundaries for it (Smith and Varzi 2000). The central point in this definition is that the organismic boundary of an organism is, by definition, an organismic part of that (and only that) organism, i.e. a part inter-subordinated (inter-regulated) with the other organismic parts of that (and only that) organism.

Obviously, it must not be expected that the organismic boundary always be a spatially «simple» part: it may well be very indented, or scattered into disjoint sub-boundaries, and so on. That is, while living bodies and organisms, modelled as topological spaces, are connected,[24] organismic boundaries, modelled as topological spaces, are almost always disjoint unions.

The suggested definition squares with the following ontological positions about boundaries in general:

- that the organismic boundary is a concrete part (rather than, e.g., a lower-dimensional geometrical surface);
- that the organismic boundary is a part (only) of the organism (rather than, e.g., of both the organism and the environment);
- that the organismic boundary involves a closed/open dichotomy (rather than, e.g. a closed/closed one), i.e. that, modelled as topological spaces, the organism is closed while its environment is open (obviously, the environment is open where it faces the organismic boundary; nothing is said about possible environmental closed boundaries elsewhere);
- that both the organism and its organismic boundary are ontologically dependent upon (though chronologically coextensive with) certain interactions between bodies. That is, it is when some bodies start to interact in a certain way that an organism is generated with its organismic boundary; equally so, it is the irreversible cessation of certain interactions between the organismic parts to constitute the death of an organism and simultaneously the corruption of its organismic boundary;
- that the organismic boundary is ontologically dependent upon (though chronologically coextensive with) the organism.[25] That is, ontologically, first there is the organism; second, the organism is composed by organismic parts; third, among these parts there is the organismic boundary.

I am perfectly aware that these ontological positions are not unproblematic, but, while being ontologically no more problematic than others, they appear biologically more sound to the biologist I am.

However, my definition leaves open the question about the spatial extension of the organismic boundary, whether it is an extremely thin layer or a thicker bed of the organism; however, it is reasonable to claim that the organismic boundary have a «thickness» considerably inferior to that of the organism itself: after all, though the organismic boundary is an important part and performs important functions of the organism, it is neither the only part of the organism, nor one which performs most

---

[24] A possible exception could be given by a living body L composed of three parts ABC, placed consecutively in the sense of its length; if A and C are inter-subordinated, they will constitute an organism O, which will result – modelled as a topological space – a disjoint union; however, it would be controversial whether AC were an organismically living *body*. Smith and Varzi (1997) say that it is reasonable to assume that all *bona fide* objects are connected; in this case, the question is about which entity is the *bona fide* object: L, or O, or both?

[25] Besides, the concept of organismic boundary is logically posterior to the concept of organism; i.e., while I can define the term 'organism' without any reference to boundaries, I cannot define the term 'organismic boundary' without a reference to the organism possessing that boundary.

of the organismic functions; so, it would be biologically implausible to think of an organismic boundary constituting the most voluminous part of the organism itself.

Acknowledgements This work is supported by a grant from the John Templeton Foundation, and is part of the Research Project 'The Organism in Interdisciplinary Context' of the STOQ Project. I thank my friend and philosopher Alberto Bertini for helpful comments and incessant encouragement, Roberto Poli for having invited me to reflect more carefully upon the links between ontology and biology, and an anonymous referee for his or her valuable suggestions.

References

Ageno, M. 1986. *Le radici della biologia*. Milano: Feltrinelli.

Ageno, M. 1992^2. *Dal non vivente al vivente. Nuove ipotesi sull'origine della vita*. Palermo: Theoria.

Allen, C., M. Bekoff, and G. Lauder eds. 1998. *Nature's purposes*. Cambridge, MA; London: MIT Press.

Atlan, H. 1979. *Entre le cristal et la fumée*. Paris: Seuil.

Bertalanffy, L. von. 1968. *General system theory*. New York: Braziller.

Boniolo, G. 2003. Che cos'è il caso in biologia? Riflessioni a partire da J. Monod, Il caso e la necessità. *Roma, Atti Convegni Lincei* 185:25–44.

Boniolo, G., and M. Carrara. 2004. On biological identity. *Biology & Philosophy* 19:443–457.

Brandon, R.N. 1997. Does biology have laws? *Philosophy of Science, Proceedings* 64:S444–S457.

Bunge, M. 1977. *Treatise on basic philosophy*, vol. 3: Ontology I. Dordrecht-Boston: Reidel.

Campbell, D.T. 1974. 'Downward causation' in hierarchically organised biological systems. In *Studies in the philosophy of biology*, eds. F.J. Ayala, and T. Dobzhansky, 179–186. London: Macmillan.

Casati, R., and A. Varzi. 1999. *Parts and places*. Cambrige, MA; London: MIT Press.

Coyne, J., and H. Allen Orr. 2004. *Speciation*. Sunderland, MA: Sinauer.

Dawkins, R. 1982. *The extended phenotype*. Oxford: W. H. Freeman.

De Rossi, P. 2006. The so-called human body. In: *The organism in interdisciplinary context*, ed. P. Ramellini, 113–127. Vatican: LEV.

Diderot, D. 1769. La rêve de D'Alembert. In: 1875–1877. *Oeuvres complètes de Diderot*, ed. J. Assézat. Paris: Garnier, t. 2.

Edelman, G.M. 1988. *Topobiology*. New York: Basic Books.

Foerster, H. von. 1960. On self-organizing systems and their environments. In: *Self-organizing systems*, eds. M.C. Yovits, and S. Cameron, 31–50. London: Pergamon Press.

Foerster, H. von. 1982. *Observing systems*. Seaside: Intersystems Publications.

Ford, N. M. 1988. *When did I begin?* Cambridge: Cambridge University Press

Foucault, M. 1966. *Les mots et les choses*. Paris: Gallimard.

Fry, I. 2000. *The emergence of life on Earth*. New Brunswick, NJ: Rutgers University Press.

Ghiselin, M.T. 1974. A radical solution to the species problem. *Systematic Zoology* 23:536–544

Gil, F. 1978. Coppie filosofiche, 1050–1095. In: *Enciclopedia Einaudi*, vol. 3. Torino: Einaudi.

Haldane, J.S. 1931. *The philosophical basis of biology*. London: Hodder & Stoughton.

Hoffman, J., and G.S. Rosenkrantz. 1997. *Substance: Its nature and existence*. London: Routledge.

Hoffmeyer, J. 1998. Surfaces inside surfaces: On the origin of agency and life. *Cybernetics & Human Knowing* 5(1):33–42.

Gibson, J.J. 1950. *The perception of the visual World*. Boston, MA: Houghton-Mifflin.

Jacquette, D. 2002. *Ontology*. Chesham: Acumen Publishing.

Johnsen, S., and E.A. Widder. 1999. The physical basis of transparency in biological tissue: Ultrastructure and the minimization of light scattering. *Journal of Theoretical Biology* 199(2):181–198.

Jonas, H. 1966. *The phenomenon of life*. New York: Harper & Row.

Kauffman, S.A. 1995. *At home in the universe*. New York: Oxford University Press.
Kauffman, S.A. 2000. *Investigations*. New York: Oxford University Press.
Keller, E.F. 2001. Beyond the gene but beneath the skin. In *Cycles of contingency*, eds. S. Oyama, P.E. Griffiths, and R.D. Gray, 299–312. Cambridge, MA: MIT Press.
Laubichler, M.D., and G.P. Wagner. 2000. Organism and character decomposition: Steps towards an integrative theory of biology. *Philosophy of Science, Proceedings* 67:S289–S300.
Luisi, P.L. 2006. *The emergence of life*. Cambridge etc.: Cambridge University Press.
Mahner, M., and M. Bunge. 1997. *Foundations of biophilosophy*. Berlin-Heidelberg-New York: Springer.
Maturana, H.R., and F.J. Varela. 1980. *Autopoiesis and cognition*. Dordrecht etc.: Reidel.
Mayr, E. 1982. *The growth of biological thought*. Cambridge, MA; London: Harvard University Press.
Monod, J. 1970. *Le hasard et la nécessité*. Paris: Seuil.
Needham, J. 1936. *Order and life*. Cambridge; New Haven: Cambridge & Yale University Press.
NIH (U. S. National Institutes of Health). 2006. Stem cell information. http://stemcells.nih.gov/. Accessed 2006-09-14.
Oyama, S. 1985. *The ontogeny of information*. Cambridge: Cambridge University Press.
Piaget, J. 1967. *Biologie et connaissance*. Paris: Gallimard.
Poli, R. 2001. The basic problems of the theory of levels of reality. *Axiomathes* 12(3–4):261–283.
Portmann, A. 1965. *Aufbruch der Lebensforschung*. Zürich: Rhein.
Ramellini, P. 2001. Dai livelli di organizzazione ai livelli biologici. *Systema Naturae* 3:203–213. http://www.biologiateorica.it/systemanaturae/art2001/Ramellini.pdf
Ramellini, P. 2002. Prolegomeni alla biologia: dalla percezione alla classificazione. *Epistemologia* 25:185–198.
Ramellini, P. 2003. L'evoluzione al tempo della postgenomica (e oltre). In *La Nuova Scienza*, vol. 4: La società infobiologica, eds. U. Colombo, and G. Lanzavecchia, 81–90. Milano: Libri Scheiwiller.
Ramellini, P. 2006a. *Life and Organisms*. Vatican: LEV.
Ramellini, P. 2006b. *Il corpo vivo*. Siena: Cantagalli.
Ramellini, P. 2007. *Temi di biologia teorica*. Roma: Pontifical University 'Regina Apostolorum'.
Rashevsky, N. 1961. *Mathematical principles in biology and their applications*. Springfield, IL: Thomas.
Rizzotti, M. ed. 1996. *Defining life*. Padova: University of Padova.
Rosen, R. 2000. *Essays on life itself*. New York: Columbia University Press.
Salthe, S.N. 1993. *Development and evolution: Complexity and change in biology*. Cambridge, MA: MIT Press.
Schiller, J. 1978. *La notion d'organisation dans l'histoire de la biologie*. Paris: Maloine.
Schuh, R. 2000. *Biological systematics*. Ithaca: Cornell University Press.
Simons, P. 1987. *Parts: A study in ontology*. Oxford: Clarendon.
Smith, B. 1994. Fiat objects. In *Parts and wholes: Conceptual part-whole relations and formal mereology*, eds. N. Guarino, S. Pribbenow, and L. Vieu, 15–23. Proceedings of the ECAI94 Workshop, Amsterdam, ECCAI.
Smith, B., and A. Varzi. 1997. The formal ontology of boundaries *The Electronic Journal of Analytic Philosophy* (online publication), 5. http://ejap.louisiana.edu/EJAP/1997.spring/smithvarzi976.html
Smith, B., and A. Varzi. 2000. Fiat and Bona Fide boundaries. *Philosophy and Phenomenological Research* 60:401–420.
Smith, B., and A. Varzi. 2002. Surrounding space: On the ontology of organism-environment relations. *Theory in Biosciences* 120:139–162.
Stroll, A. 1988. *Surfaces*. Minneapolis: University of Minnesota Press.
Thagard, P. 1999. *How scientists explain disease*. Princeton, NJ: Princeton University Press.
Thom, R. 1998. Goethe e la pregnanza delle origini. In: *Goethe scienziato*, eds. G. Giorello, and A. Grieco, 253–297. Torino: Einaudi.

Varzi, A. 2004. Boundary. In: *The stanford encyclopedia of philosophy* (Spring 2004 Edition), ed. E.N. Zalta. http://plato.stanford.edu/archives/spr2004/entries/boundary.

Wilson, J.A. 1999. *Biological individuality*. Cambridge: Cambridge University Press.

Wilson, M. 2005. *Microbial inhabitants of humans*. Cambridge etc.: Cambridge University Press.

Wimsatt, W.C. 1976. Complexity and organization. In *Topics in the philosophy of biology*, eds. M. Grene, and E. Mendelsohn, 174–193. Dordrecht-Boston: Reidel.

Winkelmann, R.K. 1959. The erogenous zones: Their nerve supply and significance. *Mayo Clinic proceedings. Mayo Clinic* 34(2):39–47.

Woodger, J.H. 1929[1]. *Biological principles*. London: Routledge & Kegan (London-New York, Routledge & Kegan-Humanities Press, 1967[2]).

Woodger, J.H. 1937. *The axiomatic method in biology*. Cambridge: Cambridge University Press.

Chapter 9
The Ontology of Perception

Liliana Albertazzi

Das Eigentümliche der Gestalt sich in Verhältnissen erschöpfe
(Gelb)

9.1 On Ontological Classification

According to Aristotle's classical distinction, *Being* is one and there is no single genus of all the categories. Moreover, being is defined in diverse senses, i.e. according to the categories, potency and act, truth and falsehood, and finally according to the individual accident (Aristotle 1983).

Of these senses, the categorial classification according to genus and specific difference distinguishes ten genera which express, in regard to being:

> its essence, quantity, quality, relation, place, time, position, state, activity, passivity. For the accident and genus and property and definition of anything will always be in one of these categories (Aristotle 1960) (*Topics*, I 9, 103 b, pp. 20–25).

This categorization, which has influenced both the grammar and the conceptualization of scientific culture and the Western languages (Nisbett 2003, Albertazzi 2007), as well as the method of the natural sciences, starts from the discretization of being into types of substances (objects) and the types of accidents inherent to them, assigning most ontological weight to substances.

The taxonomic categorization, which is broadly satisfactory for various domains of reality, from zoology to botany, is best expressed when a morphological criterion of classification is adopted. It reveals its limitations in critical cases like the duck-billed platypus (Eco 1997) and, in general, if a genetic criterion for the classification of form is adopted, or in cases like colour, whose phenomenal nature – i.e. its nature as a *quality* of visual matter, its visibility – is still unknown. We have in

L. Albertazzi (✉)
Cimec (Centre for Mind and Brain), and Department of Cognitive Sciences and Education, University of Trento at Rovereto, Rovereto, Italy
e-mail: liliana.albertazzi@unitn.it

R. Poli, J. Seibt (eds.), *Theory and Applications of Ontology: Philosophical Perspectives*, DOI 10.1007/978-90-481-8845-1_9,

fact an advanced colorimetric science (chemistry of pigments), a physics of colours (wavelengths) and a psychophysics of colour (from retinal stimulation to neuronal processing), but we do not yet have a science of colour as a *paradigmatic quality* of the objects of vision. The various hypotheses on the origin of colour put forward, for instance, in the eighteenth and nineteenth centuries, by Runge (1910), Ostwald (1917) and Goethe (1970) have lapsed into oblivion, being often classified as 'metaphysical abstrusenesses', in that they are incompatible with the Newtonian, physicalist, version of the science of colour. How can one speak of simple coloured objects (or of substances with specific inherent qualities) in the visual field, therefore, if the nature itself of *coloured quality* is still unknown from a phenomenal point of view and introduces substantial difficulties of categorization from the linguistic point of view (Berlin and Kay 1969, Rosch 1978, Kay et al. 1997, Davidoff et al. 1999, Roberson et al. 2005, Wierbicka 2006, Da Pos and Albertazzi 2010)? Furthermore, quality and form are inseparable aspects in regard to phenomenal perception (Brentano 1995b).

Classical physics, which has been and still is the dominant epistemological paradigm for large part of the natural sciences, is in fact a science of stimuli whose ontological existence is certainly *highly probable*, given the repeated verifiability of their relational connection with the corresponding percepts, but of which we do not have direct evidence – as argued both theoretically (by immanentist realism) and experimentally (by *Gestaltpsychologie* and kindred schools). Some of the best researchers in the field (Stevens 1986, Mausfeld 2002) are fully aware that the true problems of classical psychophysics are, in fact, (i) the unknown nature of the stimuli, and (ii) one-directional consideration of the causal nexus in assimilation of the stimulus to the percept.

Not only the qualities, but the concept itself of perceptive object (Meinong 1960) becomes highly problematic if one leaves the level of analysis of classical Newtonian physics and science of the brain (both pertinent to the material level of reality) (Poli 2001) to analyse that type of immediate reality, endowed with a high degree of certainty and pregnancy, which is phenomenal perception of the 'here and now' of the actual presentation. At this level, in fact, strictly speaking there only exist dynamic perceptive space-time structures (*acts*) endowed with *phenomenal correlates*; or, as Brentano argued, specifically a '*seeing* something red', a '*hearing* a loud noise', a '*touching* something smooth or rough', a '*smelling* something pleasant or unpleasant' (Brentano 1995a, pp. 78–80). The construction of *coloured objects*, rough surfaces or fruity perfumes is a more tardy and more complex construction of the mind's representational structures. It involves, for example, decomposition of the actual percept, which is instead an indivisible psychic phenomenon, into:

1. a perceiver
2. an object
3. qualities inherent to the latter (Brentano 1995b, pp. 13–15).

In other words, the classical taxonomic classification into objects and their qualities is to be considered a product of higher-order representational processes. It is certainly supported by certain structures of particular levels of reality, and by dominant and efficacious cultural and epistemological paradigms, but it is not always applicable to the immediate phenomenal reality. One wonders whether for Aristotle, who did not have Newton as a reference, also his taxonomic categorization did not have well-defined limits; and in fact, in his biological works such as *On the Parts of Animals* or in *Metaphysics*, the predominant categorization is of a different type, being by part/whole or potency/act (Aristotle 1972, 1977). In other words, Aristotle was well aware of the existence of different types, if not categories, of *transcategorial principles* concerning different aspects of reality.

What, therefore, happens to the features of the 'objects' of the ontological classification, even before their being identified as such, in the immediate construction of reality, or in the morphogenesis of actual perception? Are these the same items, and are they subject to the same principles of organization? In other words, do they have the same causes and do they arise in the same space-time of classical physics? And, above all, is the *visual corporality* of phenomenal appearances in the visual field really reducible to the matter and substance of physics? (Aristotle 1977, 10121a30, Brentano 1995b, p. 24, Metzger 1954a, 1975, Albertazzi 1998, pp. 261–310, 2002b, pp. 29–79, 2006a, pp. 3–34).

The instruments that I shall adopt to analyse this level of reality – the first, immediate and ecologically crucial one for our survival, as well the most meaningful – are:

1. An ontological theory of levels vs. a theory of categories as linguistic descriptions (Hartmann 1935, Poli 2001).
2. An inner vs. an external psychophysics, i.e. the analysis of what is 'just qualitatively perceivable' (*jpd*) instead of what is 'just noticeable difference' (*jnd*, the representative unit of classic psychophysics) (Brentano 1995a, 1988).
3. The Gestalt mereology, from whole to parts determination (Brentano 1995b, Wertheimer 1923, Metzger 1941).

My analysis will be almost entirely restricted to examples concerning visual objects, even if the argument can be transposed and documented for the other perceptive modalities as well. Moreover, I shall concentrate on the level of *presentative acts*, because these are basic acts, and also because they are mostly forgotten by the analyses – whether ontological or psychological – conducted on this level of reality. The focus, in fact, is usually on representations, judgements and emotional phenomena, which, moreover, are usually considered on a par with states of affairs, i.e. analysed according to their content.

It is understandably difficult to delineate an ontology of acts, because they do not appear to us objectively and they are not given to us as objects unless modified in reflection and memory once their presence is no longer actual, with all the 'objectual' modifications that the situation brings about. Sometimes they are not even experienced immediately and are unconscious. This does not exempt one, however, from finding the means to give them an ontology. Here, before passing to analysis of the base level, I recall that different types of acts (presentations, representations, judgements and emotions) have different objectual relations (Brentano

1995a, Husserl 1970, Fifth Logical Investigation) and that a first classification of their nature concerns egological and non-egological acts (Stein 1962). Egological acts are ones like feeling cold, warm, etc. (sensorial) or feeling bored, excited, relaxed, etc. (moods). Non-egological acts are ones like seeing, touching, hearing, imagining, reasoning, etc. (primary/secondary).

My analysis will therefore focus mainly on *non-egological acts* like seeing.

9.2 The Field of Visual Objects

By 'field of visual objects' is usually meant the field of optics: that is, the physics of wavelengths, the reflectance of light from surfaces, the metric properties of items, and so on (Albertazzi 2006a). As Gelb already noted in the 1930s, however:

> Our visual world is not built up through the operations of accessory, higher order processes imposed on an original raw material, but is constituted, rather, by the internal structural form of our visual world (Gelb 1938).

The problem is explaining what constitutes an *inner structural form* of our visual world, i.e. the primitives, the material and laws of organization of what, from Aristotle to the Gestaltists, has been called a naïve physics (Aristotle 1980, Lipmann 1923).

The first step in this direction is, *heuristically*, to bracket off classical physics and its conceptual framework and consider the subject matter of our inquiry to be *visual appearances* and their *visual quality* as such (Hering 1964), their structures, their types, etc.

Such analysis, as I shall seek to show, pertains to a theory of 'matter' as a qualitative and relational structure of the level of ontological reality of psychic acts and their inner correlates (Brentano 1981, 1988, Husserl 1991).

My analysis, therefore, as Albers would put it, does not begin with optics and the physiology of visual perception, nor with any presentation of the physics of light and wavelength (Albers 1963), because the essential task of representation seems to be given by connectedness in meaning, rather than the mechanical logic of geometrical optics (Kepes 1944).

Adoption of this point of view obviously has some consequences. For example, it enables one to avoid certain errors common in both the methodology and the epistemological assumptions of natural sciences, viz:

1. The hypostasis of classical physics as the *primary, unique and veridical* level of reality.
2. The adoption of a naïve realismus, which in its turn entails *two canonical types of error*: i.e., the so-called stimulus error, and the experience error (Boring 921, Kanizsa 1980, Chap. 5).

The *stimulus error* consists in substituting the list of the characteristics of the stimulus for the description of direct experience: in other words, what one 'knows' instead of what one 'sees' (Schumann 1904, Matthaei 1929). Consider, for example, the phenomena of transparency analysed by Metelli, where one has, *physically*, four juxtaposed opaque regions, i.e. two larger rectangles, green and red, and two superimposed smaller yellow rectangles. *Perceptively*, what one sees, however, is a transparent rectangle over two others, with the emergent property of a yellowish light spreading on the whole appearances, i.e. items which do not exist at the level of stimuli (Metelli 1941, 1967).

The *experience error*, instead, consists in attributing the characteristics of distal experience to the proximal stimulus (i.e. in the visual field, the retina) (Koffka 1935, p. 98). For example, again, in the case of the Necker cube, *physically*, we have some intersecting lines, while *perceptively* we see a 3D cube.

Briefly, there is a major difference of ontological status and qualities between physical and perceptual objects. Moreover, there are aspects which optics is entirely unable to consider, viz. the fact that:

> The things as perceived possess a *surplus* of properties which are not simply coloured surfaces and which cannot be obtained by association or inferences from other sensory properties. In fact, one directly sees tenacity, brittleness, obdurateness, bluntness and many other attributes for which we lack linguistic descriptions (Schapp 1909, emphasis mine).

This *surplus* has ecological importance for the survival of human beings, and requires a theory of its own.

Given these premises on the nature of our visual world, I shall divide my contribution into three parts:

1. Part I, on the concept of the '*real*'.
2. Part II, a short intermezzo on the concept of '*visual thing*'.
3. Part III, on the concept of '*quality*' of a visual thing.

9.2.1 Part I: The Concept of Real

Once physics has been heuristically bracketed off, the first question that arises is this: to which type of reality are we referring?

Brentano, Hartmann and Metzger marked out the boundaries of this ontological level of reality by characterizing it (i) in psychophysics as *internally bounded* (in effect an essential part of Fechner's programme, which he desired to complete but was unable), (ii) the *ontic level* (for Hartmann, an unanalysable and irrational residue of metaphysics) and (iii) the phenomenal reality of visual, acoustic, tactile, intermodal and even synaesthetic appearances.

Unlike Hartmann, who produced the best ontological and non-reductionist theory of the levels of reality in philosophy (Hartmann 1935: for a development see Poli 1998, 2001, 2002, 2006a, b, 2007 and Chapter 1, this volume; Poli and Gnoli 2004, Poli and Obrst, TAO 2), and following the canons of a psychology both descriptive (Brentano 1995b) and experimental (*Gestaltpsychologie*), my thesis here, and which I have argued elsewhere (Albertazzi 2002a, b, 2005, 2006a, b, c, 2007), is that it is entirely possible to analyse this ontological level of reality both theoretically and experimentally (Albertazzi 2003, 2002a, b, 2005, 2006a, b, c, 2007).

From a general point of view, the ontological level of phenomenal reality pertains to the *structure of the presentation* (*Vorstellung*) and comprises all the types of phenomenal appearance. *Presentation* concerns the *actual phenomenal perception*, i.e. the ongoing and deploying *acts* of perception, their structure, and their correlates. Neurophysiological aspects are not relevant to this kind of inquiry, which concerns itself only with the *modes of appearance* of perceptive objects (on this see Spillmann and Ehrenstein 2003). The fact that the 'objects' of the phenomenal field are appearances and cannot be reduced to the physical level of reality is particularly evident if one analyses their dynamic onset in the time of presentness. What one *sees*, in fact, are not so much well-defined objects with a definite outline but *unfolding patterns*, with environmental qualitative salient aspects, ruled by internal constraints given by spatio-temporal duration. In these situations, not even movement has the characteristics of physical motion, but rather that of qualitative change (Husserl 1996, Albertazzi 1999, Rensink 2002). In particular, the microgenesis of the objects of vision highlights the intrinsic connection between movement and colour in visual space (Albertazzi 2006c). As specifically regards colour, experiments from Benussi (1925) to Katz (1935) to Hoffman (2003) show that:

1. Colour appearance does not pertain to the physical nature of objects.
2. Colour is a non–independent part of a phenomenal whole (not an autonomous attribute).
3. Colour plays different roles in different presentational primitives.
4. Colour exists *in the way it appears* (Katz 1935, Kanizsa 1960, Sivik 1997, Mausfeld 2003), i.e. it has an essentially qualitative nature (see Albertazzi 2007).
5. Colour, consequently, is not a natural kind.

A presentation corresponds to the kind of information flow that takes place in a very short time, around 700 ms (the so-called specious present). The information which occurs in the spatio-temporal structure of the presentation consists in a correlation between the state of the environment and a modification of the subjective and cognitive system state, resulting in what Koffka called 'manifest' or 'non-silent organization' (Koffka 1935). From this point of view, this primary information partially corresponds to Gibson's notion of affordance. However, attention should be paid to:

1. The specific nature of the *space* and *time* which rule the information flow, and which do not correspond to physical space-time (Albertazzi 2002a, b).
2. The nature and the behaviour of the *subjective* components (the original Gestalt theory on the *Afforderungscharakter* of the tertiary qualities implied also a specific analysis of subjective processing, *Spannung*, for example See Metzger 1941, Chapter 2, and below).

There was an important body of theoretical and experimental literature on the nature on phenomenal appearances in perceptive fields at the beginning of the last century. However this literature is now almost forgotten, for several reasons, ranging from the difficulty of the texts to their neglect because they do not comply with the dominant paradigms in the natural sciences, specifically classical psychophysics, which today is largely computational (Brentano 1988, Husserl 1991, Meinong 1899, Albertazzi 2001, 2005, 2006a, Stern 1897, Lindemann 1922, Wertheimer 1923, Kopferman 1930, Sander 1930, Metzger 1930, Michotte 1963, Werner and Wapner 1952). Of course, also psychologists bear some of the responsibility for this situation.

More recent experimental studies have addressed the problem from specific points of view, and not always in the awareness that they are operating on the edges of an alternative scientific paradigm, the exception being Kanizsa, who was well aware of the presuppositions of his experimentation (Kanizsa 1991, Kubovy et al., 2002, Li and Gilchrist 1999, Rensink 2000. On this see Albertazzi 2002a, b, c, 2006a). Some examples of these non-standard approaches, which have yielded interesting results, are:

1. The difference between 'actual change' and 'perceived motion' (Rensink 2002).
2. The difference between 'continuous spatio-temporal structure' and 'object', which may also be influenced by the type of display (i.e. presentation of a few static displays (Freyd and Finke 1984) versus presentation of a continuous motion (Hubbard and Barucha 1988, Verfaille and d'Ydewalle 1991)).
3. The role of the perceptual belongingness of field components (Benary 1930), for example how the configuration of motion in the visual field influences the location of both stationary and moving stimuli (Whitney and Canavagh 2000).
4. The difference in magnitude among the moving elements used in experiments, which influences the velocity perceived (Runeson 1974, Bozzi and Bressan 1987).
5. The presence of colour, which influences the perception of motion (Nijhawan 1994, 1997).
6. The differing speeds of the elements (Müsseler and Ascherleben 1998).
7. The presence or otherwise of reference grids (as in the original Frölich effect, where it alters the data through the occlusion effect that it produces (Kammer et al. 1999)).
8. The structural difference among phenomena like the flash-lag effect (displacement between spatio-temporally aligned flashing and moving stimuli (Freyd 1987, Haber and Haber 1988, Hubbard 1999, 2004, Hubbard and Motes 2002, Khurana, Watanabe, and Nijhawan 2000, Intraub 2002), or the Frölich effect (a fast-moving line entering a window) (Frölich 1923).
9. The differing cognitive processes involved (early mechanism vs. memory or higher-order processes).
10. The different role and effect of attention (attention shift).
11. The connection among the physical motion of an object, the perceived motion, the motion of other objects in the field, and its perceived spatial location (Krekelberg and Lappe 1999, Khurana, Watanabe, and Nijhawan 2000, Whitney 2002).
12. The specific spatio-temporal structure involved in these types of events, which displays aspects of anticipation (for instance in the direction of the perceived motion).

13. The nature of the space and time involved at the phenomenal level (Koffka 1930, Albertazzi 2002a) both because of the influence that the *temporal coding* of a moving object has on the perceived position of an object, and which gives rise to a time delay in a spatial visualization (the explanation usually given for the flash-lag effect), and because of the importance that may be assumed by *where* the object is perceived, independently of the temporal mechanism (Whitney's (2002) explanation for the flag-lag effect. For more information see Albertazzi 2006a).

Generally speaking, phenomenal appearances as correlates of actual perceptions are immediately given in 3D, in an anisotropic subjective space and in a subjective duration. The aspects of these appearances show the existence of a specific causal law and a specific principle of identification. The complexity of the theory, analysable philosophically in Husserlian terms of inner consciousness of time and passive synthesis of experience (Husserl 1996, 1991), can be summarized with the following example from Metzger, revised by Massironi (Massironi and Bonaiuto 1966, Massironi 2002, p. 207) (Fig. 9.1).

We are able to describe these visual presentations in terms of 'a diamond that deforms a texture' and of 'a rectangle that deforms a different texture' because we are able to reconstruct, in the actual presentation, what Leyton has called the 'history of shape', or the form states preceding the current shape (Leyton 1992). We are also able to do so because of the intrinsically dynamic structure of the act of actual presentation, which is able to retain past phases and to anticipate future ones (Husserl 1991, Leyton 1992). These simple visual appearances, moreover, present with clarity what Schapp has called a qualitative surplus, i.e. the 'sharpness' of the diamond and the 'heaviness' of the rectangle, which are experienced in the former case as a pointed instrument and in the latter as a brick (on these aspects see below).

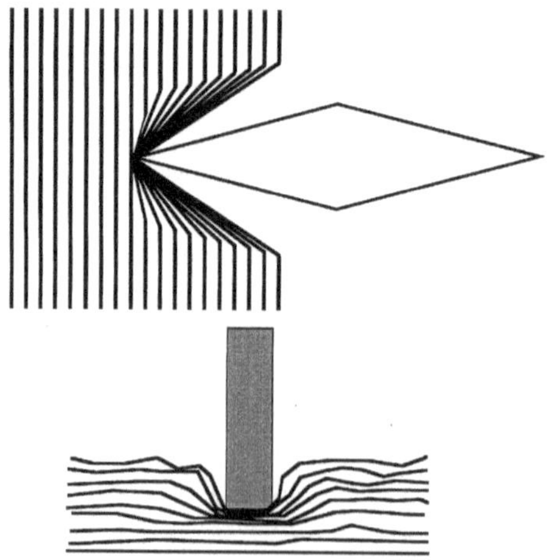

Fig. 9.1 Two presentations of causal relationships: a texture 'deformed' by a diamond and a texture 'deformed' by a rectangle (Massironi 2002, 207)

Over the centuries, the medium that has been best able to ‘give shape to’ and to represent the laws of organization of this level of reality has been art – pictorial art in particular – because of the similarity of the spaces involved and the fact that the ontological level of reference of pictorial representation is not the level of the physics but that of qualitative perception (Albertazzi 2006a, b).

By adding further complexity to analysis of visual space, pictorial space exhibits a further commitment by the perceiver to the construction of the objects of vision. Pictorial space has properties similar to those of optical space: boundaries, depth, colour, brightness, distance, and so on, which are only actualized or imagined (‘looked in’) by the perceiver (Wollheim 1970, Koenderink and van Doorn 2002, 2003), in that it has no physical support except the medium of the pictorial representation (Arnheim 1954). Considered from this point of view, an object of pictorial representation manifests diverse ontological levels, as the analyses by Hartmann and Ingarden have shown (Hartmann 1950, Ingarden 1962, 1968). Hartmann, for example, distinguishes two layers in the aesthetic object: the *foreground* layer, which comprises the physical dimensions of the object, and the *background* layer, which is the layer of the *content* embedded in the foreground layer. This background layer, however, exists only in relation to the observer who grasps the content. Ontologically speaking, therefore, the aesthetic object has two layers, and the foreground layer imposes constraints on the background layer. The background layer, however, according to the overall structure of its content, has many layers within it, depending on the type of object, for example whether this is a literary work or a painting (Hartmann 1950, on this see Albertazzi 2006a, b).

In the pictorial field, Op Art has been particularly adapt at representing the presentative structures of visual reality. Consider, in relation to Massironi’s example, Ryley’s *Untitled Fragment*.

That the perceptive qualities are not identifiable with those of physics is evident from a large series of examples. Consider, for example, the phenomena of chromatic assimilation described by Fuchs (1923) and Bezold (1874), where given a grid of intercalated red and black stripes, and a grid of red and white stripes, the red perceived is very different (see also Albers 1963, xx).

At perceptive level, the identity of a particular colour’s wavelength, in certain contexts, strictly speaking ‘no longer exists’ because the stimuli have assumed the perceptive behaviour of a non-independent part in the general context of the phenomenal appearance as a whole (Wertheimer 1923, Husserl 1970, Third Logical Investigation).

Once classical physics has been bracketed off, and analysis of phenomenal reality proper has begun, other consequences concerning its inner complexity ensue.

The phenomenal level of reality has inner layers which as a first approximation are distinguishable between:

1. layer of *perceptive presence*;
2. layer of *mental presence* (Kanizsa 1991, Chap. 1);

   both of which characterize, in different ways, the structures of the presentation.

The layer of *perceptive presence* has the quality of being encountered, of being experienced as absolutely present, before us, within immediate reach. Moreover, it comprises visual, acoustic, tactile, intermodal, synaesthetic phenomena, but also phenomena like amodal presence, hallucinations, assimilations, pictorial images, and even dreams and virtual reality (Benussi 1922–1923, Musatti 1964, Metzger 1941, Kanizsa 1991, Albertazzi 2003).

A paradigmatic example of the complexity of perceptive presence is provided by stereokinetic phenomena, which are localisable in subjective space, and dynamically unfold in actual presentation from 2 to 3D (Benussi 1925, Musatti 1924, 1928, 1953, 1955, 1964, Chap. 1, Wallach, O'Connell 1953, Ullman 1984, Zanforlin 1998a, b, 2000, 2003, Profitt et al., 1992, Tarr and Kriegman 2001, Albertazzi 2004).

Particularly expressive are those stereokinetic phenomena that also exhibit the emergent property of transparency, as in the examples provided by Metzger (1941) and Albertazzi (2004b).

The layer of *mental presence* vice versa comprises the domain of thought, or memories, unconscious mnestic traces, hypotheses, fictions, inferences, deductions, planning, etc., which is the domain of the unencountered, of what is not experienced as immediately present in actual perception. A good pictorial representation of this type of structure is Bosch's *Paradise*.

Kanizsa largely devoted himself to the analysis and differentiation of the two different presentative layers, his purpose being to prevent improper completions from being surreptitiously introduced top-downwards into the analysis of perceptive phenomena. Obviously, in conditions of natural perception, as information is being processed, the distinctive aspects of the two layers are usually co-present; but the problem is maintaining their characteristics distinct at the level of experimental analysis, and not drawing unwarranted conclusions which induce the errors mentioned above.

A classic case study of the difference between the two inner layers of presentation – which are often confused even in the experimental literature – is furnished by the relationship between a triangle given in all sensorial modalities (no. 1) and an amodal triangle (no. 2) (Fig. 9.2).

According to the structural laws of phenomenal presentation, *both* triangles are *given in perceptive presence*, i.e. the amodal triangle is not thought: that is to say,

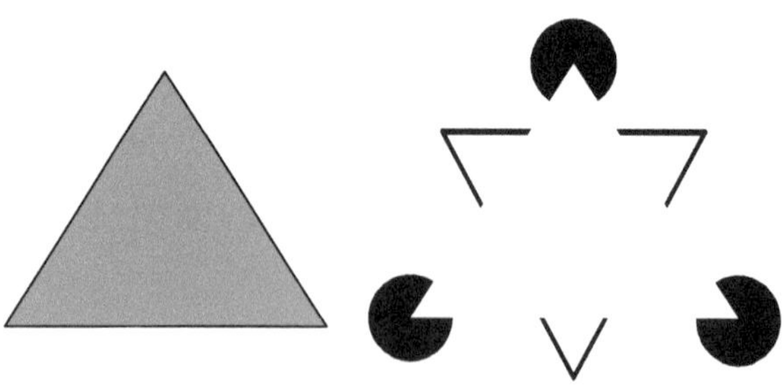

Fig. 9.2 Triangles given modally (part 1) and amodally (part 2)

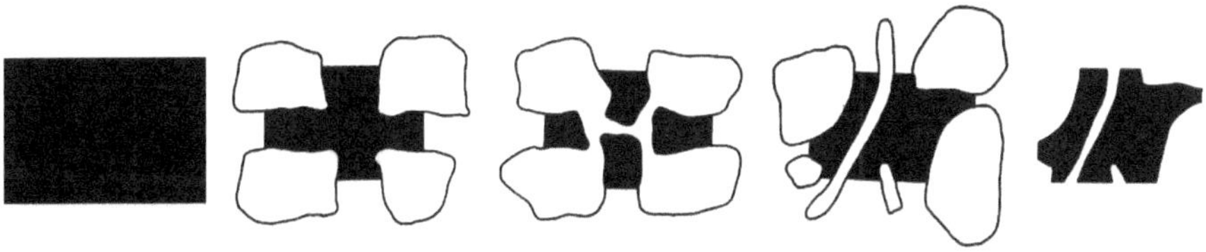

Fig. 9.3 Occlusion effect and shape completion. The occluded shape (rectangle, part 1) is still perceived (by completion) regardless of the number, size and connection of occluding shapes (parts 2–4). However, note that if the missing pieces cannot be attributed to occluding shapes (part 5), the completion effect does not occur: while the black pieces in parts 4 and 5 coincide, the perceived result is a completed rectangle only in the former case (Kanizsa 1991)

it is not given in mental presence (Kanizsa 1991, Purghè and Coren 1992). In other words, phenomenal analysis greatly reduces the ontological weight of stimuli.

There are *degrees of presence* between perceptive presence and mental presence: consider, for example, the following phenomenal appearances in regard to a rectangle and certain forms of its occlusion (Fig. 9.3).

Only in the last figure does the rectangle no longer exist perceptually and can only be thought; whilst conversely in the previous appearances it is given in perceptive presence, despite the progressively broader occlusions.

There remains the problem of continuity between the two layers; a problem which Kanizsa left unsolved, and which Benussi sought to deal with by analysing the *phases* of presentation (Kanizsa 1952, 1991, Benussi 1913. On this see Albertazzi 2001, 2003). The problem of analysis of the presence or otherwise of phases in presentation is, I believe, one of the main shortcomings of contemporary psychology. It is so for various reasons, but principally because, in the time of the actual presentation, the *processing of information consists in the assimilation and transformation of stimuli* also through forms of subjective completion.

Shannon and Weaver's classic theory of information (Shannon and Weaver 1998) does not refer to this type of complexity and in effect has no intention to do so (Albertazzi et al., eds., forthcoming; ibid., Albertazzi forthcoming). Analysis of this aspect of reality, in fact, must necessarily draw on a theory of subjective time and space and of a filling-in of an essentially qualitative nature: that is, a theory of qualities and relations which falls entirely outside the classic framework of the mathematical information.

Apart from some isolated lines of inquiry (Pöppel 1994, Libet 1982, Rosenthal 2004, Hubbard and Barucha 1988, Rensink 2000, Vicario 2005, Albertazzi 1999, 2002b, 2006a), such analysis does not seem to be a concern of current research, which is performed almost uniformly by *levels of representation*, and almost always ones of highly abstract representation, as in the case of analysis by simulation on the basis of cognitive models. In this case, too, a whole body of philosophical and experimental literature on these fundamental aspects of reality has been lost (Stern 1897, Husserl 1996, Benussi 1913, Lindemann 1922, Sander 1930, Werner and Wapner 1952, Jaensch 1909). On the concept of representation see Albertazzi 2001, 2006a, pp. 14–17.

Once again, pictorial space is one of the few representative media able to render the complexity of the structure of the time of presence, while also evincing the surplus of qualities that from time to time may be present: for instance, the properties of 'fleeting event' (Meinong 1899), of 'slow permanence', or even of ecstatic anticipation of the future (Heidegger 1953). Consider in this regard, respectively, Balla, *Dog on a Leash*, Seurat, *Afternoon on the Ile de la Grande Jatte* and Caspar Friederich, *Woman on the Shore of Rugen*.

At the beginning of the twentieth century much progress had already been achieved in analysis of qualitative salience in the temporal apprehension of acoustic intervals, temporal inversions in information processing at the qualitative level, and the inner division of the duration of the time of presence: experimental analysis that drew on Husserl's theory of inner time (Benussi 1913, Husserl 1961, Vicario 2005). The aim of these analyses was to construct a *science of consciousness on experimental bases* and grounded on a theory of the perceptive continua and on a qualitative physics (Albertazzi 2005, Chap. 7).

Metzger distinguished among diverse characteristics within the ontological level of phenomenal reality. For example, he distinguished among:

1. Presented reality and represented reality.
2. Reality given as present and reality given as presently absent.
3. Phenomenally real reality and phenomenally apparent reality.

The first distinction concerns the difference between currently *presented reality* and *represented reality*.

Consider the sporting event of a regatta, which takes place during a certain period of physical time, and which is followed 'live' with a subjective experiencing that varies its 'velocity' and 'duration' in relation to the spectator's attention, interest and emotional involvement. Then consider the event's representation on a television screen and the further graphic representation furnished by the physical coordinates of the relative distances among the boats as the regatta proceeds and in relation to the finishing line. Then consider a further form of representation of the event in a static photographic image in an instantaneous time and physical space.

Science and language thus represent the event in a quantitatively parametrized mode, but these are not exact descriptions of the presentative level of the event, nor of its unfolding and its visibility according to laws of anticipation, retention and subjective salience in the flow of consciousness. They are *representations* of it which involve structural changes in the lived experience. Besides language and mathematical formulas, other forms of representation of presentative events are sketches, caricatures, logos, graphs, television, radio, networks (for example, neural networks), etc.

A second difference within the level of phenomenal reality is given by the *present reality in its fullness*, and by the reality that is equally given but present in the form of a lack, of a void, or of an absence (Albertazzi 2000a, 2000b, Pinna and Albertazzi 2010).

Examples of this difference are almost structural at presentative level because of the organization of appearances into figure/ground, so that in the visual field there is always a 'double presentation' (Rubin 1958). Other striking examples are provided by the phenomena of occlusions, film colour, or the determinateness vs. indeterminateness of colours, or the volume of a half full and half empty glass. In regard to the figure/ground principle in particular, the science of vision has identified its fundamental components in inclusion, orientation, contrast, symmetry, convexity, and parallelism. The complexity of pictorial space in its turn reveals still further aspects, which concern the above-mentioned connectedness in meaning. The difference between reality given in all its phenomenal fullness and reality given phenomenally with the properties of absence is striking in examples like Rodin's *The Kiss* or, even more so, Michelangelo's *Slaves*. But, one may ask, *what* matter is foregrounded? The pictorial *matter* of the phenomenal level of reality must in this case resort at least to the four Aristotelian causes to explain the embedding of matter and form in sculptures that develop out of a physical material (marble in this case) and have a phenomenal visibility but, if the boundaries of the shape are not well defined, introduce a qualitative surplus of non-separateness in the forms and materials involved, each of which relates to the other (Aristotle 1980, Wertheimer 1922, Rubin 1958).

Other examples of this difference between presence/absence in phenomenal reality are provided by calligraphy in Lao Tse, whose organization takes account of empty spaces as well, and whose structural appearance is also given by components such as the texture, heaviness, roughness/softness of the sign. These appearances also inform us about the nature of 'velocity' in perceptive continua, which is given by transformation or qualitative change of the form (Brentano 1998, Albertazzi 2002b).

A further difference within the phenomenal level of reality is that between forms of reality that present themselves as *phenomenally real* and forms that present themselves as *phenomenally apparent*.

In the latter case, they have a lower degree of phenomenal reality. Examples are mirror images (Bertamini et al. 2003, 2004), after-images, and eidetic images (Metzger 1941, Chap. 1, Vicario 2005). A complex and paradigmatic example of this difference is provided by amodal shadows, such as those produced on the basis of anomalous contours in an unfolding stereokinetic truncated cone (Fig. 9.4).

In this case, one has the perceptive presence of the cone in fullness and the less real presence of the not well-defined, localized shadows that develop on the amodal conours. Another example of the difference between phenomenally real and phenomenally apparent is provided by the visibility of the continuity in the stroboscopic movement which, although perceived as continuous, presents itself as *qualitatively less real* than other non-apparent visual movements (Musatti 1924, pp. 105–120, Albertazzi 2004). A further example is the hollow mask. Currently, studies on this phenomenon are conducted in the neurosciences, and they concern the time taken to learn the configuration or where it is processed at neuronal level (Kovàcs 2000, Kroliczak et al. 2006). From the point of view of the phenomenal level of reality, however, at issue is incongruence between different sensory modalities (sight-touch) in the perception of the mask. In the case of the inverted mask, as well as in that of reverse perspective barbed wire, there is a discrepancy between physical and

Fig. 9.4 Stereokinetic phenomenon: A truncated cone on whose black base the *white dashes* float, and some sort of *shadow* which obscures stretches of the *white lines*. If the *smaller circle* is in front, the *shadows*, rather than appearing distinct for both *circles*, merge together, and in their rotating motion appear as *shadows* covering not only the base but also the mantle of the cone. In this case, the shape of the truncated cone is distorted so that it looks like a skull-cap or the segment of a sphere, across which these shadows slide (Musatti 1955)

perceived motion, i.e. the perceived movement of some objects under a change of perspective does not correspond to their physical 3D displacement, which appears to be in the opposite direction.

To sum up this first part of my contribution, thus far I have analysed the phenomenal level of reality and its layers (aspects, degrees of presence, absence and expressivity, and degrees of reality). I would stress that these matters concern the *coherence of the structure* and not the *veridicality* of the objects. The question of veridicality, in fact, is meaningful if the primary level of reference is the physical level; but most visual objects are objects operating on the presentational structures of vision, or as field objects, i.e. they have another primary level of reference, the phenomenal level of appearances. They are, indeed, as Brentano maintained, intentional objects (Brentano 1995a. See also Koenderink and van Doorn 2003).

9.2.2 Part II. Intermezzo

Once classical physics has been bracketed off, *what is to replace the object*?

In fact, we are no longer dealing with the objects of physics, but with the 'visual things' of phenomenal appearances. Kanizsa not by chance was wont to call himself a 'thingologist'! Included among visible things are phenomenal appearances, pictorial images, and the various forms of virtual reality. Visual things, moreover, can be, and usually are, analysed in two ways as:

1. *Percepts* already given and stabilized in their configurations.
2. *Processes* (and sub-processes), as in Wertheimer's definition of Gestalt:

> There are wholes, the behaviour of which is not determined by that of their individual elements, but where the part-processes are themselves determined by the *intrinsic nature* of the whole. It is the hope of Gestalt theory to determine the nature of such wholes (Wertheimer 1923, p. 3, Albertazzi 2006b).

That this aspect is fundamental for the analysis of visual things has been demonstrated by Metzger's experiments on the morphogenesis of their appearances, i.e. how a primitive situation of homogeneous *Ganzfeld* leads to the appearance of discontinuities and finally of visual things, according to the laws of organization of visual perception (Metzger 1934, Wertheimer 1938, 2002a, 2002b, p. 14, Brunswik 1934, Albertazzi 2006, Li and Gilchrist 1999).

Given that, strictly speaking, there are no static objects of vision (not even from a merely physiological point of view), I prefer to talk of them in terms of *events*, in order to underline their intrinsic dynamic character, and to avoid the linguistic opposition between percept and process which obviously has methodological consequences as well. I therefore distinguish, following Metzger, visual things into:

1. Stationary events (relative to the perception of stationary things).
2. Non-stationary events (relative to the perception of movement or change).
3. Quasi-stationary events (relative to variable stimulation in space).
4. Quasi-continuous events (relative to islands of stability in an event perceived overall in evolution in phases) (Metzger 1941, Musatti 1928, Albertazzi 1998, 2004, Vicario 2005).

Stationary events are, for example, a line which persists unchanged, or more commonly tables, chairs, buildings, statues, etc., what Aristotle called *sensibles per accidens* (Aristotle 1986, Albertazzi 2005, Chap. 2).

Non stationary events are a line which elongates or is misshapen, a surface which changes colour, the forms of pictorial perception and also multistable figures (Fig. 9.5).

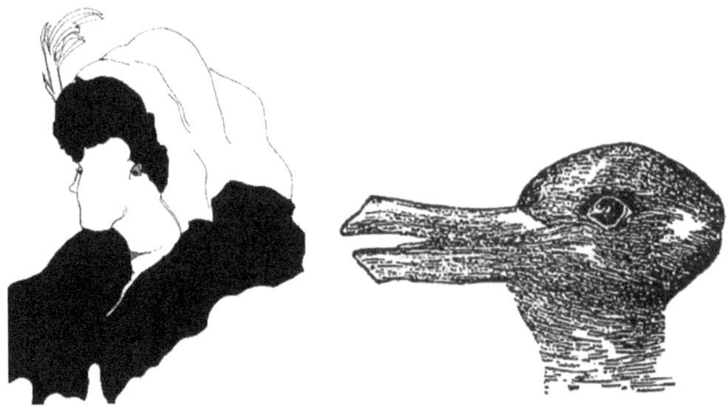

Fig. 9.5 Semantic multistable figures: the young and the old women (Hill), and the duck-rabbit (Jastrow)

They also concern the perception of movement or qualitative change (*alteratio*) (Aristotle 1980, Struber and Stadler 1999, Kress and van Leeuwen 1996).

Quasi-stationary events are events of stable patterns with island of change, for example the sea, flames, clouds, gush, vortex and, from the acoustic point of view, buzz.

Quasi-continuous events are, vice versa, visual things which present an evolving pattern with islands of stability, like fireworks. In acoustics, an analogous event is, for example, an ascending and descending musical scale which, however, maintains the distinction of individual notes at a certain pitch.

What are the qualities of these events? Are they the same for every type of event? Can they be classified in terms of viewpoint invariant features, to use an expression from the computational theory of vision (Marr 1982)?

9.2.3 Part III: The Qualities of Events

The third part of my contribution analyses the qualities of visual things or events from both (i) a general and (ii) specific point of view.

From a general point of view, one must distinguish between *properties* of the event as such (*Eigenschaften*), or the 'what' of visual appearance, and *qualities* of the visual material (*Qualitäten*) of the event, or the 'how' of visual appearance.

There then exist specific characteristics, difficult to define, which do not properly pertain to the distinction between properties of the thing and qualities of the mode of some thing's appearance: for example, qualities such as the shimmer of perceived brightness (Metzger 1930, Hochberg et al. 1951, Gibson and Waddell 1952).

A property of the first type is, for example, a *violet* parasol or a *red* apple. A quality of the second type is *crepe*, which is a characteristic of the texture of the event's material and can be present as the mode of self-manifestation of taxonomically very distant events, such as a person's hair (consider Rembrandt's *Violante*) or the sea under certain breeze conditions. An analogue of this quality from the acoustic point of view is a ripple of noise, and laughter (which may assume a very different auditory texture if it is the laughter of a child or the laughter of an adult) or a murmur, or the rustling of foliage (Metzger 1966, 733 ff, Gibson 1950).

That this aspect of visual things is important from the point of view of information has also been stressed by the ecological theory of vision. Gibson argues that the texture of vegetation, for example, cannot be graded from fine to coarse, and that the units of texture are nested with one another at different levels. He then maintains that they 'vary in form, so that they are form within forms ... and the forms of a texture escapes measurement' Gibson 1979, p. 98). That the problem of measuring the qualities of the mode of appearance of certain phenomenal events is of greater complexity than that of their underlying physical properties should not, however, exclude the possibility of its quantification in principle. The problem, if anything, is that of having a *descriptive theory* that identifies the specific components of the phenomenal level, and then looking for its suitable type of metric and modelling. A descriptive theory of the phenomenal qualities, in fact, must necessarily involve *at least partially constructivist aspects*, such as identification of the visual thing starting from aspects given in the actual presentation, in a subjective time and space, and the distribution of the attention that shifts from consideration of the objectual and three-dimensional aspects of the phenomenal appearance as percept (for instance, a tree) to aspects inherent in that specific appearance (for example the foliage of broadleaf plants). Not to speak of the successive nested properties and qualities relative to the understanding of the various percepts (for example, a certain set of trees as a wood, whose derived quality, in turn, is given by aspects like 'wooded'). Going no further than metric properties or the linguistic labels corresponding to them (usually Anglo-American) in the analysis of the qualities of the ontological level of phenomenal events is substantially a dead end, because it fails to grasp the nature of its 'object of reference'.

From a specific point of view, instead, the qualities of the appearances can be distinguished into qualities of:

1. The archi-tectonics
2. Global of the material
3. Way of being
4. Demand.

The qualities of the first type are proper to the *skeletal structure* of appearances, for example the spatial form or the figural form, the distribution of colours and lightness, the rhythm and also structural processes in change and movement. I call these formal data of the structure/joint concerning the entire realm of perceptive presence, from stationary to continuous events. Specifically, they are expressed by adjectives like straight, round, angular, elliptical, closed, symmetrical, pointed, corrugated, serrated; continuous, discontinuous, stable, unstable; or even dynamically expressed like to grow, diminish, rise, fall, flow, leap, i.e. skeletal structures in deployment. Analogous qualities in acoustics are the characteristics of melody and harmony (Metzger 1941, Chap. 2, § 8). A good example of this type of quality in the phenomenal field is the corrugated Mondrian phenomenon (Fig. 9.6).

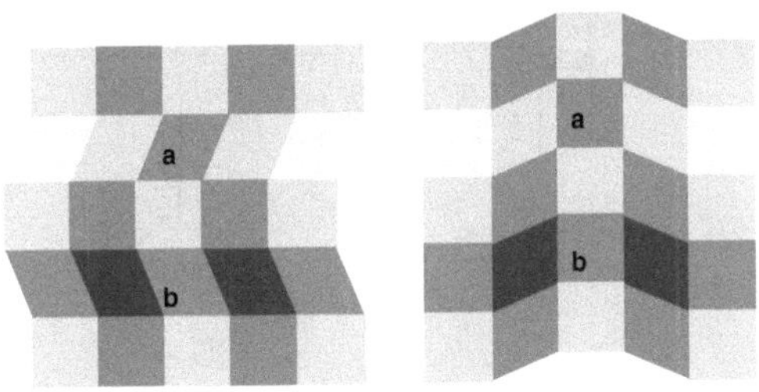

Fig. 9.6 Perceived colours are strongly influenced by perceptual organization; physically the same, to the *left* the *grey* in *a* appears very different from that in *b*, while to the *right* they are seen almost identical (Adelson 1993, 2043)

Or, in pictorial space, examples like Mondrian's or van Doesburg's paintings, where we have planned interactions among horizontal, vertical directions, straight lines, advancing and receding movements of colours; or again, the perceived visual difference between continuous movement and stroboscopic movement (I owe this last comment to Da Pos).

A sub-class of these qualities comprises the dynamic structures concerning the direction, distribution, tension, attraction, repulsion, pressure, launching, braking of events (see experiments by Michotte 1946, Burke 1952) or to arise, to transform, to end, as in gamma movement (Kenkel 1913), but which are also visible in simple geometrical figures appearing in the anisotropic visual space of vision (Lipps 1879) (Fig. 9.7).

In pictorial space examples are also provided by Boccioni's *Cyclist*, by Mirone's *Discobolus* (Pierantoni 1986), or by the structural skeleton of the square analysed by Arnheim (Fig. 9.8).

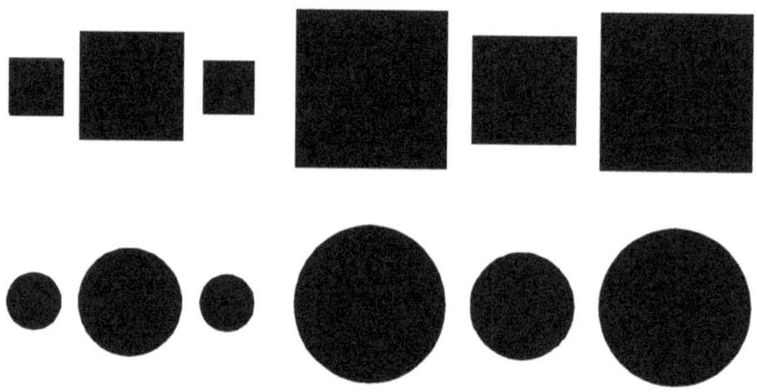

Fig. 9.7 Example of spatial extendedness. Ebbinghaus illusion: so-called apparent size of objects in distinct configurations (as parts)

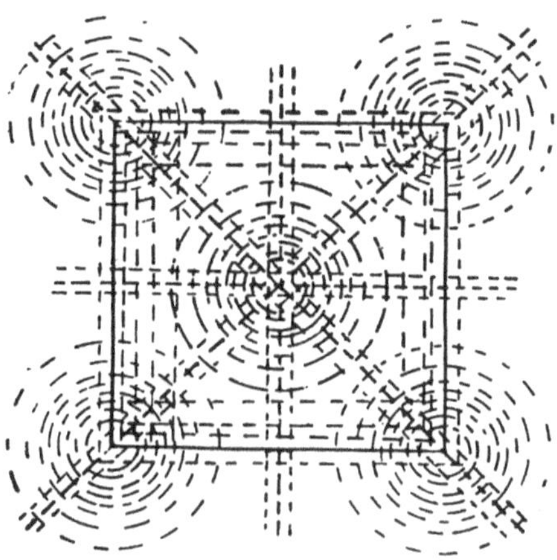

Fig. 9.8 Example of spatial extendedness. The hidden structural skeleton of the square (Arhneim 1954)

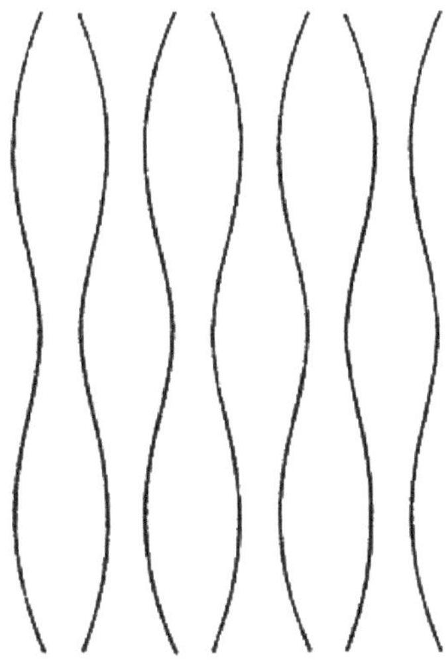

Fig. 9.9 Convexity favours the emergence of figures (Morinaga 1942)

These are qualities classified by Aristotle as *common sensibles* (see also Lewin 1926, 1929, Köhler 1933).

Other examples are given by phenomena of grouping or ungrouping by pairs, as in Morinaga's example (Fig. 9.9) where the alternative is due to the organization of the part to the left side of the series vs. the right side (Morinaga 1942, Metzger 1966, p. 713). A corresponding example in pictorial space is Riley's *Arrest*.

The second classification of qualities concerns qualities proper to the material of visual things, like transparency or glossiness. Transparency is a paradigmatic quality of this type, because it is given by the stratification of two or more objects seen one through the other and in the same direction of sight (Metelli 1941). Representation of the uncorporeal, diffuse, shadowy is marvellously apparent in Tohaku Hasegawa's *Shourinmatsu*.

As to glossiness, it is a characteristic of illumination to produce a 'non visibility' of the visual material itself of the event! (Mausfeld, in press). Other qualities of this type are those of mirror images and Chinese shadows.

The third classification concerns qualities of the way of being (*Weseneigenschaften*) of visual events, i.e. expressive and physiognomic qualities. These are qualities of character, ethos, habit, and atmosphere expressed by adjectives like merry, sad, friendly, bold, terse, pacific, vehement, gracious; or feminine, virile, infantile, senile; crackling, noisy, shrill, whining. They concern both percepts and processes, and they are usually addressed as *tertiary qualities* (Metzger 1941, Chap. 2, § 8, Klages 1942).

Paul Klee's artistic production provides numerous examples of the pictorial representation of these qualities, as in *Tweeting machine* or *Once Emerged from the Gray of Night*. Another fine representation is Muraka's *Onna* (Female).

Other qualities of this type of appearance are coarse, luminous, silky, full-bodied; tender, hard, viscous, smooth, velvety, elastic; strident (which can appear as clashing in colour), dull (which appears as sullen in character), etc. The qualities of cast shadows pertain to them as well. These qualities relate to the phenomenal real vs. phenomenal apparent (Albertazzi 2004, Mausfeld and Wendt 2006). An example in pictorial space is Boccioni's *Elastic*.

A fourth classification of qualities is that of the qualities with a demand character (*Afforderungscharakter*). They express the relation between perceived expressive qualities and the subject's way of being, and specifically, its effect on the perceiver. These qualities are expressed by adjectives like attractive, repulsive, fascinating, disgusting, pleasing, exalting, oppressive, repugnant, stimulating, calming, tempting, exciting, distressing, appetizing, etc. They are qualities given by the coordinative field (Lewin 1926, Rausch 1966).

In pictorial space, for example, Van Gogh's *Starry Night* represents the phenomenal appearance of obscurity with the surplus of a demand character quality. The same applies to expressionistic painting in general. Particularly interesting are the dynamic qualities of demand that characterize the perception of deliberate phenomena such as those of attraction or avoidance, whose meaning is given by the corresponding kinetic structure, in its turn analysable in terms of the relative velocity, distance, and magnitude of the components, which have specific behaviours in the visual space of forces (Husserl 1997, Michotte 1950a, b, Michotte et al. 1962, Heider and Simmel 1944, Kanizsa and Vicario 1968). Currently, these phenomena have been reprised in the experimental field (Schlottman 2000), but not always within a phenomenal theory of visual appearances (Scholl and Tremoulet 2000).

Finally, none of these qualities can be isolated as a feature in itself and arranged in a dictionary-type list. The qualities of phenomenal events is always given in a context, and in mutual interplay.

9.3 Towards a Theory of Internal Relations

It is not possible to provide a list of the qualities of visual appearances, owing to the intrinsic contextual dependence of items in the visual field. Different types of qualities in different configurations offer different *potential meanings* given by the diverse potential saliences in the field (for the concept of potential meaning see Koenderink 1984, Noë 2004, p. 135). Examples are the phenomenon of transparency, given by the interplay between the quality of the material and the quality of the structure, or by the phenomenon of *Pregnänz*, due to the interplay between the quality of the way of being and that of the structure.

In particular, the quality of *Pregnänz* concerns the nucleus itself of the quality of events, and more in general, of a qualitative approach to perception. In fact, for each quality of the way of being there is a specific structure *which realizes it best*, so that there is a beautiful melody, a beautiful painting, a beautiful landscape, a beautiful novel, etc. However, this 'cross higher order quality' has an intrinsic grammar of its own whose complexity has not yet been fully understood (von Allesch 1923, Wertheimer 1923, Metzger 1941, Chap. 2, § 9, Kanizsa and Luccio 1985, Hochberg and Brooks 1960, Rausch 1966, Kanizsa 1991, Chap. 4, Goldmeier 1982, Stadler et al. 1979).

Firstly, pregnancy as a phenomenal quality can be defined in terms of simple, regular, good form. For example, the structural skeleton of the square analysed by Arnheim evinces the underlying dynamics of forces due to the fact that we may have 'good' or 'bad' points on the basis of the field relations underlying the visible (Fig. 9.10).

From this point of view, the 'good' Gestalten are orderly and well-formed structures which optimally incorporate tertiary quality. Specifically:

1. They are endowed with inner coherence.
2. They are constructed according to the same principle in all of their parts.
3. They comply with the law of phenomenal membership (Benary 1930).
4. They are more resistant to transformation (Stadler et al. 1979).

Moreover, if we consider pregnancy, not as a quality of the percept 'good' as such, but as a *tendency* towards good form, we encounter problems concerning the relationship of gradualness and/or of continuity/discontinuity in pregnancy itself. From this point of view, pregnancy is the principle that regulates the economy and the simplicity of the process, whose result is the maximum equilibrium among the forces at play and the maximum stability of the configuration. From this point of view, moreover, pregnancy assumes the role of a general principle that operates alongside the other factors of unification.

We may therefore consider pregnancy as a quality to which one can gradually approximate (so that we speak, for example, of preparatory studies for a painting, or an 'almost realized' painting), highlighting gradualness (Rausch 1952, 1964, Garner 1962).

Rausch has identified seven bipolar *Prägnanzaspekte*, which range from a maximum to a minimum, are gradual, and which can be mathematically modelled, given that pregnancy is substantially a scalar property (Rausch 1966). They are regularity, independence (rectangle), completeness, structural simplicity, structural richness

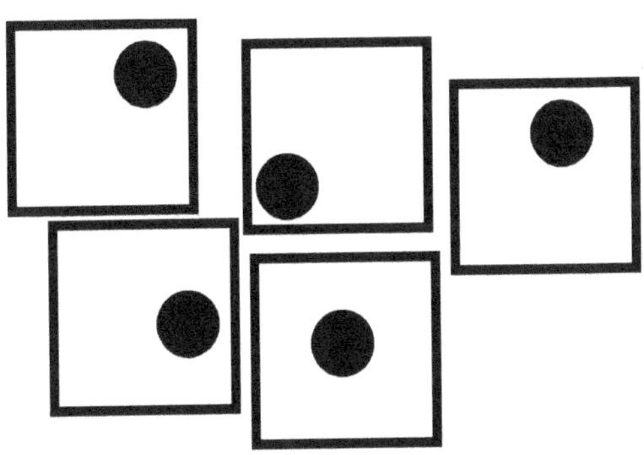

Fig. 9.10 'Good' or 'bad' points, due to the structural skeleton (see Fig. 9.8)

(symphony), expressiveness, and fullness of meaning (consider the distinction between phenomenally real and phenomenally apparent discussed above).

Or one may consider the process of approximation to good form as indeed a gradual process, but not as continuous, and which introduces zones of discontinuity rather than grades of intensity. From this point of view, there exist discontinuities, or degrees (*Stufen*) internal to the pregnancy relation. This approach, which is that of Goldmeier (Goldmeier 1982), considers the *Pregnänz* of a pattern as uniqueness, i.e. a quality missing from all the others, a unique and self-consistent pattern. If there are zones around a point of *Prägnanz*, then we can have cases of perfect realization, or unsuccessful cases of mere approximation, or even of derivation, i.e. patterns of near singularity.

As Kanizsa has stressed, however, pregnancy is more a tendency to equilibrium of the field that the achievement of an excellent (*ausgezeichnet*) form, which comes about also to the detriment of individual Gestalten with scant pregnancy (Kanizsa and Luccio 1985).

In conclusion, at present there is an unresolved tension between the concept of pregnancy as *a tertiary quality and the phenomenal result of a configuration* (singularity, figural goodness of a visual fact) and pregnancy as characteristic *of a process*, as a *principle of minimum* (Hatfield and Epstein 1985).

Once again, I believe that the problem must be framed in terms of a theory of relations, and specifically:

1. If perceptive Gestalten can somehow be incorporated into a theory of relations.
2. In what sense 'relation' must be understood.

In fact, because a Gestalt is not a sum of elements but a higher-order whole given by *components in reciprocal non-independence*, it is not possible to identify, except in abstract, the individual components and the types of relations that arise among them. For example, in a melody, one can identify parts of content (the notes), parts of apprehension of the content (the perception of acoustic and tonal intervals), parts relative to the laws of phenomenal organization (by similarity or common destiny, etc.), pre-gestalten in the phases of the melody's progress due to simultaneously and subsequently unfolding chords, as well as components related to the distribution of attention, the individual (analytical or synthetic) set, the top-down completions that may originate from culture or expertise, etc.; but these are always identified *ex post*. The relations at the basis of a perceptive configuration are seldom expressly recognized or noted as such at the *presentative level* (Kreibig 1909).

From this point of view, analysis of the *phenomenal material* of configurations, in whatever perceptive modality, best expresses the complexity of a type of relation that is internal to the figural whole. Consider the 'aspects' mentioned above as qualities of phenomenal events *in the mode of their appearance*: each of them is implicitly connected to the whole, which on their basis is dynamically reconstructed because it is *internally and structurally connected* to all the other aspects of the presentative event, of which it is an anticipation, and as such it is also *internally and structurally dependent* on all the others.

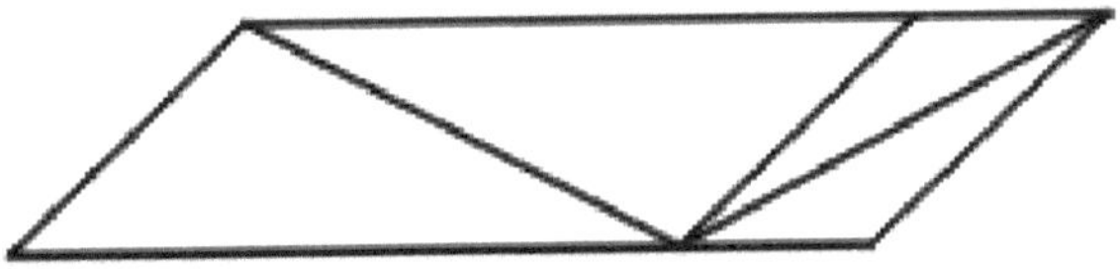

Fig. 9.11 Sander illusion. When the two sides of the isosceles triangle become the diagonals of the two parallelograms, they are no longer of equal length

It is also important to note that, from a morphogenetic point of view, the functional ordering between the parts and the whole (the so-called *Gestalt Bindung*, see Seifert 1917) is closely connected with the homogenization of the components, as in the case of Fuchs's chromatic assimilation, or musical colour (*Klangfarbe*) (Brentano 1995b, p. 95), or the visual quality of Sander's parallelogram (Fig. 9.11).

As regards in that sense in which the concept of 'relations' should be understood, since its first formulation, implicit in the *Gestaltqualität* have been the components of:

1. the quality of being *complex, homogeneous*, which concerns the whole;
2. intimacy (*Innigkeit*) of the structure's articulation.

In some way Gestalten are formed and differ from each other according to the degree of intimacy in their structure. They stand in fact midway between an *amorphous mass* of phenomenal material devoid of connections, of features, and whose totality is characterized by a *diffused* quality (see above) and the *maximum degree of the structure's articulation* into disconnected pieces (a sort of chaos).

Between the two extremes of this continuum, in which the structural properties and qualities of the structure's way of appearance are intimately connected, there unfolds all the richness of the perceptual world.

It seems that one may conclude from all this that a qualitative approach to perception strongly reduces the design of the algorithmic load of the stimulus, switches the level of complexity to a higher one, supports the understanding of visual things, and represents a *relational theory* of *visual matter*, i.e. *qualities*. Classically, *Ubi materia, ivi geometria*. A formal modelling of human perception, as a necessary step for fulfilment of Fechner's programme, and also to implement a model of complexity in artificial agents, can only be conceived in light of analysis of the eminently qualitative structure of this specific ontological level of reality, which manifests its *categorial novelty* in the emergence of meaning.

References

Albers, J. 1963. *Interaction of color*. New Haven, CT: Yale University Press.

Adelson, E.H. 1993. Perceptual organization and the judgment of brightness. *Science* 262: 2042–2044

Albertazzi, L. 1998. Form metaphysics. In *Shapes of forms*, ed. L. Albertazzi, *From gestalt psychology to phenomenology to ontology and mathematics*, 261–310. Dordrecht: Kluwer academic.

Albertazzi, L. 1999. The time of presentness. A chapter in positivistic and descriptive psychology. In *Vittorio benussi*, ed. S. Cattaruzza, special issue of *Axiomathes,* 10, 49–74.

Albertazzi, L. 2000a. Which Semantics. In *Meaning and cognition. A multidisciplinary approach*, ed. L. Albertazzi, 1–24. Amsterdam: Benjamins Publishing Company.

Albertazzi, L. 2000b. Directions and perspective points in spatial perception. In *Meaning and cognition. A multidisciplinary approach*, ed. L. Albertazzi, 123–143. Amsterdam: Benjamins Publishing Company.

Albertazzi, L. 2001. Vittorio Benussi. In *The school of Alexius Meinong*, eds. L. Albertazzi, D. Jacquette, and R. Poli, 95–133. Aldershot: Asghate.

Albertazzi, L. 2002a. Continua. In *Unfolding perceptual continua*, ed. L. Albertazzi, 1–28. Benjamins Publishing Company: Amsterdam.

Albertazzi, L. 2002b. Towards a neo-aristotelian theory of continua: Elements of an empirical geometry. In *Unfolding perceptual continua*, ed. L. Albertazzi, 29–79. Benjamins Publishing Company: Amsterdam.

Albertazzi, L. 2002c. Kinetic structure and causatives. *Axiomathes* 1:17–37.

Albertazzi, L. 2003. From Kanizsa back to Benussi: Varieties of intentional reference. In *The Legacy of Gaetano kanizsa*, ed. L. Albertazzi, special issue of *Axiomathes*, 13:239–259.

Albertazzi, L. 2004. Stereokinetic shapes and their shadows. *Perception* 33:1437–1452.

Albertazzi, L. 2005. *Immanent realism*. Berlin; New York: Springer.

Albertazzi, L. 2006a. Visual spaces. In *Visual thought. The depictive space of the mind*, ed. L. Albertazzi. Amsterdam: Benjamins Publishing Company.

Albertazzi, L. 2006b. Das rein figurale. *Gestalt Theory* 28(1/2):123–151.

Albertazzi, L. 2006c. Intentional presentations. At the roots of consciousness. In *The concept of consciousness. Integrating an emergent science*, ed. S. Jordan, special issue of *Journal of Consciousness Studies*, January 2007:94–114.

Albertazzi, L. 2007. Matrix: Schematic universals. In *Cognitive aspects of bilingualism*, eds. I. Kesckes and L. Albertazzi, 63–97. Berlin; New York: Springer.

Albertazzi, L. Forthcoming. Metaphorical information, In: *Perception beyond inference. The information content of visual processes*, eds. Albertazzi, L., G. van Tonder, and D. Vishwanath, MIT Press, Fall 2010.

Allesch, C. von 1923. *Zur nichteuklidischen Struktur des phänomenales Raum*. Jena: Fischer.

Aristotle. 1960. Topica. In *Loeb classical library* (trans: E.S. Forster). Cambridge, MA: Harvard University Press.

Aristotle. 1972. *De partibus animalium* (trans: D.M. Balme). Oxford: Clarendon Press.

Aristotle. 1977. *Metaphysics*. In *Loeb classical library*, 7th ed. (trans: H. Tredennick). Cambridge, MA: Harvard University Press.

Aristotle. 1980. Physics. In: *Loeb classical library*, 5th ed. (trans: P.H. Wicksteed, F.M. Cornford). Cambridge MA: Harvard University Press, Loeb.

Aristotle. 1983. Categories. In: *Loeb classical library*, eds. H.P. Cooke and T. Tredennick. Cambridge MA: Harvard University Press,.

Aristotle. 1986. *De Anima* (trans: W.S. Hett). Cambridge MA: Harvard University Press.

Arnheim, R. 1954. *Art and visual perception: The psychology of the creative eye*. Berkeley, CA: The Regents of the University of California.

Benary, W. 1930. The influence of form on brightness contrast. In *A source book of gestalt psychology*, ed. W.D. Ellis, 104–108. London: Routledge.

Benussi, V. 1913. *Psychologie der Zeitauffassung*. Leipzig: Hölder.

Benussi, V. 1922–1923. *Introduzione alla psicologia sperimentale. Lezioni tenute nell'anno 1922–23*, typescript by Dr C. Musatti, Fondo Benussi, Milan, Bicocca University.

Benussi, V. 1925. *La suggestione e l'ipnosi come mezzi di analisi psichica reale*. Bologna: Zanichelli.

Berlin, B., and P. Kay. 1969. *Basic color terms: Their universality and evolution*. Berkeley: University of California Press.

Bertamini, M., A. Spooner, and H. Hecht. 2003. Naive optics: Predicting and perceiving reflections in mirrors. *Journal of Experimental Psychology: Human Perception and Performance* 29:982–1002.

Bertamini, M., A. Spooner, and H. Hecht. 2004. The representation of naïve knowledge about physics. In *Multidisciplinary approaches to visual representations and interpretations*, ed. G. Malcom. Amsterdam: Elsevier.

Bezold, W. von. 1874. *Die Farbenlehre in Hinblick auf Kunst und Kunstgewerbe*. Braunschweig: Westermann.

Bozzi, P., and P. Bressan. 1987. On the perception of launched projectiles. In *Proceedings of the Fourth International Conference on Event Perception and Action*, 49. Trieste: Dec Sistemi.

Brentano, F. 1981. *The theory of categories*, eds. R.M. Chisholm and N. Guterman, Den Haag, Nijhoff (1st German ed. 1933, ed. by A. Kastil, Leipzig, Meiner).

Brentano, F. 1988. *Philosophical lectures on space, time and the continuum*, ed. S. Körner and R. M. Chisholm. London: Croom Helm.

Brentano, F. 1995a. *Psychology from an empirical standpoint*, ed. L. McAlister. London: Routledge (Translation of the 2nd ed. with an Introduction and notes by O. Kraus, Leipzig 1924) (1st German ed. 1874, Leipzig Duncker and Humblot).

Brentano, F. 1995b. *Descriptive psychology*, ed. B. Müller. London: Routledge (1st German ed. 1982, ed. by R.M. Chisholm and W. Baumgartner, Hamburg, Meiner).

Brunswik, E. 1934. *Wahrnehmung und Gegengstandwelt. Grundlegung einer Psychologie der Gegenstand her*. Leipzig: Deuticke.

Burke, L. 1952. On the tunnel effect. *Quarterly Journal for Experimental Psychology* 4:121–138.

Da Pos, O., and Albertazzi, L. 2010. It is in the nature of color...'. *Seeing and Perceiving* 23:39–73.

Davidoff, J., I. Davies, and D. Roberson. 1999. Color categories in a stone-age tribe. *Nature* 398:203–204, 402, 604.

Eco, U. 1997. *Kant e l'ornitorinco*. Milan: Bompiani.

Finke, R.A., J.J. Freyd, and G.C.W. Shyi. 1986. Implied velocity and acceleration induce transformations of visual memory. *Journal of Experimental Psychology: General* 115: 175–188.

Freyd, J.J. 1987. Dynamic mental representations. *Psychological Review* 94:427–438.

Freyd, J.J., and R.A. Finke. 1984. Representational momentum. *Journal of Experimental Psychology: Learning, Memory and Cognition* 10:126–132.

Frölich, F.W. 1923. Über die Messung der Empfindungszeit. *Zeitschrift für Sinnespsychologie* 54:58–78.

Fuchs, W. 1923. Experimentelle Untersuchungen über die Änderung von Farben unter dem Einfluss von Gestalten (Angleichungserscheinungen). *Zeitschrift für Psychologie* 92:249–263.

Garner, W.R. 1962. *Uncertainty and structure as psychological concepts*. New York: Wiley.

Gelb, W. 1938. The colour constancy of visual things. In *A source book of gestalt psychology*, ed. W. Ellis, 196–209. London, Routledge (Original 1929).

Gibson, J.J. 1950. The perception of visual surfaces. *American Journal of Psychology* 63: 367–384.

Gibson, J.J. 1979. *The ecological approach to visual perception*. Boston, MA: Houton Mifflin.

Gibson, J.J., and D. Waddell. 1952. Homogeneous retinal stimulation and visual perception. *American Journal of Psychology* 65:263–270.

Goethe, W. 1970. *Theory of colors*. Cambridge MA and London: MIT Press.

Goldmeier, E. 1982. *The memory trace: Its formation and its fate*. Hillsdale, NJ: Erlbaum.

Haber, R.N., and L.R. Haber. 1988. Eidetic imagery as cognitive skill. In *The exceptional brain: The neuropsychology of talent and special skills*, eds. L. Obler, and D. Fein, 218–241. New York: Guilford Press.

Hartmann, N. 1935. *Grundlegung der Ontologie*. Berlin: De Gruyter.

Hartmann, N. 1950. *Abriss der speziellen Kategorienlehre*. Berlin: De Gruyter.

Hatfield, G., and W. Epstein. 1985. The status of minimum principle in the theoretical analysis of visual perception. *Psychological Bulletin* 97(2):155–186.

Heidegger, M. 1953. *Being and time*. Albany: State University Press.
Heider, F., and M. Simmel. 1944. An experimental study of apparent behaviour. *American Journal of Psychology* 57:243–259.
Hering, E. 1964. *Outlines of a theory of light sense*. Cambridge, MA: Harvard.
Hochberg, E., W. Triebel, and G. Seaman. 1951. Color adaptation underconditions of homogeneous visual stimulation (*Ganzfeld*). *Journal of Experimental Psychology* 44:153–159.
Hochberg, J., and V. Brooks. 1960. The psychophysics of form: Reversible perspective drawing of spatial objects. *American Journal of Psychology* 73:337–354.
Hoffman, D.D. 2003. The interaction of colour and motion. In *Colour perception: Mind and the physical world*, eds. R. Mausfed, and D. Heyer, 361–377. Oxford: Oxford University Press..
Hubbard, T. 1999. How consequences of physical principles influence mental representation: The environmental invariant hypothesis. In *Fechner day 99: The end of 20th century psychophysics. Proceedings of the 15th Annual Meeting of the International Society for Psychophysics*, eds. P.R. Killeen and W.R. Uttal, 274–279. Tempe, AZ: The International Society for Psychophysics.
Hubbard, T. 2004. The perception of causality: Insights from Michotte's launching effect, naïve impetus theory, and representational momentum. In *Fechner Day 2004*, eds. A.M. Oliveira, M.P. Teixeira, G.F. Borges, and M.J. Ferro, 116–121. Coimbra, Portugal: International Society for Psychophysics.
Hubbard, T., and J.J. Bharucha. 1988. Judged displacement in apparent vertical and horizonthal motion. *Perception and Psychophysics* 44(3):211–221.
Hubbard, T., and M.A. Motes. 2002. Does representational momentum reflect a distortion of the length or the endpoint of a trajectory? *Cognition* 82:B89–B99.
Husserl, E. 1966. *Analysen zur passiven Syntesis*, Husserliana XI. Den Haag: Nijhoff.
Husserl, E. 1970. *Logical investigations*, ed. J.N. Findlay. London: Routledge & Kegan Paul.
Husserl, E. 1991. *Lectures on internal time*, ed. J.B. Brough. Dordrecht: Kluwer (Zur *Phänomenologie des inneren Zeitbewusstseins*, ed by R. Boehm, Den Haag, 1966).
Husserl, E. 1997. *Thing und space*. Dordrecht: Kluwer. (*Ding und Raum. Vorlesungen 1907*, ed. U. Claesges, Husserliana XVI, Den Haag, Nijhoff).
Ingarden, R. 1962. *Untersuchungen zur Ontologie der Kunst: Musikwerk, Bild, Architecture, Film*. Tübingen: Niemeyer.
Ingarden, R. 1968. *Vom Erkennen des literarischen Kunstwerks*. Tübingen: Niemeyer.
Intraub, H. 2002. Anticipatory spatial representation of natural sciences: Momentum without movement?. *Visual Cognition* 9: 1–2, 93–119.
Jaensch, E.R. 1909. Zur Analyse der Gesichtswahrnehmungen. *Erg. Band der Zeitschrift für Psychologie*.
Kammer, T., L. Lehr, and K. Kirschfeld. 1999. Cortical visual processing in tempoprally dispersed by luminance in human subjects. *Neuroscience Letters* 263:133–136.
Kanizsa, G. 1952. Legittimità di un'analisi del processo percettivo fondata su una distinzione in fasi o stadi. *Archivio di Psicologia, Neurologia e Psichiatria* 15(3):251–264.
Kanizsa, G. 1960. *Funktion der Microstruktur und des Randgefälles. Psychologische Beiträge* 5: 93–101.
Kanizsa, G. 1980. *La grammatica del vedere*. Bologna: Il Mulino.
Kanizsa, G. 1991. *Vedere e pensare*. Bologna: Il Mulino.
Kanizsa, G., and G.B. Vicario. 1968. 'La percezione della relazione intenzionale'. In *Ricerche sperimentali sulla percezione*, eds. G. Kanizsa and G.B. Vicario, 69–126. Trieste: Università degli studi di Trieste.
Kanizsa, G., and R. Luccio. 1985. La pregnanza e le sue ambiguità. *Psicologia italiana* 7: 11–39.
Katz, D. 1935. *The world of colour*. London: Kegan Paul, Trench, Trubnov and Co.
Kay, P., B. Berlin, L. Maffi, and W. Merrifield. 1997. Color naming across languages. In *Color categories in thought and language*, eds. C.L. Hardin and L. Maffi, 21–56. Cambridge: Cambridge University Press.

Kenkel, F. 1913. Untersuchungen über den Zusammenhang zwischen Erscheinungsgrösse und Erscheinungsbewegung bei einer sogenannten optischen Täuschungen. *Zeitschrift für Psychologie* 67:358–449.
Kepes, G. 1944. *The language of vision*. Chicago: Theobald.
Khurana, B., and R. Nijhawan. 1995. Extrapolation or attention shift? *Nature* 378:566.
Klages, L. 1942. *Grundlegung der Wissenschaft vom Ausdruck*. Leipzig: Barth.
Koenderink, J.J. 1984. The structure of images. *Biological Cybernetics* 50(5):363–370.
Koenderink, J.J., and A. van Doorn. 2002. Ecological optics and the creative eye. In *Perception and the physical world*, eds. D. Heyer, and R. Mausfeld, 271–304. Chichester: John Wiley.
Koenderink, J.J., and A. van Doorn. 2003. Pictorial space. In *Looking into pictures*, eds. H. Hecht and R. Mausfeld, 239–299. Cambridge, MA: MIT Press.
Koffka, K. 1930. Some problems of space perception. In *Psychologies of 1930*, ed. C. Murchison, 161–187. Worchester, MA: Clark University Press.
Koffka, K. 1935. *Principles of gestalt psychology*. New York: Harcourt, Brace, and World.
Köhler, W. 1933. *Psychologische probleme*. Berlin: Springer.
Kopferman, H. 1930. Psychologische Untersuchungen über die Wirkung zweidimensionaler Darstellungen körperliche Gebilde. *Psychologische Foschung* 13:293–364.
Kovàcs, I. 2000. Human development of perceptual organization. *Vision Research* 40(10–12):1301–1310.
Kreibig, J.C. 1909. *Die intellektuelle Funkionen. Untersuchungen über Grenzfragen der Logik*. Wien: Holder.
Krekelberg, B., and M. Lappe. 1999. Temporal recruitment along the trajectory of moving objects and the perception of position. *Vision Research* 39:2669–2679.
Kress, G., and T. van Leeuwen. 1996. *Reading images*. London: Routledge.
Kroliczak G., P.F. Heard, M.A. Goodale, and R.L. Gregory. 2006. Dissociation of perception and action unmasked by the hollow-face illusion. *Brain Research* 1080(1):1–16.
Kubovy, M., W. Epstein, and S. Gepshtein. 2002. Foundations of visual perception. In *Experimental psychology*, eds. A.F. Healy and R.W. Proctor, vol. 4, I.B. Weiner ed., *Handbook of psychology*, 87–119. New York: John Wiley.
Khurana, B., K. Watanabe, and R. Nijhawan. 2000. The role of attention in motion extrapolation: Are moving objects 'corrected' or flashed objects attentionally delayed?. *Perception* 29: 675–692.
Lewin, K. 1926. Vorsatz. *Wille und Bedürfnis: mit Vorbemerkungen über die psychische Kräfte und Energien und die Struktur der Seele*. Berlin: Springer.
Lewin, K. 1929. *Die Entwicklung der experimentellen Willenpsychologie und die Psychotherapie*. Leipzig: Hirzel.
Leyton, M. 1992. *Symmetry, causality, mind*. Boston: MIT Press.
Li, X., and A.L. Gilchrist. 1999. Relative area and relative luminance combine to anchor surface lightness values. *Perception and Psychophysics* 61(5):771–785.
Libet B. 1982. Brain stimulation in the study of neuronal functions for conscious sensory experience. *Human Neurobiology* 1:235–242.
Lindemann, E. 1922. Experimentelle Untersuchungen über das Entstehen und Vergehen von Gestalten. *Psychologische Forschung* 2:5–60.
Lipmann, O. 1923. Bemergungen zur Gestalttheorie. *Archiv für Psychologie* 44.
Lipps, Th. 1879. *Raumaesthetik und geometrisch-optische Täuschungen*. Leipzig: Barth.
Marr, D. 1982. *Vision*. San Francisco: Freeman Press.
Massironi, M. 2002. *The psychology of graphic images*. London: Elsevier.
Massironi, M., and P. Bonaiuto. 1966. Ricerche sull'espressività. Qualità funzionali, intenzionali e relazione di causalità in assenza di movimento reale. *Rassegna di psicologia sperimentale e clinica* 8:3–42.
Matthaei, R. 1929. Das Gestaltproblem. *Monatschrift für Kinderheilkunde* 29(1) (repr. 2005).
Mausfeld, R. 2002. The physicalistic trap in perception theory. In *Perception and the physical world*, eds. D. Heyer and R. Mausfeld, 75–112. Chichester: Wiley.

Mausfeld, R. 2003. Conjoint representations and the mental capacity for multiple simultaneous perspectives. In *Looking into pictures*, eds. H. Hecht, R. Mausfeld, 17–60. Cambridge MA: MIT Press.

Mausfeld, R. In press. Colour with an internalist framework: The role of 'color' in the structure of the perceptual system. In *Color ontology and color science*, eds. J. Cohen, and M. Matten. Cambridge MA: MIT Press.

Mausfeld, R., and G. Wendt. 2006. Material appearances under minimal stimulus conditions: Lustrous and glassy qualities. *Perception* 35(Suppl.):213–214.

Meinong, A. 1899. Über Gegenstände höherer Ordnung und deren Verhältniss zu inneren Wahrnehmung. *Zeitschrift für Psychologie und Physiologie der Sinnesorgane* 21:182–272.

Meinong, A. 1960. The theory of objects. In *Realism and the background of phenomenology*, ed. R.M. Chisholm, 76–117. Glencoe: The Free Press.

Metelli, F. 1941. Oggettualità, stratificazione e risalto nell'organizzazione percettiva di figura e sfondo. *Archivio di Psicologia, Neurologia e Psichiatria* 2:831–841.

Metelli, F. 1967. Zur Analyse der phänomenalen Durchsictighkeiterscheinungen. In *Gestalt und Wirchlichkeit*, eds. R. Mühler, and J. Fischl. Berlin.

Metzger, W. 1930. Optische Untersuchungen am Ganzfeld, I, II. *Psychologische Forschung* 13: 6–29.

Metzger, W. 1934. Beobachtungen über phänomenale Identität. *Psychologische Forschung* 19: 40–48.

Metzger, W. 1941. *Psychologie: die Entwicklung ihrer Grundannahmen seit der Einführung des Experiments*. Dresden: Steinkopff.

Metzger, W. 1966. Figural Wahrnehmung. In *Handbuch der Psychologie*, ed. W. Metzger, vol. I, 693–744. Göttingen: Hogrefe.

Metzger, W. 1975. *Gesetze des Sehens*. Frankfurt: Kramer.

Michotte, A. 1950a. A propos de la permanence phénoménale: Faits et theories. *Acta Psychologica* 7:298–232.

Michotte, A. 1950b. The emotion regarded as functional connections. In *Feelings and emotions*, ed. M.L. Reymert, 128–144. New York: Mc Graw Hill.

Michotte, A. 1963. *The perception of causality*. London: Methuen.

Michotte, A., et al. 1962. Causalité, permanence et réalité phénoménales. *Studia Psychologica*. Louvain: Publications Universitaires.

Morinaga, S. 1942. Beobachtungn über Grundlagen und Wirkungen anschaulich gleichmässiger Breite. *Archiv gesamte Psychologie* 110:310–348.

Musatti, C.L. 1924. Sui fenomeni stereocinetici. *Archivio Italiano di Psicologia* 3:105–120.

Musatti, C.L. 1928. Sui movimenti apparenti dovuti a identità di figura. *Archivio Italiano di Psicologia* 6:205–219.

Musatti, C.L. 1953. Luce e colore nei fenomeni del contrasto simultaneo, della costanza e dell'euguagliamento. *Archivio di Psicologia, Neurologia e Psichiatria* 5:544–577.

Musatti, C.L. 1955. La stereocinesi e la struttura dello spazio visibile. *Rivista di Psicologia* 49:3–57.

Musatti, C.L. 1964. *Condizioni dell'esperienza e fondazione della psicologia*. Florence: Editrice Universitaria.

Müsseler, J., and G. Aschersleben. 1998. Localizing the first position of a moving stimulus: The Frölich effect and an attention-shifting explanation. *Perception and Psychophysics* 60:683–695.

Nijhawan, R. 1994. Motion extrapolation in catching. *Nature* 370:256–257.

Nijhawan, R. 1997. Visual decomposition of colour through motion extrapolation. *Nature* 386:66–69.

Nisbett, R.E. 2003. *The geography of thought. How Asians and Westerners think differently...and why*. London: Nicholas Brealy Publishing.

Noë, A. 2004. *Action in perception*. Cambridge MA: MIT Press.

Ostwald, W. 1917. Der absolute System der Farben. *Zeitschrift für Phys. Chem.* 92:222–226.

Pierantoni, R. 1986. *Forma fluens*. Torino: Boringhieri.

Pinna, B., and Albertazzi, L. 2010. From grouping to meaning. In *Perception beyond inference. The information content of visual processes*, eds. Albertazzi, L., G. van Tonder, and D. Vishwanath, MIT Press, Fall 2010.
Poli, R. 1998. Levels. *Axiomathes* 9(1–2):197–211.
Poli, R. 2001. The basic problem of the theory of levels of reality. *Axiomathes* 12(3–4):261–283.
Poli, R. 2002. Ontological methodology. *International Journal of Human-Computer Studies* 56:639–664.
Poli, R. 2006a. Levels of reality and the psychological stratum. *Revue Internationale de Philosophie* 61(2):163–180.
Poli, R. 2006b. The theory of levels of reality and the difference between simple and tangled hierarchies. In *Systemics of emergence: Research and development*, eds. G. Minati, E. Pessa, and M. Abram, 715–722. New York, NY: Springer.
Poli, R. 2007. Three obstructions: forms of causation, chronotopoids, and levels of reality. *Axiomathes* 1:1–18.
Poli, R. Ontology: The categorial stance. In *TAO-theory and applications of ontology*, Vol.1 Philosophical foundations, eds. R. Poli, and J. Seibt. Dordrecht: Springer.
Poli, R., and C. Gnoli. 2004. Levels of reality and levels of representation. *Knowledge Organization* 31(3):151–160.
Poli, R., and L. Obrst. 2010. The interplay between ontology as categorial analysis and ontology as technology. In *Theory and applications of ontology*, eds. R. Poli, J. Seibt, and J. Symons, vol. 1. Berlin: Springer.
Pöppel, E. 1994. Temporal mechanism in perception. *International Review of Neurobiology* 37:185–202.
Profitt, D.R., I. Rock, H. Hecht, and J.M. Schubert. 1992. Stereokinetic effect and its relation to the kinetic depth effect. *Journal of Experimental Psychology: Human Perception and Performance* 18:3–21.
Purghè, F., and S. Coren. 1992. Subjective contours 1900–1990. Research trends and bibliography. *Perception and Psychophysics* 51:291–304.
Rausch, E. 1952. *Struktur und Metrik figural-optischer Wahrnehmung*. Frankfurt a.Main: Kramer.
Rausch, E. 1964. Einzelgegenständlisches als phänomenale Eigenschaft. *Psychologische Forschung* 28:33–45.
Rausch, E. 1966. Das Eigenschaftsproblem in der GT der Wahrnehmung. In *Handbuch der Psychologie*, ed. W. Metzger. Göttingen: Hogrefe.
Rensink, R.A. 2000. Seeing, sensing, scrutinizing. *Vision Research* 40:1469–1487.
Rensink, R.A. 2002. Change detection. *Annual Review Psychology* 53:245–277.
Roberson, D., J. Davidoff, I.R.L. Davies, and L.R. Shapiro. 2005. Color categories: Evidence for the cultural relativity hypothesis. *Cognitive Psychology* 50:378–411.
Rosch, E. 1978. *Cognition and categorization*. Hillsdale: Erlbaum.
Rosenthal, V. 2004. Microgenesis. Immediate experience on visual processes in reading. In *Seeing, Thinking and Knowing*, ed. A. Carsetti, 221–243. Dordrecht: Kluwer.
Rubin, E. 1958. Figure and ground. In *Readings in perception*, eds. D.C. Beardsley, and M. Wertheimer. New York: Van Nostrand.
Runeson, S. 1974. Constant velocity: Not perceived as such. *Psychological Research* 37:3–23.
Runge, O.P. 1910. *Farbenkugeln*. oder Construction der Verhältnisse aller Mischungen der Farben zu einander, und ihrer Vollständigen Affinität, mit angehängten Versuch einer Ableitung der Harmonie in der Zusammenstellungen der Farben. Hamburg: F. Perthes.
Sander, F. 1930. Structures, totality of experience and gestalt. In *Psychologies of 1930*, ed. C. Murchison, 188–204. Worchester MA: Clark University Press.
Schapp, W. 1909. *Beiträge zur Phänomenologie der Wahnehmung*. Frankfurt: Klostermann.
Schlottman, A. 2000. Is perception of causality modular? *Trends in Cognitive Sciences* 4: 441–442.
Scholl, B.J., and P.D. Tremoulet. 2000. Perceptual causality and animacy. *Trends in Cognitive Science* 4:299–309.

Schumann, F. 1904. Beiträge zur Analyse der Gesichtswahrnehmungen: 1. Einige Beobachtungen über die Zusammenfassung von Gesichtseindrücken zu Einheiten. *Zeitschrift für Psychologie* 23:1–32.
Seifert, E. 1917. Zur Psychologie der Abstraktion und Gestaltwahrnehmung. *Zeitschrift für Psychologie* 78.
Shannon, C.E., and Weaver, W. 1998. *The Mathematical Theory of Communication*. Urbana, IL: University of Illinois Press. (Originally published in 1949).
Sivik, L. 1997. Color system for cognitive research. In *Color categories in thought and language*, eds. C.L. Hardin, and L. Maffi, 163–192. Cambridge: Cambridge University Press.
Spillmann, L., and W. Ehrenstein. 2003. Gestalt issues in modern neuroscience. *Axiomathes* 13:433–458.
Stadler, M., L. Stegagno, and G. Trombini. 1979. Quantitative analyse der Rauschschen Pragnänzaspekte. *Gestalt Theory* 1:43–51.
Stein, E. 1962. Die ontische Struktur der Person und ihre erkenntnistheoretische Problematik. In *Edith Steins Werke* 6, 137–197. Freiburg: Herder.
Stern, W. 1897. *Psychologie der Veranderungsauffassung* Breslau: Preuss und Junger.
Stevens, S.S. 1986. *Psycho-physics. Introduction to perceptual, neural and social prospects*. New Brunswick & Oxford: Transaction Books.
Struber, D., and M. Stadler. 1999. Differences in top-down influences on the reversal rate of different categories of reversible figures. *Perception* 28:1185–1198.
Tarr, M., and D. Kriegman. 2001. What defines a view?. *Vision Research* 41:1981–2004.
Ullman, S. 1984. Visual routines. *Cognition* 18:97–156.
Verfaillie, K., and G. d'Ydewalle. 1991. Representational momentum and event course anticipation in the perception of implied periodical motions. *Journal of Experimental Psychology: Learning, Memory, and Cognition* 17:302–313.
Vicario, G.B. 2005. *Il tempo*. Il Mulino: Bologna.
Wallach, H.W., and D.N. O'Connell. 1953. The kinetic depth effect. *Journal for Experimental Psychology* 45:205–217.
Werner, H., and S. Wapner. 1952. Towards a general theory of perception. *Psychological Review* 59:324–338.
Wertheimer, M. 1923. Untersuchungen zur Lehre von der Gestalt. *Psychologische Forschung* 4:301–350.
Wertheimer, M. 1938. Laws of organization in perceptual forms. In *A source book of Gestalt psychology*, ed. W. Ellis, 71–94. London: Routledge.
Wertheimer, M. 2002a. Gestalt theory. In *A source book of Gestalt psychology*, ed. W. Ellis, 1–11. London: Routledge (Original 1925).
Wertheimer, M. 2002b. The general theoretical situation. In *A source book of Gestalt psychology*, ed. W. Ellis, 12–16. London: Routledge (Original 1922).
Whitney, D. 2002. The influence of visual motion on perceived position. *Trends in Cognitive Sciences* 6(5):211–216.
Whitney, D., and P. Cavanagh. 2000. Motion distorts visual space: Shifting the perceived position of remote stationary obiects. *Nature Neuroscience* 3(9):954–958.
Wierbicka, A. 2006. The semantics of colour: A new paradigm. In *Progress in Colour Studies*, 2 vols., ed. W. Ellis, vol. I, 1–24. Amsterdam: Benjamins Publishing House.
Wollheim, R. 1970. The work of art as object. In *On art and the mind*, 112–129. London: Allen Lane.
Zanforlin, M. 1988a. The height of a stereokinetic cone: A quantitative determination of a 3D effect from 2D moving pattern without a 'Rigidity Assumption'. *Psychological Research* 50:162–172.
Zanforlin, M. 1988b. Stereokinetic phenomena as good Gestalts: The minimum principle applied to circles and ellipses in rotation: A quantitative analysis and a theoretical discussion. *Gestalt Theory* 10:187–214.
Zanforlin, M. 2000. The various appearances of a rotating ellipse and the minimum principle: A review and an experimental test with non-ambiguous percepts. *Gestalt Theory* 22:157–184.
Zanforlin, M. 2003. Stereokinetic anomalous contours: Demonstrations. In *The Legacy of Kanizsa in Cognitive Science*, ed. L. Albertazzi, special issues of *Axiomathes* 13:389–398.

Chapter 10
Interactive Knowing: The Metaphysics of Intentionality

Mark H. Bickhard

Intentionality focuses metaphysical problems whose history extends into antiquity. I will argue, in fact, that intentionality cannot be understood without transcending the metaphysical framework that has been inherited from the Greeks – specifically, the metaphysics of substance and particle. The focus will not be on exegesis and interpretation, but, instead, on the historical conceptual heritage, the aporia created by that heritage, and a model – the interactive model – that transcends those aporia.

10.1 Substance and Particle

Heraclitus famously argued that all is flux. Parmenides argued that, to the contrary, change is not possible. Roughly, for A to change into B, A would have to disappear into nothingness and B would have to emerge out of nothingness. Because nothingness cannot exist, change cannot occur.

The argument against nothingness turned on the Greek notion that saying or thinking was akin to pointing at that which is said or thought. Nothingness cannot be pointed at, so it cannot exist, and, therefore, change cannot occur (Campbell 1992, Gill 1989). This may seem slightly quaint to modern ears, but, lest it be too easily dismissed, consider how much difficulty modern philosophers, from Russell through Fodor, have had attempting to account for false representation and representation of non-existents (Hylton 1990, Fodor 1990a, b, 1998, 2003).

In any case, the Parmenidean argument was taken very seriously by contemporaries, and attempts to were made to respond to it. The Empedoclean notion of substance – earth, air, fire, and water – attempts to resolve the problem via substances which in fact do not change, thus satisfying the Parmenidean criterion, but that can nevertheless mix and remix in varying proportions, thus accounting for the appearance of change. Similarly, Democritus proposed atoms as Parmenidean

M.H. Bickhard (✉)
Lehigh University, Bethlehem, PA, USA
e-mail: mhb0@lehigh.edu

R. Poli, J. Seibt (eds.), *Theory and Applications of Ontology: Philosophical Perspectives*, DOI 10.1007/978-90-481-8845-1_10,

wholes that did not change, but that could alter their configurations, thus accounting for appearance (Campbell 1992, Gill 1989, Guthrie 1965, Taylor 1997, Wright 1997).

Plato and Aristotle accepted these problems of change, and Aristotle proposed a sophisticated theory of substance that differed significantly from that of Empedocles, but that accepted the necessity for an underlying unchanging matter of some sort. It is via Aristotle that Western thought has been most thoroughly permeated by these issues and assumptions.[1]

10.1.1 Aporetic Consequences

The assumption of a substance (or particle) framework, however, imposes serious conceptual consequences and constraints. I will outline some of these, and argue that intentionality, among other phenomena, cannot be naturalistically accounted for within those constraints.

Three consequences in particular have become part of the presupposed background of thought:

1. Unchangingness – stasis or inertness – is the default. Change requires explanation.
2. Emergence is impossible. Change and emergence, after all, are precisely what substance and atom were introduced in order to avoid.
3. A realm of substance or atom, cause, and fact is split from a realm of intentionality, normativity, and modality.

These three suppositions can be problematic in any domain of study, but they have a special virulence with regard to mental phenomena: mentality is precisely a realm of intentionality, normativity, and modality, and cannot be understood without accounting for these properties, yet these are precisely what is split off from the 'natural' world by a substance or particle metaphysics.[2] Furthermore, so I will argue, the way to re-unite the two realms is to provide an account of the *emergence* of intentionality and normativity, but emergence is precisely what these metaphysical frameworks

---

[1]Aristotle's "elements" – earth, air, fire, and water – were not unchanging as they were for Empedocles, but he did postulate an unchanging ground (prime matter) beneath them. Also, translation vicissitudes have rendered "substance" for Aristotle as involving the problem of unity – the difference between an aggregate and a statue, a body and a living being. As will be addressed later in the text, problems of unity, of stability, are crucial, but I will not pursue any details of Aristotle's thought on this (Gill 1989).

[2]Note that, once the Parmenidean framework is accepted, the fact/norm or substance/mental split is a forced consequence. Within the framework of that split, there are only three possibilities: posit two realms, one of substance, fact, and cause, the other of mentality, intentionality, and normativity – e.g., Aristotle's substance and form; Descartes' two kinds of substance; Kant's noumenal and phenomenal; analytic philosophy's scientific world of fact and linguistic/philosophical world of normativity – or try to make do with only the mental realm – e.g., Hegel and the idealists – or try to make do with only the physical realm – e.g., Hobbes, Hume (on most interpretations), Quine, and most contemporary scientists and philosophers. Transcending this split requires emergence, but emergence is what the entire framework was introduced to avoid.

were introduced to preclude. Earth, air, fire, and water can mix, but there is no way to get a fifth substance. And, finally, emergence *is* metaphysically possible – so I will argue – within a metaphysics of *process*, a metaphysics in which *change* is the default and stability requires (special) explanation (Bickhard 2000, in preparation). So, in at least a general way, I am arguing for a return to process, a return to Heraclitus.

10.2 Process

A move to process can be argued for on several grounds. For one, virtually all sciences have undergone a historical shift from attempting to understand their subject in terms of substance to a recognition that the phenomena in question are in fact processes. We no longer attempt to model fire in terms of phlogiston, but instead recognize it as a process of combustion; nor heat in terms of caloric, but instead as random kinetic energy; nor life in terms of vital fluid, but instead in terms of special kinds of far-from-thermodynamic-equilibrium process, and so on. The remaining exception to this historical trend are precisely the sciences of the mind. One reason why the study of mentality is the last in this progression is that it is the only domain[3] for which the third presupposition is central.

Culminating this historical progression in physics is the replacement in the last century of a particle framework with a process framework in the form of quantum fields. Quantum fields are quintessentially processes, and, according to our best physics, there are no particles (Brown and Harré 1998, Cao 1999, Davies 1984, Huggett 2000, Saunders and Brown 1991, Weinberg 1977, 1995, 1996, 2000). What manifests particle-like properties is the quantization of quantum field processes, but that quantization is of wave-like processes: it is similar (including similar in its mathematical form) to the quantization of the number of wavelengths in a vibrating guitar string, but there are no guitar sound particles anymore than there are physical particles. 'Particles' are quantized excitations and interactions among excitations in quantum fields.

Finally, if the world were to consist only of point particles, the probability that they would ever encounter each other would be zero, and nothing would ever happen in the universe. The current standard 'naïve' view is that particles *do* interact – via fields of force among them. On one hand, this gives everything that I need for my further points because fields, if acknowledged at all, are processes. And, on the other hand, as mentioned, this view is not consistent with quantum field theory. It is possible, perhaps even likely, that quantum field theory will itself be overturned at some point in the future, but we have empirical evidence of multiple kinds of non-localities in interactions and process phenomena even in a vacuum that are more than sufficient to block any return to a classical particle model.[4]

---

[3]There is a partial exception to this point, and an important exception, in the normative phenomena of biological function.

[4]E.g., the Casimir effect, in which two metal plates held close to each other are pushed toward each other because the vacuum activity outside the plates is greater than that between the plates,

So, there are historical, physical, and metaphysical reasons to shift to a process framework, even before the emergence and intentionality issues are considered. The argument at this point turns to emergence, and then to normative emergence.

10.3 Emergence: The Metaphysical Possibility

Emergence is supposed to occur with (new) patterns of organization. Clearly something new comes into existence: the pattern itself. But in order for emergence to have any metaphysical significance, something new that has its own causal efficacy, some manner in which that which is new has consequences for the future of the world, must come into existence.

10.3.1 Kim and Particles

Within a particle framework, the very possibility of such causal emergence is precluded. New patterns of particles may indeed manifest new *regularities* of the causal interactions among the particles, but it is nevertheless only the particles that engage in any causal interaction. The new regularities are just manifestations of the manner in which the particles interact within such a configuration (Kim 1993).

Lest we be tempted to consider that some new causal power does emerge, consider that any purported such new causality would have to either violate the causality of the involved particles, or it would be epiphenomenal with respect to the causality of the particles, or, for a third possibility, the particle causal interactions could be such that they leave an indeterminancy of consequence that might be filled in by the causal consequences of the pattern.

This third possibility contradicts standard assumptions about the causal closure of the micro-physical world: if the world of basic particles suffices for the causality of the universe, then there is no such indeterminancy. The first possibility also contradicts assumptions about the causal closure of the micro-physical world, but in an opposite sense: instead of micro-causality leaving indeterminancies, there would be some sort of additional causal force that compelled deviations from what the causal consequences would otherwise be. If such a configuration-based additional causal influence were a product of the working out of other particles in the configuration, then it would not be an addition to or contravener of the causal interactions among the particles: on this interpretation, the alleged violation of the causality of the particles reduces precisely to the causality of those particles – it is no violation at all. On the other hand, if the purported additional causal influence is *not* a resultant of other particles then it does violate the assumption of the micro-physical causal closure

thus inducing a pressure. The vacuum activity between the plates is reduced relative to outside the plates because that activity is restricted to quantized wave-like processes that will "fit" between the plates – the plates "fix" the vacuum just like the fingers and frets "fix" the guitar string, forcing a quantization of the wave processes in between them (Mostepanenko et al. 1997).

of the world. There are two ways in which this could be understood: 1. the pattern of relationships *qua* pattern itself has causal efficacy, or 2. the additional influence derives from outside of the natural order – it is supernatural.

So, within a *naturalism* (which precludes the second possibility), the only possibility still open is that the relations, the configurations, the patterns, can themselves (at least at times) have causal efficacy. This is not a logical incoherence, but it is a violation of the micro-physical causal closure assumption. Given that assumption, all causal power is possessed by things that have no organization – particles – but that can interact with each other within configurations. Configuration, in this view, is merely the stage on which or within which the particles engage in their causal dance. Configuration has no causality itself. So, with the causality of configuration ruled out by the particle assumption, there is no remaining possibility for causally efficacious emergence (Kim 1993, 1998). QED.

But, as we have seen, there are no particles. Everything is process – quantum field process as far as we currently know. And process cannot exist without organization, organization that makes a difference in the causal influences among those processes. A point-process is not a coherent notion: process is inherently spatially and temporally organized, and the organization has causal power if anything does (there isn't anything else to be a candidate). So, to delegitimate organization as a possible locus of causal power, as the particle framework does, not only begs the question against emergence, it also, within a process framework, would drain all causality out of the entire world.

Causality, whatever it is,[5] must depend in part on configuration, on relations. So there may well be new causality with new patterns of process; there may well be emergent causality. One potential attempt to refute this point would be to claim that causality occurs within the quantum micro-realm, but that there is at best epiphenomenality at any scale above the quantum level. In this view, some privileged quantum scale separates those process organizations that are causal (the ones below the scale) from the ones that are not causal (the ones above the scale).

But there is no such differentiating scale. Organizational relations at all scales can manifest and depend upon quantum phenomena (e.g., consider superconductivity), so if the alleged supervenience base[6] is to include all (potentially) relevant relations,

---

[5]I would argue, in fact, that there is no unitary kind of phenomena that answers to our notions of causality. Causality has to do with locations of idealized intervention (Piaget 1954, Woodward 2003), but there are multifarious processes to which such a notion of potential intervention might be applied, ranging from quantum processes to billiard balls to military or corporate commands.

[6]A word is in order about the notion of supervenience. X is defined to be supervenient on its base, consisting of the base set of particles, their properties, and their relations, if there can be no changes in X without corresponding changes in the base (Kim 1993, 1998). There are multiple variants on this intuition, and hundreds of pages addressing them, but, ultimately, they have little to do with the issues for which 'supervenience' was enlisted. First, the notion is so broad that it includes almost any naturalistic framework (Kim 1998), but, worse, it does not apply at all to a rather large class of the most important phenomena in the world.

In particular, supervenience does not apply to relational 'properties'. Some pencil may be the longest pencil in the box, and cease to be so with the inclusion of a longer pencil, but the particles, properties, and relations that make up the pencil need not have changed (Teller 1992). Being the

then it will include all scales. Organization cannot be precluded as a potential locus of causal power, at any scale, without violating either the assumption of causality itself or the presumed naturalistic closure of the causal world.

The possibility of emergence, then, escapes Kim's arguments against emergence because those arguments turn on a question-begging delegitimation of organization as a potential locus of causal power, one that is motivated by a particle framework in which the bearers of causal power have no organization. A shift to a process framework undercuts these arguments.[7]

10.3.2 Hume Against Emergence

Kim's argument turns on the presumed locus of causality, particles, not having any organization. So they can participate in organization, but organization is merely a setting for the real causality.

In contrast, Hume's argument against deriving norms from facts provides an apparent logic-based argument. Hume stated it, and it is normally interpreted, as applying to normative issues per se, but, so I will argue, it applies to emergence more broadly. If that is so, then Hume's argument blocks, or appears to block, the possibility of emergence in a way that is independent of Kim's considerations. I will show, however, that Hume's argument is unsound.

Hume pointed out that it 'seems altogether inconceivable' how normative terms could be derived from premises that contain only factual terms (Hume 1978, Book III, Part I, Section I, pp. 469–470). The form of the argument that is attributed to Hume is that, if there are any terms in a valid conclusion that are not in the premises, then they must have been introduced by definitions making use of previously available terms. There may be one or more iterations of such definitions in terms of

longest pencil in the box is not of great interest to most, but other much more important phenomena are similarly relational in nature. In particular, thermodynamic phenomena are relational, and, more specifically, being far from thermodynamic equilibrium is relational to the environment – therefore, it has no supervenience base. Furthermore, even on a particle view, a candle flame, for example, is constantly and necessarily changing the particles, etc. that make it up. The candle flame is a configuration of process flow and cannot be identified with *any* base. The same holds for any living thing, as well as hurricanes, and so on. Supervenience was born of and presupposes a static Aristotelian world of substances (or atoms) and their properties. It cannot handle, except by ad-hoc stipulation, phenomena that are inherently relational (Bickhard 2000). It cannot handle process.

[7] Kim's more recent work has left relations out of the definition of the base. Relations, therefore, *do* contribute something beyond that base, because relations are not part of (the definition of) the base. This has allowed Kim to endorse a kind of emergence: new causal properties (perhaps mere regularities within his earlier framework) are now not reducible to the base because those relations are not in the base. On the other hand, a new configuration can have new properties precisely because that new system *is* the relational organization (Kim 1998). The move of placing relations in this special position is correct – relational organization is what emergence is supposed to depend upon – but it is not a well motivated shift so long as Kim stays within a particle framework. No metaphysical work can be done by such mere definitional shifts (Campbell and Bickhard, in preparation). Within a process framework, however, this move is not only motivated, it is forced.

previously defined or provided terms, but they will be finite in number. Any 'new' terms, then, can be back-translated through their definitions – substituting the defining phrase or clause for the term so defined – until the conclusion is restated only with terms that were in the original premises. Since these are by assumption all factual, then any valid conclusion must similarly be factual: it is not possible to validly derive norms from facts (Schurz 1997).

But the general form of the argument does not depend on the distinction between norms and facts per se. The broader conclusion that this argument yields is that there is no way to go beyond combinations of terms that are in the initial premises. You cannot get beyond combinations of whatever you start with. In this general form, the conclusion precludes emergence. It is a logical perspective on the impossibility of emergence within a substance or particle framework: you can get new configurations or combinations, but nothing beyond that.

Hume's argument has had enormous influence. It has been accepted and has constituted the conceptual framework for Kant, Hegel and the idealists, the logical positivists, and the post-Quinean science-ists. The divide between fact and norm – the divide initiated by Parmenides – is deeply embedded in modern thought (Rescher 1980, Larmore 1998).

But Hume's argument is unsound. It assumes that the only valid form of definition is explicit, or abbreviatory, definition. That is the kind of definition that permits back-translation. There is also, however, implicit definition, in which a set of constraints defines that which satisfies those constraints, but just what those are or might be is implicit, not explicit. Hilbert did not discover implicit definition, but he did introduce it in a major way in his axiomatization of geometry in the late nineteenth century (Hilbert 1971). The terms in the axioms were taken to be defined by the relational constraints posed by those axioms, rather than by reference to some prior items or kinds in the world. A 'line', for example, is that which is determined by any two 'points'. This approach was in strong contrast to the assumption that geometry is the mathematics of space, for example, in which the axioms were supposed to constitute the clear and obvious truths about space. Poincarè was another who advocated this 'method of postulates', while Frege and Russell were adamantly opposed.

But implicit definition, in the formal sense, is now a standard part of model theory (Chang and Keisler 1990). And a more informal notion of such definition-by-constraint-satisfaction is applicable within thought more broadly (Hale and Wright 2000).[8]

---

[8]Beth's theorem states that implicit definition and explicit definition are of equal power, and has often been used as an excuse to ignore implicit definition (Doyle 1985). But it just as easily legitimates implicit definition (Quine 1966). More deeply, however, Beth's theorem holds only in certain combinations of kinds of logic and kinds of models considered for those logics. In some combinations, for example, first order predicate logic with finite models, implicit definition is *more* powerful than explicit definition. In general, implicit definition has always been found to be at least as powerful as explicit definition, and, in many cases, more powerful (Kolaitis 1990). It has never been found to be less powerful. Implicit definition cannot be ignored.

The important point for my current purposes is that implicit definition is a valid form of definition, and that *it does not permit back-translation*. Implicit definition does not specify what is implicitly defined: it is implicit. So there is nothing available to be substituted for the defined term in a back-translation. Implicit definition, therefore, *does* permit valid conclusions that *cannot* be stated using only the terms in the premises.

Hume's argument is unsound: it makes a false assumption about definition. The apparent logical barrier to the possibility of emergence, therefore, is removed. Furthermore, it should also be noted that the possibility of introducing meaning in a way that is not dependent on the elements in the premises undercuts the background empiricism in Hume's argument: implicit definition can go beyond combinations of 'input' terms, so meaning in general is not restricted to constructions out of such input elements.[9]

10.4 Normative Emergence

In sum to this point, we are forced by multiple considerations to adopt a process framework, and we find that doing so enables the possibility of emergence – that which substance and particle approaches were designed to eliminate in the first place. I turn, then, to the emergence of normativity, and find that normative emergence follows naturally from certain considerations about the possibility of stable processes. Processes are inherently changing, so the assumptions of stasis and inertness as defaults that are made by Parmenidean inspired approaches are overturned, and we must address specifically how process organizations could possibly be stable.

10.4.1 Stabilities of Process

There are two general forms of process stability. The first constitutes much of our familiar furniture of the world: it is organizations of process that are in some kind of energy well, in the sense that the process will continue in that organization unless sufficient energy impinges on it to disrupt it. These are the stabilities of atoms, for example.

The second kind is central to my current purposes: these are organizations of processes that are far from thermodynamic equilibrium. There is a basic asymmetry between these two kinds of stabilities. Energy-well stabilities survive quite well even when isolated. They simply go to equilibrium and stay in their energy well. Far-from-equilibrium stabilities, however, cannot be isolated (for any extended

[9]It seems clear, in fact, that *no* meanings are derived as constructions out of basic empiricist inputs, in spite of valiant efforts to show how this is or could be done by, for example, Carnap.

time). If they are, they go to equilibrium and *they thereby cease to exist*. Far-from-equilibrium organizations of process require ongoing exchanges with their environments in order to maintain their far-from-equilibrium conditions. Far-from-equilibrium processes require *maintenance* in order to be stable; energy well processes do not.

Such maintenance may be external to the far-from-equilibrium process, such as when pumps keep a supply of chemicals being introduced into a container, perhaps for the purpose of exploring the self-organizational processes that ensue. An important subclass of far-from-equilibrium processes for current purposes is that of process organizations that make contributions to their own conditions of far-from-equilibrium stability: *self-maintenant* systems.

A canonical example of a self-maintenant system is a candle flame. A candle flame maintains above combustion threshold temperature; it vaporizes wax in the wick so that it is available for combustion; it melts wax in the candle so that it can percolate up the wick; and it induces convection, which brings in fresh oxygen and gets rid of waste products. A candle flame is self-maintenant in several ways.

A candle flame can only do one thing – burn. But in more complex self-maintenant systems, there may be an ability to shift activity in accordance with environmental conditions so as to (self-)*maintain* the condition of being *self-maintenant* across those environmental conditions – they may be *recursively*self-maintenant. A bacterium, for example, may swim, and continue swimming if it is heading up a sugar gradient toward more sugar, but tumble if it finds itself heading down a sugar gradient. Swimming is a contribution to self-maintenance if it is headed in the right direction, but detracts from self-maintenance of it is headed in the wrong direction (Campbell 1974). By being able to switch between swimming and tumbling in appropriate circumstances, the bacterium maintains its condition of being self-maintenant across variations in those circumstances: it is, to that extent at least, recursively self-maintenant.

It is in terms of far-from-equilibrium systems, and most especially self-maintenant and recursively self-maintenant systems, that I will address the crucial emergence of normativity. This is initially in the form of normative function, and then in the form of intentionality – representational truth value and aboutness – as emergent in a special kind of function.

10.4.2 Normative Function

The central point of departure is that the existence of a process makes a difference in the world, and that continued existence of far-from-equilibrium systems requires maintenance. So, it makes a difference whether a far-from-equilibrium system is maintained or not. Contributions to that maintenance are contributions to that existence, and are in that sense functional relative to that existence.

The point is not that a system (necessarily) has an intrinsic interest in its own existence, but, rather that the world has an intrinsic 'interest' in whether or not a system continues to exist, because that existence or lack thereof makes a difference in how the world proceeds. So, the perspective or consideration of continued existence is a natural one, that is relevant for the rest of the world. Functional contributions to that existence, therefore, are also relevant to the rest of the world.

This notion of function is thin for far-from-equilibrium systems per se, but becomes more interesting for self-maintenant systems and recursively self-maintenant systems. Self-maintenance is a kind of serving one or more functions for the system itself. Note that the system-relatedness of function can have one and the same process serving a function for one system while being dysfunctional for another: the heart beat of a parasite is functional for the parasite but dysfunctional for the host.

This is function as *usefulness*, rather than function as *design* as is more commonly addressed in the literature. The currently dominant conception of normative function is etiological: an organ has a function insofar as the ancestral organs have had the right kind of selection history for doing whatever satisfies that function (Millikan 1984, 1993, 2005). A kidney's function of filtering blood is constituted in ancestor kidneys having been selected for filtering blood: evolution has 'designed' kidneys for doing that.

It is useful to compare further these two models of function. A (partial) corollary of the differences between the approaches in terms of design versus usefulness is that the etiological approach focuses on *organs having functions* while the far-from-equilibrium model focuses on *serving functions*, whether or not anything has those functions. This difference yields reciprocal promissory notes for each to account for the other. The etiological approach has a very natural way of addressing the serving of a function: if an organ that has a function succeeds in performing that function, then it is serving that function. This is almost trivial, except for the consequence that, within this framework, it is at best awkward to account for any function being served if there is nothing that has that function.

And this consequence has further consequences. It precludes, for example, the functioning of muscles to help blood circulation on long plane flights – certainly they cannot have an evolutionary selection history for that function. It also makes it difficult to handle distributed functions for which there is no single organ, or, conversely, multiple functions served by a single organ (Christensen and Bickhard 2002) – can it be 'designed' by selection in two contrasting, perhaps even competing, ways?

There are two deep problems with the etiological approach that I would like to focus on, however. The first is a circularity with regard to the emergence of normativity. If kidney ancestors have been selected for filtering blood, that means that those ancestral kidneys have been useful to the organisms involved – they contributed to the continued existence of the far-from-equilibrium living systems in which those kidneys did their filtering. By definition, this kind of usefulness is not called functional within the etiological framework because it does not have the definitionally required evolutionary history. But it is difficult to deny that it is, whatever it is called, *normative* relative to the organism, normative precisely in the sense focused on by the far-from-equilibrium model (Christensen and Bickhard 2002). In this respect, etiological models account for a kind of normative phenomena, if at all, in terms of another kind of normative phenomena. This is not only a circularity with regard to normativity, it is a circularity that rests upon the far-from-equilibrium account being outlined here. So, if the far-from-equilibrium account fails as an account of normativity, then so also does the etiological account.

The second problem is a failure of naturalism in the etiological account. Having a function, according to this approach, is constituted in having the right kind of history; it is constituted in some kind of history having taken place in the past – or not. So, having a function per se is constituted in the past – the right history, if it exists at all, is in the past. In particular, having a function, on this account, is *not* constituted in current state of the organism or system.

This point is manifest in some examples and thought experiments that have attracted considerable attention. Suppose a lion were to pop into existence in the corner that, by assumption, is molecule by molecule identical to a lion in the zoo. Or, for a less science fictional example, consider the first time something appears in evolution and is useful for the organism in which it occurs. The lion in the corner has no evolutionary history, therefore certainly not the right kind of evolutionary history, therefore its organs do not have any functions. The lion in the zoo, in contrast, does have the right history and its organs do have functions. Similarly, the first-time-appearing useful 'organ' does not have an evolutionary history, therefore not the right kind of evolutionary history, and, therefore, does not have a function, while some descendent may have identical causal processes but now does have the right history and, therefore, does have a function.

These kinds of examples are generally considered to be counter-intuitive, but worth that cost for the sake of the overall power of the etiological model. After all, if we're not accustomed to counter-intuitive consequences in today's world of quantum theory, we're not keeping track. Nevertheless, they do attract attention with regard, for example, to how many generations the selection history has to proceed before 'having a function' comes into being, or whether all such generations should be weighted equally – what if the selection history changed in relevant ways more recently, for example (Godfrey-Smith 1994).

An aspect of such examples that is not commonly remarked, however, is that in both cases we have two systems that are by assumption identical in relevant current state, but one has functions and the other does not. Causality, however, is mediated *only* by current state; two systems or organisms in identical current states are identical in causal or dynamic properties. So, in both examples, having or not having functions makes no difference in the causal, dynamic properties of the organisms. Etiological function is causally epiphenomenal – it fails a fundamental criterion of naturalism: it doesn't make any difference in how the world proceeds. Having the right history may explain etiology, but it doesn't constitute a causally efficacious normativity.

In contrast, the far-from-equilibrium model *is* defined in terms of current state, so it is causally efficacious. And, as an account of emergent normativity, it is presupposed by the etiological account – and it is not itself circular.

10.4.2.1 Having a Function from Serving a Function

I turn now to the promissory note to account for *having a function* in terms of far-from-equilibrium *serving a function*. As mentioned, success in serving a function may depend in the appropriate conditions holding. Swimming serves a function if oriented up a sugar gradient. Serving a function, then, is context dependent, and the activity of serving a function *functionally presupposes* that the relevant conditions hold.

Those presupposed relevant conditions may include that other functions are being served. In some cases, internal to an organism, there may be multiple cross dependencies among various functional activities, some of which *may* presuppose that some supporting function will be served at a particular location by a particular organ. In such a case, that organ *has* that function (perhaps among others) relative to the functional presuppositions of the rest of the organism. Thus we have *having a function* in terms of *serving a function* in a manner that is normative and causally efficacious.

10.4.3 Representation: Normativity and Intentionality

There is much more to develop regarding function, but I will now turn to the emergence of representation, with its normativity of truth value and intentionality of 'aboutness'. Recursively self-maintenant systems – living systems in general – are autonomous (Christensen and Bickhard 2002), in the Aristotelian sense: 'Autonomous entities rely on themselves both for the realization of their capacities and for their persistence' (p. 213). 'An organism's activity is much more than an expression of what it is; it is also the means by which the organism preserves itself from deterioration' (p. 219). 'Self-maintenance is the preservation that results from an organism's self-directed behavior.' (Gill 1989, p. 227).

They are process organizations that are organized around maintaining that organization. Activities that they engage in that succeed in being functional, then, are in that sense 'true' to their nature, to their autonomy. Those that fail to be functional are not.[10] Furthermore, to engage in an activity is to presuppose that that activity will be functional, which, among other things, presupposes that the conditions for it to be functional do in fact hold. So, to engage in activity that is in interaction with the environment is to functionally presuppose that that activity, that interaction, is appropriate for this environment. It constitutes an implicit predication that this is one of those environments in which this kind of interaction is appropriate, will be functional. That predication might be true, or might be false: *truth value*.

Still further, to engage in an activity that is in interaction with the environment involves functional presuppositions about that environment – presuppositions that

[10] Such "truth in action" is the original meaning of truth. It has undergone major historical transformation, and, arguably, degeneration, since ancient times (Campbell 1992, in preparation).

environmental conditions that would support such an interaction hold. This constitutes an implicit *content* to the predication – an attribution of some sufficient conditions for the interaction to the environment in which the interaction is taking place. If sufficient conditions do in fact hold, then the predication will be true, and the interaction will be functional. So, we find truth value and content emergent in the function of triggering or selecting interaction in recursively self-maintenant, autonomous, systems. Truth value and content emerge as concomitants to the normativity of what it is (or would be) to be a successful autonomous being.[11]

10.4.3.1 Resources for Greater Complexity

The emergence of truth value and intentionality in such simple systems is interesting and a powerful support for the general ontological shifts that underlie it, but such interaction representation doesn't look much like familiar representation. The general task of interaction selection, however, becomes more complex in more complex organisms, and these complexities provide the resources needed for the emergence of more complex forms of representation.

In simple autonomous systems such as the bacterium, the (functional) task of interaction selection can be similarly simple. In the bacterium, swimming is or is not simply triggered if the right conditions are satisfied. In more complex organisms, the task of interaction selection splits into two complementary parts: (1) indications of what interactions are possible, and (2) selection among those possible of that which is most in keeping with the organism's current state and goals. A frog, for example, might have two flies that it could flick its tongue at in attempts to eat, and a worm somewhere else, and the shadow of a hawk flying overhead that would suggest jumping into the water in order to escape. None of these interactions are triggered – the frog must choose among them, and, in order to be able to choose, the frog must have some sort of functional indications of what those possibilities are.

It is crucial to note that such indications of interaction potentiality, even if not engaged in, still bear the properties of being, or failing to be, true to the organism, true or false as predications about the environment, and having implicit contents attributed to that environment. This point is important because the split of interaction selection into indication and selection among indications is the beginning of the elaboration of resources that allow this primitive emergence of truth value and intentionality to account for, to emergently generate, more complex and familiar kinds of representations, such as of objects.

---

[11] Elsewhere I argue that it is this implicitness of content that creates the frame problems (Bickhard and Terveen 1995): in being implicit, the content is unbounded relative to any attempt to explicitly exhaust it. The satisfiers of an implicit definition, whether formal or dynamic, cannot be simply enumerated because there is no bound on what needs to be included in the enumeration. A (meta-) perspective on an implicit definition might be able to derive a bound or to prove that the implicit definition is categorial (i.e., all models are isomorphic), but this requires examining the implicit definition itself, not just examining or enumerating its extension.

In particular, this split permits the branching of potential interaction indications – indications of multiple possibilities. A further resource emerges in the ability to iterate indications of interaction potentiality, so that, for example, engaging in interaction X may create the conditions required for interaction Y to become possible.

The necessary conditionality of interaction indications is already present even in the simplest cases. The bacterium continues swimming *if* it finds itself swimming up a sugar gradient; the frog sets up an indication that it could flick its tongue in a certain manner followed by eating if it has detected a moving speck at a particular location and moving in a certain direction. These conditionalities are inherent in the organization of the processes of the organism, even when they are not being engaged. If the frog *were* to detect a fly in a certain location etc., then it *would* set up and indication of interaction potentiality of appropriate sort. With sufficient learning and memory capability, an organism can link such conditionalities in iterated links. Together with the possibility of branching indications in multiple 'directions', this yields the possibility of *webs* of conditionalized interaction indications, webs perhaps of large complexity.

It is within such webs of interaction indications that we find the possibility of more complex representation. These webs constitute the organism's knowledge about its current situation – its *situation knowledge*. Such potentialities will, in general, vary over time, both as a result of the organism's activity, and as the result of goings-on in the environment, so the webs require ongoing maintenance and updating. I call such processes of maintaining and updating situation knowledge *apperception*. Interactions that are engaged in primarily for the sake of their influences on apperception are *perceptual interactions* (Bickhard and Richie 1983, Bickhard and Terveen 1995).

10.4.3.2 Representations of Objects

Consider now a child's toy block. It offers multiple possibilities of visual scan, manipulation, chewing, dropping, and so on. Furthermore, in the apperception based on any one such visual scan, for example, an entire subweb of interaction indications can be apperceptively constructed. These 'object' subwebs can have special properties. First, every point in such a subweb is reachable from any other – every scan potentiality is reachable from every other, for example, with appropriate manipulations shifting from one to another. Second, such an internally reachable subweb remains invariant under an important class of other activities and changes. It is invariant, for example, under changes in the location of the block – perhaps in the toy box – and the child – perhaps moving into the next room, and so on. It is not universally invariant, however: crushing or burning the block would destroy the interaction potentialities. As the child learns to keep track of such invariances, it thereby learns to keep track of parts of its environment that are out of perceptual reach – the toy block in the toy box in the next room, for example. Such object permanence capabilities constitute an important kind of memory.

Primitive indications of interaction potentiality, therefore, can become more complex in ways that can address much more complex kinds of representation. Thus, that such interaction-based forms of representation might constitute the framework within which *all* representation has evolved remains a viable possibility. Demonstrating that general capacity of the model, of course, requires addressing multifarious kinds of representation and cognition – I will not pursue that task further here, but turn instead to examining some further properties of representation, and comparisons with other models.[12,13]

10.4.4 Criteria of Emergence and Normativity

Interactive representation has multiple interesting properties, some familiar, some not so familiar. These include, for example, that it is inherently embodied, situated, deictic, and indexical. It is future oriented, rather than oriented toward the past: it is not a 'spectator' model, in which the organism is attempting to peer into the past of the input stream. It is inherently modal, with interaction indications being of *potential* interactions, and content consisting of implicitly attributed sufficient interaction-supporting conditions that *might* hold, rather than the exclusive focus on the actual-past of most models.

10.4.4.1 Representational Emergence

The two properties that I will focus on in this discussion, however, are those of being emergent, and of being representationally normative. Interactive representation is emergent in the organization of system processes, most especially of control processes that determine which other activities will be engaged in. That is, it is emergent out of non-representational phenomena. The possibility of such emergence undercuts arguments for innatism that turn on the inability of learning and development to create new, emergent, representation.[14] Here we have a model of representation that is emergent, and, therefore, that can be generated in learning and development: we

---

[12]This model of the representation of a small manipulable object is basically the translation into the interactive model of Piaget's model of such objects (Piaget 1954). Such borrowing is possible because both models are interaction based; both are within a general pragmatist framework (Rosenthal 1983). The answer to the challenge of how such an interaction model could account for abstract representation, such as of number, is also roughly Piagetian, though in this case with wider divergences (Campbell and Bickhard 1986, Bickhard and Campbell 1989). Models of much wider ranges of representational and cognitive phenomena can be found elsewhere (Bickhard 1980, 2002, 2003, 2004b, 2005, 2006, in preparation; Bickhard and Richie 1983).

[13]Physiological textbooks commonly have several chapters on "sensory encoding". Doesn't that mean that there are basic "perceptual" encodings? A good question, but the answer is "No". For this and other discussions, see Bickhard (2004, in preparation).

[14]Such arguments do not work in any case: if there is no process that can generate emergent representation, then evolution cannot do it either, and neither can cosmology, so representation cannot exist. On the other hand, if there is such a possibility, then there is no argument showing

do not have to have an innate base of representations that combinatorically suffice for all representation (Bickhard 1993, in preparation).

Furthermore, the possibility of emergent representation opens the possibility of new kinds of cognitive dynamics, such as a non-representational dynamics that generates a 'froth' of emergent representations, some of which might be supported and further activated by relevant constraints and considerations, while others may simply fade for lack of support. This would constitute a kind of internal variation and selection process, an internal evolutionary epistemology (Bickhard, in preparation). It is vastly different from the processing of inert symbols or of vectors of activations, for example.

10.4.4.2 Representational Normativity

The normativity of interactive representation is constituted both in the property of having truth value, and in the property of having system detectable truth value. The anticipatory nature of indications of interactive potentiality renders both properties, at least as possibilities (some species are not capable of making full use of them), inherent in the nature of representation. Indications of future potentialities can be true or false in that those indicated potentialities may in fact be potentialities or they may not. Those truth values can be system detectable, at least potentially and fallibly and for some sufficiently complex creatures, because engaging in such an indicated interaction potentiality that does not proceed as indicated not only falsifies the indication, it also does so in a way that is internally functionally accessible to the organism – the internal processes don't go as indicated. This is a normativity that is emergent in and for and by the organism itself, not just the analytic or stipulative perspective of an external observer. I will use these two normative criteria as a primary framework for analyzing alternative models in the literature: none satisfy them.

Traditional models of representation stem from the underlying substance or particle framework, and, originally, from the Greek notion that like-represents-like. One of the purest examples is the Aristotelian notion that perception is akin to a signet ring pressing its form into wax. The form in the wax that represents the form of the ring is an instance of exactly the same form that it is representing. This is among the tightest 'correspondence' models of representation, in which something in correspondence with something else is taken to represent that something else precisely in virtue of that correspondence – it is taken to encode it. In this case, the correspondence is that of identity (as form).

As forms were 'fractured' and abandoned (Campbell 1992). the purported representational encoding correspondences became less direct. The mental phenomena that were supposed to be representational might still be taken to be 'similar' to that

why evolution might be capable of it but learning and development not capable of it (Bickhard 1993).

which they represent (such as a statue or painting is similar to that which it portrays), but similarity too was found to be wanting – what does or could it mean to be similar to all chairs or all triangles or numbers or justice? Out of this heritage has evolved notions of representational correspondences that are constituted as informational relationships, causal relationships, or lawful relationships (Dretske 1988, Fodor 1990a, b, 1998, 2003), and notions of structural similarity (isomorphism) are also still to be found (Cummins 1996).

These constitute continuing attempts to account for the normative phenomenon of representation in terms of the non-normative world of substances or particles, causes, and facts, but without, in general, recognizing the deep problems of emergence that are involved. Such models are all either atemporal or past oriented; they are based on correspondence, rather than on interaction; they focus on the actualities of the past, not on the modalities of the future. They all presume that some special kind of correspondence constitutes an encoding of what is on the other end of the correspondence. Because they suppose that all representation has the nature of encoding, I have called such positions versions of *encodingism.*

Problems with Encodingism. Encodingism suffers from many problems, some of ancient provenance, some more recently discovered. That is not because encodings do not exist – they clearly do exist, but real encodings cannot solve any basic epistemological problems. Consider, for example, that '. . .' encodes 's' in Morse code. That is a perfectly good encoding, and it is very useful because '. . .' can be sent over telegraph wires while 's' cannot. But that encoding exists only insofar as people already know, already represent, the dots and dashes, the characters, and the relationships among them. The encodings are stand-ins, and they must have other logically prior representations to stand-in for. They cannot account for emergent representation.

Morse code is conventional, but none of these points turn on that. Consider, for a different example, the neutrino count in some gold mine that encodes properties of fusion processes in the sun. In this case, all of the relationships are natural, not conventional, but still the encoding relationship exists as an epistemic relationship only insofar as people already know, already represent, the neutrino counts, the fusion processes and properties, and the relationships among them. In this case, a natural informational relationship, based on underlying nomological relationships, supports the encoding relationship, but *only for those who know about all this*. Strictly factual informational or causal or lawful relationships do not constitute representational relationships in themselves.

Another perspective on that point derives from recognizing that there are myriads of informational, causal, nomological relationships in the universe, and at least almost all of them are not representational – so what makes the difference between those that are and those that are not? Also, any purported instance of such a foundational encoding relationship, such as the causal, lawful, informational relationships that might hold between retinal activity and light, are accompanied by myriads of additional such relationships – with the surface of the table, with the quantum processes in the surface of the table, with the table a millisecond ago, the table a week ago, the trees out of which the table has been constructed, the activities in the sun that fueled the growth of those trees, and so on – again, which of those is the crucial representational relationship, and how is the organism to determine which one, and how is the organism to know or represent the other end of the crucial one. Note that the last question is the representational problem all over again. Such circularities are rife in encodingist approaches to representation.

The basic normativity problem is manifest in the following problem: if the purported encoding correspondence exists, then the representation exists (at least by stipulation of the model), and it is correct. While if the special encoding correspondence does not exist, then the representation does not exist. But there is a third possibility that must be accounted for: the representation exists, but it is incorrect. Unfortunately, the correspondence existing or not existing would seem to exhaust the modeling possibilities within such a framework. Note again that the future oriented interactive representation has no difficulties with this criterion: the anticipatory indication may exist or not, and, if it does exist, it may be correct or not – there is nothing problematic here.

System Detectable Error. There has been a great deal of activity in the last decades attempting to resolve this problem, but, so I argue, without success. I will not rehearse those arguments here (see Bickhard 2004a, in preparation), but turn to the strengthened normativity issue, that of system detectable error. It might appear that system detectable error is too strong a criterion. Perhaps it is one that should be postponed till it can be addressed from a stronger, richer, base of representational models. Perhaps it is too unusual or special or a high level sophisticated variation that has nothing much to do with the basic nature of representation.

But system detectable error is required for error guided behavior and it is required for learning. We know that error guided behavior occurs and that learning occurs, so any model that cannot account for the possibility of system detectable error is thereby refuted. It is not a criterion that can be set aside. Furthermore, we know that simple versions of system detectable error, guiding behavior, if not learning, occur in very simple systems, such as the bacterium detecting that it is swimming *down* a sugar gradient.

Still further, system detectable error is precisely what the radical skeptical argument concludes is impossible. In order to determine the truth value of our own representations, so the argument goes, we would have to somehow step outside of ourselves to compare our representation with what we are in fact representing to see if they fit or not. But we cannot step outside of ourselves, so we cannot make that comparison, so we cannot determine the truth or falsity of our own representations. System detectable error is impossible.

The Radical Skeptical Argument. The radical skeptical argument has been around for quite a long time, and has survived many attempts to refute or transcend it (e.g., Sanches1988). So much so that a common response is to ignore it as something that cannot be solved, so don't waste time trying. But, if the argument were sound, if it has a true conclusion, then error guided behavior and learning are not possible. This is not a mere arm-chair problem. We know that error guided behavior and learning occur, so we know that something must be wrong with the radical skeptical argument. What's wrong with it is that it is a perfectly valid argument that is based an encodingist assumption about the nature of representation, and that assumption is false, even though almost universal throughout history. That assumption is a 'natural' concomitant of the underlying substance and particle framework. Fodor's transductions are just technologically updated versions of signet ring impressions, and neither one of them has a clue about how the normativities of representation can be accounted for within the factual model outlined (e.g., Fodor 1987, 1990b). In particular, so long as representation is construed as a special encoding correspondence, then the only access to what is being represented is via that or a similar correspondence – you cannot step outside of yourself to check, and any check from 'inside' is circular: it simply makes use of such correspondences again.

Nevertheless, there is important insight in the common response that you may not be able to check the correspondence per se, but you can check its consequences. If those consequences are themselves external, then they too require such encoding correspondences to check on them, and we are back to a circularity. But if those consequences are internal, such as the internal flow of interaction with the environment, then checking them to find out if they fit within the anticipated boundaries of the future course of the interaction does *not* require representing them. They can be checked functionally, not epistemically. There is no circularity. The anticipations of interactive representation can be in error, and such error can be system detectable. The radical skeptical argument does not get a grip in this model because the error checking does not itself have to be externally epistemic, it can be internally functional.

If we check models in the literature, however, they do not even address system detectable error, and cannot account for its possibility even in principle.

Millikan. Millikan's etiological model, for example, would not only render representation causally epiphenomenal along with function, function along with representational content would be constituted in the past, thus not accessible to the organism, thus not available for comparison with what is currently being represented. And any such comparison would require epistemically accessing that which is being represented anyway, and that is the representation problem over again – the basic circularity inherent in such models.

Fodor. Fodor's model attempts to address the possibility of representational error with an asymmetric dependency criterion for error. If a representation is evoked in error, perhaps a cow representation in response to a horse on a dark night, then, so argues Fodor, such an errorful evocation is dependent on the correct evocations in the sense that such horses on dark nights would not evoke the cow representation if cows did not, but that that dependency is not reciprocated: cow representations could be evoked correctly by cows even they were never evoked by horses on dark nights.

This criterion picks out a kind of parasiticness of error on correctness, but it is not even specific to representation, and does not address system detectable error. Consider, for the first point, the counterexample of a poison molecule, perhaps crank, docking on a transmitter receptor, thus mimicking a genuine neurotransmitter, perhaps dopamine. The errorful instance is asymmetrically dependent on the correct instance, but there is no representation at all (Levine and Bickhard 1999). At best we have an instance of functional error, not representational error.

When we turn to system detectable error, again the model cannot even address it. First, the content of representation in this model will depend on relationships of asymmetric dependencies among various counterfactual possibilities of evocation. No organism has access to such a structure, therefore no organism has access to its own contents. Therefore no organism could compare those contents to what is purportedly being represented, and any such comparison would require independently representing the purportedly represented anyway, and that, as should be familiar, is the representation problem yet again. Circularity, again.

Dretske. Dretske's model (1988) is also an etiological model, though the relevant etiology is a learning etiology, not an evolutionary etiology. In consequence, it too is epiphenomenal, the content is not accessible by an organism, and any comparison of the content to what is being represented would in any case require independently representing the object of representation. The circularity of the radical skeptical argument yet again.[15]

In general, attempts to model the normative phenomena of representation within the non-normative realm of substance, particle, cause, and fact, do not succeed. Modeling the normative phenomena of representation within a mental realm, on the other hand, is circular, and leaves the two realms split. Emergence is what is required, but emergence is not possible within a presumed framework of substance, particle, cause, and fact.

10.5 Conclusions

One conclusion from this framework of analyses is that the problems of substance and particle metaphysics, the impossibility of emergence, the split between the 'natural' world and the world of mentality, Hume's argument against deriving norms from facts, the failure of naturalistic attempts to account for representation, and the radical skeptical argument, all constitute (part of) a deeply interrelated package of both metaphysical and epistemological issues. It is a strongly interrelated heritage of conceptual aporia, in which the interrelationships are not at all perspicuous – or, perhaps, one single aporetic heritage with multifarious aspects. To resolve any of them in a coherent, consistent way requires transcending all of them.

---

[15] Cummins' model of representation makes a fundamental distinction between the representational content and that which is represented – between content and target – and, therefore, can account for the possibility of error per se more readily than Fodor's, for example, in which the content is prima facie determined by that which is being represented. Millikan's' model too has this positive characteristic: the content is determined in the past, while the represented is in the present, so the possibility of mismatch is not inherently problematic. But neither model can address system detectable error, and Cummins' model does not address crucial normativity issues that determine what a content is, and certainly not as involved in system detectable error. See, e.g., Bickhard (2004, in preparation).

The converse conclusions are that returning to a process framework enables emergence. Addressing the problem of process stability yields a model of normative emergence. The normativity of the task of interaction selection is the locus of the emergence of representational normativity out of functional or pragmatic normativity. And that emergence is of a nature that can naturally account not only for the possibility of error, but also for the possibility of system detectable error, and, thus, for error guided behavior and learning – thus confounding the radical skeptical argument.

Multitudinous and multifarious problems have been generated over centuries by substance and particle frameworks, and resolving and transcending them is required to understand the world, including, most especially, minds. A return to the metaphysics of process is the core to that resolution.

References

Bickhard, M.H. 1980. *Cognition, convention, and communication.* New York, NY: Praeger Publishers.

Bickhard, M.H. 1993. Representational content in humans and machines. *Journal of Experimental and Theoretical Artificial Intelligence* 5:285–333.

Bickhard, M.H. 2000. Emergence. In *Downward causation*, eds. P.B. Andersen, C. Emmeche, N.O. Finnemann, and P.V. Christiansen, 322–348. Aarhus: University of Aarhus Press.

Bickhard, M.H. 2002. Critical principles: On the negative side of rationality. *New Ideas in Psychology* 20:1–34.

Bickhard, M.H. 2003. An integration of motivation and cognition. In *Development and motivation: Joint perspectives*, eds. L. Smith, C. Rogers, and P. Tomlinson, 41–56. Monograph Series II. Leicester: British Psychological Society.

Bickhard, M.H. 2004a. Process and emergence: Normative function and representation. *Axiomathes – An International Journal in Ontology and Cognitive Systems* 14:135–169. Reprinted from: Bickhard, M.H. 2003. Process and emergence: Normative function and representation. In *Process theories: Crossdisciplinary studies in dynamic categories*, ed. J. Seibt, 121–155. Dordrecht: Kluwer Academic.

Bickhard, M.H. 2004b. The social ontology of persons. In *Social interaction and the development of knowledge*, eds. J.I.M. Carpendale, and U. Muller, 111–132. Mahwah, NJ: Erlbaum.

Bickhard, M.H. 2005. Consciousness and reflective consciousness. *Philosophical Psychology*18(2):205–218.

Bickhard, M.H. 2006. Developmental normativity and normative development. In *Norms in human development*, eds. L. Smith, and J. Voneche, 57–76. Cambridge: Cambridge University Press.

Bickhard, M.H. 2009. The interactivist model. *Synthese* 166(3): 547–591.

Bickhard, M.H. (in preparation). *The whole person: Toward a naturalism of persons – contributions to an ontological psychology.*

Bickhard, M.H., and R.L. Campbell. 1989. Interactivism and genetic epistemology. *Archives de Psychologie* 57(221):99–121.

Bickhard, M.H., and D.M. Richie. 1983. *On the nature of representation: A case study of James Gibson's theory of perception.* New York, NY: Praeger Publishers.

Bickhard, M.H., and L. Terveen. 1995. *Foundational issues in artificial intelligence and cognitive science: Impasse and solution.* Amsterdam: Elsevier Scientific.

Brown, H.R., and R. Harré. 1988. *Philosophical foundations of quantum field theory.* Oxford: Oxford University Press.

Campbell, D.T. 1974. Evolutionary epistemology. In *The philosophy of Karl Popper*, ed. P.A. Schilpp, 413–463. LaSalle, IL: Open Court.

Campbell, R.J. 1992. *Truth and historicity*. Oxford: Clarendon.
Campbell, R.J. in preparation. *Doing the truth*.
Campbell, R.J., and M.H. Bickhard. in preparation. Physicalism, Emergence and Downward Causation.
Campbell, R.L., and M.H. Bickhard. 1986. *Knowing levels and developmental stages*. Contributions to Human Development. Basel: Karger.
Cao, T.Y. 1999. Introduction: Conceptual issues in quantum field theory. In *Conceptual foundations of quantum field theory*, ed. T.Y. Cao, 1–27. Cambridge: University of Cambridge Press.
Chang, C.C., and H.J. Keisler. 1990. *Model theory*. Amsterdam: North Holland.
Christensen, W.D., and M.H. Bickhard. 2002. The process dynamics of normative function. *Monist* 85(1):3–28.
Cummins, R. 1996. *Representations, targets, and attitudes*. Cambridge, MA: MIT Press.
Davies, P.C.W. 1984. Particles do not exist. In *Quantum theory of gravity*, ed. S.M. Christensen, 66–77. Bristol: Adam Hilger.
Doyle, J. 1985. Circumscription and implicit definability. *Journal of Automated Reasoning* 1:391–405.
Dretske, F.I. 1988. *Explaining behavior*. Cambridge, MA: MIT Press.
Fodor, J. 1987. A situated grandmother? *Mind and Language* 2:64–81.
Fodor, J.A. 1990a. *A theory of content*. Cambridge, MA: MIT Press.
Fodor, J.A. 1990b. Information and representation. In *Information, language, and cognition*, ed. P.P. Hanson, 175–190. Vancouver: University of British Columbia Press (now Oxford University Press).
Fodor, J.A. 1998. *Concepts: Where cognitive science went wrong*. New York: Oxford.
Fodor, J.A. 2003. *Hume variations*. Oxford: Oxford University Press.
Gill, M.-L. 1989. *Aristotle on substance*. Princeton: Princeton University Press.
Godfrey-Smith, P. 1994. A modern history theory of functions. *Nous* 28(3):344–362.
Guthrie, W.K.C. 1965. *A history of greek philosophy vol. II: The presocratic tradition from Parmenides to Democritus*. Cambridge: Cambridge University Press.
Hale, B., and C. Wright. 2000. Implicit definition and the a priori. In *New essays on the a priori*, eds. P. Boghossian, and C. Peacocke, 286–319. Oxford: Oxford University Press.
Hilbert, D. 1971. *The foundations of geometry*. La Salle: Open Court.
Huggett, N. 2000. Philosophical foundations of quantum field theory. *The British Journal for the Philosophy of Science* 51(supplement):617–637.
Hume, D. 1978. *A treatise of human nature*. Index by L. A. Selby-Bigge; Notes by P.H. Nidditch. Oxford: Oxford Unioversity Press.
Hylton, P. 1990. *Russell, idealism, and the emergence of analytic philosophy*. Clarendon Press: Oxford.
Kim, J. 1993. Epiphenomenal and supervenient causation. In *Supervenience and mind*, ed. J. Kim, 92–108. Cambridge: Cambridge University Press.
Kim, J. 1998. *Mind in a physical world*. Cambridge, MA: MIT Press.
Kolaitis, Ph.G. 1990. Implicit definability on finite structures and unambiguous computations. In *Proceedings of fifth IEEE annual conference on logic in computer science*. Philadelphia, PA, 168–180.
Larmore, C. 1998. Scepticism. In *The cambridge history of seventeenth-century philosophy, Vol. II*, eds. D. Garber, and M. Ayers, 1145–1192. Cambridge: Cambridge University Press.
Levine, A., and Bickhard, M.H. 1999. Concepts: Where Fodor went wrong. *Philosophical Psychology* 12(1):5–23.
Millikan, R.G. 1984. *Language, thought, and other biological categories*. Cambridge, MA: MIT Press.
Millikan, R.G. 1993. *White queen psychology and other essays for alice*. Cambridge, MA: MIT Press.
Millikan, R.G. 2005. *Language: A biological model*. Oxford: Oxford University Press.
Mostepanenko, V.M., N.N. Trunov, and R.L. Znajek. 1997. *The Casimir effect and its applications*. Oxford: Clarendon Press.

Piaget, J. 1954. *The construction of reality in the child.* New York: Basic.
Quine, W.V.O. 1966. Implicit definition sustained. In *The ways of paradox*, ed. W.V.O. Quine, 195–198. New York: Random House.
Rescher, N. 1980. *Scepticism.* Totowa, NJ: Rowman and Littlefield.
Rosenthal, S.B. 1983. Meaning as habit: Some systematic implications of Peirce's pragmatism. In *The relevance of Charles Peirce*, ed. E. Freeman, 312–327. La Salle, IL: Monist.
Sanches, F. 1988/1581. *That nothing is known.* Cambridge: Cambridge University Press.
Saunders, S., and H.R. Brown. 1991. *The philosophy of vacuum.* Oxford: Oxford University Press.
Schurz, G. 1997. *The is-ought problem : An investigation in philosophical logic.* Trends in Logic, vol. 1. New York: Kluwer Academic.
Taylor, C.C.W. ed. 1997. *From the beginning to plato.* London: Routledge.
Teller, P. 1992. A contemporary look at emergence. In *Emergence or reduction? Essays on the prospects of nonreductive physicalism*, eds. A. Beckermann, H. Flohr, and J. Kim, 139–153. Berlin: Walter de Gruyter.
Weinberg, S. 1977. The search for unity, notes for a history of quantum field theory. *Daedalus* 106(4):17–35.
Weinberg, S. 1995. *The quantum theory of fields. Vol. 1: Foundations.* Cambridge: Cambridge University Press.
Weinberg, S. 1996. *The quantum theory of fields. Vol. II: Modern applications.* Cambridge: Cambridge University Press.
Weinberg, S. 2000. *The quantum theory of fields. Vol. III: Supersymmetry.* Cambridge: Cambridge University Press.
Woodward, J. 2003. *Making things happen.* Oxford: Oxford University Press.
Wright, M.R. 1997. Empedocles. In *From the beginning to plato*, ed. C.C.W. Taylor, 175–207. London: Routledge.

Chapter 11
The Role of Logic and Ontology in Language and Reasoning

John F. Sowa

11.1 The Search for Foundations

Natural languages are the most sophisticated systems of communication ever developed. Formal ontologies are valuable for applications in science, engineering, and business, but they have been difficult to generalize beyond narrowly defined *microtheories* for specialized domains. For language understanding, formal systems have only been successful in narrow domains, such as weather reports and airline reservations. Frege, Russell, and the Vienna Circle tried to make formal logic the universal language of science, but that attempt failed. Only the final results of any research can be stated formally, never the vague hunches, intuitive explorations, and heated debates that are necessary for any creative advance. Scientists and engineers criticized formal methods with the pithy slogans 'Physicists don't do axioms' and 'All models are wrong, but some are useful.' Even Aristotle, who invented the first formal logic, admitted that his syllogisms and categories are important for stating the results of research, but that informal methods are necessary for gathering and interpreting empirical evidence.

Aristotle's logic and categories still serve as a paradigm for the ontologies used in modern computer systems, but his grand synthesis began to break down in the sixteenth century. Aristotle's physics and cosmology were demolished by the work of Copernicus, Galileo, Kepler, and Newton. In philosophy, the skeptical tradition of antiquity was revived by the publication in 1562 of a new edition of the works of Sextus Empiricus, whose attacks on Aristotle were popularized by the essays of Michel de Montaigne. In responding to the skeptics, Descartes began his search for certainty from the standpoint of universal doubt, but he merely reinforced the corrosive effects of skepticism. The British empiricists responded with new approaches to epistemology, which culminated in Hume's devastating criticisms of the foundations of science itself. Two responses to Hume helped to restore the legitimacy of science: Thomas Reid's (1785) critical common sense and Immanuel Kant's three

J.F. Sowa (✉)
VivoMind Intelligence, LLC, Rockville, MD, USA
e-mail: sowa@bestweb.net

R. Poli, J. Seibt (eds.), *Theory and Applications of Ontology: Philosophical Perspectives*, DOI 10.1007/978-90-481-8845-1_11,

major *Critiques*. Kant (1787) adopted Aristotle's logic as the basis for his new system of categories, which he claimed would be sufficient for defining all other concepts:

> If one has the original and primitive concepts, it is easy to add the derivative and subsidiary, and thus give a complete picture of the family tree of the pure understanding. Since at present, I am concerned not with the completeness of the system, but only with the principles to be followed, I leave this supplementary work for another occasion. It can easily be carried out with the aid of the ontological manuals. (A:82, B:108)

Two centuries later, Kant's 'easy' task is still unfinished. His *Opus postumum* records the struggles of the last decade of his life when Kant tried to make a transition from his *a priori* metaphysics to the experimental evidence of physics. Förster (2000) wrote 'although Kant began this manuscript in order to solve a comparatively minor problem within his philosophy, his reflections soon forced him to readdress virtually all the key problems of his critical philosophy: the objective validity of the categories, the dynamical theory of matter, the nature of space and time, the refutation of idealism, the theory of the self and its agency, the question of living organisms, the doctrine of practical postulates and the idea of God, the unity of theoretical and practical reason, and, finally, the idea of transcendental philosophy itself.'

Unlike Aristotle, who used logic as a tool for analyzing language, Kant assumed that logic is a prerequisite, not only for language, but for all rational thought. Richard Montague (1970) pushed Kant's assumption to an extreme: 'I reject the contention that an important theoretical difference exists between formal and natural languages.' That assumption, acknowledged or not, motivated much of the research in artificial intelligence and formal linguistics. The resulting systems are theoretically impressive, but they cannot learn and use ordinary language with the ease and flexibility of a 3-year-old child. But if logic is inadequate, what other foundation could support linguistics and AI? What kind of semantics could represent the highly technical formalisms of science, the colloquial speech of everyday life, and the requirements for sharing and reasoning with the knowledge scattered among millions of computers across the Internet? How would the research and development change under the assumption that logic is a derivative from language, not a prerequisite for it?

One major change would be a shift in emphasis from the rigid views of Frege, Russell, and Carnap to the more flexible philosophies of Peirce, Whitehead, and the later Wittgenstein. As logicians, those two groups were equally competent, but the former considered logic to be superior to language, while the latter recognized the limitations of logic and the power of language. Peirce, in particular, was a pioneer in logic, but he included logic within the broader field of semiotics, or as he spelled it, *semeiotic*. That broader view relates the precise formalisms of grammar and logic to the more primitive, yet more flexible mechanisms of perception, action, and learning. Language is based on vocal signs and patterns of signs, whose more stable forms are classified as vocabulary and grammar. But instead of starting with formal precision, the first signs are vague, ambiguous, and uncertain. Precision is a rare state that never occurs in the early stages of learning, and absolute precision is unattainable in any semiotic system that represents the real world. Grammar, logic, and ontology describe stable patterns of signs or *invariants* under transformations of perspective. Those stable patterns, which are fossilized in formal theories, develop as each individual interacts with the world and other creatures in it.

Although formal logic can be studied independently of natural language semantics, no formal ontology that has any practical application can ever be developed and used without acknowledging its intimate connection with NL semantics. An ontology for medical informatics, for example, must be related to medical publications, to a physician's diagnoses, and to the discussions among general practitioners, specialists, nurses, patients, and the programmers who develop the software they use. All these people are constantly thinking and using NL semantics, not the formal axioms of some theory. Frege (1879) hoped 'to break the domination of the word over the human spirit by laying bare the misconceptions that through the use of language often almost unavoidably arise concerning the relations between concepts.' Wittgenstein agreed that language can be misleading, but he denied that an artificial language could be better. At best, it would be a different *language game* (Sprachspiel).

These philosophical observations explain why large knowledge bases such as Cyc (Lenat 1995) have failed to achieve true artificial intelligence. An inference engine attached to a large collection of formally defined facts and axioms can prove theorems more efficiently than most people, but it lacks the flexibility of a child in learning new information and adapting old information to new situations (Sowa 2005). Two computer scientists who devoted their careers to different aspects of AI have concluded that the goal of a fixed formal ontology of everything is both unattainable and misguided. Alan Bundy, who developed formal methods for theorem proving and problem solving, proposed *ontology evolution* as a method for systematically relating smaller domain ontologies and adapting them to specific problems (Bundy and McNeill 2006, Bundy 2007). Yorick Wilks, who developed informal methods of *preference semantics* for natural language processing, maintained that the lexical resources used in language analysis and interpretation are sharply distinct from and should not be confused with formal ontologies (Wilks 2006, 2008a, b). These two views can be reconciled by using linguistic information as the basis for indexing and relating an open-ended variety of task-oriented ontologies.

Instead of a static ontology, this article develops a dynamic approach that can relate the often vague and shifting meanings of ordinary words to the formal ontologies needed for computer applications. Section 11.2 surveys semiotic theories from Aristotle to Saussure with an emphasis on Peirce's contributions. Section 11.3 summarizes twentieth-century theories of language, the more recent recognition of their limitations, and the relevance of Peirce and Wittgenstein. Section 11.4 reviews a computational approach to language developed by Margaret Masterman, a former student of Wittgenstein's. Section 11.5 presents a method of mapping language to logic based on Wittgenstein's notions of *Satzsystem* and *Beweissystem*. Section 11.6 shows the underlying relationships between the formal methods of deduction, induction, and abduction and the informal methods of analogy. The concluding Section 11.7 develops a foundation for ontology that supports both formal and informal methods of reasoning. The formal theories necessary for precise reasoning are embedded in a framework that can accommodate the open-ended flexibility of natural languages.

11.2 A Semiotic Foundation for Ontology

Without vagueness at the foundation, the words and syntax of our stone-age ancestors could never have been adapted to every innovation of modern civilization. The evolution of language over millions of years is recapitulated in a dozen years as an infant grows to a teenager and in another dozen years to a PhD. The growth in precision of the second dozen years, although valuable, is almost trivial in comparison to the achievements of the first dozen – or even the first three. The key to understanding how language works lies in the first 3 years from infancy to early childhood – alternatively, in the past three million years from *Australopithecus* to *Homo sapiens*. The signs of language are rooted in the prelinguistic signs of the infant and the ape, which in turn have evolved from more primitive signs generated and recognized by every living thing from bacteria to humans. The signs of every ontology, formal or informal, are derived from those same roots.

Aristotle began the study of signs by *psyches* at every level from the vegetative to the rational. His treatise *On Interpretation*, one of the most influential books on language ever written, begins by relating language to the psyche, while avoiding *psychologism*. The following passage relates language to internal processes, whose existence is not in doubt, but whose nature is unknown. As he said, the psyche is a different subject.

> First we must determine what are noun (*onoma*) and verb (*rhêma*); and after that, what are negation (*apophasis*), assertion (*kataphasis*), proposition (*apophansis*), and sentence (*logos*). Those in speech (*phonê*) are symbols (*symbola*) of affections (*pathêmata*) in the psyche, and those written (*graphomena*) are symbols of those in speech. As letters (*grammata*), so are speech sounds not the same for everyone. But they are signs (*sêmeia*) primarily of the affections in the psyche, which are the same for everyone, and so are the objects (*pragmata*) of which they are likenesses (*homoiômata*). On these matters we speak in the treatise on the psyche, for it is a different subject. (16a1)

In this short passage, Aristotle introduced ideas that have been adopted, ignored, revised, rejected, and dissected over the centuries. By using two different words for sign, Aristotle recognized two distinct ways of signifying: he adopted *sêmeion* for a natural sign and *symbolon* for a conventional sign. With the word *sêmeion*, which was used for symptoms of a disease, Aristotle implied that the verbal sign is primarily a natural sign of the mental affection or concept and secondarily a symbol of the object it refers to. That triad of sign, sense, and object constitutes the *meaning triangle*, which Ogden and Richards (1923) drew explicitly.

From the twentieth to the sixteenth centuries, the Scholastics developed semiotics in great depth and subtlety. They observed the distinction between natural and

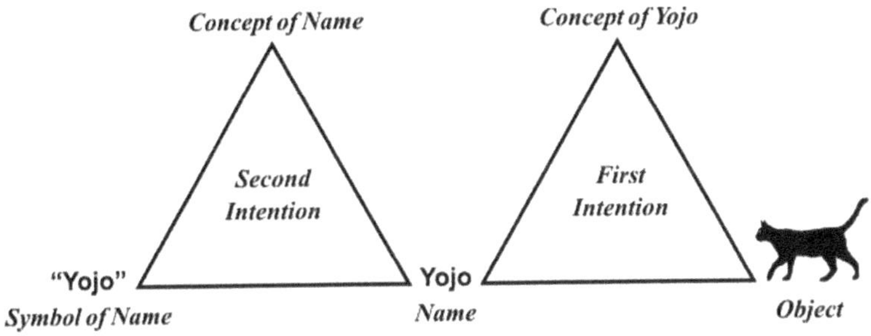

Fig. 11.1 Scholastic meaning triangles

conventional signs, but they applied the generic term *signum* to signs of all kinds. For the other two vertices of the meaning triangle, they coined the terms *significatio* for the sense of a sign and *suppositio* for its intended object. They recognized that the supposition of a sign might not exist: one example would be a mythical beast or chimera, but more often the intended object would be the result of a future action. They also recognized that the supposition could be another sign and coined the terms *prima intentio* for a sign whose supposition is a physical entity and *secunda intentio* for a sign whose supposition is another sign (Fig. 11.1).

For the signification at the top of a triangle, a common Latin term was the translation *passio animae* of Aristotle's *pathêma* or a mental term such as *intellectus conceptio*. The sign at the lower left could be a word, an image, or a concept. The supposition at the lower right could be an existing thing, a spoken sign, or an imagined sign of something sought, feared, planned, or otherwise intended. The Scholastic semiotics with a Tarski-style semantics by Ockham (1323) provided a more structured and robust foundation for language and logic than the loose associations proposed a few centuries later by Locke, Condillac, and others. Franz Brentano (1874) had studied Scholastic logic, and he adopted the word *intentio* as the basis for his theory of *intentionality*, which he defined as the directedness (*Gerichtetheit*) of thought toward some object, real or imagined.

Not all linguists and logicians recognized the sign relation as triadic. For his *sémiologie*, Saussure (1916) defined a sign as a dyadic relation that excludes the object at the lower right of the meaning triangle: 'The linguistic sign unites, not a thing and a name, but a concept and a sound-image. The latter is not the material sound, a purely physical thing, but the psychological imprint of the sound, the impression that it makes on our senses.' Tarski, Quine, and many other logicians ignored the top of the triangle and focused on the dyadic link between the sign and object. The dyadic versions by Saussure and Tarski have complementary weaknesses: Tarski had a clear criterion for truth, but no recognition of intention; Saussure's dyads permitted multiple levels of interpretation, but they did not relate words and sentences to objects and events. A complete theory of meaning must recognize the full triad.

Frege had a triadic definition of sign with the labels *Zeichen, Sinn,* and *Bedeutung*, usually translated *sign, sense,* and *reference*, which correspond to the Latin *signum, significatio,* and *suppositio*. In comparing Frege and Husserl,

Mohanty (1982, p. 57) observed that they had similar definitions and similar difficulties with context-dependent indexicals, such as *I, you, this,* or *that*:

> Husserl refers to indexicals and their like as threatening 'to plunge all our hard-won distinctions back into confusion.' These are what he calls 'essentially occasional' expressions, in their case 'it is essential to orient actual meaning to the occasion, the speaker, and the situation.'

Those 'hard-won distinctions,' as Mohanty explained, included 'objective, self-subsistent, ideal meanings.' Ordinary words, such as *green* or *tree*, could have an objective sense, independent of speaker or context. But the meaning of the word *I* would vary with each speaker, and the meaning of *this* would vary at each occurrence. Frege's triangle, which assigned a single objective sense to each word, could handle *green*, but not *I*. Husserl suggested that sense could be a function of both the word and its use, but that solution conflicted with Frege's goal of context-independent meaning.

In the *Tractatus*, Wittgenstein (1921) observed Frege's restrictions, but in the preface to his second book, he called them 'grave errors.' In his later philosophy, Wittgenstein (1953) focused on usage in context, especially in the social activities that give language its meaning. Syntax is valuable for precise, concise, fluent speech, but with enough context, the syntax can be garbled without destroying comprehension. For an infant, a foreigner, or an instant-message addict, context is more important than syntax.

Peirce handled context with a more general definition of sign, which includes the triangles of Aristotle, the Scholastics, and Frege as special cases. In the 1860s, he discovered a metalevel principle for generating triads when he and his father were studying Kant. To derive his twelve categories, Kant started with four major groups: *Quantity*, *Quality*, *Relation*, and *Modality*, each of which he divided in three. Relation, for example, produced the triad of *Inherence*, *Causality*, and *Community*. While searching for a deeper principle underlying Kant's categories, Peirce noticed that Inherence could be defined by a monadic predicate that characterizes an entity by what it has in itself, independent of anything else; Causality requires a dyadic relation that characterizes some reaction between two entities; and Community requires a triadic relation that relates an entity (1) to a community (2) for some purpose (3). He generalized that observation to his trichotomy of *Firstness*, *Secondness*, and *Thirdness*.

For his theory of signs, Peirce adopted the trichotomy as the unifying theme that relates signs of all kinds to language and the world. Every sign is a triad that relates a perceptible *mark* (1), to another sign called its *interpretant* (2), which determines an existing or intended *object* (3). Following is one of Peirce's most often quoted definitions:

> A sign, or *representamen*, is something which stands to somebody for something in some respect or capacity. It addresses somebody, that is, creates in the mind of that person an equivalent sign, or perhaps a more developed sign. That sign which it creates I call the *interpretant* of the first sign. The sign stands for something, its *object*. It stands for that object, not in all respects, but in reference to a sort of idea, which I have sometimes called the *ground* of the representamen. (CP 2.228)

A pattern of green and yellow in the lawn, for example, is a mark, and the interpretant is some type, such as Plant, Weed, Flower, SaladGreen, or Dandelion. The guiding idea that determines the interpretant depends on the context and the intentions of the observer. The interpretant determines the word the observer chooses to express the experience. As Peirce noted, a listener who is an expert in the subject matter can sometimes derive a richer interpretant than the speaker. Mohanty (1982, p. 58) remarked 'Not unlike Frege, Husserl would rather eliminate such fluctuations from scientific discourse, but both are forced to recognize their recalcitrant character for their theories and indispensability for natural languages.' Fortunately for science, theoreticians like Einstein and Bohr could often derive more meaning from scientific language than the authors intended.

Unlike Aristotle's categories, which represent types of *existence*, Peirce's *phenomenological* categories represent aspects of how something is perceived, conceived, or described. Any phenomenon can be described in all three ways. An object, for example, can be recognized as a dog, cat, man, or dandelion by directly observable properties of the individual (Firstness), but it cannot be recognized as a pet, stray, owner, or salad green without some evidence of an external relationship (Secondness). The corresponding Thirdness involves intentions that are indicated by signs, such as a contract or a habitual pattern of behavior.

Like nouns, verbs can also be classified by what aspect they describe: a directly observable event (Firstness); a causally related effect (Secondness); or a mediating intention (Thirdness). The next three sentences describe the same event in each of those ways:

1. Brutus *stabbed* Caesar.
2. Brutus *killed* Caesar.
3. Brutus *murdered* Caesar.

An act of stabbing can be recognized at the instant it happens. That is a classification by Firstness, since no other events or mental attitudes are involved. But an act of stabbing cannot be called killing unless a second event of dying occurs. Murder involves Thirdness because the stabbing (1) is related to the dying (2) by the intention (3). Determining whether an act of stabbing that resulted in killing should be considered a murder depends on subtle clues, whose interpretation may require a judge, a jury, and a lengthy trial.

On the surface, Peirce's triads seem similar to Aristotle's and Frege's. The difference, however, is that each of the three terms – the sign, the interpretant, and the object – can be further analyzed by the same metalevel principle. By analyzing the method by which the sign determines its object, Peirce (EP 1.1) derived the triad of *icon, index* and *symbol*: an icon refers by some similarity to the object; an index refers by a physical effect or connection; and a symbol refers by a habit or conventional association. Figure 11.2 shows this *relational* triad in the middle row.

After thinking about signs for another 30 years, Peirce discovered deeper patterns of relationships. He realized that the relational triad is based on Secondness – the relationship between a sign and its object. He therefore searched for two other triads.

	1. Quality	2. Indexicality	3. Mediation
1. Material	**Qualisign** *A quality which is a sign.*	**Sinsign** *An actual existent thing or event which is a sign.*	**Legisign** *A law which is a sign.*
2. Relational	**Icon** *Refers by virtue of some similarity to object.*	**Index** *Refers by virtue of being affected by object.*	**Symbol** *Refers by virtue of some law or association.*
3. Formal	**Rheme** *A sign of qualitative possibility.*	**Dicent Sign** *A sign of actual existence.*	**Argument** *A sign of law.*

Fig. 11.2 Peirce's triple trichotomy

The signs in the first or *material* triad signify by the nature of the sign itself; those in the third or *formal* triad signify by a formal rule that associates sign and object. The labels at the top of Fig. 11.2 indicate how the sign directs attention to the object: by some quality of the sign itself, by some causal or pointing effect, or by some mediating law, habit, or convention. The following examples illustrate nine types of signs:

1. *Qualisign* (material quality). A ringing sound as an uninterpreted sensation.
2. *Sinsign* (material indexicality). A ringing sound that is recognized as coming from a telephone.
3. *Legisign* (material mediation). The convention that a ringing telephone means someone is trying to call.
4. *Icon* (relational quality). An image that resembles a telephone when used to indicate a telephone.
5. *Index* (relational indexicality). A finger pointing toward a telephone.
6. *Symbol* (relational mediation). A ringing sound on the radio that is used to suggest a telephone call.
7. *Rheme* (formal quality). A word, such as *telephone*, which can represent any telephone, real or imagined.
8. *Dicent Sign* (formal indexicality). A sentence that asserts an actual existence of some object or event: 'You have a phone call from your mother.'
9. *Argument* (formal mediation). A sequence of dicent signs that expresses a lawlike connection: 'It may be an emergency. Therefore, you should answer the phone.'

Peirce coined the term *indexical* for the words or *deictics* that have the effect of a pointing finger or other kind of index. Instead of being troublesome exceptions, as they were for Frege and Husserl, indexicals become an integral part of a systematic framework.

The nine categories in Fig. 11.2 are more finely differentiated than most definitions of signs, and they cover a broader range of phenomena. Anything that exists can be a sign of itself (sinsign), if it is interpreted by an observer. But Peirce (1911, p. 33) did not limit his definition to human minds or even to signs that exist in our universe:

> A sign, then, is anything whatsoever — whether an Actual or a May-be or a Would-be — which affects a mind, its Interpreter, and draws that interpreter's attention to some Object (whether Actual, May-be, or Would-be) which *has already* come within the sphere of his experience.

The mind or quasi-mind that interprets a sign need not be human. In various examples, Peirce mentioned dogs, parrots, and bees. A dog, like its owner, could experience ringing as a qualisign and recognize it as a sound from a particular source (sinsign). By a kind of Pavlovian conditioning, a dog could be taught a legisign to answer a specially-designed telephone. But an intelligent dog might discover for itself that a ringing phone is an index of its owner's habit (another legisign) of running to answer it. In fact, there is anecdotal evidence that some parrots imitate a phone ring in order to summon their owners. Higher animals typically recognize icons and indexes, and some might recognize symbols. A language of some kind is a prerequisite for signs at the formal level of rhemes, dicent signs, and arguments. Whether dolphins or trained apes have a language adequate to express such signs is still an open question.

By building on and extending the semiotics of Aristotle and the Scholastics, Peirce avoided the dangers of psychologism. As he said, 'Thought is not necessarily connected with a brain' (CP 4.551), but every thought is a sign, and every sign depends on some mind or quasi-mind. In the following definition, Peirce emphasized the independence of signs on any particular implementation:

> I define a sign as something, A, which brings something, B, its interpretant, into the same sort of correspondence with something, C, its object, as that in which it itself stands to C. In this definition I make no more reference to anything like the human mind than I do when I define a line as the place within which a particle lies during a lapse of time. (1902, p. 235)

As an example, Fig. 11.3 illustrates the concept of representation by means of two meaning triangles. The first-intentional triangle at the bottom shows that the name Yojo refers to a cat illustrated by an image at the bottom right. The peak of that triangle is a concept illustrated by the same image enclosed in a balloon. The second-intentional triangle at the top, shows that the symbol **Cat: Yojo** refers to the same concept that is shared with the peak of the first-intentional triangle. The uppermost balloon illustrates a concept of representation that relates the symbol **Cat: Yojo** to the concept of the same cat. To explain how language is learned and used, this article includes many second-intentional statements that express such concepts.

Of the five signs shown in Fig. 11.3, three have physical marks and two are mental concepts, which are shown in balloons. Although the mental concepts are internal, no introspection is needed to infer their existence. The triangles are based on semiotic principles, which, as Peirce said, would hold for 'any scientific intelligence' – human, nonhuman, extraterrestrial, or even artificial. Humans and apes can understand one another because they have similar bodies and live in similar environments. Dolphins, however, are intelligent mammals with an utterly different

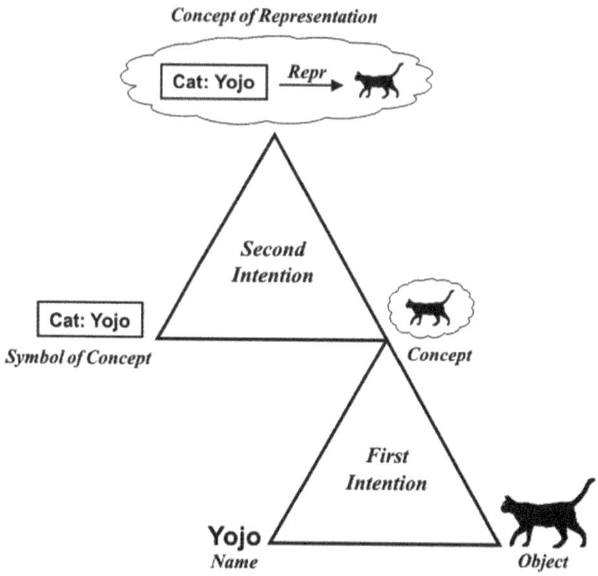

Fig. 11.3 Meaning triangles for the concept of representation

method of communication about a radically different environment. But if they are capable of thinking about their signaling system, diagrams such as Fig. 11.3 would characterize their thoughts. The same principles would hold for beings from another galaxy whose biology had no resemblance to anything on earth. The meaning triangles are as formal as mathematics, which is independent of psychology, biology, and physics.

As these examples show, Peirce's theory of signs provides a more nuanced basis for analysis than the all-or-nothing question of whether animals have language. Unlike the static meaning triangles of Aristotle or Frege, the most important aspect of Peirce's triangles is their dynamic nature: any node can spawn another triad to show three different perspectives on the entity represented by that node. During the course of a conversation, the motives of the participants lead the thread of topics from triangle to triangle. Understanding the interconnections of themes and motives requires a map of those triangles.

11.3 Twentieth-Century Theories of Language

In the *Tractatus*, Wittgenstein began the practice of treating natural language as a version of logic, but he rejected that view in his second book. Chomsky (1957) revived the formal approach by defining a language as the set of sentences generated by a formal grammar. Besides a formal grammar, Montague (1970) added a *formal semantics* that was much richer than Wittgenstein's early version. That kind of formalization was ideal for the artificial languages of logic and computer science, but many linguists rejected it as a distortion of natural language. Some logicians were also skeptical about attempts to formalize the notoriously ambiguous natural languages. Peter Geach, a logician and former student of Wittgenstein's, derided Montague's system as 'Hollywood semantics.'

The logical positivists renamed the traditional language arts – grammar, logic, and rhetoric – with the terms *syntax*, *semantics*, and *pragmatics*. Of the three, syntax is a relatively compact subject, although there are many theories about how to represent it. Semantics and pragmatics, however, raise controversial issues about the meaning of 'meaning' and the endless variety of uses for language:

1. Syntax defines grammar by some sort of rules or patterns. Around the fifth century BC, Panini produced one of the most detailed grammars of all time, with nearly 4,000 rules for the syntax of Sanskrit. Bharati et al. (1995) claimed that Panini-style grammars have important advantages for highly inflected languages with a free word order, such as the languages of modern India. In the early part of the twentieth century, Ajdukiewicz (1935) invented rule formats for *categorial grammar*, Tesnière (1959) invented *dependency grammar*, and Post (1943) developed *production rules*, which are used to specify *phrase-structure* grammars. Harris (1951) combined a phrase-structure base with *transformation rules*, which Chomsky (1957) adopted and elaborated in several variations. Finally, Chomsky (1995) settled on a *minimalist program*: express grammar as a set of constraints that determine the simplest mapping from a *conceptual-intentional* representation to the spoken forms of a language. Yet the early hopes for formal grammars that could define all and only the grammatical sentences of a language were never realized. For a more flexible and extensible method of accommodating novel patterns, Fillmore (1988) and Goldberg (1995) developed *construction grammars* as an open-ended system of form-meaning pairs.
2. Semantics, loosely speaking, is the study of meaning. But the meaning triangle (Fig. 11.1) has three sides, and different studies typically emphasize one side or another: the link from words to the concepts they express; the link from words and sentences to objects and truth values; or the link from concepts to percepts of objects and actions upon them. In different books, Aristotle addressed all three aspects: expression (*lexis*), reason (*logos*), and thought (*dianoia*). Modern approaches also address them in different books, usually by different authors:

    - *Lexical semantics*, according to Cruse (1986), is a 'contextual approach,' which derives 'information about a word's meaning from its relations with actual and potential linguistic contexts.' That definition corresponds to the left side of the meaning triangle, which omits the connection between words and the objects they refer to. It is compatible with Saussure's definition of language (*langue*) as 'the whole set of linguistic habits, which allow an individual to understand and be understood' (1916). Lexicographers analyze a corpus of contextual citations and catalog the linguistic habits in lexicons, thesauri, and terminologies.

- *Formal semantics* studies the logical properties of words and sentences and relates them to objects and configurations of objects. The first logic-based systems were designed as computer implementations (Bohnert and Backer 1967, Woods 1968, Winograd 1972), but Montague's theories were more influential among philosophers and logicians. Other formalisms include *discourse representation theory* (Kamp and Reyle 1993) and *situation semantics* (Barwise and Perry 1983). Yet despite 40 years of sustained research, none of the implementations can translate one page from an ordinary textbook to any version of logic. Lexical semantics covers a broader range of language than the formal versions, and it addresses more aspects of syntax and vocabulary that affect meaning. But unlike the logic-based theories, lexical semantics does not define a mapping from language to objects or a method of reasoning about them.
- *Cognitive semantics* studies the concepts and patterns of concepts that relate language to perception and action. Locke's associations influenced many nineteenth-century psychologists, but Kant's *schemata* led to more structured theories by Selz (1913) and Bartlett (1932). Other versions included *Gestalt theory* (Wertheimer 1925), *activity theory* (Vygotsky 1934), and *cognitive maps* (Tolman 1948). The earliest computer implementations, called *semantic networks*, were designed for machine translation; among the first were the *correlational nets* by Ceccato (1961). Other highly influential computational versions include *conceptual dependencies* by Schank (1975), *chunks* by Newell and Simon (1972), who cited Selz as an inspiration, and *frames* by Minsky (1975), who cited Bartlett. Robotics applications use concepts and cognitive maps to relate a robot's language interface to its sensory and motor mechanisms. Among linguists, Lakoff (1987), Langacker (1999), Talmy (2000), and Wierzbicka (1996) devoted their careers to analyzing cross-linguistic cognitive patterns and their relationship to extralinguistic objects and activities. The term *conceptual structure* is commonly used for those patterns, both in linguistics (Jackendoff 1983) and in artificial intelligence (Sowa 1976, 1984).

3. Pragmatics or rhetoric analyzes the use of language for some purpose. Like semantics, pragmatics can be studied from different perspectives: the structure of a text or discourse; the intentions of the speaker or author; or the function of language in its social context. Unlike the single semantic triad, the intentions of two or more participants in a social setting can entangle the pragmatic triad with more triads and subtriads, as in Figs. 11.2 and 11.3. The plots of literary and historical narratives illustrate the complexity that can develop from a clash of multiple perspectives and motivations. Following is a brief summary:

   - *Discourse*, *narrative*, and *argumentation* depend on structural patterns that organize strings of sentences into a coherent whole that may range in length from a paragraph to a book. Aristotle began the systematic study of such patterns in his books *Rhetoric* and *Poetics*. Propp (1928) classified the thematic patterns of folktales. Lord (1960) and Parry pioneered the study of oral epics, related them to the classical epics, and demonstrated the formulaic patterning at every level from short phrases to global themes. With their theory of *scripts*, Schank and Abelson (1977) developed methods for representing thematic patterns and analyzing them in computer programs. Despite many centuries of analysis by literary critics, the technology for automatically recognizing these patterns or generating them from a knowledge base lags far behind the work on syntax and semantics.

- *Motivation*, which depends on feelings and emotion, determines the direction of discourse and the choice of patterns to accomplish the desired effect. Aristotle considered desire (*orexis*) the ultimate source of direction, but he distinguished three kinds of desire: appetite (*epithymia*), passion (*thymos*), and will (*boulêsis*). He classified appetite and passion as feelings shared with beasts and will as the result of rational thought. In classifying emotions, Arieti (1978) proposed three categories, which resemble a Peircean triad: First-order or *protoemotions*– tension, appetite, fear, rage, and satisfaction – are feelings that arise from basic mechanisms, such as hormones. Second-order emotions associate protoemotions with imagined objects and events: anxiety, anger, wishing, and security. Third-order emotions are mediating processes that relate feelings of all kinds to past experiences and future expectations: love, hate, joy, and sadness. Without emotions, an intelligent system, no matter how logical, would have no reason to do or say anything. To design computational mechanisms that could provide some direction, Minsky (2006) proposed an *emotion machine* that would integrate intelligence with motivation.
- *Social interaction* is the ultimate ground of communication, and language develops in social activity. One of the most significant insights into language development and use was Wittgenstein's view of language games as an integral part of behavior. It had a strong influence on many later developments, including *speech acts* (Austin 1962), *conversational implicatures* (Grice 1975), and *relevance* (Sperber and Wilson 1986). One of the linguists influenced by Wittgenstein was Halliday (1978, 1999), whose *systemic-functional* approach was implemented in Winograd's early logic-based system and in *rhetorical structure theory* (Mann and Thompson 1988), which is widely used for discourse analysis and generation.

As this summary indicates, many aspects of syntax and semantics can be formalized, but no current formalism is as dynamic and flexible as language. The far more complex subject of pragmatics, however, is key to understanding the nature, origin, and function of language. Infants use language to satisfy their needs with their very first words, the protolanguage of early hominins probably had little or no syntax, and foreigners with a rudimentary knowledge of the local language can communicate effectively with gestures and isolated words. The idea that syntax is the foundation began with the logical positivists, who focused on written symbols as concrete 'observables.' To avoid the complex relationship of language to the world, they replaced the world with abstract sets, which serve as surrogates for the messy objects, events, and people. They left pragmatics as an afterthought, which was almost totally ignored in the writings by Carnap, Tarski, Montague, and Quine. Yet any formal definition that cannot be adequately explained in the semantics and pragmatics of ordinary language is destined to be misunderstood by the people who need it the most.

11.4 A Neo-Wittgensteinian Approach

In the *Tractatus*, Wittgenstein claimed that 'the totality of facts' about the world can be stated clearly in language or logic, and 'Whereof one cannot speak, thereof one must be silent.' That book set the agenda for formal semantics in the twentieth century. Yet those formal systems were also brittle, inflexible, and incapable of representing the kinds of language that people normally speak and write. In his later philosophy, Wittgenstein replaced the monolithic logic and ontology of his first book with an open-ended family of language games. As an alternative to definitions by necessary and sufficient conditions, he used the term *family resemblance* for the 'complicated network of overlapping and criss-crossing similarities, in the large and the small' (1953, §66). Unlike his mentors, Frege and Russell, he did not consider vagueness a defect in language:

> One might say that the concept 'game' is a concept with blurred edges. — "But is a blurred concept a concept at all?" — Is an indistinct photograph a picture of a person at all? Is it even always an advantage to replace an indistinct picture with a sharp one? Isn't the indistinct one often exactly what we need?
> Frege compares a concept to an area and says that an area with vague boundaries cannot be called an area at all. This presumably means that we cannot do anything with it. — But is it senseless to say: "Stand roughly (ungefähr) there"? (§71).

Frege's view is incompatible with natural languages and with every branch of empirical science and engineering. Vagueness is not the result of a careless use of language, and it cannot be eliminated by replacing natural languages with artificial languages. Its ultimate source is the attempt to describe the continuous physical world with a finite vocabulary of discrete symbols. For representing vagueness, fuzzy logic (Zadeh 1975) and logics of ambiguity (van Deemter and Peters 1996) have been useful for some applications, but they don't address the core issues. Vagueness caused by semantic discrepancies cannot be remedied by context-independent syntactic rules.

Natural languages can be as precise as any formal language or as vague as necessary in planning, negotiation, debate, and empirical investigation. In a formal language, the meaning of a sentence is completely determined by its *form* or syntax together with the meaning of its components. In this sense, natural languages are informal because the meanings of nearly all sentences depend on the situation in which they're spoken, the background knowledge of the speaker, and the speaker's assumptions about the background knowledge of the listeners. Since nobody ever has perfect knowledge of anyone else's background, communication in natural language is an error-prone process that requires frequent questions, explanations, objections, concessions, distinctions, and stipulations. Precision and clarity are the goal of analysis, not the starting point. Whitehead (1937) aptly summarized that point:

> Human knowledge is a process of approximation. In the focus of experience, there is comparative clarity. But the discrimination of this clarity leads into the penumbral background. There are always questions left over. The problem is to discriminate exactly what we know vaguely.

During his career as an experimental physicist and a practicing engineer, Peirce learned the difficulty of stating any general principle with absolute precision:

> It is easy to speak with precision upon a general theme. Only, one must commonly surrender all ambition to be certain. It is equally easy to be certain. One has only to be sufficiently vague. It is not so difficult to be pretty precise and fairly certain at once about a very narrow subject. (CP 4.237)

This quotation summarizes the futility of any attempt to develop a precisely defined ontology of everything, but it offers two useful alternatives: an informal classification, such as a thesaurus or terminology designed for human readers; and an open-ended collection of formal theories about narrowly delimited subjects. It also raises the questions of how and whether the informal resources might be used as a bridge between informal natural language and formally defined logics and programming languages.

A novel theory of semantics, influenced by Wittgenstein's language games and related developments in cognitive science, is the *dynamic construal of meaning* (DCM) proposed by Cruse (2002). The fundamental assumption of DCM is that the most stable aspect of a word is its spoken or written sign; its meaning is unstable and dynamically evolving as it is used in different contexts or language games. Cruse coined the term *microsense* for each subtle variation in meaning. That is an independent rediscovery of Peirce's view: sign types are stable, but each interpretation of a sign token depends on its context in a pattern of other signs, the physical environment, and the background knowledge of the interpreter. Croft and Cruse (2004) suggested an integration of DCM semantics with a version of construction grammar, but their definitions are not sufficiently detailed for a computer implementation.

A computable method directly inspired by Wittgenstein's language games was developed by Margaret Masterman, one of six students in his course of 1933–1934 whose notes were compiled as *The Blue Book*. In the late 1950s, Masterman founded the Cambridge Language Research Unit (CLRU) as a discussion group, which became one of the pioneering centers of research in computational linguistics. Her collected papers (Masterman 2005) present an approach with many similarities to DCM:

- A focus on semantics, not syntax, as the foundation for language: 'I want to pick up the relevant basic-situation-referring habits of a language in preference to its grammar' (p. 200).

- A context-dependent classification scheme with three kinds of structures: a thesaurus with groups of words organized by areas of use, a *word fan* radiating from each word type to each area of the thesaurus in which it occurs, and dynamically generated combinations of fans for the word tokens of a text.
- Emphasis on images as a language-independent foundation for meaning with a small number (about 50–100) of combining elements represented by ideographs or monosyllables, such as IN, UP, MUCH, THING, STUFF, MAN, BEAST, PLANT, DO.
- Recognition that analogy and metaphor are fundamental to the creation of novel uses of language, especially in the most advanced areas of science. Maxwell's elegant mathematics, for example, is the final stage of a lengthy process that began with Faraday's analogies, diagrams, and vague talk about lines of force in electric and magnetic fields.

Figure 11.4 shows a word fan for *bank* with links to each area in Roget's *Thesaurus* in which the word occurs (p. 288). The numbers and labels identify areas in the thesaurus, which, Masterman claimed, correspond to 'Neo-Wittgensteinian families.'

To illustrate the use of word fans, Masterman analyzed the phrases *up the steep bank* and *in the savings bank.* All the words except *the* would have similar fans, and her algorithm would 'pare down' the ambiguities 'by retaining only the spokes that retain ideas which occur in each.' For this example, it would retain 'OBLIQUITY 220 in *steep* and *bank*; whereas it retains as common between *savings* and *bank* both of the two areas STORE 632 and TREASURY 799.'

Although Masterman's work is over 40 years old, it has some claim to be a more plausible cognitive theory than systems of 'mentalese' for a private language of thought:

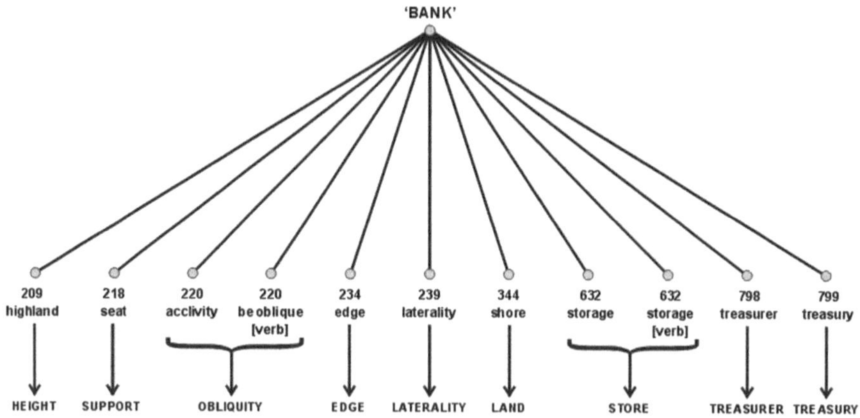

Fig. 11.4 A word fan for *bank*

1. Emphasis on images as the primary semantic representation.
2. Actual English words as the units of meaning rather than abstract or artificial markers, features, or categories.
3. Language games as the basis for organizing and using patterns of words.
4. A context-dependent organization of word senses by usage (thesaurus style) instead of the more common dictionary style of grouping all senses of each word type.
5. Word fans as a secondary (context-independent) method for finding all senses of a word type when the area of usage is not known.

These principles are compatible with Wittgenstein's later philosophy, but more is needed to capture the dynamics of the games, the way they mutate and evolve, and their relationships to one another. Halliday was a cofounder of CLRU who explored other aspects of language games with his emphasis on the use of language in social interactions. Yet neither Masterman nor Halliday addressed the language games of mathematics and logic, which were Wittgenstein's starting point and a topic he addressed repeatedly in his later teaching, writing, and notebooks. To support both formal and informal languages, Masterman's word fans must be extended with links to logic, but in a flexible way that permits an open-ended variety of options.

11.5 Steps Toward Formalization

In his *Philosophical Remarks* from the transitional period of 1929–1930, Wittgenstein analyzed some 'minor' inconsistencies in the *Tractatus*. His analysis led to innovations that form a bridge between his early system and the far more flexible language games. Shanker (1987) noted two new terms that are key to Wittgenstein's transition:

1. *Satzsystem*: a system of sentences or propositions stated in a given syntax and vocabulary.
2. *Beweissystem*: a proof system that defines a logic for a Satzsystem.

Formally, the combination of a Satzsystem with a Beweissystem corresponds to what logicians call a *theory* – the deductive closure of a set of axioms. Informally, Wittgenstein's remarks about Satzsysteme are compatible with his later discussions of language games. In conversations reported by Waismann (1979, p. 48), Wittgenstein said that outside a Satzsystem, a word is like 'a wheel turning idly.' Instead of a separate mapping of each proposition to reality, as in the *Tractatus*, the Satzsystem is mapped as a complete structure: 'The Satzsystem is like a ruler (Maßstab) laid against reality. An entire system of propositions is now compared to reality, not a single proposition.' (Wittgenstein 1964, § 82).

For a given logic (Beweissystem), each Satzsystem can be formalized as a theory that defines the ontology of a narrow subject. The multiplicity of Satzsysteme implies that any word that is used in more than one system will have a different sense in each. For natural languages, that principle is far more realistic than the monolithic logic and ontology of the *Tractatus*. Yet Wittgenstein illustrated his *Philosophical Remarks* primarily with mathematical examples. That *turning point*, as Shanker called it, implies that the goal of a unified foundation for all of mathematics, as stated in the *Principia Mathematica*, is impossible. The implication alarmed Russell, who observed 'The theories contained in this new work of Wittgenstein's are novel, very original, and indubitably important. Whether they are true, I do not know. As a logician who likes simplicity, I should wish to think that they are not.'

From the mid 1930s to the end of his life, Wittgenstein focused on language games as a more general basis for a theory of meaning. But he continued to teach and write on mathematical topics, and he compared language games to the multiple ways of using words such as *number* in mathematics: 'We can get a rough picture of [the variety of language games] from the changes in mathematics.' These remarks imply that Satzsysteme can be considered specialized language games. The crucial addition for natural language is the intimate integration of language games with social activity and even the 'form of life.' As Wittgenstein said in his notebooks, language is an 'extension of primitive behavior (For our language game is behavior).' (Zettel, §545) The meaning of a word, a chess piece, or a mathematical symbol is its use in a game – a Sprachspiel or a Beweissystem.

A formal definition of language game is probably impossible, primarily because the games are integrated with every aspect of life. Even an informal characterization is difficult because Wittgenstein traversed many different academic boundaries in his examples: syntax, semantics, pragmatics, logic, ontology, speech acts, scenarios, sublanguage, and genre. As he admitted, 'the very nature of the investigation... compels us to travel over a wide field of thought criss-cross in every direction... The same or almost the same points were always being approached afresh from different directions, and new sketches made' (1953, Preface). In effect, each Satzsystem uses a formal logic to define a formal ontology that may be used in one or more language games. But even a simple language game, which might use the ontology of a single Satzsystem, has a pragmatics that integrates the moves of the game with human behavior in a social setting. Chess, for example, is a game that can be formalized and played by a computer, but no computer experiences the struggle of combat, the joy of winning, or the disappointment of losing. Those experiences determine human intentionality, which might be represented in an ontology or *metalevel* ontology of a language game for talking about language games and the people who play them.

As formal theories, Satzsysteme require a metalevel theory to support reasoning about theories and their relationships with language games. The basis for such reasoning is generalization and specialization: a theory can be specialized by adding detail (more axioms) or generalized by deleting axioms. For example, a theory that describes properties of all animals is more general than a theory that describes mammals, because any true statement about all animals must also be true about mammals. Similarly, a theory about dogs or cats is more specialized than a theory about mammals. The generalization-specialization operator defines a partial ordering of theories, which happens to form a *lattice*. General theories near the top of the lattice are, in Peirce's terms, 'sufficiently vague' to characterize a wide range of subjects. Specialized theories at lower levels are sufficiently 'narrow' to be 'pretty precise and fairly certain' No formal logic can be truly vague, but the axioms of a theory may be underspecified to accommodate multiple options. When precision is necessary, a theory may be specialized by tightening the constraints and adding detail.

Theories in the lattice may be large or small, and they may be stated in any version of logic. For most practical applications, the ISO standard for Common Logic is sufficient (ISO/IEC 2007). If $\boldsymbol{L}$ is the set of all possible theories expressed in a given logic, then the lattice over $\boldsymbol{L}$ is specified by a partial ordering $\leq$ and two dyadic operators $\cap$ and $\cup$. Let x, y, and z be any theories in the lattice $\boldsymbol{L}$:

- If the theory x is true of a subset of the cases or models in which y is true, written $x \leq y$, then x is said to be a *specialization* of y, and y is said to be a *generalization* of x. Every theory is a generalization and a specialization of itself.
- The *supremum* of x and y, $x \cup y$, is their most specialized common generalization: $x \leq x \cup y$; $y \leq x \cup y$; and if $x \leq z$ and $y \leq z$, then $x \cup y \leq z$.
- The *infimum* of x and y, $x \cap y$, is their most general common specialization: $x \cap y \leq x$; $x \cap y \leq y$; and if $z \leq x$ and $z \leq y$, then $z \leq x \cap y$.
- The top of the lattice $\top$, called the *universal theory*, is a generalization of every theory. It contains all tautologies, and it is true of everything.
- The bottom of the lattice $\bot$, called the *absurd theory*, is a specialization of every theory. It contains every statement expressible in the given logic (including all contradictions), and it is true of nothing.

For every imaginable subject, every true or false theory x lies somewhere between the top and the bottom: $\bot \leq x \leq \top$. Even inconsistent theories are in the lattice, because they collapse into the absurd theory at the bottom. The complete lattice of all possible theories is infinite, but only a finite subset can ever be implemented in an actual system.

To relate language to logic, Masterman's word fans can link each word type to multiple word senses, each represented by a *monadic predicate* or *concept type*. Figure 11.5 illustrates a word fan that maps word types to concept types to *canonical graphs* and finally to a lattice of theories. In this article, the canonical graphs are represented as *conceptual graphs* (CGs), one of the three standard dialects of Common Logic. Equivalent operations may be performed with any notation for logic, but graphs have important formal advantages (Sowa 2008).

The fan on the left of Fig. 11.5 links each word to an open-ended list of *concept types*, each of which corresponds to some area of a thesaurus in Masterman's system. The word *bank*, for example, could be linked to types with labels such as `Bank799` or `Bank_Treasury`. In various applications or language games, those types could be further subdivided into fine-grained subtypes, which would correspond to Cruse's microsenses. The selection of subtypes is determined by canonical graphs, which specify the characteristic patterns of concepts and relations associated with each type or subtype. Figure 11.6 illustrates three canonical graphs for the types `Give`, `Easy`, and `Eager`.

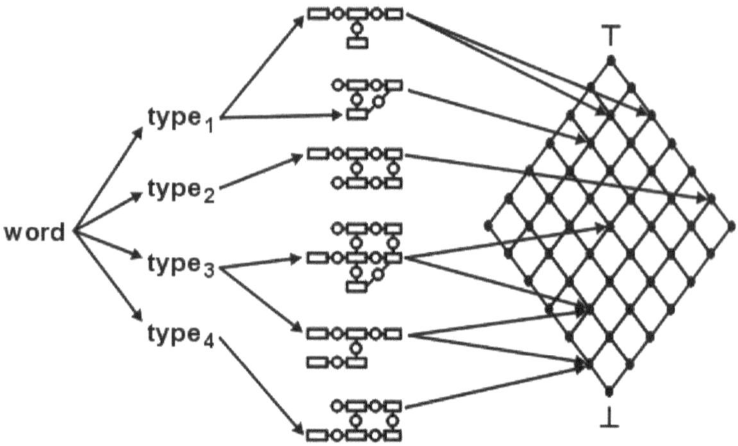

Fig. 11.5 Words → concept types → canonical graphs → lattice of theories

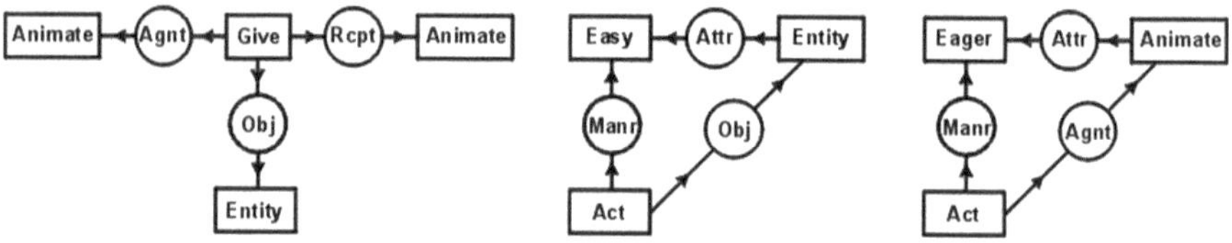

Fig. 11.6 Canonical graphs for the types `Give`, `Easy`, and `Eager`

A canonical graph for a type is a conceptual graph that specifies one of the patterns characteristic of that type. On the left, the canonical graph for `Give` represents the same constraints as a typical *case frame* for a verb. It states that the agent (`Agnt`) must be `Animate`, the recipient (`Rcpt`) must be `Animate`, and the object (`Obj`) may be any `Entity`. The canonical graphs for `Easy` and `Eager`, however, illustrate the advantage of graphs over frames: a graph permits cycles, and the arcs can distinguish the directionality of the relations. Consider the following two sentences:

Bob is easy to please. *Bob is eager to please.*

For both sentences, the concept `[Person: Bob]` would be linked via the attribute relation (`Attr`) to the concept `[Easy]` or `[Eager]`, and the act `[Please]` would be linked via the manner relation (`Manr`) to the same concept. But the canonical graph for `Easy` would make Bob the object of the act `Please`, and the graph for `Eager` would make Bob the agent. The first sentence below is acceptable because the object may be any entity, but the constraint that the agent of an act must be animate would make the second sentence unacceptable:

The book is easy to read. * *The book is eager to read.*

Chomsky (1965) used the easy/eager example to argue for different syntactic transformations associated with the two adjectives. But the canonical graphs state semantic constraints that cover a wider range of linguistic phenomena with simpler syntactic rules. A child learning a first language or an adult reading a foreign language can use semantic constraints to interpret sentences with unknown or even ungrammatical syntax. Under Chomsky's hypothesis that syntax is a prerequisite for semantics, such learning is inexplicable.

Canonical graphs with a few concept nodes are adequate to discriminate the general senses of most words, but the canonical graphs for detailed microsenses can become much more complex. For the adjective *easy*, the microsenses occur in very different patterns for a book that's easy to read, a person that's easy to please, or a car that's easy to drive. For the verb *give*, a large dictionary lists dozens of senses, and the number of microsenses is enormous. The prototypical act of giving is to hand something to someone, but a large object can be given just by pointing to it and saying 'It's yours.' When the gift is an action, as in giving a kiss, a kick, or a bath, the canonical graph used to parse the sentence has a few more nodes. But the graphs required to understand the implications of each type of action are far more complex, and they're related to the graphs for taking a bath or stealinga kiss.

The canonical graph for *buy* typically has two acts of giving: money from the buyer to the seller, and some goods from the seller to the buyer. But the canonical graphs needed to understand various microsenses may require far more detail about the buyers, the sellers, the goods sold, and other people, places, and things involved. Buying a computer, for example, can be done by clicking some boxes on a screen and typing the billing and shipping information. That process may trigger a series of international transactions, which can be viewed by going to the UPS web site to check when the computer was airmailed from Hong Kong and delivered to New York. All that detail is involved in one microsense of the verb *buy*. In a successful transaction, the buyer can ignore most of it, but somebody must be able to trace the steps if something goes wrong.

11.6 Formal and Informal Reasoning

Historically, Aristotle developed formal logic and ontology as an abstraction from the arguments and patterns of reasoning in ordinary thought and language. In his pioneering work on symbolic logic, Boole (1854) continued the tradition by calling his version *The Laws of Thought*. Frege (1879) developed a complete system of *first-order logic* with a tree notation, but Peirce (1880, 1885) extended Boolean algebra to a version that Peano adopted for *predicate calculus*. Although Peirce gave equal attention to applications in language and mathematics, most twentieth-century logicians emphasized mathematics to the almost complete exclusion of other uses for logic. Montague tried to force natural language semantics into the same deductive forms, and other logicians extended his approach. Finally, Kamp (2001), a former student of Montague's, admitted

> Natural language semantics increasingly takes on the complexion of a branch of a general theory of information representation and transformation. The role of logical inference

> in the processes of linguistic interpretation indicates an interleaving of inferential and other representation-manipulating operations. This suggests that the inferential relations and operations that have often been considered the essence of logic are better seen as an integral part of a wider repertoire. Thus logic comes to look much more like a general theory of information, than as a discipline concerned more or less exclusively with deduction.

Although Peirce knew that deduction is important, he realized that it can only derive the implications of already available premises. Without some method for deriving the premises, deduction is useless. He observed that two other methods, induction and abduction, are required for deriving the starting assumptions:

1. *Deduction.* Apply a general principle to infer some fact.
   Given: *Every bird flies. Tweety is a bird.*
   Infer: *Tweety flies.*
2. *Induction.* Assume a general principle that subsumes many facts.
   Given: *Tweety, Polly, and Hooty are birds.*
   Tweety, Polly, and Hooty fly.
   Assume: *Every bird flies.*
3. *Abduction.* Guess a new hypothesis that explains some fact.
   Given: *Vampy flies. Vampy is a bat. Vampy and Tweety have wings.*
   Guess: *Every animal with wings flies.*

Deduction, which is the most precise and disciplined method of reasoning, is the only method that is certain. But as Peirce observed, discipline is 'purely inhibitory. It originates nothing' (CP 5.194). The patterns of induction and abduction, which can derive new premises, are, at best, methods of plausible reasoning. Aristotle listed those methods among the fallacies, but he admitted that they were necessary for deriving theories from empirical data. In his skeptical writings, Sextus Empiricus noted that deduction in mathematics could be certain, but any generalization about the physical world, such as *Every bird flies*, would have to be derived by induction from observations. Any conclusion derived by deduction would be just as uncertain as the premises derived by induction and abduction.

Figure 11.7 shows the source of vagueness and uncertainty in the discrepancies between the physical world and Tarski-style models about the world. On the left is an illustration of the world. On the right is a theory stated in some version of logic. In the center is the kind of model Tarski (1933) assumed: a set of entities, represented by dots, and relationships between entities represented by lines. For each sentence in the theory, Tarski's evaluation function would determine a unique truth value in terms of the model. Scientific methodology, including theories of probability or fuzziness, would evaluate the degree of approximation of the model to the world.

Thee evolution of Wittgenstein's thought can be summarized by the way the model is related to the world. In the *Tractatus*, he considered the model to be an exact picture of some aspect of the world: the dots and lines are isomorphic to objects in the world and atomic facts that relate objects. Each true sentence is a Boolean combination of atomic facts that makes a true statement about the world:

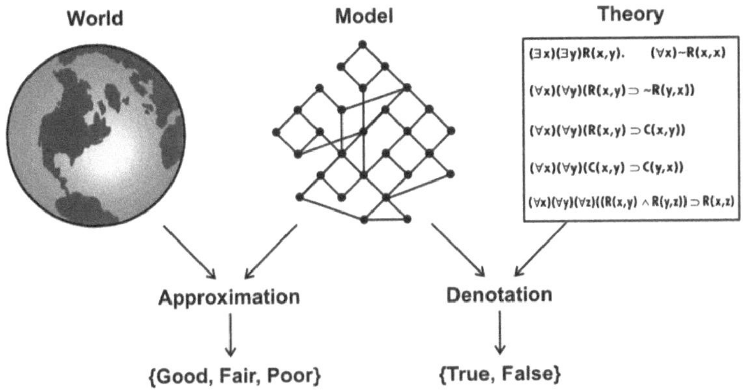

Fig. 11.7 The world, a model, and a theory

'Everything that can be said can be said clearly' (§4.116), and 'Whereof one cannot speak, thereof one must be silent' (§7.0). In his transitional period, Wittgenstein weakened the assumption by claiming that the theory as a whole (the Satzsystem) can be mapped to the world, but not each sentence by itself. That implies that the model is a good picture of the world, but not all parts of the model have a one-to-one correspondence with objects and relations in the world. A vague imperative, such as 'Stand roughly there,' could be meaningful in a language game, even though the phrase *roughly there* does not determine a unique object. In his late philosophy, he dropped the requirement that words and sentences need any referents outside the pattern of behavior associated with the language game. Language games involving prayers, singing, or even nonsense syllables would acquire their meaning solely from the associated behavior, even though many words might have no observable referents. The new language games could accommodate all the sentences of the early philosophy, but as special cases, not as the mainstream.

Of the three methods of reasoning, induction draws a generalization from instances, but only abduction can introduce a truly novel idea. In Peirce's semiotics, abduction is the basis for creativity, and there is no need for Descartes's innate ideas or Kant's synthetic *a priori* judgments. In a computer implementation, abduction can be implemented by a process for selecting appropriate chunks of information from memory and reconfiguring them in a novel combination. It can be performed at various levels of complexity:

- *Reuse*. Search for a previous fact, rule, pattern, theory, or chunk that approximately matches the current context, problem, or goal.
- *Revise*. Modify any promising chunk from an approximate match to an exact match.
- *Combine*. Revise and combine as many theories and chunks as needed to solve the problem or reach the goal. If a new chunk is consistent with the current theory, conjunction is appropriate. If it is inconsistent, revise it.

These steps can be iterated indefinitely. After a hypothesis is formed by abduction, its implications must be tested against reality. If the implications are not confirmed, the hypothesis must be revised or replaced by another abduction. In Peirce's logic of pragmatism, the novel ideas generated by abduction are constrained at the two 'gates' of perception and action:

> The elements of every concept enter into logical thought at the gate of perception and make their exit at the gate of purposive action; and whatever cannot show its passports at both those two gates is to be arrested as unauthorized by reason. (EP 2.241)

Abduction reassembles previously observed elements in novel combinations. Each combination is a new concept, whose practical meaning is determined by the totality of purposive actions it implies – in Wittgenstein's terms, by the language games associated with those actions. As Peirce said, meanings grow as new information is received, new implications are derived, and new actions become possible. Unlike other logicians, Peirce put learning at the center of his system and assumed a continuity from an infant's early experience to the most sophisticated theories of science. There are three kinds of learning, each of which modifies an old theory to create a new theory:

1. *Rote*. Rote learning accumulates information by adding low-level facts about instances. With only rote learning, each fact is a new axiom, no deduction is possible, and the number of propositions in the theory is equal to the number of axioms.
2. *Induction*. The number of axioms is reduced when a general principle derived by induction subsumes multiple instances that can be derived as needed by deduction. In effect, a generalization, such as 'Every bird flies,' compresses the data and reduces the memory load by enabling a smaller set of axioms to imply all the old statements.
3. *Abduction*. Like induction, abduction can also reduce the number of axioms. Unlike induction, which does not change the vocabulary, abduction can introduce new terminology for concepts that are not mentioned in the old axioms. Induction, for example, might lead to the generalization 'Every bird and bat flies.' Abduction, however, forms new kinds of connections, which may require new terminology: 'Every animal with wings flies.'

The lattice of theories provides a framework for analyzing and relating all the methods of learning and reasoning. Classical deduction is the only method that stays within the bounds of a single theory. All other methods can be viewed as plans or strategies for walking through the lattice of theories. Each step along the path adds, deletes, or changes some axiom to make a new theory that is more suitable for some purpose. Every method of learning specializes the starting theory by adding new axioms. Pure rote learning accumulates facts without relating them. In effect, each new fact adds a new axiom to the old theory, but it doesn't form connections to the previous axioms. Induction and abduction add general principles, which may make some old axioms redundant, but they increase the number of implications.

For reasoning about defaults and exceptions, nonmonotonic logics introduce new kinds of operators and rules of inference. Methods of belief revision achieve the same results by changing the theories instead of changing the logic (Makinson 2005, Peppas 2008). Like learning, belief revision can be treated as a walk through the lattice to select an appropriate revision of the current theory. The parallels between learning and nonmonotonic reasoning are appropriate because defaults and exceptions add new information that had not been incorporated in the old theory. Unlike learning, which always specializes a theory by adding axioms, belief revision may generalize a theory by deleting axioms or move sideways in the lattice by changing axioms. Figure 11.8 shows the four basic operators for navigating the lattice: *contraction, expansion, revision,* and *analogy*.

The operators of contraction and expansion follow the arcs of the lattice, revision makes short hops sideways, and analogy makes long-distance jumps. The first three operators obey the AGM axioms for belief revision (Alchourrón et al. 1985). The analogy operator (Sowa 2000) relabels one or more types or relations. If the original theory is consistent, any relabeled version is guaranteed to be consistent, but it may be located in a remote branch of the lattice. To illustrate the moves through the lattice, suppose that A is Newton's theory of gravitation applied to the earth revolving around the sun and F is Niels Bohr's theory about an electron revolving around the nucleus of a hydrogen atom. The path from A to F is a step-by-step transformation of the old theory to the new one. The revision step from A to C replaces the gravitational attraction between the earth and the sun with the electrical attraction between the electron and the proton. That step can be carried out in two intermediate steps:

- *Contraction.* Any theory can be contracted to a smaller, more general theory by deleting one or more axioms (and their implications). In the move from A to B, axioms for the gravitational force would be deleted. Contraction has the effect of blocking proofs that depend on the deleted axioms.
- *Expansion.* Any theory can be expanded to a larger, more specialized theory by adding one or more axioms. In the move from B to C, axioms for the electrical force would be added. The result of both moves is a substitution of electrical axioms for gravitational axioms.

Unlike contraction and expansion, which move to nearby theories in the lattice, analogy jumps to a remote theory, such as C to E, by systematically renaming the

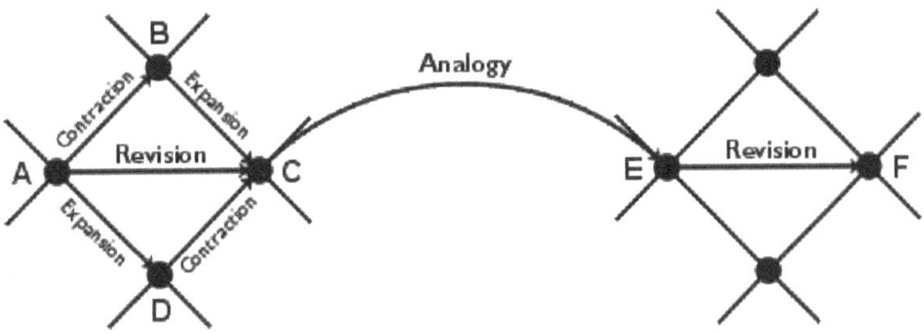

Fig. 11.8 Four operators for navigating the lattice of theories

types, relations, and individuals that appear in the axioms: the earth is renamed the electron; the sun is renamed the nucleus; and the solar system is renamed the atom. Finally, the revision step from E to F uses a contraction step to discard details about the earth and sun that have become irrelevant, followed by an expansion step to add new axioms for quantum mechanics.

Formal and informal reasoning should not be considered incompatible or conflicting. Instead, formal reasoning is a more disciplined application of the techniques used for informal reasoning. Analogy, the process of finding common patterns in different structures, is the foundation for both. The logical methods of reasoning by induction, deduction, and abduction are distinguished by the constraints they impose on analogy:

- *Deduction.* A basic rule of deduction is *modus ponens*: given an assertion p and an axiom of the form p implies q, derive the conclusion q. In most applications, the assertion p is not identical to the p in the axiom, and a version of analogy is necessary to *unify* the two ps before the rule can be applied. The most time-consuming task is not the application of a single rule, but the repeated use of analogies for finding patterns that may lead to successful rule applications.
- *Induction.* When every instance of p is followed by an instance of q, induction may derive the general principle that p implies q. Since the ps and qs are rarely identical in every occurrence, the generalization requires a version of analogy that subsumes all the instances.
- *Abduction.* The operation of guessing or forming an initial hypothesis by abduction uses the least constrained version of analogy, in which some parts of the matching structures may be more generalized while other parts are more specialized.

According to Peirce (1902), 'Besides these three types of reasoning there is a fourth, analogy, which combines the characters of the three, yet cannot be adequately represented as composite.' The basis for analogy is pattern matching, which is also used in more disciplined versions of reasoning. But analogy is also used in *case-based reasoning*, which can have the combined effect of deduction, induction, and abduction.

11.7 Foundations for Dynamic Ontology

In every science, the vocabulary and theories are developed in close connection with the data on which they are based. Although they may be distinguished during the analysis, the data and the vocabulary influence one another inextricably. No ontology, formal or informal, is independent of the vocabulary and the methodologies (i.e., language games) used to analyze the data. Natural language terms have been the starting point for every ontology from Aristotle to the present. Even the most abstract ontologies of mathematics and science are analyzed, debated, explained, and taught in natural languages. For computer applications, the users who enter data and choose options on menus, think in the words of the NL vocabulary. Any options that cannot be explained in words the users understand are open invitations to mistakes, confusions, and system vulnerabilities. Therefore, every ontology that has any practical application must have a mapping, direct or indirect, to and from natural languages.

These observations imply that any foundation for applied ontology must support a systematic mapping to and from natural languages. Yet both logicians and linguists recognize that Montague's claim that there is no difference between the semantics of formal and natural languages is false. In a series of studies with a strong Wittgensteinian orientation, Wilks (2006, 2008a, b) has shown that the widely used linguistic resources such as WordNet (Miller 1995) and Roget's *Thesaurus* are fundamentally different from and irreconcilable with the axiomatized ontologies expressed in formal logics. The linguistic resources blur distinctions that are critical for the ontologies. Even worse, translations from language to logic based on them introduce contradictions that would make a theorem prover unusable. Furthermore, there is no way to 'correct' them in order to align them with formal ontologies because any such correction would make them unusable for their primary purpose of interpreting a broad range of natural language texts. Attempted alignments merely blur critical distinctions and introduce contradictions in the formal systems. Using WordNet to align independently developed ontologies is as futile as using it to align Linux with Microsoft Windows and Apple's OS X.

The comparison with operating systems is significant because every program or collection of programs is a formal system that could be described by some theory in the infinite lattice. Such a theory would be a detailed formal specification of the program, with preconditions and postconditions for every change to the data. Every revision or update to the programs would be described by a different theory somewhere in the lattice. Even a fix to a bug creates another program described by another theory. For minor revisions, all the programs would be described by theories located close to one another in the lattice. The lattice operators could be used to organize and relate different versions of the systems. For example, suppose that some program X has multiple versions distinguished by numbers such as 4.1, 4.2, 4.21:

- In usual practice, version 4.x would be more similar to version 4.y than either would be to any version 3.z.
- For any version X.Y, let ThX.Y be the theory that describes it.
- For any two versions X.Y and Z.W, the supremum ThX.Y∩ThZ.W would be a generalization that correctly describes all the features common to both versions and was silent about their differences.
- For a major version number, such as 4.x, the least common generalization of Th4.0, Th4.1, ..., Th4.9 would be a theory that describes all and only those features common to every version. Any other program that uses only those features would be guaranteed to run correctly with every version from 4.0 to 4.9.

This summary, which characterizes common programming practice, is just as applicable to any application of formal ontology. The lattice of theories is key to implementing the approach.

The words used in programming illustrate the variations in terminology that typically occur in all engineering applications. The word *file*, for example, is commonly used to describe a collection of data managed by an operating system. But every version of every operating system has a different definition. In Linux and other UNIX-like systems, a file contains an ordered list of character strings separated by newline characters. In Apple's operating systems, the strings of a file are separated by carriage-return characters. In all versions of Windows, the strings are separated by two characters – a carriage-return followed by a newline character. In IBM's mainframe operating systems, the strings are called *records*, and a file with fixed-length records might have no character strings between records. This example is just one way in which the meaning of the word *file* differs among systems, and each version of every operating system for the past half century has added new microsenses to the meaning of all such terms, including the term *operating system* itself. Yet a typical English dictionary lumps them all under a single word sense, such as definition 2c of the *Miriam-Webster Collegiate*: 'a collection of related data records (as for a computer).' In computational linguistics, assigning word sense 2c to an occurrence of *file* is considered 'disambiguation,' but it is only the first step toward mapping it to a formal ontology.

The problem of matching language to logic is unsolvable if the two are considered totally different, irreconcilable systems. Montague simplified the problem by adopting Wittgenstein's early assumption: both language and logic can have a monolithic model-theoretic semantics, along the lines developed for formal logics. Forty years of research in logic, linguistics, and AI has not produced a successful implementation: no computer system based on that approach can read one page of a high-school textbook and use the results to answer the questions and solve the problems as well as a B student. Wittgenstein's later philosophy makes the semantics of formal logic a special case of the much richer semantics of natural languages. Instead of a monolithic semantics, each language game has its own semantics that is intimately connected with the more general methods of perception and behavior. The diversity of mechanisms associated with language is a reflection of the diversity involved in all aspects of cognition. In his book *The Society of Mind*, Minsky (1987) surveyed that diversity and proposed an organization of active processes as a computational model that could simulate the complexity:

> What magical trick makes us intelligent? The trick is that there is no trick. The power of intelligence stems from our vast diversity, not from any single, perfect principle. Our species has evolved many effective although imperfect methods, and each of us individually develops more on our own. Eventually, very few of our actions and decisions come to depend on any single mechanism. Instead, they emerge from conflicts and negotiations among societies of processes that constantly challenge one another. (§30.8)

This view is radically different from the assumption of a unified formal logic that cannot tolerate a single inconsistency. Minsky's goal is to build a flexible, fault-tolerant system out of imperfect, possibly fallible components. Different processes supported by different components could implement different language games or even different aspects of the same language game. Versions of analogy would support the reasoning methods used by most or all of the processes, some of which might use the more disciplined methods of analogy called formal logic.

A foundation for ontology inspired by Peirce, Wittgenstein, and Minsky sounds intriguing, but any implementation would require more detailed specifications. The infinite lattice of theories is formally defined, but no actual implementation can be infinite. A less ambitious term is *open-ended hierarchy*, which implies that only a finite subset is ever implemented, the implemented theories do not form a complete lattice, but there is no limit to the possible revisions and extensions. Following is a proposed foundation for a dynamic ontology that would relate natural language terminologies to a hierarchy of formal theories related by generalization and specialization:

1. Separate, but related lexical and formal resources: *lexical resources* for natural language terminologies, syntactic information, informal semantic information, and links to the formal types and relations; and a *hierarchy of formal theories*, represented in any dialect of Common Logic, including subsets such as RDF(S) and OWL.
2. A *registry* for recording all the resources of point #1 and a *repository* or a distributed collection of repositories for storing them.
3. *Metadata* about the resources, including who developed them and used them for what purposes and evaluations of the results.
4. The lexical resources could contain a variety of terminologies, dictionaries, lexicons, grammars, and resources such as WordNet. The links to logic could be represented as word fans and canonical graphs, as in Figs. 11.5 and 11.6, but they could use any dialect that could be mapped to Common Logic, including frame-like notations.
5. The hierarchy of formal theories would be organized in a partial ordering by generalization and specialization, but the full set of lattice operations need not be fully implemented. As time goes by, more gaps would be filled in and more of the implications of the partial ordering would be discovered.
6. The theories in the hierarchy could be of any size. Some would represent the *microtheories* of Cyc, which are devoted to specialized subjects, and others would resemble typical upper-level ontologies. Many of them would represent useful mathematical structures or standard relationships for times and dates, weights and measures, or geographical coordinates. Others might contain large mergers of a variety of other theories that can be used together. In general, any useful ontology of any size that is represented in any dialect of Common Logic could be contributed to the hierarchy.
7. The generalization hierarchy would be especially valuable for stating interoperability constraints and version controls. If the interfaces to two programs are compatible with theory X in the ontology, then they would be compatible with anything stated in any ontology that is a generalization of X. If one program is compatible with theory X and another with a different theory Y, then they could

interoperate on anything stated in an ontology that is a common generalization of X and Y.

Nothing in this proposal requires any further research, since parts of every point above have been implemented in one or more working systems. This proposal does not require a unified upper-level ontology, but it allows any ontology with such an upper level to be registered in the hierarchy as one among many. It also allows specialized low-level theories, such as an ontology of times and dates, to be placed in the hierarchy as a specialization of many different upper levels. A program that uses times and dates, but no other specialized information, would then be able to interoperate with other systems that used different upper-level ontologies.

For linking lexical resources to formal ontologies, the hierarchy provides the mechanism for resolving the multiple microsenses. As an example, the dictionary definition 2c for the word *file* cannot distinguish the multiple microsenses for every operating system. That word sense could be linked to a simple, general theory about file systems as collections of records or strings without any detail about how the records are represented. Theories about the multiple versions of file systems for Unix, Microsoft, Apple, and IBM mainframes would be specializations of that theory further down in the hierarchy. The word *file* in the context of a Microsoft manual would narrow the meaning to a subtype in a theory several levels deeper in the hierarchy. The single definition 2c in the English dictionary would correspond to hundreds of different microsenses for every version of every operating system that ever used the word *file*.

The sharp distinction between lexical resources and a hierarchy of theories enables multiple agents to use them concurrently without requiring a prior merger into a single consistent theory. Majumdar and Sowa (2009) take advantage of that option in the VivoMind Language Processor (VLP), which implements a society of heterogeneous agents as suggested by Minsky (1987, 2006). During the process of language analysis and reasoning, different agents can use different dictionaries and ontologies to analyze different parts of the same text or even the same sentence. To avoid inconsistency, deductive reasoning must be restricted to a single theory with a single ontology. For abduction, however, different agents, using different ontologies, may propose new hypotheses derived from any resource of any kind. Other agents can then test those hypotheses on competing interpretations of the current text. The VLP system does not yet implement the full range of ideas discussed in this article, but the framework has proved to be highly flexible and efficient for language analysis and reasoning.

References

Ajdukiewicz, K. 1935. Die syntaktische Konnexität. *Studia Philosophica* 1:1–27; translated as Syntactic Connexion. In *Polish logic 1920–1939*, ed. S. McCall. Oxford: Clarendon Press, 1967.

Alchourrón, C., P. Gärdenfors, and D. Makinson. 1985. On the logic of theory change: Partial meet contraction and revision functions. *Journal of Symbolic Logic* 50(2):510–530.

Arieti, S. 1978. The psychobiology of sadness. In *Severe and mild depression*. eds. S. Arieti, and J. Bemporad, 109–128. New York, NY: Basic Books.

Aristotle, *Works*, Loeb Library, Cambridge, MA: Harvard University Press.

Austin, J.L. 1962. *How to do things with words*, eds. J.O. Urmson, and M. Sbisá, 2nd edn. Cambridge, MA: Harvard University Press.

Barwise, J., and J. Perry. 1983. *Situations and attitudes*. Cambridge, MA: MIT Press.

Bartlett, F.C. 1932. *Remembering*. Cambridge: Cambridge University Press.

Bharati, A., V. Chaitanya, and R. Sangal. 1995. *Natural language processing: A Paninian perspective*. New Delhi: Prentice-Hall of India.

Bohnert, H., and P. Backer. 1967. Automatic English-to-logic translation in a simplified model. Technical report RC-1744. Yorktown Heights, NY: IBM.

Boole, G. 1854. *An Investigation into the laws of thought*. Reprinted. New York, NY: Dover.

Brentano, F. 1874. *Psychologie vom empirischen Standpunkte*. translated as *Psychology from an empirical standpoint* (trans: A.C. Rancurello, D.B. Terrell, and L.L. McAlister). London: Routledge.

Bundy, A. 2007. Cooperating reasoning processes: More than just the sum of their parts. *Proceedings of IJCAI-07*, 2–11.

Bundy, A., and F. McNeill. 2006. Representation as a fluent: An AI challenge for the next half century. *IEEE Intelligent Systems* 21(3):85–87.

Ceccato, S. 1961. *Linguistic analysis and programming for mechanical translation*. New York, NY: Gordon and Breach.

Chomsky, N. 1957. *Syntactic structures*. The Hague: Mouton.

Chomsky, N. 1965. *Aspects of the theory of syntax*. Cambridge, MA: MIT Press.

Chomsky, N. 1995. *The minimalist program*. Cambridge, MA: MIT Press.

Croft, W., and D.A. Cruse. 2004. *Cognitive linguistics*. Cambridge: Cambridge University Press.

Cruse, D.A. 1986. *Lexical semantics*. New York, NY: Cambridge University Press.

Cruse, D.A. 2002. Microsenses, default specificity and the semantics-pragmatics boundary. *Axiomathes* 1:1–20.

Fillmore, C. 1988. The mechanisms of construction grammar. *Berkeley Linguistics Society* 35: 35–55.

Förster, E. 2000. *Kant's final synthesis: An essay on the opus postumum*. Cambridge, MA: Harvard University Press.

Frege, G. 1879. *Begriffsschrift*. English translation in J. van Heijenoort, ed. 1967. *From Frege to Gödel*. Cambridge, MA: Harvard University Press. 1–82.

Goldberg, A.E. 1995. *Constructions: A construction grammar approach to argument structure*. Chicago, IL: University of Chicago Press.

Grice, H.P. 1975. Logic and conversation. In *Syntax and semantics 3: Speech acts*, eds. P. Cole and J. Morgan, 41–58. New York, NY: Academic Press.

Halliday, M.A.K. 1978. *Language as social semiotic: The social interpretation of language and meaning*. Baltimore: University Park Press.

Halliday, M.A.K. and C.M.I.M. Matthiessen. 1999. *Construing experience through meaning: A language-based approach to cognition*. London: Cassell.

Harris, Z.S. 1951. *Methods in structural linguistics*. Chicago: University of Chicago Press.

ISO/IEC. 2007. *Common logic (CL)—A framework for a family of logic-based languages*. IS 24707. Geneva: International Organisation for Standardisation.

Jackendoff, R. 1983. *Semantics and cognition*. Cambridge, MA: MIT Press.

Kant, I. 1787. *Kritik der reinen Vernunft*. *Critique of pure reason* (trans: N. Kemp Smith). New York, NY: St. Martin's Press.

Kamp, H. 2001. Levels of linguistic meaning and the logic of natural language. http://www.illc.uva.nl/lia/farewell_kamp.html

Kamp, H., and U. Reyle. 1993. *From discourse to logic*. Dordrecht: Kluwer.

Lakoff, G. 1987. *Women, fire, and dangerous things*. Chicago: University of Chicago Press.

Langacker, R.W. 1999. *Grammar and conceptualization*. Berlin: de Gruyter.

Lenat, D.B. 1995. CYC: A large-scale investment in knowledge infrastructure. *Communications of the ACM* 38(11):33–38.
Lord, A.B. 1960. *The singer of tales*. Cambridge, MA: Harvard University Press.
Majumdar, A.K., and J.F. Sowa. 2009. Two paradigms are better than one and multiple paradigms are even better. In *Proceedings of ICCS'09*, LNAI 5662, eds. S. Rudolph, F. Dau, and S.O. Kuznetsov, 32–47. Heidelberg: Springer.
Makinson, D. 2005. *Bridges from classical to nonmonotonic logic*. London: King's College Publications.
Mann, W.C., and S.A. Thompson. 1988. Rhetorical structure theory: Towards a functional theory of text organization. *Text* 8(3):243–281.
Masterman, M. 2005. *Language, chohesion and form*. ed. Y. Wilks. Cambridge: Cambridge University Press.
Miller, G.A. 1995. WordNet: A lexical database for English. *Communications of the ACM* 38(11):39–41.
Minsky, M. 1975. A framework for representing knowledge. In *The psychology of computer vision*, ed. P. Winston, 211–280. New York, NY: McGraw-Hill.
Minsky, M. 1987. *The society of mind*. New York, NY: Simon & Schuster.
Minsky, M. 2006. *The emotion machine: Commonsense thinking, artificial intelligence, and the future of the human mind*. New York, NY: Simon & Schuster.
Mohanty, J.N. 1982. *Husserl and frege*. Bloomington: Indiana University Press.
Montague, R. 1970. English as a formal language. reprinted In *Formal philosophy*, ed. R. Montague, 188–221.New Haven: Yale University Press.
Newell, A., and H.A. Simon. 1972. *Human problem solving*. Englewood Cliffs, NJ: Prentice-Hall.
Ockham, William of (1323) *Summa logicae*, Paris: Johannes Higman. 1488 (the edition owned by C.S. Peirce).
Ogden, C.K., and I.A. Richards. 1923. *The meaning of*meaning, 8th edn, 1946. New York, NY: Harcourt, Brace, and World.
Peirce, C.S. 1880. On the algebra of logic. *American Journal of Mathematics* 3:15–57.
Peirce, C.S. 1885. On the algebra of logic. *American Journal of Mathematics* 7:180–202.
Peirce, C.S. 1902. *Logic, considered as semeiotic*. MS L75, ed. J. Ransdell, http://members.door.net/arisbe/menu/library/bycsp/l75/l75.htm
Peirce, C.S. 1911. Assurance through reasoning. MS 670.
Peirce, C.S. (CP) *Collected papers of C. S. Peirce*, ed. C. Hartshorne, P. Weiss, and A. Burks, 8 vols., 1931–1958. Cambridge, MA: Harvard University Press.
Peirce, C.S. (EP) *The essential Peirce*, ed. N. Houser, C. Kloesel, and members of the Peirce Edition Project, 2 vols., 1991–1998. Bloomington: Indiana University Press.
Peppas, P. 2008. Belief revision. In *Handbook of knowledge representation*, eds. F. van Harmelen, V. Lifschitz, and B. Porter, 317–359. Amsterdam: Elsevier.
Post, E.L. 1943. Formal reductions of the general combinatorial decision problem. *American Journal of Mathematics* 65:197–268.
Propp, V. 1928. *Morfologia Skazki*. translated as *Morphology of the folktale*, 1958. Austin: University of Texas Press.
Reid, T. 1785. *Essays on the intellectual power of man*. Edinburgh: Edinburgh University Press.
de Saussure, F. 1916. *Cours de Linguistique Générale. Course in general linguistics* (trans: Baskin, W., 1959). New York, NY: Philosophical Library.
Schank, R.C., ed. 1975. *Conceptual information processing*. Amsterdam: North-Holland Publishing Co.
Schank, R.C., and R.P. Abelson. 1977. *Scripts, plans, goals and understanding*. Hilsdale, NJ: Erlbaum
Selz, O. 1913. *Über die Gesetze des geordneten Denkverlaufs*. Stuttgart: Spemann.
Shanker, S.G. 1987. *Wittgenstein and the turning point in the philosophy of mathematics*. Albany: SUNY Press.
Sowa, J.F. 1976. Conceptual graphs for a data base interface. *IBM Journal of Research and Development* 20(4):336–357.

Sowa, J.F. 1984. *Conceptual structures: Information processing in mind and machine.* Reading, MA: Addison-Wesley.
Sowa, J.F. 2000. *Knowledge representation: Logical, philosophical, and computational foundations.* Pacific Grove, CA: Brooks/Cole Publishing Co.
Sowa, J.F. 2005. The challenge of knowledge soup. In *Research trends in science, technology, and mathematics education,* eds. J. Ramadas, and S. Chunawala, 55–90. Mumbai: Homi Bhabha Centre.
Sowa, J.F. 2008. Conceptual graphs. In *Handbook of knowledge representation,* eds. F. van Harmelen, V. Lifschitz, and B. Porter, 213–237. Amsterdam: Elsevier.
Sperber, D., and D. Wilson. 1986. *Relevance: Communication and cognition.* Oxford: Blackwell.
Talmy, L. 2000. *Toward a cognitive semantics, Volume I: Concept structuring systems, Volume II: Typology and process in concept structure.* Cambridge, MA: MIT Press.
Tarski, A. 1933. Der Wahrheitsbegriff in den formalisierten Sprachen. English edition: The concept of truth in formalized languages. In *Logic, semantics, metamathematics,* ed. A. Tarski, 152–278, 2nd edn. Indianapolis, IN: Hackett Publishing Co.
Tesnière, L. 1959. *Éléments de Syntaxe structurale,* 2nd edn, 1965. Paris: L.C. Klincksieck.
Tolman, E.C. 1948. Cognitive maps in rats and men. *Psychological Review* 55(4):189–208.
van Deemter, K., and S. Peters. 1996. *Semantic ambiguity and underspecification.* Stanford, CA: CSLI.
Vygotsky, L.S. (Original work published 1934) 1962. *Thought and language.* Cambridge, MA: MIT Press.
Waismann, F. 1979. *Ludwig Wittgenstein and the Vienna circle: Conversations recorded by friedrich waismann.* Oxford: Blackwell.
Wertheimer, M. 1925. Über Gestalttheorie. Gestalt theory (trans: Ellis, W.D., 1938). *Source book of Gestalt psychology.* New York, NY: Harcourt, Brace and Co.
Whitehead, A.N. 1937. Analysis of meaning. *Philosophical review,* reprinted In *Essays in science and philosophy,* ed. A.N. Whitehead, 122–131. New York, NY: Philosophical Library.
Wierzbicka, A. 1996. *Semantics: Primes and universals.* Oxford: Oxford University Press.
Wilks, Y. 2006. Thesauri and ontologies. In *Perspectives on cognition: A Festshrift for Manfred Wettler,* eds. S. Rapp, and G. Zunker-Rapp. Lengerich: Pabst.
Wilks, Y. 2008a. The semantic web as the apotheosis of annotation, but what are its semantics? *IEEE Transactions on Intelligent Systems.* May/June 2008.
Wilks, Y. 2008b. What would a wittgensteinian computational linguistics be like? *Proceedings of AISB'08,* Workshop on Computers and Philosophy, Aberdeen.
Winograd, T. 1972. *Understanding natural language.* New York, NY: Academic Press.
Wittgenstein, L. 1921. *Tractatus logico-philosophicus.* London: Routledge & Kegan Paul.
Wittgenstein, L. 1953. *Philosophical investigations.* Oxford: Basil Blackwell.
Wittgenstein, L. 1964. *Philosophische Bemerkungen.* ed. R. Rhees, *Philosophical remarks* (trans: Hargreaves, R., and White, R., 1980). Chicago: University of Chicago Press.
Woods, W.A. 1968. Procedural semantics for a question-answering machine. *AFIPS Conference Proceedings.* 1968 FJCC, 457–471.
Zadeh, L.A. 1975. Fuzzy logic and approximate reasoning. *Synthése* 30:407–428.

Chapter 12
Ontologies in the Legal Domain

Laurens Mommers

12.1 Introduction

Ontologies are conceptual models of a specific domain. This use of the term 'ontology' in the context of computer science and artificial intelligence differs from the use of the term in a philosophical context (cf. Mommers et al. 1997). Gruber (1993) defines an ontology as a specification of a conceptualisation, and, more specifically, as a description of concepts and relations that exist for an individual or a community of individuals. A conceptualisation is a representation of the world that is both simplified and abstract (ibid.). In artificial intelligence, ontologies are primarily meant to provide a basic framework for knowledge representation: the entities and relations distinguished in an ontology provide a user with the means to represent knowledge in the domain that the ontology covers. Ontologies were considered to be able to establish the missing link between legal theory and AI & law by Valente and Breuker (1994).

The rise of ontologies in the domain of artificial intelligence and law (AI & law) can be seen as both the almost inevitable consequence of developments in computer science and artificial intelligence in general, and as a recognition of the necessity of building maintainable, scalable models that do justice to the structure of legal domains. An inherent problem for legal ontologies, however, is that legal systems that underlie such ontologies vary according to time and place. The general concepts and relations of a top-level ontology can rarely accommodate all the peculiarities of legal systems. In order to address the specific problems bound to appear in legal ontology building, this chapter provides an (incomplete) overview of ontologies built in the past decades of AI & law research.

Not all the ontologies discussed were named as such by their creators. We assume that any model – regardless of its name – that makes implicit or explicit claims regarding the existence of entity types and relation types amounts to an ontology.

L. Mommers (✉)
Centre for Law in the Information Society, Leiden University, Leiden, The Netherlands
e-mail: l.mommers@law.leidenuniv.nl

R. Poli, J. Seibt (eds.), *Theory and Applications of Ontology: Philosophical Perspectives*, DOI 10.1007/978-90-481-8845-1_12,

This chapter also critically assesses the claims of ontologies, it provides an overview of the tasks attributed to legal ontologies, and it summarizes developments expected in the near future. For a different overview of legal ontologies and their applications, please refer to Breuker and Winkels (2003), focusing mainly on a specific set of projects, but still indicative for the field.

This paper sets out by discussing legal ontologies, classifying them through a classic distinction between semantics, epistemology and ontology (Section 12.2). It subsequently discusses the applications of ontologies in the legal domain (Section 12.3). Then, it continues to explore future opportunities of the application of ontologies in legal domains (Section 12.4). Finally, it provides conclusions. However, we first elaborate on principled problems in building legal ontologies, arising from the nature of legal domains.

The legal domain is – as many other domains – dominated by the use of natural language. Although legal language use often has a particularly formal nature, and contains a lot of jargon, it is still natural language – not the formal kind of language we find in programming languages or logics. This means that there is neither a formal syntax nor a formal semantics for legal language. Any attempt to represent parts of a legal domain will encounter this lack of formal syntax and semantics, as representation languages require – at least – a formal syntax in order to be usable for automated reasoning, and a formal semantics in order to disambiguate meaning. The mapping from natural language – by far the important representation language for legal knowledge – towards (semi-)formal languages introduces so many principled and practical problems that one could wonder if building formal representation frameworks actually is a sensible thing to do.

Principled problems are, first, the nature of natural language meaning in general. The revolution that the later Wittgenstein (1953) started in philosophy of language was the denial of being able to fix natural language meaning in terms of necessary and sufficient conditions. This revolution has been translated to the legal domain by, among others, Hart (1961), by introducing the notion of open texture concepts (cf. also Bix 1991). Modeling a domain almost necessarily assumes a low degree of change if the representation is required to give a correct picture of that domain. Any changes in the domain have to be modeled to keep the representation up to date. As legal concepts change through time (they are either replaced by new concepts, or their meaning or interpretation changes through judicial decisions), their place in the ontology should change as well.

Second, modeling a domain assumes that a domain *can* be represented. However, many branches of legal theory actually concern those acts that 'mould' the law: judicial reasoning for instance, making new 'things' (decisions) on the basis of incomplete information about facts and rules that are not conclusive. Although there is discussion on the matter whether this problem concerns only hard cases (cf. Hage et al. 1993, Leenes 1998) – and consequentially, how to establish whether a case is actually a hard case – the problem will probably always apply to simple cases to a certain degree.

Third, representing a legal domain often includes representation of relevant parts of the 'real world'. Therefore, legal ontologies generally contain a mix of legal concepts and real-world concepts. There are major differences in the accommodation of the legal and the legally relevant types in legal ontologies. For instance, McCarty's (1989) Language of Legal Discourse (see below) contains largely legally relevant concepts. Van Kralingen's (1995) frame-based ontology of law (see below) contains mostly legal concepts. Mommers' (2002) knowledge-based ontology of law makes an explicit distinction between the two types.

Elaborating a bit further on natural language meaning – the first principled problem stated above – meaning is a subject of major importance to modelling in the law, as so many legal issues arise from the meaning and interpretation of natural language terms and sentences. In this respect, some logico-philosophical history is necessary. Frege (cf. Frege 1892) developed a theory of meaning that distinguishes between two components of meaning: sense (Sinn) and reference (Bedeutung). The sense of an expression consists of the conditions under which it obtains: if we call an unmarried man a bachelor, then the concept 'bachelor' has as conditions: being a man and being unmarried.

The presence of each of these conditions is necessary, and the presence of both of these conditions is sufficient for a person to be a bachelor. The reference of an expression consists of the set of all objects that fulfil the conditions that are part of its sense: 'bachelor' refers to all unmarried men. The sense of an expression determines its reference, and two expressions with the same sense have the same reference. Meaning may change, i.e., for instance, the conditions that determine the sense of a concept may change through time. This is sometimes referred to as the 'open texture' of a concept.

The open-texture nature of legal concepts can be more precisely defined as the possibility that elements of the definition of some concept may change, may be left out, or may be added at some point in time, from which point in time the new set of elements will constitute the definition of that concept. In other words: the sense of an open texture concept changes through time. The concept of open texture is not a purely legal phenomenon. It was introduced by Waismann (1952, p. 120), who distinguishes between open texture and vagueness of empirical concepts. If we consider vagueness to be the unclear (or missing) demarcation lines of application of a concept, then open texture can be defined as the *possibility* of vagueness. Vagueness may apply to both the intension (sense) of a concept, in which case there is no (clear) set of necessary and sufficient application conditions for the concept, and to the extension (reference) of a concept, in which case we cannot (completely) determine the set of objects the concept refers to.

The view of meaning as use, introduced by Wittgenstein (cf. Wittgenstein 1953), always is subject to the danger of becoming a slogan rather than a serious idea. It has to be more strictly defined (or rather, explained by examples, as Wittgenstein did) to make sense, because otherwise, it raises questions such as: whose use constitutes meaning? and: what kinds of use constitute meaning? Putnam (1975, p. 145) has an approach that may clarify the 'use' aspect of meaning:

> [E]veryone to whom gold is important for any reason has to acquire the word 'gold'; but he does not have to acquire the method of recognizing if something is or is not gold. He can rely on a special subclass of speakers. The features that are generally thought to be present in connection with a general name – necessary and sufficient conditions for membership in the extension, ways of recognizing if something is in the extension ('criteria'), etc. – are all present in the linguistic community considered as a collective body; but that collective body divides the 'labor' of knowing and employing these various parts of the 'meaning' of 'gold.

The question whose use constitutes meaning becomes acute when only a small part of the community is able to determine whether some substance is really gold. Is only their use of the term 'gold' relevant? The majority of people, who do not distinguish gold from many other substances that look like gold, use the term 'gold' in a way that makes it impossible to determine its reference. Should we then exclude reference from our understanding of meaning?

Any definition of meaning that is related to use yields such problems. In the determination of the meaning of 'meaning' we can employ the approaches to the concept itself. For an intensional approach, this would mean that we can define the meaning of 'meaning' in terms of necessary and sufficient conditions. As 'meaning' itself is an open-textured concept, we need to consider the possibility of changes in this set of necessary and sufficient conditions. Meaning regarded as use also enables us to integrate open-texturedness into the concept of meaning. Because the use of the concept of meaning varies through time and through communities, we should incorporate use in its definition. The meaning of 'meaning' thus becomes dependent on the actual occurrence of the concept in natural language use, or, more specifically, in the legal domain, or even in the domain of the employment of legal information systems. The concept of meaning forms the core of legal ontologies: any ontology that does not take into account the peculiarities of legal meaning – the meandering of legal meaning between fixed criteria ensuring legal certainty and open texture enabling proper responses to unforeseen situations and unfair consequences – will render itself useless in little time.

12.2 A Selection of Legal Ontologies

Despite the name 'ontology', legal ontologies are actually quite different in their approach to legal domains. For clarification purposes, I distinguish between three different approaches. Semantically oriented approaches focus on the semantic interpretation of a representation of elements and relations in a certain domain. Epistemically oriented approaches focus on the (acquisition of) knowledge in a domain. Ontologically oriented approaches stress the entities and relations that constitute a domain. It goes without saying that these approaches tend to overlap to a certain extent with respect to their semantic, epistemic and ontological claims. Still, the distinction helps to classify ontologies on the basis of their assumed relation to reality: through the relation between language and reality (semantics), between knowledge and reality (epistemology) or through claims regarding existence (ontology). What the examples below have in common, is that they are based on a top–down approach, starting from very abstract concepts, and trying to apply these on concrete domains. There is one notable exception to this: the LOIS WordNet, which can be considered as a (lexical) ontology, was partly built from the viewpoint of individual legal concepts. The bottom–up approach, however, seems promising, and is further discussed in Section 12.4.

12.2.1 Semantically Oriented Theories

Many logical languages used in AI & law tend to make ontological assumptions if their syntax and semantics are deemed to be representative of certain legal classes. Deontic logics that distinguish between different types of norms make such underlying assumptions as well – unless any relation between the logic and the 'real world' is denied. An example of a semantically oriented theory is McCarty's Language of Legal Discourse. It is both a semantic and an ontological framework. The categories that McCarty distinguishes in one of his articles about LLD are space, time, mass, action, permission, obligation, causation, purpose, intention, knowledge, belief (McCarty 1989, p. 180). These categories give a clear indication of the common-sense character McCarty ascribes to the legal domain: there is little attention for its typically legal characteristics.

A different, less formal (in terms of lacking a formal semantics) approach is found in applications of WordNet in the legal domain. WordNet is a framework of relations between concepts. In WordNet, concepts are represented by a set of synonyms (synset) with an accompanying explanation of its meaning. These synsets are linked to each other by a fixed set of relations that are part of the WordNet framework (Fellbaum 1998). These include causality and specificity. JurWordNet is an extension of a generic Italian WordNet that contains legal terms and their meanings, linked up to the generic WordNet (cf. Gangemi et al. 2003). The LOIS WordNet is a legal WordNet for six European languages that is partly based on JurWordNet and contains around 5,000 legal concepts per language (cf. Dini et al. 20055). These WordNets enable, for instance, linking layman's search terms with the legal professional's language, thereby enabling search actions in legal documents without the need to know legal terminology beforehand. As WordNet is such a widespread semantic framework, it enables linking up legal WordNets to the generic ontologies that have been modelled in WordNet.

12.2.2 Epistemically Oriented Theories

Epistemically oriented theories contain claims on knowledge of the legal domain. As the law is generally regarded – at least partly – a human-constructed phenomenon, it makes sense to approach it from the viewpoint of knowledge: it consists largely of agreements between people; it is not tangible, and thus, it resides 'in the head' for the better part. A clear example of an epistemically oriented theory is Valente's (1995) 'functional ontology'. It models an ontology of law from the perspectives of both information science, following the definition of 'ontology' given by Gruber, and of legal theory, following such legal theorists as Kelsen and Hart. The functional ontology distinguishes between six different basic types of knowledge: normative knowledge, meta-legal knowledge, world knowledge, responsibility knowledge, reactive knowledge, and creative knowledge.

Normative knowledge is regarded the most obvious kind of legal knowledge. It consists of the elements of the legal domain prescribing the behaviour of the people constituting a society, and a description of the way social reality should look. Meta-legal knowledge consists of the entities not directly regulating behaviour. These entities are empowering and derogating norms, and norms regulating the mutual relations among primary norms. World knowledge consists of elements telling us what the world looks like. Responsibility knowledge consists of the knowledge that links normative knowledge to reactive knowledge: in case some agent causes a certain event, responsibility knowledge helps to establish the extent to which the agent can be held responsible for what he did. Reactive knowledge consists of the sanctions imposed if an agent breaches a norm and is held responsible for that. Creative knowledge, finally, consists of information about newly created institutions and other entities that arise from the application of the law.

12.2.3 Ontologically Oriented Theories

Ontologically oriented theories make claims about reality. Such a theory will, for instance, make a claim about the existence of individual norms. Ontologically oriented theories will be the most 'ontological' from a philosophical viewpoint: they make implicit or explicit claims about existence.

An early ontologically oriented theory was that of Van Kralingen 'frame based ontology' (1995). He distinguishes between three main types of entities: acts, norms and concepts. For representation purposes, each of these entity types is represented by a so-called frame, each containing a number of slots filled with characteristics of a specific occurrence of the entity. An act frame consists of fourteen elements: an act identifier, promulgation, scope, agent, act type, means, manner, temporal aspects, spatial aspects, circumstances, cause, aim, intentionality, and final state. The slots of a norm frame are a norm identifier, promulgation, scope, conditions of application, subject, legal modality, and an act identifier. The third type of frame, concept frames, consists of a concept, concept type, priority, promulgation, scope, conditions, and instances. Concept types distinguished are definitions, deeming provisions, factors or meta-concepts.

Verheij and Hage (1997) developed a model consisting of three main elements: states-of-affairs, events, and rules. States-of-affairs are (possible or real) situations that can be described by descriptive sentences. Events bring about changes in the current states-of-affairs. Rules express direct relations among states-of-affairs. Thus, there are two different relations among states-of-affairs: either the transition from one state-of-affairs into another is *caused* by an event, or the transition from one state-of-affairs into another is the result of the application of a rule, which makes the former *constitute* the latter. The model is inspired by institutional theories of law. By accommodating the temporal aspects of relations between states-of-affairs and events, the supervenience relation between states-of-affairs, and the different modalities of states-of-affairs, the authors introduce a very abstract approach towards modelling legal phenomena.

LRI-Core, developed by, among others, Breuker and Winkels (2003) is a core ontology specifically aimed at the legal domain, but with a clear connection to the physical world. The main entity classes distinguished in the physical world are objects (e.g., documents) and processes (e.g., actions). Mental objects and processes often relate to the physical world. Social organization is attained by imposing roles on agents, partly regulated by (legal) norms. It has been used as top-ontology in several practice-related projects, such as the CLIME project (Winkels et al. 1998), in which a question–answerring system was based on an ontology-oriented representation of a certain domain.

12.2.4 Mixed Approaches

Mommers' (2002) 'knowledge-based ontology of law' focuses merely on the ambiguous perspective that one can have on legal domains. By distinguishing between ontological status layers and empistemic roles, he accommodates both the epistemic and the ontological viewpoint in a single ontology. Although the author includes some semantically oriented categories (sentences, statements) in his ontology, the main focus is on accommodating views on the existence of legal systems and their constituents, and knowledge of the law. Ontological status layers are efficacy (the degree to which a law has the intended effect), validity (has a law been issued by the proper authorities in a proper way) and recognition (has a law been recognized as a law by its addressee). They each reflect, for instance, a view on the existence of legal rules. An epistemic role is a role that an entity (a belief, a statement) can take in the acquisition or justification of knowledge. Epistemic roles include reasons, defeaters ('arguments' that attack a reason or a relation between a reason and a conclusion) and knowledge. By including such epistemic roles, there is also a clear place for legal argumentation in the ontology.

12.3 Applications of Legal Ontologies

Applications of legal ontologies range from information systems to knowledge-based systems. The more 'intelligence' is requested from a system, the more detailed knowledge representation the ontology should support. Examples of applications of legal ontologies are:

(a) Information retrieval. By encoding knowledge about the meaning of concepts and the relations among them, it becomes possible to empower users of information retrieval systems. A seminal version of an ontology, a *thesaurus*, can encode relations between terms and concepts, for instance hierarchical relations. Information about less and more specific concepts can help the user to find information relevant to his query. Examples of relevant publications and projects are Matthijssen (1999), who introduces an interface between the lay user and a legal database, LOIS (which stands for 'Lexical Ontologies for legal Information Sharing', cf. Dini et al. 2005) and BEST (which stands for 'Batna Establishment using Semantic web Technology', cf. Van Laarschot et al. 2005).
(b) Translation of legal documents. Making explicit the meaning of legal terms can help in (manually!) translating legal documents from one language into another one. A framework for this specific purpose has been developed by Termorshuizen-Arts (2003). Although her work was not done from the perspective of artificial intelligence & law, it is certainly relevant to that discipline.
(c) Automated classification and summarizing. Parallel to information retrieval, automated classification is meant to facilitate finding documents. Ontologies, combined with statistic techniques and natural language processing techniques, can support classification techniques as well. The same goes for making summaries of documents automatically (cf. Moens et al. 1997, Moens 2004).
(d) Question answering. Automatic question answering requires thorough representation of knowledge in order to let a system 'understand' both a question and the sources of knowledge on which to base automatic answering. Cf., e.g., the CLIME project. CLIME stands for 'Computerised Legal Information Management and Explanation', cf. Winkels et al. (1998).
(e) Decision support and decision making. Legal (procedural) regulations often contain decision structures that allow making certain decisions or qualifications. Although such structures can be modelled in relatively simple decision trees, such decision trees still require user intervention on making a choice in each step. An ontology can be used to encode not only the decision steps, but also the contents of the decision rules. Advantages of using an ontology in such a case are supposed to include consistency of the modeling activity result and the re-usability of the underlying ontology for other modeling activities. Although the models underlying case-based systems are seldom called 'ontologies', they can be regarded as such. The model underlying a sentencing system described in Oskamp (1998) is just one example of this. It contains a model with two main constituents: facts and factors. Factors are subjective qualifications of (sets of) objective facts. By the nature of these entities, they constitute an 'ontology' of the arguments underlying sentencing decisions.
(f) Agent technology. Although still largely a theoretical exercise, agents are assumed to allow for intelligent autonomous communication between different computer systems. For such communication, the modelling of rules governing that communication is necessary. As in the case of decision support and decision making, such modelling can be supported by an underlying ontology. Potential

practical applications of agents in the legal domain are automated dispute resolution by negotiation and the controlled exchange of sensitive data, for instance in electronic legal dossiers

Of these different applications of ontologies, information retrieval still remains the most widely found application of ontologies – especially if we count those frameworks that are regularly not *called* ontologies, such as thesauri. In this respect, the legal domain does not really differ from many other domains.

12.4 New Developments

Large-scale information systems and knowledge-based systems have stimulated the development of ontologies in recent years. Unlike the earlier top–down approach towards ontology construction seen in the discussions in Section 12.2, a bottom–up approach towards the generation of ontologies has gained attention, by following the structure of legal sources themselves. The result of generating such a model can be coined a 'bottom–up ontology'. The development of interactive internet applications has triggered the generation of 'folksonomies': classification schemes that are the result of the joint participation of many users. This development will play a growing role in the legal domain. For instance, Wikipedia (the internet encyclopaedia; cf. www.wikipedia.org) currently contains many legal entries, and the references between these entries indicate a structure. The same will be seen for Jurispedia – a legal variant of Wikipedia.

How the process of bottom–up construction of ontologies can be best facilitated, is largely unknown. Most platforms that could support such construction are still in their infancy – policies for the proper use of on-line collaborative environments (such as wikis, enabling the joint production of texts) are subject of trial and error in their actual use. Use of such platforms in the legal domain is still quite rare, so little is known about suitable policies for collaboration among lawyers. Still, this bottom–up approach could be very promising as it involves domain specialists to a much higher degree, putting more specialist knowledge into legal ontologies.

As a response to top–down, legal-theoretically oriented ontology building, more pragmatic and positivist approaches have been developed. From the viewpoint that general classification schemes will always be largely normative in nature, the awareness arose that the most important basis for ontologies can be found in formal sources of law: in legislation, case law etc. This insight was used in the LOIS project, in which roughly half of the multi-lingual WordNet is constituted by concepts directly derived from definitions in European directives (cf. Dini et al. 2005, Mommers and Voermans 2005). A similar approach was suggested in Després and Szulman (2005).

Folksonomies are classification schemes developed on the basis of user interaction. They have become widely known through services such as FlickR.com, that enable users to classify, for example, their own photos with self-selected 'labels'. A more or less coherent system or taxonomy of labels can thus come into existence.

The opportunities offered by folksonomies are especially interesting with respect to information retrieval. Current legal information systems are often either based on full-text retrieval, statistic-based retrieval, or thesaurus-based retrieval. Full-text retrieval does not offer meaningful connections with synonyms or related terms. Statistics-based information retrieval generally provides only access to documents with 'associated' terms, which makes these less reliable than search engines based on thesauri or ontologies, the latter providing more rigid connections between concepts.

Thesaurus-based retrieval is based on a pre-built thesaurus, which includes the views of the builders on the legal domains included. This view can clash with the users' expectations of synonymy and related terms. It would be interesting to see the type of user-initiated classification schemes applied in legal information retrieval. Little work has been done on this matter in the legal domain. A somewhat related attempt to model user interaction in the quality assessment of legal documents and legal institutions is found in Mommers (2003) and (2005). A collaborative approach of legal knowledge dissemination is found in Hoorn (2005). A more complex collaborative approach would allow for establishing, for instance, WordNet relations between different items.

12.5 Conclusion

Although a considerable number of legal ontologies has been developed in the past two decades, there are still few large-scale applications. Apart from an apparent lack of dissemination activities by the AI & Law community in the legal domain, this could be attributed to the gap between the state-of-the-art in AI & Law and the situation in legal publishing, one of the main (potential) users of legal ontologies. It seems that the more profound type of modeling in legal ontologies is still too advanced for legal information retrieval, in which traditional taxonomies, thesauri and keyword lists are still prevalent. Additionally, an important cause for a lack of 'deep' modeling can be found in the enormous effort that has to be made for it.

Also, there is a tendency in AI & Law to build generic models that do not really fit in with large parts of the legal domain, which in itself is very complex and diverse, and thereby very hard to classify. A bottom–up approach is seldom found, which is a pity, because it could yield very interesting insights in the nature of legal concepts: how they can be defined, how they relate to common-sense concepts (if they do), and what legal relations there are among legal concepts. The most important development in this respect comes, in my opinion, from outside AI & law. Folksonomies and on-line collaborative environments create great opportunities in distributing the modelling effort needed for large-scale ontology-based legal information systems among many persons. All kinds of incentives (for instance, reputational rewards) could be used in order to unleash the massive knowledge present in the population of lawyers in order to build semantic networks.

References

Bix, B. 1991. H.L.A. Hart and the open texture of language. *Law and Philosophy* 10:51–72.

Breuker, J., and R. Winkels. 2003. Use and reuse of legal ontologies in knowledge engineering and information management. *Proceedings of the ICAIL 2003 workshop on legal ontologies & web based legal information management*, 1–35. Edinburgh, Scotland.

Després, S., and S. Szulman. 2005. Merging of legal micro-ontologies from european directives. *Proceedings of the LOAIT workshop*. June 6, Bologna.

Dini, L., D. Liebwald, L. Mommers, W. Peters, E. Schweighofer, and W. Voermans. 2005. Cross-lingual legal information retrieval using a WordNet architecture. *Proceedings of ICAIL'05*, 163–167, ACM, New York.

Fellbaum, C. ed. 1998. *WordNet: An electronic lexical database*. Cambridge, MA: MIT Press.

Frege, G. 1892. Über sinn und bedeutung. *Zeitschrift für Philosophie und Philosophische Kritik* 100: 25–50.

Gangemi, A., M.T. Sagri, and D. Tiscornia. 2003. Jur-Wordnet, a source of metadata for content description in legal information. In *Proceedings of the workshop on legal ontologies & web based legal information management, part of The international conference of artificial intelligence and law (ICAIL 2003)*, Edinburgh, June 24, 2003.

Gruber, T.R. 1993. A Translation Approach to Portable Ontology Specifications. Knowledge Acquisition 5:199–220.

Hage, J.C., R.E. Leenes, and A.R. Lodder. 1993. Hard cases: A procedural approach. *Artificial Intelligence and Law* 2(1):113–167.

Hart, H.L.A. 1961. *The concept of law*. Oxford: Oxford University Press (ninth impression 1978).

Hoorn, E. 2005. JurisPedia en de zichtbaarheid van de rechtswetenschap. In Nederlands Juristenblad, 4 November 2005.

van Kralingen, R.W. 1995. *Frame-based conceptual models of statute law*. Leiden University, Ph.D. thesis.

van Laarschot, R., W. van Steenbergen, H. Stuckenschmidt, A.R. Lodder, and F. van Harmelen. 2005. The legal concepts and the layman's terms. *Proceedings of the 18th annual conference on legal knowledge and information systems*. IOS Press, Brussels, December 8–10, 2005.

Leenes, R.E. 1998. *Hercules of karneades, hard cases in recht en rechtsinformatica*. Dissertatie UT, Enschede: Twente University Press.

Matthijssen, L.J. 1999. *Interfacing between lawyers and computers: An architecture for knowledge-based interfaces to legal databases*. Den Haag: Kluwer Law International.

McCarty, L.T. 1989. A language for legal discourse, I. basic features. *Proceedings of the second international conference on artificial intelligence and law*, 180–189, Vancouver, BC.

Mommers, L., A.H.J. Schmidt, and E.W. Oskamp. 1997. Controversies in the ontology and law debate. In *Proceedings of the 1st international workshop on legal ontologies*, eds. P. Visser, and R. Winkels, 1–5, Melbourne, Australia, July 4 1997.

Moens, M.F., C. Uyttendaele, and J. Dumortier. 1997. Abstracting of legal cases: The SALOMON experience. *Proceedings of the 6th international conference on artificial intelligence and law*. 114–122, Melbourne, Australia.

Moens, M.F. 2004. Innovative techniques for legal text retrieval. *Artificial Intelligence and Law* 9(1):29–57.

Mommers, L. 2002. *Applied legal epistemology: Building a knowledge-based ontology of law*. Leiden University: Ph.D. thesis.

Mommers, L. 2003. Application of a knowledge-based ontology of the legal domain in collaborative workspaces. In: *Proceedings of the ninth international conference on artificial intelligence and law*, 70–76. Edinburgh.

Mommers, L. 2005. Promoting legitimacy: Feedback in dispute resolution. In: *Artificial intelligence and law*. Netherlands: Springer.

Mommers, L., and W.J.M. Voermans. 2005. Using legal definitions to increase the accessibility of legal documents. In *Legal knowledge and information systems. Jurix 2005: The 18th annual conference*, eds. M.F. Moens, and P. Spyns, 147–156.

Oskamp, E.W. 1998. *Computerondersteuning bij straftoemeting. De ontwikkeling van een databank*. Arnhem: Gouda Quint.

Putnam, H. 1975. The meaning of 'meaning'. In *Language, mind, and knowledge*, Minnesota studies in the philosophy of science, vol. VII, ed. K. Gunderson, 131–193. Minneapolis: University of Minnesota Press.

Stamper, R.K. 1991. The role of semantics in legal expert systems and legal reasoning. *Ratio Juris* 4(2):219–244.

Termorshuizen-Arts, M. 2003. *Juridische Semantiek. Een bijdrage tot de methodologie van de rechtsvergelijking, de rechtsvinding en het juridisch vertalen*. Nijmegen: Wolf Legal Publishers.

Valente, A., and J. Breuker. 1994. *Ontologies: The missing link between legal theory and AI & law*. In Legal Knowledge Based Systems Jurix 1994, eds. H. Prakken, A.J. Muntjewerff, and A. Soeteman. Lelystad: Vermande

Valente, A. 1995. *Legal knowledge engineering: A modelling approach*. Amsterdam: IOS Press.

Verheij, H.B. and Hage J.C. 1997. States of Affairs, Events, and Rules: an Abstract Model of the Law. Oskamp, A, de Mulder, R.V., van Noortwijk, C., Grütters, CA.F.M., Ashly, K. and Gordon, T. 1997. Legal Knowledge Based Systems. Jurix: The Tenth Conference, Jurix: 3–19.

Waismann, F. 1952. Verifiability. In *Logic and language (first series)*, ed. A. Flew. Oxford: Basil Blackwell.

Winkels, R.G.F., Boer, A., Breuker, J.A. and Bosscher, D. 1998. Assessment Based Legal Information Serving and Co-operative Dialogue in CLIME. Proceedings of the eleventh Jurix conference on artificial intelligence and law.

Wittgenstein, L. 1953. *Philosophical investigations*. Oxford: Blackwell, translated from *Philosophische Untersuchungen* by G.E.M. Anscombe.

Chapter 13
Ontology in Economics

Jason Potts

13.1 A New Chapter in Economic Philosophy

Economics is the study of the 'economic world' of human action in relation to material resources. The economic world is therein composed of objects: including economic agents (e.g. *Homo Oeconomicus*, firms), resources (e.g. commodities), economic institutions (e.g. markets, money, central banks); yet is also composed of knowledge (e.g. technology, expectations, routines, preferences) and is thus in significant part subjective. The fusion of object and subject, and the complexity this raises (for example in the theory of value), however, is just the beginning of the vast ontological complexity of the economic world. For the economic world is also an emergent (and massively parallel) process of socially-coordinated individual knowledge. This knowledge is pragmatic, conjectural and mostly inductive. The organizations and institutions that coordinate economic behavior are themselves subject to self-organization and evolution. There is manifold supervenience and protean sets. The question 'What is the economic system made of?' or 'What are the constituents of economic reality?' has a great many possible answers that harbor substantial incommensurability. The upshot, then, is that the economic world is ontologically complex in a profound way.

For the most part, this complexity has been ignored in economics, or subsumed under the heading of economic methodology when dealing with theory-specific concerns such as the meaning of aggregate variables, the nature of the economic agent and rationality, or the treatment of causality. The philosophy and methodology of economics has therefore largely focused about epistemic concerns that relate to the nature of economics as a science and the nature of economic knowledge. In particular, this centers on the nature of economic theories and models and the status of economic laws and mechanisms, and, as such, is predominantly concerned with

J. Potts (✉)
School of Economics, University of Queensland, Brisbane, QLD, Australia; ARC Centre of Excellence for Creative Industries and Innovation, Queensland University of Technology, Brisbane, QLD, Australia
e-mail: j.potts@uq.edu.au

R. Poli, J. Seibt (eds.), *Theory and Applications of Ontology: Philosophical Perspectives*, DOI 10.1007/978-90-481-8845-1_13,

the legitimate domain of economic analysis and its proper relation to other sciences (see, e.g., Hausman 1992, Backhouse 1997). There have been occasional concerns with ethics, but by and large, ontology has not been a priority area in the philosophy of economics.

The neoclassical approach to economics largely dominated economics in the twentieth century, and because its theoretical foundation was based substantially on mechanistic equilibrium analysis, it had little use for a descriptive ontology of economic reality as a basis for theory or for theory development. Instead, the ontology of modern economic analysis was effectively shipped wholesale from nineteenth century mechanics and operationalized through set-theoretic foundations (Mirowski 1989, Potts 2000). Economic analysis thus became the study of economic models and ontological questions were neutralized. They niggled on, of course, in distant corners, but with seemingly no practical relevance to modeling, such 'metaphysical' concerns were never a priority for serious economists (although with some notable exceptions, e.g. Georgescu-Roegen 1971).

But then something happened. New sciences began to emerge in the various forms of general systems theory, synergetics, autopoesis, open-system thermodynamics, non-linear dynamics, complexity theory, and, by the late twentieth century, the enormous growth in the significance of evolutionary biology and computer science had become clear. Thus a new kind of economics began to re-emerge under the broad rubric of *evolutionary economics* which included the schools of Behavioural, Austrian, Computational, Institutional, Post-Keynesian, Constitutional and Schumpeterian economics (Potts 2000). And while much of this work was directed at the development of new theoretical and empirical analysis, it also demanded a fresh ontological inquiry due to the manifest implication that the mechanistic ontology was no longer appropriate.

Ontology thus re-entered economics at the level of fundamental analytic critique and the attempt to re-construct economic analysis based on realism. This was a *revisionary* and not just descriptive ontological turn (Vromen 2001, 2004). For the past few decades, ontology in economics has begun a minor resurgence in the endeavour to describe the constituents of economic reality in an *open system*.

Conventionally, economic ontology had largely focused on the obvious problems of a mechanistic ontology in a world with emergent categories, such as the nature of coordinated behavior, economic aggregates and suchlike (see Mäki 1995, 2001c, Davis et al. 2004 in overview). It is entirely natural, however, that new open system understandings of 'how the world works' should provoke ontological re-examination in economics. Indeed, beginning with Adam Smith's invisible hand resolution of the mystery of decentralized coordination, economics was surely the first complex systems science. The modern analysis of economic growth and evolution is now largely framed in terms of open-system growth of knowledge processes in historical time and as conditioned by a complex structure of institutions. It is hardly surprising, then, that ontology has re-emerged as a valuable basis for the development of analysis and theory in relation to what exists in such a world.

13.2 Ontological Commitments in Modern Economics

As indicated above, economic ontology largely spills over from concerns with economic epistemology and methodology. Ontology is in theory practiced as an exercise of direct description of what is believed to be the fundamental nature of the economy, but in practice it is shot through with analytic concern in relation to the nature of theories, models and evidence. This is not untoward, and certainly befits the proper subject of an applied philosophy of science; yet it is also not an ontology *qua* ontology. It is not, in other words, constructed from ontological axioms, but rather (largely) in response to or as an addendum to methodological critique.

This pragmatic view of ontology then serves as a way to highlight potential mismatches between the subject matter of scientific investigation and the method chosen to investigate it. This is of particular significance in the social sciences, which are indelibly immersed in natural language and ontic subjectivity, to say nothing of endemic complexity and existences made of human activity. Metaphor is an inescapable concomitant in such an analytic context that is freighted with many direct although more often tacit expressions of ontological convictions and commitments. There are many such developments, but I will consider just three.

First: agents and agency. Individuals exist in economic analysis as the locus (or agents) of action, an ontological commitment known as *methodological individualism*. Causality in mechanistic ontology is assigned as the outcome of environmental interaction (via incentives) subject to the universal rule of rationality. In evolutionary economic analysis, however, agency is the outcome of rules that are selected for rationality, and causality is historical. Both of these perspectives hews to methodological individualism, but the evolutionary view also permits a mereological dual by way of *methodological populationism*. This view, which will be considered further below, develops agency ontologically beyond a naturalistic interpretation of intentionality (and the problems with the meaning of collective intentionality) toward an evolutionary consistent view (Dopfer 2004, 2006).

Second: wholes, parts, and populations. There has been much renewed concern with the most appropriate decomposition of the economic system into its component parts and the proper re-construction of those into whole units of analysis. The reality of macroeconomic constructions is a prime concern (e.g. Hoover 2001, who argues that macro supervenes on micro, but does not reduce to it), as is the proper meaning of the existence of an institution (such as the rule of law, money and property) in relation to mereological supervenience, emergence and process. The common property of such philosophic concern is the duality of part–whole relations, such that what is a whole at one level is a part at another, and vice–versa. Furthermore, populations naturally express variety within the actualizations of a rules (due to different space-time context) and in the carriers of rules (due to the presence of other rules). Both of these aspects are awkwardly treated in a mechanistic ontology, in which emergent levels and variety (along with selection and self-organization processes) do not naturally exist. Yet these properties are naturally composed in a bimodal evolutionary ontology. There are many signs that a new open system computational universe of interacting whole and parts is beginning to displace an ontologically flat mathematic universe of set theory and topology (Dupre 2001, Mirowski 2002, Dopfer 2005).

Third: models and theory. The ontological contribution to the models and theory debate has concerned the connection between theory and reality with respect to the value of theory. This began as a squarely methodological debate about the necessity of realism in assumptions (e.g. Friedman 1953) when the true test of a theory was what was useful for prediction. General equilibrium theory, for example, was not realistic, but it worked and was therefore methodologically warranted (even if ontologically opaque, Rosenberg 2001). This debate continued through the second half of the twentieth century picking up, along the way, the question of probability in both agent expectations and in the performance of models, which in turn fractured into many lines of ontic approach (e.g. frequentist versus Bayesian, e.g. Runde 2001).

Yet, arguably, the most interesting line of development concerns the meaning of change in the process of economic coordination as centered about the various ontological conceptions of economic evolution that range from strong Darwinism (Hodgson 2002, Hodgson and Knudsen 2004) to epistemic continuity (see Vromen 2004 in review of this revisionary ontology in economics, also Dupre 2001, Davis 2001, Pettit 2001, and Zuniga 1999). A revisionary ontology (cf. a descriptive ontology) attempts to change the prevailing ontological categories and analytical presuppositions for which the major ontological issue in modern economics concerns the status of non-mechanistic ontology. This is the *new realism* (see Mäki 1990, 1995, 2001) which has sought to re-examine the ontic foundation of modern economics.

13.3 New Realism

New realism arrived in economics largely through the work of the Tony Lawson's (1997, 2003) *critical realism* which followed the work of Roy Bhaskar's (1975, 1998) *transcendental realism*. In essence, Lawson sough to explain the inadequacies of mainstream economics in terms of inadequate concern with ontology. His basic critique was that any attempt to identify regularities on the surface of economic phenomena is doomed to failure. Instead, explanation must lie with the identification of underlying causal tendencies and mechanisms, of which there are many.

In critical realism, then, ontology is a pre-scientific first principle that sets the conditions for scientific analysis. It is intended, in this sense, to be constitutional. And in this constitution, processes and structures exist. Critical realism thus functions as an ontological critique of neoclassical economic theory and of the paucity of its ontological commitments. The ontological commitments of neoclassical economics are not just opaque in this view, but manifestly wrong, for they fail to account for the existence of the multiplicity of deep economic causes.

Critical realism thus seemingly offers a new (social) ontology for economic analysis by highlighting both the knowledge and institutional dimension of the economic system in terms of a social ontology of social practices, social rules and social positions (See also Searle 1997, 2005 on the construction of social reality and its role in the ontology of economic institutions). The objects of social reality, in his view, are structural, processual and emergent phenomena (Lawson 2004). This makes clear that social analysis cannot meaningfully explain surface phenomena in terms of themselves but only in terms of 'deep' or underlying conditions that are multiple, open and not generally separable, thus forming tendencies, not mechanisms. The main limitation of critical realism, however, is that it is mostly silent on the mechanisms and processes by which novel ideas are originated and the processes by which they are adopted and retained for ongoing economic reality. Critical realism thus provides a coherent ontological account of economic mechanisms, but not of the mechanisms by which they change (Klaes 2004).

The ontology of evolutionary analysis, however, has been significantly conducted as a development not of mechanistic analysis, but of biological analogy. The credentials for this approach have significant pedigree in economics, and include the work of such economic luminaries as Thomas Malthus, Thorstein Veblen, Alfred Marshall, Edith Penrose and Joseph Schumpeter. The path breaking works of Nelson and Winter (1982) and Hodgson (1993) have since advanced this ontological perception so as to account for skills, habits, routines, rules and institutions as the elementary units of economic analysis. Yet they have still failed to offer an axiomatic treatment of the ontology of open economic systems. For this, we require *evolutionary realism* (Dopfer and Potts 2004).

Evolutionary realism is an approach to the ontology of evolution based on three ontological axioms. Evolutionary realism is therefore an axiomatic approach to economic ontology. An ontological axiom is to be understood not just as a *mathematically* consistent set of theoretical propositions, but as an *empirically* consistent set of analytical propositions. The three axioms of evolutionary realism are: (1) bimodality; (2) association; and (3) process. All analytically relevant existences in the economic world are constituted as bimodal associative processes in the form of an idea and its actualizations (bimodality) that have particular connections and structure with respect to other ideas (association) and which exists in time as a process. These axioms describe the primary analytical dimensions of economic evolution.

Axiom 1 – bimodality – asserts that all existences are composed of an *idea* and a matter-energy *actualization*. This (pre-scientifically) defines the generic dimension of economic reality (rules and populations) that underpins the operational dimensions of production, consumption, transactions, commodities, and the like. Axiom 2 – association – asserts that all ideas are differentially associated, and so the connectivity of an economic system has generic structure. Axiom 3 – process – asserts that all ideas are located in both space and time and so economic evolution is real in the sense that history both exists and matters.

The first axiom of evolutionary realism is *bimodality*, which proposes that the elementary unit of existence in an economic system is a idea (or generic rule) and its population of actualizations (as operations). This is fundamentally different to a mechanistic ontology in that it accounts not just for (Platonic) ideas, but also for their space-time of actualizations and the inherent variety within this (Dopfer 2005). This recognizes not just knowledge, but the individual operations of knowledge, and thus gives rise to the concept of the (meso) population, which is an analytical building block of much economic structure, including markets, institutions and even the concept of history. This defines the ontological existence of the economic world.

The second axiom of evolutionary realism is *association*, which means that economic reality is composed of information, in the form of specific connections. Ontologically, this means that rules associate in some ways, but not in others (economic space is non-integral, Potts 2000), and that these ways are the origin of value. The structure of an economic system is a bimodal composition of these associations in terms of generic rules and populations of actualizations. This defines the ontological *structure* of the economic world.

The third axiom of evolutionary realism is *process*, which locates the reality of the economic system in both space and irreversible time. A process is a path of existence by which a novel idea becomes an economic constituent as it is originated, adopted and retained as a generic rule in an entropy governed world. This ontological open system process is the analytic basis of economics as an historical science.

Economic evolution, therefore, is: (1) a bimodal associative process of generic change in the existence of generic rules; (2) the associative structure of rules; and (3) the process by which generic rules form into the institutional populations that compose the economic system. In other words, economic reality is generically composed of rules and their populations of actualizations as process-structures. Economic analysis in an open system is therefore properly constructed about this ontological foundation. The generic approach to ontology, in turn, seeks to identify and describe the building-blocks of economic reality in the rules (and their populations, structures and processes) that constitute the economic system. This is the sense in which it is a realism. But unlike critical realism, the generic approach to economic ontology offers a constructive realism that lays foundations for the study of the structure and process of coordination and change in generic economic reality (Dopfer and Potts 2007).

13.4 The Evolutionary Reality of Economic Systems

Economic ontology is the study of what exists in the economic system. This involves more than just an extension of methodological concern with a mechanistic ontology, but the endeavour to create a new methodology that is based on the ontological precepts of an open system and in the analytical context of an evolutionary process (Popper 1972, Ziman 2000). As such, the central concept in the ontological analysis of economic systems is, currently, the evolutionary question of the nature and meaning of existence in an open system. The three axioms of evolutionary realism provide an ontological foundation for such a general evolutionary analysis of social phenomena.

This is not a new question. Biology has also been effected by these same ontological reconceptions of the nature of the world order (e.g. Kauffman 1993), as has physics (e.g. Haken 2005). Economics has developed ontological sophistication along these same lines (Potts 2000, Vromen 2004, Dopfer 2005). Moreover, the new generic ontology in economics offers an analytically smooth transition to concern with the generic systems that compose the human agent (biology, psychology) as well as social structures (politics, sociology, cultural studies) that form the natural (and artificial) environment of the economic agent. The generic ontology is analytically general in this sense.

Economic ontology therefore seeks to describe the constituents of the economic world order, and ideally to put these into set-theoretic classifications. But unlike ontology in computer science, which is ultimately an artificial affair, ontology in social science is natural in both discovery and synthesis as generic objects (explained by an evolutionary ontology) rather than as external events (accommodated by a weakened mechanistic ontology). An interesting line of intersection, however, occurs in the agent-based computational approach to economics and the study of artificial economies (e.g. Tesfatsion 2002, Mirowski 2002, Castronova 2005). These experimental ontological domains have proven to be very interesting platforms for the experimental formalization of the necessary conditions for an economic world (or part thereof, e.g. a market) to exist. By the process of creating new categories of understanding, social science continues to build new ontologies through the identification of new generic rules, structures and processes. Ontologies are discovered in the physical sciences – a quintessentially Kantian point – but they are constructed in the social sciences – as Wittgenstein explained.

Economic reality is ultimately composed of the ideas (rules) for operations that are adopted and retained by generically evolving economic agents (i.e. humans). Philosophers and theologians have long debated the prospect of moral evolution, and epistemic evolution is fundamentally inductively constrained, but ontological evolution is entirely normal in an open social system, for this is the basic generic structure and process of economic growth and development.

Economic ontology, therefore, is ultimately a practical project that comprises the identification and description of the new realities of an evolving economic system, and in as timely a fashion as possible. Yet this requires an ontology. This analytical economic tool used to be called philosophy, but that was eventually captured by methodology. Nowadays, fortunately, novelty has once again become the dynamic building block of economic reality as open-system processes have reasserted themselves as the proper ontological basis of economic theory. Change is normal – indeed, it is the cause of growth and development. Thus not only is economic ontology complex in the extreme, but economic ontology also evolves. The future development of economic ontology will therefore necessarily be engaged further with the spade-work that reveals the analytic building blocks of the economic system as it is now. This is the economic meaning of practical ontology.

References

Backhouse, R. 1997. *Truth and progress in economic knowledge*. Cheltenham: Edward Elgar.

Bhaskar, R. 1975. *A realist theory of science*. London: Verso.

Bhaskar, R. 1998. *The possibility of naturalism: A philosophical critique of the contemporary human sciences*, 3rd edn. London: Routledge.

Castronova, E. 2005. *Synthetic worlds*. Chicago: University of Chicago Press.

Davis, J. 2001. Agent identity in economics. In *The economic worldview*, ed. U. Mäki, 114–131. Cambridge: Cambridge University Press.

Davis, J., A. Marciano, and J. Runde.eds. 2004. *The elgar companion to economics and philosophy*. Cheltenham: Edward Elgar.

Dopfer, K. 2004. The economic agent as rule maker and rule user: Homo sapiens oeconomicus. *Journal of Evolutionary Economics* 14:177–195.

Dopfer, K. 2005. Evolutionary economics: A theoretical framework. In *Evolutionary foundations of economics*, ed. K. Dopfer, 3–55. Cambridge: Cambridge University Press.

Dopfer, K. 2006. A unified ruled theory for economics: Integrating self-organization and evolution. MPI papers.

Dopfer, K., and J. Potts. 2004. Evolutionary realism – a new ontology for economics. *Journal of Economic Methodology* 11(2):195–212.

Dopfer, K., and J. Potts. 2007. *The general theory of economic evolution*. London: Routledge.

Dupre, J. 2001. Economics without mechanism. In *The economic worldview*, ed. U. Mäki, 308–358. Cambridge: Cambridge University Press.

Friedman, M. 1953. The methodology of positive economics. In *Essays in positive economics*, ed. M. Friedman, 3–43. Chicago: Chicago University Press.

Georgescu-Roegen, N. 1971. *The entropy law and the economic process*. Cambridge, MA: Harvard University Press.

Haken, H. 2005. Synergetics: From physics to economics. In *Evolutionary foundations of economics*, ed. K. Dopfer, 70–85. Cambridge: Cambridge University Press.

Hausman, D. 1992. *The inexact and separate science of economics*. Cambridge: Cambridge University Press.

Hodgson, G. 1993. *Economics and evolution*. Cambridge: Polity Press.

Hodgson, G. 2002. Darwinism in economics: From analogy to ontology. *Journal of Evolutionary Economics* 12(2):259–281.

Hodgson, G., and T. Knudsen. 2004. General selection theory and economic evolution: The price equation and the genotype/ phenotype distinction. *Journal of Economic Methodology* 11(2):147–173.

Hoover, K. 2001. Is macroeconomics for real? In *The economic worldview*, ed. U. Mäki, 225–245. Cambridge: Cambridge University Press.

Kauffman, S. 1993. *The origins of order: Self-organization and selection in evolution*. Oxford: Oxford University Press.

Klaes, M. 2004. Ontological issues in evolutionary economics. Special issue of *Journal of Economic Methodology* 11(2):121–124.

Lawson, T. 1997. *Economics and reality*. London: Routledge.

Lawson, T. 2003. *Reorienting economics*. London: Routledge.

Lawson, T. 2004. *A conception of ontology*. Mimeo: Cambridge.

Mäki, U. 1990. Scientific realism and Austrian explanation. *Review of Political Economy* 2:310–344.

Mäki, U. 1995. Special issue of *The Monist* 78(3):235–385.

Mäki, U. 2001a. Economic ontology: What? How? Why? In *The economic worldview*, ed. U. Mäki, 3–14. Cambridge: Cambridge University Press.

Mäki, U. 2001b. The way the world works (www): Towards an ontology of choice theory. In *The economic worldview*, ed. U. Mäki, 369–389. Cambridge: Cambridge University Press.

Mäki, U. ed. 2001c. *The economic worldview: Studies in the ontology of economics*. Cambridge: Cambridge University Press.

Mirowski, P. 1989. *More heat than light: Economics as social physics*. New York, NY: Cambridge University Press.
Mirowski, P. 2002. *Machine dreams: How economics became a cyborg science*. New York, NY: Cambridge University Press.
Nelson, R., and S. Winter. 1982. *An evolutionary theory of economic change*. Cambridge, MA: Harvard University Press.
Pettit, P. 2001. The virtual reality of Homo economicus. In *The Economic Worldview*, ed. U. Mäki, 75–97. Cambridge: Cambridge University Press.
Popper, K. 1972. *Objective knowledge: An evolutionary approach*. Oxford: The Clarendon Press.
Potts, J. 2000. *The new evolutionary microeconomics: Complexity, competence and adaptive behaviour*. Cheltenham: Edward Elgar.
Rosenberg, A. 2001. The metaphysics of microeconomics. In *The economic worldview*, ed. U. Mäki, 174–188. Cambridge: Cambridge University Press.
Runde, J. 2001. Chances and choices: notes on probability and belief in economic theory. In *The Economic Worldview*, ed. U. Mäki, 132–155. Cambridge: Cambridge University Press.
Searle, J. 1997. *The construction of social reality*. New York: Penguin.
Searle, J. 2005. What is an Institution? *Journal of Institutional Economics* 1(1):1–22.
Tesfatsion, L. 2002. Agent based computational economics: Growing economies from the bottom-up. *Artificial Life* 8:55–82.
Vromen, J. 2001. The ontological commitments of evolutionary economics. In *The economic worldview*, ed. U. Mäki, 189–224. Cambridge: Cambridge University Press.
Vromen, J. 2004. Conjectural revisionary economic ontology: Outline of an ambitious research agenda for evolutionary economics. *Journal of Economic Methodology* 11(2):213–47.
Ziman, J. 2000. *Technological innovation as an evolutionary process*. Cambridge: Cambridge University Press.
Zuniga, G. 1999. An ontology of economic objects: An application of Carl Menger's ideas. *American Journal of Economics and Sociology* 58(2):299–312.

Chapter 14
Ontology and Phenomenology

Angela Ales Bello

14.1 Introduction

The phenomenological school, which counts as one of the most important movements of the twentieth century, is most famous for the methodological 'turn' upon which it based itself. This, the so-called 'phenomenological turn', is characterized by the following two core aspects:

(1) The first one consists in 'starting from the given'. According to Edmund Husserl, the founder of the school, the philosopher has to perform his investigation starting from what is given to him, bracketing his own ideas or theories of reality, or those of the community. On the contrary, he or she must grasp the given as it appears, through a complete absence of prejudice and openness of mind.

It is not only possible, but also necessary to do so, because each aspect of the reality or object of the field of research that manifests itself to us – and for this reason becomes a 'phenomenon' – reveals thereby, in a direct or indirect way, its proper sense or, using a term well known in the philosophical tradition, its 'essence'. The investigation of essence is made possible by the thing itself, and then complexes of the things themselves (*Sachen selbst*), which disclose a necessary property in as much as every individual has something as its own *quid*. As Husserl wrote: '*At first* "essence" designated what is to be found in the very own being of an individuum as the What of an individuum. Any such What can, however, be *put into an idea*. Experiencing, or *intuition of something individual* can become transmuted into *eidetic seeing* (*ideation*) – a possibility which is itself to be understood not as empirical, but as eidetic' (Husserl 1977, § 3, p. 8). Eidetic, here, comes from *eidos*, that is the Greek word for essence.

This is the 'essential reduction' which constitutes the first step of the phenomenological method, meaning that it is possible to put apart, or bracket what is not necessary in order to pinpoint the What, which is necessary to it to be what it

A.A. Bello (✉)
Lateran University, Piazza S. Giovanni in Laterano 4, 00120 Città del Vaticano, Italy
e-mail: alesbello@tiscali.it

R. Poli, J. Seibt (eds.), *Theory and Applications of Ontology: Philosophical Perspectives*, DOI 10.1007/978-90-481-8845-1_14,

is. Husserl called this bracketing the *epoché*, and, as we shall see, it is a crucial Husserlian move. The acknowledgement of the essences allows us to discover the complexity and the stratifications of 'phenomena', however they are categorized: as natural, human, social, scientific, etc. The important thing is that they can all be understood according their What in an essential way. *This is the common feature of the phenomenological school. When the phenomenologists speak of 'essence', they are using Husserl's definition.*

(2) The second step, according to Husserl consists in a change of perspective: *what is factually given must be put into parentheses in order to grasp the sense of what exists, which enables us to have insight into the presence of a residuum; in fact, we must regard the identity of who performs the reduction, who discovers the essence, as an open question.* Here phenomenology opens up a new territory, in which our subjectivity is to be understood as the 'transcendental' region of pure lived experiences (*Erlebnisse*), with the implication that intentionally carries within it the 'real' and the 'possible' universe, and that these can be subject to phenomenological analysis on an essential level.

Husserl paid particular attention to how sciences, both human sciences and natural sciences, are built as intellectual products and how they know their objects. Thus, the main task of the phenomenological project as it reconstructed ontology was to understand it with relation to the foundations of scientific knowledge. The term 'ontology' refers to the set of things whose existence is acknowledged by a particular theory or system of thought. These sets of things refer to material genera or to formal categories. This kind of analysis permits us to pinpoint the 'ontology' of the different spheres of reality.

> The understanding of ontology as category theory has become the standard view in present-day analytical ontology, as, for instance, in Roberto Poli's definition: : «Ontology deals with what, at least in principle, can be categorized (objectified, i.e. subsumed under distinguishable categories)». [Poli, 2010] It should be noted that Husserl was the first who proposed this approach. According to Husserl, inside the process of objectivation we can make a distinction between formal and material ontology, with the former designating an absolute ontology that is delineated, in its proper sense, as soon as one discovers "Something in general" or the "Object in general". This is immediately and irreducibly expressed through categories.

In this paper, as noted, we deal not only with Husserl, but also with the other first generation phenomenologists who were his students and were in direct contact with him: Adolf Reinach, Jean Hering, Hedwig Conrad Martius and Edith Stein. Their works give us ontology as it was constructed in the first phase of phenomenology. Further, we can see how they applied this phenomenologically liberated ontology in different fields of research.

By reconstructing Husserl' s initial approach to ontology, we can understand why his followers went along two different direction: a realistic and a transcendental path. These paths correspond to the first and the second step of the phenomenological method. Indeed, after his transcendental turn, Husserl was left almost alone; only Edith Stein followed him for a long while, turning at last to metaphysics, but never forgetting what she learned from him. The others remained linked up with the essential description of reality, which is, in any case, the mark of the school.

In both lines of research we find an analysis of ontology, to be understood as category theory. Briefly, we can describe the contributions of the first phenomenologists as follows:

Reinach developed both a general and categorical ontology, which is important from two points of view: from a theoretical perspective, his ontology provides a description of the general structure of 'states of affairs'; while from a practical point of view, it is at the basis of law and social philosophy insofar as it gives us a sense of actions.

Hering offered an ontological interpretation of the levels of reality by analysing, as key to their differentiation and constitution, the themes of 'essence', 'essentiality' and idea.

Conrad-Martius' contribution is directed toward ontology of nature. In a wider perspective, particularly interesting is Conrad-Martius' analysis regarding the complex systems according the quantum theory. She opened also a path leading to many current applications of ontology in the field of the living systems and anticipatory systems.

Edith Stein sought to clarify the difference between 'ontology' as the description of Being according to the metaphysical tradition, and ontology as it is used in category theory. Accordingly, we can grasp the main features of the contemporary ontology and compare it with ones proposed in the past, or at least the metaphysical tradition, and even translate features from the later.

Hedwig Conrad Martius and Edith Stein both sought to capture the complexity of the human being as revealed in its stratified levels. They analysed the traditional orders, 'body' and 'soul', so as to show that under these labels it is possible to find many intersecting aspects. At a first approach we can notice that, if corporeity is a very fundamental level, it is necessary to admit psychic and mental-spiritual dimensions into one's ontology.

14.2 Edmund Husserl's Ontology: Between Logic and Science

Edmund Husserl's view of ontology should be contextualized within the framework of his interests in logic and his focus on how the distinctions of types of knowledge find their origin in modernity. These distinctions are organized in a series of disciplines that define their diverse fields with reference to the material and formal aspects of the reality of their objects. In particular, I refer to four major moments of Husserl's philosophical career, which correspond to a progressive expansion and deepening of his research. It is necessary to follow the development of Husserl's phenomenological analyses to understand his ontological assumptions, because, even if ontology as category theory is a constant premise for Husserl, its meaning can be refracted in different ways according to different perspectives.

(a) Formal and Material Ontology. Whole and Parts

In the *Logical Investigations* one can trace the path that leads Husserl to his interpretation of ontology. The initial step in his ontological turn derives from his claim that the 'thinking of evidence' (*Evidenzgedanken*) in a logical sense is not only a subjective necessity but that the subjective incapacity-to-represent-things-otherwise corresponds to the objectively ideal necessity of an inability-to-be-otherwise. This, by its essence, is given to our consciousness as *apodictically self-evident*, so that we are obliged to assert that such an objective necessity is correlated to a 'pure law'. In this way we can speak of an essential lawfulness (*Wesensgestzlichkeit*), that is, of an ideal necessity that comes to consciousness in apodictic evidence and is constituted by laws (law is nothing concrete and perceptible). This evidence presents itself as completely different from empirical necessity, which *means that there are two levels of reality: the empirical one and the essential one; and, furthermore, it is possible to discover the laws according to which what is essential constitutes itself. In other words, the laws governing the process of categorization.*

In order to explain what ontology is and whether there are different ontological levels, it is worthwhile to approach a theoretical question of great importance, namely, how we are to conceive the essential relation between whole and parts or even the essential relation between parts coordinated within a whole (*The Third Logical Investigation*), given our preliminary distinction between empirical and essential. Gaining a clear description of wholes and parts relations gives us some understanding of the structure that we obtain when we submit a field of inquiry to an ontological analysis.

The relation between wholes and parts is founded apriori on the idea of the 'object', understood not as *real* in the sense of empirically real, but as *reell*, in the sense of being a possible content of a presentation. Even though the presentation is a subjective moment and can be expressed with the word 'think', Husserl insists on the 'ideal objective necessity of not-being-able-to be-*otherwise*', affirming that a pure lawfulness belongs to the essence of this objective necessity, where 'pure' means we are in front of a necessity which is, a., established in itself, b., valid in any possible case, and c., does not depend on empirical fact. The lawfulness belonging to non-independent objects consists in establishing that they are objects of a pure species, existing as parts of more comprehensive wholes. This is the case when one affirms that the parts cannot be thought of as existing in themselves. This schema operates within the distinction between independent ideas and dependent ones and, therefore, between a pure genus of the highest order and the hierarchy of species (Husserl 1984, § 7).

There exists a multiplicity of laws that concern the diverse modes of non-independence. An important distinction should be made between 'material' and 'formal' laws. Attaching themselves to materiality, concepts like 'house', 'tree', and 'colour' are quite different than those that encompass 'something', 'object', and 'quality'. The former are ordered within the highest material genera, material categories; *material ontologies* are based on these. The latter, however, are articulated in *formal* ontological categories in such a manner that the two spheres are inherently distinct. *One sphere is materially essential and the other is formally essential.* These lead back to laws and, therefore, to disciplines that are both synthetically apriori and analytically apriori. Examples of pure analytic generalities are: 'a whole cannot be without parts' insofar the correlative elements are reciprocally postulated, whereas 'If we set beside these any definite propositions of the opposite sort, e.g., "A color cannot exist without something coloured" or "A colour cannot exist without some space it covers" etc. – the difference leaps into view. "Colour" is not a relative expression, whose meaning includes the idea of a relation to something else. Though colour is "unthinkable" without something coloured, the existence of the latter, and more definitely that of a space, is not "analytically" founded on the notion of colour' (Husserl 1984, § 11, pp. 19–20).

The independence or non-independence of content has a character of relativity that stems from its dependence on the relationship with the whole. Husserl gives, as an example of such dependence within the flow of consciousness, every 'now' that passes into a 'having been'; it is possible that a fraction within a momentary visual intuition be independent, but the colour that is related to this momentary intuition is not independent (Husserl 1984, § 13).

In order to justify this Husserl introduces the concept of 'foundation' (Husserl 1984, § 22), maintaining that the unity of independent objects is realized only through the foundation, insofar as one is founded upon the other, and they, in turn, found other contents.

In the *Third Investigation*, the term foundation is introduced with regard to the description of regions, that is, those areas that are the objects of the sciences of particular givens of fact, or empirical sciences. Each region has a theoretical, essential foundation in its ontology. Husserl clarifies what he means by giving the example of those disciplines that are central in the natural sciences. To each one there corresponds an eidetic science of a general physical nature, since an essence corresponds to factual nature. As we pointed out in the introduction, eidetic science gets its name from *eidos* (this is the Greek word that means essence), and the essence of nature is that which is intuitively graspable in its purity (Husserl 1984, § 25). That means that the general 'ontology' of nature is given, going beyond all the ideas of a nature that we can grasp empirically. In other words, Husserl is making a distinction between two levels of knowledge: empirical knowledge, which gives us some ideas linked to our experience and an 'ideal' knowledge, that is the idea of nature 'in general' with its own ideas of what is an 'empirical whole in general' or what is 'independent in general'. If we put all these ideas together, we obtain the ontology of nature. We are presented here with two kinds of ideas: the first consists of those that are directly connected with our empirical experience; the second, of those that are 'general', up to and including what is empirical 'in general'. The connection between them is enacted in, and characteristic of, the ontology of nature.

To repeat, Husserl takes the general position that there are two levels that are encountered in ontology, one being the empirical, the other being the essential; but it turns out in Husserl's analysis that the latter can be further divided, so we can more precisely say that there are really three levels: firstly, our empirical and factual experience of nature, which are condensed in our empirical and factual concepts;

secondly, ideas that are connected with a general ontology of nature; and thirdly, a formal ontology, based on a law. For example, in the case of whole and part: 'the Idea of unity or the Idea of a whole is based on the idea of 'Founding', and the latter Idea upon the Idea of a Pure Law' (Husserl 1984, p. 39). That means that a founded whole is a categorical notion whose content is determined by a material specificity, and whose categorical status is because this law, definite in its content, gives the whole its unity. At this point it is necessary to analyze what kind of links there are among these levels.

(b) The Constitution of the Sciences: from Objectivity in General to the Individual

Husserl in his *Ideas pertaining to a pure Phenomenology and to phenomenological Philosophy* takes up this theme, and radicalizes it with reference to 'natural' knowledge upon which the sciences, dealing with experience linked to givens of fact, are founded; these can be called sciences of the world. They can be those sciences that deal with 'matter', understood as that which is inorganic, and they can also be those that concern themselves with the psycho-spiritual nature, including physiology, psychology, and even the human sciences like history, and sciences of culture like sociology (Husserl 1977, I). The radicalization proposed by Husserl consists in showing that pure factuality is insufficient in order to construct a science. An eidetic necessity must be seen as concomitant to factuality because to every factual given belongs an essence that is ascertainable intuitively through the vision of essence (*Wesenserschauung*), which constitutes an 'object' of a new species that is non empirical. As we have already seen in the Introduction, the reduction to essence consists of this and is the first step of the phenomenological method.

Judgments about essences, eidetic propositions and eidetic truths are connected to the operation of making evident the evidence of essence, recalling that *eidetic* is the Greek word that stands for the essential. Husserl always claimed that in such a fashion we can establish a difference between sciences of factual givens and sciences of essence, in which the former depends on the latter, while the latter exists autonomously with respect to the former. In fact, it can be observed that every fully developed science enters into a 'relation' with formal ontological disciplines, which include, in addition to formal logic, the disciplines of *mathesis universalis*, that is arithmetic, pure analysis and the doctrine of multiplicity (Husserl 1977, I §8).

The eidetic 'regional' ontologies, which construct the foundation of every empirical science, are delineated in a similar fashion. Husserl gives the same example that he gave in the Third Logical Investigation, the one related to the ontology of nature. He does so because 'factual' nature corresponds to a graspable purity, that is, the essence of nature. The making-real of a completely rational science of nature is founded on a formal *mathesis* that concerns all sciences, including ontological material disciplines. If one examines the birth of physics, one notes that geometry, understood since Plato as the classical example of a pure science, is involved in the methodology of physics. Geometry as an ontological discipline, therefore, concerns itself with the essential moment of the thing, understood as *res extensa*, that is, its spatial form (Husserl 1977, § 9).

Husserl proceeds next to the distinction between formal and material regions. All material regions come under a formal region, which is empty and prescribes for it a communal formal lawfulness. Recalling the distinction between the analytic and synthetic already laid down in the Third Logical Investigation, Husserl maintains that formal ontology, understood as pure logic (with logic, here, being construed as the eidetic science of the object in general), contains immediate and fundamental truths, logical categories that function as 'axioms' in the disciplines of pure logic. *The fundamental concepts of pure logic are defined as logical categories and are considered analytic concepts as opposed to synthetic ones. Examples of logical categories can include those of properties, characteristic determinations, states of affairs, relations, identity, similarity, togetherness, number, whole and parts, genus and species.* Once again Husserl takes up the last two pairs, already investigated in the Third Logical Investigation. He argues that every essence, be it material or empty, inserts itself in a hierarchy of genera and species. For example, number in general is the highest genus with respect to single numbers just as the thing is the highest with respect to contents or material singularities (Husserl 1977, I, § 10).

The formal region of 'objectivity in general' is divided into syntactical categories and ultimate substrates. If material objectivities are taken into consideration, one reaches the ultimate substrates and the *tode ti* of Aristotle – the presence of the *Organon* of Aristotle can be felt in everything Husserl has presented so far. It is true that the Greek expression *tode ti* can be translated as 'individual'. Husserl prefers to preserve the *tode ti*, 'this here', however, in order to avoid the sense of indivisibility that the term 'individual' possesses (Husserl 1977, I, §14).

The concept 'individual' is further determined in reference to independent and non-independent objects, already investigated in the Third Logical Investigation. In this case, however, he introduces the formal categorial concepts of the individuum that is 'concrete and abstract'. 'A non-self sufficient essence is called an *abstractum*, an absolutely self sufficient essence a *concretum.* A This-here, the material essence of which is a concretum, is called an *individuum*' (Husserl 1977, I, § 15, 29).

Eidetic singularities derive from this and are divided into abstract and concrete, as we have seen. These, in turn, are systematized in terms of *genera and species* and, therefore, are divided accordingly, each slotting into their separate highest genera with respect to ultimate differences. For example, in a thing, the figure leads to the highest genus, namely, spatial figure but also to that of a seeable quality in general. All of this is fundamental for the formation of material regions. *The domain of the 'region' comprehends the ideal totality of the highest genera, whereas the domain of the individual comprises all the possible individuals that fall under those concrete essences.* This is the key point of analysis. Here is where Husserl applies the distinction of synthetic and analytic, already elaborated in the Third Logical Investigation. In fact, every essential region contains essential synthetic truths, which are founded upon each regional essence. It is possible to find a link between regional ontology and formal ontology, but they are also independent. The link is due to the fact that formal ontology contains the general concept of a regional object, but is quite apart from the regional ontologies (Husserl 1977, I § 16). In this sense formal ontology is the third level, as we mentioned above, at the end of paragraph (a).

Pure logic, then, serves to determine all individuals according to objects or laws under the rule of synthetic apriori principles. *All empirical sciences, therefore, must be founded on respective regional ontologies.* From the viewpoint of a theory of knowledge, the task is to determine, on the basis of the intuition of individuals, the regions of being upon which the single eidetic and empirical sciences may be founded. 'The problem of a radical 'classification' of the sciences is, in the main, the problem of separating regions; and this, in turn, requires antecedent investigations in pure logic like those which were conducted here along some lines' (Husserl 1977, I § 17, 32)

(c) Absolute Universal Apriori Ontology as the Basis for a Formal Ontology and an Ontology of All the Forms of the Reality

Husserl's analyses are amplified and deepened in his *Formal and Transcendental Logic*, which coincides with the mature phase of his phenomenological research. Firstly, the logical dimension is no longer accepted as a factual given. Rather, it is now necessary to understand how it is constituted. Secondly, *there appears the problem of an absolute ontology that may serve as the basis for a formal ontology and an ontology of all the forms of the reality. The novelty consists in the acknowledgment of the importance of mathematics in order to understand what such an ontology is.*

Husserl maintains that the ancients (Husserl 1974, § 26a) did not know that the concept 'cardinal number' could be emptied of any concrete content in such a way as to enter into the territory of the 'Something' in general and that the apophantics, (that is the sphere of the judgments, according to the traditional logic) can thus be formalized. Aristotle remained very much in the domain of ontology of reality and he considered it as 'first philosophy'. It is only with modernity, and specifically through the algebra of Viéte and, above all, Leibniz, that a *mathesis universalis* is delineated, albeit an imperfect one. Only when the internal connection between mathematics and logics was discovered could the meaning of logic-formal formations be understood (Husserl 1974, § 26b). Even Bolzano, who outlined the possibility of an apriori general ontology, did not distinguish material ontology from the formal ontology of the 'Something' in general. It was the discovery of the new non-apophantic mathematics – mathematics of the wholes, of the cardinal and ordinal numbers etc., which displaces the traditional logic use of judgments as fundamental concepts – that led to individuating the empty universe of the 'Object in general', or 'Something in general'. This made possible the elaboration of a new formal ontology (Husserl 1974, § 24). Regarding the distinction between the second level of ontology, for example a general ontology of nature, and the third level, a formal ontology based on a law, we can say that he goes more deeply into the third one, trying to explicate more and more what 'formal' consists of.

The third level, the level of formal ontology, is better delineated in the first part of *Formal and transcendental Logic* than in the *Ideas*. Husserl claims to have presented the idea of a pure logic in his *Logical Investigations*, even if he did not yet call it a formal ontology. *However, it is only in Formal and Transcendental Logic that he claims to have realized the full idea of the formal logic, which can be called the formal ontology of 'Something in general'*

At this point Husserl's problem it that of connecting the ontological-formal apriori with the apophantic priori, namely, propositional meanings. This connection, however, entails a distinction between objective formal categories (object, state of affairs, unity, plurality, cardinal number, relation, connection, etc.) and the categories of signification (that is all the concepts that concern the formation of judgments). The laws of such domains are divided between *objective categories (formal ontology) and categories of signification (formal apophantic)* (Husserl 1974, § 27b).

If the formation of the sciences is examined, one notes that the categorial objectivities in relation to pure form are the theme of analytic logic as the formal doctrine of science, which is the same as formal ontology, since it gives us the rules for salient information concerning the objects in themselves (Husserl 1974, § 43).

If Husserl's analytic is a formal ontology, this does not mean it isn't also a formal apophantic. It retains this apophantic aspect because of the necessary relation between judgments and propositions. In fact all of the objectivities are nothing other than judgments. It is necessary, therefore, to proceed to an analysis of judgments. The person who makes judgments not only turns to objects that she or he wishes to determine but also to their determinations. This turning involves a reflection of a secondary nature that individuates an intended substrate insofar as it is intended (Husserl 1974, § 48). Judgments are objects of a particular region, which is a field of objects closed in itself. So it is possible to establish a difference between simple and direct judgments and second degree judgments, in the latter of which we find what is judged in itself, that is intended objectivities. The latter constitutes a new region, that of meaning or sense.

On this point, Husserl returns to the phenomenological investigations of consciousness already developed in the *Ideas.* Here, we refer to the second stage of his method, namely, the transcendental reduction. In the *Ideas*, his logical analyses demonstrate how every lived-experience (*Erlebnis*) is intentionally linked to something perceived, every 'I remember' is connected to something remembered, every valuing act is linked to something valued. Reflection upon 'perceived', 'remembered', 'valued' is also possible, which is to say, reflection upon intentional objectivity as such. This type of reflection is called doxic (the term doxa etymologically is linked to 'opinion', but in this case describe this kind of reflection) and presents the intended object as such. It presents the sense of the perceived content, the meanings of the value, and so forth. Also, insofar as every attitude has its own evidence, one can speak of doxic evidence.

Every positional sphere has its proper syntactic categories and its proper modalities of something and, therefore, its proper formal and analytic logic (Husserl 1974, § 50). The pure formal analytic has these senses as its thematic sphere. It refers to the morphology of the pure senses and to non-contradiction. In this way we can understand how it is possible to perform a *mathesis universalis*, of which Husserl has already spoken: it is the analytic of the possible categorial elements and it has nothing to do with concrete reality. One concludes, therefore, that judgments, understood as senses or meanings, have a formal lawfulness that is contained within them, and they contain no information about the possible being of their objectivities. The realm of judgments presents us with a purely formal logic. The idea of a purely formal mathematics, constructed solely from the rule of non-contradiction and its analytic consequences, is founded on this.

Viewing concrete possible truth (Husserl 1974, § 54a) as an adequation of the same possible things forces one into formal ontology. In fact, formal ontology is the apriori science of the possible objects in general and if a logic orients itself *epistemologically*, that is, if it aims at being a science of possible formal categorials, it cannot be a pure formal apophantic logic. Rather, it is a formal ontology, in which the possibility of the substrate objectivities is given in a veridical sense. If the objectivity has received a categorial confirmation, we do not find ourselves facing apophantics, rather we face ontology. What is the epistemological meaning of the new ontology?

A double orientation of formal logic corresponds to the above-mentioned doubleness, that is *mathesis universalis* on one hand (A) and concrete possible truth on the other hand (B).

(A) This involves apophantic logic, as it orients itself towards judgments and, as it is extended to the categorial forms of sense, its configuration of itself as a *mathesis universalis*. (B) We are in the ontological-formal camp, if our formal logic orients itself towards possible categorial objectivities; even if it instrumentally employs the meanings of its judgments as its objects, it has its 'objects' as its final intention (Husserl 1974, § 54b).

The first section of *Formal and transcendental Logic*, in which he deals with formal logic, concludes with these last clarifications, but Husserl at this point turns once again to a programmatic observation that he made at the beginning of the book about logic's dual character. If, on one hand, we are given an objective sphere that has its proper objective validity, and, on the other hand, we find, upon inquiring into the origin of these objective formations, that we return to the subjective sphere, then Husserl's *basic point consists in the fact that objectivity, as a subjective operation, has never been investigated adequately. This takes us to the problem of the transcendental sphere, which Husserl intended to analyze through his phenomenological research. This is, in fact, an epistemological turn, that is it deals with the problem of our way of knowing and tackles the theme of the origin of the logical formations.*

(d) The Epistemological Turn: from the Knowledge of Objectivity to Subjectivity

In the wake of Kant, but with a radicalism unbeknownst to him and with different results, Husserl tackles the theme of *transcendental logic*. His first move consists of ridding the theme of subjectivity of logical psychologism in order that we may here confront the question that is fundamentally connected to the peculiarity of phenomenology.

This question focuses a new terrain of research targeting the distinction between psychic acts and conscious lived-experiences. The former are psychic realities, whereas the latter possess their own ideality concomitant with their own evidence. The general ideality of all intentional unities with respect to the multiplicities that constitute them is delineated, be it relative to external or internal experience (Husserl 1974, § 62). Particularly interesting is Section 62, where a long analytic discussion concerning the distinction between immanence and transcendence is synthesized. Not only external objects are transcendent, but there also exists an internal transcendence between the real psychic dimension and the conscious lived-experience of these. The sphere of the conscious lived experiences is a *medium* between external reality and internal psychic reality. The conscious lived experiences configure the immanent sphere of the multiplicity of consciousness in referring both to external objects and the internal psychic dimension.

The transcendence of the real constitutes itself in the immanent sphere in the particular form of ideality. In this sense, we can understand how logical formations occur in consciousness. There is a spontaneous and originary activity that produces irreal objects that are given in real psychic processes, but which are distinguishable from them. This involves an originary act of production of ideal objectivities that possess their own evidence and which constitute themselves intentionally in judgment (Husserl 1974, §63). *The systematic examination of the connections and the distinctions between reality and irreality, the real and the possible, configures itself as a universal, absolute ontology that serves as the basis for both formal and real ontology* (Husserl 1974, § 64).

> At this point, Husserl proceeds with a very detailed description of the subjective genesis of all the objectivities that have been in question in the Formal and Transcendental Logic from a formal point of view, making evident the apriori nature of subjective structures correlate to objective apriori structures. Practically, this entails focusing on the theme of the constitution of ideality, on the analytic principle of contradiction, of formal ontology as truth, and so on.

For example, from the subjective perspective, the fundamental formal law of the pure analytic involves the apriori structure of evidence insofar as subjective essential situations correspond to objective ones. One discovers that subjective structures have an apriori function that must be investigated (Husserl 1974, § 75). With regard to the logic of truth as the basis to justify the meaning of formal ontology, one runs across idealized presuppositions that are at the basis of the principle of contradiction and the law of the excluded middle. In the final analysis, one realizes that through the operation of 'variation', we can go from a concrete fact to an ideally possible fact, which, in general, defines the process of idealization (Husserl 1974, § 80). On the other hand it is possible to descend from what is ideally made through a process that is like an archaeological excavation to understand the way in which something ideal has been produced. In the case of judgments, every real and possible judgment leads back to ultimate nuclei that have greater syntactic value. Hence, one regresses back to the ultimate substrates, ultimate subjects (and not nominal predicates), ultimate predicates (not predicates of predicates), and ultimate relations.

All of this does not concern the *mathesis universalis*, or formal mathematics, as we have already seen. Rather, this relates to *the logic of truth* because the objects of the ultimate substrate are individuals. Every truth relates to these, and it is necessary to lead back every analytic proposition to the ultimate individual nuclei until each proposition is understood (Husserl 1974, § 82). Then it is possible to establish apriori that every judgment leads back to something individual that has a relation to a real universal and to a world in which it has value (Husserl 1974, § 83).

As we regress along the *series of evidence* whose judgments are the finished products of the genesis of sense, which has its own history (Husserl 1974, § 86), we continue until we reach the antepredicative level, or, in other words, the *non-predicative evidences* that constitute true and proper experience (Husserl 1974, § 86). The result consists in becoming aware that logic postulates a theory of experience which, in order to be formally well ordered, requires logic itself. All of this indicates that preparatory work on our way of knowing is necessary. *Evidence is the key point of this analysis, because evidence is the universal modality of intentionality, linked to the totality of consciousness. This is why the category of the Object as such is in correlation with evidence.* If we want understand how the ontology of the Object in general can be achieved we have to explore the meaning of evidence.

(e) The Subjective Foundation of Logic as a Transcendental Problem

The transcendental terrain develops, according to Husserl, into the new terrain of formal ontology that is no longer about a possible world, but concerns every being in every sense (Husserl 1974, § 102). It involves leading the two formal sciences, that is, formal ontology as the analytic of new generalities and the new ontology that configures itself as the form of totality of reality, to transcendental subjectivity, the place of the originary foundation of all sciences. Phenomenology insofar as it is philosophy is the unique authentic science that analyzes transcendental subjectivity as such (Husserl 1974, § 103).

Through phenomenological analysis we have the tools to reach from the antepredicative dimension on the bottom to the objectivity of the formal analytic on the top. We also formally understand all that is entrusted to a theory of knowledge, which in turn is connected to a transcendental logic. Together they will let us clarify the meaning of a constituting subjectivity.

Transcendental logic is not a secondary logic, in the sense of a different logic that flanks the first; it is traditional logic radically understood as the absolute logic of science and, therefore, as absolute ontology. All the disciplines of mundane ontology fall under its rule and they find their justification in it. The most radical point reached, here, is that of transcendental aesthetics, understood as the analysis of the sphere of pure experience. Using it as a point of departure, we discover the justificatory grounds for geometry, then physics as exact natural sciences operating through the construction of ideal models, and, lastly, the human sciences that require normative concepts that move beyond them.

Looked at in this way, we have the key to the various themes successively developed in *The Crisis of European Sciences and Transcendental Phenomenology*, including the birth of geometry (Husserl 1976, Beilage 9a) and the ontology of the life-world. *Mundane ontology, which includes all cultural formations, needs, as we saw previously, an apriori universal ontology in order to be understood.* This involves returning to the apriori life-world by way of the transcendental epoché, to arrive at the transcendental correlation of world and consciousness of the world, of subject and object, which consists of that intentional life by means of which our world acquires sense (Husserl 1976, § 51). Intentionality and evidence mutually refers each other, as we have already seen. In fact, evidence is one of the universal modes of intentionality. Intentionality and evidence disclose the universal teleological structure of consciousness, to which one must regress in order to collect the apriori universal of the life-world in the transcendental correlation of subject-object, understood as the ultimate terrain upon which all objective sciences ground themselves.

An apriori universal and absolute ontology is founded on the essential description of transcendental subjectivity; its status as ontology is discovered by understanding its categorial nature, in that it is possible to subsume everything under distinguishable general categories: of something in general, object in general and, as an aspect of the latter, being in general.

This recognition, this sense given to the absolute, universal apriori ontology, is central to the novelty of Husserl's ontology. It is possible, then, to discover the link between the *Third Logical Investigation* and the universal apriori ontology; Husserl's goal was to find a 'foundation'. In the first case the unity of foundation was based on a Pure Law. In the second case the theory of foundation is developed as far as an absolute, universal apriori ontology, gained through the universal science of the transcendental subjectivity, i. e. phenomenology. This is why it is necessary to start from *Logical Investigation* to understand how Husserl progressively elaborated the new ontology.

Using these premises, he moves through the following stages:

1. The empirical is distinguished from the essential;
2. The content of the essential delimits a field of inquiry and enables us to construct an ontology;
3. Ontology subdivides into a material and a formal ontology;
4. Both are grounded in an absolute and apriori formal ontology;
5. Absolute apriori ontology is gained through the essential description of transcendental subjectivity characterized by intentionality and evidence;
6. And, finally, the universal science of transcendental subjectivity, i.e. phenomenology, is used as the basis to understand the main structures of the life-world, the ontology of the life-world.

The life-world is the terrain of our cultural products, in particular natural sciences and human sciences. We can accept it in a naïve and natural attitude, as sciences usually do, or we can to start from the distinction between empirical and essential (1) to go through all the process that we already described, from the top to the bottom and from the bottom to the top (2, 3, 4, 5). This is the task of phenomenology as far as it assumes an epistemological attitude.

Logic is obviously invoked on a number of levels in this process, showing itself under two aspects: formal logic, supporting formal ontology, and transcendental logic as logic of truth, which is the inquiry into the forms of judgments as they conform to the 'things themselves'. Transcendental logic deals with the essential description of transcendental subjectivity, which is necessary to understand the meaning of the life-world (6).

14.3 Adolf Reinach's Apriori Essential Connections

As we said in the introduction, our intent is to show how Husserl's original students received and used his phenomenological program. The text I should like to consider, at first, is Reinach's *Über Phänomenologie* (*On Phenomenology*) (1914), in which Reinach declared his allegiance to the phenomenological method. His reason for doing so was expressly not to deal with the problem of existence, but rather with the problem of essence. However, by the logic of following the phenomenological method, Reinach accepts that that his essential analysis should have as its terrain consciousness with its lived experiences, according to Husserl's position. Also for Reinach, *Wesenserschauung*, that is 'seeing of an essence' is necessary to apprehending the significance of other disciplines, especially mathematics. Reinach appropriated Husserl's term, to which he gave approximately the same sense as Husserl when he wrote: '. . .essence designated what is to be found in the very own being of an individuum as the What of an individuum. (. . .) Experiencing, or *intuition of something individual* can become transmuted into *eidetic seeing* (*ideation*)' (Husserl 1977, § 3).

Reinach, however, does not see the analysis of essence as an end, but rather as a means for arriving at laws that are valid for all the facts and for all the interconnections of which we are made aware by sense perception. Reinach follows Husserl in hooking the validity of these laws to their having to be as they are, or, in other words, to the impossibility of their being different. *The task of philosophy is precisely that of highlighting these essential connections that are given a priori and are not connections of thought, but connections of being, independent of the human subject, who could also not be there* (Reinach 1989a, p. 545). *Indeed, they are Seinsverhältnisse, relationship in being. This is the meaning of ontology according to Reinach.*

The question therefore is how can we come to know them? Reinach agrees that there is no evidence of the existence of things, but, seeing that empirical judgments are involved, their validity cannot be called into question; for example, the judgment 'I see a house' cannot be doubted, while 'a house exists there' can be called into question (Reinach 1989a, p. 546). For Reinach *Sein* (being) and *Existenz* (existence) are not really connected; when one speaks of *Sein*, one is referring to a 'state of affairs' in essential rather than existential terms.

The validity of a priori lawfulness, linked to the discovery of the essential level, enables Reinach to obtain two results: to continue to keep existence between parentheses – a Husserlian theme – and to hold that the essential connections are not the work of thought, but rather of intuiting the essential structure of being – a motive that in his opinion leads away from Husserl's position, since he seems to hold that Husserl's a priori is a necessity of thought, but not a necessity of being. Whether or not this is a good interpretation of Husserl's position, we should notice that for Husserl the essential sphere does not depend on subjectivity. Still, Husserl believes it is necessary to examine subjectivity to understand better in which way human beings grasp what is essential. Reinach's critique, especially with reference to Husserl's analysis of consciousness as the locus of the analysis of essence as it is elaborated in *Ideas pertaining to a pure phenomenology*, led to the school being split into two currents that were referred to as, respectively, 'realist', for those who accepted only the 'essential reduction' proposed by Husserl, and 'idealist', for those who accepted the 'transcendental reduction' too, the reduction to subjectivity.

The deepening of the theory of the phenomenological a priori, obtained through the 'seeing of essence', is the main result of Reinach' s work. A priori is the field of the essential connections, but it is not only linked up with propositions and acts of judgment, that is with something that is linked to the subject, but also and primarily with states of affairs (*Sachverhalte*), which are objects of judgment and recognition.. States of affairs are what is correlative to judgments.

When we say, for instance: 'The tree blooms', we can examine this proposition according to many aspects:

a) the proposition, that is the meaning of these group of words, that is what we mean with them and that is out of time;
b) the act of the judgment, which is in time;
c) the act of judgement in general;
d) the state of affair: in the case of 'the tree blooms' the state of affairs in time, in the case of $2+2 = 4$ the state of affairs out of time;
e) the object of the judgment that can be real or ideal, it exits or not.

Because judgements constitute themselves in time and states of affairs are out of time, the concept of a necessity independent from experience belongs only to the states of affairs, which, therefore, are apriori (Reinach 1989b, p. 351). Being in time is meant in two ways: it is possible to be in time without constituting oneself in time, as for example in the case of the *state of affairs that* 'the tree blooms'; or to constitute oneself in time and this is the case of the *judgment* 'the tree blooms'.

Reinach, describes the relationship between the level of judgment and that of states of affair, that is between the epistemological and ontological levels, in his essay entitled *Zur Theorie des negativen Urteils* (*On the Theory of negative*

Judgment) (1911). While propositions can be true or false, states of affairs can be (*bestehen*) or not (Reinach 1989b, p. 116).

To grasp the meaning of a state of affairs, we must not only examine the positive judgments, but in particular, the negative ones, as the latter are more problematic to a logical inquiry. Reinach argues that the latter ones refer themselves to the positive ones, and that in fact they cannot exist alone, but need the connection between positive judgment and a state of affairs, their existence being due to such peculiar operations as questioning or doubting (Reinach 1989b, p. 123). He offers this example: to say that 3 is not less than 2, it is necessary to know that 3 is more than 2 (Reinach 1989b, p. 124). This is the case of ideal objects, but it is possible to examine particular concrete experiences in the same way. Positive states of affairs can be 'grasped' by beginning with the perception of a thing and using this as a springboard to determine a true belief (*Überzeugung*). If a rose is red, the state of affairs is positive and evident; if we say that it is not yellow, we understand this statement as holding out a contrast with which we grasped the colour of the flower. Our negative evidence comes to the fore and given the force of this, we cannot believe in the proposed new state of affairs, i.e., that the rose is yellow. That means that our negative conviction is based on a contrast and that it comes from a negative state of affairs, because there is at the bottom a positive state of affairs (Reinach 1989b). In this way we can obtain a priori essential connection (*apriorische Wesenzusammenhang*) which may be stated in this way: every conviction of positive or negative state of affairs presupposes positive evidence (Reinach 1989b, p. 125).

Reinach deepens the meaning of negation by posing the question of whether questioning or doubting are grounded in pure subjectivity. According to him, the answer is no. If assertion (*Behauptung*) is linked up to conviction in such a way that it truly belong to subjectivity, we would be logically forced to believe in negative convictions, but from the side of what is objective we find the positive belief in negative states of affairs (Reinach 1989b, p. 137). This means that negativity is on the objective side of judgment. The result is that the apriori is an ontological category first, and only secondarily an epistemological one.

Reinach especially applied his method to 'law'. In his work *Die apriorischen Grundlagen des bürgerlichen Rechts* (*Apriori Foundations of Civil Law*) (1913) he described the root of law, beginning with certain primitive 'social acts', such as claim, connection and promise. Promising is considered the source of the first two others (Reinach 1989c, Chap. I). On these bases, according to him, one can establish the doctrine of law as an apriori level (*die apriorische Rechtslehre*), distinguishing it from the laws and statutes laid down, contingently, by the legislator, and which may depart from it and even turn against it (Reinach 1989c, Chap. II). Rather, this a priori level of law should be considered as a purely ontological field, one that is quite different from those natural laws finding which legislative law finds its roots (Reinach 1989c, Chap. III). Reinach's work, here, gives him a claim to be a forerunner of deontological logic or the ontology of normative domains.

14.4 Jean Hering's Early Phenomenological Ontology

Jean Hering's *Bemerkungen über das Wesen, die Wesenheit und die Idee* (1921) (*Observations on Essence, Essentiality and Idea*) foregrounds Conrad-Martius' analytic work, as well as that of the later Edith Stein. In Hering's *Observations*, he focuses not so much on the scholastic tradition but, instead, on Greek philosophy, especially Plato and Aristotle. According to Hering, they were the first who pinpointed the importance of the discovery of the *What* in an individuum.

Hering's *Bemerkungen* can be charted in the following way. In the first chapter, he sustains the position that every object has just one – and no more than one – essence (*Wesen*), i.e. the fullness of the *Eigenart*, or the distinctive character that constitutes it. This means that the essence of something is non-independent. Essence is individual in the sense that two individual objects can have similar but not identical essences; consequently, though it is legitimate to speak of an essence of all similar things, and therefore in terms of universality (the essence of all the 'a's), this always presupposes an individual essence. Using an Aristotelian expression, one might say, according to Hering, that the essence is the *to ti en einai*. As an example of what the Greek phrase *to ti en einai* means, imagine it a house that can be painted successively with different colors, but always remains the same. It responds to the question regarding the *poion einai,* the 'being thus' of an object (*das Sosein eines Gegenstandes*) (Hering 1921, p. 496). In a note added to § 1, Hering specifies that 'being thus' has to be distinguished from *poion*, the way in which a thing is, for example its particular color, and from the 'state of affairs' (*Sachverhalt*) 'S is p', that can be affirmed or denied, while p, from the point of view of *poion einai*, belongs essentially to S (Hering 1921, p. 497).

Dealing with the theme of constitution and affection, Hering distinguishes 'being thus' from 'doing' (*poiein*) and 'suffering'(*paschein*). To explain the difference he gives an example: the German poet Konrad Gessner used for the first time the hexametron in his poems. From this use we cannot gain the *Sosein* of the hexametrom, because it was completely accidental, totally different from the 'being thus' of the hexametron which does not depend on the circumstances in which it is used. Rather, the relationship is the inverse, with the hexametron's fitness for epic poetry and not for lyric poetry depending on the hexametron itself (Hering 1921, p. 499). In order to go deeper in the 'being thus' we have to seek the 'essential nucleus' (*Wesenkern*), which is the immanent foundation of the essence (Hering 1921, p. 503).

In the second chapter, Hering poses the question – as Aristotle had already done – regarding the 'whatness', the *ti,* the *was*. Here Hering speaks of *Washeit* or *Washaftigkeit*, which is different from 'being thus'. To be red is different from 'red' as a color in itself: the first is 'what', the second 'being thus'. The first therefore identifies a form, *morphe*, of a particular object (Hering 1921, p. 509). It is necessary then to separate the 'being thus' of a thing, and its 'whatness', or immediate *morphe.* When this *was* is considered in itself, as, for instance, in the case of the horse, not as 'being horse' in relation to a horse, but as 'being horse as such', one is in a sphere quite apart from an object, so one can speak of essentiality (*Wesenheit*) or of *eidos*, which constitutes the *prote ousia*, the primary substance (Hering 1921, p. 511).

To know an individual object it is necessary therefore to know its ideal quality (*ti*) and its 'being thus'. That is why 'whatness' can be considered as the primary substance. This identification was later contested by Edith Stein, who declared that the Aristotelian meaning of 'substance' is totally different, because it is something in itself that contains and develops its own essence within it, and is by no means just an ideal quality.

In any case *prote ousia,* the 'ideal quality', must not be confused with the sphere of ideal objects, which are to be considered as a secondary substance, *deutera ousia*: red as ideal object is determined according to its *ti einai* through its essentiality.

When primary substance and secondary substance refer to the empirical object, the result of the analysis can be grasped even better; in fact, in both cases one can speak of a singularization (*Vereinzelung*), but, though the singularization of an ideal object is the object itself, the same cannot be said in the case of essentiality, because its realization is the Whatness of the object; the real object is therefore only a 'realizer' of essentiality, whereas an ideal object cannot be indicated as a realizer or, better, as a concretizer, because the empirical object is itself reality (Hering 1921, p. 514).

Hering then shows that there are immediate and mediate *eidoi.* 'Redness' is immediately grasped in itself, while it has a mediate relationship with a rose that is red. There are also simple and complex forms, so it is possible to distinguish 'originary *morphe'* (*Ur-morphe*) and complex ones. Hering takes his base for studying their relationship from Husserl's *On the Theory of Whole and Parts,* contained in *Logical Investigations* (Hering 1921, p. 515). Different forms can belong to the same object, so that they constitute a teleological unity (Hering 1921, p. 516). It is possible that there is a 'fusion' (*Verschmelzung*) of forms*;* they can be separated one another, but also internally connected, as it happens in the case of 'colourness' and 'redness', in this case they create a new *morphe,* 'a red' (Hering 1921, p. 518).

After having made the distinction between essence (*Wesen*), essentiality (*Wesenheit*) and object (*Gegenstand*), Hering turns to the analysis of the ideational sphere. Ideas do not represent a class of what is by the side of objects or essentialities, but participate in the various spheres of what is, because among them are ideas of object, of *eidos*, and so on; these can be identified and studied as a particular sphere of objects (Hering 1921, p. 526). In this connection, it is right to insist on the very wide significance attributed to the term 'object', so much so that it has to be specified on each occasion: real or empirical object, for example, or ideal object, and so on.

At this junction the difference between Hering and Husserl becomes most noticeable, even though Hering offers his critique merely as addition to and elaboration on what Husserl had maintained in *Ideas pertaining to a Pure Phenomenology.*

Hering writes that for many years past, Husserl's lectures had distinguished a double nature of ideas, namely a nature they have in things and a nature they have in themselves. The thing in idea already has a *hic et nunc*, that is to say, the idea of this lamp, for example, is something like a space-time representation, even though the idea itself, the idea as such, exists neither here nor now (Hering 1921,p. 530).

It is precisely this indeterminacy characteristic of the idea as a generality that distinguishes it from essentiality, which latter, according to Hering, is wholly determinate, so that Husserl's eidetic intuition had gone no further than the identification of the idea (ideational act or ideation) (Hering 1921, p. 527), without grasping the distinction between essentiality, as a class of what is, and the idea, as an instrument for identifying the classes of what is.

At this point one has to make a terminological distinction that is not merely formal, but serves to further clarify the question: in *Ideas pertaining to a pure Phenomenology*, indeed, Husserl uses the expression *eidos* to signify the essential moment and no longer uses the word idea – as he had done in the *Logical Investigation* – because this word tends to have, not least for Husserl himself, a regulative function in the Kantian sense. Hering concedes that Husserl's ideative act or ideation identifies the particular act by means of which the idea presents itself to us (Hering 1921, p. 527); yet in his opinion Husserl does not sufficiently develop the distinction between essence, particular and universal essentiality, as a class of what is, and on the other side idea, as an instrument for identifying the classes of what is – a distinction that, as we have already seen, Hering deems to be important. Thus, he cannot grant that the terms *eidos* and *Wesen* are equivalent, as Husserl believes (Hering 1921, p. 533).

The discussion with Husserl is important in order to understand the realistic point of view maintained by Hering. Together with Adolf Reinach, and preceding Hedwig Conrad Martius, he intended the phenomenological description to pertain exclusively to the intuition of essences. Recognizing that reality shows itself in a complex way, Hering distinguished the various levels in which 'essence' (*Wesen*) can be given, which are always in relationship with the existence of things. At the end of his long essay he renews his theme using the example of a singular thing, a lamp or an animal, in particular a lion and a wolf, and discovers a new series of starting points, necessary to understand the ways in which a thing can be approached. This series is made by five couples of opposites (*Gegensatzpaare*): exemplar and idea, particular and universal, individual and genus, singularity and universality, real and ideal. Exemplar, particular, individual, singularity, real belongs to what is individual; on the other side we find what belongs to universal (idea, universal, genus, universality, ideal). All this is said and done in order to show how it is possible to go up and down in the essential description of the levels of reality.

14.5 Hedwig Conrad-Martius' Interpretation of Reality and the Constitution of Nature

14.5.1 Realontologie

The position of Conrad-Martius is rather different from that of Husserl. Nevertheless, her movement away from the maestro was a gradual process.

Notwithstanding her protest of fidelity to Husserl, in actual fact her analysis was conducted in such manner as to move away from his assumptions at several points, even though her results – at least in broad principle – are compatible with Husserl's.

She accepted the first step of Husserl's method, that is the reduction to essence, essence being interpreted as what can be grasped through intuition, showing the property or the *quid* of a thing in a wide sense, (a physical thing, fact, event, cultural phenomenon and so on). The differences concern first and foremost her insistence on essence, which Conrad-Martius takes to have aspects far more complex than the Husserlian model. Second, she poses the central metaphysical question, 'why there is something rather than nothing?', which takes her in the direction of the questions raised by existence, which is a question that never guided Husserl's own work in such a direct and radical manner. Certainly, the development of this metaphysical question cannot be likened to that of many philosophies of the past; Conrad-Martius uses a phenomenological approach consisting in the peculiar attitude of 'paying attention' to aspects and dimensions of reality, grasped just as they present themselves, but not so as to interrogate their presence in the factual sense. Rather, on the contrary, Conrad-Martius seeks the essential aspect, tracing a never fully exhaustible totality, which is to be recomposed by means of analyses of partial ambits of being, i.e. by means of the description of their peculiar 'ontology'.

The 'realism' of this position springs precisely from the desire of following the manner in which 'things' give themselves rather than forcing them into conceptual categories that frame and determine them; here we have the phenomenological attitude, rendered concretely operative by means of an inquiry that proceeds by incrementally gaining greater insight. Thus, Conrad-Martius rejects Husserl's transcendental turn, and his consequent construal of subjectivity. Conrad-Martius' novelty and originality deserves a finer grained analysis than she has gotten from philosophers so far.

Conrad-Martius' long essay published in 1923, *Realontologie*, (*Real Ontology*), bears a title indicative of the object of the inquiry and the point of view assumed by the author. It is a question of coming to grips with a problematic of the cognitive type, that is to say, asking oneself in what manner and up to what point one may be sure of the reality of this or that givenness. Conrad-Martius notes that the solipsist philosopher identifies consciousness, with which this question has been paired since Descartes, with his own I, his positivist counterpart with a complex of sensations, and the idealist metaphysician with God or the Absolute. Nevertheless, the question regarding the reality of every partial ambit implies the significance of the whole of reality; in fact, if one wants to pinpoint the ambit of being subjected to inquiry in order to grasp the sense of this ambit – for this is the way in which one can understand, initially, the term 'ontology' – this ambit is not partial, but rather coincides with reality. The question thus becomes immediately radical: what is reality itself? And therefore, why is there being rather than nothingness? Examining the matter in essential terms, we have to analyze the relationship between *Essenz* (essence) or *Washeit* (whatness) and the existence or the forms of existence that are different from essence (Conrad-Martius 1923, p. 162).

At this point, the inquiry becomes oriented towards a realistic unfolding (Conrad-Martius 1923, § 8). Returning to the theory of knowledge, Conrad-Martius asks what distinguishes a hallucination from real existence. A hallucination is given 'bodily' (*leibhaft*) in its 'personal' actuality for him/her who has it, even though it is not factually given; it is therefore necessary to distinguish what one understands by 'givenness in its 'personal' actuality the body' and the 'being in of real existence': thus, the chair in the next room is not *leibhaftig* 'given' to me, but exists as such and must therefore be considered to be *leibhaft* (Conrad-Martius 1923, § 9). What, then, does being 'in its 'personal' actuality consist of?

Here Conrad-Martius puts forward the theory that what characterizes reality is the existence of a 'substrate' (*Träger*) that is 'laden' with a whatness, so that a real entity is the totality of the two moments (Conrad-Martius 1923, § 11). This substrate is signified by the Greek term *hypokeimenon,* but it must not be understood as something underlying, because the substrate and the whatness constitute one unit. Since existence is distinguished into ideal and real, on can say that the number three is the formal substrate of a whatness that determines the number three as number three (Conrad-Martius 1923, § 12). The ideal substrate is constituted in such a way as to show that it is substantively determined by its whatness, while the real substrate factually takes over whatever essentially determines it; consequently, even those that are not factually configured are real entities.

In general, reality is given to us when an essentially determined substrate and something that determines it in an essential manner behave like a true substrate and a 'laden' whatness (Conrad-Martius 1923, § 14).

Though we are summarily outlining Conrad-Martius' ontology, we can see that her general intention is to discover the fundamental constitution of what is determinant for the world of the real in all its configurations, with which and in which this world becomes possible in the first place. This ontology as pure objectivity is counterposed by Conrad-Martius to Kant's subjective point of view. In this sense, therefore, one may speak of a 'real' ontology that discovers the constitution of real being in all its configurations.

The detachment from Kant implies coming closer to Scholasticism, especially as regards the effectuality of what is real; since what is real (*das Reale*) is the 'realizer' in a positive and personal manner of its whatness, one speaks, like the scholastics, of reality as effectuality (*Wirklichtkeit*) or actuality (*Aktualität*). Nevertheless, Conrad-Martius considers the scholastic concept of reality (*Wirklichtkeit*) to be connected to natural real entities, whereas she deems it to be ontologically important to distinguish natural real entities from real entities *tout court*, among which she includes, for example, the state, the home, etc. On the other hand, what distinguishes the scholastic approach even more thoroughly from the one here assumed is the methodical use of intuition; in other words, the type of vision employed, the type of analysis that tends towards the primary, originary phenomenon (*Urphänomen*) of reality, without concerning oneself with its factual realization in the given world (Conrad-Martius 1923, p. 174, note 1).

One may wonder what coordinates describe this philosophical position, in as much as she does not seem to be presenting us with an ingenuous form of realism, nor is she applying themes derived from the Husserlian transcendental dimension in terms of some recognizable idealism.

Yet it is precisely this nucleus, for the moment identified only by the exclusion of other positions, that we need to identify if we want to understand her realistic phenomenology – which is not an easy task. From Husserl's phenomenological analysis she appropriates the descriptive, intuitive method, which essentially tends to highlight the significance of the *Sache*, that is the 'object' of the analysis, this *Sache* being reality: and at this point she begins to move away from Husserl.

The various texts of Conrad-Martius here mentioned trace out a phenomenological tradition that goes back to the *Logical Investigation,* which Husserl already revised and perfected in his *Ideas* of 1913. Why, however, does Conrad-Martius, in 1923, 10 years later, still refer to Husserl without taking account of his turn in a transcendental direction? In fact, one has to remember that Conrad-Martius had already raised the issue of her selectivity at the beginning of the *Realontologie*, aligning her project with analysis in Husserl's eidetic sense; in other words, retaining the eidetic moment of the reduction, and rejecting the transcendental one.

In the course of more than 30 years of research, one can see the profile of a realistic phenomenology become ever clearer in Conrad-Martius' work. And ever more explicitly, she counterposes her theory to Husserl's phenomenology, yet always with the nuance that that this was a family quarrel or, rather, a quarrel that concerned the best way of carrying out an analysis that can be called truly phenomenological.

14.5.2 Science and Philosophy as Aspects of the Inquiry into Nature

Nevertheless, what motivates Conrad-Martius is the project of reconciling contemporary scientific research and philosophical inquiry. The guiding thread is represented by her 'realism', which consists of recognizing a reality configured 'substantially' in a plurality of modes that can all be traced back to some fundamental 'principles'.

In the *Realontologie,* Conrad-Martius devoted a considerable portion of her analysis to nature, beginning with the phenomenological sense of 'what' appears, an analysis of which presents us with an instrument of knowledge that furnishes something real, as opposed to something dreamt or hallucinated. In fact, her entire analysis seeks to trace materiality, understood in its embodiment, substantially. Certainly, even 'what appears' has a lifelike quality and a substance, but the problem that Conrad-Martius sets herself concerns the fact that something can be 'real' not only in the sense that it appears, but also in the sense that it is 'material'. The entity or material unity is in itself, reposes, is to be found in 'existence', and all this is demonstrated by sense experience, which cannot indicate something that does not exist, so that whatever announces itself in it does exist. One therefore has to turn upside down the relationship that the phenomenologist – and here I would add phenomenologist of the Husserlian school, even though this is not said explicitly – postulates between what appears and what is factual: the former is not more certain than the latter, but – quite the contrary – is of itself empty. It is of the mode of being of pure fluctuation and possesses an inferior degree of reality. Nevertheless, the initially disconcerting originality of her stance is to force us to recognize the existence of a continuity that ranges from matter to light, so that the formations that appear are light formations, i.e. they have a substantiality that consists of light, their matter is light.

The profound reason underlying this interpretation is to be found in the fact that through the examination of light, gaseous formations, matter with its 'heaviest' concretizations – an examination carried out with the help of the physical and chemical sciences, which for the moment are in the background – one arrives at a surprising ascertainment: everything is material, but there are different degrees of materiality, so that it is possible to establish a profound correlation between what is solid, fluid and gaseous in nature and the constitution of the essential components the human being, corporeity understood as living corporeity, psychicity and spirituality, the triad which had been previously highlighted by Husserl. We are here concerned with symbols and analogies: gas and light are symbols of the spirit and correspond to the fact that the spirit is free, but the resemblance is not only external, for in actual fact some constitutive forms of matter and some fundamental movements ontologically characterize the whole of reality.

The most interesting of Conrad-Martius' texts regarding her position vis-à-vis the history of science is represented by *Naturwissenschaftlich-metaphysische Perspektiven* (*Natural scientific and metaphysical Perspectives*) (Conrad-Martius 1949, p. 6), which contains three lectures she gave in Heidelberg in 1946; these lectures bear witness to her profound knowledge of scientific thought in its contemporary development and achievement in the fields of physics and biology.

14.5.3 The Constitution of Living Nature

These lectures take a stance on the epistemological debates of the day and propose a philosophical interpretation of nature taking full account of the discoveries of the natural sciences as its starting point. As already noted, Conrad-Martius, without acceding to a positivism that would give science the last word, wants, still, to recognize science as the source of precious information, According to Conrad-Martius, even contemporary scientists are beginning to doubt the certainty that nineteenth century physicists demonstrated vis-à-vis the results of their research. In the contemporary age, science, according to its own intrinsic logic, must forego the claim of possessing the essential and real explanation of the world.

Conrad-Martius extended her lecture remarks in her most taxing work dedicated to the study of nature: *Der Selbstaufbau der Natur – Entelechien und Energien*, (*The Auto-constitution of Nature – Entelechies and Energies*) published in an enlarged second edition in 1961 (Conrad-Martius 1961, p. 339). This complex book is a synthesis of the long research road covered by Conrad-Martius not only as regards the study of nature, but – on account of the profound connection between philosophy and science – also as regards the metaphysical investigation of reality.

Conrad-Martius holds that hers is an ontological inquiry that preserves its fundamental links with the phenomenological method, the only one that can arrive at an essential analysis; and, further, that everything valid to be found in experimental science can be efficacious grasped only by means of an intuitive attitude, and it seems to her that the proposal of Hans Driesch regarding the presence of an entelechy in organisms is, in fact, supported by intuition (Conrad-Martius 1961, p. 55, footnote 43).

We have already referred to Conrad-Martius' interest in biology and, as we may here add, more specifically in embryology. In this book she bases herself on the work of Wilhelm Roux, who made a start with physiological research regarding organisms in 1881, and Hans Driesch, who in 1891 studied the embryo of the sea urchin.[1] Starting from this research work, Conrad-Martius, just as she had done for the physical theories, draws generally valid consequences on a wider metaphysical level, trying to come to the grips with the question of the origin and development of life.

In the 1930s, following in the path his research work seemed to point to, Driesch had insistently spoken of an entelechy of organisms that represents a typical plan or project, capable also of intervening to correct the organism in the course of its development, a kind of artificer that could not be traced to either a psychic (*seeliche*) or a spiritual (*geistige*) activity. To deal with this, he had therefore introduced a new concept: 'psychoid' (Conrad-Martius 1961, p. 58).

Taking her cue from this proposal, Conrad-Martius adds that the entelechy is not only the causal factor that conserves the typical identity of a living organism, but also the one that constructs the organic body in accordance with a typical essential mode and always regenerates it, so that in this sense entelechy is this selfsame typical modality (Conrad-Martius 1961, p. 63). We can thus understand Driesch's entelechy not as separate from an ideal plan, which it follows, but as embodying itself that ideal plan; it is clear, however, that in this way we have passed to a metaphysical consideration of the essence.

But there remains the question as to how an essence can be received in a physico-material compound and one therefore has to distinguish two different types of entelechy, an entelechy that controls the formation and development of the organism, *Bildungsentelechie*, and an entelechy that characterizes in an actual manner the typical individual identity, the true essence, *Wesensentelechie*. The former may be defined transphysical and is a model that guides the organism, accompanying it in its various degrees of development and presenting itself as an instrument for realizing the latter, which constitutes the ultimate causal factor of a metaphysical type (Conrad-Martius 1961, p. 77).

As regards the origin of life, Conrad-Martius resolves the metaphysical question of morphogenesis by means of the hypothesis of two forms of entelechy, plus

[1] Hans Driesch (1867–1941), a German biologist and philosopher, following his research work on sea urchins, maintained the theory of dynamic vitalism against Darwinist determinism. From the philosophical point of view he affirmed the presence of an entelechy in organic development that he conceived as having a finalistic orientation.

discovery of two powers within the generative entelechy, defined respectively as imaginoid and spermatoid, whose synthesis gives rise to the capacity of orienting the vital development of the organism; the first is connected with the genetic constellation of the embryo, while the second is the one that furnishes the type of organization that will guide the actualization of the body from within (Conrad-Martius 1961, p. 239). All this is supported by experimental research carried out – in particular – on amphibians, which Conrad-Martius considers in some detail.

When morphogenesis is examined from an ontological point of view, one must concede that the essential entelechy depends on the material conditions. This means that every material constellation possesses a mechanism that controls the possibility of union of a particular essential entelechy, identified by means of this passage, with a particular 'part' of living matter. This occurs in such a way that the latter can become configured as an ovule capable of developing (Conrad-Martius 1961, pp. 276–277).

The dependence of the entelechial essence on the structural conditions of matter does not indicate a materialist solution, because in the last resort it is precisely the entelechial essence that constitutes the foundation of the entire organization. Conrad-Martius' analogy for the relationship between the material conditions and the entelechy is that the material conditions could be regarded as the provisional construction of the first floor of a house that needs new foundations before a more complex structure can be completed (Conrad-Martius 1961, p. 280). But chaos rather than cosmos would result if there were no control; if, that is, there were to be a struggle of all the entelechies against each other (Conrad-Martius 1961, p. 281).

Conrad-Martius shows how quantum theory can, at this juncture, support this connection between essence and matter by demonstrating that it is possible for matter to change in such a way as to render possible the encounter with different essences, since it is fundamental to quantum theory to throw into crisis the idea of a space-time continuum governed solely by mechanical laws. In this new approach, chemical processes are likewise due to factors that can no longer be specified by means of the interpretation of energy given by classical physics. Processes now reveal themselves as transpatial and transtemporal or, to use a new terminology, as pre-physical (Conrad-Martius 1961, p. 287).

The criterion of discontinuity thus becomes fundamental in many directions, representing our most scientifically advanced knowledge of the real. Starting from the phenomenon of electromagnetism and the analysis of light, the quantum theory – by means of which space-time discontinuity could be pinpointed – makes it possible to highlight the transphysical factors, the ether for example, thus not only enlarging the vision of the cosmos, but also explaining the phenomena of life in such a way as to go beyond a narrow materialism.

However, contrary to that one might expect from what has been said up to now, it is not even a question of accepting vitalism. In actual fact Conrad-Martius holds that one can understand the scientific hostility to vitalism, though not for the reasons the scientists adduce. When Driesch, for example, a supposed vitalist, speaks of entelechy, one has to delve somewhat deeper and anchor this intuition by assigning it a place in the plan of being. This gives it a sense, whereas otherwise it will effectively remain 'in the air', i.e. will not be justified. For Conrad-Martius, then, the issue is not the insufficiency of the quantitative scientific attitude, but that of delineating an ontological setting, which is what the very concept of entelechy calls for (Conrad-Martius 1961, p. 441).

In this way Conrad-Martius counters both the substantially positivist conception and anti-positivist organicism or vitalism, in as much as the latter limits itself to opposing the former, remaining always on an exclusively scientific level.

Notwithstanding the bold originality of Conrad Martius' position, it should be kept in mind that her work was developed before the dawn of chaos and complexity theory. The latter in particular shows how the bewildering variety of living forms can be understood in terms of emergent, self-organizing phenomena (Goodwin 2001). Furthermore, the seminal work of Rosen on anticipation theory (Rosen 2007 (1st edn. 1985)) opened the way for higher-order complexity theory, coordinating not only the emergence of life but also the higher-order emergence of brain, mind and behavior, each with own specific kinds of dependency and autonomy from supporting lower levels (Baianu 2006, Baianu and Poli 2007). In this regard, Conrad-Martius was able to foresee that living and higher-order complex systems present quantum features. Details apart, the deep value of her work lies in making us aware that all scientific developments need ontological scrutiny and more generally in calling for an ontological interpretation all aspects and forms of reality.

14.6 Edith Stein's Ontology: Between Phenomenology and Metaphysics

Edith Stein addresses the theme of ontology when she brings mediaeval philosophy into dialogue with phenomenology. She considers ontology important and her approach difficult, starting with the polyvalence of the very term, 'ontology'. Focusing her attention on Thomas Aquinas and Husserl, she underlines the fact that phenomenologists distinguish between ontology and metaphysics. The former takes essences as its domain, whereas the latter concentrates on existence. For Aquinas, however, ontology refers to this latter sense of existence. Also, Husserl refers to material and formal possibilities, but not in a specific way as related to existential realities (Stein 1974).

This theme is taken up in her book *Potency and Act*, where the two modes of understanding ontology are interwoven. Edith Stein refers to Husserl's most significant research on this matter, closely reading the *Formal and Transcendental Logic*, which maintains that formal ontology is to be understood from a logical viewpoint that refers to 'something in general', or, in other words, to empty generality – a viewpoint that draws inspiration from the intuition of then-contemporary mathematics. Aquinas, on the contrary, moves in the direction of the fullness of being, which is given in our experience. Stein adopts a middle way, which draws inspiration from both positions. She wishes to examine the concepts of potency and act, studying them with reference to formal and material ontology. Following this path, material ontology is the doctrine of being in its fullness and the doctrine of the existent in its different genera (Stein 2005, Chap. 3, § 3). In order to achieve this result Stein investigates the two great regions, that is, the material and formal, already studied by Husserl. She returns to anthropological themes viewed from a phenomenological perspective, including the I, subject, soul and person. She adds to these, in a complementary fashion and not in any oppositional way, the Thomistic concept of spiritual substance (Stein 2005, Chap. 5, § 2).

It is best to proceed by having a firm grasp on the organic unity of Stein's work, which can be lost among connections and themes which at times seem too disparate. The starting point of her work is the simple factual given of being, discovered, in the first instance, as the fact of my own existence. Building on Augustine, Descartes and Husserl, she maintains that this point of departure opens a series of paths that lead us beyond this fact.

Because the fact of being is linked to the subject, we must inevitably start from Husserl's philosophic-transcendental modality to pass, by means of a necessity encoded in the structures of consciousness themselves, from immanence to transcendence. The development of this position concerns the precise value of this transcendence: whether it is strictly linked to a constituting consciousness (and this seems to be the position taken by Husserl according to his students, including Reinach and Conrad-Martius) or whether there is an autonomous world. Edith Stein does not want to reduce consciousness to an accessory fact, as it is, in any case, necessary to know the world, but Stein also wants to do justice to the world's own consistency. If the indispensable subjective point of departure is the *quoad nos*, an intermediate feature for obtaining access to the other spheres, its value in itself is relativized. It cedes, in the first place, to a formal ontology, understood as an all-embracing investigation of being from which one can begin a concrete analysis (Stein 2005, Chap. 1, § 3).

The allusions to Husserl and Thomas' positions, which manifest themselves in the individuation of a territory 'of something that is', become clearer at this juncture. From a formal point of view, this territory cleaves into 'something', or 'object' and 'in being', understood as a *fullness* of the object itself. For this reason, the fundamental ontological forms are: *aliquid, quod quid est, esse*, to which is necessary to attach *quale* that is inseparably connected to *quid* (Stein 2005, Chap. 2, § 1). Logical forms correspond to these ontological structures, which Husserl also interested himself in. Grades of universality that advance from the object in general to the individual are distinguished within ontological forms. The individual is also an empty form, alternating between differentiation and specification. If the empty forms are filled by content, we are on the slope of being and, in this case, the individual exists as a concrete being, as something singular, and in that sense a unique thing, a being that does not refer back to an other, or, finally, a primary object (Stein 2005, Chap. 2, § 2).

It is possible to distinguish three types of being: that of concrete individuals, that of empty forms, and that of material ideas. Working on the basis of 'fulfillment', understood in the phenomenological sense, Stein maintains that an 'individual' is wholly fulfilled; empty forms are fulfilled through the individuals to which they refer, and the material ideas remain in need of fulfillment. At this level, one finds examples of colours, sounds, and geometric forms. They are, on the one hand, related to more universal forms and, on the other hand, related to individuals and, therefore, can be called 'ideal objects' (Stein 2005, Chap. 2, § 2).

At this point, Stein tackles the question of independence and non-independence in relationship to the whole and the parts, turning her attention to themes present in Husserl's *Logical Investigations*. Moving from the observation that universality and formality are not the same thing, she underlines that in the formal domain one moves from something to the individual, passing through the forms of genus and species. But, if we focus on the other empty forms like *being* and *that which is*, we note that even these are ordered according to grades of universality, under which falls a new subdivision, namely, that of independence and non-independence. If we examine being, only being that has no relation is independent, whereas the being of all empty forms is non-independent. Concrete objects alone are independent, and their forms ground independence. Also, at this point, one can introduce the opposites of whole and part, and simple and composite. Only the whole can be independent. Universal forms are simple, but non-independent because they depend upon a possible whole. More specific forms are composites and all individuals are independent and simple. In the extreme case, this is true for God, who is a non-dependent simple individual (Stein 2005, Chap. 2, § 3).

In order to present the collective objects of material ontology, it is necessary to analyze first the necessary cognitive modality in which that presentation is formed; that is, the being held in a formal or a material intuition. Material intuition requires a sensory collection that permits one to grasp the 'something' that fills the empty forms. Intuition is fundamental because only on this basis is it possible to proceed to the activity of judgment, passing through abstracting intuition, which can be ideating or generalizing. If I pay attention to the color of a thing through an ideating abstraction, I grasp the color in its species, but from the specific shade I can grasp red in general and color in general. One reaches, in such a way, ultimate ideas, ideas of sound or colour, which make possible objects of science like the doctrine of pure colour or sound. This involves partial fields of material ontology. If I, then, take into consideration individuals, I reach the *essentia rerum*, that is, the structure of things or *quidditas* – the full and concrete *whatness* of the thing.

In establishing the relation between formal and material ontology Stein asks herself whether it would be possible to imagine a *mathesis universalis*, that is to say, a formal ontology, which could include all forms of material ontology inside itself as a closed system. Her response is that this is intrinsically impossible, since such a formal ontology would neither be able to satisfy all the criteria of material ontology in itself, nor generate an ordering procedure going reciprocally from the bottom to the top. The proof of this lies in the fact that neither experience nor science is closed in on itself. That which can be indicated, given the systematic nature of the various forms of knowledge, consists in the fact that human beings advance on the path of knowledge by moving from experience of concrete individuals through ideation to variation and generalization. It is possible to carry out formalization at each of these levels. An example of an ontology that can clarify the relationship between the formal and the material proceeding is the Euclidean geometry that moves from a few principles and permits a closed axiomatics. The same thing has not been done for colours – notwithstanding Goethe's doctrine of colours – and sounds.

The material idea or the fundamental category that governs the domain of the material thing is not, in fact, material. It is only comprehensible from the vantage point of the spirit (*Geist*). It is, therefore, necessary to determine what the 'spirit' might be.

The spirit is divided into the objective and subjective spirit. Here, the centrality of the anthropological theme is taken up once again with respect to the advancement of Stein's research, which is always carried out by human beings. The difference between subject and object is not only logical, but also ontological; it is not only *hypokeimenon* (what underlies) but also *hypostasis* (what subsists). Subjectivity is the objective form of the spiritual, and the subject is the *bearer* of the spiritual life and in this sense is a substance. In this way, Stein passes in a non-traumatic way from phenomenological analysis to metaphysical determination, avoiding the stark dualism of Descartes. The subject is not only the pure I, but also a spiritual substance. Its status of being-separated is graspable from consciousness and is different than any other thing; it alone can call the I itself an I (Stein 2005, Chap. 5, § 2).

Remaining on the phenomenological plane, Edith Stein again takes up the themes of intentionality, temporality, the spiritual life as the intellectual life, the cognitive process that founds itself on the relation noesis-noema, and the play of the movement between exteriority and interiority (Stein 2005, Chap. 5, § 4, 5, 6).

The *Geist* discloses the seat of the operations of will and intellect within the double domain of cognition and morality as we assimilate the consequences of the phenomenological reduction, and in this sense we can understand *Geist* as something 'mental and spiritual'.

The necessity to return from the ontology of the 'mental-spiritual' to the ontology of matter arises from the analysis itself, which is produced in a double movement from material ontology to what is spiritual-mental and from this to the material again. This is so because material things carry within themselves something that is objectively spiritual. The encounter, however, is complex; it is articulated throughout different levels of reality, including plants, animals, human beings, angels, and demons. Stein seeks the aid of Conrad-Martius in order to help her map out these levels. Stein discusses them by examining in which way, always understood as a sense-bearing way, the world of living beings and the inorganic matter that belongs to them could be understood in its levels of existence.

14.7 The Ontology of the Human Being

14.7.1 Hedwig Conrad-Martius

14.7.1.1 The Origin of the Human Being

In order to delineate Conrad-Martius' approach to the structure of the human being, it is necessary to begin with her standpoint on evolutionism.

Using her considerable knowledge regarding classical Darwinism and Neo-Darwinism, Conrad-Martius addresses with the question of the origin of the human being, discussing the thesis of the so-called missing link in the evolution of man from the monkeys. In some lectures given between 1949 and 1950 she concentrates her attention on two significant aspects: the discovery of the Australopithecus, held to represent this particular link, and the way in which one can explain, starting from this link, the behavior changes characteristic of an attitude that could be defined as eminently human, for example, the overcoming of the fear of fire (Conrad-Martius 1965).

This behavior reveals itself as certainly not secondary in the distinction between animal and man, but is it possible to accept the Neo-Darwinian interpretation that attributes the overcoming of this fear to a mutation? Furthermore, could a 'compromise' position be right, according to which the human body was prepared by evolution in such a manner as to accept the psychological capacities we consider human?

According to Conrad-Martius, it is precisely the most recent scientific discoveries that throw into crisis the principle of continuity in nature, something that was noted in connection with the quantum theory. And it is this theory that constitutes the guiding thread of analysis also in the case of the origin of man. It is therefore pointless to look for the missing link, for the simple reason that such a link does not exist. And, what is more, cannot exist; indeed, it is precisely by reflecting about the fear of fire that one comes to admit that, if Australopithecus does not fear fire and makes use of it, he is no longer an animal, but if he has this fear, he remains at the animal level and one cannot consider the fact that 'he is not yet' man, but could become so, as if he were half man and half monkey.

Undoubtedly, when man appeared, there was a change or, better, a mutation (to use a scientific term), but it would not be proper to invoke a 'chance' genetic mutation to justify the qualitative difference. Such a mutation would not be consistent with the continuous development that is sustained by evolutionism, and therefore cannot be interpreted in a purely biological sense. It is precisely scientific observation that tells us that we are face to face here with something different, that invites us to pass to a new level, because we are faced with a mystery as far as its viewpoint is concerned, in as much as it cannot resolve this fact.

All this leads to considering the human being as a living totality (*Lebenstotalität*) that cannot be examined from just a single point of view, neither morphological, nor physiological, nor psychological, and not even ethological or theological. These perspectives are interwoven and complementary and furnish a false image when considered in isolation; their complementary nature is demonstrated by the fact that each one of them reveals a schematic insufficiency that requires one to jump to a different sphere of inquiry.

Since Conrad-Martius admits that there are transformations of the human being in the course of natural history but still maintains that the soul is always there, she puts forward a suggestive interpretation of the development process of humanity in order to reconcile these claims.

How should one judge the erect Sinanthropus or Peking man from the standpoint of philosophical anthropology? How is it possible for them to have a human and an animal nature at one and the same time? Undoubtedly, if that is so, they are already men, but how can one explain their nearness to apes, the paradoxical fact that they have both human and monkey traits?

To answer this, Conrad-Martius turns to meaning of the 'original sin'. It is possible to discover in the scientific narrative an accordance with the Holy Bible, and this can be considered as mutually validating science and religion. If man has fallen, his body must likewise have undergone a regressive process, so that his soul and body bear the signs of a fall into a quasi-animal condition. It is difficult to say how this regression occurred in concrete terms, whether there already existed hominid forms ready to gather the human being or whether they were formed specifically for this purpose, but these questions are not fantastic when one bears in mind that mammals appeared in the Tertiary, when Sauria still predominated. How can one explain this seemingly sudden appearance. Did they come from the Sauria by means of a new entelechy and a total transformation of these latter, or did they come into being in some other manner? If these questions are legitimate in reference to animals, why not also for human beings?

Man's animal origin is excluded also by another consideration of a strictly scientific order. His embryo demonstrates that the human being has 'virtually' always been such; this embryo is characterized by the fact that the organs are not specialized and this prevents its ontogenic development through a clearly determined series of phylogenic animal species. One may speak of a kind of 'primitivism' that – as Arnold Gehlen underscores – is not a sign of inferiority with respect to animals, but simply of non-specialization, so that the relationship with animals could even be inverted: in fact, monkeys do better – as it were – than the human embryonic stage with their specific formation (Conrad-Martius 1965, p. 447).

In the human embryo it is already possible to trace the erect posture, the relationship between the upper and the lower limbs, the configuration of the feet, all characteristics that distinguish it from the other primates and determine the 'open' attitude vis-à-vis the surrounding world, as Joseph Kaelin, a Swiss paleontologist puts it.

This evolutionism, which Conrad-Martius calls creative, differs from the classical one, which she considers 'banal', because it succeeds in demonstrating the reason for the 'regenerative' phenomena that characterize the development of organisms, tracing them back not to a purely physical transformation, but to powers that, as we have already noted, are defined as transphysical (Conrad-Martius 1948); the use of this term is justified by the fact that these powers are not beyond nature and therefore meta-physical, but rather immanent within nature but non-reducible to a purely physical level. In order to understand this kind of interpretation, it is necessary to remember what Conrad-Martius has written on 'entelechy' (Conrad-Martius 1961, p. 77).

According to her it is true that inside an organism one can find a plan of development that can be called 'entelechy', but there two kinds of entelechy, one is the *Wesensentelechie*, that is the true essence of the thing, which needs to activate another entelechy, a second one that can be defined *Bildungsentelechie.* The latter can be called trans-physical, because it a model which informs all the organism through all the degrees of its development and shows itself as an instrument of realization of the first one.

14.7.1.2 The Constitution of the Human Being

All this is fundamental for understanding a particular problem, namely, the constitution of the human being. Two components are traditionally distinguished, the soul and the body; it is precisely the inquiry into nature that serves as the necessary condition for the comprehension and valuation of this ancient idea, always contested, but continuously reborn. It is not be chance that the question body-soul relationship it is treated, for example, in the book *Bios und Psyche* (Conrad-Martius 1948) after the question of the constitution of nature and the discussion of evolutionism.

Indeed, the background against which Conrad-Martius is moving is the one already proposed by Husserl, even down to the terminology. Particularly in the second volume of *Ideas pertaining to a pure Phenomenology,* but also in all the other writings in which he faces up to this theme, Husserl distinguishes three moments or aspects of the human being: the *Leib*, which we could translate with the expression 'living body' (in distinction from the *Körper,* i.e. the body in the general sense), the *Seele*, psychic activity, and the *Geist*, spiritual activity; the distinction of these three components therefore makes it possible to grasp the complexity of the constitution of the human being, the different aspects of our reality. By means of the methodical approach theorized in the first volume of *Ideas*, Husserl recuperates the traditional partition of soul and body in order to delve more deeply by identifying the functions and moments that remained unexplicated in it. Thus the definition of the corporeity as 'living' corporeity referred to profound bond with psychic activity, *Seele*, which must not be confused with the strictly spiritual moment.

By virtue of their souls, all living beings, plants included, show a form that is corporeal; but precisely the comparison of the various vegetal and animal realities makes it possible to underscore that, in the case of plants, we are not concerned with an affective soul that has sentiments, and even less so with a spiritual soul. Here we have a clear reference, which becomes explicit as well in the case of Conrad-Martius, to entelechy in the Aristotelian sense as making possible the formation and the development of the living being, the harmonic agreement of the structures and the functions in a totality in accordance with a principle that is superordinated with respect to matter (Conrad-Martius 1948, pp. 83–84).

When one proceeds to consider animals, one notes that already in the amoeba there can be found bodily movements and sensations, for example in hunting for prey or escaping from an enemy, just as in an organized animal; all this demonstrates that animals have experiences and can learn; nevertheless, we have to be cautious in making these distinctions, in other words, it is essential to separate a capacity of having purely living (*leiblich*) sensations, and therefore also corporeal sensations, from sentiments and sensations that suggest an affective psychic (*seelich*) life. This capacity appears in fish and is manifested progressively also in reptiles, birds and mammals: we are here concerned with a bifurcation that determines the distinction between body, understood as 'living body' (*Leib*), and soul (*Seele*); and this, in turn, in human beings divides into three moments, the psychic-corporeal moment, which is concerned with corporeity, the affective moment, which turns to itself, and the mental-spiritual moment, which issues from within itself to return to itself (Conrad-Martius 1948, pp. 92–93).

One may therefore say that the entelechial soul has a fourfold organization: corporeal, corporeal-psychic, affective and spiritual. Human beings have five fundamental principles grouped in a manner such that what is defined as soul (*Seelegrund*) is in its turn differentiated into two further ambits, the affective and the mental-spiritual, and, as far as the body is concerned, by the side of corporeity (*Leib*) one can trace a corporeal souls (*Leibseele*) that could be defined as psychic (Conrad-Martius 1948, pp. 93–94).

The entelechial soul, which is a fundamental principle, or the essential entelechy, is like the artificer of the entire living organism, the *logos* or the plan of the species. It constructs its body, becomes incarnated in it; naturally, this entelechial soul remains profoundly and organically bound to its body. Thus, all the functions, even the vegetative ones, have their roots in the soul, so we are not introducing a supervenient dynamic principle on a ready-made physical nature. Instead, the physiological processes can take place precisely thanks to this entelechial factor that is the profound, constitutive root, but of a pre-physical (*vorphysisch*) order (Conrad-Martius 1948, pp. 98–99).

As always, the justification of these results of the inquiries are furnished by the studies of physiology concerning, in particular, the nervous system; the distinction between 'cortical' and 'basal' within the brain indicates in the first case that control of the entire periphery of the body is exercised through the cerebro-spinal nervous system, while the second case refers to the vegetative nervous system; it is thus clear that the capacity of animals to have sensations and to move has its foundation in the cortical region, and that everything that is performed 'unconsciously' has its roots in the profound vegetative sphere present also in plants. And this grounds Conrad-Martius' distinction between the *Leib-seelich* (psychic-corporeal) region characteristic of animals, and the *leiblich* (living corporeal) region peculiar of plants. Through the nervous vegetative system there is founded a level of being (*Seinsschicht*) that is more profound than the one constituted by the animal nervous system; in fact, while the latter commands a mechanically controllable materiality, the former grafts the vegetative stimuli into the innermost and constitutive regions of the body (Conrad-Martius 1948, pp. 101–102).

The profound unity of these parts of the organism is borne out by the fact that that what can be controlled is not just what depends on the cortical region – as one would conclude after a merely superficial consideration – but also the vegetative function and this is further strengthened by the experiences that spring from different historical and cultural phenomena that range from magical practices to yoga and, lastly, the therapeutic methods of autogenous training.

By means of these analyses, Conrad-Martius attains substantially two ends. Philosophically, she provides a phenomenologically grounded answer to the question theorized in the modern age by Cartesianism concerning the soul-body relationship. Culturally, she comments on the convergence of explanations seemingly far removed from each other in disciplinary space (for instance, the theological and the biological), which is rendered possible by a certain manner of understanding the unity of the organism notwithstanding the complexity of its constitution.

What distinguishes Conrad-Martius is her ability to inhabit the scientific discourse while also inhabiting wholly alternative discourses, such as yoga, in such a manner as to utilize elements from many disparate domains without employing science as an absolute filter; indeed, everything that physiology tells us about the nervous system corresponds to what concretely happens in autogenous training, which is inspired by yoga, and makes it possible to come to grips with the philosophical problem of the will as a control instrument of corporeity. These very techniques support the thesis of the quadruple nature of the vital ambits present in the totality of the human being; in fact, if the voluntary act is what permits the beginning of these practices, it is equally true that the subsequent control of the members and the internal organs of the body is due to verbal or imaginative self-suggestion phenomena, a concentration that is not active, but rather passive as in dreams and therefore reveals regions and dimensions that can be brought to light thanks to the 'placing within parentheses' of both consciousness and conscience (Conrad-Martius 1948, pp. 104–105).

14.7.1.3 The Ontological Levels of the Human Being

By means of her analysis Conrad-Martius has enlarged the traditional concept of soul. We have noted that the quadruple nature characteristic of the human being consists of the vegetative dimension (*leiblich*), the corporeal-psychic dimension (*leib-seelisch*), the affective dimension (*affektiv-seelisch*) and the mental-spiritual dimension (*geistig*). However, these English translations don't completely correspond to those proposed in German; in fact, the word *Seele* cannot be generically translated by soul, because the term *Geist* refers more properly to the traditional concept of the spirit, and this would justify the use of psychic to convey *seelisch* and of spiritual- mental to convey *geistig*, thereby separating two aspects of the soul that characterizes both men and animals.

In this way one clarifies the further distinction that Conrad-Martius proposes between an affective dimension and a spiritual dimension; it is here, in her opinion, that there comes to the fore the dualism that was proposed by tradition, because it is precisely in the life of affections and feelings that one grasps a distinction between interiority and exteriority and notes an absolutely internal moment. This does not mean, however, that there is no connection between the two aspects. On the contrary, it seems clear that joy, fear and worry concern the soul and the body, and this is possible because they find themselves in 'polar contraposition', so that they can react in an analogous and parallel manner (Conrad-Martius 1948, pp. 108–109).

In fact, we have to concede, here, that in an ontological sense there exists a psychic 'space' and also a 'psychic' matter, irreducible to 'extensive' physical matter but, instead, to be defined as 'intensive' matter. This shift problematizes the location of the feelings (sentiments), which still, to a certain extent, exists – fear, love, joy are felt at the centre of the body, while understanding is to be found in the head, but is bound up with the spiritual moment we shall discuss further on (Conrad-Martius 1948, p. 111).

In Conrad-Martius the dualism is thus configured as polarity between a visible exterior body and an interior soul that possesses the same characteristics as corporeity, but as a self-contained internal analogue of the external body; in any case, unity is preserved, because it manifests itself in the fact that the whole of affective life stands in need of corporeity to express itself (Conrad-Martius 1948, p. 116). One may speak of a psychic energy similar to C. G. Jung's notion, which commands and directs physical energy. Also, according to Conrad-Martius, one has to recognize that it is possible for corporeity to block the sentiments and the affects, as is demonstrated by autogenous training, and one may therefore conclude that 'The body is the field of manifestation of the soul' (Conrad-Martius 1948, p. 119).

The question of the duality or unity of the human being returns with even greater insistence in the case of the relationship between corporeity and spirituality. The sign of the presence of the spiritual soul (*Geistseele*) is given by the fact that we discover a double interiority within ourselves, one in relation to the body and the other in relation to ourselves; in other words, we transcend ourselves from within in two modes, thus demonstrating that we possess the freedom of placing ourselves 'in front of' our body and 'in front of' ourselves (Conrad-Martius 124).

But the strong objection here is that, notwithstanding all the distinctions that can be theorized, we see that the spirit seems to depend on the integrity of the brain, implying a relationship between the spirit and brain which has to be accounted for, philosophically (Conrad-Martius 1948, p. 126). It is here that Conrad-Martius re-introduces the concepts of potency and act.

Undoubtedly spiritual acts, inasmuch as they are acts, stand in need of being exercised through an instrument – we have already noted this in the psychophysical processes – nevertheless, we confront a seemingly irresolvable question in terms of the framework we have used so far to analyze spiritual syntheses, categorical thought, memory, the capacity of intellectual reproduction: how does it happen that all this depends on the cerebral circuits? It is at this point that the problem of the distinction between *res extensa* and *res cogitans* becomes justified and one can understand the dualist proposal made by Descartes.

But it is possible to go deeper in understanding the link between the spiritual ego and the brain on the analogy of the relation between a performer and his or her musical instrument. Nevertheless, there are two distinctions that have to be made. The first concerns the quality of the products in the two cases. The sounds emitted by a musical instrument, even though not material in the strict sense, have a sensitive quality, while the thoughts, the spiritual acts, do not possess this characteristic. The second distinction deals with the difference between the virtuoso and the artist: one has to distinguish between a performer who tries to utilize all the potentials of an instrument and a performer who creates something new and then uses the instrument only as a means, as a vehicle of manifesting his interior world (Conrad-Martius 1948, pp. 128–129).

Nevertheless, it is necessary to find the point of organic connection between spirit and body, because one may also play the instrument as a virtuoso and not just as an artist. Also, by the logic of the analogy, we are here concerned with an instrument to which we are bound without any possibility of subtracting ourselves, but which in other respects can be considered as provisional and which we can therefore do without. Here, as at other points already indicated, there comes into play Conrad-Martius' theological moment: it is a question of inquiring into the significance of death; indeed, on the basis of the movement of the argument, one can see that death is not generically a separation of soul and body, but more precisely that of the body and the psyche. There occur, at death, changes of a physical order that can be studied from a scientific point of view and no longer permit the soul to exert mastery over the body. All this, however, cannot be understood as a natural fact. It is 'a fact', but not a natural fact, because from a natural point of view there is a body that belongs to the psyche, so that one can conclude that we 'deprive' ourselves of one body in order to assume another (Conrad-Martius 1948, pp. 132–137).

In conclusion, one may note that Conrad-Martius does not exclude the support provided by any inquiry or any discipline in her approach to the soul-body relationship. On the one hand, she strongly associates the genesis and constitution of man with nature, without reducing man to a natural entity, that is to say, in the sense of banal naturalism. This non-reducibility demonstrates that comprehension of nature and its most profound processes cannot be entrusted only to a superficial scientific reading, because such a reading, coming up against questions that it is incapable of resolving, indicates the need for trans-physical analysis. On the other hand, because of the failure of the naturalistic framework to reduce man to a natural entity, the traditional opposition between science and theology must be overcome even from a scientific point of view; in fact, the acceptance on the part of the philosopher of the results of inquiries and proposals deriving from different sources is determined by the coherence of these results as brought out when these selfsame phenomena are appropriately investigated: indeed, these phenomena indicate the possibility of agreement between the different perspectives.

One may note that the analysis of the soul is carried out by Conrad-Martius with meticulous care by delving into its internal articulations and potentialities and, further, that comprehension of this specific phenomenon is possible only by inserting it in the whole; the emergence of the human being from nature points to a trans-physical dimension from which it can be understood. There re-emerges the idea of a microcosm profoundly bound to all parts of the cosmos and connected with levels that cannot be physically perceived and yet are very real.

In Conrad-Martius' analysis on human being as a living system, we can find the main lines of the 'anticipatory systems' as proposed by Robert Rosen. According to him 'anticipation concerns the capacity exhibited by some systems to tune their behavior according a model of the future evolution of the environment in which they are embedded' (Rosen, Anticipatory Systems, 1985 (2nd edn. 2007), p. 341). But what distinguishes anticipation theory from the other theories of the future is that anticipation is a property of the system and can work below the threshold of consciousness. This is why anticipation is the principal feature not only of biological living systems, but of psychological and sociological systems as well (Baianu, 2006; Baianu and Poli, 2007).

The difference between the non-living natural systems and the living natural system is linked up with two layers of organization, which are able to govern the interactions and to modify the rules of interactions, so that the systems can be adaptive. A complex system requires the bottom-up type and the top-down type of composition, autopoiesis and autonomy. To be super-complex it must be provided by the theories of levels of reality, by its own spatio-temporal and causal structure, by interactions and anticipation. Given the complexity, anticipation is still the main feature of a living system, understood as a whole with a multiplicity of levels of organizations. If we compare the structure of the living systems as described by Conrad-Martius, we can discover that her analysis containes the presupposition for such a development. Another aspect of the description is important. According to Rosen all these characteristics are in the system itself and do not depend on the observer: this is a point of view that we can define 'realistic', as that one sustained by Conrad-Martius.

14.7.2 Edith Stein

14.7.2.1 The Identity of the Human Subject

In the attempt to delineate the map of the human being and the complexity of its constitutive moments it is necessary to start with the new region of being, which Husserl has spoken of: pure consciousness with its lived experiences. In the wake of Husserl, Edith Stein writes as follows in her *Einführung in die Philosophie* (*Introduction to Philosophy*): 'consciousness is not a box that collects the lived experiences within it, but rather these experiences, continuously merging with each other, do themselves constitute the flow of consciousness' (Stein 1991, p. 111). To be conscious must not be understood as an act of reflection, inasmuch as this latter is itself a lived experience, but rather as 'an interior light that illumines the flow of experiencing and by this very flowing clarifies it for the experiencing Ego without being directed onto it' (Stein 1991, p. 128).

One should note that the fundamental thing for both Husserl and Edith Stein is evidently the correlation between consciousness and the Ego, and in this connection there are three aspects of the Ego to be considered. First of all, there is the pure Ego. This aspect of the Ego does not regard somatic features, but is grasped in the correlation with such lived acts as perceiving, remembering, judging, feeling, willing, etc., and with reference to the objects in various ways depending on the acts it performs. The Ego under this aspect can grasp and perceive itself. The flowing of consciousness constitutes the last moment of immanent temporality and that is the road to be followed if one wants to grasp the significance of identity. 'Its identity is an identity throughout this immanent time', writes Husserl in connection with the pure Ego, meaning that the Ego remains in this or that act of consciousness even though it is not a real moment or a constitutive part thereof (Husserl 1989, p. 109).

The difference between reality and pure Ego is strongly stressed by Husserl and is what makes it possible to grasp the identity of the Ego, its non-dispersion, because the Ego or the pure subject is neither generated nor transient, because otherwise we would stumble into an absurdity, that pure intuition grasps an essential possibility characterized by non-essential traits of generation and transience. On the contrary, therefore, the pure Ego enters and leaves the scene, but 'the only way that it is possible for the pure Ego not to encounter itself is for it not to reflect on itself' (Husserl 1989, p. 110).

Nevertheless, the theme of reality is not neglected; one may say that the pure Ego and consciousness interact throughout the lived experiences that derive their content from the reality of the psyche and the mental-spiritual. Edith Stein examines this with great acuity in the analysis contained in *Beiträge zur philosophischen Begründung der Psychologie und Geisteswissenschaften* (*Contributions to the philosophical Foundation of Psycholoy and Human Sciences*). Husserl, too, speaks of the real structure of the human being having real dimensions that have to be recognized as such, inasmuch as these are the dimensions of awareness (of the consciousness and pure Ego) that make a transcendental inquiry possible .

14.7.2.2 The Ego and the Person

Husserl's analysis of the 'real' structure of the human being in *Ideen II* tells us that the lineaments of the personal Ego depend on corporeity, with a pre-given base that can be said to be psychic, but configures itself as a really unitary person in a superior sense inasmuch as it is subject to the positions assumed by the will, actions and thought. This is Husserl's way of construing the relationship between the pure Ego and the personal Ego. In short, the personal Ego functions as a free Ego. The pure Ego mirrors these processes and thus becomes the way we can access the bodily, psychic and spiritual reality that constitutes the personal Ego.

Edith Stein resumes this analysis in her *Contributions,* where she takes it further and arrives at identifying a core of the personality in which there resides the immutable consistency of its being. This is not the result of a development, but rather imposes a certain tendency upon this development. Since it is the unitary moment of the human being, this core has both a psychic and a mental-spiritual aspect, in keeping with the two fundamental dimensions out of which the human being is constituted. Stein says that the spiritual life of an individual is determined by the singularity of this core, and yet this core is something new with respect to this spiritual life and not even a complete knowledge of the spiritual or the psychic life would be sufficient for grasping it in its entirety.

The core would rather seem to coincide with the soul, because neither the core of the personality nor the being of the soul determined by this core displays any development capacity, whereas both the psychic and the spiritual capacities are capable of development.

Stein's treatment of the soul involves her in a number of complexities for several reasons. Firstly, because the term *Seele* is used by Edith Stein with a multiplicity of meanings, sometimes indicating the psyche and sometimes the combination of psyche and spirit; and there are also times when *Seele* denotes a wholly autonomous dimension, as we saw above. The analysis attains such subtlety and such lyrical expression as to astonish and seduce the reader. The pages dealing with this topic in *Contributions*, Part II, 2.3 c, which is dedicated to *the specific character qualities, 'soul' and 'core of the person'*, should be read with particular care.

Let me draw attention to a passage that may be considered, if not a summary, at least a conclusion drawn from a series of analyses, according to which the human personality, observed as a whole, presents itself to us as a unity of qualitative characteristics formed by a core, a formative principle. It is made up of soul, body and spirit, but it is only in the soul that the individuality expresses itself in a wholly pure manner, free of all admixtures. Neither the material living body nor the psyche, understood as a substantial unity of every sensitive and psycho-spiritual human being, nor the life of the individual are wholly determined by the core (Stein 1970, p. 215).

The core is supremely important for gaining access to the world of values, but account must also be taken of other forces or capacities peculiar to the psyche (the senses, the memory, the intellect and the will), and of course these must be explicated with regard to the external conditions, which also contribute greatly to the formation of the personality.

14.7.2.3 The Ego and the Self

Der Aufbau der menschlichen Person (*The Consitution of the human Person*), which brings together the lectures Edith Stein gave at the Münster Institute of Scientific Psychology in 1932, represents the work in which she explicitly begins to compare the results of phenomenological analysis with the philosophical reflections of Thomas Aquinas on the anthropological theme.

However, the author also confronts contemporary positions, most notably Heidegger's reading of *Dasein* and Jung's deep psychology, even though Stein doesn't mention Jung by name. She carefully sifts these interpretations and does not reject them prejudicially. Heidegger's analyses do not convince her, because his existential ones remain on the surface of the phenomenon of the 'human being' without ever penetrating to a sufficient depth, and as regards depth psychology – and in this direction she recognizes precursors both among the Romantics and the Russian writers Tolstoy and Dostojevski – she accords them the merit of having journeyed into an 'interior' dimension ignored by German idealism, by Lessing, by Herder, by Schiller, and by Goethe.

Particularly interesting is the relationship she established between the Ego and the self, thus coming to grips with a question that is still of considerable importance in our own day, because Jung's interpretation of the human being represents a rather common cultural model. In her opinion the self is to be identified with the bodily and psychic capacities of the human being that are given, but have to be formed. It is precisely the spiritual activity that has to intervene in the formation process and therefore the Ego manifests itself as a mental-spiritual and free person. Edith Stein's analysis proceeds in a predominantly phenomenological manner. The question that attracts her attention is that of the relationship between the Ego and the self, and namely the paradox that they are and are not the same thing. They are the same thing in view of the unity of the human being with which Edith Stein finds herself faced when examining human reality; but they are also not the same thing, because this unity reveals itself of such a complexity as to make it impossible for one element to be reduced to the other. And therefore in what relationship does the Ego that forms the self stand in relation to corporeity? It is situated in the body, but cannot be identified with it: 'Attempts have been made to do this in the past: but, even though the cerebral anatomy could also indicate a particular part of the brain ten destruction of which could comport a diminution of the "consciousness of the Ego" and of the entire personal-spiritual structure, we could not affirm that the Ego is situated in this part' (Stein 2004, p. 130). The proof of all this consists of the fact that the Ego is bound up with the lived experiences: 'I can go to any part of my living body and be present in it, even though some parts, the head and the heart for example, are closer to me than others' (Stein 2004, p. 130).

14.7.2.4 The Levels of the Human Being

Ego, soul, spiritual life, person – these terms are evidently closely related in *Ewiges und endliches Sein* (*Eternal and finite Being*) (Stein 2006). Here the author proposes a final and definitive delineation of the map of human interiority, and the different levels that constitute it are further specified and inserted in a unitary framework. As far as the methodological aspects are concerned, one may note that – ever since her earliest works – Stein proceeds concentrically, with circles that tend to become ever wider and reach greater profundities.

The centrality of the Ego is underscored; she arrives at the following definition: the Ego is the entity whose being is life. It dwells in the body and in the soul and is present in every part of the body and the soul, but, in particular, (here Stein takes up a theme introduced by A. Pfänder) the Ego seems to reside specifically behind the eyes at the center of the head – one might even compare it with the third eye present in the oriental tradition – and this is brought out by the fact that not only the looks of human beings are directed towards this point, but also those of some animals. This Ego is also conscious of itself, pervades the soul from surface to the depths, and is living, personal and spiritual in its manifestations.

'Surface' and 'profundity' are the guiding thread of an inquiry that takes into account the contributions made by both depth psychology, and phenomenological analysis. The two themes converge in delineating the map of human interiority, each contributing and adding a piece, a detail. Also in this case we gain an essential description of the various levels of which the human being is constituted.

The human being is not alone. Through the lived-experience of 'empathy' we can establish a link with other human beings, whom we recognize 'like' us. With them it is possible to live at different intersubjective levels, corresponding to our psychic attitude or mental-spiritual attitude. Collectively, we can live just as 'mass' or develop up to the level of 'community'. The description of community is one of the original aspects of Edith Stein's analysis. She believes that every human association that is well organized must be based on community level; this is the case of family, society, people and even State. Her ideas could clarify the meaning of community, a topic of current interest to many political scientists and sociologists.

Conrad-Martius' and Edith Stein's anthropological ontology should be better known within the human sciences. In particular, Edith Stein's purpose was to give a theoretical basis for the research in the field of psychology, psychopathology regarding subjectivity, and in the field of sociology, history, political sciences and all the human sciences in general that encompass our multiple intersubjective links.

References

Baianu, I. 2006. Robert Rosen's work and complex systems biology. *Axiomathes* 16:1–10 (Introduction to Axiomathes' special issue on Robert Rosen).

Baianu, I., and R. Poli. 2007. Simple, complex, super-complex systems: A paradigm shift towards non-abelian systems dynamics. In *TAO Theory and Application of Ontology*, eds. R. Poli, M. Healy, and A. Kameas, vol. 2, Computer Applications.

Conrad-Martius, H. 1923. Realontologie. *Jahrbuch für Philosophie und phänomenologische Forschung* VI:159–333.

Conrad-Martius, H. 1961. *Der selbstaufbau der natur*. Munich: Kösel Verlag.

Conrad-Martius, H. 1949. *Naturwissenschaftlich-metaphysische perspektiven*. Heidelberg: F. H. Kerle Verlag.

Conrad-Martius, H. 1948. *Bios und psyche*. Munich: Kösel..

Conrad-Martius, H. 1961. *Der selbst aufbau der natur*. Munich: Kösel.

Conrad-Martius, H. 1965. Die abstammung des menschen nach heutiger naturwissenschaft und der biblische schöpfung. In *Schriften zur Philosophie*,ed. E. Avé-Lallemant, vol. III. Munich: Kösel.

Goodwin, B. 2001. *How the leopard changed its spots. The evolution of complexity*, 2nd ed (1st edn 1994). Princeton, NJ: Princeton University Press.

Hering, J. 1921. Bemerkungen über das Wesen, die Wesenheit und die Idee. In „*Jahrbuch für Philosophie und phänomenologische Forschung*„ IV, Halle 1921, 495–543.

Husserl, E. 1989. *Ideas pertaining to a pure Phenomenology and to a phenomenological Philosophy*, vol. I. (trans: R. Rojcewicz and A. Schuwer). Dordrecht: Kluwer.

Husserl, E. 1984. *Logische Untersuchungen*. Zweiter Teil. Untersuchungen zur Phänomenologie und Theorie der Erkenntnis. In *zwei banden*. ed. Ursula Panzer. Halle: 1901; rev. ed. 1922. Husserliana 19, Dordrecht: Kluwer.

Husserl, E. 1977. *Ideen zu einer reinen Phänomenologie und phänomenologischen Philosophie*. Erstes Buch: Allgemeine Einführung in die reine Phänomenologie 1. Halbband: Text der 1.-3. Auflage – Nachdruck. Edited by Karl Schuhmann. Husserliana 3-1, Dordrecht: Kluwer.

Husserl, E. 1982. *Ideas pertaining to a pure phenomenology and to a phenomenological philosophy*, First Book. General Introduction to a Pure Phenomenology. Translated by Fred Kersten. Dorrdecht: Kluwer, 1982.

Husserl, E. 1974. *Formale and transzendentale Logik.* Versuch einer Kritik der logischen Vernunft." ed. Paul Janssen. Husserliana 17. Dordrecht: Kluwer.

Husserl, E. 1976. *Die Krisis der europäischen Wissenschaften und die transzendentale Phänomenologie.* Eine Einleitung in die phänomenologische Philosophie. ed. Walter Biemel. Husserliana 6. Dordrecht: Kluwer.

Mulligan, K. ed. 1987. *Speechact and Sachverhalt. Reinach and the foundations of realist Phenomenology*. Dordrecht: Martinus Nijhoff Publishers.

Poli, R. 2010. *An introduction to the ontology of anticipation*. Future 2010 (in press).

Reinach, A. 1969. *Űber Phänomenologie*, in Sämtliche Werke, herausgegeben von K Schuhmann und B. Smith, Philosophia Verlag, München. *Concerning Phenomenology*, "The Personalist" 50:194–221 (trans: D. Willard).

Reinach, A. 1989. *Notwendigkeit und Allgemeinheit im Sachverhalt* in Sämtliche Werke, herausgegeben von K. Schumann und B. Smith. München: Philosophia Verlag.

Zur Theorie des negativen Urteils, in Sämtliche Werke, herausgegeben von K. Schumann und B. Smith, Philosophia Verlag München 1989. *On the Theory of the negative Judgment*, in *Parts and moments: Studies in logic and formal ontology*. ed. B. Smith. München: Philosophia Verlag, 1982.

Reinach, A. 1983. *Die apriorischen Grundlagen des bürgerlichen Rechtes.* In Sämtliche Werke, herausgegeben von K. Schuhmann, and B. Smith. München: Philosophia Verlag. The a priori foundation of the civil law. *Aletheia* 3:1–142.

Reinach, A. 1989a. In *Űber Phänomenologie*, ed. S. Werke. herausgegeben von K. Schuhmann und B. Smith. München: Philosophia Verlag. Concerning Phenomenology. *The Personalist* 50: 194–221 (1969). Translation D. Willard.

Reinach, A. 1989b. In *Zur Theorie des negativen Urteils*, ed. S. Werke. herausgegeben von K. Schumann und B. Smith. München: Philosophia Verlag . [*On the Theory of the negative Judgment*, in *Parts and Moments: Studies in Logic and formal Ontology*, ed. by B. Smith, München: Philosophia Verlag (1982)].

Reinach, A. 1989c. In *Die apriorischen Grundlagen des bürgerlichen Rechtes*, ed. S. Werke. herausgegeben von K. Schuhmann and B. Smith. München: Philosophia Verlag. [The a priori Foundation of the civil Law. *Aletheia* 3: 1–142 (1983)].

Rosen, R. 2007. *Anticipatory systems. Philosophical, mathematical and methodological foundations*, 2nd edn. Polimetrica, Monza, (1st edn. Pergamon Press, 1985).

Stein, E. 1970. *Beiträge zur philosophischen Begründung der Psychologie und der Geisteswissenschaften,* Tübingen: Max Niemeyer Verlag.

Stein, E. 1974, *Husserls Phänomenologie und die Philosophie des heiligen Thomas von Aquin. Versuch einer Gegenüberstellung*, Festschrift Edmund Husserl zum 70. Geburtstag, Ergänzungsband zum Jahrbuch für Philosophie und Phänomenologische Forschung, Max Niemeyer Verlag, Tübingen, pp. 315–338.

Stein, E. 1991. *Einführung in die Philosophie,* ESGA, vol. 8. Freiburg i.Br.: Herder.

Stein, E. 2004. *Der Aufbau der menschlichen Person*, ESGA, vol. 14. Freiburg i.Br.: Herder.

Stein, E. 2005. Potenz und Akt: Studien zur einer Philosophie des Seins. In *Gesamtausgabe*, ed. K. Mass, and H.R. Sepp, vol. 10. Freiburg: Herder.

Stein, E. 2006. *Endliches und ewiges Sein. Versuch eines Aufstiegs zum Sinn des Seins*, ESGA, vol. 11/12. Freiburg i.Br.: Herder.

Chapter 15
Phenomenology and Ontology in Nicolai Hartmann and Roman Ingarden

Nicoletta Ghigi

15.1 Phenomenology and Ontology in Hartmann

15.1.1 The Neo-Kantian Phase and the Scientific Foundation of Philosophy

After having abandoned medical school for studies in philosophy and philology at the University of St. Petersburg, Hartmann met one of his most important Russian professors, Nikolaj O. Losski,[1] who can be seen as an important precursor of Hartmann's future philosophical outlook, especially because of his intuitivistic conception of knowledge and his affirmation of the connection between gnoseology and ontology. Transferring to Marburg in 1905 to pursue the neo-Kantian school, Hartmann became the student of Hermann Cohen and Paul Natorp. Here began the neo-Kantian phase of his early oeuvre, with works such as *Platos Logik des Seins* (The Platonic Logic of Being) and *Über des Proklus Diadochus philosophische Anfangsgründe der Mathematik* (On the Philosophical Fundamentals of the Mathematics of Proclus Diadocus), written to obtain his certification for university teaching. The general approach of these works strongly reflects the neo-Kantian influence in the form of themes such as 'pure thought' and 'logic of origin'.[2]

As Cohen asserted, ideas, the fulcrum of Platonic metaphysics, are not real entities but logical functions of knowing, and it is the task of philosophy to establish

N. Ghigi (✉)
University of Perugia, Perugia, Italy
e-mail: nicoletta.ghigi@unipg.it

[1]For the influence and importance of Hartmann's Russian professors on his thought, see Harich 1983, pp. 1303–1322.

[2]Hartmann acknowledges that his study of Plato seeks "traces of the logical elements in order to demonstrate their determining function, as explained by Plato, where it is possible to find them [. . .]. In this sense, the logic of being, as we are trying to interpret the doctrine of ideas [. . .] does not claim to be the only point of view possible, but rather the decisive one for the purposes of philosophical evaluation» (Hartmann 1965a, pp. V-VI).

R. Poli, J. Seibt (eds.), *Theory and Applications of Ontology: Philosophical Perspectives*, DOI 10.1007/978-90-481-8845-1_15,

the conditions and possibilities for such a cognitive act. The Platonic idea is thus only a scientific hypothesis and has no reality; the penetrative force of intuition is consequently abandoned because it is a re-opening to metaphysics, which, because of its logical groundlessness, is defined as poetic and mythic and thus non-scientific and dogmatic (Hartmann 1965b, pp. V–VI).[3]

The logical interpretation of Platonism and the anti-metaphysical structure of these first two works shows us a young Hartmann whose perspective – although its contents will change – corresponds with an exigency that will remain constant in his future philosophical production: the fact that, for him, 'authentic philosophy,' Barone observes, 'must move, even though it maintains its original task, in accordance with the scientific orientation' (Barone 1963).

15.1.2 The Entrance of Phenomenology into the Neo-Kantian Framework

In the works that follow his teaching certification, *Philosophische Grundfragen der Biologie*, *Systematische Methode* and *Systembildung und Idealismus* (1912), Hartmann begins progressively distancing himself from the principal themes of the Marburg school, though the departure from neo-Kantianism is not a sharp and definitive one. While he remains interested in a scientific foundation for authentic philosophical reflection, it is also true that once the fundamental neo-Kantian conviction that identified being with pure thought is traced to its origins in the categorial forms of judgment, he sees an evident limitation that jeopardizes its very scientific and universal legitimacy. The same attains with the rejection of metaphysics, understood as synonymous with dogmatism and abstractness. If the premise of neo-Kantian philosophy is consigned to the categorial logical closure of judgment by which its scientificity is relative to 'pure thought' and, thus, to the limitations that, as has been said, this scientificness, the non-dogmatic legitimacy of philosophy itself is undermined.

Thus it is necessary to develop a new concept of this scientificness as well as to reconsider what is *truly* dogmatic, strictly speaking. During these years, Hartmann moves closer to Husserl, in particular to the works of this time, such as *Die Philosophie als strenge Wissenschaft* (1911) (*Philosophy as rigouros science*) and *Ideen zur einer reinen Phänomenologie* (1913) (*Ideas for a pure phenomenology*), articulating a new concept of authentic philosophy as scientifically rigorous, that is, founded on carefully evaluated bases and premises, and also a reconsideration

[3]Notwithstanding Hartmann's profession of faith in Cohen's outlook, Sirchia observes: "In accepting the logical-methodological meaning of the idea, he does nothing other than appropriate as a "working hypothesis"[...] that which in Cohen instead was a sure point of departure for a whole long-range autonomous theoretical reconstruction" (Sirchia, 1969, p. 28). See also: Werkmeister (1990).

of metaphysical science and of phenomenologically founded philosophy as 'access routes to the authentic metaphysics of nature, the spirit, and ideas' (Husserl 1987, p. 37). Precisely in opposing the neo-Kantian categorial limitation of being to a merely logical-conceptual definition, the phenomenological re-evaluation of the premises of knowledge itself, and, even more fundamentally, of the very possibility of knowing, enables Hartmann to re-think the ontological question from a new point of view, free from the cramped limits of 'pure thought.'

However, Hartmann feels that phenomenology, precisely because it is tied to the phenomenon, to the given, and, above all, to a 'placing in parenthesis' of the worldly being, remains far from the true being, and thus slips into a superficial reconstruction of the phenomenical datum, albeit on the basis of a critical reassessment. Thus for these reasons he sees phenomenology as just the first, albeit necessary, step toward the construction of a science of being, and certainly not the point of arrival. What is given is what is offered to the subject; but in this givenness there is evidently something that is present, with or without the representation of the object itself. In this sense, Hartmann writes, phenomenology 'stops at the phenomena described as such, believing that it has reached the essence of the thing by 'showing' the general element, and calls this absolute. Thus it ignores the problems inherent in phenomena'. In reality, instead, if it intends to be the science of authentic being, the description for phenomenology should be only 'a preliminary step in the search, an entranceway, a way for regaining, in their originality, the great fundamental interrogatives' (Hartmann 1955, pp. 129–130).

For this reason, once the problems that derive from phenomena have been identified, there is a need for an aporetics, a reflection of philosophy on 'what has not been comprehended in the phenomena' in order to 'clearly identify the natural aporias. In this stage [philosophy] constitutes the aporetics. Only in a third step can it attempt a solution of aporias, that is, to go toward a theory' (*ib*., p. 130).

In this sense, the contribution of phenomenology is essential but insufficient for reaching the truth about the knowledge of being. Even though its objective is scientific clarification of the assumptions underlying knowledge, it stops at the description of the phenomenical datum and does not even manage to foresee the difficulties arising from such a representation. Phenomenology thus does not see that residue that remains in the givenness of the phenomenon. It does not understand that in the aporeticity of this residue, in the irrepressible transcendence that, even so, it had encountered in its own analyses, there is hidden an immense patrimony, the fundamental element for authentic knowledge. In other words, being cannot be reduced to phenomenicity. What remains, beyond the perception of the datum is something too essential to set aside and suspend with an epoché.

While phenomenology 'can know only phenomena', Hartmann resolutely affirms, 'one must nevertheless conduct a particular inquiry on the character of being. It is in this inquiry that the work of ontology consists. Real being 'as such' is never being 'as it shows itself' (as phenomenon), but being 'as it is in itself' (as apparent behind the phenomenon)'(*Ib.*, p. 222).

15.1.3 The Overcoming of Phenomenology: the Metaphysics of Knowing

Phenomenology is thus the premise of ontology. It indicates how the object of knowledge is constituted. But, in the light of these capacities, in describing and analysing the phenomenological datum, phenomenology fundamentally also has another function: bringing to light the metaphysical foundation of knowing (Hartmann 1965).[4] If in fact knowledge of the phenomenic datum is knowledge of the transcendence of the being, it is at the same time the unknowability of what is not representation. And this 'residue' is indicated by phenomenology. Hartmann maintains that knowledge is not a creating, a producing, a 'bringing the object to light,' but is rather the comprehension that there is something that precedes knowledge and that is totally independent of it.

Consciousness thus attained knowledge of the object when it understood the insurmountable limitation of the *transobjective* and hence in the moment in which it *objects to* the latter as unintelligible. The awareness of this limitation represents for consciousness its gnoseologic possibility, or better, the metaphysics of knowledge. In fact, he writes that 'knowledge is neither a psychological nor a logical problem, but fundamentally, a metaphysical one' (*ib.*, p. 3). Thus constructing a new metaphysics, with knowledge as its foundation, is unnecessary; vice-versa, what is required is to lay the groundwork for a theory of knowledge, founded upon metaphysics.

Therefore one understands the meaning of metaphysics in relation to knowledge: metaphysics is the conscious knowledge of the gnoseological limit imposed by the transcendence of the given object, of reality. The problem of reality is thus a metaphysical one: for this reason, there is a need for a metaphysical knowledge able to comprehend the reality's structure, a critical metaphysics as inquiry into the nature of real being. In the realization of this objective, phenomenology enters into play, above all bringing to light the development of the cognitive process and the metaphysical sphere to which the object belongs, from which the images and knowledge are formed. In fact, the 'content of the phenomenon' is metaphysical. The aporeticity of the relationship between knowing subject and known object is thus of a transcendent nature; the being in itself of the subject's wanting and desiring is transcendent; it is not depleted in the gnoseologic dimension. The being of the object represented is transcendent; it hides in its nature a necessary and structural precondition. The transobjective in the subject, on the one hand, and the transobjective of the object, on the other, form the so-called 'aporias.' 'The subject and the object are more than knower and known; they are both transcendent, both have a being in itself, so there is also a need for the relationship of knowledge as transcendent' (*ib.*, p. 61).

The immediate aporia presents quickly itself between the object known and the image we have of it, before which one immediately asks oneself how much this

---

[4]But, he warns, "a phenomenology of knowing as essential analysis of the metaphysics of the cognitive phenomenon is not yet present to date" (Hartmann 1965b, p. 38).

is real or not. The gnoseological possibility thus assumes the aporetic character, because the cognitive subject also presents its own knowledge of the object (ideal or fruit of the image) that claims to be real. The solution that Hartmann proposes for this aporeticity regards seeing whether 'the enigma of knowledge' becomes more or less comprehensible through the metaphysical hypothesis, whether it resolves into a smaller or greater enigma (*ib.*, pp. 125–128).

Thus the goal of critical metaphysics is to resolve this principle aporia considering the common foundation underlying the two spheres of the knower and the known: being is the common ground to which the individual parts must refer. Knowledge is one, the same that belongs to being. For this reason, subject and object can no longer call themselves separate but part of a unity forming their foundation.

'The aporia of immanence-transcendence, writes Barone, is no longer an impediment, inasmuch as consciousness also belongs to the same ontic sphere of the transcendent object and is the point in which being reflects on itself' (Barone 1963, p. 21). The object in its reality participates in the categorial formation, just as the subject participates in unrevealing the transcendent peculiarity of the object.

In this way, the metaphysics of knowledge solves the aporia and, therefore, attains a true theory of knowledge that has in being, in the ontological sphere, its point of departure, its original terrain.

15.1.4 'Critical ontology' and Realism

Since the experimental sciences say nothing, but only assume reality, the objective of a philosophical theory is to recover everything that goes beyond their sphere (everything that is fundamentally unknowable for knowledge) and therefore give rise to a 'metaphysics of knowledge'; that is, as Vanni Rovighi writes, to a science that can 'grasp these unknowable realities in their most universal aspect of entities', from which it is possible, according to Hartmann, 'to formulate a theory of entity as entity. This, in fact, is ontology [. . .] Hartmann thus distinguishes ontology, which is metaphysics in the broad sense, from metaphysics strictly speaking, which is speculation on the ultimate foundation of being, on *Weltgrund*, which, according to him, is not rationally possible' (Vanni Rovighi, p. 176).

Ontology is therefore the metaphysics that focuses attention on the intellectually attainable entity. But it is distinguished from metaphysics, which instead draws from that which is rationally unknowable, that is, the ultimate foundation of being. In this way, the metaphysics of knowledge means nothing other than the clarification of that which philosophy can consider its cognitive patrimony, and what instead lies beyond the province of its possibilities. In addition, ontology moves in a completely different plane than that of true metaphysics, that is, from the reality with which it is concerned. While metaphysics examines the ultimate foundation of being, ontology stops at being, at the entity in itself, independent of its phenomenicity, from that appearing that phenomenology considered the authentic reality of the object.

Against idealism, Hartmann sustains therefore that knowing means having to do with an itself ('an sich') that is transobjective: 'For the givenness of the being in itself, he explains, the entrance into action of the cognitive phenomenon has a decisive meaning' Hartmann 1965b, p. 162). Neither idealism nor realism were able to recognize the metaphysical character of the entity. In fact, like the idealistic theories, the realistic ones also seek to 'comprehend the essence of the so-called real world, and its way of reality. And if they explain this world as pure 'phenomenon,' or for that matter as empty appearance and illusion, it nonetheless is precisely an interpretation of the phenomenon, an explanation; it's not so much an exclusion of the problem of being, as a theory for facing it' (*ib.*, p. 37).

So then, the two positions provide a definition of being that excludes its transcendent consideration, its being in itself from which the phenomenon itself originates. In the same way, phenomenology, 'exiting' empirical consciousness with the consideration of an extra-subjective reality such as the transcendental 'I', has done nothing other than postpone the problem of reality, without finding any possibility for a solution.

Therefore, granting that being in itself also precedes the formation of the phenomenon, it is necessary to reckon with its modality of revealing itself. «Among the transcendent acts, writes Hartmann, knowledge is the most transparent, pure, and objective. However, it is not the most important testimony to being in itself» (*ib.*, p. 163). For Hartmann, knowledge is not the only thing able to give us the trace of being in itself; above all, the emotional states, such as sentimental states, volitions, and actions are what enable us to deduce the presence of a reality in itself.[5]

'The gnoseologic act always arises only from an interwoven set of acts that are more deeply rooted and just as transcendent; more often than not, it does not even emerge from them, but remains entangled among them[...]But this rootedness is fundamental for the problem of being: in the vital connection of acts, it pushes more deeply into the totality of the entity' (Hartmann 1965b, p. 163).

These acts are the emotional-transcendent acts, that is, forms with which man 'feels' even before knowing, independently of his will for choice. For Hartmann, this direction offers another, even deeper way of reaching being, reaching the transcendence of the real in its unfolding.[6] Again, against idealism, Hartmann tries to re-vivify the validity preceding the gnoseologic activity in the emotional acts. As clearly noted in Husserl's *Ideas II*, this is a way to take into account the spiritual life and the non-categorial acts, like an autonomous set of truths that explicitly speak of real being.

---

[5]This approach differs from Husserlian metaphysics: "Hartmann's metaphysics, explains Vanni Rovighi, is realistic, while that of Husserl is idealistic, but the position of the problem of knowledge is idealistic in Hartmann, realistic in Husserl, because for Hartmann, I know some facts of my consciousness and from these I have to deduce a reality in itself, while for Husserl, I know some realities, even though he then concludes that these realities are created by a transcendental 'I'" (Vanni Rovighi 1939, p. 181).

[6]He also deals with this problem in Hartmann 1931.

In this order of ideas, the metaphysical counters the idealistic, that is, it counters all that grants privilege to the subjective sphere (understood as rational and logical) over the impulsive and sentimental, irrational one. According to the 'pre-critical' philosophy that Hartmann seems to want to follow, the irrational fact must be recovered and inserted into ontological science (into the metaphysics of knowledge), and in contrast to the classical ontology that favoured the aprioristic and deductive character, and also to all that was unable to draw from the thematized experience all the implicit consequences. Contrary to the position of Platonism, Hartmann holds that the real being is not inferior to the ideal being: equal importance should also be given in a foundation of ontology to the *pure un-reales* (*reine Irreale*) that are not ideal forms, but transcend toward a being in itself, that of reality.

The phenomenological framework, implemented by a vigorous renewal of the theme of reality in itself as reality not idealistically understood in a subjective way, also draws attention to the so-called irrational aspects of life and of human reality. At the same time, the metaphysics of knowledge overcomes the phenomenological framework, which remains trapped in a construct of idealistic reality, offering instead of reality emotional states and emotional acts that are receptive of their irrational structure, from which emerges, in all its force, being 'in itself,' 'independently of knowing, never exhausted by knowing, constantly transcending the cognitive sphere and not at all 'correlated' to it' (Penati 1975, p. XVII).[7]

15.1.5 The Theory of the Levels of Reality

In terms of the problem of reality, Hartmann observes that there are multiple overlapping strata of being that are reciprocally placed in relation by various laws and governed by categorial structures. Within so-called nature, he felt it was necessary to set a line of demarcation between that which is living and that which is not, or in other words, between the organic and the inorganic. Similarly, in the spirit it is possible to distinguish between psychic phenomena and objective contents given by man's communitarian life. Thus four principle strata build the real world, intertwining on the basis of physical or material being, which is the basis of everything, and subsists independently from everything.

Now, for Hartmann, as for Husserl, reality (*Realität*) and effectuality (*Wirklichkeit*) are not the same thing. 'In the realm of the real there are also real possibility and real necessity: this realm comprises the modes of being, which for that matter also re-present themselves in eventual other realms of the entity [. . .]. Inasmuch as the essences have a being, albeit not real, their possibility and their necessity are

[7]Hartmann writes in regard to emotional acts such as loving, hating, living, etc., "that all these emotional acts have a counterpart to whom they are directed, and the real world consists precisely in the totality of these counterparts, in the measure in which it is conceived (and becomes an object for us). The transcendent acts represent the ways of relationship between consciousness and the world in which it finds itself. One could also say: such acts represent this staying-inside itself" (Hartmann 1982, p. 17).

equally ontic' (Hartmann 1965b, p. 68). Therefore, to his mind, it is not possible to exclude from this realm the ideal being. Reality is thus marked by different qualifications that can be identified by a 'categorical' analysis of we intend in terms of 'being'.

In the work, *Der Aufbau der Welt* (*The constitution of the world*), Hartmann provides his ontological proposal about the *determination* of effectual reality. To his mind, though this categorial analysis it is possible to reach the constitution of reality. In Hartmann, as in Aristotle, the categories mean not only the substance but also the connotations of substance. In addition, unlike Aristotle, they are fundamental structures of the real world, principles immanent to the world and, therefore, entirely anti-subjectivistic (to pick up Husserl's critique) and necessary (Hartmann, 1964, p. 2). The prerequisite for this categorial analysis is the *stratification* of the world into a series of levels. As stated above, there is inorganic nature, organic nature, psychic nature, and spiritual being. Now, the categories refer to all these strata: there are modal categories (that emerge from the reflection of *Möglichkeit und Wirklichkeit*), for which possibility and need are only relative modes of being, meaningless outside the fundamental mode, or in other words, outside the mode of effectuality (Hartmann 1964, p. V); the categories linked to couples (or *bipolar* categories, such as unity-multiplicity, quality-quantity, continuous-discrete, form-matter, etc.) that cross through all the strata of being, and the categories that express the fundamental laws of real being and therefore the determination of effectual reality. The categories common to all the strata are existence, temporality, and processuality.

The categories in turn are divided into four groups that underlie the principle of value, coherence, planning and dependence. The laws of value clarify that value is not the equivalent of normativity (legality), but rather of the laws of nature of or mathematical laws. For this reason, their universality is guaranteed. The planning laws express the relationship and degrees among the various levels of reality. In this direction, for Hartmann, the lower categories return to the higher ones, but not vice-versa. Every level of being therefore implies a new categorial moment that cannot be reduced to the lower elements or their synthesis (laws of the *novum* by which every successive stratum is born from a 'new' categorial moment.)

In this regard, he distinguishes over-forming (*Überformung*) from building-above (*Überbauung*) (Hartmann 1962, pp. 66–69). The latter occurs when the upper level does not conserve the categories of the lower level; the former happens when there is a relationship within which the successive stratum comes to be the form of the preceding one, that is, that constitutes its '*external basis of existential support*' (Poli 1998, p. 203). In this principle of dependence by which every higher stratum implies the preceding one, Hartmann indicates various laws: the law of strength (the highest category always presupposes the lower categorial series); the law of indifference (the lower stratum is indifferent to being the foundation of the next one); the law of matter (in over-forming the lower category is the material for the next one); the law of freedom (the highest categories are founded on the lowest, but unlike them, have their own autonomy).

In terms of the psychic level, one can say that compared with the organic one, it is a building-above in which there is no longer the category of space that dominates in the organic being. The objective spirit is an over-forming because it raises itself up above consciousness exactly as much as consciousness raises itself up above the organism. Just as consciousness leaves outside itself the organic world's spatiality and materiality, so the objective spirit raises itself up above an impersonal horizon that elevates itself above the spiritual being. However, the autonomy of the psychic from the inorganic is of another type and order than that of the organic from the material.

Instead, this relationship which like over-forming can be called building-above, or in other words: 'From the lower stratum and resting on it, it elevates to a higher stratum in which not all the categories of the first return [. . .] almost as if they were made of a different material' (Hartmann 1962, p. 68).

The objective spirit, inasmuch as it is a *novum* compared to the level of personal consciousness, is not a jumble of individuals, but rather, a set of forms, contents, and principles. The 'different material,' or in other words, the reality of the spirit, is that which gives form to literature and the arts, etc. The reign of the spirit is a world unto itself, above the psychic life that permits the constitution of the human reality. But there is also a 'common spirit,' the living spirit. Thus for Hartmann, the three forms of the spiritual being are connected in a reciprocal relationship: 'The personal spirit and the objective one share a relationship of profound heterogeneity, so that taken by themselves, they reveal no common bond. However, they are connected in the objective spirit: in fact, both, albeit in very different ways, are connected to it' (*ib.*, p. 71).

The three forms of the spirit (personal, objective, and objectivated), however, in the stratified structure of the world and of its categorial laws, neither build-above nor over-form each other, but belong to the concrete and indivisible unity of an identical ontic stratum of being; better still, in their intertwining they are precisely what constitute this stratum. Thus they are in the same relationship in terms of psychic, organic, and material being. 'Together and in the same mode, 'they rest upon' the same stratum; they are not afloat and, if we remove their real foundation from under their feet, they will collapse' (*ib.*, p. 76).

Resting upon reality, upon the stratum of being that precedes it, the objective spirit is the protagonist of history and in its interpenetration with the spirit of the person gives rise to the living spirit. In this sense, for Hartmann, in the determination of being mentioned above, the human person in his individuality maintains his freedom of action. However, in this categorial form (in the interpenetration of the objective spirit and personal consciousness) that constitutes the living being, there re-appears the necessitating determination of each category, and thus, also the determination to which the individual consciousness is necessarily subjected.

15.2 Phenomenology and Ontology in Roman Ingarden

15.2.1 Phenomenology as a Point of Departure

Roman Ingarden also followed the teaching of Edmund Husserl. Having studied mathematics and philosophy at Lvov with Kazimierz Twardowski (who was also a student of Brentano's) he moved to Göttingen where Husserl was, and attended seminars and lessons from 1912 to 1915. When the latter transferred to Freiburg, Ingarden followed him, writing his doctoral dissertation on 'Intuition und Intellekt bei Henri Bergson' (Intuition and intellect in Henry Bergson). Having obtained his certification for teaching in 1925, he taught at both the high school and university level. During a long journey in this period, he wrote the work that made him famous, *Das literarische Kustwerk* (The literary Work of Art), which was published in 1930 and enabled him to obtain a position at the University of Lvov. The reflections of this period, influenced by the political tragedy of the war, flowed into the principle work: *The Controversy on the Existence of the World*, completed in 1945 in Cracow and subsequently revised and translated into German as *Der Streit um die Existenz der Welt*.

The main objective of the young Ingarden, student of Husserl, is to comprehend the value and meaning of transcendental phenomenology in terms of a foundation of the concrete world, of concrete worldly experience. 'Quite early on, he confessed in *The Controversy on the Existence of the World,* I realized that inquiries oriented only subjectively were insufficient [...]. More in particular, it was necessary to clarify the meaning of the 'categories' and the fundamental structures of the real object' (Ingarden 1960, I, p. 5).

Like Hartmann, Ingarden[8] also acknowledged phenomenology has the merit of coming close to the problem of the constitution of the objective world, but judged that it failed to succeed, because of the fact that intentionality, read as the principal aspect for the transcendental constitution of objective reality, impedes effectively 'seeing' real objects in their existence, rather than in their revelation to consciousness. According to his point of view, phenomenology comes close to philosophical problems and represents a sort of method and theoretical system by which the fundamental problems of reality are approached from the point of view of their essence and their constitution. But, against the absolutization of the real world, writes Ingarden, Husserl considers that 'the existence which is only 'for' the conscious subject and does not possess its own essence is not to be considered as a being 'in itself' which is endowed with its own effective essence» (Ingarden 1975, p. 5).

In other words, with the objective of achieving a philosophy as a 'rigorous' science, Husserl applies to consciousness the transcendental reduction, eliminating the real consciousness and its acts in order to substitute it with an impersonal subject, the transcendental 'I' for which reality is the object of its constitution. In this way the 'in itself' of the world is no longer of value and is thus subjected to a suspension of judgment regarding its existence. But even the conscious acts, realistically directed toward an objective reality, with the inclusion of the intentional object, remain a

[8]Also from Ingarden's same school in Göttingen was Conrad-Martius who, in his *Realontologie* (1923), called attention to the themes of an ontology understood as science of being, and thus criticized as idealist the position of his professor after *Ideas*.

simply transcendental fact, and thus enter in a framework of idealistic immanentization. Transcendence and the 'in itself' of the world undergo a harsh change in the idealistic phase of phenomenology. For Ingarden, this suspension of the natural attitude and the suspension of judgment that leads to transcendental phenomenology impede philosophy from becoming a science (*ib.*, pp-38–43).

As Hartmann asserted, in fact, Husserlian phenomenology does not take into account this 'in itself,' which it relegates to the natural attitude, to be 'overcome' through transcendental reduction. Therefore it does not explain the fact that there is a reality 'in itself' toward which our consciousness 'has some limits'. 'The term 'phenomenology' has different meanings in Husserl himself and in his students, meanings that have never been articulated with precision' (Ingarden 1960, I, p. 60, note 1). Among these are ontology and metaphysics, as sciences concerned with the existing being and the world in a rigorous and scientific manner, something that Husserl's phenomenology, according to Ingarden, did not bring to a proper conclusion.

The problem of fundamental Husserlian phenomenology is that of having passed from a realistic position (that of *Logical Investigations,* in which objective reality had its own value independently of the cognitive factor that the eidetic reduction allowed to survive) to transcendental idealism, in which objective reality is that to which the subject is intentionally directed, and is thus its representation, constitution of the subject.[9] In this way, however, the initial realistic framework was completely abandoned to the detriment of a possible interpretation of the 'existing' and 'existence' of the concrete world.

15.2.2 'Ontic Moments' and Existential Analysis

Before beginning his analysis of ontology as existential ontology and thus dealing with the question of the existence of the world, Ingarden intends to clarify the meaning of the term existence: 'Existence or the mode of existence is always existence or the mode of existence of something, never something separate *per se* [. . .] therefore there exists uniquely the idea of the existence of *something* (in this or that mode)' (Ingarden 1960, I, p. 79). This is meant to reaffirm that, as Husserl had already asserted, the modality of existence, the themselves-giving of things, is foundational to their existential possibility. In this regard, Ingarden shows the possibility for analyzing existence, affirming that 'the reality itself of something (in the sense of the real 'being') is only one of the modes of existence, that can be opposed to other modes of existence' (*ib.*, p. 81). The objective that he sought, then, was

[9]Ingarden recalls that the difference in position between Husserl and the Göttingen school that gathered his ex-students of that university, began precisely with the publication of *Ideas I*. During the lesson following discussion of some sections that should have been read at home, "very lively discussions arose because many of Husserl's older students advanced various objections against the idealistic tendencies that surfaced in *Ideas I,* as well as in reference to the sense and function of the transcendental reduction" (Ingarden 1968, p. 113).

to clarify the relationship between the modes of existence and the moments that he defines as 'ontic moments'. Ontic moments are «something that can be distinguished in the individual modes of existence of something, but because of its essence will not let itself be separated from the mode of existence in which it is distinguished» (*ib*., p. 92).

In other words, while the mode of existence will not let itself be separated from the object to which it 'belongs,' 'the ontic moment is characterized however by an inseparability of a higher degree' (*ibidem*). In fact, no ontic moment is sufficient in and of itself for the existence of an object in some mode of existence, while in every mode of existence of something 'many different ontic moments can be distinguished intuitively' (*ib*., p. 93). Now, since the ontic moments are real, precisely of the real world of existence, then, as said above, they belong to the mode of existence to which they refer, and, according to Ingarden, head three pairs of opposites: ontic autonomy and heteronomy, self-sufficiency and ontic non-self-sufficiency, and finally, ontic dependence and non-dependence.

Now, writes Ingarden, 'something exists in autonomous mode if [...] it has in itself its own ontic foundation. And it has this foundation in itself if it is determined in itself immanently' (*ib*., p. 94). This divergence from phenomenology that distances him from Husserl's transcendental turning point, obviously also bears upon the consideration of reality and intentionality. In this regard, Ingarden writes, 'to this end I have sought an object whose pure intentionality was beyond any doubt and on the basis of which one could study the essential structures and the mode of existence of purely intentional object without being subject to suggestions stemming from considerations of real objectivities. The literary work seemed to me an object of investigation particularly suitable for this purpose. As I concerned myself with it in greater detail, however, specific problems of literary theory opened up to me, and their treatment, in conjunction with the basis goals mentioned above, produced the present book' (Ingarden 1973, pp. LXXII–LXXIII).

Thus the problem of ontic modes and modalities of reality, form and the mode of existence, take on substance in the study of the literary work as 'mode of existence.' Its heteronomous nature, inasmuch as objective and subjective at the same time, enables the work of art to be a structure with a 'polyphonic character.' In this sense, it is a formation composed of four different strata that are heterogeneous but in interaction: 'That is to say [...] each of them is visible in its own way within the whole [...]. In particular, each of these strata has its own set of properties which contribute to the constitution of specific aesthetic value qualities. There thus arises a manifold of aesthetic value qualities in which a polyphonic yet uniform value quality of the whole is constituted' (*ib*., p. 30).

The first stratum is that 'of *word sounds* and the *phonetic formation*' such as simple and complex propositions, words, and temporal scansions (time and rhythm). This stratum is essential as the foundation for the other three (hence the similarity with Hartmann in his differentiation between over-forming and building-above in the different strata of being (cf. Poli 1998, p. 205 and ff.).

The second stratum is that of the '*meaning units* of various orders', such as words, propositions, and sets of propositions (Ingarden 1973, p. 30). Its function is to provide the structural framework of the whole work and thus presupposes all the other strata that have in this stratum their ontic bases (cf. *ibidem*, p. 29). Now, this stratum does not have an autonomous ideal existence. Rather, the meaning of a noun is given by what the word intentionally designates, by the 'intentional object projected' that constitutes the intentional correlate of a given verbal sound.

The third stratum is that of the 'manifold schematized *aspects*' (*ibidem*, p. 30). The schematic mode in which a given object is thematized from an individual does not exhaust the qualities of the object in question: thus many qualities remain unrealized. This stratum, then, highlights the unity of realized and unrealized qualities that can potentially be 'filled' through the contents that the reader has previously taken in, and thus through the framework with which we portray the object through the qualities realized. For Ingarden, this is the context for the problem of the *points of indetermination,* according to which each work of art contains parts for which the text provides no details. He considers this question useful in distinguishing the object of the empirical world from the object created intentionally within a work, because here aspects are constituted that lie beyond the author's intentionality and hence develop different determinations of the object represented. But the finality of this theory does not stop here, because, as Poli observes, it 'is generalizable to the ontologically and cognitively fundamental problem of the degrees of freedom of the object represented' (Poli 1998, p. 206)

The third stratum is that of '*represented objectivities* and their vicissitudes' (*ibidem*), and is constituted of objects such as things, persons, states of things, etc., that are intentioned by the units of meaning that derive from words and propositions, which are the aspect that most interest the reader. They are the objects represented by a proposition, the significance (intentionality) of which depends on the conscious act of the reader, and thus constitute a unified ontic sphere where the objects (represented as existent) are operating.

Through these stratifications present in the literary work, Ingarden comes to philosophical reflection on the reality of such moments, and, establishing the degrees of possibility of the same intentional object according to the points of indetermination, thus arrives at the point of defining the borders of ontology. Thus before dealing with the problems concerning the real existence of the world, that is, the metaphysical problems, Ingarden intends to address the meaning this existence can have in relation to the request for meaning to which humanity in and of itself is called constitutively to give an account.

Drawing upon the eidetic theme of Husserlian phenomenology, Ingarden understands ontology as the '*a priori*' analysis of the content of the idea, regardless of the existence of the object in question. For this reason, ontology must be the 'premise' for dealing with the themes of metaphysics and, therefore, the problem of existence. Ontology, because of its character as *a priori* analytics (just as in the stratifications present in the approach to literary work), is the foundation of metaphysics that addresses the question of the real existence of the objects that ontological analytics examines in various moments. This point of view renders comprehensible Ingarden's distinctions of an *existential, formal* and *material* ontology, from which it is possible to set up the fundamental metaphysical problems as premises.

Existential ontology, first of all, leaving to metaphysics the task of establishing whether an object exists or not, has the objective of comprehending the kind of existence that it is assigned by its essence. This requires 'a purely ontological analysis of the idea of existence in general' (Ingarden 1960, p. 69). *Formal ontology* has the goal of analyzing the form of the object in order to establish which it is (if it is a thing, a proposition, a relation, etc.). Finally, *material ontology* studies the object as a complex of material moments, that is, of the qualities that compose and determine it.

Therefore, having clarified the formal-ontological aspects of the question about existence, it is now possible to return to the issue of the value that existence itself has for humanity and thus, to deal with the material question of the world, starting from the material ontology Husserl spoke of, and referring to it the acquisitions of an existential ontology, as an openness to metaphysics, that is beyond the controversy between idealism and realism.

15.2.3 Ontology as Recovery of the World

'Husserl's world, writes Ingarden, is a simple creation of acts of consciousness' (Ingarden 1960, I, p. 171). For him, the existence of the world is always an existence for a transcendental subject, or for a plurality of monads that represent it. But Husserl also affirms that the real object manifests in its realization a transcendence, and this transcendence, he believes, is the key to the transcendental dimension, because it is in this way that the inclusion of the intentional object happens, and thus the structuring of transcendental experience.

However, Ingarden believes that precisely in defining this objective transcendence, Husserl shifts reflection from the merely ontological level (of the concrete objective being) to the metaphysical one (merely subjective and abstract), and in doing so, moves away from any probable realistic solution, embracing instead the idealistic stance in regard to the gnoseologic position. This solution could be avoided, should it prove possible to have «a return to the objects given and the retention of the proper character of their existence» (Ingarden 1975, p. 37). This would mean abandoning the idealistic position wanted by Husserl.

The transcendental idealism that Ingarden rejects is the formulation by which the so-called 'real world' depends on the acts of the consciousness for its existence and essence[10]: that the real world is nothing outside such acts. Transcendental reduction facilitates this undertaking, leaving to consciousness just the task of making notable and analyzable that which it excludes from the 'placement in parenthesis'. But actually, according to Ingarden, doing so does not confer on phenomenology its most

[10]Cfr. the study of Haefliger 1994, which deals analytically with the possibility of an existential theory in Ingarden, conducting a wide-ranging, thorough analysis of his ontology, beginning with the problem of meaning of Husserlian logic and of Frege, to produce what, to his mind, are the modalities of being of the Ingardian ontology.

authentic purpose, that of clarifying the difference between the way of existence and the way of presentation, so as not to confuse a gnoseologic argumentation with the ontological sphere from which the possibilities of existence itself begin.

'Why, explains Ingarden, could it not through retaining that form be something existing in itself and independently of individually performed perception?' (Ingarden 1975, p. 46).

Ingarden's position regarding Husserlian phenomenology, above all regarding transcendental idealism, does not seem very far at all from that of Hartmann, with the substantial difference that Ingarden accentuates the existential factor of the real world, while Hartmann is more directed at formulating a gnoseology, a theory of knowledge (a metaphysics of knowledge) on the basis of a critical ontology.[11]

The transcendental idealism into which Hartmann's analyses delve is rejected by both philosophers, above all in relation to the question of the transcendental reduction that would block reference to the reality of the natural world. In fact, in this regard, Ingarden asks: 'How are things with real existence and with the meaning of that existence? After completing the reduction, doesn't the meaning of reality remain unchanged?' (Ingarden 1974, p. 206).

In fact, once the epoché has been applied, one proceeds in a terrain no longer in contact with reality. But, asks Ingarden, what contact does this new reality maintain with the old reality, the originating one from which the existence of a real world was formed? Also, if we apply the transcendental reduction, doesn't the ontology subsequently proposed undermine the very foundation of the reduction?[12] If, in fact, one stops talking about ontology through this reduction and abandons the eidetic reduction that refers only to pure essences, what then does the reduction return to refer to? Doesn't it in turn admit a parallel, non thematized world, but that is necessary in

[11] Cf. in this regard the brilliant study of Tymieniecka (1957), highlighting the differences and similarities between the two ontoloiges regarding their respective conceptions of existence (*Dasein*) and essence (*Sosein*). From Tymieniecka's point of view, both give rise to an ontology in opposition to dogmatic ontology ; but, while for Ingarden this "analyzes the structures and the laws of being as pure possibilities, independenly of all existential theorems, Hartmann, in contrast, seeks being as being without an existential opening" (ivi, p. 180). In this sense, the existential that Ingarden does not know of lies in the fact that he, concerning the foundation of an ontology, is interested in identifying the eidetic aspect of the phenomenological reduction, while Hartmann strives to analyze the structures and stratifications of being in order to find being's existential meaning, of which transcendental phenomenology had known nothing.

[12] According to Ingarden, it is wrongheaded to consider the transcendental reduction as a scientific method to attain a rigorous science. "By suspending (in one or another way) the belief in the existence and determination of the objects of knowledge of certain investigated kind, e.g. of the outer perception, it is to prevent prejudging in a positive manner the cognitive validity of the investigated cognition at the moment when this validity is still to be disclosed or evaluated in the very epistemological investigation [...]. We meet here the principal difficulty how not to make use, in the investigation on knowledge of objects of a certain type, of the justified knowledge of these obiects without losing cognitive contact with reality which concerns the given cognition" (Ingarden 1975, pp. 39–40).

order to speak of these essences? Finally, what would be the relationship between these essences and the existence of the real world?[13]

Ingarden writes in this regard, 'On the terrain that has been subjected to transcendental reduction, one cannot affirm, depending on the intuitive comprehension of the essence of a certain object, that the object is ontically transcendent in respect to pure consciousness' (Ingarden 1974, p. 181). What is needed in order to be able to make such an affirmation is the thematization of the ontic level, or in other words, of the real word from which the analyses of a transcendental reduction start out.

Therefore the problem comes down to clarifying what essence consists of. If essence approaches what Husserl called *species* in his *Logical Investigations*, in Ingarden it seems at the same time different because of the fact that it does not have to do with a quality, but rather a set of predictabilities, of meanings, of determinations that are attributed to some thing. Thus the pure *species* are the ideal qualities that present themselves in experience, but do not appear there in their purity. From here, the process of ideation becomes possible, founded on perception, but also independent from it, because, for example, in the act of seeing, once we close our eyes we know the existence (the 'an sich') of the thing, and at the same time its essence in the act of our seeing it. In the process of ideation we do without existence, because we do not need an immediate recourse to it, but this does not mean that our conscious acts are what constitute it. In this fact, Ingarden's ontology of ideas overcomes Husserlian idealism, because unlike Husserl, who in the transcendental reduction 'does without' the world, Ingarden restores to the world its existence, and conducts for philosophy an ontology of the pure ideal qualities.[14]

The Husserlian distinction between 'pure consciousness' and 'real world' must be re-thought, according to Ingarden, in the light of a re-evaluation of the problem. 'For Edmund Husserl's 'pure' sense of consciousness one must intend all living beings and the conscious sets that are found within the reach of a possible 'immanent perception,' and one must take them precisely in that form in which they appear in this position, after the elimination of any conception extraneous to it' (Ingarden 1960, p. 19). In this way, it is possible to neutralize consciousness as

[13]In regard to the question of ontology and knowledge, Ingarden propsed in *The Controversy on the Existence of the World* a gnoseology that holds tight to the eidedic (the constitution of ideas) but that contemporaneously opens to a recovery of the existential dimension in every format. In addition, the theory of knowledge must aim at an objectivity. However, such an objectivity must not merely address current events, the current status revealed by scholars. Like Husserl, Ingarden holds that one must begin from the pre-scientific state of knowledge in order to give a valid definition that corrects previous stages (cfr. in this regard Chrudzimski 1999).

[14]"In his ontological and phenomenological inquiries into Husserl, writes Tymieniecka, Ingarden follows two roads: one recognizes the role of ideas in the constitution of concrete being inasmuch as concrete, *in linea entis*; the other, the directive role that aims at ideas in their development, from their origin to their decline [...] the critical analysis – formal, material, essential – the second aspect of the role of ideas is what Ingarden considers the key that permits access to the permanent structure of being" (Tymieniecka 1959, pp. 162–162). Cf. in addition: Id. "Analecta Husserliana" 4 (1976); Id. 1989; Id. "Analecta Husserliana" 30 (1990); Id. "Analecta Husserliana" 33 (1991); Mitscherling 1997.

real process, but at the same time it is possible to maintain the existence of the real world. Existence and essence thus confirm their autonomy and, at the same time, their possibility in the different fields of manifestation. Something, writes Ingarden, exists autonomously 'if it has in itself its own ontic foundation. It has in itself that foundation if in itself it is determined immanently' (*ib.*, p. 94). However, this does not mean setting the world 'outside discussion' as if not existing 'in itself,' thus reproducing the dispute between idealists and realists, and hence re-proposing the critique of Husserl.

Rather, it means restoring to ontology not only the formal and material aspect of the being, but fundamentally also the existential aspect of the real world. In fact, Ales Bello writes, 'in his [Ingarden's] opinion, Husserl runs the risk of affirming a presumed or feigned existence, the kind of existence that effectively characterizes artistic production, the only ones to which Ingarden deems intentionality to be applicable' (Ales Bello 2004, pp. 99–100). In other words, according to Ingarden, if the reduction has ontological meaning, it must remain eidetic and thus stop in order to establish an ontology of essences. Instead, should it seek to impose itself as transcendental, it would completely change the meaning of the ontological consideration of existence (which would be cut out of ontology itself) and thus its value for life.[15]

References

Ales Bello, A. 2004 *The Controversy about the Existence of the World in Edmund Husserl's Phenomenological School.* A. Reinach, R. Ingarden, H. Conrad-Martius, E. Stein, in "Analecta Husserliana" LXX.

Barone, F. 1963. *Il pensiero di Nicolai Hartmann.* Introduzione a *La fondazione dell'ontologia (The Thought of Nicolai Hartmann.* Introduction to *The Foundation of Ontology*). Milan: Fabbri.

Chrudzimski, A. 1999. *Die Erkenntnistheorie von Roman Ingarden (The Theory of Knowledge of Roman Ingarden*). Dordrecht: Kluwer Academic Publishers.

Conrad-Martius, H. 1923. *Realontologie (Realontology*). in "Jahrbuch für philosophische und phänomenologische Forschung" VI.

Haefliger, G. 1994. *Über Existenz: die Ontologie Roman Ingardens (On the Existence: Roman Ingarden's Ontology*). Dordrecht/Boston/London: Kluwer Academic Publishers.

Harich, W. 1983. *Nicolai Hartmann und seine russischen Lehrer (Nicolai Hartmann and his Russian Professors*), in "Sinn und Form", 35.

Hartmann, N. 1931. *Zum Problem der Realitätsgegebenheit (On the Problem of the Givenness of Reality*). Berlin: Pan-Verlagsgesellschaft.

---

[15]For Ingarden, constitution must stop at the eidetic level and deal with essences (ideas and their formation) beginning with the lived experience of consciousness. It cannot become constitution of the objective world because it would invalidate the transcendence of the world that is irrepressible. The experience of transcendence must then remain as for Hartmann the limit with which gnoseology must always return to settle accounts. For its part, the reduction can call itself scientific, that is, give rise to a "rigorous science" only when it deals with the eidetic sphere without claiming to reach the constitution of the objective world.

Hartmann, N. 1955. *Systematische Selbstdarstellung (Sistematic Selfpresentation)*. In *Kleinere Schriften*, ed. W. de Gruyter, 1–51, vol. I. Berlin.
Hartmann, N. 1962. *Das Problem des geistigen Seins (The Problem of Spiritual Being)*. Berlin: De Gruyter.
Hartmann, N. 1964. *Der Aufbau der realen Welt (Construction of the Real World)*. Berlin: De Gruyter.
Hartmann, N. 1965^5. *Platos Logik des Seins (The Platonic Logic of Being)*. Berlin: A. Töpelmann.
Hartmann, N. 1965a. *Grundzüge einer Metaphysik der Erkenntins (Principles of a Metaphysics of Knowledge)*. Berlin: W. de Grutyter.
Hartmann, N. 1965b. *Zur Grundlegung der Ontologie (Foundation of Ontology)*, Berlin: De Gruyter.
Hartmann, N. 1982. *Die Erkenntnis im Lichte der Ontologie (Knowledge in Light of Ontology)*. Hamburg: Felix Meiner.
Husserl, E. *Philosophie als strenge Wissenschaft (Philosophy as Rigorous Science)*, in Husserliana XXV, edited by T. Nenon, H. R. Sepp, Kluwer Academic Publishers, Dordrecht/Boston/Lancaster 1987.
Husserl, N. 1975–2002. *Logische Untersuchungen (Logical Investgations)*. In *Husserliana XVIII*. ed. E. Holenstein. The Hague: Nijhoff; XIX/1, XIX/2 (edited by U. Panzer), Nijhoff, The Hague 1984; XX/1 (edited by U. Melle). Dordrecht/Boston/Lancaster: Kluwer Academic Publishers.
Ingarden, R. 1960. *Spór o istnienie świata (Controversy on the Existence of the World)*, PWN, Warsaw 1960.
Ingarden, R. 1968. *Erinnerungen an Husserl*, in *Briefe an Roman Ingarden (Letters to Roman Ingarden)*. Den Haag: M. Nijhoff.
Ingarden, R. 1973. *Das literarische Kunstwerke (The Literary Work of Art)*, English translation, Evanston: Northwestern University Press.
Ingarden, R. 1974. *Wstęp do fenomenologii Husserla (Introduction to Husserl's Phenomenology)*. Warsawa: PWN.
Ingarden, R. 1975. *On the Motives which Led Husserl to Trascendental Idealism*. Den Haag: M. Nijhoff.
Mitscherling, J. 1997. *Roman Ingarden's Ontology and Aesthetics*. Ottawa: University of Ottawa Press.
Penati, G. 1975. *Traduzione, introduzione e note a (Translation, introduction, and notes to)* N. Hartmann, *Nuove vie della ontologia (New Ways of Ontology)*, Brescia: La Scuola.
Poli, R. 1998. Levels. "Axiomathes" 1–2,:197–211.
Rovighi, S.V. *L'ontologia di Nicolai Hartmann (The Ontology of Nicolai Hartmann)*. In "Rivista di Filosofia Neo-Scolastica", XXXI (March 1939-XVII), fasc. II.
Sirchia, F. 1969. *Nicolai Hartmann. Dal neokantismo all'ontologia. La filosofia degli scritti giovanili, (1909–1919), (Hartmann. From Neo-Kantism to Ontology. The Philosophy of His Early Writings, (1909–1919)*. Milano: Vita e Pensiero.
Tymieniecka, A.-T. 1957. *Essence et existence. Essai sur la Philosophie de la de Nicolai Hartmann et Roman Ingardens (Essence and Existence. Essai on the Philosophy of Nicolai Hartmann)*. Paris: Aubier.
Tymieniecka, A.-T. 1959. *L'Analyse de l'Idée et la Partecipation (The Analyse of the Idea and the Partecipation)*. In AA.VV., For Roman Ingarden. *Nine Essays in Phenomenology*. Den Haag: M. Nijhoff.
Tymieniecka, A.-T. 1976. *Ingardeniana: A Spectrum of Specialised Studies Establishing the Field of Research*. Analecta Husserliana 4.
Tymieniecka, A.-T. 1989. *On the Aesthetics of Roman Ingarden: Interpretations and Assessments*, ed. D. Bohdan and M. Peter. Dordrecht: Kluwer Academic Publishers.
Tymieniecka, A.-T. 1991. *Ingardeniana III: Roman Ingarden's Aesthetics in a New Key and the Independent Approaches of Others: The Performing Arts, The Fine Arts, and Literature (vol. III)*. *Analecta Husserliana* 33.

Tymieniecka, A.-Y. 1990. Ingardeniana II: New Studies in the Philosophy of Roman Ingarden, with a New International Ingarden Bibliography, ed. Hans H. Rudnick. *Analecta Husserliana* 30.
Werkmeister, W.H. 1990. *Nicolai Hartmann's New Ontology*. Tallahassee: The Florida State University Press.

Chapter 16
Ontology and Methodology in Analytic Philosophy

John Symons

16.1 Introduction

From a certain perspective it is remarkable that a tradition which regards Rudolf Carnap, Ludwig Wittgenstein, and John Austin as central figures in its recent history, currently devotes so much of its intellectual energy to basic metaphysical questions. Given the prominence of anti-metaphysical doctrines and arguments, espoused by positivists, pragmatists and ordinary language philosophers, the fact that ontology is flourishing among analytic philosophers in the early twenty first century deserves some explanation.[1] Ontology is a slippery business which is usually characterized via the claim that it is the inquiry into the nature of existence or the attempt to determine the kinds of things that exist. It sometimes seem to lack enough real content to be considered a meaningful enterprise, but clearly many familiar areas of philosophical inquiry involve ontological questions and demand arguments on behalf of, or against ontological theses. With the revitalization of analytic metaphysics in recent decades there has been a gradual convergence towards a cluster related ontological problems and methodological assumptions. The purpose of this essay is to introduce some highlights of recent ontology in their proper conceptual and historical context.

In their *Oxford Handbook of Metaphysics*, Michael Loux and Dean Zimmerman describe the generational shift which coincided with the emergence of modern analytic ontology as follows:

> By the mid-1980s a new generation of philosophers was coming to the study of metaphysics. These philosophers had no first-hand knowledge of the positivist or ordinary language attacks on metaphysics. For them, the attacks were quaint episodes from a distant past rather

J. Symons (✉)
Department of Philosophy, University of Texas, El Paso, TX, USA
e-mail: jsymons@utep.edu

[1] The development of analytic ontology over the past three decades deserves extended discussion. There are a number of introductory anthologies which cast a broad net, including Barry Smith and Hans Burkhardt (1991) and Roberto Poli, and Peter Simons (1996). Two examples of recent work in analytic ontology which provide a solid introduction to the contemporary debates are Trenton Merricks (2007) and Theodore Sider, (2003). Dale Jacquette makes a case for the importance of logic in ontology in his (2002).

R. Poli, J. Seibt (eds.), *Theory and Applications of Ontology: Philosophical Perspectives*, DOI 10.1007/978-90-481-8845-1_16,

> than serious theoretical challenges. Accordingly, they were not in the least apologetic about doing metaphysics, nor were they content with a piecemeal approach to metaphysics. Unlike their predecessors they were willing to attempt the construction of comprehensive ontological theories, building upon the work of such trailblazers in the rehabilitation of systematic metaphysics as Roderick Chisholm, David Armstrong, and David Lewis. (2003, p. 4)

One of the goals of this essay is to explain why philosophers, beginning in the 1970s and 1980s rejected the standard theoretical challenges to ontology and how the contemporary ontological landscape took shape. Very briefly, the story I will tell runs as follows: Ontology reemerges in a very robust and unapologetic manner thanks to a confluence of developments in the 1950s and 1960s. These include Quine's criticism of the analytic-synthetic distinction, Strawson's presentation of the metaphysical assumptions underlying our ordinary ways of talking and thinking, and Barcan Marcus' defense of modal reasoning. By the early 1970s, Saul Kripke's account of necessary aposteriori truth and David Lewis' analysis of counterfactuals had the important effect of encouraging philosophers to entertain the possibility that metaphysical theses should be evaluated independently of theses in the philosophy of language or epistemology.

It is relatively uncontroversial to point out that Kripke's arguments in his 1970 lectures, later published as *Naming and Necessity* were especially important in the revival of metaphysics. Developments in late twentieth and the early twenty-first century metaphysics, including David Lewis' defense of Humean supervenience, the explosion of work in the philosophy of mind, the deep and ongoing discussions of modality, and the emergence of a two-dimensionalist approach to language and metaphysics can all be read as either reactions to, or developments of Kripke's insights in those lectures.[2]

In very general terms, Kripke's work allows for a principled distinction between metaphysics and epistemology; a distinction between the study of the world itself and the study of how we come to know the world. Kripke's arguments undermine a broadly Kantian approach to philosophy according to which, we are unable to know the world apart from our experiential or epistemic apparatus. Thus, according to this Kantian perspective, we are unable to begin a metaphysical investigation without first determining the scope and limits of our cognitive or experiential access to the world.

In the twentieth century it was common for philosophers to regard language as playing this mediating role between minds and worlds. Such philosophers often dismissed ontological investigation as naively ignoring the mediated character of understanding and experience. As we shall see, this anti-metaphysical posture not so easy to sustain in our time and, in fact, it was not universally shared by pre-Kripkean analytic philosophers.

[2]Scott Soames (2005) has argued persuasively for the centrality of Kripke's work in the revival of metaphysics.

The early days of analytic philosophy were relatively friendly to ontology. Bertrand Russell and (the early) Ludwig Wittgenstein espoused versions of logical atomism which can be understood as attempts to provide a fully general account of the ontological characteristics of reality. Furthermore, one of the main features of Gottlob Frege's philosophy is his view that concepts and objects should be regarded as basic ontological categories. Among the other important facets of the ontological discussion in early analytic philosophy were Frank Ramsey's criticism of the distinction between universals and particulars and his analysis of the ontological commitments of scientific theories. (Ramsey 1931) Even in the Vienna Circle, in the midst of what we might see as the least friendly environment for ontology, discussions of ontological questions were lively and productive. Gustav Bergmann's effort, beginning in the 1940s to create a realistic ontology was informed by developments in the Vienna Circle and is perhaps the most constructive product of those discussions for ontology.[3]

The most important methodological principles guiding contemporary analytic ontology are continuous with the concerns and approach we find in these early figures. A broadly realist approach to ontological questions, a preference for parsimony, and an emphasis on common sense methodological conservatism are foremost among the features which contemporary philosophers share with those at the origins of the tradition. Thus, the ontological and methodological commitments of these early figures are worth reviewing in any attempt to understand the development of contemporary metaphysics.[4]

While the roots of contemporary ontological investigation run deep in the history of analytic philosophy, the tradition's focus on language and logic has sometimes proved detrimental to progress with respect to ontological questions. Historically, an increased focus on the philosophy of language in the middle of the century was accompanied by a general distrust of ontology. So, while Frege, Russell and the early Wittgenstein made maximally general claims concerning the categorial structure of reality, many mid-century philosophers urged their readers to abandon ontological inquiry entirely.

In his later work Wittgenstein, John Austin and their followers rejected ontological disagreements as at best misguided and at worst an utterly meaningless or misleading enterprise. In recent years, criticisms of ontology have continued along roughly similar lines. While it was popular in the 1980s and 1990s to speak, in somber fin de siècle terms, of the death of philosophy, recent decades have actually seen an increasing level of activity and energy focused on the most basic questions in metaphysics, moral philosophy, philosophy of logic and the philosophy of mind.

---

[3]While this essay will not discuss Bergmann's ideas, his struggle to reconcile positivism and ontology is a fascinating example of the more general problem, in analytic ontology of reconciling common sense presuppositions with formal and scientific insights. Herbert Hochberg provides a very informative discussion of Bergmann's views in his (1994).

[4]Two books which examine the ontological views of early analytic philosophers are Jan Dejnozka (1996) and Gideon Makin (2001)

Ontology has figured prominently in this return to fundamental questions in philosophy. Critics of metaphysics like Hilary Putnam and Richard Rorty called, in the 1980s and 1990s, for a broadly pragmatic approach to philosophy and an end to analytic philosophy.[5] While Putnam and Rorty were advocating some form of post-metaphysical thought, metaphysicians had been engaged in interesting and fruitful work. Philosophers in the 1980s and 1990s have been busily sharpening our understanding of basic notions related to modality, mind, causality, individuation, free will, and the like. In fact, it is probably fair to say that many of the richest, clearest and most detailed studies of these topics have been written in recent decades.

Relatively recently, philosophers have begun to examine some of the methodological assumptions underlying work in analytic metaphysics and epistemology. There has been an increasingly self-conscious reflection on the assumptions and techniques which govern philosophical work. In addition to a range of articles and books on conceivability, possibility and intuition, philosophers have begun to develop important analyses of the relationship between purely conceptual investigation and formal methods drawn from logic and mathematics.[6]

In recent analytic philosophy, ontological investigations are conditioned by at least three competing principles. In imprecise terms, the most important of these can be characterized as a conservative approach to philosophical methodology which, as touched on above, aims to preserve as many common sense theses and explanations as possible. The second principle is far crisper, namely the rejection of epistemic criticisms of metaphysics and the adoption of a realistic approach to basic philosophical questions. A third principle involves commitment to the view that attention to the structure of language or logic should inform ontological investigations. Clearly, these principles are not adhered to universally. In fact, depending on how strictly one interprets them, these principles, they may even be mutually incompatible. In any event, it is a relatively easy to find prominent examples of philosophers who reject one or more of them. In this essay these principles are offered as a way of introducing the contemporary state of ontology in very general terms and as a way of connecting contemporary developments with some of the guiding themes in early analytic ontology.

The complicated relationship between ontology, logic and language is one of the topics which this essay will discuss from a variety of perspectives. As is well known, the ontological views of early analytic philosophers were closely connected

[5]Most recently, in his *Ethics Without Ontology* Hilary Putnam argues that ontology has had disastrous consequences for philosophy of mathematics and moral philosophy. Like Carnap, he argues that moral and mathematical reasoning can be conducted apart from debates concerning the foundations of these endeavors, arguing in effect, that ontology factors out of our moral and mathematical reasoning. Given his earlier criticisms of logical positivism, it is striking that Putnam comes so close to the anti-ontological arguments which we find in the *Aufbau* and in *Pseudoproblems of Philosophy*.

[6]By way of examples, the see the papers collected in Szabo Gendler and Hawthorne (2002) and Vincent Hendricks' *Mainstream and Formal Epistemology*.

to the development of modern logic. Theses in the philosophy of logic and language continued to shape attitudes towards ontology well into the second half of the twentieth century. However, in the work of the later Wittgenstein and the ordinary language philosophers, reflection on language and logic were deployed as part of a critical posture towards traditional ontology. In the mid-twentieth century, many of the most prominent criticisms of ontology and arguments against metaphysics were motivated by claims about the nature of language and the relationship between metaphysical theses and our epistemic capacities.

For Russell and Frege, logic and ontology were intimately entangled and it is not always a simple matter to determine which of the two has priority in their philosophical work. It is often difficult to separate the strands of their arguments into distinctively formal and distinctively metaphysical types. In fact, many of the most important interpretive questions in the study of Frege's work involve the problem of determining the relative importance he attached to ontological and logico-linguistic considerations in philosophical reflection. In Russell's early work, abstract entities are invoked in order to support the possibility of logic, but as we shall see below logical techniques like the theory of descriptions and methods like logical construction also serve to inform us with respect to our ontological commitments. While there are a range of difficult interpretive questions which can be raised here, there can be little doubt that ontology is inextricably related to logic in the thought of these early figures.

In a somewhat different vein, G.E. Moore's deeply influential account of common sense in philosophical reasoning, gave a central role to the ontological claims that are part of our ordinary experience of the world. Moore encourages us to be highly suspicious of any attempt to abandon common sense theses for what he saw as exotic theoretical reasons. Following Moore, a conservative emphasis on common sense in philosophical methodology has been one of the near constant features of ontological investigation in the analytic tradition. As we shall see below, the methodological conservatism that Moore's work inspires has played an important role in the development of contemporary ontology.[7]

Ontological questions have played a central role in recent analytic metaphysics. Among the themes which explicitly engage with the kinds of concerns which ontologists share are the debates between perdurantist and endurantist views, debates over the existence of specific aspects of reality or specific kinds, such as numbers, ordinary objects, minds etc. Investigations into the character of vague predicates, the reality of natural kinds, the nature of causal powers and dispositions are also of direct importance for the development of a meaningful ontology. In contrast with the kind of ontological work in mainstream analytic metaphysics (the kind of work which we might associate with philosophers like Kit Fine, Ted Sider, Trenton Merricks, Amie Thomasson, Clifford Elder and others), there is also a variety of stand-alone efforts to develop complete ontological frameworks. Prominent among

[7] Scott Soames makes a compelling case for the centrality of Moore's thought in the development of analytic philosophy in the twentieth century in his (2005)

these is E.J. Lowe's four category ontology which will be discussed briefly below. In a chapter-length contribution, it is very difficult to provide even a brief treatment of the many important views and proposals which ontologists have generated in recent decades. The purpose of this chapter is not to provide an encyclopedic account of the history of ontology in the analytic tradition, but rather to provide a sketch of some of the defining figures and approaches to ontological questions.

16.2 Ontology and Logic for Frege

Standard accounts of the history of analytic philosophy see the tradition as starting with the work of Gottlob Frege, Bertrand Russell and G.E. Moore. In the present context, Frege is striking insofar as his ontological views play such a central role in his philosophical system. Frege understood concepts and objects to constitute ontologically fundamental categories. His ontology is coordinated directly with some of the key features of the logic that he presents in *Begriffsschrift*. In that book, Frege not only articulates the central advance that defined modern logic – the logic of polyadic quantification – but also prepares the way for the ontological claims articulated in later essays like 'Function and Object' and 'Concept and Object'. Moreover, *Begriffsschrift* contains the first statement of Frege's description of the misleading effect of ordinary language in philosophical reflection. Frege's criticism of ordinary language is well-known. However, understanding his view of the proper role played in philosophical reflection by language involves a high level of interpretive complexity. This circumstance has led to divergent readings of Frege's philosophy.

While some important points in Frege's philosophy of language continue to be debated, there is no interpretive doubt concerning his view of the inadequacy of natural language. In this respect, his complaints have set the tone for many philosophers who favored formal philosophical reasoning in the twentieth century. Bertrand Russell, for example, exemplified the Fregean insistence that ordinary language is a source of error for philosophers. In sharp contrast with the later Wittgenstein, Austin and others, Russell argued that 'an obstinate addiction to ordinary language' is 'one of the main obstacles to progress in philosophy'. (Schlipp 1944, p. 634) While the view that ordinary language is an inadequate guide to philosophical investigation has been an ongoing feature of more formally-oriented thinkers, it has faced opposition from philosophers who argue that we must rely on common sense, ordinary language or more recently on our intuitions. This tension between common sense and formal or scientific reasoning continues to be an ongoing feature of philosophical practice.

Fregean and Russellian criticisms of ordinary language were due, at least in part, to the perception that formal techniques provide insights which would otherwise be difficult to achieve. Specifically, Frege and Russell were impressed by the insight that comes via a clear view of the interplay of quantifiers, variables and predicates. For both Frege and Russell, the surface features of ordinary language distract us from a clear view of logical and ontological matters. Rather than looking to the surface syntax of natural languages, Frege turns instead to the mathematical notion of the function as a starting point in his project to reform philosophy. For Frege, refashioning logic in terms of quantifiers, variables, names, and functions allows us to avoid the philosophically misleading features of natural language. In Frege's view, if one did not have access to the new logic and relied solely on ordinary language to grasp the implications of complex expressions involving embedded generality, one would be at a profound disadvantage.

Throughout his career, Frege believed that the 'logical imperfections' in 'the language of life' stand in the way of philosophical investigation. (1979, p. 253) Frege believed that his new logic could liberate us from the thrall of language. He writes, for instance, '[i]f it is a task of philosophy to break the power of words over the human mind, by uncovering illusions that through the use of language often almost unavoidably arise concerning the relations of concepts, by freeing thought from the taint of ordinary linguistic means of expression , then my Begriffsschrift, [. . .] can become a useful tool for philosophers.' (1967, pp. vi–vii) According to Frege, the reason that language taints our thought is that its grammar does not reflect the underlying structure of our judgments. Attachment to the superficial grammatical features of natural language blocks philosophers from achieving a clear view of the structure of valid reasoning.

This view of ordinary language is not simply a mark of his early enthusiasm for logic. In Frege's posthumous writings we find this criticism of grammar repeated in uncompromising terms. In his *Logic*, he writes, for instance: 'We shall have no truck with the expressions 'subject' and 'predicate' of which logicians are so fond, especially since they not only make it more difficult for us to recognize the same as the same, but also conceal distinctions that are there. Instead of following grammar blindly, the logician ought to see his task as that of freeing us from the fetters of language.' (1979, p. 143) As Frege saw it, the central step in the creation of a proper logic (which on his view is one which allows for multiple, embedded expressions of generality) involved drawing our attention away from grammatical subjects and predicates and towards arguments and functions (1967, p. 7). This step is emphasized throughout Frege's entire body of work. It was pivotal to the development of modern logic and it shapes his view of ontology.

In his 1925 paper 'Universals' Frank Ramsey extended the spirit of Frege's attitude towards grammar and ordinary language by showing that the grammatical distinction between subject and predicate does not, by itself, support the distinction between universals and particulars (1931). This claim is somewhat at odds with the Fregean distinction between objects and concepts described below, but it is consonant with Frege's criticism of the role of grammatical distinctions in ontological investigation.

Ontology has, as one of its major topics, the study of identity and difference. From Frege's perspective, ordinary language is an obstacle to our capacity to form true judgments concerning identity and difference and one important task of the logician is to remove these obstacles. Frege was justified in thinking that his logic offers a more accurate representation of distinctions and identities than analyses based solely on the grammatical distinction between subject and predicate permit. It is well known that if the words 'all' or 'some' appear in the predicate place in a traditional syllogistic logic, then invalid inferences can be shown to follow straightforwardly. Syllogistic reasoning provides no insight into the logical structure of multiply embedded statements of generality and is often positively misleading. It can be shown easily that by introducing polyadic quantification in the *Begriffsschrift*, Frege was able to express a range of judgments which had eluded previous attempts to formalize logic.[8]

The formal features of *Begriffsschrift* itself are directly related to one of the core philosophical insights in Frege's work, namely his application of the mathematical idea of the function. Specifically, the mathematical concept of the function inspires Frege's characterization of the structure of judgment. Ordinarily, functions can be understood as taking arguments and giving values, some function, for example $f(x) = 2x$, gives the value 4 when it takes 2 as its argument. The variable 'x' in this context plays the role of an empty slot or placeholder, which, in this context is filled by numbers. On Frege's view concepts play a similar role.

Concepts, by themselves, are incomplete expressions or, as he sometimes puts it, they are 'unsaturated'. This incompleteness is filled by singular terms. Singular terms name objects and when singular terms are placed in the gaps of an incomplete expression, (in the same way that a number can serve as the argument for a function) then concepts and singular terms combine to give a truth value. For Frege, truth values are special kinds of objects: 'The true' and 'the false' are singular terms which name those objects. So, continuing the analogy with functions in mathematics, concepts have as their codomain, two objects; the true and the false. Their domain is (with some important qualifications) the set consisting of every object.

The division of everything into two ontologically fundamental categories; concepts and objects, is motivated by Frege's view that no deeper analysis of these notions is possible and that these two categories suffice to generate the logic presented in *Begriffsschrift.*

In his 1892 paper 'Concept and Object' Frege recognizes a counterintuitive consequence of his ontological view. If we claim, for instance that the concept 'x is a horse' is a concept, then given Frege's view of concepts and objects, we have actually said something false. This is because the claim in question treats the concept term as a singular term. On Frege's view, only objects can be referred to using singular terms. Since the sentence 'the concept 'x is a horse' is a concept' is false, it surely seems as though Frege is driven to accept the paradoxical judgment that 'the concept 'x is a horse' is an object'. While a great deal of interpretive effort has been devoted to understanding this problem, it is important to note that Frege regards this situation as the result of the inadequacy of ordinary language and does not waiver from his ontological thesis.

Frege's ontological commitments, I would argue, are such that he is willing to accept that the sentence 'the concept *horse* is a concept' is false! However, the apparent strangeness here is not as serious as some have worried. Anthony Kenny alerts

---

[8]For a more expansive and detailed account of the advantages of Frege's logic over syllogistic logic, see Anthony Kenny (1995, 12–26).

us to a footnote in 'Concept and Object' where Frege points to a way of resolving the apparently paradoxical implication of his account (1995, p. 124). Frege points out that there a range of cases in natural language in which we make strange sounding statements as a result of the awkwardness of ordinary language. He describes, for example how, by explicitly calling some predicate a predicate, we deprive it of that property. In modern terms we would say that Frege is pointing out that ordinary language is subject to possible use/mention confusions of the kind which we try to avoid via devices like quotation marks or italicization.

Kenny suggests that the expression '"the concept..." is really meant to serve the same purpose for our talk of "concepts as is served by quotation marks in relation to predicates.' (1995, p. 125) Without examining the details of this resolution, it is enough here to note that on Frege's view, any fault which might exist, lies with language rather than with his ontological thesis.

Note also that in the employment of devices like quotation marks we are attempting to make our language conform to our intentions with respect to the ontological state of affairs under consideration. If one writes, for instance, ''the mailbox' contains ten letters' the quotation marks do not indicate that there are ten pieces of mail in the physical mailbox, but rather that the string of two words in the quotation marks contains ten letters. If one intends to talk about relatively abstract things like letters of the alphabet rather than letters in envelopes, one can easily indicate this intention via artificial typographic devices. It is more difficult (but not impossible) to make the same kinds of ontological distinctions in unaided spoken language. The introduction of the typographical conventions discussed here assumes that there is a level of insight into ontological facts which leads us to supplement natural language with various kinds of formalism. I would argue that Frege assumed that we do have such insight.

Formal devices, from quotation marks to quantifiers are employed in order to expand the expressive power of our language. Specifically, the function of these devices is to capture genuine distinctions and identity claims which language would fail to encompass in their absence. Frege's view of the significance of these extensions is clear.[9] In the *Begriffsschrift*, for example, he draws an analogy between his logical notation and the microscope which, while lacking the versatility of our eyes, proves useful for matters where scientific precision is demanded (1967, p. 6). Frege sees his logical formalism as a supplement to natural language which permits philosophers a more precise view of the nature of judgment and which is more faithful to the ontological facts than the superficial grammar of ordinary language.

As I have described them so far, Frege's views on logic and ontology are intertwined with his criticisms of ordinary language. By emphasizing Frege's ontological commitments, the present discussion is somewhat at odds with at least one

[9]He writes that "the mere invention of this ideography has, it seems to me, advanced logic" (1967, 7)

prominent interpretation of Frege's philosophy.[10] Frege's foremost contemporary interpreter, Michael Dummett has argued that the central innovation in Frege's philosophy is his conversion of questions about ontology into questions about the nature of meaning. According to Dummett, traditional ontological questions become 'part of the theory of meaning as practised by Frege' (1981, p. 671). Dummett not only regards this as one of the most important features of Frege's philosophy by also as a general principle which helps form the distinctive methodology of the ensuing analytic tradition. For Dummett and like-minded readers, the lingua-centrism of much of analytic philosophy is due to Frege's own commitment to transforming philosophy into the philosophy of language.

The present essay is not the appropriate venue to tackle Dummett's claim about the origins or the distinguishing features of analytic philosophy in detail. Instead, it suffices to note that alternative readings of the relative fundamentality of ontology and language can be justified. Clearly, Frege's ontological theses cannot be separated completely from his views on the nature of language and human epistemic capacities. However, the interpretive challenge is to understand precisely how he believes ontology and language are related. According to Dummett, traditional ontological questions are completely subsumed within Frege's larger theory of meaning. There is some evidence to the contrary which I will discuss very briefly.

Frege recognizes that he cannot provide a purely formal account of, for example, the distinction between concept and object; that he must move beyond the formal language of *Begriffsschrift* and must appeal to hints or elucidations that depend on his readers' grasp of the roles of names and predicates in ordinary language.[11] However, readers have disagreed on the manner in which he regarded the argument for accepting his ontological taxonomy of concepts and objects as dependent on an understanding of language.

As Joan Weiner argues and as we saw in our discussion of 'Concept and Object' above, Frege's ontological claims did not arise via a slavish adherence to the surface properties of language. As Weiner notes, he was alert to sentences in ordinary language like 'The horse is a four-legged animal' where the grammatical structure indicates a simple predication but where Frege argues that it should not be understood as such (1990, 249 footnote). As we saw above, Frege's own account of, for example, the difficulties involved with talking about 'the concept *horse*' support interpreting him as seeing ontological commitments as more fundamental than theses in the philosophy of language. While it runs counter to the mainstream reading of Frege, I believe that it is consistent with the textual evidence to see him as placing primary importance on ontological rather than linguistic theses. At the very

---

[10]Although Gideon Makin (2000) makes a strong case for the seeing both Frege and Russell's work as fundamentally oriented towards metaphysical questions rather than attempting to replace metaphysics with philosophy of language.

[11]See Anthony Kenny's discussion of the 'unbridgeable gulf between concepts and objects' and Frege's reliance on common sense acquaintance with the distinction between predicates and names in his (1995, 121). Joan Weiner has an extended reading of the distinction between definition and elucidation for Frege in her (1990), especially pp. 99–104 and 227–280.

least, it seems clear that Frege believe that ontological considerations should guide our understanding of grammatical categories and logical formalism rather than vice versa. For example, as we saw above, Frege regarded 'the concept *horse*' problem as a product of the inadequacy of ordinary language rather than as a symptom of a problem with his ontology.

As Claire Oritz Hill has noted (1997) Frege's goal of creating a language free from the imprecision and systematically misleading features of ordinary language, was forced to face the ontological challenge of accounting for identity. Ortiz Hill addresses Frege's views on the nature of identity with special focus on the ambiguity which Frege found in identity statements. She quotes the following striking remark in § 8 of *Begriffsschrift* 'thus along with the introduction of the symbol for equality of content, all symbols are necessarily given a double meaning: the same symbols stand now for their own content, now for themselves'. (Quoted in 1997, p. 5) Concerns over the nature of the equals sign in Section 16.8 of the *Begriffsschrift* involve ontological considerations and are not merely a matter of the nature of signs. Since Frege's reflection on the nature of identity claims motivates his pivotal distinction between the sense and the reference of a sentence, we can understand the problem of identity as motivating, at least in part, his account of how the content of a sentence is determined. In this sense, pace Dummett, one can read Frege's ontological concerns as motivating his interest in philosophy of language.

16.3 Logical Construction in Russell, Ramsey and Carnap

After Frege, one of the most significant points of origin for twentieth century analytic philosophy is Russell and Moore's reaction against what they saw as the speculative excesses of British Idealism. This reaction is often seen as a turn towards Humean empiricism or positivism.[12] However, reading Russell and Moore as anti-metaphysical and as narrowly empiricist is a profoundly mistaken approach to their work. For the purposes of this essay, the most significant problem which results from an empiricist reading of Russell and Moore is that it distracts attention from the importance of ontological considerations on their early thought. As we can see from the careful studies of Russell's early philosophy provided by Peter Hylton (1990) and others, it makes more sense to read the anti-idealist turn in Russell and Moore as the developments of a conservative methodological stance with respect to common sense judgments and ordinary experience.

Russell and Moore famously rejected the views of their neo-Hegelian teachers. For Russell, this turn only takes place once he had already completed work on the

[12]David Pears' *Bertrand Russell and the British Tradition in Philosophy* (1972) is a prominent example of the empiricist reading of Russell's turn away from British Idealism. Peter Hylton's *Russell, Idealism and the Emergence of Analytic Philosophy* (1990) presents a more accurate and detailed analysis of the early philosophy of Russell and Moore which notes the centrality of abstract entities in Russell's thought. In his early work, Russell often had recourse to abstract entities in ways which do not comport with the kind of empiricism that Pear and others have in mind.

first part of his plan to produce an encyclopedic synthesis of scientific and political thinking in the spirit of Hegel's philosophy (Russell 1897). Both Russell and Moore were driven to abandon Idealism because of their inability to reconcile it with a common sense attitude towards the reality of objects, the truthfulness of propositions and the objectivity of judgment. While Russell's conversion to Moore's common sense realism was pivotal to his philosophical development, his encounter with modern logic in the work of Frege and Giuseppe Peano provides the technical backbone and content for many of the most important developments which followed.

The influence of the newly developed formalism on Russell's ontological views is well known. Among Russell's seminal achievements is his theory of descriptions. Perhaps the most important feature of the theory of descriptions was its implications for ontological reasoning. Russell describes how we can formalize sentences in such a way as to permit us to see more clearly what the ontological commitments of our assertions are. So, for example, when one hears the assertion that the present King of France is bald, one might be concerned about the ontological status of the monarch under consideration. At the moment, France is free of kings. However, one might worry that denying or assenting to claims about the King's baldness commits one to an ontology which includes the non-existent King of France.

Alexius Meinong had understood judgments concerning non-existent objects as committing us to a realm of objects, including impossible objects, which do not exist in the ordinary sense. Whether an object exists is a question which is distinguishable, according to Meinong, from questions concerning its properties. The fact that an object does not exist, on this view, is not a barrier to our making true claims concerning that object. For Meinong, there is a variety of properties that a non-existent object can possess. Consequently, he regards part of the task of ontology to involve cataloguing the characteristics of nonexistent objects as they relate to our reasoning and discourse. Meinong's ontology is extremely rich and generates a range of interesting and fertile questions.[13] However, Russell's theory of descriptions has had an important role insofar as it allows a principled way of blocking the move from judgments about objects like the present King of France to claims about their exotic ontological status. Russell's strategy is simply to unpack the implicit embedded quantification relation in the sentence:

$$(\exists \mathrm{x})\ (\mathrm{Kx}\ .\ ((\forall y)\ ((\mathrm{Ky} \rightarrow (x = y))\ \ .\ \mathrm{B}x)$$

As such, it becomes clear that, whether the King is said to be bald or not bald that the sentence is straightforwardly false because it is making a false existence claim. This is a simple, yet critically important step in our thinking about ontology. The theory of descriptions shows how our sentences cannot always be taken at their face value and do not automatically license ontological claims. Instead, logic allows us (at the very least) an alternative analysis of our ontological commitments, such that we do

[13] See John Findlay's (1963) for a very clear presentation of some of the subtleties of Meinong's ontology.

not mistakenly regard judgments concerning Kings of France and golden mountains as forcing us to make exotic ontological claims. There may be other reasons for accepting a Meinongian ontology, but Russell shows one very important reason for pausing before taking this step.

Like Frege, Russell saw logic as permitting us a way of getting clearer on the ontological presuppositions of our theories and in *Our Knowledge of the External World* he proposes the principle that 'Wherever possible, logical constructions are to be substituted for inferred entities.' (1914, p. 112) Russell's application of logic to ontological questions provided a new way of thinking about how we approach investigations in ontology. Russell exemplified a strategy in metaphysics whereby one could show that the apparent ontological commitments of some sentence or theory could be reconsidered while maintaining the relevant content of the theory or sentence. Again, like Frege, Russell is clarifying the fact that our ordinary ways of talking and thinking about existence need not compel us to follow the grammatical structure of our sentences blindly. Russell believed that with this technique we could legitimately hold that there are no unreal objects.[14]

Frank Ramsey would extend Russell's insight in two important ways. As mentioned above, Ramsey's criticism of the distinction between universal and particular, takes aim at the idea that the subject predicate structure of judgments in ordinary language compel us to adopt an ontology consisting of universals and particulars. In addition to his criticism of universals, Ramsey applies the technical apparatus set forth by Russell in his account of the relationship between the structure of theories and their ontological commitments. Ramsey's account of theories had profound ramifications for philosophy in the late twentieth century and would shape the core ontological presuppositions of functionalist theories in philosophy of mind and philosophy of biology.

Ramsey asks us to consider some scientific theory T where T ranges over unobservable properties $A1 \ldots An$, observable properties $O1 \ldots On$ and individuals $a1 \ldots an$.

$$T(A1 \ldots An, O1 \ldots On)$$

The ascription of some unobservable property (say the property of being a neutron) to some individual or region of space-time *a* can be carried out via a sentence containing a higher-order existential quantifier along the following lines:

$$(\exists A1) \ldots (\exists An)\ [T\ (Al \ldots An,\ O1 \ldots On) \text{ and } Aia)]$$

[14]One could argue that because the theory of descriptions makes all claims about fictional or unreal objects false, it is thereby too restrictive and potentially self-undermining. This objection forces Russell to introduce the distinction between primary and secondary occurrence of a term which fails to denote. The secondary occurrence of the term 'Hamlet' in a sentence like 'Hamlet was a prince' allows us to claim that what is really intended here is the true sentence 'The play tells us that Hamlet was a prince'. Names for unreal or fictional objects can still play a role in true sentences in this sense.

This definition characterizes unobservable theoretical terms based solely on existential quantification, observables and the structure provided by the theory. If we understand our theory T as providing a unique ordering of properties, then reference for problematic terms; things like neutrons, beliefs, or market forces can be fixed via their relationships with one another and with the observable phenomena described by the relevant theory. The structure of relationships between the elements of a theory is presented by the theory *T* and to say that some individual has some property can be converted into a claim about relative placement within the structure described by T, in this case that *a* has the *i*th of A*1*... A*n*.

Ramsey's work would have important ramifications later in the century, especially in the development of functionalism in the philosophy of mind and the philosophy of biology. David Lewis' application of Ramsey's technique to characterizations of functionally individuated concepts (1972) was widely understood to simplify the ontological status of claims made, for example, in folk psychological discourse. Treating such concepts as existentially bound variables specifies the role of theoretical terms via the system of relationships defined by the structure of the theory (1931, pp. 212–236). Given some psychological theory, the Ramsey sentence can serve as a way of providing definitions for mental terms that do not themselves include mental terms.

Metaphorically speaking, we can say that the Ramsey sentence serves to provide non-question begging definitions of mental terms by treating them as locations in the network provided by a theory. If our theory provides a unique ordering of properties, then reference for theoretical terms is fixed via their relationships with one another and with the observable phenomena described by the relevant theory. The structure of relationships between the elements of a theory is presented by the theory and to say that some individual has some property can be converted into a claim about relative placement within the structure described by the theory.

Ramsey elimination does not make any significant difference in the development of a scientific theory of mind since it assumes the existence of a theory that is both finished and true. It tells us nothing about how one might settle on a causal structure appropriate to particular explanations: It assumes an ordering without saying anything about what it is, or how one might decide between alternatives. Of course, Ramsey's account was not originally intended to answer such questions and so this defect does not matter for his purposes. His goal was to account for the meaningfulness of theoretical terms in an established theory. Lewis's use of Ramsey faces the well known threat that even if a part of the folk psychological theory turns out to be false, the statement of the theory in terms of a Ramsey sentence will also be false. Additionally, as Jaegwon Kim points out, even if the folk psychological theory has false non-mental consequences, the whole Ramsey sentence turns out false (1996, p. 108).

If we ignore these threats and settle *apriori* on a particular psychological taxonomy and decide that it is not subject to revision, then functionalism suffices as a theory of mind in the sense that it provides a way of resolving the meaningfulness of our talk of mind without encountering ontological worries. This was Lewis' strategy insofar as mental states are 'physical states of the brain, definable as occupants of certain folk-psychological causal roles.' (1999, p. 5) By deferring to folk psychology, Lewis' position denies the relevance of progress in psychology to philosophy of mind. This might be a defensible position if it could be shown that we have access to folk psychology in a way which resists correction or refinement via inquiry. Elsewhere, I have argued that Lewis' use of Ramsey sentences is undermined by the assumption that it is possible to improve our understanding of psychological terms. (Symons, forthcoming)

The approach to ontology which is pioneered by Russell in 'On Denoting' and which we find developed in Ramsey's work involves embracing the idea of logical construction mentioned above. The idea of a network of relations defining a theory and the possibility that these relations can be thought of in lieu of inferred entities, had profound effects in the philosophy of mind and the philosophy of biology in the late twentieth century. Functionalism can be seen, in large part, as a development of the ontological insights which we find in early analytic philosophy.

Most importantly, the ability to characterize complex and interdependent systems of relations via multiply embedded statements of generality, changed the manner in which terms behave in our theories and led to a fundamental rethinking of the place of mental and other nonphysical terms in our ontology. The other major effect of the Russellian approach to logical constructions was the development of a profoundly anti-ontological line of thinking in Rudolf Carnap's work. While this is not the place to provide detailed account of Carnap's philosophy, his anti-metaphysical position has had a profound influence in twentieth century thought. Carnap's major works are less well known to philosophers than some of his more provocative and readable articles. As Philipp Frank notes, the paper which brought Carnap most attention and have the widest consequences was 'The elimination of metaphysics through logical analysis of language' Frank describes the effect of that paper as follows:

> People who have always had an aversion against metaphysics felt an almost miraculous comfort by having their aversion justified by 'logic'. On the other hand people for whom metaphysics had been that the peak of human intellectual achievement have regarded Carnap's paper as a flagrant attack upon all 'spiritual values' from the angle of a pedantic logic. Logical positivism got the reputation of being cynical skepticism, and simultaneously, intolerant dogmatism. (1963, p. 159)

Analytic philosophy is occasionally criticized for being narrowly focused on language, logic or conceptual analysis to the detriment of ontological or metaphysical investigation. More commonly, analytic philosophy has been accused of an excessively deferential attitude to mathematics and the natural sciences.[15] This line of criticism obscures the historical reality and contemporary diversity of the analytic tradition. However, it is true that analytic philosophers have generated some of the severest criticisms of traditional metaphysics. Many early analytic philosophers, in particular those who were part of or influenced by the Vienna Circle, tended to

[15]One of the most explicit general criticisms of analytic philosophy as a movement is Stanley Rosen (1985). While Rosen's discussion of the history of analytic philosophy is not reliable, his criticisms exemplify widely held complaints against mainstream philosophical practice.

identify metaphysics with obscurantist or reactionary cultural tendencies.[16] By contrast with traditional metaphysics, philosophers like Carnap, Neurath, and Schlick were motivated by a modernist ideal of a reformed philosophical practice which was guided by the kinds of intellectual virtues which they believed were exemplified by the natural sciences. Science offered a more appealing and progressive example of intellectual activity than the kinds of traditional philosophy with which they were familiar.[17] The sciences, they believed, offer a model of clarity, openness and internationalism which stood in stark contrast to, for example, the ontological rumblings that members of the Vienna circle heard coming from Heidegger's hut.[18] Heideggerian forms of ontology, were anathema to the refugees from fascism who helped to shape philosophy in the second half of the twentieth century.[19]

Historical, social and political factors partly explain some of the strongly anti-metaphysical rhetoric which we read in the Vienna circle. Nevertheless, in spite of this apparent hostility to metaphysics, ontological questions have always been central to the enterprise of analytic philosophy. For example, Wittgenstein's *Tractatus* was held in the highest esteem by the members of the Vienna Circle. Few books tackle ontological questions as directly as the *Tractatus*. Today, metaphysical debates are at the heart of philosophy and these debates are guided, perhaps more so than ever in the history of philosophy, by basic ontological questions.

In the pages that follow I will introduce briefly some of the general background to Carnap's criticism of metaphysics. Specifically, it is important to grasp his view of the role of logical construction in philosophy. Carnap's approach to ontology was influenced, to a very great extent by Russell's theory of descriptions and his account of relations. In his *Logical Structure of the World,* Carnap describes his project as '[a]n attempt to apply the theory of relations to the analysis of reality' (1967, p. 7) and asserts that his own work is a radicalization of the major

---

[16]Richard von Mises (1951) provides an introduction to positivism which emphasizes its cultural implications and contrasts prior philosophical orientations with the liberal model of inquiry and social progress to which the positivists aspired.

[17]In his criticism of analytic philosophy Avrum Stroll emphasizes what he sees as the scientistic mainstream of analytic philosophy. He contrasts the vices of scientism with the virtues of the those philosophers who would draw a sharp distinction between science and philosophy (in his view this was Wittgenstein and Austin) One problem with this view is, among other things, the centrality of the distinction between science and philosophy in the work of the Vienna circle and specifically in Carnap's distinction between scientific and non-scientific propositions. Stroll, like Rosen and other critics often seem more concerned with philosophical style or tone, than with any specific philosophical point.

[18]See Michael Friedman's *A Parting of the Ways* (2000) for a detailed discussion of the political and cultural background to Carnap's criticism of Heidegger. The resolute opposition to metaphysics is more easily understood in historical context.

[19]As Friedman (2000, 11–13) and others have noted, Carnap's well known criticism of Heidegger's account of nothingness; Heidegger's notorious claim that "Nothing itself nothings [*Das Nichts selbst nichtet*]" is not a crude application of verificationism. Instead, Carnap sees Heidegger's usage as violating the logical form of the concept of nothing. Heidegger's vice is less a matter of metaphysics than of misology

direction of Russell's philosophy *(ibid*, 8). However, unlike Russell, Carnap's attitude towards metaphysics is profoundly critical. For Carnap, metaphysics tended to generate meaningless statements. In *The Logical Syntax of Language* (1934) he presents this critical attitude as follows: 'In our Vienna Circle' as well as in kindred groups... the conviction has grown and is steadily increasing, that metaphysics can make no claim to possessing a scientific character. That part of the work of philosophers which may be held to be scientific in its nature...consists of logical analysis' (1959, p. xiii). According to Carnap, philosophy was to be purged of metaphysical claims by means of the development of a logical syntax which was to serve as the logic of science: 'The aim of logical syntax is to provide a system of concepts, a language, by the help of which the results of logical analysis will be exactly formulable. *Philosophy is to be replaced by the logic of science.* That is to say, by the logical analysis of the concepts and sentences of the sciences, for *the logic of science is nothing other than the logical syntax of the language of science'* (1934, p. xiii). [italics in the original] In *The Logical Syntax of Language* (1934) he writes: 'By the logical syntax of a language we mean the formal theory of the linguistic forms of that language'.

Carnap distinguishes between sentences of two types: 'real' (empirical sentences) and 'auxiliary' (logico-analytic sentences). On Carnap's view, empirical inquiry provides the former while philosophy is restricted to the latter. Strictly speaking, according to Carnap, the logico-analytic sentences with which philosophers are concerned have no empirical content.

In his early work, Carnap arrives at his criticism of metaphysics via an attempt to understand the nature of philosophical disagreement. His earliest major philosophical work begins with an attempt to provide an analysis of disagreements over the nature of space and specifically, an analysis of distinct frameworks within which the term 'space' functions. This work diagnoses philosophical disagreements as resulting from confusions of physical, perceptual, and mathematical frameworks. These distinguishable frameworks each employ 'space' in legitimate, but incommensurable ways. This early analysis gives way to a more sweeping dismissal of all metaphysical claims in the years which followed.

Carnap's view of the nature of metaphysical disagreement is very straightforward. He argues repeatedly that metaphysical disagreements simply factor out of meaningful discourse altogether. Metaphysical considerations, on Carnap's view, are simply irrelevant to inquiry. Before describing this move in his work, it is instructive to consider the following biographical comment:

> in my talks with my various friends I had used different philosophical languages, adapting myself to their ways of thinking and speaking. With one friend, I might talk in a language that could be characterized as realistic or even materialistic... In a talk with another friend, I might adapt myself to his idealistic kind of language... With some I talked a language which might be labeled nominalistic... I was surprised to find that this variety in my way of speaking appeared to some objectionable and even inconsistent... When asked which philosophical position I myself held, I was unable to answer. I could only say that in general my way of thinking was closer to that of physicists and of those philosophers who are in contact with scientific work. (1963, pp. 17–18)

Carnap describes his way of thinking is 'neutral with respect to traditional philosophical problems'. This stance is formulated as the principle of tolerance in *The Logical Syntax of Language.*

In his *Pseudoproblems of Philosophy* Carnap imagines two geographers engaged in a disagreement concerning the reality of the external world. Given the task of discovering whether some mountain in Africa is only legendary or whether it really exists, the realist and the idealist geographer will some to the same positive or negative result. According to Carnap, in all empirical questions 'there is unanimity. Hence the choice of philosophical viewpoint has no influence upon the content of natural science... There is disagreement between the two scientists only when they no longer speak as geographers but as philosophers' (1967, p. 333).

In *The Logical Structure of the World* (1928) Carnap presents an attempt to show how the structure of the world is derivable from the moments or time points of experience by means of a single relation. The relation he employs is that of 'partly remembered similarity'. Carnap's thesis is that science deals only with the description of the structural properties of objects. Proof of the thesis depends on demonstrating the possibility of a formal constructional system containing all objects in principle. What Carnap meant by 'formal' in this context is given by the following definition: 'A theory, a rule, a definition, or the like is to be called *formal* when no reference is made in it either to the meaning of the symbols (for example, the words) or to the sense of the expressions (e.g. the sentences), but simply and solely to the kinds and order of the symbols from which the expressions are constructed' (1934, p. 1). The notion of construction which Carnap favored shares many important features in common with Russell's.

Carnap is often read as attempting to reduce all of reality to perceptual experience along the lines of a deductive model of reduction of the kind we find later in Ernst Nagel's work for example (1961). While Carnap uses the term 'reduction' throughout the *Aufbau,* the purpose of his reductions is not ontological in the sense of showing that the physical facts or facts about perception are exhaustive of all the facts. Instead, reducibility in Carnap should be understood as transformation. Thus, for example, one of his examples of the kind of transformations which he has in mind is the interdefinability of fractions and natural numbers. Statements about fractions can be transformed into statements about natural numbers without any loss of content thereby. Carnap's account of reductions as transformations or logical constructions is clearly stated:

> To reduce *a* to *b, c* or to *construct a* out of *b, c* means to produce a general rule that indicates for each individual case how a statement about *a* must be transformed in order to yield a statement about *b, c.* This rule of translation we call a construction rule or constructional definition. (1967, p. 6)

Scientific knowledge, according to Carnap, consists solely in the presentation of systems of relations. The structural features of the systems permit possible transformations of various kinds such that we gain insight into essential character of scientific inquiry and are no longer distracted by non relational features of scientific discourse.

The task of the *Aufbau* is to demonstrate the possibility of a complete constructional system the goal of which would be to provide a unified system which would permit us to overcome the separation of unified science into special sciences. More deeply, such a system would allow us to move from the 'subjective origin of experience' however such an origin is to be understood, to something like an intersubjective basis for objectivity. Carnap writes that the constructional system will show how to 'advance to an intersubjective, objective world which can be conceptually comprehended and which is identical for all observers' (1928, p. 7). Carnap's thesis is that science deals only with the description of the structural properties of objects. The intersubjectively objective world that science provides consists of a set of relationships which can be grasped in them selves and apart from any specific subjective experience. What Carnap proposes is a purified structural characterization of scientific knowledge which can be conveyed to readers via the kind of formal strategies which Russell had already pioneered. On Carnap's view, logic provides a way of tackling all problems of the pure theory of ordering without much difficulty (1928, p. 7).

The burden of the *Aufbau* is to provide something like an existence proof for the very possibility of a constructional system. More specifically, proof of his thesis depends on demonstrating the possibility of a formal constructional system which could in principle contain all objects.

Rather than focusing on properties and objects, Carnap's logical construction is concerned with the purely formal properties of relations between objects. It is worth noting, for instance that Carnap rejects the Fregean distinction between concepts and objects. On the contrary Carnap claims that '[i]t makes no logical difference whether a sign denotes the concept or the object' (1928, p. 10). Carnap's concerns are formal and his account of 'formal' means involves the claim that formal characterizations can be understood apart from the specifics sense or meaning that we assign to the subject matter or to the objects or to the terms involved. By formal properties of a relation, he means those that can be formulated without reference to the meaning [inhaltlicher Sinn] of the relation and the type of objects between which it holds. These formal properties of relations can be presented in quantificational terms (they are the subject of the theory of relations). Carnap lists some of the formal properties of relations, such as symmetry, transitivity, reflexivity, connectivity etc. and then begins to consider the possibility of comparing relations in purely formal terms. He asks for instance that we consider relations in terms of arrow diagrams. The arrow diagram for Carnap is a way of visualizing relations stripped down to their most basic characteristics.

> If two relations have the same arrow diagram, then they are called *structurally equivalent*, or *isomorphic*. The arrow diagram is, as it were, the symbolic representation of the structure. Of course the arrow diagrams of two isomorphic relations do not have to be congruent. We call two such diagrams equivalent is one of them can be transformed into the other by distorting it, as long as no connections are disrupted (topological equivalence)

For contemporary readers, this passage seems to substantially anticipate some of the goals and strategies of the branch of mathematics known as category theory. His focus on capturing the most general features of relations has a strikingly modern flavor and, arguably, indicates the general direction of his work.

The final step in the development of the constructional system is the move from relation descriptions to structure descriptions. Structure descriptions are intended by Carnap to capture precisely what it is that makes scientific claims objectively intelligible. We can derive structure descriptions from the properties of relation descriptions such that the intelligible core of scientific inquiry is laid out in its most objective form. Carnap describes the move from individuals to relation descriptions to structure descriptions as a process of dematerialization, by which he means a removal of the specific or subjective component of knowledge in order to reveal an intersubjective reality underlying our knowledge claims.

> It was possible to draw conclusions concerning the properties of individuals from the relation descriptions. In the case of structure descriptions this is no longer the case. They form the highest level of formalization and dematerialization (23)

For Carnap, many prominent traditional ontological disputes, disputes between phenomenalists and materialists were between idealists and realists were a distraction from more productive lines of inquiry. On the view presented in the *Aufbau* the genuine content of knowledge lies in its structural features. These structural features are preserved no matter whether the scientists in question adopt a realist or an idealist ontological perspective.

As many recent interpreters of Carnap have noted, it is extremely difficult to read his work without being influenced by Quine's depiction of his views in papers like 'Two Dogmas of Empiricism'. However, in recent years, there has been an increasingly sophisticated return to Carnap's philosophy and a growing appreciation of its depth.[20] Michael Freidman (1989, 1992) and Alan Richardson (1998) have provided some especially compelling readings of the *Aufbau* and have clearly demonstrated the ambitious nature of Carnap's attempt to uncover the intersubjective core of inquiry.

While Carnap was a harsh critic of metaphysics, it is possible to read him (at least in his early work) as offering something akin to a version of structural realism as a replacement for traditional ontology. Contemporary advocates of structural realism will occasionally cite his work as anticipating some of the problems under consideration today (See for example Cao 2001). In a certain sense, Carnap's criticisms of traditional metaphysics occupy far less space in his work than his constructive efforts. While these criticisms have drawn the most attention, they tend to be somewhat weakly argued when compared with the effort invested in some of his more constructive projects. Strikingly, for instance, his criticisms of ontology tend to be restricted to examples drawn from realism/anti-realism debates and likewise, his criticism of metaphysics points to classic cases of obscurantism and confusion. The

---

[20]The best discussion of Carnap's constructional system is Alan Richardson's *Carnap's Construction of the World.* In general terms, my presentation owes a great deal to Michael Friedman's reading of the *Aufbau* in, for example, "Carnap's *Aufbau* Reconsidered" and his "Epistemology in the *Aufbau*"

most fruitful interpretation of Carnap's work for the purposes of ontology are likely to begin from his characterization of logical construction and his account of the possibility of an intersubjectively accessible system of relations.

In Carnap's later work, it is possible to detect a shift in his attitude towards ontological questions. Rather than maintaining a hypercritical stance towards all metaphysical claims, Carnap admits the necessity of ontological commitment as a part of inquiry. Inquiry depends, in an important sense on having at least some ontological commitment. In his 'Empiricism, Semantics, and Ontology' (1950). Carnap presents a pragmatic conception of ontological questions as having meaningful answers within specific linguistic frameworks. While external questions, which ask for example whether some linguistic framework has the properties that framework defines, are still regarded as meaningless by Carnap, the kinds of ontological questions which scientists might ask are regarded as internal questions. Carnap's adopts a fallibilist attitude towards ontological questions, such that any ontological commitments are subject to revision in light of new evidence.[21]

16.4 Quinean Naturalism and Ontological Commitment

For much of the late twentieth century, Carnap's work was overshadowed by W.V. Quine's approach to philosophy. Quine's most widely read article 'Two Dogmas of Empiricism' is a sustained critique of attempts to draw the kind of distinction between analytic and synthetic truths that Quine claims is required in order to support Carnap's distinction between questions that are internal and external to science. Quine's work served to undermine the Carnapian criticism of ontology and set in its place a compellingly simple worldview known as philosophical naturalism. Naturalism has been one of the dominant currents in late twentieth century thought. The relationship between ontology and naturalism is complicated and deserves further exploration. However, for the purposes of this essay it will suffice to show how Quine's criticism of Carnap helps to make room for the modern revival of ontology and also how Quine's account of ontological commitment is connected to some of the developments in early analytic philosophy which we have already touched upon above.

Naturalism is a simple doctrine to introduce. Naturalists argue that science and philosophy should not be sharply distinguished; that they are continuous theoretical enterprises. For Quine, philosophy does not stand apart from our engagement with the natural world. There is no privileged standpoint, or 'first philosophy', that can permit us to discover or determine the rules for natural science, for aesthetics, politics or even ethics apart from an engaged practical acquaintance with these pursuits.

Philosophers, according to Quine and other naturalist thinkers, simply do not have access to the kinds of *a priori* truths (propositions that are true apart from

---

[21] Thanks to Stephen Elliot for pointing me towards "Empiricism, Semantics, and Ontology".

experience) that can allow us to regulate or legislate the scope and content of human knowledge. Carnap believed that philosophers are primarily in the business of analyzing and explaining the meanings of important concepts and, as we saw above with showing how structural features of scientific inquiry can be transformed without loss of content. Conceptual analysis of various forms, it was taught, could be practiced without the need for experimental results of any kind. While the topic of conceptual analysis, on Carnap's view, was science, the practice and results of philosophical analysis per se did not have any genuine content.

Quine's work had the effect (at least among philosophers in the United States during the 1950s and 1960s) of undermining the notion that philosophers working on the meanings of concepts were engaged in a qualitatively different kind of enterprise from scientists working in their laboratories. Quine focused his criticism on what he saw as Carnap's notion that philosophers uncovered analytic or purely conceptual truths as opposed to the synthetic or empirical truths of the natural sciences. The assumption that certain statements were analytically true (true by virtue of their meanings alone) had seemed to provide a way for philosophers to carve out a useful niche for themselves in the service of science. For example, a statement like 'all bachelors are unmarried males' seemed like the kind of truth that one could discover apart from any scientific research. The concept 'unmarried male' seems included in the concept 'bachelor' in such a way as to render the statement 'all bachelors are unmarried males' true by meaning alone. Quine depicts his philosophical predecessors as seeing philosophy as purely a matter of investigating and discovering such analytically true statements.

In 'Two Dogmas of Empiricism,' (1954) Quine argued that no non-circular account of analyticity can be provided that would justify the claim that a statement can be true by virtue of its meaning alone. For, if one claims that analytic truths are sentences that are true on the strength of their meanings, then the question shifts to the definition of meaning? Quine argued that an attempt to pin down the notion of meaning leads us back to analyticity and that there is therefore no non-circular definition of analytic truth. According to Quine, this means that the notion of analytic truth crumbles. Through his criticism of the 'analytic-synthetic' distinction, Quine understood his work as having brought the traditional dream of a distinctly philosophical kind of knowledge to an end.

According to naturalists, philosophers and scientists are engaged in the collective human project of inquiry. This continuity has the practical effect of allowing philosophers to apply empirical results to the solution of traditional philosophical problems. More specifically, the naturalist believes that all of reality, including mental life, ethics and culture, can be understood as part of a single natural order. Nothing in nature, according to the naturalist needs to be explained by reference to something that falls outside of the causal order of nature. Naturalists reject the idea that we have access to *a priori knowledge*, which cannot be corrected or rejected in light of future evidence. All knowledge comes to us through our dealings with the natural world and there are no divine revelations or philosophical intuitions that can underpin our claims.

Quine's views of ontology should be understood in the context of this broader naturalist framework. However, naturalist sloganeering, by itself was not responsible for the influential account of ontology which Quine's work provides. Instead, as we shall see, his account arises directly out of his consideration of the role of existential quantification in formal theories.

Quine's theory of ontological commitment states that if a thing exists it will be the value of the variable in a theory once that theory is construed in logical terms: 'To be is to be the value of a variable.' As was the case for Ramsey and Carnap, Russell's theory of descriptions serves as the basis of Quine's analysis. Unlike Carnap, Quine sees no principled away of distinguishing scientific from philosophical investigation and does not accept Carnap's rejection of ontology. For Carnap, ontological disputes do not have any bearing on genuine scientific inquiry. As we saw above, Quine's naturalism challenged the sharp distinction between analytic and synthetic propositions. Since this distinction licensed Carnap's claim to be able to see ontology as otiose with respect to meaningful inquiry, one of the effects of Quine's argument was to encourage a reconsideration of the nature of metaphysical and more specifically of ontological claims. In this respect, Quine's work was one of the catalysts for the revival of ontology in the second half of the century.

Like Carnap, Quine's views on the nature of ontology were directly informed by Russellian reflections on the relationship between logic and ontology. Quine's initial work on ontological questions concerned the notion of the proposition as it relates to sentences in logic. He first published on the topic of ontology in 1934. In his paper 'Ontological remarks on the propositional calculus' Quine challenges what had, by then become a widely shared view, namely the idea that sentences denote propositions. Quine's argument rests on the idea that we can do without the notion of the proposition insofar as propositions are taken as the denotata of sentences while still maintaining the identity of the components of our discourse. He argues, quite simply, that we can simply conflate sentences and propositions without losing anything of significance. Any role which might have been played by propositions understood as independent entities, for example, the maintenance of sameness of meaning, can be accomplished via convention or via the sameness of structure of written marks. Quine's first foray into ontology was very much in the spirit of Russell, Ramsey and Carnap, insofar as it sought to eliminate otiose objects from our ontological inventory.

Quine's engagement with ontological questions undergoes a dramatic shift once he begins to reflect on the nature of quantification. In particular, the nature of existential quantification becomes central to the development of Quine's perspective on ontology. The goal of his account of ontological commitment is to specify as precisely as possible, the nature of existence claims. His ontological position is articulated most famously in his essays 'On what there is' and 'Ontological Relativity'.

Quine's holistic account of language commits him to a picture of existence claims such that they cannot be understood apart from consideration of the background language in which those claims are made. Usually, his discussions of ontology connect existence claims to the claims made by theories. However, whenever we begin to analyze Quine's account of ontology, it is always entangled to an important extent with his views of the nature of language and truth. It is extremely difficult to untangle, for instance, the Quinean doctrine of the inscrutability of reference from his account of the relativity of ontology.

The subject matter of some theory is, presumably, that set of objects or processes that the theory is about. In order for the theory to be true those objects or processes must exist. The implicit existence claim of that theory is what Quine calls its ontological commitment. The ontological commitments of the theory are readily apparent once the theory is articulated in terms of first-order logic. Specifically, for every existentially quantified sentence that the theory mentions there must exist some object which could go in for the variable which is bound by the existential quantifier such that the sentence would be true. Roughly speaking, we can say that if the theory is committed to or implies a statement involving existential quantification, then the theory can only be made true given the existence of some object such that the open sentences corresponding to the existentially quantified sentences are made true by the object. Peter Hylton (2004) cites the following presentation of Quine's account of ontological commitment:

> The theory is committed to those and only those entities to which the bound variables of the theory must be capable of referring in order that the affirmations made in the theory be true.[22]

It is important to recognize that for Quine ontological questions only arise in any meaningful sense once a regimented language is in place. Moreover, for Quine, the very possibility of reference only arises once some coordinate system is in place. Ontological considerations are, for Quine, always preceded by some notion of reference or truth. Insofar as reference and truth are connected to some coordinate system, it should come as no surprise that Quine's ontological views will make our choice of such a system central to our analysis of ontological commitment.

Quine admits that a range of possible formal languages or methods of regimentation can be applied to scientific language and that as a result of variety of possible ontological interpretations of the theory are admissible (1969, p. 86). This is one sense in which Quine admits the possibility of ontological relativity. Like everything else in Quine's philosophy our ontological commitments are subject to revision and refinement. Moreover, on occasion Quine emphasizes how specifying the universe of discourse for some specific theory is relative to the choice of background theory. Ontological relativity is the result of relativity with respect not only to choice of background theory but also, according to Quine, with respect to the truce choice of how to translate from some object theory into the terms of the background theory. Unlike Carnap's principle of tolerance, Quine's claims about ontological relativity do not amount to the idea that we're free to choose any one system of regimentation over another. For Quine, we have no neutral standpoint from which to make such a

[22]'On what there is', in *From a logical point of view*, second edition. Cambridge: Harvard university press, 1961 1–19

choice. Instead, we always find ourselves embedded within some preexisting world theory or background to theory which we inherit from our scientific community.

Quine's view of ontology is inextricably bound up with his broader naturalist framework. This naturalism has had considerable influence on late twentieth century thought, in a variety of ways. In one sense, as discussed above, Quine's criticism of Carnap opened the door to the revival of ontological and metaphysical investigation. On the other hand, Quine's criticism of modal reasoning, as we shall see below, was an obstacle which metaphysicians were obliged to overcome. In the remaining pages of this section, I will describe the relationship between naturalism and ontology in slightly more general terms.

Put in its simplest possible terms naturalism is the combination of two basic notions: that the natural world is all there is, and that we do not possess any non-natural sources of knowledge. Put in slightly more Quinean terms, for the naturalist, there is no super-scientific or transcendent standpoint that allows us to know more than our latest, best science tells us. The essence of his view is that 'it is within science itself, and not in some prior philosophy, that reality is to be identified and described' (1981, p. 21). All of Quine's philosophy can be understood as a reflection and an elaboration on this simple insight.

While many philosophers have contributed to naturalism and have agreed with Quine's general position, his view has created significant critical response. In fact, much of the most interesting and important philosophy in the second half of the last century was written in direct opposition to Quine's view. A list of philosophers critical of Quine would include Saul Kripke, Jaakko Hintikka, Ruth Barcan Marcus, David Lewis, Jerry Fodor and Hilary Putnam. To varying extents, these philosophers have objected to the implications of Quinean naturalism.

Quinean naturalists stand in opposition to philosophers who contend that we can take some set of common sense intuitions as starting points in philosophical reflection. As we shall see, this puts Quine's view in opposition to much of the mainstream of philosophical opinion. Quine's opponents have, for the most part, objected to the radical consequences of his view. For instance, Quine's strict behaviorism with regard to mental life and his apparent rejection of notions like possibility and necessity have struck some philosophers as so contrary to common sense as to be completely implausible. As we shall see in the next section, the mainstream of opinion in the analytic tradition is committed to the idea that philosophy should be guided by our common sense intuitions and that these intuitions are, at least to some extent insulated from the results of the natural sciences.

While some might contend that we have a special set of intuitions or insights that allow us to step outside of science and judge it from some superscientific vantage point, naturalists see all human knowledge as subject to the same basic standards. Eschewing transcendence, naturalists prefer to see both philosophy and science as a set of all-too human activities conducted by scientists and philosophers who are themselves parts of the natural world. Both philosophy and science are communal endeavors which take as their starting point the world view we inherit. 'I philosophize' he admits 'from the vantage point only of our own provincial conceptual scheme and scientific epoch, true; but I know no better' (1958, p. 7). While the inherited world-view is a starting point, the naturalist argues that continued scientific investigation and discovery improves and revises our inheritance. The scientific wisdom of our age is held to be provisionally true and none of our knowledge claims are held to be sacred or beyond modification.

At its best, according to the naturalist, philosophy is the practice of thinking through the consequences of our inherited scientific worldview. It is the informed reflection of science on its own workings. Rather than attempting to determine the principles or logical framework that scientific research must obey, the naturalist philosopher sees herself as an active participant in the scientific practice of her community. Part of this participation involves the criticism of certain scientific practices or research programs, but this criticism, if it is to be worthwhile, should be informed by our best scientific evidence. Philosophy and science are, as Quine put it, *reciprocally contained.*

> There is thus reciprocal containment, though containment in different senses: epistemology in natural science and natural science in epistemology. . .We are after an understanding of science as an institution or process in the world, and we do not intend that understanding to be any better than the science which is its object. This attitude is indeed one that Neurath was already urging in his Vienna Circle days, with his parable of the mariner who has to rebuild his boat while staying afloat in it. (Quine 1969, p. 84)

Quine avoids the trap of fixing his naturalism to a particular conception of nature or mind, insofar as it rests instead on a way of understanding scientific inquiry and explanation rather than on any fixed image of what nature or the knower must be. Furthermore, for Quine, human knowledge itself is a matter best investigated via natural science. Epistemology itself is naturalized; it becomes a set of problems that we can investigate using whatever means are available to us, including the techniques of psychology and neuroscience. By contrast with the kind of aprioristic reasoning that characterizes most epistemology, Quine's willingness to admit the fallibility of all inquiry is one of the defining characteristics of his philosophy.

So, for example, it would run counter to the spirit of philosophical naturalism to take a particular materialist or physicalist ontology as a starting point on purely metaphysical grounds. Rather, if we accept a physicalist ontology it is because we have strong scientific or empirical grounds supporting our view. From the naturalist perspective, physicalism with respect to most aspects of the natural world happens to be the best ontological position we have found to date, better than idealism, vitalism and dualism for example. Physicalism, for Quine is the notion that a difference in a matter of fact is 'a difference in the fulfillment of the physical-state predicates by space-time regions.' (178, 166) It is difficult to imagine how one could specify a *change* in any other way.

While Quine is takes a physicalist position on most questions, he famously denied that physicalism was a complete ontology. So, for example, Quine's attitude towards mathematics is strikingly Platonist. For Quine, physics provides our best scientific understanding of the natural world. However, physics requires measurement and measurement requires mathematics (or at least set theory). In order for our mathematical (or set-theoretical) propositions to be true, Quine claims that sets must exist as abstract entities. Physics, he argues, is the most accurate account of the natural world we currently have. Mathematics is indispensable for physics and realism about mathematics is entailed by the truth of our mathematical propositions.

Quine briefly flirted with nominalistic solutions to ontological problems in work with Nelson Goodman (1948). However, Quine soon recognized the inability of nominalism to make sense of scientific generalizations, in particular quantitative reasoning. Not only does Quine maintain a naturalistic attitude towards his ontological commitment, he also recognizes that the meaning of notions like 'physical' is the product of scientific deliberation. What it means to be a physical thing is not something we can know *apriori*. Rather, 'physical' is a term that we come to know via our latest, best science. The naturalist will happily agree that the physics of his era, and the conception of physical thing that it assumes, is likely to contain errors. Of course, the only way to show the flaws of our latest, best science is by engaging in a better science and if such changes result in our having to adjust our metaphysical presuppositions, so be it. For Quine, as we have seen claims about ontology are ultimately simply questions about the ontological commitments of our theories.

16.5 Barcan Marcus and Kripke on Modality

Where Quine seems most at odds with contemporary ontology is in his attitude towards questions of possibility and necessity. Quine famously rejects any consideration of possibilities that fall beyond the way the world actually is. For Quine, talk of possible worlds, counterparts and counterfactuals is simply misguided. While certain features of Quine's naturalism have become relatively standard parts of philosophical practice in contemporary philosophy, his Quine's views of logic and modality remain deeply controversial. Quine's rejection of the notions of necessity, possibility and essence, placed him in clear opposition to some of the most prominent metaphysicians in the second half of the twentieth century. Contemporary metaphysics is, in large part, a matter of reasoning about the consequences of basic beliefs about necessity and possibility.

Quine's opposition to modal logic and modal metaphysics rested on arguments whose validity has been challenged repeatedly in recent decades. As we come to understand some of the shortcomings of Quine's criticisms of modality, it is possible that we will be able to separate the broader naturalistic perspective from the anti-modal arguments that defined much of Quine's perspective on metaphysics. While Quine's specific criticism of modality may have been mistaken, his general philosophical position has a number of important implications for metaphysics.

Naturalism came of age prior to the heyday of modal metaphysics over the past three or four decades. As a result, Quine's work is largely disconnected from analytic metaphysics as it is currently practiced. The work of philosophers like Kripke, David Armstrong, David Lewis and Alvin Plantinga set the stage for some of the most important work in contemporary metaphysics. Kripke, Lewis and

Plantinga develop metaphysics around certain features of ordinary terms like 'can', 'must', 'possible', 'necessary' etc. These modal notions can be understood in formal terms using the techniques of modal logic. Since the late 1960s philosophers have developed sophisticated accounts of traditional metaphysical notions like identity, essence and causality via the use of modal logic.

Unfortunately, Quine defined his own position in opposition to philosophers who explored modal notions using the techniques of formal logic. He famously denied that notions like necessity and possibility can play any significant role in philosophical or scientific investigation. Against philosophers like Jaakko Hintikka, Ruth Barcan Marcus and Kripke, Quine argued that realistic interpretations of notions like possibility and necessity lead to incoherence. As we shall see, Quine mistakenly believed that realistic interpretations of modal notions have no place in legitimate discourse. One of the most unfortunate consequences of Quine's denial of modality was its effect on the development of a sophisticated naturalistic metaphysics. Historically, it can easily look as though Quinean naturalists were on the wrong side of the development of contemporary metaphysics.

Quine's criticism of modality rested on a view of language which was closely tied to the Russellian descriptivist tradition. Ruth Barcan Marcus was one of the first philosophers to recognize that once we consider an alternative approach to language, the core objection to modal reasoning is circumvented. Rather than thinking of names in descriptivist terms, Barcan Marcus suggested that we consider names on the model of what she called 'tags' (1961). These tags can be understood as picking out objects directly in some sense. Rather than seeing the naming relation as somehow including or involving descriptions which mediate between the words and their reference, for Marcus, tags can be seen as simply attaching to objects directly and arbitrarily. Her insight paved the way for Kripke to provide a full exposition of the metaphysical implications of what he called 'rigid designation'. Once Barcan Marcus' response to Quine was in place, his criticisms of modal reasoning could be understood as unnecessarily restrictive. Quine's resistance rested on the failure of substitutivity in modal contexts.

Quine's reasoning runs along the following lines: Sentences which involve modal claims do not meet one of the necessary conditions on legitimate scientific discourse, namely the requirement that replacing a term in a sentence with a different term referring to the same object as the original term should have no bearing on the true value the original sentence. If for instance the terms 'Farookh Bulsara' and 'Freddie Mercury' pick out the same man then replacing one for the other in some sentence should not alter the truth value of that sentence. Quine argued that both modal terms and the propositional attitudes were useless for science. Consider the following sentence:

(a) 'If Freddy Mercury comes to town there will be a commotion'

Notice that this sentence contains no propositional attitudes, no mention of belief, desire, thought and the like, nor does it make any reference to the necessity or possibility of the truth of the sentence. Given this statement as part of my wider theory I can make a number of perfectly reasonable predictions and inferences. Despite its strangeness, this little law of nature in our imaginary theory has the same logical structure as:

(B) 'If water is brought to 100° Centigrade it will boil'

or

(C) 'If enough snow falls on that branch it will break'

However, as soon as I introduce propositional attitudes or modal qualifiers into the statements of my theory, trouble ensues. The reason is simple. Given for instance:

(D) 'Jean believes that Freddy Mercury was the lead singer for Queen'

We cannot infer with certainty that

(E) 'Jean believes that Farookh Bulsara was the lead singer for Queen'

This is the case despite the little known fact that Freddy Mercury and Farookh Bulsara were the same person. As all die-hard fans know, Bulsara changed his name to Freddy Mercury in order to make himself more acceptable to a British audience. Jean, of course, may not be a fan and may never have heard the name Farookh Bulsara, therefore (E) may not be true. So, (D) and (E) are not interchangeable, by virtue of containing propositional attitudes. But now consider our original statement (A) above, the one that contained no mention of propositional attitudes:

(A) 'If Freddy Mercury comes to town there will be a commotion'

If this is true, then it will also be true that

(A*) 'If Farookh Bulsara comes to town there will be a commotion'

In (A) and (A*) we are referring to a particular physical object – a man – whose presence is likely to cause a commotion, whereas in (D) and (E) we are referring to a something far more problematic, the propositional attitude belief that. Quine argued that this failure of substitutivity in (D) and (E) is enough to vitiate all theories that include propositional attitudes and that, if we want good science, the very least we can ask for is that the law of substitutivity hold. Therefore, according to Quine we should eliminate talk of propositional attitudes from our science.

A similar problem obtains in the case of modal notions. If I say for instance that

(F) Necessarily, nine is greater than seven

and

(G) Nine is the number of planets

I cannot replace 'the number of planets' with 'nine' in the modal context without generating the false claim that

(I) Necessarily, the number of planets is greater than seven.

The failure of substitutivity in modal contexts is the principal reasons for his rejection of modality. Barcan Marcus points out that Quine's argument is undermined by what she sees as his confusion with respect to the nature of identity and by his failure to recognize the possibility of a non-descriptivist account of names.[23]

---

[23]See her classic paper 'Modalities and Intensional Languages' in *Modalities: Philosophical Essays*, Oxford University Press, 1993. pp.3–39

In terms of identity, she argues, Quine fails to distinguish between the 'is' of predication and the 'is' of identity. So for example to make the claim that nine is the number of planets is to invoke the 'is' of predication whereas claims like 'nine is nine' or 'nine equals nine' are meant to indicate identity rather than predication. The 'is' of predication involves ascribing properties or characteristics to objects whereas the 'is' of identity makes a metaphysical claim concerning the objects themselves/itself.

When one makes the assertion that 'Her shoes are purple,' the word 'are' serves to indicate a relationship of predication. Obviously since other things are purple one cannot say that her shoes are related to purple via an 'is' of identity because if one claims that her shirt is also purple one is committed to saying that her shoes are her shirt since identity is a transitive relation. Now, clearly, the 'is' of predication does not have the property of transitivity, by contrast, transitivity is a defining characteristic of the 'is' of identity.

The two different ways in which we use the word 'is' shed some important light on the notion of reference. In addition to problems related to identity, Quinean objections to the introduction of modal terms involve confusing tags with the objects picked out by those tags. Once this confusion is removed, then Quine's claim that substitution fails in modal contexts can be overcome. The price, according to Quine is a return to what he calls 'Aristotelian essentialism'.

Ruth Barcan Marcus' response to Quine sets the stage for Kripke's treatment of modality. Kripke's *Naming and Necessity* is widely appreciated as central to the recent history of philosophy insofar as it clarifies the distinction between logical, epistemological and metaphysical notions of necessity. The implications of this distinction are deep and far reaching. Most strikingly, it allows for Kripke's recognition of aposteriori necessary truths. By untangling necessity from apriority and analyticity, Kripke shows how metaphysical investigation can avoid traditional epistemological criticisms.

The argument of the lectures is well-known: Kripke follows Barcan Marcus in arguing against a descriptivist view of reference and for a direct-reference model of names. Direct reference is intended to capture the way proper names and natural kind terms serve to track objects across possible states of affairs. In this context, names serve as rigid designators. While Kripke's claims concerning rigid designation are widely regarded as providing a new theory of reference, it is important to recognize the function of notions like rigid designation in support of his more basic metaphysical argument. Insofar as there is a new philosophy of language in Kripke's work his account of language is secondary to the more basic metaphysical purpose of the lectures.

Naming and Necessity begins with some relatively straightforward metaphysical assumptions. For example, identity is understood to be a relation. Identity, he claims, never holds between two things and if it holds, it always holds of necessity. From here, the claim that if a is identical with b then it is necessarily identical with b is the result of a very simple semi-formal argument which runs as follows: If we accept the necessity of self-identity, then for all x, necessarily $x=x$. If we accept the principle of the indiscernibility of identicals then, for all x and for all y, $x=y \rightarrow \forall \varphi\ (\varphi x \text{ « } \varphi y)$.

Now, if *a* is identical with *b* and if *a* is identical with *b* then whatever is true of *a* is true of *b*, then it is necessarily the case that *a* is identical with *b* since it is true of *a* that it is necessarily identical with *a* and whatever is true of *a* is also true of *b*.

However, accepting the result leads to some odd sounding claims. As Kripke points out, it seems to entail, for instance that if Ben Franklin is the first postmaster general, then it is necessarily the case that Ben is the first postmaster general. There is an apparent mismatch between the formal reasoning (which led us to the necessity of identity) and our ordinary ways of using the word *is*.

Kripke's lectures criticize descriptivist approaches to language replacing it with his account of names as rigid designators. The elaboration of Kripke's so-called 'new theory of reference' in *Naming and Necessity* serves to reconcile the formal or semi-formal insights with respect to modality and identity with ordinary identity statements. Kripke's arguments in these lectures are designed to lend some commonsense plausibility to the underlying metaphysical argument.

In *Naming and Necessity*, the notion of intuition is deployed in three distinguishable ways. Intuition is connected to the meaningfulness of certain terms and concepts, it is taken as indicating the conclusiveness of arguments and it serves as a way of distinguishing between formal and informal reasoning in philosophy. Distinguishing the various roles played by intuition in Kripke's work is important insofar as it clarifies our own uses of this notion in philosophical investigation.

Carrying the heaviest argumentative burden in Kripke's defense of modal reasoning is the idea of intuition as the means by which we connect to the 'ordinary' or 'commonsensical' meanings of our words. So for example, he stresses the familiarity of modal discourse when he writes:

> When you ask whether it is necessary or contingent that *Nixon* won the election, you are asking the intuitive question whether in some counterfactual situation, *this man* would in fact have lost the election. (1980, p. 41)

Modal questions can be intuitive and presumably, he believes, ordinary questions. That modal questions have some connection to ordinariness is intended as a means of certifying their meaningfulness; on this view, ordinary sentences and questions are meaningful sentences and questions. While neither 'Is it contingent that Nixon won the election?' nor 'Is it necessary that Nixon won the election?' sound like ordinary questions to my ear, Kripke is less concerned with these particular examples and is focused instead on leading us to recognize that we ask a range of modal questions in ordinary daily life. He is specifically interested in counterfactual reasoning – 'Would Nixon have lost his bid for re-election had he not followed Kissinger's advice?' and the like.

Kripke's notion of meaningfulness here is informed by the ordinary language tradition in philosophy. His confidence that the meaningfulness of words and questions is grounded in their ordinary usage as we see in the following passage, where Kripke writes:

> It is very far from being true that this idea [that a property can meaningfully be held to be essential or accidental to an object independently of its description] is a notion which

> has no intuitive content, which means nothing to the ordinary man. Suppose that someone said, pointing to Nixon, 'that's the guy who might have lost'. Someone else says 'Oh no, if you describe him as 'Nixon', then he might have lost; but, of course, describing him as the winner, then it is not true that he might have lost.' Now which one is being the philosopher, here, the unintuitive man? It seems to me that obviously the second. The second man has a philosophical theory. (1980, p. 41)

Kripke's characterization of meaningful and meaningless questions introduces the notion of 'intuitive content'. If an idea has 'intuitive content' then, according to Kripke, it is meaningful to the 'ordinary man.' The reference to the ordinary man here is connected with the idea of intuition or commonsense which is operative. By adding 'intuitive' to 'content', he means to distinguish contexts where the content of a term might be due to some stipulation or some unusual specialist usage. The ordinary man is contrasted with the philosopher, who in this passage is characterized as the 'unintuitive man'. Here, Kripke is deploying commonsense or intuition in a manner very close to that of the ordinary language philosophers. Intuitive content contrasts with content derived via formal or technical considerations. In Kripke's thinking, formal considerations are distinguished from and perhaps even subordinated to intuitive content. In terms of justificatory force, one clear impression is that intuitive content plays a more central role in philosophical deliberation than theories generated by 'unintuitive men'.

Kripke's account of possible worlds marks a break with Quine's naturalism in terms of its methodological emphasis on common sense or intuition. As indicated above, Kripke's philosophy owes a great deal to ordinary language philosophy insofar as it rests on the idea of familiar intuitions which serve as guides in our ontological or philosophical reflection.

16.6 Common sense, Ordinary Language and Categorial Ontology

Quine's naturalism runs counter to the emphasis on common sense and ordinary experience in twentieth century analytic philosophy. The interplay between formal considerations and intuitive common sense principles is an ongoing theme of analytic ontology. This section traces that emphasis from the early work of Russell and Moore through the ordinary language philosophers to the revival of ontology in the work of Strawson, Barcan-Marcus and Kripke.

In Russell's early work, we saw how logic serves as a means to organize ontological investigation while at the same time (according to Russell) logic requires support, in some sense, from ontology. Thus, abstract entities are invoked in order to support the possibility of logic, and logical techniques like the theory of descriptions while methods like logical construction also serve to inform us with respect to our ontological commitments. Russell was sensitive to both the corrigibility of common sense and the limitations of formal reasoning. In this sense, his work sets the tone for much of the best work in ontology which followed.

Like Frege, Russell regarded the developments in modern logic as centrally important to progress in philosophy. At the same time, Russell's early work is shaped by his rejection of Idealism and by the influence of Moore's account of the nature of judgment.[24] The rejection of Idealism and his adoption of some of Moore's central doctrines are both motivated by his common sense ontological commitments.

The connection between logic and ontology is obvious in his *Principles of Mathematics* from 1903. As Peter Hylton has described in detail, Russell's most important early achievements, and especially his work in the *Principles* were influenced by Moore's arguments against Idealism (Hylton 1990). Both Moore and Russell reject the Idealist doctrine of internal relations, the notion that propositions can have degrees of truth, and what they saw as the psychologistic features of the transcendental method. The reaction to Idealism generated a diverse and complicated range of positions, but its motivation was simple. Russell and Moore saw their work as a straightforward turn away from what they saw as Idealism's denial of the reality of familiar objects and towards what these philosophers saw as a commonsensical form of realism.

Reflecting on his concern with the ontological implications of Idealism in *Our Knowledge of the External World,* Russell asserts that this view 'condemns almost all that makes up our everyday world: things and qualities, relations, space, time, change, causation, activity, the self. All these things, though in some sense facts which qualify reality, are not real as they appear. What is real is one, single indivisible, timeless whole called the Absolute' (1914, p. 16). Russell's concern with the ontological inadequacies of Idealism led him to attempt to develop a form of realism which he believed would save us from having to reject the truthfulness of virtually all our judgments and which would allow us to avoid rejecting the reality of the objects of ordinary experience.

In his *Principles of Mathematics,* he presents in his bluntest and most extreme form, the realistic approach to metaphysics and logic which marks much of his most important work. He famously states, for instance, that discoveries in mathematics have the same character as Columbus' discovery of the West Indies. '[W]e no more create the numbers' he writes 'than he created the Indians' (1903, p. 427). Russell's realism undergoes significant modification in his later work. However, at this stage, his ontological commitments are clear and staggeringly direct. He writes for instance (in a passage which is quoted in Hylton 1990, p. 172): 'The number two is not purely mental, but is an entity which may be thought *of.* Whatever can be thought of has being, and its being is a pre-condition, not a result, of its being thought.' (ibid)

While this is not the place to examine Russell's arguments in detail, it is worth considering the turn to common sense in his and Moore's philosophy. Moore's work encourages us to pause before settling into a preferred set of methods or theses, and to begin instead by thinking about the place from which our investigations start, namely from ordinary experience. Moore asserts that anyone engaged

---

[24]Moore's break with Idealism is defended in his article 'The Nature of Judgment', (1898)

in theorizing can be assumed to hold a set of implicit beliefs along the following lines:

> There exists at present a living human body, which is *my* body. This body was born at a certain time in the past, and has existed continuously ever since, though not without undergoing changes; it was, for instance, much smaller when it was born, and for some time afterwards, than it is now. Ever since it was born, it has been either in contact with or not far from the surface of the earth; and, at every moment since it was born, there have also existed many other things, having shape and size in three dimensions (in the same familiar sense in which it has), from which it has been *at various distances* (1925, p. 107)

He goes on to claim that he knows with certainty that many people have known things concerning themselves and their bodies corresponding to propositions described in the above paragraph.

Moore reasons along the following lines: Any attempt to deny these propositions seems to involve some implicit acceptance of their truth; to actively deny these propositions is in some sense implicitly self-undermining. As Moore points out, these propositions are not necessary truths. They are conceivably false. So, while he has not directly countered the skeptic's position, he has called on the background beliefs of participants in any argument as evidence that the skeptic is likely to be either insincere or implicitly self-contradictory. Those propositions of common sense that Moore points to as implicitly at play in any argument are difficult to deny coherently, but such a denial is clearly possible.

If a theory implied that I was not born at some point in the past, it would require an extremely high degree of evidence in order for me to accept it. The readjustment in my set of beliefs demanded by this claim would be so fundamental that the evidence required would have to be extraordinarily strong. What makes denying Moore's propositions of common sense so uncomfortable is that these propositions are often precisely what we rely on when deciding between competing theories. As we shall see below, the commitment to common sense has been a central feature in analytic discussions of ontology. In later analytic ontology, the term 'intuition' comes to play the role that 'common sense' had played for Moore. There is an important difference between the role played by intuition in more recent philosophy and the realist employment of common sense in Moore and the early Russell. For more recent philosophers, intuition serves as a methodological guide which can orient our investigations without determining the conclusions of those investigations. As we shall see, methodologically conservative ontologists like David Lewis can be led to counterintuitive conclusions.

One component of inquiry that all ontologists are likely to accept is the notion that common sense or ordinary experience has an important role in our ontological deliberations. Ontologists will disagree with respect to the nature of the role which common sense should play. Some contemporary ontologists, like Mark Heller, will move from the manifest or ordinary starting point to the conclusion that that familiar objects do not really exist.[25] Heller, for example, argues only subatomic particles

[25] See for example his *The Ontology of Physical Objects* (1990),

exist. Heller's conclusion is that we can only legitimately individuate at the most basic physical level and from there the best we can do is to talk about hunks of subatomic particles. Other philosophers, e.g. Amie Thomasson and Crawford Elder contend that familiar objects are just as real as subatomic particles.[26] Thomasson and Elder begin from the recognition that there is something counterintuitive and potentially self-undermining about the denial of familiar objects for exotic theoretical reasons. The challenge for readers of debates like this is to determine the degree to which our common sense intuitions about familiar objects ought to outweigh strong arguments to the contrary. Ontology is subject to risks on both sides: Either a dogmatic attachment to familiar objects on the one hand or costly philosophically extravagances on the other.

Common sense plays an important regulative role in all forms of inquiry, but it has special importance for philosophy. Common sense helps the philosopher avoid asserting views that are unreasonable and guides her towards more plausible lines of inquiry. Its role should be especially important in ontological theorizing, where we have fewer of the guideposts that help orient inquiry in other areas of philosophy. One role that common sense has played in twentieth century philosophy is in support of a critical posture towards philosophical investigation per se.[27] Common sense informs us that a philosopher who denies the reality of familiar objects is indulging in a potentially self-undermining form of philosophical extravagance.

Philosophical extremism, according to ordinary language philosophers like John Austin, can be cured by careful attention to the way philosophical terms of art are originally used in ordinary language. So, for example, with respect to ontological questions, rather than worrying about the reality of chairs and tables, Austin argued, philosophers should look to common sense and attend to the role of terms like 'real' in ordinary language. Philosophical problems, according to Austin, lose their grip on us once we understand their origins. The basic idea of the ordinary language tradition in philosophy is that philosophical theories and more specifically the philosophical use of terms can be evaluated through a comparison with ordinary usage.

The Austinian reaction to philosophical analyses of the word 'real' assumes (in a way which I think is highly problematic) that common sense is never in conflict with itself in any philosophically interesting way. Instead, according to Austin it is philosophers who, in his words, have led us up the garden path as the result of their misunderstanding. 'Real', Austin writes 'is what we might call a *trouser-word*... it is the negative use that wears the trousers' (Austin 1964, p. 70).

---

[26]See Amie Thomasson's 'Artifacts and Human Concepts' (forthcoming). And Crawford Elder's *Real Natures and Familiar Objects* (2004)

[27]Wittgenstein described the project this way: "When philosophers use a word – "knowledge", "being", "object", "I", "sentence", "name" – and try to grasp the *essence* of the thing, one must always ask oneself: is the word ever actually used in this way in the language-game which is its original home?

What *we* do is to bring words back from their metaphysical to their everyday use." *Philosophical Investigations* § 116

> 'A real duck' differs from the simple 'a duck' only in that it is used to exclude various ways of being not a real duck – but a dummy, a toy, a picture, a decoy and c.; and moreover I don't know *just* how to take the assertion that it's a real duck unless I know *just* what, on that particular occasion, the speaker has it in mind to exclude. This, of course, is why the attempt to find a characteristic common to all things that are of could be called 'real' is doomed to failure. (Austin 1962, p. 70)

He might be correct to claim that fakes and decoys originally cause us to notice the problem of determining what counts as real. As far as it is a genealogy of philosophical problems, his account might have some merit. However, it is worth asking whether this kind of genealogical criticism has any relevance to ontological questions in science and metaphysics. For instance, consider how a working scientist might approach questions of whether 'mental maps', the Freudian superego or genes are real. Each of these examples would involve a sense of 'real' which is not parasitic on 'fakes' in the same way as questions concerning decoy ducks and leather couches.

The ordinary language philosopher misses the point with respect to what motivates contemporary ontological investigations. For instance, as we have already seen above, one important problem for contemporary metaphysics is that familiar objects seem to be rendered epiphenomenal by the assumptions of scientifically informed common sense. Such problems are especially pressing for the ontology of the special sciences. If those objects mentioned by the special sciences are not really real then the truth value of those sciences is in jeopardy. Thereby, in psychology for instance, we would have no objective reason for preferring one ontology over another. In the case of psychology, the ontological challenge relates directly to our understanding of ourselves. Do we have ideas? Are we conscious? Are we best modeled as connectionist or classical systems? etc. All such questions are empty if our non-physical ontologies are irrelevant and illusory. Whatever its virtues as a description of the sources of philosophical problems, the Austinian or ordinary language strategy provides no response to this and most other kinds of ontological concern.

It is not enough to claim that the philosophical problem is the product of a misunderstanding, since, even if this were true, leaving the philosophical problem unresolved or worse still denying that the problem can be solved generates another problem, namely it leads to the inability to decide between theories in the special sciences. Even granting the possibility that philosophical questions have their origins in confusion, debates over individuation and reality are not *merely* artifacts of philosophical misunderstanding. They figure centrally in a range of familiar disputes in the history of science. Prominent examples include the units of selection problem in evolutionary biology, the question of the reality of atoms in late nineteenth and early twentieth century physics, the nature of mental images in psychology, etc. Debates over the ontological status of a particular scientific term can take a variety of forms. In some cases, the question is not whether the objects in question exist, but rather, whether they constitute a kind. So, for instance, we can find instances of misfolded proteins, without knowing whether these things really constitute a class of infectious agents-prions that are responsible for brain diseases. By contrast, some physicists and philosophers doubt that there really are strings of the kind that we read about in string theory. Ontological questions arise in scientific inquiry in contexts where traditional skeptical concerns of the sort which interest philosophers are simply not in play. Furthermore, ontological challenges result from and have direct bearing on scientific practice.

We do not have to draw our examples from natural science. For instance consider the question as to whether shadows are real. It is not the case that the use of 'real' in this question parasitic on the notion of 'fake'. Instead, we may be engaged in a very different kind of reasoning. The question as to whether shadows or holes are real would not be a straightforward question of the relationship between appearance and reality. If an ontologist is deciding whether to include shadows or holes in her inventory of the real, she is not engaged in a purely skeptical inquiry and is not necessarily denying the existence of shadows or questioning their apparent reality, she is asking instead what kind of existence they have. She might ask, for instance, whether it is right to see shadows as being on an ontological par with the objects that cast shadows.

We can assume that ordinary language philosophers would not wish to take all objects as being on a par ontologically, consequently we can assume that they would permit us to inquire into degrees of existence. Is my being an uncle, more or less real than my being human? I am really a teacher, (not a fake teacher) and I am really human (not a mannequin) but could it not make sense to say that I instantiate the property of being human in some stronger sense than I instantiate the property of being a Texan? Can I instantiate the property of being an Irish citizen and also be a Texan? Ontologists can begin to make sense of such claims and questions in a variety of ways. It is certainly not the case that all questions having to do with reality are reducible to the familiar themes of appearance and skepticism.

Even if Austin were right about the origins of ontological questions, his diagnosis itself is infected with a genetic fallacy. Just because the philosophical problem was born out of some original confusion, does not mean that it should not be taken seriously in its current form.

Ordinary language philosophy was a relatively short-lived movement. However, it has had deep influences on some of the most important philosophers who followed. One of the more interesting followers of the ordinary language tradition was Strawson. Unlike the ordinary language philosophers who preceded him, Strawson actively engaged in what we would recognize as ontological investigation. Strawson described metaphysics as the finding of reasons for what we believe on instinct. Rather than stopping at ordinary language, Strawson's goal was to provide an explanation for some of its more prominent and philosophically significant features. In his 1959 book *Individuals* he undertakes an analysis of the fundamental categories which he believes underlying human reasoning. It provides an argument for the fundamentality of space and time and suggests that bodies in space and time should be considered the basic particulars of our ontological framework.

Strawson provides a fascinating criticism of process-based ontologies arguing that demonstrates the priority the notion of object over process in our thinking. Strawson's approach has a pronounced Kantian flavor. He presents it as a scheme-dependant ontology, meaning that the philosopher's task is to uncover the ontological categories presupposed by the conceptual scheme in question. It is our ordinary way of talking and thinking that serves as the basis for this analysis. Thus, like the ordinary language philosophers Strawson rests the authority of his claims on the authority of everyday experience, language, and thought. The categorial approach to ontology which we find in contemporary ontologists like E.J. Lowe can be traced directly to Strawson's methodological exam example in works like *Individuals.*

The Strawsonian project of descriptive metaphysics shares important characteristics in common with both ordinary language philosophy and the realism of the early Russell and Moore. As we saw above, Moore saw the Common Sense view of the world as embodied in a set of propositions whose denial (while not flatly contradictory) leads to absurdity. The attempt to deny these propositions, he claimed, seems self-undermining since claiming and arguing for anything seems to involve some implicit acceptance of the truth of a whole range of Common Sense propositions. So, according to Moore, to actively deny these propositions is in some sense implicitly self-undermining. Rather than directly confronting skeptical arguments he provided a description of the background beliefs of participants in an argument. As an antidote to what he saw as the speculative excesses of his British Idealist predecessors, Moore's arguments are intended to support a view of philosophical practice in which speculative exuberance is restrained by the modesty of Common Sense. Strawson takes this Moorean starting point and develops a categorial account of its ontology.

16.7 Common Sense Conservatives and Their Counterintuitive Conclusions

While there is still broad acknowledgment of the importance of commonsense in philosophy, intuition often figures in support of metaphysical theses which do not seem consonant with the kind of modesty that Moore advocated. It is common for contemporary metaphysical arguments to deduce counterintuitive conclusions from some relatively plausible set of intuitions or platitudes. Consider David Lewis' famous arguments for modal realism. While Moore might have joined philosophers who stare incredulously at the strangeness of modal realism, Lewis' arguments consistently make appeal to commonsense and he follows Moore in his emphasis on theoretical conservatism as a methodological principle for philosophers.

Lewis was perhaps the most influential philosophical ontologist of recent decades. He argues for a position which has come to be known as Humean supervenience. While Lewis's views concerning modality have gained notoriety, and contrast in significant ways with Quine's, his overall approach to philosophy shares some common features with Quinean naturalism. Lewis regarded scientific inquiry, and specifically physical science, as the most promising path to truth. Given this picture of scientific inquiry Lewis regards it has virtually inevitable that physics will eventually provide an account of the fundamental constituents of the natural world. If we know the basic constituents of the natural world then on Lewis's view all other facts will follow as supervenient on the physical facts. The claim that the physical facts; the spatio temporal account of the natural world, suffice to account for all the truths is known as Humean supervenience. A great deal of contemporary ontology involves the development of objections to Lewis's view or the extension and refinement of his position.

In spite of its occasionally extravagant and exotic appearance Lewis's philosophy is organized around the principle of frugality and methodological conservatism. However Lewis' attitude towards the propositions of commonsense themselves stands in contrast with Moore's. In *On the Plurality of Worlds*, for example, Lewis's argument for modal realism amounts to the presentation of reasons for accepting some commonsense theses at the expense of others. For example, in his defense of modal realism, he explains his conclusion by way of showing which of three commonsense intuitions he accepts and which he rejects.[28]

Unlike Moore, Lewis distinguishes the significance of commonsense for philosophical methodology and its significance with respect to the evaluation of the results of inquiry. Commonsense has no veto power over the latter. It 'has no absolute authority in philosophy... It's just that theoretical conservatism is the only sensible policy for theorists of limited powers who are duly modest about what they could accomplish after a fresh start' (1986, p. 134). It is likely that the British Idealist targets of Moore's criticism would have agreed with Lewis' methodological point. Thus, common sense figures prominently in Lewis' work, but not in the way that Moore would have recognized.

In ontology, commonsense has taken a decidedly un-Moorean turn. For instance, Moore argued that we ought to accept truisms with respect to the existence of familiar objects. By contrast, as Crawford Elder points out, in the years that followed, ontologists have almost universally lost faith in the existence of ordinary things. Familiar objects 'have been crowded out by sleeker rivals unheard of by common sense – objects having crisper extinction conditions, or characterized by properties not susceptible to sorites arguments, or objects whose causal efficacy traces to far cleaner laws than would ever fit common-sense objects'(2004, p. x).[29] One of

---

[28] He writes:
"Suppose we interviewed some spokesman for common sense. I think we would find that he adheres firmly to three theses:
(1) Everything is actual
(2) Actuality consists of everything that is spatiotemporally related to us, and nothing more (give or take some 'abstract entities'). It is not vastly bigger, or less unified than we are accustomed to think.
(3) Possibilities are not parts of actuality, they are alternatives to it.
[...] I speak as party to the conventions of the community in question. [...] I am within my rights in standing with common opinion about the unification and the extent of actuality, at the expense of common opinion that everything is actual, I do of course disagree with common opinion. I acknowledge that as a fair objection." (1986, 99–100)

[29] Williamson (2004, 112) makes a similar point, noting examples of philosophers (van Inwagen 1995, Horgan 1996) who deny the existence of mountains.

the reasons for Elder's complaint is that many ontologists follow Lewis in attempting to provide conditions for individuation which do not violate the restrictions of Humean supervenience and physicalism. It is striking that the kind of methodological conservatism which Lewis's philosophy encourages, has the consequence of abandoning the familiar objects of common sense ontology. As we saw above, for Moore, the truisms of common sense are thoroughly entangled with the reality of familiar objects. Figuring prominently among these are his body, his clothes, the furniture in his study, his pen, etc. It is precisely the Idealist denials of familiar objects and ordinary experience that his essay is intended to correct.

It is worth distinguishing the kind of methodological conservatism that Lewis associates with commonsense from the evaluation of conclusions. This methodological role is relatively straightforward and involves the recognition that we usually cannot make a completely fresh start in inquiry and that attempts to do so are usually not very successful. Philosophical inquiry, according to Lewis, ought to begin modestly by provisionally accepting commonsense starting points. This general principle says nothing, of course, about where inquiry might take us or how we ought to evaluate its results.

In recent philosophy, when common sense is playing the role of the methodologically conservative guide to inquiry, it has tended to morph into the slippery notion of intuition. Intuition plays a prominent role in contemporary ontology. Many philosophers, especially those working in ontology, epistemology and moral philosophy, want to claim a role for intuition in the generation or in the support of our beliefs about basic philosophical problems. Intuition is usually characterized in propositional attitude terms; agents are described as having the intuition that *p*, or as intuiting that *p*, where *p* is understood to be some proposition. While intuition is widely regarded as a source of belief, the manner in which intuition plays this role is obscure. Broadly speaking, the idea is that something akin to a faculty of intuition might support our accounts concerning basic conceptual matters insofar as it somehow serves as a guide for the agent in deciding between accepting and rejecting propositions. In addition to serving a variety of evidential roles in philosophical arguments, intuitions are sometimes thought of as hypotheses or as marks of conclusiveness. At bottom, most contemporary accounts of intuition characterize it as an especially authoritative way of *seeming that*. Contemporary accounts of intuition oscillate between the folksy and the rarefied: Intuition is sometimes understood to be a peculiarly aprioristic faculty while elsewhere it is portrayed as the most ordinary, commonsense level of thinking; accessible to all of us.

George Bealer describes intuition as a *sui generis* propositional attitude which, at the same time, serves as the source of all (non-stipulative) a priori knowledge (2002, p. 73). Elsewhere, we find 'intuition' and 'commonsense' being used interchangeably. Kripke, for example, contrasts intuitions with 'philosopher's notions' and regularly identifies intuitive content as the kind of thing to which the folk would readily agree (1980, p. 42). The connection to the traditional uses of the notion of common sense is also complicated somewhat by contemporary views which identify intuition with various kinds of competence. Ernest Sosa, for example, characterizes philosophical intuition as roughly equivalent to competence with respect to the relevant subject matter while distinguishing intuitive insight from conceptual analysis (Sosa, 2007).

I have argued elsewhere, that conflating the content of favored propositions with the feelings which lead us to favor those propositions figures frequently in the literature and is the source of unnecessary obscurity (Symons 2008). The salutary effect of distinguishing between intuitions and propositions is that it clarifies the sources of justification in an argument. So, for instance, it would allow us to distinguish arguments which rest on the truth of propositions from those which rest on the authority of something like a faculty of commonsense or intuition. While those propositions which are favored by commonsense are true or false independently of their relation to commonsense, a proposition's having the property of being favored by commonsense or intuition might count as a reason to believe that it is true. However, we could only reasonably believe that this property is a guide to truth by virtue of some additional set of propositions concerning the reliability and nature of the faculty of intuition or commonsense. For instance, we might argue that the intuitions of a specialist in some domain can be trusted. A specialist has acquired what philosophers had once called tacit knowledge through years of training and experience such that his or her 'gut feelings' about some topics in the discipline ought to be given serious consideration. We might have reasons (which can be articulated and defended) to trust the intuitions of some specialist. Similarly, we can imagine reasons for taking a more generalized and widely distributed form of commonsense seriously.

To say that we need reasons to heed the voice of commonsense is not equivalent to an epistemic principle to the effect that we ought to have evidence in all cases for the propositions that commonsense provides. Instead, by focusing on our reasons for heeding the faculty of intuition, we would undertake a general (largely empirical) project to give an account of the faculty and its place in the philosophical enterprise.[30]

16.8 Explanatory Adequacy and Parsimony

Commonsense has played a central role in ontological reasoning. In recent years, the role of intuition or commonsense in philosophical reasoning has come under scrutiny from self-described experimental philosophers and there has been a number of attempts to provide a precise articulation of the role of intuition in argumentation.[31] However, there are a range of competing criteria according to which one can evaluate an ontological system. In addition to its degree of consonance with commonsense, one might argue that a parsimonious ontological framework is preferable

---

[30]For a more complete discussion of the role of intuition in contemporary philosophy, see Symons (2008)

[31]Among the first paper to make an experimental case against the assumed consensus with respect to some philosophical intuition is Jonathon Weinberg, Shaun Nichols, Steven Stich (2001) on normative intuitions. In a recent paper Swain, et al, (forthcoming) conduct experiments on epistemic intuitions to similar effect. See their blog at http://experimentalphilosophy.typepad.com

to one which adds categories or types of entities ad hoc. At the same time, it is reasonable to prefer an ontological system which is less parsimonious while providing a more adequate explanation. For some ontologists, faithfulness to common sense and scientific investigation should be the principal determinants of our ontological claims. If one adopts this third stance, ontology is relegated to a relatively secondary role in relation to the account of the world which is on offer at any particular moment from our current, best science.

One recent project provides a useful test case for some of the competing factors that contribute to our evaluation of an ontological system. E.J. Lowe, in his recent book (2006) proposes an ontology consisting of objects, kinds, attributes, and modes. According to Lowe, this four category ontology captures the fundamental features of reality in way which provides explanatory resources for other metaphysical questions. What Lowe means by calling some category fundamental in this context is '...that the existence and identity conditions of entities belonging to that category cannot be exhaustively specified in terms of ontological dependence relations between those entities and entities belonging to other categories' (2006, p. 8). Like the logical property of the independence of axioms in some system, Lowe sees the ontological project as being one in which we propose independent and fundamental categories. Any proposed set of fundamental categories is then evaluated in terms of its ability to provide explanations or clarifications in other areas of philosophy. So, for example, he claims that his four category ontology has the virtue of explaining natural laws and causal relations.

Lowe follows Aristotle by emphasizing two major distinctions, the distinction between universals and particulars and between terms which refer to substantial and non-substantial entities. These two pairs form the vertices of what Lowe calls an ontological square, which forms the basis of his four category ontology: Substantial particulars, non-substantial particulars, non-substantial universals, and substantial universals. Objects (substantial particulars) have modes (non-substantial particulars). A mode is simply a way that a specific object bears a property; for example, the brownness of this chestnut. Attributes (non-substantial universals) would include, for instance, brownness; brownness, over and above the particular brownness of this chestnut. Finally natural kinds, like the kind 'chestnut tree' would count as a substantial universal for Lowe. Thus, objects have modes, modes are particular instances of attributes, kinds are defined in terms of their attributes and kinds are instantiated by objects. The members of this interlocking set of categories are each, according to Lowe, fundamental, in the sense of being independent of one another. He contends that the manner in which they relate to one another is such that it constitutes an exhaustive framework for describing all of reality.

Evaluating a framework of this kind involves comparison with alternative systems and the application of criteria such as its consistency, its commonsense acceptability (does the framework lead to counterintuitive consequences), its level of parsimony, and finally its explanatory adequacy. Lowe's ontology is less parsimonious than its contenders and must therefore justify itself in terms of its explanatory strength.

Deciding whether Lowe's ontology possesses the kind of explanatory power that he claims is beyond the scope of this essay. However, the burden for ontologists like Lowe is two-fold. The first involves justifying each of his fundamental categories as well as the relations which he posits between them. The second involves showing that the explanatory payoff with respect to problems such as laws of nature or the dispositional-categorical distinction is far higher than one receives with competing ontological systems. Armstrong's ontology, for instance, provides a considerably slimmer framework for addressing many of the same problems. Ryan Wasserman's insightful review of Lowe's *The Four Category Ontology* provides an example of how one might demonstrate the pitfalls of an expanded ontology (Wasserman 2006).

Lowe claims that his ontology provides an explanation of laws and dispositions. He takes Armstrong's ontology as his principal opponent. Armstrong's work can be seen as an attempt to understand the modal features of notions like cause, law and disposition within a broadly naturalistic framework. It is worth considering the way in which Armstrong's naturalism plays a role in his ontology.

Armstrong's materialist account of mental life extended and deepened Gilbert Ryle's blend of behaviorism and ordinary language philosophy. However, Armstrong's investigations were always more directly concerned with the broader metaphysical implications of questions about the mind than Ryle's. Stephen Mumford (2007) argues that Armstrong's later interest in universals and laws of nature emerged directly from reflections on the nature of dispositions in behaviorist models of mind.

Armstrong is a realist about universals, but in the spirit of naturalism, he argues that there are no uninstantiated universals. For Armstrong universals are real, but their reality depends on the reality of their instances. So, whereas Lowe's four category ontology sees them as equally fundamental features of reality, for Armstrong, universals are revealed to us via scientific inquiry into particulars. Lewis, by contrast, takes universals or properties to be something like sets (or perhaps classes) of possibilia. Andy Egan has criticized the Lewisian approach to properties for failing to permit things to have different properties in different possible worlds (2004).

Armstrong's metaphysics is one of the most detailed attempts to provide a systematic alternative to Lewis' Humean supervenience approach. It has been criticized by Alex Bird (2007), Mumford (2007) and others as sharing many of the same basic commitments as Lewis' view with respect to basic notions like the role of dispositions and their relation to the fundamental ontological constituents of nature. Bird, Ellis and other scientific essentialists, advocate a foundational role for dispositions in ontology. While the details of these debates are beyond the scope of the present essay, the resolution of these questions involves (at least in part) competing sets of commitments to the goals and presuppositions of ontology.

16.9 Concluding Remarks

In this essay, I have tried to indicate how some of the features of analytical ontology arise from the interplay of logic, language, and commonsense. In very general terms, it is possible to claim that throughout the history of analytic ontology we see the competition between formal insight and common sense. As we have seen, this tension persists, insofar as the ubiquity of the notion of intuition in contemporary ontology stands in sharp contrast with the frugality and precision to which Lewisian metaphysics aspires. Current debates reflect the ongoing struggle between these competing principles.

As we have seen, the revival of ontology and metaphysics after a significant wave of criticism in the mid-twentieth century has a variety of sources and causes. Centrally important are the arguments of four figures; W.V. Quine, Peter Strawson, Ruth Barcan-Marcus and Saul Kripke, all of whom were pivotal in the transition from a linguistically-oriented approach to philosophy to the realistic orientation that characterizes much of contemporary ontology. I hope that the foregoing sketch has indicated at least some of the reasons supporting the revival of ontology. While no single argument or text was uniquely responsible for bringing about the revival of ontology, it is clear that the reaction against the limitations of ordinary language philosophy, the development of modal logic, the criticisms of Carnap's attempt to separate philosophy and science, and Kripke's defense of necessary a posteriori truths all combined to clear the way for contemporary ontology.

Acknowledgments This essay was made possible in part thanks to support from the John Templeton Foundation's individual research awards program. I am also very grateful to two anonymous reviewers for their helpful suggestions. In addition I would like to thank Pablo Zavala, Stephen Elliott, and Roberto Poli for reading a draft of this manuscript and for offering some useful corrections

References

Austin, J. 1964. *Sense and sensibilia.* ed. G.J. Warnock. New York: Oxford University Press.

Bealer, G. 2002. Modal epistemology and the rationalist renaissance. In *Conceivability and possibility*, eds. T. Szabo Gendler and J. Hawthorne. Oxford: Oxford University Press.

Bird, A. 2007. *Nature's metaphysics: Laws and properties.* Oxford: Oxford University Press.

Bishop, M., and J.D. Trout. 2005.. *Epistemology and the psychology of human judgment.* Oxford: Oxford University Press.

Cao, T.Y. 2001. Philosophy of science: Retrospect and prospect. *Studies in Dialectics of Nature* 17(11):5–17.

Carnap, R. 1928.*Der logische Aufbau der Welt.* Berlin-Schlachtensee: Weltkreis-Verlag (trans. R. George, 1967) *The logical structure of the world.* Berkeley: University of California Press.

Carnap, R. 1934. *Logische Syntax der Sprache*. Springer Vienna. (trans. A. Smeaton, 1937) *The logical syntax of language.* London: Kegan Paul, Trench, Trubner & Co.

Carnap, R. 1950. Empiricism, semantics and ontology. *Revue Internationale de Philosophie* (Bruxelles) 11:20–40.

Carnap, R. 1963. 'Intellectual autobiography' and 'replies and systematic expositions'. In *The philosophy of rudolf carnap*, ed. P.A. Schilpp, 3–84. La Salle, IL: Open Court.

Dejnozka, J. 1996. *The ontology of the analytic tradition and its origins. Realism and identity in Frege, Russell, Wittgenstein and Quine*. New York, NY: Rowman & Littlefield.

Dummett, M. 1981. *Frege: Philosophy of language.* Cambridge: Harvard University Press.

Egan, A. 2004. Second order predication and the metaphysics of properties. *Australasian Journal of Philosophy* 82(1):48–66.

Elder, C. 2004. *Real natures and familiar objects*. Cambridge: MIT Press.
Findlay, J. 1963. *Meinong's theory of objects and values*. Oxford: Clarendon Press.
Frege, G. 1967[1879]. Begriffsschrift, a formula language, modeled upon that of arithmetic, for pure thought. In *From Frege to Gödel: A source book in mathematical logic, 1879–1931*, ed. J. van Heijenoort. Cambridge: Harvard University Press.
Frege, G. 1979. *Posthumous writings*, ed. H. Hermes, F. Kambartel, and F. Kaulbach (trans: Long, P. and White, R.). Chicago: University of Chicago Press.
Friedman, M. 1992. Epistemology in the aufbau. *Synthese* 93:15–57.
Friedman, M. 2000. *A parting of the ways: Carnap, Cassirer and Heidegger.* La Salle, IL: Open Court Press.
Frank, P. 1963. The pragmatic component in carnap's elimination of metaphysics. In *The philosophy of Rudolf Carnap*, ed. P.A. Schilpp, 159–164. La Salle, IL: Open Court Press.
Heller, M. 1990. *The ontology of physical objects*. Cambridge: Cambridge University Press.
Hochberg, H. 1994. From Carnap's Vienna to Meinong's Graz: Gustav Bergmann's ontological odyssey. *Grazer Philosophischen Studien* 48:1–50.
Hogran, T. 1996. Kim on the Mind–Body Problem, *British Journal for the Philosophy of Science* 47:579–607.
Hylton, P. 1990. *Russell, idealism and the emergence of analytic philosophy.* Oxford: Clarendon.
Hylton, P. 2004. Quine on reference and ontology. In *The cambridge companion to Quine*, ed. R. Gibson, 115–180. Cambridge: Cambridge university press.
Jacquette, D. 2002. *Ontology.* Montreal, QC: Mc-Gill-Queens's University Press.
Kenny, A. 1995. *Frege: An introduction to the founder of modern analytic philosophy*. Malden, MA: Blackwell
Kim, J. 1996. *Philosophy of mind*. Boulder, CO: Westview.
Lewis, D. 1972. Psychophysical and theoretical identifications. *Australasian Journal of Philosophy* 50:249–258.
Lewis, D. 1986. *On the plurality of worlds*. Oxford: Blackwell.
Lowe, E.J. 2006. *The four-category ontology: A metaphysical foundation for natural science.* Oxford: Oxford University Press.
Loux, M., and D. Zimmerman. 2003.*Oxford handbook of metaphysics*. Oxford: Oxford University Press.
Makin, G. 2001. *Metaphysicians of meaning: Russell and Frege on sense and denotation*. London: Routledge.
Marcus, R.B. 1961. Modalities and intensional language. *Synthese* 13:303–322.
Merricks, T. 2007. *Truth and ontology*. Oxford: Oxford University Press.
Moore, G.E. 1898. The nature of judgment. *Mind* 8(30):176–193.
Moore, G.E. 1925. A defence of common sense. In *Contemporary british philosophy* (2nd series), ed. J.H. Muirhead, 193–223. London: Allen and Unwin. Reprinted in *Philosophical papers* and in **G. E. Moore: Selected Writings* (1959) 106–133.
Mumford, S. 2007. *David Armstrong*. Durham, NC: Acumen.
Nagel, E. 1961. *The structure of science*. New York, NY: Harcourt Brace.
Hill, O.C. 1997. *Rethinking identity and metaphysics: On the foundations of analytic philosophy*. New Haven, CT: Yale University Press.
Pears, D. 1972. *Bertrand Russell and the British tradition in philosophy*. London: Fontana.
Poli, R., and P. Simons. eds. 1996. *Formal ontology*. Dordrecht: Kluwer.
Quine, W.V. 1934(1966). Ontological remarks on the propositional calculus. In *The ways of paradox and other essays*, 57–63. New York, NY: Random House.
Quine, W.V. 1948. On what there is. *Review of Metaphysics* 2:21–38.
Quine, W.V. 1960. *Word and object*. New York, NY: Wiley.
Quine, W.V. 1969. *Ontological relativity and other essays.* New York, NY: Columbia University Press.
Ramsey, F.P. 1931. *The foundations of mathematics and other logical essays,* ed. R.B. Braithwaite. London: Routledge & Keegan Paul.

Richardson, A. 1998. *Carnap's construction of the world.* Cambridge: Cambridge University Press.
Rosen, S. 1985. *The limits of analysis.* New Haven, CT: Yale University Press.
Russell, B. [1897] 1956. *An essay on the foundations of geometry.* New York, NY: Dover.
Russell, B. [1903] 1992. *The principles of mathematics*, 1937, 2nd edn. London: Routledge.
Russell, B. [1914] 1993. *Our knowledge of the external world.* London: Routledge.
Schlipp, P. ed. 1944. *The philosophy of Bertrand Russell.* La Salle, IL: Open Court.
Schlipp, P. ed. 1967. *The philosophy of Rudolf Carnap.* La Salle, IL: Open Court.
Sider, T. 2003. *Four-dimensionalism: An ontology of persistence and time.* Oxford: Oxford University Press
Strawson, P.F. 1959. *Individuals: An essay in descriptive metaphysics.* London: Methuen.
Symons, J. 2008. Intuition and philosophical methodology. *Axiomathes* 18:67–89.
Symons, J. forthcoming. Functionalism and fallibility. *Southwest Philosophical Studies*
Smith, B., and H. Burkhardt. eds. 1991. *Handbook of metaphysics and ontology.* Munich: Philosophia Verlag.
Soames, S. 2005. *Philosophical analysis in the twentieth century*, vol. 2. Princeton, NJ: Princeton University Press.
Sosa, E. 2007. Experimental philosophy and philosophical intuition. *Philosophical Studies* 132:99–107.
Swain, S., J. Alexander, and J. Weinberg. Forthcoming. The instability of philosophical intuitions: running hot and cold on truetemp. *Philosophy and phenomenological research*
Gendler, T.S., and J. Hawthorne. eds. 2002. *Conceivability and possibility.* Oxford: Oxford University Press.
Thomasson, A. forthcoming. Artifacts and human concepts. *Creations of the mind: Essays on artifacts and their representation*, ed. S. Laurence, and E. Margolis. Oxford: Oxford University Press.
van Inwagen, P. 1995. *Material beings.* Ithaca, NY: Cornell University Press.
von Mises, R. 1951. *Positivism: A study of human understanding.* Cambridge: Harvard University Press.
Wasserman, R. 2006. E.J. Lowe's the four-category ontology. *Notre dame philosophical review* (2006.04.11) http://ndpr.nd.edu/review.cfm?id=6341 (last accessed November 28, 2008).
Weiner, J. 1990. *Frege in perspective.* Ithaca, NY: Cornell University Press.
Williamson, T. 2004. Philosophical 'intuitions' and scepticism about judgement. *Dialectica* 58(1):109–153.

Chapter 17
Hermeneutic Ontology

Daniel O. Dahlstrom

17.1 Historical Presuppositions

17.1.1 The Perils of Traditional Ontology

Ontology is traditionally conceived as the investigation of what there is or, a bit more precisely, the attempt to determine the most basic and general ways of being. This endeavor typically entails the project of articulating the fundamental kinds of beings, frequently with the aim of sorting them into a taxonomic order (where some kinds are superordinate or structure the others).[1] The aim of the investigation is to provide inventories corresponding to these sorts and levels of being, inventories that are as complete and ordered as possible, based upon an understanding of the characteristics essential to whatever is, both generally and specifically.

D.O. Dahlstrom (✉)
Department of Philosophy, Boston University, Boston, MA, USA
e-mail: dahlstro@bu.edu

[1]Though the coinage of the term 'ontology' is relatively modern, investigation of this sort is akin to medieval philosophers' preoccupation with determining the basic categories or predicates (*praedicamenta*) of things, the basic ways of being able to predicate one thing of another (*praedicabilia*), as well as those terms like 'thing' or 'being' itself that are predicated across the basic categories, the so-called 'transcendentals'. The discipline of ontology also has obvious roots in Aristotle's metaphysics or, more precisely, in disambiguating Aristotle's sometimes confusing remarks about the subject matter of metaphysics. This confusion led Islamic philosophers, at least as they were read by Latin authors, to differing accounts of that subject matter, depending upon whether theology or what was subsequently deemed 'ontology' is its center of gravity. Telling in this connection is the question with which Duns Scotus opens his commentary on Aristotle's *Metaphysics*: "Utrum subiectum metaphysicae sit ens inquantum ens, sicut posuit Avicenna, vel Deus et intelligentiae sicut posuit Commentator Averroes?" See Scotus (1893, p. 11). In this traditional context, ontology corresponds to the sort of discipline entailed by the metaphysical investigation of *on he on* (ens inquantum ens) which might be translated 'being as being' or, perhaps more clearly, 'beings insofar as they exist.' This translation, for which I am indebted to John Tomarchio, complements Aristotle's differentiation of metaphysics from other disciplines, including mathematics, that study only parts of beings, in detachment from their existence; see *Metaphysics* Γ, 1 (1003a21-31).

R. Poli, J. Seibt (eds.), *Theory and Applications of Ontology: Philosophical Perspectives*, DOI 10.1007/978-90-481-8845-1_17,

There are considerable obstacles to the pursuit of this objective. Not least of these difficulties is the fact that ordinary and even scientific discourse is often notoriously profligate or, at least, uninhibited in assigning reality to a host of candidates in ways that, upon further examination, are not always evidently compatible. Perhaps not surprisingly, the history of ontology itself reflects considerable difference of opinion as to whether the fundamental sorts of being are substantial individual entities (relatively permanent 'things' in a more prosaic sense), structures, classes, properties (e.g., quantities or qualities), relations, collections, composites, dispositions, functions, events, processes, and/or any number of other determinations of beings. The options here are multiple but seemingly not unlimited, since no ontology dispenses with hierarchies. Nor can it, given the fact that the prospects of theoretical explanation largely determine the scope and granularity of ontological investigations. For similar reasons, inasmuch as the scientific enterprise of theoretical explanation provides the horizon for descriptions of what there is (as it has since Aristotle), no ontology is purely descriptive.[2]

Debate over the basic ontological categories typically turns on the explanatory horizon informing the determination of the categories. The explanatory power of any ontology depends upon the effectiveness of its differentiation of certain basic categories of being (including categories of their interrelationships) and its capacity to demonstrate the derivativeness of less basic categories (or of even a sub-categorial level). At the same time, ontology is faced with the considerable dilemma of justifying this pretension (its categorical account of what is) for the inaccessible future. Closely connected to this last difficulty is the problem of determining suitable constraints. In the process of trying to get a handle on what is and what is not the case, ontology inevitably and quite reasonably issues constraints. While the aim of formulating these constraints is to facilitate further investigation, ontology must guard against rendering the constraints so restrictive that they serve as impediments to research, pre-emptively foreclosing the emergence of different categories of beings or modes of access to them.

17.1.2 Regional and Formal Ontologies

Husserl responds to these difficulties by insisting on two (complementary) distinctions. He distinguishes essential (purely conceptual or theoretical) from factual (empirical or existential) characteristics of being. Only essential characteristics are the proper subject matter of ontology. Husserl is by no means the first ontologist to articulate and endorse this distinction. What Husserl contributes, in addition to making the distinction precise, is the requisiteness of a phenomenology as the method for ascertaining the essential characteristics of things. Ontology, he submits, can lay claim to determining such essential characteristics only as the product of a discernment of properly reduced contents of consciousness or, more

---

[2]Insofar as a description is made with a view to possible explanation, the description has an explanatory bias.

precisely, the properly reduced contents contained in a corresponding form of consciousness.[3]

This last qualification is necessary since, given the complexities among beings, there is reason to be skeptical that one method and the determination of a single, overriding sort of being suits all subject matters. The second crucial distinction introduced by Husserl is based upon an appreciation of the fact that our access to essential characteristics of being differs from one region to another and across such regions. One region of beings may seem to dictate one approach, while another region appears more open to a different approach (photosynthesis is measurable only in vegetation; you can ask human beings but not spiders how a particular food tastes). Some regional characteristics may prove more general than others and, indeed, such that they subsume more particular regional characteristics (e.g., a capacity to initiate one's movements in contrast to possession of a vertebrate). Research within a region may take the form of specialization or generalization accordingly. At the same time, researchers move from region to region in a way that presupposes a common logical space. Within a given region, for example, it may be possible to differentiate those aspects of being that are generic (e.g., being animate) and those that are particular (e.g., being ambulatory), as well as those aspects of being that correspond to ways of speaking of them across the particular/generic distinction (e.g., as parts and/or wholes). In other words, the movement across regions supposes the possibility of considerations so formal (neutral with respect to their content) that they can pertain to any and all regions. The generalizations within one or more regions (e.g., taxonomies forming 'trees' in the mathematical sense) are not to be confused with determinations of a formal nature that apply equally across regions and across generic as well as more specific levels.

These sorts of considerations prompted Husserl to distinguish generalization from formalization as well as regional from formal ontologies (Husserl 1968, 252ff; Husserl 1980, pp. 23–27, 304–313). Regional or material ontologies are synthetic a priori disciplines about particular regions of objects. Each region is constituted in one way or another in accordance with consciousness and thus delineates in advance (a priori) our modes of access to it (or, equivalently, its manner of presenting itself to scientific scrutiny). On this material or regional level, then, Husserl's working hypothesis is that of an ontological pluralist. He does not assume or look to establish a superordinate set of synthetic a priori statements, with different regional ontologies in a subordinate relationship to it.

Formal ontology is, by contrast, an analytic a priori discipline, basic parts of which are, not identical, but equivalent to formal logic, a discipline that focuses on the essential possibilities of inference (including its various elements, e.g., concepts, judgments, assertions, the truth of assertions). Such principles of formal logic can be transformed into "equivalent' formulations of formal ontology, as focus shifts,

---

[3]Husserl (1980, 115ff, 139ff). As the cited sections make clear, the essences described in transcendental phenomenology are fundamentally distinct from those of other eidetic disciplines, such as mathematics.

for example, from principles governing judgments to principles governing states of affairs (*Sachverhalte*), about which judgments are made. So, too, the attention shifts from assertions and their capacity to convey the truth about objects and states-of-affairs to what it is to be an object or state-of-affairs (akin to the shift from *de dicto* to *de re*) as well as what it is to refer to them. However, formal ontology not only entails and thus parallels formal logic but, in another sense, also includes it since propositions and inferences (as well as references) exist no less than objects or states-of-affairs. One of the principal structures of the purely formal relations of objects among themselves and across regions is mereological, with the crucial distinction between dependent and independent parts (Husserl 1968, pp. 216–293).

17.1.3 Phenomenological Ontology and the Task of Grounding

Ontological considerations at both regional and formal levels make up the presuppositions and the aims of Husserl's phenomenological project. Ontology in regional and formal senses presupposes not only its subject matter but also access to that subject matter, some way of thinking and speaking about beings and the types of beings, in short, a method. As the relation of formal ontology to formal logic and semantics illustrates, an ontology entails some account of its ways of identifying and sorting out the essences of various kinds of beings. Husserl conceives phenomenology as the project of investigating the evidence for the ontological descriptions of the essential features of particular regions and across regions. The principle of all principles, as Husserl puts it, is the need to ground all theoretical claims in intuition (*Anschauung*), a term signifying the adept observations and discernments of – in some cases even the expert insight into – the essential features of the domain about which those claims are made (Husserl 1980, 43f). But observations and discernments are clearly not all of a single stripe.[4] It remains incumbent on a phenomenological ontology, as Husserl conceives it, to take into account essential features of being and our access to those features both on and across various regions, for example, from micro to macro levels and everything in between. While each ontology of this sort is a self-contained sphere unto itself, marked by a certain conceptual closure, Husserl does not set any limits on the number or scope of such regional ontologies. Husserl's differentiation of formal and regional ontologies, together with the open-endedness of the latter, stands in sharp contrast to any traditional ontological pretension to some sort of single taxonomic order ('tree') of beings.

[4]Husserl in effect follows Aristotle's advice that the subject matter dictates the method and mode of knowing it. See Smith and Smith (1995, p. 32): "In the three books of the *Ideas*, Husserl argued that to every domain of objects there is correlated a form of 'intuition' (*Anschauung*) through which we come to know the given objects in the most adequate achievable way. Observations in nature are known through perception, acts of consciousness are known through phenomenological reflection, values are known through emotions, other people's experiences are known through empathy, ideal species or essences are known through 'eidetic variation,' and so on."

This last observation suggests a 'bottoms-up' strategy of working from the accounts of what there is in or across domains, afforded by the respective experts. The same 'bottoms-up' strategy holds for formal ontology, though the domain from which the formal ontologist works is universal, namely, formal logic and the aspects of things entailed by formal logic. Immersing herself in the ongoing work of developing scientific accounts of particular regions or across regions, the phenomenologist attempts to identify and describe the essential possibilities at each level on the basis of intuitions or discernments of them or, in other words, in terms of the manners in which those features are given and accessible – and not constructed – in consciousness. Although material reality underlies all other realities for Husserl, he does not consider those other realities reducible to complexes of material reality, arguing instead that each distinctive type of reality has 'its own constitutive phenomenology' (Husserl 1980, p. 319). In keeping with his brand of ontological pluralism (noted above), the aim of his phenomenological method is to disclose 'the complete system of the formations of consciousness constituting the original givenness of all such objectivities [*Objektitäten*] and thereby make intelligible the equivalent in consciousness to the respective type of 'reality'' (Husserl 1980, p. 319). Even if phenomenology for Husserl, at least in the order of knowing, takes its cues from particular disciplines, the grounding of the formal and regional ontologies underlying those disciplines is the work of phenomenology.[5]

One of the many morals of Husserl's deliberations is the mutual dependence of an ontology and its method. Identifying what there is and identifying our mode of access to it are equivalent (albeit not identical) to one another. There is considerable reliable evidence that many entities exist quite independently of the ways in which we attend to them, use them, think about them, and so on. But this sort of ontological realism is itself based upon evidence, evidence that necessarily reflects ways in which human beings relate to the entities. Once again, the sense of the subject matter is inextricably tied to the method of relating to it. For Husserl the job of phenomenology is to secure the intuition of the essential formal and regional possibilities of being. In other words, the aim of Husserl's phenomenology is ontology, based precisely upon the discernment (eidetic intuition) of essences or, equivalently, a determination of what is fundamentally and essentially given in and to the correspondingly perceptive consciousness. Far from supplanting scientific explanation, these descriptions are supposed to articulate what make it possible. Phenomenological ontology, the pursuit of ever-revisable inventories of essential possibilities, is a process of distilling, unifying, and thereby abetting the work of science.

---

[5]Husserl (1980, p. 323). Robert Poli advances a related but more comprehensive distinction between domain-dependent and domain-independent as well as between descriptive and formal ontologies. Poli also helpfully distinguishes a formalized ontology from formal ontologies, labeling the latter 'categorial' ontologies in order to avoid confusion of them with formalized ontologies; see Poli (2003).

17.2 The Hermeneutics of Fundamental Ontology

Heidegger critically appropriates Husserl's phenomenological approach to ontology, sketched in the foregoing section. Like Husserl, he is interested in phenomenology as a method for ontology in general and, indeed, a basic, reflexive method that underlies but does not itself generate the content of other ontological investigations. Heidegger follows Husserl in not supposing that there is some overarching ontological discipline from which ontological determinations of every region of being might be derived. However, unlike Husserl he conceives his phenomenological method as hermeneutical and, in fact, refers to Husserl's phenomenology as non-hermeneutical. Further departing from Husserl's project, Heidegger conceives this hermeneutical phenomenology as the method, not of a formal or regional ontology, but as the method of what he deems 'fundamental ontology.'

17.2.1 The Critique of Husserl's Unhistorical Ontological Method

Among his objections to Husserl's phenomenology is what Heidegger deems the insufficiency of its manner of determining and demonstrating ontology at either the regional or categorical level. According to Heidegger, Husserl's phenomenology ultimately fails to explain sufficiently why certain contents are ontologically significant.[6] In other words, he faults Husserl's phenomenological approach to ontology for not providing an adequate grounding of ontological criteria or, equivalently, for not subjecting to critical analysis the conception of being that he employs. In this connection, Heidegger chastises Husserl for taking it for granted that ontology is an *ancilla scientiae*, an attendant or auxiliary to the sciences, one that facilitates *normal* scientific investigation.[7] For this reason, Heidegger questions whether Husserl's account of the foundation of ontology, namely, the discernment, proper to an underlying consciousness (the so-called 'transcendental ego'), of essential features that present themselves within and across scientific pursuits, is as radical and self-critical as it needs to be. Traditional scientific investigations, at the regional and formal level, with an all too ready-made distinction between essences and facts, constitute the unquestioned horizon of Husserl's phenomenological ontology. As such, it can neither guide science to new avenues and domains of investigation nor explain its commitment to conceptions specific to certain domains (regional ontology) or to the trans-regional categories that make up its conception of formal ontology.

---

[6]This criticism is interesting given the fact that Husserl does take pains to demonstrate how one would proceed to arrive at essential features (namely, the method of free variation) and given the paucity of argumentation provided by Heidegger for his own choice of the themes relevant to his fundamental ontology.

[7]This is a recurrent theme of Heidegger's first Marburg lectures where he criticizes Husserl's appropriation of the Cartesian tradition and a concern with securing "already known knowledge" (Heidegger 1994, pp. 56–59). By contrast, Heidegger attempts to link his own version of phenomenology to the "productive logic" of Plato and Aristotle (Heidegger 1972, p. 10).

In Heidegger's mind, this obsequious traditionalism on Husserl's part extends not only to normal science, but also to the ontological legacy presupposed by it. Heidegger contends that Husserl's phenomenological ontology, like the sciences that it is meant to serve, takes over uncritically a traditional and excessively reductive understanding of ontology's most basic concept, i.e., its conception of being. Precisely in this connection, Heidegger presses the need for a historical and, as we shall see below, hermeneutical turn in the method of pursuing ontology. For just as a science's normal and normative dimensions only become evident through consideration of its history, so, too, the ontological legacy presupposed by it can only be gathered properly from consideration of the history of philosophy. The ontological legacy in question is a product of the history of Western metaphysics, namely, its conception of being as the essential presence or accessibility of things. Heidegger is convinced that the conception is ill-advised, not least because it is strikingly at odds with a suitably analyzed understanding of the manner of being proper to humans.

Another shortcoming of Husserl's phenomenological ontology, intimately connected in Heidegger's view to the shortcoming just noted, is its location of the founding, reflexive center of ontology in consciousness (*Bewußt-sein*) without an adequate, foregoing account of what sort of being it is that is conscious. Heidegger's particular misgivings in this connection can be gathered, at least in part, from his query to Husserl, during their quickly aborted collaboration on the 'phenomenology' entry to the *Encyclopedia Britannica*: 'Does not the pure ego have a world?' (Husserl 1962, p. 274, note 1). The question reveals Heidegger's basic contention that modes of being, both human and non-human, most basically disclose themselves, not to an observing or perceiving consciousness, but to a manner of being in the world, a manner of being that is presupposed by observation and perception.

In sum, then, Heidegger identifies two principal deficiencies with Husserl's phenomenological ontology, namely, its lack of an historically critical analysis of two central conceptions that it works with: its conception of being in general and its conception of the sort of being who is conscious. These deficiencies are interrelated, in Heidegger's eyes, inasmuch as Husserl uncritically takes over a traditional conception of being as the essential presence or accessibility of things to a conscious observer or perceiver, capable of reflecting on her observations and perceptions. These deficiencies motivate Heidegger's efforts to develop a hermeneutical ontology or, better, a fundamental ontology by way of a hermeneutical phenomenology. In hermeneutic phenomenology, the work of dispositions, understanding, and the ongoing, shared and communicated interpretation of them (including the self-interpretation that such work entails) takes the place of observation or intuition, eidetic or categorical. The work of interpretation, moreover, is required precisely because absences and inaccessibilities of what is interpreted, no less than its presence and accessibility, fundamentally determine its manner of being.[8]

---

[8]While there is much to recommend this critique, it is in some respects disingenuous inasmuch as Husserl himself emphasizes the horizonal, never fully adequate character of perception, an emphasis upon which Heidegger undoubtedly draws when he insists that being is not to be equated with

17.2.2 *The Fundamental Question and the Reason for Beginning with Human Existence*

For Heidegger the question of what there is cannot be divorced from the question of what it means to say of something that it is. Neither of the two questions that Aristotle poses, among others, for scientific inquiry – the question of whether something is and the question of what it is (*Posterior Analytics*, II, 89b24) – is identical to this fundamental question.[9] A fundamental ontology is the ontology that provides a foundation for other possible ontological investigations, precisely by virtue of addressing this question.[10] But the question itself and any prospects of addressing it presuppose that there is some entity to whom this meaning is disclosed, some entity whose distinctive manner of being-here entails an understanding of being. Heidegger accordingly attempts to ground the prospects for ontology properly by giving an account of how the sense of being is disclosed in and to human existence as mattering to it.

Heidegger's account can be put in the form of a modus ponens argument. Human existence incorporates or realizes qualities specific to it (= *p*). Heidegger identifies four equally primary qualities of this sort, regarding them as 'basic existentials': (1) a foregoing, emotionally charged disposition towards beings, including itself; (2) a corresponding, i.e., predisposed understanding of them in the sense of knowing (more or less) how to deal with them; (3) a shared or common means of expressing and communicating that predisposed understanding; and (4) a struggle over taking possession of (and thus responsibility for) its unique manner of realizing these qualities. Human existence incorporates or realizes these qualities specific to it only if being matters to it (*p only if q*). Hence, being matters to human existence (*q*) and, indeed, does so by way of being disclosed in and to the predisposed understanding, forms of expression, and struggle for authenticity, all of which uniquely characterize human existence. As noted above, Heidegger refers to these fundamental characteristics as 'existentials,' an expression that is meant to capture both (a) the fact that they are ways of being, enacted or performed by us in a constitutive manner (other actions and practices can be regarded as types and instantiations of them) and

---

presence; see Husserl (1950, p. 62); for a balanced treatment of Heidegger's critique of Husserl in this connection, see Gadamer (1972, pp. 241–250).

[9] In other words, if ontology is the study of what is, it presupposes not only an account of what there is and the various ways of approaching the subject matter, but also an understanding of what it means to say that something is or exists. Precisely at this juncture Heidegger introduces his notion of fundamental ontology, the path to which is an existential analysis conducted as a hermeneutic phenomenology. In the 1930s Heidegger makes this distinction more perspicuous, distinguishing Western metaphysics' leading question of what there is from the basic question of what being is.

[10] It bears emphasizing that addressing this question, far from ruling out traditional ontological considerations of what there is, entails considerations of this sort, a point that Heidegger comes to concede, at least in lectures, in the years immediately following the publication of *Sein und Zeit*; see his discussion of 'metontology' in his 1928 lectures (Heidegger 1990, p. 199). I return to this issue which concerns the precise nature of a fundamental ontology, relative to other ontologies, in the final paragraph of this study.

(b) the fact that this enactment is itself disclosive of what it means for us to be (and thus self-disclosive).

Although the characteristics listed above are equally basic (such that their serial treatment in the order given is merely a concession to the demands of exposition), there is also a sense of 'understanding' that coincides with all four existentials. Indeed, this primary sense of 'understanding' is distinct from at least three other, derivative senses.[11] The primary sense of 'understanding' refers to understanding what it means to be, an understanding signified by the expression that 'being matters.' This sense is preontological; in other words, we typically do not reflect or make explicit to ourselves the sense of being that is disclosed by the very fact that we exist and thereby realize the qualities specific to us. Nevertheless, this *preontological understanding of being* motivates various predispositions towards what we find in the world around us and our ways of dealing with and, in that sense, understanding them, i.e., projecting possibilities of how to deal with them. In other words, this preontological understanding of being underlies our ways of understanding and coping with all that enters into our concrete, individual fates. Heidegger famously characterizes understanding in this first derivative sense as a kind of know-how, a tool-wielding facility; let us call this sense of 'understanding' – corresponding to (2) in the list of basic existentials given above – a *practical, ontic understanding*.

Neither that primary, preontological understanding of being nor this practical understanding of how to deal with beings is to be identified with a theoretical or even proto-theoretical act of consciousness such as observing or perceiving. Observation and experiment constitute a derivative sort of predisposed understanding, the sort that attempts – sometimes quite successfully – to maintain a distance between itself and what it observes and thereby to exercise a measure of deliberate control over its dispositions, understanding, and modes of publicly registering what it understands. Focusing on the constant, iterated or iterable presences of things (presences typically expressed in law-like formula) facilitates this attempt considerably. Let us call this second sort of derivative understanding a *theoretical, ontic understanding*.[12] The requisite distance and control demanded by theory are necessarily absent from the more basic sort of predisposed understanding indicated above, the sort of understanding that is intrinsic to the way a human being exists.

The task of fundamental ontology corresponds to a fourth sense of understanding (the third derivative sense), namely, a *theoretical, ontological understanding*. What distinguishes fundamental ontology from traditional ontology, including regional

[11] For Heidegger, these different senses correspond to his differentiation of a primary, existentially pre-ontological sense of 'understanding' from derivative, existentielly ontic (practical and theoretical) senses and a derivative, existentially ontological sense (the formal ontology to be derived from the existential analysis of *Sein und Zeit*).

[12] In Heidegger's eyes, one of Husserl's central 'mistakes,' a mistake that he shares with most traditional ontologists in the history of philosophy, consists precisely in privileging this derivative sense of understanding over the practical understanding of entities and the primary preontological understanding of being that it supposes. Theoretical understanding, nevertheless, has, in Heidegger's eyes, "the legitimate task of grasping what is on hand" (Heidegger 1972, p. 153).

and formal ontologies, as Husserl conceives them, is precisely its attempt to retrieve the sense of being that matters in human existence and, indeed, to retrieve it as the sense of being that is fundamental to ontology in general. In Heidegger's jargon, fundamental ontology presupposes existential analysis, i.e., the analysis of the basic qualities distinctive of human existence (the basic existentials) with an eye to interpreting or making explicit the primary understanding of being – the more or less inchoate understanding of what it means for us to be at all – that accompanies, motivates, and reveals itself in those very qualities.[13]

It bears noting that the different senses of 'understanding' in Heidegger's analysis are not exclusively disjunctive. We understand at multiple levels at once, understanding things other than ourselves in view of an understanding of our relations to them and thus in view of an understanding of ourselves. Moreover, these understandings of things, our relations to them, and ourselves are at once ontic and ontological. For example, in understanding something as a fork (the specific ontic conception of it), I also understand it as being-handy (the implicit ontological category of *Zuhandensein*, in Heidegger's jargon).

Our human existence is fundamentally marked for Heidegger, as already noted, by basic predispositions towards and a corresponding understanding of things within a world that we share (and share principally through talking with one another). The manner of being that is disclosed in and to these basic existential characteristics is (a) a worldly existence (entailing an array of relations to things other than ourselves as individuals) that is both (b) settled (present, complete) and (c) unsettled (absent, incomplete). For example, our experience of being disposed or 'undergoing' fears, desires, moods, and the like at once establishes and reveals (a) our concrete way of feeling towards something, (b) the fact that what is feared, desired, and so on, like these dispositions themselves, are already part of the inherited situation in which we find ourselves, and (c) the unresolved character of the situation, i.e., of our relation to what is feared, desired, and the like. We find a similar manner of being disclosed in the possession and exercise of a know-how (the second basic existential and the first derivative sense of 'understanding' noted above). As a degree of competence in using things that we find within the world and using them for our purposes, this know-how establishes and reveals (a) the world that we call our own. At the same time, while (b) reflecting more or less settled and effective practices, this know-how also makes eminently clear (c) that our projects and, indeed, potential-to-be are essentially incomplete. A similar dynamic tension of settled and unsettled possibilities pertains to the discourse or talk by means of which we make that worldly

[13]Since it is an understanding that coincides with how being matters to us as existing in a world, it also discloses and even expresses senses of being of various entities within the world and, indeed, does so in terms of how we relate to them. But here, too, they are senses of being that cannot be equated with the presence or accessibility of things. For example, being pre-disposed to one's environment we find things fearful, accommodating, alluring and the like, precisely inasmuch as they are not fully present or on hand. Something is ominous only as long as it remains impending; something is desirable only as long as the desire for it is not fulfilled.

existence and any parts of it more or less intelligible and communicable to others and to ourselves. Our ways of speaking are means of sharing a world with one another, but they have only proven themselves in and for the world from which they have been inherited. Just as dispositions and practical understanding only exist in our moods and acquired know-how, so talk only exists insofar as we talk to ourselves and one another, and there is no guarantee, without creative intervention on our part, that 'tried and true' ways of speaking are genuinely suited for making intelligible and communicating what lies ahead for us.

The foregoing reprise of the analysis of each of these basic existentials is highly truncated, not least because it misleadingly suggests that they can be treated in relative isolation from one another. Nevertheless, the analysis reveals, in keeping with the distinctiveness of existentials noted above, how human existence is at once a distinctive manner of being and self-understanding (or understanding of that very manner of being). Moreover, what is distinctive about that manner of being and the understanding of it is the fact that possibilities in a certain sense, far more than anything actual, define who we are.[14] These possibilities are, on the one hand, the possibilities of the world into which we have been thrown. Such possibilities correspond to the fact that we are already outfitted with certain predispositions and in certain relationships, that we have already acquired capabilities and beliefs requisite for continuing membership in that world, that we are born with certain genetically and environmentally determined possibilities as well as with the inevitability of death. Yet these possibilities must be enacted or projected by us, some of them deliberately, and our projections of one set of possibilities eliminates another set. To be sure, we are thrown into the world and thrown precisely to project possibilities (as exemplified by our moods and know-how) but that projecting, as far as we know, is not determined – or, better, not overdetermined, i.e., deterministically determined – by the thrownness of our existence. So, too, the world itself, while already historically constituted before we find ourselves in it, is as historically incomplete and rife with possibilities as we are.[15]

The manner of being that is disclosed by the existential analysis is that of a thrown projection (intimated by the expression 'predisposed understanding'). For Heidegger the horizon or sense of being that is presupposed by this manner of being

[14]To translate this characteristic into the framework of modalities: Possibility in the existential sense of the term is more fundamental than actuality or necessity. Death itself has a singular, existential significance for us, not as something actual, but as the possibility of the end our possibilities.

[15]The sort of individual discernment, expert knowledge, and intuitive insight so fundamental to Husserl's phenomenological method is not discarded but reinscribed in an emotive, shared understanding, in Heidegger's analysis. Intuitions, observations, discernments are part of a process by which human beings, like other animals, orient themselves in their environments with one another for the sake of certain aims; so the intuitions of individuals are always derivative of an emotive process of coping with the environment and understanding how (having the know-how) to do so as a member of a family or group. Heidegger accordingly urges this sort of reinterpretation of intuition, removing it and its variants from a foundational position and placing it in the historical lived experience of human beings.

is a mode of temporality in which a distinctive union of absences – the absence of the past and the future – yields the present. He contends that the traditional conception of being as a present presence trades on a neglect of the way time, so construed, underlies our understanding of what it means to be.

17.2.3 The Reflexivity of the Hermeneutical Circle and Taking Responsibility

Our review of Heidegger's project of fundamental ontology has so far shown how he departs from Husserl's phenomenological approach to ontology by arguing that the theoretical discernment driving that approach is derivative of a more basic manner of disclosing what it means to be, a self-disclosure characteristic of the essential qualities (existentials) of human existence. Analysis of these qualities reveals a manner of being (and being disclosed to itself) that is defined by possibilities and, indeed, such that time forms the horizon for any understanding of being. The foundation of fundamental ontology, the manner of being and understanding being that is proper to human existence, is not so much something actual or actually present as it is the temporal interplay of presences and absences that gives meaning to the possibilities that define human existence. This temporality is the nexus of presences and absences, a nexus that, like the past and future, is never fully present.

Left unexplained up to this point is why Heidegger characterizes his phenomenological approach to ontology as 'hermeneutical.'[16] But the key to the explanation lies in the connection that has been drawn between the defining possibilities of human existence and their temporal significance. Human existence is, in Heidegger's jargon, a being-in-the-world, an entity whose understanding of being is inseparable from the possibilities that it projects for itself in the historical situation of the discursively shared world into which it has been thrown. While circumstances, typically in the form of crises, can bring this understanding brusquely to the surface as the presupposition for theory and practice, this understanding is largely inchoate, tacit, pre-reflective – and in need of interpretation.

Heidegger emphasizes repeatedly that the two operative senses of human existence – being 'thrown' into the world and being itself a throw or projection of possibilities – belong together (Heidegger 1972, pp. 181, 192, Gadamer 1972, p. 249). There is a basic, irresolvable tension between the possibilities into which human existence has been thrown and the possibilities that it itself projects and thus understands ('projecting' and 'understanding' are metonyms in Heidegger's existential analysis). The possibilities that we project and the projecting itself – from the

[16]In keeping with the history of the term, I take 'hermeneutics' to designate a theory, practice, and art of interpretation. Theoretical hermeneutics (the ontology of interpretation) provides an account of what constitutes an interpretation, while 'hermeneutical practice' designates a mode of interpreting informed by some conception of what constitutes an interpretation, and 'hermeneutical art' the mastery of a hermeneutical practice.

preontological and practical to the theoretical and ontological senses of understanding – are all a function of having been thrown into the world. We have been cast into the world in such a way as to have to project possibilities and the possibilities that we project, like the projecting itself, bear the stamp of what Heidegger calls the thrownness or facticity of human existence. We sustain our biological states precisely by projecting or, better, continuing to project possibilities that already constitute a necessarily eccentric movement towards and within a particular environment. We do this for the most part without thinking about what we are doing, and something similar holds for a considerable portion of the exercises of predisposed understanding (know-how) that allow us to cope with our world. Even when we manage to keep firmly in mind the purpose of an activity (e.g., driving a car or carrying on a conversation), most of the possibilities that we project in performing that activity are not the product of deliberation or conscious effort. In all these senses, the possibilities that we project and the projecting itself are pre-reflective, testimonies to what Heidegger deems the thrownness of human existence.[17]

Yet the projection itself also delimits the range of possibilities of our being-in-the-world and with this delimitation comes the possibility of making or not making the projected possibilities one's own and of taking or not taking responsibility for them. But in order to assume responsibility for these possibilities, we have to make them explicit or, in some cases, more explicit by unpacking their historical conditions. Making explicit the possibilities that we project in understanding is what Heidegger deems the task of interpretation.[18]

For every interpretation, there is something to be interpreted and, to that extent, something that the interpretation presupposes. Interpretation accordingly remains always a step behind. We typically single out interpretation as an activity that we engage in when something eludes our ordinary ways of understanding, not least when something seems to be other than it is or when it has been taken for something other than it is. But this activity presupposes some acquaintance with what is to be interpreted.

Heidegger accordingly maintains that interpretation trades on a forestructure – the domain that we have in advance before us (*Vorhabe*), a foregoing perspective

[17]According to Gadamer, Heidegger recognizes that the thrownness and facticity of one's being form the bedrock of all understanding, a recognition that accounts for his break with Husserl's transcendental phenomenology (Gadamer 1972, 249f).

[18]The activity is an attempt to disclose or unpack what is understood more or less vaguely or, at least, inattentively and unthematically, perhaps even improperly. A great deal of our everyday behavior is, as has already been stressed, rote, marked by a tacit understanding of what we are doing, the things of which we avail ourselves in order to do it, and the setting within which we do it. We understand what we are doing in the course of doing it precisely by way of projecting possibilities realized and realizable by the actions. The respective possibilities, like the actions themselves, are typically ordered in some purposive way (e.g., I pick the hammer up by the handle, lifting it at a certain angle, relative to the nail between my fingers, and the wood beneath them, and so on) and, of course, they can turn out to be quite harmful or inappropriate. To paraphrase Kant's old saw, interpretation without understanding is empty, understanding without interpretation is blind.

(*Vorsicht*), and preconception (*Vorgriff*) – implicit in every understanding. For example, when we use a hammer, there is a forestructure to the way we understand/project possibilities for ourselves and it, a forestructure in terms of which the hammer and the hammering have their particular significance. Thus, to continue the same example, within a workshop (*Vorhabe*), we regard certain things and disregard others (*Vorsicht*), thanks to our conception of what hammering can achieve and what the hammer is for (*Vorgriff*). To interpret something is to take it a certain way, for example, to take something *as* a hammer or an activity *as* hammering. But this structure of interpretation (taking *x* as *y*), Heidegger maintains, is founded upon the forestructure of understanding (Heidegger 1972, 149ff, Gadamer 1972, pp. 250–256).

In this account of the relation of interpretation to understanding, I have been relying upon the practical, ontic sense of understanding as know-how. But the basic relation of interpretation to a foregoing structure of understanding holds generally and thus also for the interpretation of what it means to be. Here we see at least one reason why, after identifying phenomenology as ontology, Heidegger insists that the phenomenology of human existence is 'a *hermeneutic* in the primordial signification of this word, where it designates the business of interpreting' (Heidegger 1972, 37). Phenomenology is the method of attending to a phenomenon precisely insofar as this phenomenon presents itself of itself. However, the phenomenon in question (human existence) essentially presents itself to itself and does so in the form of a tacit, prereflective understanding that shapes and is shaped by its predispositions and know-how. In short, the phenomenon presents itself as an understanding in need of interpretation – a hermeneutic – in order to be rendered responsibly explicit.

Heidegger has two further reasons for qualifying his phenomenology as hermeneutical, each of which has a bearing on any project of hermeneutical ontology. To the extent that the meaning of being in the case of human existence provides the horizon for further ontological study of other sorts of entities, the study is also hermeneutical, he submits, in the sense of elaborating the conditions of the possibility of any ontological investigation (Heidegger 1972, 37). Presumably, what Heidegger has in mind is the fact that the interpretation or hermeneutic elaboration of the forestructure of the understanding (constitutive of being-in-the-world) doubtlessly has a bearing on the interpretation of the manner of being of other entities as well.

In recounting Heidegger's critique of Husserl, we already alluded to the third reason why he conceives his phenomenology as hermeneutical. Each of us is his or her past in the sense that we assimilate traditional beliefs and practices, and, not least, ways of interpreting what it means for us to be. We may even be said, as Heidegger puts it, to 'fall prey' to such beliefs when the apparent self-evidence of tradition blocks our access to original sources of those beliefs and, indeed, even to the fact that they have a history. From this 'our own essential historicality' as well as our tendency to cede control of ourselves to settled traditions, it follows that inquiry into what it means to be must be an historical inquiry, 'inquiry into the history of that inquiry itself' if we are 'to go back to the past in a positive manner and make it our own' (Heidegger 1972, 20ff).

As the sentence just cited makes quite clear, Heidegger's hermeneutic phenomenology as the method for fundamental ontology is motivated by a sense of responsibility (corresponding to the fourth basic existential mentioned above), a need to take responsibility for the interpretation. The aim of the hermeneutic is, he insists, not to relativize or undo traditional ontology but to take its measure and, if relevant, even take responsibility for making it one's own. Yet this responsibility for the interpretation is itself both facilitated and limited by the peculiar recursive relation of interpretation to understanding. Insofar as interpretation presupposes understanding, in the sense of making explicit what is always already implicitly understood, interpretation moves reflexively in a kind of circle.

Yet the point of Heidegger's hermeneutical reflections in this regard, as Gadamer stresses, is to demonstrate, not the existence of a circle, but that 'this circle has an ontologically positive sense' (Gadamer 1972, p. 251). Far from disabling, this circular structure is what makes a genuine interpretation possible, i.e., an interpretation that aims at making explicit its own conditions of interpretation. Nor is interpretation in this sense something free-floating or arbitrary; it is, instead, 'the expression of the existential *fore-structure*' of our being-here. Heidegger accordingly insists that, within the circular structure of interpretation, 'a positive possibility of the most primordial kind of knowing' affords itself, a possibility that we genuinely take hold of 'only when the interpretation has understood that its first, constant, and final task is never to allow the domain that we have before us, our foregoing perspective on it, and our preconceptions to be presented to us by fancies and popular conceptions, but instead to make the scientific theme secure by working out these forestructures in terms of the matters themselves' (Heidegger 1972, 153). The final words of this text echo the phenomenological demand to return to *den Sachen selbst*. While making clear that this return can only be hermeneutical, i.e., an ongoing task (*erste, ständige und letzte Aufgabe*) of interpretation, the matters themselves are supposed to serve as the constraint for the elaboration of the fore-structure of understanding.

17.3 Hermeneutic Ontology: an Outline

In the preceding section we sketched what is, in effect, Heidegger's interpretation of interpretation, as he presents it in *Sein und Zeit*. Interpretation or, equivalently, hermeneutics is essential to his phenomenological method for arriving at the manner of being that is disclosed in and to human existence, the manner of being that can alone serve as the basis for a fundamental ontology. Whatever measure of control and responsibility that we can exercise over our manner of being is dependent upon an interpretation of the very possibilities, not least the discursive possibilities, that we inherit and project for ourselves in the world that we share with one another.

Heidegger does not speak of a 'hermeneutic ontology' explicitly, though his student, Hans-Georg Gadamer, does (Gadamer 1972, p. 415). The remainder of this study attempts to outline such an ontology by drawing on three themes from his project of developing a fundamental ontology through hermeneutic phenomenology.

First, hermeneutic ontology is based upon the notion that what, among other things, enables interpretation to succeed is its essentially historical character. Second, hermeneutic ontology requires an ontological determination of interpretation itself. I accordingly offer an account of interpretation as an activity, relative to an ongoing process of self-interpretation constituted by what I dub 'the interpretive helix.' Third, hermeneutic ontology entails not only an ontology of interpretation but also an interpretation of ontology, since the historical process to which interpretation belongs is itself an object of interpretation. Finally, in light of the foregoing outline, I sketch Gadamer's hermeneutic ontology and his remarks on language as its horizon.

17.3.1 The Historicity of Interpretation

The expression 'historicity of interpretation' is meant to convey the fully and essentially historical character of interpretation. This historical character encompasses the interpreter (*interpretans*), the experience, event, object, text, etc. to be interpreted (*interpretandum*), and the concepts and proto-concepts by means of which they are to be interpreted (*modi interpretandi*). Insisting that the historicity of interpretation applies to the interpreter herself is another way of underscoring that every interpretation is a self-interpretation and every responsible or authentic interpretation is so self-consciously.

The completeness of this historical character is to be understood in three complementary senses or modalities. First, by the time that anyone gets around to interpreting, what constitutes the experience, the ways of registering (describing, classifying) it, and those undergoing the experience are all discursive carriers of a tradition. To take a homely example, the very way we eat and what we take to be eating are traditional in this sense. Something similar holds for an entire range of interpretable events and interpreting activities, not least the more narrowly discursive activities of registering, classifying, discussing matters, and the like. Interpretation inevitably works on a subject matter that has already been interpreted or, at least, avails itself to the interpreter from a standpoint already interpreted and accessible to the interpreter (see the discussion of the *Vorstruktur* above). The interpreter, the interpreted, and the modes of interpretation all have a history, i.e., a past that is intrinsic to their manner of being.

At the same time (and this is the second sense of the historicity of interpretation), the interpretation would not be historical if it failed to appreciate the potential import of the difference between what it can no longer touch (as Robert Lowell, with a poet's gift, dubbed the past of memory) and the present. Affirming this potential difference does not, by any means, entail that the present is never – especially for theoretical or practical purposes – more than a carbon copy or facsimile of the past. Hempel was right; general laws have a function in history and they could not have that function if there were not sufficient similarities between historical events. But even a carbon copy is a copy and the historically-minded interpreter, i.e., the interpreter cognizant of her ontological status as interpreter, is precisely concerned with the possibility of determining whether the difference between the past and the present makes a difference.

The third sense or modality of interpretation's historicity is its open-ended, future horizon. The interpreter as well as what is interpreted have such horizons, both in the sense of what they might deliberately and non-deliberately project and in the sense of what they are coming to. These future horizons in both senses determine the interpretation no less than do its past and its present.

In all three modalities, there is an inescapable mix of determinacy and indeterminacy, presence and absence, that is the mark of the ontology of interpretation.

The foregoing senses of the historicity of interpretation, it bears noting, also inform Gadamer's own, self-described hermeneutical ontology. Gadamer stresses how attempts to objectify matters or, equivalently, to discount the interpreter's historical horizon forfeit the historical dimension of the hermeneutic experience. His hermeneutical ontology is accordingly a plea for the historical reality of interpretation as something antecedent to any differentiation of perspective and content (or, equivalently, subject and object, interpreter and tradition, language and world) (Gadamer 1972, pp. 434–439).

17.3.2 The Interpretive Helix

Given its historical nature, the reflexive character of interpretation is never simply recursive. When the interpreter reflects back on the conditions of the interpretation, they are not simply iterated in the sense of being available to her in exactly the same way as they functioned pre-reflectively or in an earlier reflection. The return is not so much a turn back as it is a turn forward to the conditions as they are considered in the present (conditions deemed similar and accordingly memorialized) in view of something projected (hoped for, feared, awaited, etc.) as the future. In other words, interpretation is a process that is better pictured as a helical than a circular motion. Like a helix, interpretation moves forward by moving back to consideration of the conditions of understanding but it does not and cannot move back literally; rather it moves back in the sense that it moves in the direction it already traversed and perhaps even continues to traverse, precisely in moving forward. The interpreter is engaged in this process as part of her effort to make explicit what she already understands of the subject to be interpreted. This image of the interpretive helix captures a central idea of the ontology of interpretation offered here. Encompassing at once the interpreter, what is interpreted, and the dynamics of their interaction, interpretation is an activity of making explicit the conditions and directions of a process in which the interpreter is already engaged.

Why do interpretations move in helical patterns and why do they move in the directions they do? Though answers to these questions in particular cases depend on the particular arena of interpretation, the historicity of interpretation entails its helical and forward-moving character. Indeed, the helical and forward motion of interpretation is a way of making more explicit the self-interpretation involved in interpretation – though, for reasons already discussed, it would falsify matters to construe self-interpretation as the provenance exclusively of the interpreter or the interpreted.[19] Taking a further page from Heidegger, moreover, we may add that interpretation generally is subject to alethic constraints. That is to say, the movement is constrained by the ways that concrete possibilities present and absent themselves to the interpreter along the path of the interpretive helix. What is at work in interpretation is neither subjective nor objective but rather, as Gadamer puts it, 'the interplay [*Ineinanderspiel*] of the movement of tradition and the movement of the interpreter' (Gadamer 1972, p. 277).

17.3.3 The Ontology of Interpretation and the Interpretation of Ontology

The foregoing sections have hopefully made clear the sense in which interpretation is a fundamentally historical activity with a certain structure (the interpretive helix) that encompasses the situation of the interpreter, the subject matter to be interpreted, and the modes of interpreting that subject matter. Since this situation is historical in the open-ended sense noted above (Section 17.3.1), hermeneutic ontology entails that an honest or authentic interpretation be self-consciously fallible and inveterately self-correcting, without pretensions to articulating universal and necessary conditions of what is. A hermeneutic practice or even a theoretical hermeneutics can be formal and rule-governed, but with inherent limits that preclude a full and definitive disclosure.[20] Interpretation is necessarily incomplete because what is in need of interpretation, existence, is inherently dynamic and unfinished and because it is exposed and open to horizons beyond its determination.[21] Again, Gadamer makes a similar point with his stress on the 'absolute openness of the meaning-event,' on the tradition-bound character of any measure, and on the fact that 'there is no possible consciousness in which some handed-down subject matter [*Sache*] might appear in the light of eternity' (Gadamer 1972, p. 448).

Hermeneutic ontology is the sort of ontology that, in the tradition of Heidegger's fundamental ontology, is concerned with not only what sorts of entities there are and can be, but also with the various ways in which entities are said to be. A hermeneutic ontology, in other words, attempts to determine the senses of 'being' that have been and continue to be presupposed in identifying and determining what there is and can

---

[19]The forward movement of interpretation is not the same as either a teleological or a teleonomic movement.

[20]For this reason, this account of the ontology of interpretation, as noted earlier, does not exclude the ascertainment of covering laws of explanation and other iterable patterns, but entails the notion that their measure of validity is tied to a convention-driven abstractness and ideality relative to the helical character of interpretation.

[21]There is a sense in which, given the historicity of interpretation and the interpretive helix, hermeneutic ontology – much like Heidegger's hermeneutic phenomenology of human existence – is a distinctive form of possibilism, where the possibilities that are fundamental are existential.

be. Its aim is, of course, not merely to determine senses of being that have been presupposed, but also determine the appropriate senses and to do so in light of our own prospects. Given the interpretive helix and its own historical character, hermeneutic ontology as the ontology of interpretation entails an interpretation of ontology, conceived as attempt to retrieve ontological legacies that are operative in the historical situation lived by the hermeneutical ontologist herself. The interpretation of ontology is an interpretation of the history of interpretations of ontological concepts, precisely as they inform the language of the interpreter. The mutual entailment of the ontology of interpretation and the interpretation of ontology and its history forms its own interpretive helix.

Hopefully, it is obvious by now that the import of this emphasis on the historicity of interpretation is anything but antiquarian. Precisely by taking seriously that all interpretation is self-interpretation, hermeneutic ontology situates the interpreter and her task of interpretation in a historically determinate but underdetermined situation with the aim of making evident to the interpreter the decisions that she makes and can make in the course of interpreting. Herein lies a major advantage or contribution that hermeneutic ontology can make to the study of ontology. A hermeneutic ontology attempts to understand, interpret, and formulate necessary conditions of formal and regional ontologies by establishing the historicity of the interpretations underlying them. Hermeneutic ontology looks, as we have seen, to the condition of the possibility of understanding. Inasmuch as this understanding underlies in turn the possibility of description and explanation, hermeneutic ontology is necessarily not simply descriptive (there is no such thing) or explanatory, at least in the reductionistic manner that explanation is often understood (e.g., the covering law model).[22] Hermeneutic ontology's contribution is precisely to make explicit or more explicit, as the case may be, the historicity, fallibility, and promise of formal and regional ontologies.

Hermeneutic ontology is not a fundamental ontology in the sense that it subsumes, and cannot be subsumed by, other sorts of ontological investigations. Hermeneutic ontology makes *prima facie* use of categories employed across various regions of being as well as categories restricted to particular regions. Hermeneutic ontology is accordingly dependent upon formal and regional ontologies. However, it

[22]Hermeneutic ontology does address a phenomenon that contains in some sense the conditions of the possibility of explanation, including scientific explanation. These conditions are historical, i.e., they are received but precisely in the course of being enacted and this enactment (projection of received possibilities as one's own) can but need not take the form of a theoretical reflection. Hermeneutic ontology cannot be conceived in a purely theoretical manner if theory is presumed to be able to abstract from traditions received or from the aims of the theory, i.e., the extra-theoretical purposes that the theory serves and, indeed, perhaps is meant to serve. For this reason hermeneutic ontology also views suspiciously conceptions of ontology as a purely descriptive not explanatory enterprise, at least inasmuch as those descriptions are designed to serve the purposes of explanation, purposes typically but not exclusively attributable to the conscious or unconscious intentions of the theoreticians themselves. See Heidegger's critique of Husserl along these lines; descriptions for the sake of explanation are no more pure descriptions of things than description for the sake of persuasion.

is not so dependent that it cannot take the measure of the ontological commitments of these investigations, systematically and historically. Indeed, as argued above, it is incumbent upon hermeneutic ontology, in its pursuit of the task of determining the ontological make-up of interpretation, to do so. Moreover, it is capable of doing so. For every ontology, including hermeneutic ontology, is in the end an interpretation. Every ontology accordingly supposes an adequate articulation of what it means to be an interpretation and, in that sense, every ontology is beholden to hermeneutic ontology.

17.3.4 Gadamer on Language as the Horizon of Hermeneutical Ontology

In his major work, *Truth and Method*, Gadamer pleas for the universality of hermeneutics by way of considering the distinctiveness of art, history, and language – the truth of which is irreducible to scientific method. Just as truth, so construed, is bound to interpretation, so 'the speculative constitution of being that underlies hermeneutics has the same universal scope as reason and language' (Gadamer 1972, p. 452). Indeed, it is precisely language, on Gadamer's account, that forms the horizon of what he calls 'hermeneutical ontology' and introduces by emphasizing the co-dependency of the language and the world. 'Language's primordially human character signifies at the same time the primordially linguistic character of human being-in-the-world' (Gadamer 1972, p. 419). Whereas animals are constrained in a certain sense by and to their habitat or *milieu*, humans have a freedom with respect to their worlds and environment, precisely due to language.

Moreover, it is language not primarily as assertions about things but as a process – and not mere means – of communication. Gadamer accordingly distinguishes artificial languages designed as means of conveying information (*Mittel zu Informationszwecken*) from the communication in the actual language community (the *Sprachwelt*) that those designer languages presuppose. In keeping with this priority of hermeneutical ontology to the regional ontologies underlying science, Gadamer contends that the natural experience of the world through language does not make it 'available and usable' since the world's manner of being is different from the sorts of things that are available, through objectification, to science.[23] The world is only experienced in the historical act of communicating and there is no meaningful way to distinguish what the world is (ontology) from the interpretation (hermeneutic) inherent in this linguistic act.

---

[23]While disputing talk about the 'world in itself' (including scientific claims to objectivity), Gadamer's hermeneutical ontology espouses the fundamental character of "the linguistic character of our experience of the world, prior to everything that is recognized and articulated as being" (Gadamer 1972, p. 426).

References

Gadamer, H.G. 1972. *Wahrheit und Methode*. 3., erw. Auflage. Tübingen: Mohr.
Heidegger, M. 1972. *Sein und Zeit*. 12. Auflage. Tübingen: Niemeyer.
Heidegger, M. 1990. *Metaphysische Anfangsgründe der Logik*. Hrsg. Klaus Held. *Gesamtausgabe*, Bd. 16. Frankfurt am Main: Klostermann.
Heidegger, M. 1994. *Einführung in die phänomenologische Forschung*. Hrsg. F. von Herrmann. *Gesamtausgabe*, Bd. 17. Frankfurt am Main: Klostermann.
Husserl, E. 1950. *Cartesianische Meditationen*. Hrsg. S. Strasser. *Husserliana*, Bd. 1. Haag: Nijhoff.
Husserl, E. 1962. *Phänomenologische Psychologie*. Hrsg. W. Biemel. *Husserliana*, Bd. 9. Haag: Nijhoff.
Husserl, E. 1968. *Logische Untersuchungen*. Zweiter Band, erster Teil. 5. Auflage. Tübingen: Niemeyer.
Husserl, E. 1980. *Ideen zu einer reinen Phänomenologie und phänomenologischen Philosophie*. 3. Auflage. Tübingen: Niemeyer
Poli, R. 2003. Descriptive, Formal and Formalized Ontologies. In *Husserl's Logical Investigations Reconsidered*, ed. D. Fisette, 183–210. Dordrecht: Kluwer.
Scotus, D. 1893. *Quaestiones subtilissimae supre libros Metaphysicorum Aristotelis*, Book 1, q. 1. *Opera Omnia*, vol. 7. Paris: Vives.
Smith, B., and D.W. Smith. 1995. *The Cambridge companion to Husserl*. Cambridge: Cambridge University Press.

FSC
www.fsc.org
MIX
Papier | Fördert
gute Waldnutzung
FSC® C083411

Kolibri 360 GmbH
Ferdinand-Jühlke-Straße 7
99095 Erfurt, Deutschland
produktsicherheit@kolibri360.de